MW01010488

THE LAW OF GOD

THE LAW OF GOD

The Philosophical History of an Idea

RÉMI BRAGUE

Translated by Lydia G. Cochrane

The University of Chicago Press
Chicago & London

Rémi Brague is professor of philosophy at the Université Paris I–Panthéon Sorbonne and at the University of Munich. Five of his books, including *The Wisdom of the World* (2003), have been previously published by the University of Chicago Press. Lydia G. Cochrane has translated a number of books for the Press, most recently Piero Melograni's *Wolfgang Amadeus Mozart: A Biography* (2006).

The University of Chicago Press, Chicago 60637
The University of Chicago Press, Ltd., London
© 2007 by The University of Chicago
All rights reserved. Published 2007
Printed in the United States of America

16 15 14 13 12 11 10 09 08 07   2 3 4 5

Originally published as *La loi de Dieu: Histoire philosophique d'une alliance.* © Éditions Gallimard, 2005.
Published with the support of the National Center for the Book—French Ministry of Culture.
Ouvrage publié avec le soutien du Centre national du livre—ministère français chargé de la culture.

ISBN-13: 978-0-226-07078-0 (cloth)
ISBN-10: 0-226-07078-6 (cloth)

Library of Congress Cataloging-in-Publication Data

Brague, Rémi, 1947–
    [Loi de Dieu. English]
    The law of God : the philosophical history of an idea / Rémi Brague ; translated by Lydia G. Cochrane.
        p. cm.
    Includes bibliographical references and index.
    ISBN-13: 978-0-226-07078-0 (cloth : alk. paper)
    ISBN-10: 0-226-07078-6 (cloth : alk. paper)
    1. Religion and law—History. 2. Law (Theology). 3. Christianity. 4. Islam. 5. Judaism.
I. Title.
    BL65.L33B6813   2007
    208'.4—dc22

                                            2006029906

♾ The paper used in this publication meets the minimum requirements of the American National Standard for Information Sciences—Permanence of Paper for Printed Library Materials, ANSI Z39.48-1992.

Contents]ॐ··

Preface

What I propose to do in this book is to study the idea of divine law. That idea supposes that human actions are guided by norms received from the divine. At certain times and in certain regions, the law that regulated human conduct was characterized as divine. The two ideas of law and of divinity have each been understood in very different ways, which increased the ambiguity of the formula associating them.

By exploring that alliance between law and divinity, I have attempted to return to an approach that I had already used in an earlier work, *The Wisdom of the World*, which was a history of Western ideas over the long term. In the two works, I compare the three cultural areas of the medieval world by resetting them on their two common bases, the thought of antiquity (Greek antiquity in particular) and biblical revelation, while keeping in mind the great river-system civilizations of the ancient Near East, and with the hope of arriving at a better comprehension of our own modernity.

I have chosen as a unifying thread the notion of "divine law," because the idea—or in any event, the expression—can be found in the three worlds, Jewish, Christian, and Muslim, that I will need to investigate in order to grasp the choices, basic and successive, that each civilization made. Divine law, in fact, reveals what Judaism, Islam, and Christianity think and know about themselves.

❖

The Wisdom of the World studied how human action had been conceived of as being in phase with cosmological realities that were presumed to furnish humankind with a model, a metaphor, or at least a guarantee, of right conduct. The present book examines how human practice was understood as dependent on laws and rules of a theological nature. Both works show how that human practice broke away from the two domains, cosmological and theological, with which it had been associated.

Those two domains form what might be called two sides of the same history. The first imagines the law on the basis of the physical world, a vision for which I was obliged to coin the neologism *cosmonomy*.[1] In the second, the relationship of the law to the divine might be rendered by the term *theonomy*, a term that already has a long history but that should not be understood as foisting on it more than its etymology indicates.[2] If the two models had to be embraced within a common term to be opposed to a rival term, I might borrow the term *heteronomy*—receiving one's law from another—in opposition to *autonomy*—giving oneself one's law.

These opposed terms, which Kant placed at the center of moral reflection, have come to define a project: autonomy defines the ideal to be realized in an ever more radical manner; heteronomy designates the enemy that must be eliminated. In fact, the modern world, in the morality that it claims and that is its foundation, flatters itself that it has sent packing everything tainted with heteronomy, and it is pleased to understand itself as constructed on the idea of autonomy. By studying the two adversaries of autonomy more closely, I hope to have contributed—indirectly—to making the project underlying modernity more visible. A more exact idea of premodern *heteronomy* contributes, in fact, to elucidating the question of modernity, both in the objective and the subjective meanings of the term. For one thing, that more exact idea will permit us a better understanding of what modernity reproaches in the ages preceding it and with which it claims to break; for another, it also throws light on what is dubious in the modern project itself.

❖

Even more than in *The Wisdom of the World*, I have had to focus on the premodern era in my remarks here. It is at that time, it seems to me, that decisions were made that our modernity has simply inherited. Hence our own day will be treated here only as a sort of rapid epilogue.

In carrying out my investigations I have used the works of historians of philosophical, juridical, political, and religious thought without claiming to add much of my own that is new: I have limited myself to philosophical reflection on givens that others before me had often elaborated from their own points of view.

I have used the forms of proper names that are most frequently found in the literature, and I have transcribed foreign words in the simplest manner, which is not always the most rigorous one. The bibliography is limited to titles that I have actually used, and I cite the editions consulted.

❖

The bibliography was compiled with the aid of Marie-Isabelle Wasem, who used it as the topic for her dissertation for the École Nationale Supérieure des Sciences Bibliothèques (Lyon). In Munich both my assistant Hans-Otto Seitschek and Gregor Soszka brought many documents to my attention, thus sparing me a good deal of travel.

I have presented this topic at a number of conferences and in courses, above all, in my graduate seminars at the Université Panthéon-Sorbonne (Paris-I) and Charles Leben's graduate seminar in the Philosophy of the Law (Paris-II), but also abroad: in the universities of Lausanne, where I replaced Ada-Babette Neschke-Hentschke, and Boston, on the invitation of Charles Griswold, where I presented an early version of the current work. Finally, a course at the University of Munich offered a synthesis of the book.

My editor, Ran Halévy, has read this book very attentively and offered me thousands of highly useful suggestions. The final version once again benefited from painstaking review by Irène Fernandez and my wife. Dedicating it to them is the least I can do.

My American translator, Lydia Cochrane, has checked all of my citations, identifying a certain number of errors in the process. I have shared the list of corrections with other translators and will take them into account for an eventual new edition in French. May this serve to express my gratitude to her.

Translator's Note

This translation of Rémi Brague's *La loi de Dieu* has benefited enormously from the author's review. He has been unfailingly patient, supplying information on the sources he cites and correcting the translator's misinterpretations, major and minor. Working with him has been a great pleasure, and he has my heartfelt thanks.

Introduction]ᵌ᠁

The question of divine law can be posed in several ways. In investigating the connection between the notions of law and divinity, one might move in one of two directions. The first would be to begin with the notion of law to ask: What is a law that is presented at a given place and time as divine? What does that divinity consist in? Is it a point of origin or a property? What characteristics does that divinity confer on the law? If, on the other hand, we begin with the notion of divinity, the questions become: What does the fact that a god is presented as lawgiver tell us about his divinity? What relationship with the divine, and what type of religion, emerge from such an idea?

These first questions give rise to a second and more practical series of questions that lend themselves, to some extent, to an empirical approach: How can we describe societies in which human behavior is regulated by laws characterized as "divine"? In what ways are such societies affected by the different ways in which the idea of the divinity of the law has appeared? What is the relationship between such societies and the law: submission, adaptation, more and less creative interpretation? What social groups administer those various relationships?

But a third sort of question appears on the horizon, one that surpasses the resolutely premodern framework within which I have chosen to operate here. In modern societies, law, far from being conceived of in any relation with the divine, is quite simply the rule that the human community gives itself, considering only ends that it proposes for itself. Hence we might ask: What has permitted, or even caused, the rupture with the premodern relationship with the law and the transition to the modern version of that relationship?

Lurking behind the themes of divine law is a triple articulation that both links and separates philosophy and religion, philosophy and the political, and religion and the political, forming what philosophers have called "the theologico-political problem."[1] What follows are a few brief remarks on the topic.

The question is most often treated exclusively within the European framework, a procedure that limits it both in space, by confining it to what is known as the "Judeo-Christian" world, and in time, by restricting it to "only" what has occurred in the last three thousand years. In point of fact, the two recognized sources of European culture, "Athens and Jerusalem," the Greeks and the Bible, and their oldest written documents go back, at the limit, to some one thousand years before our own era. Even that is only a thin slice of time. First, in relation to the immensity of prehistorical time. Here lack of evidence makes our knowledge extremely scanty. Everything perishable has been lost; everything that made language possible—even just oral language—has disappeared. Indeed, neither political organization nor religion, in the broader sense of the terms, has an identifiable origin. In order to understand the origins of religion, we would have to be able to pinpoint practices comparable to rites. Scholars often cite burial of the dead, a custom that dates back a hundred thousand years, and the habit of covering the body with flowers, ascertainable by the presence of fossil pollens around the skeletons. But we have no idea why this was done: did it symbolize some sort of rebirth or, more practically, was it to mask the odor?

Even without venturing on to the infinite ocean of prehistory, history, properly speaking, also begins well before Homer and the Bible. The invention of writing, an event chosen as indicative of history's beginning, occurred around 3000 BCE. Hence the history of Western thought, as it is usually studied, robs us of over two millennia to concentrate on only three-fifths of history's span. There is every indication, however, that a large number of decisively important cultural choices were made during that earlier period.

We also need to reach beyond a focus on Europe that prevents us from seeing even that region in perspective. An appreciation of the singularity of what occurred there requires comparative study of the various traditions of political thought. The usual procedure is to examine only the European gallery of great ancestors from St. Augustine to Hegel, after which, remarkably enough, the major thinkers seldom really grapple with questions of political philosophy. We also need to study the political thought of such Muslims as Alfarabi and Averroes and such Jewish scholars as Maimonides, to mention only the leading names, on whom monographic studies are available.[2] What remains to be done is to investigate the ways in which their cultural milieus made their political thought differ from the tradition that is more familiar to us.

An examination of medieval political and legal thought also requires us to reach beyond the Middle Ages in an attempt to reappropriate, at least on an elementary level, the common sources of the three traditions. Those sources are, as we have seen, Athens and Jerusalem. That seemingly simple statement implies several serious questions: the very fact that there are *two* sources is not automatic. To speak of "Athens and Jerusalem," an opposition that has become an old refrain, leaves unanswered the question of why there should be two sources instead of one.[3]

On the one hand, there is the Greek source, the principal origin of political philosophy. Here we need to ask what the medieval traditions knew of the Greek theoreticians of the polis, and at what point in time those Greek authors were read. The more important question is, of course, to know *how* those texts were read.

On the other hand, there are the sacred texts, the Bible (Old and New Testaments), and the Qur'an, works that require a philosophical reading. This has not been the most frequent approach, and even when it has been attempted the reading has been unilateral. The sacred text, considered as absolutely true, can be used in support of a philosophical argument. In practice, however, it usually serves to illustrate a conviction acquired by other means, as is the case with the Fathers of the Church or the medieval thinkers. In the modern era—and to quote only the best examples—I am thinking of Fichte's use of the Gospel According to St. John or, more recently, that of Michel Henry.[4] Conversely, the text can also be the object of a philosophical critique of religion. This was the case in the early modern age in Machiavelli, for whom the example of Moses is central;[5] in Hobbes, a good half of whose *Leviathan* (1650) is biblical exegesis; and in Spinoza, who presents a critical reading of the Old Testament in an entire treatise, the *Tractatus Theologico-Politicus* (1670), a title that has become the name of a problem. Later philosophers, because of the emergence of biblical criticism as a historico-philological specialty (among other reasons), have shown little interest in the technical aspects of biblical interpretation, relying instead on the works of specialists. Nietzsche, for example, discusses St. Paul, but although he was trained as a philologist, he shows little interest in literal exploration of New Testament texts.[6]

While I shall try to avoid both naive acceptance and polemics, my purpose is to follow Machiavelli and read the Bible "judiciously" (*sensatamente*).[7] Machiavelli was intent on contesting the authority of biblical texts by destroying the theological interpretation of them. My goal is more sober: to lead the Bible and the Qur'an to a neutral, philosophical reading.

⟡

European reflection on the relationship between the political and the religious is dominated by one of what Jean-François Lyotard calls the *grands récits*—the grand narratives—in which modernity tries to explain itself: an escape of the political from the domain of theology. The two are supposed to have gone their separate ways after an original unity. In order to express that unity, modernity reinterprets the past and distributes it into *ad hoc* categories. In doing so, the movement of disengagement from the past has received various names: the secularization of a world supposed to have been "enchanted"; the laicization of a supposedly clerical society; the separation of church and state, supposed to have been originally one.

The most authoritative application of this way of reconstituting reality to the juridical domain is Max Weber's. In his great and posthumous *Wirtschaft und Gesellschaft* (1923), he proposes the concept of "sacred law," a notion that embraces Jewish and Islamic law, Hindu law, and medieval canon law. He creates a four-part overall scheme for the evolution of the juridical domain, the first stage of which is the charismatic revelation of the law by "prophets of the law." The three following stages are: the creation and empirical discovery of the law by special "dignitaries" of the law; the vouchsafing of the law by the temporal *imperium* and the theocratic powers; and finally the "systematization" of the law, henceforth regulated by specialized jurists.[8] Weber was quite aware that this sort of reconstruction is fictional. His schema follows the evolution of Western law, however: three of the stages that he sketches correspond roughly to the law of the Roman jurists, then the law of a Middle Ages dominated by conflict between the Empire and the papacy, and finally the juridic positivism of modern societies. What propels evolution is the rationalization of societies, a notion that Weber held dear. My only quarrel with Weber's interpretation lies in the unity of the concept of "sacred law," a notion that seems to me to include heterogeneous phenomena.

When it comes to applying that concept to the political domain, the categories under which the unity with which modernity is supposed to have broken are in fact quite recent. The "divine right of kings" had barely been formulated before the seventeenth century; the "alliance of the throne and the altar" goes back no further than the Restoration in France. Categories that permit a more particularized grasp of events—"caesaropapism," for example—acknowledge that there already existed two discrete elements whose shifting relations reflect a history. Not everywhere, however, was there a pope and a Caesar—or two poles bearing other names supposed to be present and distinct.

The terms for designating a tendency to set the religious at a distance are both paradoxical and dubious. "Laicization" is a truly odd term, given that "lay" is a Christian notion. The noun *laos*, from which the adjective *laikos* is derived, in fact signifies the people as the people of God and it originates in a Homeric term picked up in Greek translation in the Septuagint. The layman—as distinguished from the individual, the subject, or the citizen—is a man called by God to be one of his people and to assume the dignity of one who knows himself to be promised an eternal destiny. Moreover, do not modern democracies, with their idea of the "citizen," rely on an anthropology that makes use of the consequences of Christian ecclesiology, but without accepting the premises that render that anthropology consistent?

As for the idea of "secularization," the term hints at what it is supposed to explain, namely, that there exists something like a "secular" domain distinct from the religious domain; a "pro-fane" that defines its position at the temple parvis (*fanum*).[9]

Finally, the idea of a "separation of church and state" is even less adequate, if that is possible, because it takes the phenomenon of "the church" as a given. Where are we to seek for "the church" in the ancient city? Do the Jewish people or the Islamic nation (*umma*) constitute a church or a society? The community is indissolubly religious and political for both of these. In Christianity, that supposed separation is thus made possible, in a certain sense, because it never occurred at any assignable moment but has always existed.

In all societies certain phenomena can be described as religious and others as political. Still, the articulation between the two does not necessary occur in the same manner from one society to another. It would be better not to tie down the idea of desacralization and to consider the inverse movement, from the profane toward the sacred, as well. More generally, the time has come to contest the explicative principle that underlies all of these so-called evolutions, which is the idea that societies always and constantly drift in the same direction—from the sacred to the profane—through an inexorable withdrawal of the sacred. In order to accomplish this task, we need to begin before the Bible, which represents a sacralization of phenomena that were originally political.

◈

These considerations have led me to enlarge the "theologico-political problem," and even to move beyond its boundaries. I shall have two remarks to make on this subject, one about the term and the other about the thing itself. The term has a double heritage. The adjective comes, as we have seen, from Spinoza. In more recent years, the ancient idea of a political theology (Varro; Eusebius of Caesarea) has been rejuvenated, first in a much-discussed work to which Carl Schmitt gave the title *Political Theology* (1922), then by the works of the theologian Johann Baptist Metz in the 1970s.[10] In its designation as a problem the term has the drawback of suggesting a connection between two academic disciplines, theology and political science. It is not the coexistence of two fields of knowledge that is bothersome, however. As the word indicates, "theo-logy" is already a way for the divine to pass through the prism of discourse (*logos*). Much more disturbing is the divine's claim to strike the field of the political with full force and no rational mediation. This is why, at the risk of creating a neologism, it might be better to speak of a *theo-political* problem.

This is not just pedantic affectation. After all, the very existence of a discipline such as "theology" is not to be taken for granted. It constitutes the particularity of one specific religion, Christianity, and is absent from other religions. There are of course ritual, juridical, and mystical "religious sciences" in those other religions, which can reach a very high level of elaboration and technicality. But the project of a rational elucidation of divinity, the dialectic of "to believe" and "to understand," *fides quaerens intellectum,* "faith in search of understanding"—the program of Anselm, and still of exemplary importance for Hegel—is specific to Christianity.[11] We would have no right to force on Judaism or Islam—let alone the religions of the ancient world or the Far East—a problematic that is by definition foreign to them. We should even ask whether the coming of a theology within Christianity was not made possible by the way that religion effected and reflected the articulation of the divine onto human action.

Still, I have no intention of stopping at what I have just dubbed the "theopolitical." I would like to add an *iota* and speak of the *theio-political,* the prefix "theio-" to indicate that we are speaking of the *divine* (in Greek, *theios*) and not of one or several *gods* (in Greek, *theos*). My preference for this neologism over the more widely accepted "theo-" corresponds to a concern that a highly revolutionary event not be turned into something banal: the divine emerged from its neutrality (*to theion*) to present itself as God (*ho theos*), thus taking on a personal figuration or, if God transcends our idea of personality, becoming suprapersonal rather than impersonal.

These are considerations of terminology; a second series of remarks applies to the thing itself. The theio-political is, at most, simply an articulation onto the divine, not only of the political, but of the entire genre of the *practical,* as it is classically divided into three parts: self-government (ethics), "government of the household" (economics), and government of the city (politics).[12] As it happens, the divine can also be pertinent to the two other arts of government, the ethical and the economic, and in fact it has, throughout history, asserted its claim on them just as strenuously as it has on the political. I would thus to suggest the appearance, on the horizon of the theio-political, of what I shall call here the *theio-practical*.

One important consequence of an enlargement of perspective of this sort that deserves to be stressed is that an eventual solution to the theio-political problem, no matter how satisfactory it may seem, would never be better than partial. It would concern only one species, the political, and would leave aside the genus of that species, which is the practical. That is not necessarily a drawback: a discipline, a field of knowledge, or a technique can—in fact must—keep within a particular domain and opt to ignore other domains. But the genus (the practical) imposes on the species (the political) certain specific properties. As long as the theio-practical problem remains unresolved, any statement or resolution of the theio-political problem remains unbalanced and resolved in a wobbly manner.

This is precisely what traditional political philosophy does in the European world: more often than not it supposes that the theio-practical problem has already been resolved, and that it has received one particular solution, the Christian one. Historiography undergoes a parallel shrinkage: more often than not, it defines as "theologico-political" the way in which a political authority claims to draw its legitimacy from the invocation of a divine instance. The divine thus governs indirectly. The demand for authority and the real exercise of authority are the property of the leader who claims to represent the divine principle. The power of God over man passes through the power of one man over another. This idea—the idea of sacred kingship—has given rise to an immense literature, almost an entire literary genre, that forms an imposing mass that includes several outstanding masterpieces.[13] I have no intention of adding my own reflections to that mass, and even less of competing with those authors.

All of those works limit their examinations to the West, however, and to the "political" species of the "practical" genus. In the long run this dual restriction becomes just one: the historiography of sacred kingship takes as its object the result of a prior history, which it recounts only marginally. Hence insufficient consideration has been given, up to now, to placing the political within the context of the practical genus of which it is but a species. I have attempted to do just that, and I present my results here.

The idea of divine law constitutes precisely the "theio-practical" idea *par excellence*. To take divine law as an object of inquiry is to set oneself, from the start, on the theio-practical level, and even to make it appear for what it is, with all its constraints. The idea of divine law implies that *human action, in its full breadth, receives its norm from the divine.* It is within this framework—and only within this framework—that we can speak of "theocracy" with any rigor. The word, incidentally, was forged by Flavius Josephus to describe the Jewish regime, which is distinct from all other human regimes in that it represents the reign of the Law alone.[14]

Hence I propose to follow the historical path of the notion of divine law. I shall show how that notion, present in Greece as a metaphor for natural law, took on new meaning with Israel. In the Middle Ages Judaism, then Islam, each in its own fashion, elaborated that notion and gave it a different foundation. Christianity soon gave up the idea of a revealed legislation. Instead, it approached the Greek idea of a law that was divine because natural, while introducing a relation to God that went beyond the framework of legislation. The modern era represents a departure from the Christian solution, both in the sense of denying it and of abandoning it as a source of law, often going so far as to reject any idea of a law that is not of human origin.

PART I

Origins

1

Prehistory

There is nothing self-evident about "divine law." The expression establishes a connection between two notions, thus supposing that those two notions already exist. Its appearance in history requires a double evolution in how power is conceived: social power—the power of society over itself—must present itself in the form of laws; divinity, for its part, must have appeared as the locus of a power, and of a power susceptible of exerting a normative function.

The Idea of Law

The idea of "law" is not clearly perceptible in ancient societies. Our word "law" derives from the Latin *lex*, which expresses a Roman notion. When we use it to render the Greek term *nomos* or the Hebrew *hoqq* (and for even greater reason, the term *torah*), we make an arbitrary choice. It is out of the question blithely to apply our use of the term "law" to stages in social and intellectual evolution that have preceded our own and that at times occurred elsewhere than in Europe. Quite to the contrary, we will need to review the entire series of those stages during the course of this investigation. But first let me offer a rapid sketch of the genesis of the idea of law.

The idea of law expresses only one portion of the normative domain, which is much vaster than the law. To be sure, we know of no society without rules. Any society exerts a degree of pressure on its members. It suggests to them a certain type of response to the fundamental questions of human life, as men and women, overshadowed by the divine and immersed in the natural, carry on permanent negotiations concerning their relations with one another and with their surroundings. Those rules do not always have to be spelled out objectively. Take the rules of language: the individual does not perceive them as something external, which means that the constraints that assure their respect are never felt as an external pressure. Where more ritualized behaviors are concerned—courtesy, for example—social pressure suffices to insure compliance. In the worst cases, ridicule functions as a call to order.

It may happen that the norm is expressed, becoming conscious. This process simply formulates what had been implicit until then. Formulation does not necessarily imply a constraining authority. Its authority may be limited to that of long-standing acceptance, and it may remain oral, indeed without an assignable author. This is the "voice of the people," the source of proverbs and of the implicit value judgments with which language is saturated. At that level, counsel and commandment are still indivisible.

A norm that has been made explicit can be the object of an obligation. In that case, we can begin to speak of law. In order for there to be a law, there must be not only explicit statement but also imposition. This is what is expressed by the Latin *ferre*, still present in French in the verb *légi-férer,* like the *setzen* included in the German *Gesetz*. The idea is even redoubled in the word *Gesetzgebung,* or legislation.[1] That laws are the source, and the only source, of law as a system, and that every law derives from a positive act of legislation rather than being the crystallization of a habitual social practice, seem to us axiomatic. This is not to be taken for granted, however. Similarly, choosing to call "law" only prescriptions accompanied by a statement of the punishment involved (in contrast to what then appears as *lex imperfecta*) occurred relatively late in history, and it is a presupposition that I shall take care to avoid.

The early civilizations were well acquainted with decisions that were issued by some authority, hence had "force of law." These can be separated into two groups: decisions with juridical value and sentences laid down in particular cases, on the one hand, and, on the other, general rules determining sentences to be applied in all cases. The idea of an objective and stable rule according to which such decisions would be made was at first quite unclear, however. Concrete judgments, handed down in particular circumstances, require explicit formulation, for their only existence is within and by means of that formulation. In contrast, principles that have been infringed upon do not have to be explicitly defined and can remain tranquilly implicit. The law appears as such only in situations in which harm has been done by a transgression and may require punishment. In ancient China one of the terms for the law was "punishments" (*hsing*).[2]

The law takes a decisive step forward when it is set down in writing. The redaction of laws permits their conservation independently of their memorization by a guild of specialists; it gives the laws an objective and public status; and it facilitates comparison among different systems of laws and invites investigation of their coherence. The invention of the state and the invention of writing are closely connected, and—by definition—it is with writing that history begins. Authority becomes independent of the people, issuing rules that, expressed and formulated as such, are imposed on the people as coming from an external entity.

Later stages concern my theme less directly. Among them, however, there is one that needs to be touched on, which is that of *codification*. With this step, laws are not only written down but also assembled and organized into one corpus, at times given material form as a book or an inscription. Beyond this stage of assembling laws, and called into being by it, there is *systemization*, or the placement of the laws within a system that aims at exhaustiveness and coherence. When this occurs, an individual law takes on its full meaning only within an entire set of legal dispositions.

Power and Divinity

The notion of "divine," although not distinct, is decisively present from the start in the civilizations that interest me here. Belief that some sort of beings, or at least a higher region of being, exists above humankind is present everywhere. The connection between power and divinity, in contrast, is less automatic. The God of certain of the Greek philosophers, Aristotle's unmoved Prime Mover or Epicurus' gods far off in space, exercise no power, properly speaking: they may be models or objects of desire, but not efficient causes. The fact remains, however, that such views pertained among a very small elite who were reacting against widespread popular beliefs, and that for the better part of the populations the connection between power and the gods was more the rule than the exception. The Greeks were accustomed to calling their gods "those who are more powerful [than we are]" (*hoi kreittones*). Moreover, divinity was at first attributed to natural sites of power: above and around us, the stars and sources of water; among us, the fertility of plants or the sexuality of animals. Here the divine power is mute. It weighs on humankind or animates it from the inside, but it does not address humans.

A further step, which is, again, by no means self-evident, was to attribute to the divine the particular modality of power that affects humans as such—that is, insofar as the *logos* present in man makes him capable of comprehending an order and obeying it. That modality is the political. That something that defines humans as human can derive from the divine is a paradox. The link between the divine and the political involves so many difficult conflicts of jurisdiction that one might think it exceptional. That said, it is a fact that the connections between political power and divinity are both ancient and common.

Divinity is often credited to the holder of concrete political power—for simplicity's sake, the king. This relationship is no more necessary that those we have already seen, of which it is a particular case. But as before, it is widespread. In Egyptian, the word for "king" (n[y]-sw.t) is accompanied by the same determinative as the word for the gods. On occasion, the king is invested with a purely human role. When he has a relationship to the divine, it can take several forms, depending upon how the divine is represented in a given society. He can be viewed as the image of the cosmos, the spouse of the supreme goddess, or the son of a god. In the last case, he may have been engendered miraculously by that god or adopted by him. This is why the king in the Near East is represented as the elect of one or more gods, perhaps by adoption. In Psalm 110, for example, the god of Israel says to the king, "Before the daystar, like the dew, I have begotten you." Finally, the king's reign may be ushered in with a special ceremony of investiture in which he crosses the frontier between the profane and the sacred. One such act in ancient Israel was unction with oil by a prophet, an act that left an inherited trace in the anointing of kings in the Western tradition.

The gods also assist the king throughout his life. As a sacred personage, he is in contact with the divine and participates in the ambiguity of all things holy.[3] Certain prerogatives (such as inviolability) derive from this contact, as do certain special powers, such as the power to heal.

The relationship with the divine, finally, is not only a source of power: it also determines a function. The elements are connected, because the familiarity that derives from the divine origin of power facilitates access to the sphere of the divine. Thus it often happens that the king is also a priest. Even in Athens, which was reputed to be desacralized, the archon, called the "king," still played this priestly role.

Law and Divinity

Within the various dimensions of the political, however, legislative activity was not necessarily a part of the connection with the divine. A relationship between the juridical in general and the divine is not a basic given. That relationship seems to be totally absent, for example, in Chinese civilization. Ancient China had an extremely elaborate system of laws, but "in China no one at any time has ever hinted that any kind of written law—even the best written law—could have had a divine origin."[4] I shall leave China aside, however, and concentrate on the civilizations to which Western Europe is the heir, all of which established a connection between law and divinity.

In those civilizations there is a discernable triangular structure connecting the divine, the political power (the king), and the law. Those three constituent elements can be structurally related in three ways. The divine can affect the king directly and the law only indirectly, or it can affect the law directly and the king only indirectly. In the first case, the relation of the king to the law will be legislative: the king, divinely chosen or inspired, makes the laws. In the second case, that relation is one of execution: the king applies laws that are intrinsically divine and have no need of him to exist. The third possibility is that of a direct association between the political power and the law that leaves the divine completely outside the entire sphere of the juridical and the political. That last structural arrangement, which appeared at a relatively late date, bears some resemblance to our own situation. The other two, in contrast, were the two alternatives available to the ancient world.

The Law of the Divine King: Egypt

Egypt represents what is probably the clearest example of the first arrangement. It was quite possibly in Egypt that something resembling a state appeared for the first time in history. State power as an abstract entity ceased to coincide with the persons who gave that power material form. With the XIIth dynasty (1994–1781 BCE) a distinction between the wealth of the state and the personal fortune of the king first appears.[5]

In Egypt, terms such as *hp* or *wj* can be translated as "law." They designate "a universally valid rule, usually decreed by the king (or by a god) and concerning singular and concrete states of fact," and they originally specified a punishment.[6] The law is a collection of individual cases, to the point that the plural *hpw* is attested before the singular *hp*, which figures as an abstract term only very late and in demotic texts.[7]

The law was the word of the pharaoh: "Thus says the law of Pharaoh (*hr.f m p3 hp n pr-'3*)."[8] The literal meaning of the word "pharaoh" (*pr-'3*), a term that has become familiar to us through the Bible and the Qur'an, is the "big house," or the royal palace. It becomes the title of the sovereign beginning in the XVIIIth dynasty, hence relatively late in the course of Egyptian history. The term does not designate the king in general, however, as Egyptian has other words for that, but rather the sovereign who is reigning at a given moment. If the laws are presented as the pharaoh's words, he must have had to ratify his predecessors' decrees.[9]

Did ancient Egypt write down its laws? That depends on what is meant by "write." The determinative of *hp* is a roll of papyrus, but this is also true of all terms that designate abstractions.[10] Some scholars have identified as written laws bands represented in a fresco depicting a trial on the wall of the tomb of Rekh-mi-Re in Thebes, but this interpretation has been disputed.[11] In any event, we have no monumental inscription with a juridical content. Ancient Egypt had two modes of writing, paralleling the two styles of architecture, in stone and in mud brick. The first writing style corresponds to a desire for a permanent record; the second reflects immediate needs.[12] If the Egyptians redacted laws, it is interesting that they did so exclusively on perishable materials. Their laws may have been written, but they were never inscribed.

In Egypt there seems not to have been any attempt to systematize the law into a code organized according to principles from which rules could be derived. This probably reflects a more general aspect of the structure of Egyptian thought, which prefers parataxis and the juxtaposition of elements to syntax, which organizes such elements according to a determinate point of view.[13]

Egypt opted for the second solution regarding the law: juridical decisions come from men and are not dictated by the gods. It may be that the king, who is a divine being, issues a decree, but that does not mean that the law itself is divine. Thus the king is the source of law because he is a god, the "perfect god" (*ntr nfr*) living on earth. The idea that a king might stray from the law and merit punishment as a consequence seems not to appear before the "Demotic Chronicle" in the third century BCE. That did not prevent the king from presenting himself as obedient to the gods, who give him formal instructions rather than counsel.[14]

Thus men are not delivered over to arbitrary choice; they are subordinate to something other. Nonetheless, this is not to say that they regulate their actions according to principles external to themselves; rather, they are inspired from within by a divine wisdom, the *ma'at*. This central concept of Egyptian thought can be translated as "justice" as well as "truth." The law thus depends on a instance higher than itself, which could, if desired, be characterized as divine.[15]

The law, so defined, is simply an overall framework, within which the divine is not responsible for details: "The *ma'at* is the 'generating principle' of legislation, but it is never a codified law. What comes from God is only the general directive, not the details of content. The *ma'at* is a 'canon'—in the original, Greek, sense of the word—that orients all legislation in the fashion of a generative and regulating principle, but it is never the explicit and total content of codified juridical dispositions."[16]

With the idea of *ma'at* Egypt came close to the notion of natural law. The "Protests of the Eloquent Peasant" include a formula that lends credence to that supposition. The plaintiff asks the judge to render justice, appealing to the lord of justice-truth (*ma'at*), in this case the god Thoth. He adds an obscure phrase (*ntj wn ma'at nt ma'at.f*), for which various translations have been proposed, but all of which assert, in varying degree, that the justice of that god is justice itself.[17] Whatever the case may be, if *ma'at* is the superior instance that measures the justice of the laws, that means that it is not itself a law.

The Law of the Divine King: Mesopotamia

Although ancient Mesopotamia differs from Egypt in that it has transmitted law texts to us, it too has left no code. Even what has long been called "The Code of Hammurabi" is not a code at all. We possess texts of judgments, contemporary and of a later date, that make no mention of that supposed "Code." Hence it must be something more like an anthology of exemplary juridical decisions.[18]

In the ancient Middle East the divine aids the sovereign in his lawmaking activities. The oldest text of a law that we possess, the Ur-Nammu edict, which dates from the mid-eleventh century BCE, includes a theological prologue.[19] Similarly, in the inscription on the famous stele where he boasts of his activities as a judge, Hammurabi (ca. 1750 BCE) presents himself as operating under the protection of Anum and Enlil.[20] Still, although the god is described as assisting the king, thus lending legitimacy to his legislation, the god is not considered as being himself the origin of the enacted laws. The religious and the political are juxtaposed rather than merged. There are two signs of this. First, the "theological" prologues are written in a different style from that of the laws that follow them, and were probably provided by palace poets rather than by jurists. "Prologues and epilogues are above all religious documents, which distinguishes them from the juridical rules, which are almost exclusively profane in character." And second: "It is remarkable that for the crimes mentioned at the end of the epilogues (on the destruction or modification of the text or the stele), no threat other than divine punishment is offered. No judiciary pursuit, backed by the laws, is expressed, even though these are crimes against the authority of the sovereign. Perhaps the laws promulgated by the king had only a limited value in the sacred sphere."[21]

Divine Law

The first of the alternatives just outlined is to attribute divinity to the king, who supposedly dictates the law; the second is, precisely, the idea of divine law. As this is the topic of the present book as a whole, I shall offer only a brief summary here. The idea of divine law represents a shortcut: divinity applies to the law itself and not to a living person who "makes the law." At first sight, it seems odd to attribute divinity to an abstraction incapable of putting itself into effect. In reality, the one may compensate for the other here: it is precisely because the law is incapable of imposing itself unaided that it needs divine legitimation. We shall see this movement in operation in the Old Testament with the idea of Torah.[22] It is to some extent analogous to the decisive turning point reached in Greece in roughly the same period with the idea of Nature. In both cases, something resembling an objectification takes place: a third term appears, independent of human partners, that permits communication. To describe a law as divine is to refuse to reduce it to the conditions of its formulation.[23]

The process of setting up a dual relationship between the idea of law and that of divinity can be observed in both Greece and ancient Israel, and hence the idea of divine law appears in the two sources of Western civilization. "This notion," Leo Strauss writes, "the divine law, it seems to me is the common ground between the Bible and Greek philosophy. . . . The common ground between the Bible and Greek philosophy is the problem of divine law. They solve that problem in a diametrically opposed manner."[24]

Greek divine law is divine because it expresses the profound structures of a permanent natural order; Jewish Law is divine because it emanates from a god who is master of history. In both cases, it is external to the human and transcends the quotidian.

Divinity can be the origin of the law: the law comes from the divine, in ways that remain to be determined, such as dictation or inspiration. Divinity can also be an intrinsic characteristic of the law, which is then supposed to possess such divine characteristics as perfection or eternity. Finally, it can be a mixture of the two: the law comes from the divine *and* reflects the divine, which means that the law can be traced back to the Lawgiver. These responses to the question of the divinity of the law can be ranged between two extremes: at one extremity there is a law with no particularly intrinsic character but that is divine simply because it is taken as commanded by God; at the other extreme, and in symmetrical fashion, there is a law that is perfect but not necessarily dependent on a divine origin, or for which the question of origin has disappeared from view.

Now that we have cleared the way, all that remains to be done is to set off.

The Greek Idea of Divine Law

We need to begin with a few words to recall what constitutes the *degré zéro*—square one—of the connection between the political and the religious: classical Greece. The history of the emergence of Greek thought has been written as the laicization of a religious mentality to the advantage of the "positive"—that is, of the profane. In politics, the "Oriental" figure of the sacred king was eclipsed by democracy. At the same time, and in a parallel development, the vision of the world of the Ionian cosmogonies presents a "desacralization of knowledge, the advent of a kind of thought foreign to religion."[1]

If Greece loosened the connection between power and divinity, it also formed the idea of "divine law" and—even at that early date—that of law itself, the genus of which divine law is a species. The idea of law is by no means self-evident, however. The same is true of the words that designate it. Studying these will help us understand the underlying materials from which Greece managed to disengage the idea of law.

Law and Custom

Along with the term *nomos*, Greek has words formed on the radical **dh,* such as *thesmos* or *themis.*[2] It also reserves a special term, *psephisma,* for measures that a political body decides to adopt in determinate circumstances and by vote, in decisions that are immediately branded as being of human origin.

The Word Nomos

In the word *nomos,* the notion of law is not immediately detached from that of mores. *Nomos* designates positive laws as well as usages or customs. Plato draws a distinction: among the "laws" (*nomos*) are "what are commonly termed 'unwritten laws' (*agrapha nomima*)."[3] The etymology of the word, derived from the verb *nemo*, refers to the idea of pasturage, thus permitting wordplay about the lawgiver as shepherd.[4] The term is a relatively late one, not found in Homer. This fact has been used for apologetic purposes to defend the anteriority of Moses over Greece's most ancient poet.[5]

In Hesiod, where *nomos* is first attested, the word designates custom, a manner of acting, a "way" in the broadest sense. The use of terms that belong to the juridical vocabulary to designate the manner of being of a thing is not exclusive to Greece: such terms include the Akkadian *urtu*, the Latin *pactum* (*hoc pacto*), and the Greek *dike* (accusative *diken*). In the Bible the word for "judgment" (*mishpat*) also designates what we would call a being's "natural" manner of behaving.[6] Thus Hesiod writes that "the son of Cronos has ordained this law (*nomos*) . . . that fishes and beasts and winged fowl should devour one another."[7] Obviously, here *nomos* does not designate a commandment or even, more generally, an activity endowed with value. Quite to the contrary, immediately following this, the poet insists on man's duty to avoid similar acts. Animals have no *dike*; Zeus has given that to humankind alone. The poet knows this *dike* and teaches it.[8]

With the advent of Athenian democracy, the idea of a norm passes from the *thesmos* imposed by an external agent to the *nomos* accepted by a group. The latter term changes meaning: once equivalent to "custom," laws come to be defined as "all the rules approved and enacted by the majority in an assembly, whereby they declare what ought and what not ought to be done."[9]

Law and Divinity

The normative and the divine are associated at first under the figure of the goddesses of the law, Themis and Dike.[10] The divine appears as the origin of the normative when Homer speaks of Zeus as conferring on the king the scepter and "judgments" (*themistes*). This gift permits him to rule and "take counsel for his people" ("lead the deliberations": *bouleusthai*).[11] This process does not imply dictating a rule of behavior, any more than it does later for Hesiod.

Some authors came to attribute divinity to the *thesmoi*. Thus Aeschylus has one of the Erinnyes (Furies) speak of their perfect *thesmos*, "the ordinance ratified unto me by Fate under grant made by the gods."[12] But this may be explained by the position in the universe granted to those divinities of vengeance by the gods. The mention of fate reminds us that the laws are imposed on the gods rather than produced by them. For Xenophon, the prayers of those who ask the gods for things not in conformity with those rules (*athemita*) are no more answered than are men's demands of one another for things contrary to human laws (*paranoma*). All action is subject to a simple requirement of internal coherence.[13] Solon viewed the ideal of *eunomia* as something like a divine order, but if an order is divine, it is not because it allegedly comes from a mythical act on the part of the divinity but rather because it is inspired by the legality and the necessity immanent in man's political being.[14] A number of authors attach the vague concept of "unwritten laws" to the gods and ascribe them to the gods and the ancestors. Thus Demosthenes, in a much-quoted passage, writes that "every law (*nomos*) is an invention and gift of the gods."[15]

Sophocles alone, however, makes us understand the significance of the divinity of a law. In a well-known passage in the play of the same name, Antigone says of the laws to which she appeals, against Creon's decree, that "none knows when first they were." This is because they have, in fact, never appeared at all: they are manifest to such a degree that they need no point of emergence.[16] In a chorus in *Oedipus Rex*, perhaps in response to the Sophists' attacks on the divine origin of the laws, Sophocles speaks of laws "that live on high; laws begotten in the clear air of heaven, whose only father is Olympus; no mortal nature brought them to birth, no forgetfulness (*latha*) shall lull them to sleep, for God is great in them and grows not old."[17] The mention of "the clear air of heaven" bears an implicit comparison: because the laws are divine, they are as visible as the brightness of a calm sky. The divinity of the laws signifies the permanence of their manifestness.

As it happens, this status is precisely that of the divine. Our idea of a "hidden god" has not always existed. It is formulated for the first time in a passage in Isaiah (45:15) that is as famous as it is unclear: "Truly with you God is hidden; the God of Israel, the savior!" The notion is already implicit in texts older than the Bible, however. It may have appeared in Egyptian theology in the age of Ramses, as a reaction to Akhenaton's idea that god is manifest in the living disk of the sun.[18] For the Greeks, what has no assignable origin is divine. This is the case with rumors: they spread without anyone's knowing who began them; they are attributed to "someone," and they are believed with no other authority than themselves, or else simply because everyone is repeating them. According to Homer, such rumors (*ossa* or *pheme*) come from Zeus; according to Hesiod, "Talk is in some ways divine." The same idea lies behind the proverb, *vox populi, vox dei*.[19] In this perspective, the divine is in no way hidden, hence has no need to be revealed. Thus Pindar associates what is divine with what is manifest, to the point of calling a goddess of his invention (as an explanation of the source of the visible) the "mother of the Sun" and naming her simply Theia, "the divine."[20]

The Gods Do Not Make Laws

It is because the divine laws are manifest that they do not have to be made known: they require no promulgation. More than the absence of written form, it is the absence of proclamation in general that is most characteristic of the so-called "unwritten" law.[21] In this context, unwritten laws are associated with the gods, as in *Antigone*, where Sophocles mentions "God's ordinances (*theōn nomima*), unwritten (*agrapta*), and secure."[22] For Sophocles, "written" and "divine" are mutually exclusive: either a law is "written," in which case it is human, or else it is divine, hence cannot be written. Other authors risk the same association, but the "writing" they speak of seems essentially metaphorical. Thus a pious young man, Euripides' Ion, asks the gods: "How is it right that you who prescribe [write? *grapsantas*] laws for mortals should yourselves be guilty of lawlessness (*anomia*)?"[23] It is never the gods who compose the oracular verses delivered by the Pythia.[24]

To be sure, the gods are invoked as guaranteeing sworn rights, and they punish the guilty.[25] But they are not the source of law. A god never issues a commandment. Of course, the Olympian gods do not hesitate to intervene to instruct one person or another about what he or she should do in a specific situation. They like to give advice, as Athena often does to her favorite, Ulysses. And the Delphic Apollo ceaselessly delivers oracles. One god, Hermes, does so in a special fashion: he gives warnings to men, as in a famous passage at the beginning of the *Odyssey*, which provides an excellent example of the way in which the gods behave in relation to the law. The context is the story of Agamemnon, killed by his wife's lover, then avenged by his son. The divine messenger has no need to state that adultery and murder are detestable in the eyes of Zeus. He does not cite the commandments of the Decalogue. He simply states a hypothetical imperative: do not give in to temptation, for vengeance will follow. A philosophical transposition of the idea can be found in a lapidary formula of Aristotle: "The god is a governor not in prescriptive fashion."[26]

Rome's conception of "divine law" (*ius divinum*) was similar in sentiment to the Greek. It even presupposed something like a desacralization: divine law was not law revealed by the gods but was rather the right of humans to establish with the gods a system of predictable relations.[27] When Rome and Hellenism combined forces, they both considered (or would have considered) ridiculous the Jewish idea of the gods dictating a path of action to be followed and behavior to be observed—the *halakhah* of the Jews or the *sharia* of Islam—as a matter of principle and in all circumstances. In the third century Galen mocked, not the content of the laws of Moses, but the manner in which Moses gave them to the Jews, without offering the slightest proof, simply stating: "This is what the LORD has commanded" (Exodus 35:4). Galen's contemporary, Alexander of Aphrodisias (ca. 198) makes fun of the Stoics, whom he caricatures as disputing such grave questions as: Should one cross one's legs when listening to a philosopher lecture? Can one take the biggest portion when dining with one's father?[28]

The Philosophers

The birth of philosophy introduced the concept, indissolubly connected with it, of nature (*physis*). The appearance of this notion upset the entire sphere of reflection. Henceforth, the "law" had to be situated in relation to "nature," either in opposition to it, becoming pure convention, or in articulation with it, as "natural law." The philosophers proposed various formulations of the relationship between "law" and "nature": for them, the idea of divinity operated within that relationship.

The Earliest Philosophers

In what has come down to us from ancient Greece, the expression "divine law" is first found in Heraclitus, in a fragment that declares that "all the laws of men are nourished (*trephontai*) by one law, the divine law."[29] As is often the case, the meaning of this dictum is highly obscure. Since in the Greek the word "law" is not repeated here, one might conclude that human laws take nourishment from the divine. But of what does that "nourishment" consist? Is it a derivation from a source? Or is it a consolidation, according to another sense of the verb in question, or even a tutelage? What role is played by the ambiguity of the word *nomos*, which also designates a source of nourishment?

Heraclitus does not speak of the gods, but of the divine. All the philosophers in fact tend to neutralize divinity. And the divinity of the laws, according to them, depends on the fact that they come, not from the gods, but from the divine. We need to distinguish between the gods and the source from which they hold their divinity, or, to put it differently, between the divine and what of the divine is crystallized in one concrete figure or another, such as the Olympian gods.[30] The adjective "divine" thus takes on a broader extension than the gods themselves and can be used to describe, for example, what is "natural." The archaic opposition between nature and custom (*physis/nomos*) gives way to a harmony: one can speak of a *nomos* of *physis*. Thus the law must come from what is the most divine in us, which is the intellect. The idea can be found in Plato: "Of all studies, that of legal regulations, provided they be rightly framed, will prove the most efficacious in making the learner a better man; for were it not so, it would be in vain that our divine and admirable law (*nomos*) bears a name akin to reason (*nous*)."[31] Plato makes no distinction between laws that are divine and laws that are not: according to him, the law is intrinsically divine.

The same play on words can be found in Aristotle: "He therefore that recommends that the law (*nomos*) shall govern seems to recommend that God and reason (*nous*) alone shall govern, but he that would have man govern adds a wild animal also." It follows that those who are subject to that "law" which is as if divine, and even more so, those who might be said to be a law unto themselves, are like gods among men. The idea of natural law appears in Aristotle, who distinguishes between the law proper to a specific city and the common law. The first of these may or may not be written; the second is according to nature (*kata phusin*). The passage in question refers to Sophocles' *Antigone* and to Empedocles.[32]

Hellenistic Theories

The Stoics were apparently the first to make systematic use of the expression "divine law." The content of the phrase is seldom explicit, but is there really any need that it be so? Epictetus defines the law of God as "To guard what is his own, not to lay claim to what is not his own, but to make use of what is given him, and not to yearn for what has not been given."[33] Here the expression designates the eternal reason of God, and of a god who is not distinct from nature. The idea is often present among the Stoics, as are the words. In Stoic thought the law is the expression of the immanent divine, present in the world and animating it. Natural law is divine; it is identified with Zeus.[34] It is divine because the city that it governs is, first and foremost, the dwelling of the gods, and only secondarily the city of men, just as children qualify as citizens because their fathers are citizens.[35] The laws of human cities are thus relative, to the benefit of cosmopolitanism. The laws do not draw their authority from being the voice of the city; there is another source of authority, which is no longer the state, but reason. This is why Stoicism is situated more on the level of morality than on that of law.[36]

According to Cicero, who follows the Stoics here, law is "the highest reason, implanted in Nature" (*ratio summa insita in natura*); nature is governed by the gods and *ratio* creates a primary society between man and the gods; the universe is a city common to the gods and men. Law and divinity are not connected directly, but through reason. The divinity of the law does not reside in its nature as commandment. The law is eternal: it is the mind of God (*mens dei*). It has been given by the gods to humankind: "The true and primal (*princeps*) law, applied to command and prohibition, is the right reason of supreme Jupiter (*ratio est recta summi Iovis*)." The world obeys God as it obeys a law.[37]

This vision of things competes with the idea that the king is the "living law." This ancient idea, according to Musonius Rufus, may be of Persian origin, passed on by Euripides with a negative cast to it—the king holds the law in his hands—and by Aristotle with a more positive slant: the best are themselves law.[38] The "Pythagorean" theorists of kingship provide a sweeping orchestration of the theme, with a cosmological parallel: the king is to the political community what God is to the universe.[39] In Pseudo-Archytas, the idea of "living law" replaces the notion of divine law as the opposite of inanimate law, which is the letter of the law.[40] The formula comes into the Roman world with Cicero, for whom the magistrate is a "talking law," and with Ulpian it finds a place within systematic law.[41]

From Divine Law to the God-Law

We encounter the expression "divine law" among later thinkers, but the meaning of the adjective "divine" remains fluid. With them as well, no specific law is decreed by a god or by the supreme God. Plotinus speaks of "divine law" in connection with the destiny of souls, perhaps echoing an expression from Plato's *Phaedrus*.[42] Hierocles speaks of man as an amphibious animal placed between two levels of being who, according to the ethical choices he makes, can rise or fall, which he does by neglecting the divine laws and stripping himself of his innate dignity.[43]

Porphyry distinguishes three sorts of law: divine, mortal, and conventional. "The divine law is unknown to the soul that folly and intemperance have rendered impure, but it shines forth in self-control and wisdom. It is impossible to transgress this, for there is nothing in man that can transcend it. Nor can it be despised, for it cannot shine forth in a man who will despise it. Nor is it moved by chances of fortune, because it is in truth superior to chance and stronger than any form of violence. Mind alone knows it, and diligently pursues the search thereafter, and finds it imprinted in itself."[44]

Certain expressions suppose the taking of a further step to state that law and god can be one and the same. More often, however, the affirmation that the laws are gods is little more than a figure of speech. One unidentified tragic poet asserts that the law is the greatest god for men; Plato states that the law is the god of temperate men; and the Stoic Hierocles declares that the laws of the land must be respected as if they were second gods.[45] Other texts are to be taken more seriously. Thus Plutarch asserts that "Zeus does not have Justice to sit beside him, but is himself Justice and Right (*Themis*) and the oldest and most perfect of laws."[46] One can even follow Themistius, for one, and speak of God as the law of the world.[47]

Plato

The idea that the divine law could also be the law of a polis, or, to put it the other way around, that the law or the laws of a human community might be divine, is almost absent in the ancient world. Plato represents a conspicuous exception to the rule. This is one of the reasons for treating him apart from the other philosophers, another being his strong influence in the Islamic and Jewish Middle Ages.[48]

The Divine Origin of the Laws?

The Platonic dialogue that is central to the question that concerns us here is obviously the *Laws*. The question of origin is posed in it. Other, earlier dialogues prepared the way for this work, which is very probably the last one that Plato either wrote or sketched out. In the *Meno*, divine characteristics are attributed, probably with a touch of bitter irony, to the statesman who, without really knowing why, succeeds in his enterprises. In the *Republic*, it is the ideal model of the city that is characterized as divine. By extension, those who participate in it by imitation—the philosophers—are also worthy of being called "divine." The laws and customs of existing cities are evaluated by the level of "the divine" or "the bestial" that they contain.[49]

In the *Laws*, the problem of the connection between the theological and the political is presented in light of human legislation: the argument concerns the laws of a particular city, the foundation of which is a human task, entrusted to actual men. In this, the city is different from earlier cities, where the inverse was true: their concrete existence in incontestable, but their foundation is attributed to heroes or demigods supposed to have lived in an indeterminate past. Moreover, because the foundation of the city in question is still to come, it is appropriate to raise questions, not about a specific city, but about the best city possible. This necessarily leads to discussion of the ultimate presuppositions of the civil existence of humankind, which must come to the fore and can be taken into account precisely as such.

The adjective "divine" appears often in the *Laws*, and the very first word of the dialogue is "God," who appears, precisely, in the role of a lawgiver. Did a god or a man create the laws of Crete and of Sparta? Thus divinity puts its stamp on the entire dialogue, which will insist on the scant importance

of human affairs in comparison with the divine realities and on the normative role that is the gods', not men's. The measure is no longer dialectics but
theology, which determines the order of what is worthy of honor: God, then
things divine, and finally, among the latter, the soul.[50]

Plato retains the idea that it is the divine that must command. Human
nature is not capable of governing itself without aid: it needs divine sovereignty, which operates through the mediation of the *nomos*. Plato begins
with a simple constatation of fact: no man has ever created a law: what creates the laws are instead encounters (*tukhe*) and coincidences (*sumphora*).
Montesquieu might subscribe to just this sort of remark, and with him the
entire sociological tradition. Far from stopping here, however, Plato notes
that one can also opt for another point of view and state that a god steers all
things, accompanied by encounter and the occasion (*kairos*), to which competence (*tekhne*) is added. Thus the laws are indeed the result of divine inspiration, and the opinions regarding the origin of the laws with which the
dialogue opened are confirmed, but on a higher level.[51] The idea of a divine
law resulting from a legislative act is thus attested in the *Laws*, just as it in
the *Minos*, if in fact that dialogue is indeed Plato's.[52]

The Laws as a Substitute for the Reign of the Gods

If the divine holds power, is the resulting law positive law? A passage quoted
above states that the judge must study the *letter* of the law in order to become a better judge, thanks to the close connection between the law (*nomos*)
and the intellect (*nous*). The city that is founded is thus a "divine regime"
(*theia politeia*). But its laws must be preceded by prologues capable of
persuading the citizens of the legitimacy of the laws. The very existence of
those prologues, however, excludes the possibility that the laws that follow
them can have been revealed. Taking the contrary position, Posidonius regrets Plato's addition of prologues to his laws, declaring that he himself
prefers laws to be "a voice, as it were, sent down from heaven."[53]

For Plato, the very fact that laws exist proves, by implication, that man is
no longer immediately tied to the divine. If the divine had any influence
over the city, it would exercise it through an intermediary, a political figure
whom it would inspire, and that inspiration (*theia moira*) would render all
law superfluous. However, we do not even know whether "the Good wishes
us well"; whether there is a providence for civil communities. Where the
Republic supposes that such a providence does not exist, the *Laws* let us understand the contrary by providing an example: Sparta is the very type of a
city saved by god—that is, by the good fortune of having its two first kings
born as twins—and producing such inspired men as Lycurgus.[54]

The myth of the reign of the god Cronus relates, in any event, that in his love for humanity he placed it under the care of divinities (*daimōn*): it is that government that we should imitate, "giving to reason's ordering (*dianome*) the name of 'law.'"[55] The political is thus the imperfect substitute for superior beings in the government of men: the political is rendered necessary by the departure of those superior beings, leaving humankind to its own devices. The political becomes secularized when the law (*nomos*) replaces the divine shepherd (*nomeus*).[56]

The divine is the presence of a sovereign principle too lofty to be pinned down in an explicit statement of any kind, and in particular in written form. Ideally, the divine that is to command is not external; it is the intellect, lodged both deep within every human being and at the inner depths of the structure of the physical universe. The gods are not the lawgivers of cities, but they are of the cosmos. The demiurge of the *Timeus* may be a worker, but he is also a lawgiver.[57] In book 10 of the *Laws*, the argument that attempts to establishing the existence of the gods results in a reversal of the commonly admitted order between the natural and the artificial. It is commonly accepted that art (*techne*) comes after nature (*phusis*); what one must understand is that the soul is anterior to anything that is body, consequently, what is supposed to be nature is nothing other than a divine art.[58]

Legislation about the Divine

Although the divinely inspired political man remains an exception, the representatives of the divine that really exist—the priests—must be decisively kept away from power. Plato exorcises the image of the priest-king and imputes it to Egypt.[59]

For Plato, the laws are not divine in origin, but they must nevertheless pay attention to the divine. The new Magnesia, the city still to be founded, will have laws relating to temples, sacrifices, hymns, and the honor paid to the dead. This is necessarily so, because all cities have an implicit relationship with the divine. The Athenian Stranger states that a city of atheists is impossible. Theology is the foundation of the state. Reaction against that supposition and the forms derived from it that were fashioned many centuries later laid the groundwork for Bayle's famous paradox about the possibility of a society of atheists.[60] For Plato, the laws must punish those who believe that the laws can do everything, including create gods; the atheist imagines, in fact, that the gods exist in virtue of certain laws.[61] Thus the laws must defend against gods that they have not created, but which exist by nature. Law comes to the aid of nature and, according to a dictum that Aristotle applied to the arts, "on the basis of Nature," they "carry things further than Nature can." In doing so, the law manifests its status as an artificial object.[62] By the same token, rejection of the idea of a civil theology, such as Varro was to define it several centuries later, leads Plato to something resembling a penal theology.

The classification of impiety that Plato attempted to outline met with an extraordinary success: Montesquieu declared, "Plato says there all of the most sensible things that natural enlightenment has ever said on the subject of religion."[63] There are three levels of impiety: believing that there are no gods; believing that the gods exist, but care nothing for humankind; believing that they exist and care about men, but that they can be swayed by prayers and sacrifices. The three levels are interconnected, as they are in Gorgias' treatise on *Non-Being*, both formally and, up to a point, in their content (existence, awareness, communication).[64] For the Athenian Stranger, the task is to counter all forms of impiety by asserting the existence of the gods, their providence, and their moral incorruptibility. The three errors of impiety must be eradicated by both persuasion and force, which is conceived as a prolongation of persuasion by other means.

⟡

In Greece and for everyone subjected to the influence of Greek thought, the idea of "divine law" is thus quite familiar—indeed, much more so than the idea of a "law of God." When it qualifies the law, the adjective "divine" indicates no trace of an origin in a god designated by a substantive, even less by a proper noun. It is the sign of a divinity that presents itself effectively only as an adjective, ready to be applied to just about anything: to the natural world and its marvels, including the immortal ones; among human things, to what has always been present and can be found everywhere; and to whatever it is within man that has access to the highest realities.

As for the second term, the idea of "law" is not presented as the expression of an explicit will, but rather as issuing from the intimate depths of things, as an emanation of what is most inherent to them. On occasion this applies to what has occurred within a given territory from time immemorial, thus merging law with custom; conversely, it can operate at the other extreme of the universal, extracted by philosophical reflection from deep within reality, In both cases, the law expresses something like the *nature* of what is.

Where the divine describes a law or a group of laws, it does so as an element operating within the physical world, in the context of what Jan Assmann calls "cosmotheism."[65] In contrast, as we shall see, the divine law of postbiblical and medieval thought appertains to a god outside the world, but who intervenes in it.

3

Historical Conditions of Alliance

In Greece, divine law was an idea with a regulatory function: at the most, it could complete or correct human legislation. In the Middle East, it acquired the force of operative law, regulating a real society. Classical Hellenism had no holy books, no authoritative sacred texts. There were authors who were universally respected, even widely committed to memory. Homer is perhaps the educator of Greece, the figure that formed its *Volksgeist,* and as such, the author of an almost sacred work, but that does not mean that his works should be put on the same plane as revealed documents. Mythology never crystallized into a system permitting the discrimination of authentic, canonical versions from possible additions. It was only at a quite late date that Hellenism attempted to give itself sacred books, at times awkwardly, as with the *Chaldean Oracles,* which—and the detail is telling—were supposed to have originated in the East.

What I intend to examine now are the real divine laws—that is, the books that were presented as containing a legislation divine in character. I shall recall the historical conditions of appearance of such systems. For methodological reasons, rather than treating the content of these sacred books, I will focus on their context alone. The texts will of course make an appearance, but uniquely as historical documents, to be investigated for the information they can provide about their redaction.

Israel

Situated in a region of a tormented geography that can shelter only small groups of humans, the land of Israel lay between two river basins favorable to the creation of vast empires. Both a route to elsewhere and a battlefield, Israel was tossed about by the two dominant civilizations—Egypt and Mesopotamia—whose influence and even domination it underwent.

A Brief Encounter

Unlike those two great river civilizations, Israel had only a limited experience of life under a genuine state, which meant, given the time and the place, under a king. Royalty began with Saul (d. 1010 BCE), and continued with David (d. 970) and Solomon (d. 931). The latter two succeeded in creating a unified state with all the accouterments of power: a fixed capital, a permanent army, and a bureaucracy.[1] Soon after, however, the kingdom divided in two. The experiment had lasted for a century. Each half had a ruling dynasty until the collapse of the Kingdom of Israel (with its capital in Samaria) in 722 BCE and that of Judah (capital, Jerusalem) in 587.

The situation before the creation of kingship was presented as anarchy. In fact, the redactor of the Book of Judges ends his text with the words, "In those days there was no king in Israel; everyone did what he thought best."[2] This image is a retrospective projection, however: in reality, the situation was perhaps one of a federation of the Twelve Tribes.[3] At worst, this was a regulated anarchy that ceased the moment the existence of the people was threatened. When that occurred, a chief (*shōfet*, traditionally translated as "judge") was named; remaining in power for a certain period and returning to private life once the danger had passed, like a Roman *dictator*.

It is everything that goes beyond fulfilling this immediate function that differentiates a king from a judge. The shift from the one to the other took place in stages: a first attempt by Abimelech, the son of Gideon, proved unsuccessful (Judges 9), and royalty "took" only with Saul. Almost never did Israel manage to assemble and possess, simultaneously, all the elements of a mature royal system: a stable royal line, ruling over a unified people, that outlasted the king. Saul was in fact king for life and reigned over all of Israel, but his reign ended dramatically in something like a suicide. The reign of David was marked by the revolt of Absalom (2 Samuel 13–20); Solomon's accession was the result of harem intrigues, recounted in a perfectly demythologized style (1 Kings 1–2). Primogeniture was not established, at least as a principle, until Solomon, who was succeeded by his son Rehoboam. The kingdom was immediately divided, however, and precisely for reasons connected with the harsh and authoritarian fiscal extractions of the state (1 Kings 12:4).

After the Judean elite had returned from exile in Babylonia (538), Judea became a Persian protectorate with only limited autonomy. It retained that status under the Hellenistic sovereigns, first the Ptolemies of Egypt (333–197), then the Seleucids of Syria (197–142). The revolt of the Maccabees against the latter opened a period of greater autonomy, modified only slightly under Roman domination, a period that ended in 63 BCE with Pompey's capture of Jerusalem. Sporadic revolts led to the destruction of the Second Temple in 70 CE, and to the Romanization of Jerusalem itself in 135.

Between the Desert and the Messiah

This historical situation was not without consequences for thought: in Israel, the state did not have enough time to become well established, and Israel always remained doubly uncomfortable with state institutions.

First, Israel had never shaken off nostalgia for an earlier period, either that of nomadic life in the desert or that of "liberty" under the Judges. Such texts could hardly have been produced in the age of the kings. Moreover, that sort of society was not so much pre-state as anti-state, in reaction against a Canaanite or Egyptian state model. One indication of this is that the Hebrew word for "free man" (*hofshi*) means "slave" in Canaanite.[4] Israel remembered the event of the Exodus as a passage from servitude into liberty. The founding event, the "primitive scene," was the Exodus—that is, the break with the state (in this case, the Egyptian state). Memory of that event was periodically revived, in snatches in the prophets, then as a unified narration in the Pentateuch.[5]

Second, Israel elaborated its thought in the painful awareness of having lost something valuable that it had hardly enjoyed, and it compensated for that loss by the messianic dream. The idea of Messiah transposes that of the ideal king into the historical dimension. In the literary genre of "Mirrors for Princes" the ideal king is presented as a permanent type; in the messianic idea, in contrast, the ideal king is yet to come. Thus the political is held within a tension between the pre-political and the meta-political, if not laminated between the two.

Christianity

Once it had moved beyond Palestine, Christianity seemed a private affair. The earliest communities, as both St. Paul and the opponents of the new faith remarked, were made up largely of humble folk. They formed associations centered on works of charity (burying the dead, for example), working on the edges of "proper society" in what represented a "new theocratic secession."[6]

Persecutions

These groups operated not only at the margins of society but also in opposition to the Roman Empire. The imperial cult—sacrificing to the statue of the emperor—was above all an expression of a form of loyalty. Judaism was a "permitted religion" (*religio licita*), and it benefited from an exemption from the imperial cult. Leaving the synagogue meant giving up the Jewish umbrella and exposing oneself to persecution, which was in fact launched at various times and places and first by the Jewish authorities. For the first time people who observed the Law were persecuted as heretics (*minim*) for reason of their belief.[7] Acts 12:1–2 tells us that between 41 and 44, Herod Agrippa persecuted the primitive community. In Matthew 5:10 and Mark 13:9–13 Jesus announces persecutions. There is an allusion to the expulsion of the early Christian community from the synagogue in Luke 6:22. These were followed by the executions of Stephen and James, "the brother of Jesus" around 62 CE.[8] The most famous persecutor was of course Paul of Tarsus.

The Romans then took up the task. It is in the context of Roman persecutions that we find the earliest pagan mentions of Christians, for example, in a letter of Pliny the Younger to Trajan of about 111. A few years later, around 115, Tacitus speaks of Nero's persecutions of the Christians, adding, "Christus, the founder (*auctor*) of the name [of the Christians], had undergone the death penalty in the reign of Tiberius, by sentence of the procurator Pontius Pilate." This dry mention is important, because it supposes the existence of an official document that Tacitus may have consulted in the archives. Suetonius, writing around 120, speaks of a certain "Chrestos."[9] He may easily have taken the adjective *christos*, a word that he probably did not understand, for a proper noun, Chrestos ("good").

The first Roman persecutor of Christians seems to have been Nero, who accused Christians of setting fire to Rome in 64. There were sporadic and localized persecutions under other emperors: Domitian in 96, Marcus Aurelius in Lyon in 177, Trajan in 211. Persecution of Christians became systematic policy only with Decius in 249. In 296, Diocletian purged the army of Christians and, beginning in 303, he launched a general persecution. That did not stop Christian propaganda. Galerius decided to put an end to Christian persecution in 311.

Constantine

A few years later Constantine went one step further than Galerius: the edict of Milan of 313 guaranteed Christians a tolerance that almost amounted to official recognition of Christianity. The founding of the city of Constantinople in 324 responded to a desire for an entirely Christian capital city without pagan temples.

It is hard to know what led the emperor to these decisions. Christian historiography has attributed his actions to a late but sincere faith; in contrast, historians of the Enlightenment saw them as a sordid political calculation. Whatever his motivations, Constantine recognized an obvious political reality, drawing the inevitable conclusions: Christians represented a large proportion of his subjects, if not the majority in certain regions. Constantine recognized an objective situation, but he was by no means the cause of it. Nor did his acts limit Christianity: to the contrary, the elimination of persecution contributed to the rising tide of conversions.

Two generations after Constantine, Theodosius made Christianity the *sole* authorized religion. He imposed obligatory acceptance of a credo (380), then prohibited the cult of the pagan gods (392). Judaism remained a *religio licita*, however, which the state was at times obliged to protect against popular sentiment. From that time on, the Roman Empire thought of itself as Christian: its history and that of Christianity were bound together. This does not mean that those two histories would continue to be considered identical, nor that the church and the state were always merged into one.

Islam

Although Islam cannot be reduced to a political act, it was in a political guise that it made its entry onto the stage of history. Once we stray from the traditional narrative, which dates from more than a century after the events themselves, the beginnings of Islam are extremely hard to reconstruct: the social and cultural context of those who narrated those events is totally different from the one in which those events are supposed to have taken place.[10]

The Conquerors

The oldest event that can be dated with certitude is the Arab conquest of the Middle East and the southern shores of the Mediterranean in the seventh century, even though we do not know what were the causes of that conquest, and perhaps never will.[11] There is nothing in the Qur'an that corresponds to the missionary call that closes the Gospel according to St. Matthew: "Go, therefore, and make disciples of all the nations" (Matt. 28:19).[12]

That conquest, which was less rapid than Alexander's, was vaster than his, and, above all, more durable. Muslims are ceaselessly reminded of it as the story of a miraculous success that propelled near-starving Bedouins from a miserable life "of sand and lice" (*raml wa-qaml*) to a fantastic opulence. It is recalled as tangible proof of the truth of religion and, in particular, of its dividends. If I may be permitted a brutal expression, Allah pays.[13] At a later date, Islam was quite conscious of the highly relative purity of the conquerors' motives. ʿUmar is quoted as saying, "You call [So-and-so] a martyr, but he had perhaps already filled up his two sacks of loot."[14] In any event, it is significant that the oldest datable document in all of Islamic history, an Egyptian papyrus, is a receipt (*entagion*) in Greek and Arabic recording a certain fellah's payment of a tax to the conquerors in the year 643.[15]

The connection between Islam and the political is perhaps still tighter than is commonly thought. The political is not only intrinsic to Islam but a constitutive part of it. The beginnings of Islam can be narrated as the birth of a state; as the transfer of functions exercised by the tribal lineage to the apparatus of a state power.[16] Islam created an original type of social organization, just as Christianity had done before it. But in the case of Islam, this was not the church but rather the "nation" (*umma*). The nation came to substitute for the social bonds traditional in pre-Islamic Arabia, based above all on blood ties: "Islam has erased the alliances."[17] Traditional ties were broken and replaced by a community of a quite different type.

In fact, the Arabian conquests brought about a redistribution of inequalities by means of expulsion from the community: the hierarchies that had distinguished one Arab from the other tended to disappear, ceding to a distinction, no longer internal to the Arab community, between conquerors and conquered. The latter were granted a status of second-class citizens, on occasion attached to agreements supposedly drawn up between Muhammad and certain groups of Jews or Christians.[18]

Thus a state based on plunder and spoils—an "État butin"—came to be formed.[19] Because the conquerors lived on the labor of the conquered, they needed to manage their dependents carefully, exploiting them wisely. At times they were even aware of this. According to an expression attributed to ʿAli, those under their protection were "the matter of Muslims." Similarly, the calif ʿUmar is supposed to have written to Abu Obeyda: "If we took those who are subjected to us and divided them among ourselves, what would be left for the Muslims who will come after us? By heaven, they would have no one left to talk to, nor any labor to profit from!"[20]

This situation mitigated internal tensions. The unity of the first community that took refuge at Medina had been created by shared pillage of caravans traveling to or from Mecca. Unity among the community of the conquerors was formed in their common exploitation of the conquered lands and peasants. Certain later jurists built a theory to explain that the non-Muslims were not the legitimate owners of their possessions. Using force of arms was simply a way to oblige them to make restitution.[21]

Throughout the initial expansion period, the struggle against a common enemy furnished an outlet for ancestral rivalries between tribes, thus providing one of the sources of the dynamism of the conquest.[22]

The Crystallization of a Religion

Conversely, it is possible that Islam as a religion explicitly different from the two other monotheistic religions dates from only shortly before the unification of Islam by ʿAbd al-Malik, the first Ummayyad caliph of the Marwān dynasty (from 685 to 705). Arabic inscriptions before that time invoked one God, but not yet a specifically Islamic God.[23] An Islamic God, distinct from the Christian Trinity and singularized by reference to Muhammad, appears clearly only at the end of the seventh century. This was when the reforms instituted by ʿAbd al-Malik imposed, among other measures, the Arabization of the administration and a nonfigurative coinage bearing Islamic inscriptions. The construction in Jerusalem of the Dome of the Rock (691) gave concrete form to Islam's dual claim to originality: in relation to Judaism by occupying the Temple Mount, and in relation to Christianity, because the Islamic building imitated the design of the Holy Sepulcher as it appeared at the time and bore anti-Trinitarian inscriptions in Qurʾanic style.

The Three Religions and Their Relation to the Political

In the medieval period all three religions had a connection with the political, but the latter was given concrete form in only two of them. The Christian religion formed Christendom, and the religion of Islam had became Islam the civilization. Judaism, on the other hand, had no state dimension. It had gone in the opposite direction, losing its political reality, first as it passed under protectorate status, then with the suppression of even the illusion of autonomy. With the destruction of the Second Temple it even lost its geographic base, instantly becoming, precisely, "Judaism," a term that, although it refers to the land of the tribe of Judah, designates by its suffix a behavior that is universally applicable.

Moreover, the two religions with a "political" dimension did not acquire it in the same way. Christianity gained ground in the ancient world against the political power of the Roman Empire, which had persecuted Christians for almost three centuries before itself adopting the Christian religion.

Islam, after a brief period of trials, triumphed during the lifetime of its founder. It then conquered, by warfare, the right to operate in peace, and even the right to dictate conditions of survival to the adepts of other religions "of the Book." In modern terms we might say that *Christianity conquered the state through civil society; Islam, to the contrary, conquered civil society through the state.*

Thus from the start Christianity set itself outside the political domain, and its founding texts bear witness to a mistrust of things political: the political terms used in the New Testament are attached to persecutors and to those who eventually crucified Christianity's central figure. Certain "Western" propositions taken to be self-evident have their roots here. God and Caesar are separate (Matt. 22:17); the cities of God and the cities of the devil are two sorts of comportment, not two political entities; the city of men is to be guided by moral rules, at times inscribed in the law, but their organization does not derive from a religious law.

A "political" dimension is instead coextensive with the Qur'anic revelation. At Mecca, the message was centered on announcement of impending Judgment, a reminder of the sorry fate of disobedient peoples, and an appeal to a conversion in which the moral and the social are inseparable. But once Muhammad settled in the city of Yathrib, subsequently named Medina ("The City [of the Prophet]"), he was surrounded by a community, the life of which required organization. What is separate in the traditional prophets was joined in Muhammad, who is both prophet and king.[24] The Qur'an set itself to laying down laws, in particular regarding marriage and inheritance. In it, it is God—not the Prophet, who is a mere instrument—who is supposed to be speaking. Political regulations bear the weight of definitive revelation, which is the revelation of a law. The same is true of the words and acts of the Prophet (*hadith*), which are taken as examples for all to adopt.

After the death of Muhammad, the caliphate "takes the place" of the Prophet, thus prolonging the way in which God, in the most widespread (although probably twisted) interpretation of a famous verse, gave the world into Adam's care.[25] Islamic political power was to continue to strive for beatitude in both this world and the next.[26] Disagreements about religious practice or belief continued to interfere with (or even coincide with) those concerning the choice of the legitimate leaders of the community (*imāmat*), thus introducing into the religious domain questions that, in our eyes, do not belong there. Conversely, the political included dimensions that Westerners take to be foreign to it. The first of these is prophetism, which also had the function of making possible the ideal city by imposing on it the Law revealed by God.

For Islam, the separation of the political and the religious has no right to exist. It is even shocking, for it appears as an abandonment of human affairs to the power of evil or a relegation of God to a place outside of his proper sphere. The ideal city must be here below. In principle, it already exists: it is the Muslim city.

PART II

The Divine Law

4

The State and the Law: Ancient Israel

Ancient Israel revolutionized the relations between the normative and the divine. But it only parted company with the world of the representations of the ancient Middle East after accompanying it for a good stretch of the road, and it is that joint voyage that we need to retrace here. One particular aspect of that world was a close and two-way connection between the divine and kingship: the divine was considered to reign; the legitimacy of the human king was thought to derive from the divine's special interest in him.

Divinity and Kingship

The link between divinity and kingship is nearly ubiquitous. The lands of Canaan were no exception: god was king (or the gods were kings), and the king participated in the divine.

The God as King

In Canaan the gods reigned in two different ways, according to whether the god in question was El or Baal. El, the supreme god and creator, ruled from the beginning; Baal, the virile god, lord of fertility and rain, was at first homeless and had to seize power by force.[1] YHWH, the god of Israel, combined the two manners of reigning. In the Bible, a group of Psalms begin with the phrase "The LORD is king" (Psalms 93, 97, 99; see also the end of Psalm 24), leading some to suppose that there was once a feast of the solemn enthronement of YHWH as God of Israel, and that these canticles were part of the liturgy for those rites.[2] The hypothesis is not indispensable, but we can in any event say that the Psalms transpose the dynamic myth in which a god accedes to power by triumphing over his rivals to a static description of a domination that he has possessed from the beginning of time.[3]

The idea according to which it is the god who reigns is ambiguous. It also occurs in Egypt, but there God reigns by an intermediary, his earthly representative, the pharaoh.[4] This solution influenced Israel, where divine investiture appears in Psalm 2:6–7: "I myself have set up my king on Zion, my holy mountain. . . . 'You are my son; this day I have begotten you.'" In Israel, however, the idea of a reign of god is exclusive: it signifies that there is no other king than YHWH, and the only legitimate regime is a theocracy. A third, and dual, interpretation supposes a sharing of responsibilities in which divine kingship counterbalances state power, thus anticipating the Christian division of roles.

The Divine Legitimation of the King

God's designation of the king is given material form by particular acts and signs, such as the unction with oil that the prophet Samuel performs for Saul, then for David. The strategies for the legitimation of the royal power and the signs that attest to it are not exclusive to Israel, but it is through Israel that they are transmitted to Christian Europe, notably in the anointing of kings.

The Greeks posed the problem of the natural or divine origin of the qualities of the ruler. The question is sometimes presented by means of the counter-image of the beehive: incontestable physical criteria make the queen bee (whom the Greeks took for a "king") stand out from the other bees.[5] It is interesting to note, however, that the usual models of natural kingship are absent from the Bible. What we do find, on the other hand, is the image of the ant as a model of a society with no authority figure, that of armies without officers, or that of locusts, which have no ruler (see Proverbs 6:7; 30:27). There is a certain piquancy in the attribution of the first of these observations on the possibility of anarchy to no less a king than Solomon (the second is attributed to Agur). The Greeks offered several sorts of response to the question of the origin of princely qualities: Xenophon, for example, mentions the king's genealogy, the nature of his body and his soul, and his upbringing.[6] Does the Bible contain narrations of how a prince acquires knowledge? Is there a biblical *Cyropaedia?*

A first response to that question centers on becoming permeated by the divine spirit. This does not always occur in the same fashion but follows the person's functions. The spirit "comes upon" the judge, "is upon" him, or "clothes" him in particular circumstances and for a limited period of time. This occurs at the outset of a military campaign in the cases of Othniel,

Gideon calling to arms, and Jephthah. It can happen simply in order to put a warrior in a trance when a private affair demands it, as with Samson (Judges 3:10; 6:34; 11:29; 14:6, 19).

Saul experienced this sort of inspiration ("the spirit of God rushed upon him"), which the author of the book of Samuel follows with an explanatory and somewhat rationalizing transposition: "and he became very angry" (literal translation: "his nose greatly heated up": 1 Sam. 11:6). Permeation by the spirit is also associated with spectacular manifestations such as prophetic delirium or is made explicit by a transformation: Saul is told, "You . . . will be changed into another man" (1 Sam. 10:6). Is this an ephemeral or a permanent transformation? The verb used can have both meanings. With King David, the infusion of the spirit is linked to his function, hence it is permanent: after being anointed by Samuel, the text tells us, "from that day on, the spirit of the LORD rushed upon David" (1 Sam. 16:13), which implies that it stayed there.

With Solomon we take another step forward. The Bible relates the scene of Solomon's dream in Gibeon, during which God gives him his wisdom (1 Kings 3:5–14). More precisely, the king asks for "an understanding heart to judge your people and to distinguish right from wrong" (3:9). In more modern terms: he asks for political and moral wisdom. In his response, God speaks of "a heart so wise and understanding that there has never been anyone like you up to now" (3:12). This is followed by the famous episode of the judgment of Solomon, an example of wisdom. The people, seeing the cleverness of the king when he solves a seemingly impossible problem, exclaim that "the king had in him the wisdom of God for giving judgment" (3:28).

This leads me to three observations. First, in this case, wisdom is not poured into a previously unenlightened vessel, as seems to be the case for the inspired artists called on to build the sanctuary (Exod. 35:31, 35; 36:1). The recipient stands prepared: wisdom is thrust into the depths of the king's heart, as seen in the expression "the king had in him." Moreover, the "wisdom of God for giving judgment" tells us two things: (a) wisdom is "divine" (which is less an indication of its source than it is a superlative); and (b) it is truly appropriated by the person who receives it: we can correctly speak of the wisdom *of* Solomon, not just of the wisdom of God *in* Solomon. Second, such wisdom has no specific content. It is not a body of knowledge but rather the means for acquiring knowledge. The knowledge for which Solomon was famous, and which involved above all questions of botany and zoology, is not innate (1 Kings 5:9–14). Finally, such wisdom is functional. It is a wisdom "for." It is not private. The idea of the state begins to appear here. The wisdom of Solomon is a wisdom of state, as one speaks of a "reason of state."

Criticism of Kingship

Ancient Israel stands out from the countries that surrounded it for having produced and transmitted texts that offer a critique of the institution of kingship, and even of the state in itself.

The Trauma of the State

On rare occasions people witness, or even participate in, a revolution—that is, a change in the conformation of the state that leads to a new form of state in which the power apparatus of state remains unchanged but falls into new hands. In contrast, it is quite exceptional to observe the birth of a state from a pre-state situation. The origins of states are usually shrouded in mystery and are often related in mythic style. The founders are heroes—Romulus, Theseus, Lycurgus—men who cannot possibly be set in the same temporal frame as ordinary mortals. As a consequence, the shift to the state leaves little trace in human history, even though it is the "main event" in that history.[7] Nor could things be otherwise. Because writing—the invention of which defines the borderline between prehistory and history—appears (or at least becomes widespread) within the framework of a bureaucratic system, it must follow the founding of the state and consequently cannot offer a historical record of that event. The only traces left by state foundation will be those of a trauma.

It is precisely that trauma that is described in the tirade that the Bible places in the mouth of the prophet Samuel when the elders of Israel come to him to ask him to appoint a king. Samuel warns them that a king will subject the people to military service, forced labor, and tithing, and oblige them to maintain his house. He will tear asunder the organic unity of the people by creating a class of functionaries (1 Sam. 8:11–17).[8] This text is a *vaticinium ex eventu:* under the guise of prophecy, it presents a retrospective summary of the reign of Solomon, to whom it alludes on several occasions. It offers a reverse image of Israel's *Grand Siècle.*

The text in 1 Samuel contains one phrase of capital importance: "He will tithe your crops and your vineyards, and give the revenue to his eunuchs and his slaves" (8:15). The objection is an old one: the manual worker complains that he has to feed others who "do not sweat through their shirts" and who, in his eyes, do nothing. The word given as "eunuch" may designate a non-castrated functionary, but I take it to be in the literal sense. The role of eunuchs in the administration of a state is a well-attested sociological fact occurring, for example, in the China of Confucius's day, in Sassanian Persia, and in Byzantium. Mention of them in this concrete sense receives an extraordinary depth if we consider the letter of the Hebrew, which speaks of "your seed (*zera*) and your vines." The state gives seed to those who produce no "seed"; it places the fertile in the service of the infertile, assuring the latter of an artificial posterity. This mention announces nothing less than the appearance of a nonbiological temporality. In the same way that the eunuch cannot reproduce, the state renounces the cyclical temporality of biological rhythms and dedicates itself to a rational temporality that overrules those rhythms. The natural time of sowing and harvest—that is, of reproduction—cedes to the abstract and cumulative time of archives and chronicles. The trauma connected with this shift, which is the birth of the state, is felt as a form of castration.

The state is also the source of trauma for its highest-ranking servant. The Bible places before us the idea of the state and of reasons of state in a passage that offers an admirable tragic scene: the loyalist army, led by its general, Joab, has just vanquished and killed Absalom, who had rebelled against his father, David. The king, absorbed by his private grief, refuses to review the victorious soldiers, who steal into Jerusalem as if they were returning "shamed by flight in battle." At that point Joab demands that David show himself to the army (2 Sam. 19:1–9). This scene has justly been called an *ecce homo*.[9] It also provides an image of the heroism of the servant of the state and the martyr to reasons of state: we need to imagine the king in tears as he tries to put on a royal countenance before the troops who march by acclaiming him.

Criticism of Kingship as Criticism of the State

Criticism of the ways in which the biblical kings formed the state occurs throughout the Old Testament, even up to a very late date.[10] Moreover, attacks on the monarchy take on a dual function, targeting both the genus and the species. Monarchy was just about the only type of state known in the ancient Near East. In reality, however, arguments against the monarchy of Saul are aimed more at the state in general than at the monarchic regime as such. In Greece the various political regimes were subjected to critical examination, for example by Herodotus, in the famous debate supposed to have taken place in Persia after the overthrow of the Magians between the partisans and the adversaries of various forms of government, in which Otanes offers a critique of monarchy and defends democracy.[11] Still, global criticism of the state is much more likely to appear in Israel than elsewhere, whereas the redactors of the Bible show little interest in the arguments raised for and against monarchy as a particular system of government.

Whereas in Egypt only the force by means of which the strong oppress the weak is seen as bad, in Israel it is the power of the state itself that seems immediately suspect.[12] Criticisms addressed to a particular sovereign can be found everywhere, but only in Israel does a criticism of the very institution of monarchy appear. This criticism accompanies each step in the establishment of the state like its shadow or its bad conscience. Thus the episode of the abortive kingship of Abimelech leads to Jotham's recounting of the old fable of the trees who decide to give themselves a king. All of the useful trees—the olive tree, the fig tree, the grape vine—refuse to leave off their function to "go to wave over the trees," and only the unproductive buckthorn tree accepts the crown (Judges 9:7–15).[13]

The opposition to kingship can even be heard in the account of how it was first instituted (1 Sam. 8:12). The passage seems to merge two versions, one favorable to monarchy, the other hostile to it. It is remarkable that the final redactor of the text combined the two elements without eliminating one or the other. Thus we zigzag between the "negative" account of the failings of the sons of Samuel, which lead the people to demand a king whose drawbacks are soon apparent (chapter 8), and the "positive" account of the lost asses of Saul's father, the anointing of Saul by Samuel, and the trance ("prophetic state") into which Saul subsequently enters (9:1–10, 16). Again, the "negative" account tells how Saul is elected by lot (10:17–24), and the "positive" tells us how, after his victory over the Ammonites, Saul was made king at Gilgal (11:15). Finally, the entire chapter 12 of 1 Samuel, which regards monarchy negatively, gives Samuel final authority and formulates the rule of loyalty to YHWH. Arguments in favor of Saul's legitimate claim to be king include his good looks and stature (9:2; 10:23); his distinguished birth (the son of a *gibbor hayl*) (9:2);[14] his military victory (11:1–11); his anointing (10:1); his participation in the trance-like "prophetic state"; and his acclamation by the people (10:24). After the experience of the "prophetic state," Saul is a different man (10:6); God has given him "another heart" (10:9).

If we classify these legitimating factors by the positive or negative tendencies of the narration, it is hardly surprising to find that most of what is to the credit of the king appears in the account favorable to monarchy. It is interesting that one justification, Saul's imposing physical appearance, occurs in both accounts, and that another detail, acclamation by the people, occurs only in the negative account. The reference to the people indicates that the source of legitimacy is not considered to be on high but to come from the base. In the account unfavorable to monarchy, this is tantamount to usurping the role of God.

To want to have a king is to want to be like the other nations (1 Sam. 8:5, 20). The expression occurs elsewhere (Deut. 17:14). Israel must constitute an exception: the "anti-monarchist" version insists on the point that the only true king of Israel is YHWH (8:7; 12:12). Gideon says as much: "The LORD must rule over you" (Judg. 8:23–24). Israel is distinctive in having conceived of human kingship as not only distinct from divine kingship but even opposed to it. In this fashion Israel planted seeds of democracy that proved just as fertile as the Greek traditions, even though they are cited less frequently.[15]

The Rules of Kingship

Kingship is not just the quality of an empirical individual. It forms a system of rules, for which Hebrew uses the term *mishpat*. These rules are first presented as the right (*mishpat*) of the king, a right that he imposes on the people as law, within the context of a critique of monarchy and the system of the state in general. It is this right that sums up a caricature of the state demands that we have seen above.

The heavy constraints of the state are compensated by rules (also *mishpat*) imposed upon the king (Deut. 17:14–20). Such rules, in the optative, are of course of another order than the ones preceding: the earlier version reflected a sad reality; these rules paint an ideal image of a zealous king. Interestingly, the passage in Deuteronomy is hypothetical: "should you then decide to have a king over you . . ." these will be the rules that must be respected. Having a king is by no means a commandment. Certain of the rabbis of the Talmud were to recall this, and an anti-monarchist tradition continued up through Abravanel, the first Jewish philosopher to undertake a systematic critique of kingship. In the Christian world as well, certain biblical commentators also presented arguments against monarchy.[16]

These rules are of two sorts. First, they determine how to choose a king. Then they indicate (and in this order) what a king must not do and what he must do. The first of these also has two parts: on the one hand, the king must be chosen by YHWH; on the other hand, he must be chosen from among his brothers and not be a foreigner. The text does not say *how* YHWH will choose the king, but in any event the question was hypothetical. Moreover, it is difficult to reconcile the first rule with the second: if it is YHWH who chooses the king, either his power to choose is unlimited and his choice cannot be questioned, or he will make it a rule to ratify his election of the Jewish people by choosing a king from among them. One might imagine a lottery (which is often the meaning of a choice on the part of YHWH) to which only members of the community are admitted.

The second group of rules contains three warnings and one positive commandment. The warnings concern excesses: the king must not own "a great number of horses," for fear that he might take the people back to Egypt to obtain them; he must not have too many wives, "lest his heart be estranged"; nor should he "accumulate a vast amount of silver and gold," a stricture for which no reason is given, but that may be a critical reference to Solomon, whose wealth, chariots, and cavalry are mentioned, along with the foreign women who urged him to combine the cult of YHWH with that of other gods (1 Kings 10:14–25, 26–27; 11:1–8).

The final clause states that the king must have a copy of the law, a requirement that had important long-term consequences.[17] Once enthroned, "he must have a copy of this law made from the scroll that is in the custody of the Levitical priests" (17:18), which means that the priests dictated the law. At first sight, this seems to be a simple justification of a social group—which was of course the same as the circles that redacted Deuteronomy. We have traces of this sort of legitimation. For one, the priests of Jerusalem had a monopoly on sacrifices, and the Levites had a similar monopoly on justice (Deut. 21:5). There is more, however: the law was made objective; it was separated not only from the person of the king but also from any specific person: the priest "dealt with the law" (Jer. 2:8), but he judged according to it. Even more, the king must not only judge according to the law; he will be judged according to it. It this spirit, with the books of Samuel and Kings, the Deuteronomist school produced a historiography that evaluates sovereigns by their loyalty to the cult of YHWH, hence according to a principle exterior to the political.

In order to render the law fully objective, it must be written. This constitutes, as is known, an important step in civilization. The idea was in the air throughout the Mediterranean area. In Athens, written law is traced back to Draco.[18] It is amusing to note that Draco's code is dated around 624 BCE, or two years before the "discovery" of Deuteronomy in 622 (2 Kings 22).

The Law and the King / The Law Is the King

Jews experience the Law as a collection of commandments (*mitzvōt*): 613 of them in all, 248 positive and 365 negative.[19] From a historical point of view, however, the Law does not immediately appear as *commandment* but rather as *teaching*. The priests, "those who dealt with the law," are the holders of the *torah* (Jer. 2:8). This *torah* is not a written text but an oral teaching referring to the priestly domain: for example, it covers ritual questions, such as what is pure or impure (Hag. 2:11–13), or the proper sort of sacrifice to offer (Zech. 7:2–3). This teaching is supposed to come from YHWH in person. The priests must be obeyed: "You shall carry out the directions (*torah*) they give you (*yorukha*) and the verdict (*mishpat*) they pronounce for you" (Deut. 17:11). "Before YHWH" was equivalent to "in the presence of the priests and the judges" (Deut. 19:17). The law was thus YHWH's law, and God is continually represented as speaking about "his" commandments.

The Legislator

From what does the law derive its divinity? Concretely, the divinity of the law is represented as resulting from the fact that it was written by YHWH himself. What is new in the Bible is precisely that a divine law can be delivered in writing, and that a law can be both written and divine (Exod. 24:12; Deut. 4:13; 5:22). This is why the writing of the law is the work of the very finger of God (Exod. 31:18; 32:16; Deut. 9:10), an unpleasant anthropomorphism that some have sought to allegorize.[20] The divine writer is not represented in a pose like that of an Egyptian scribe with reed pen and ink, nor like a Babylonian with his stylus: he writes with his finger, as one writes in the sand, without any mediating instrument. This use of the body expresses a personal engagement: in giving the Law, God gives of his own and of himself.

The first tables of the law were broken by Moses in a fit of anger before the infidelity of the people dancing about the golden calf (Exod. 32:19). Who wrote the second tables? God seems to have intended to write them anew himself (Exod. 34:1), but he ends up asking Moses to write them down (Exod. 34:27, 28b).

In Israel the very nature of the law differs from what was typical in the world of the Middle East of the time. The ancient juridical texts are collections of decisions actually handed down rather than codes. Even the famous "Code of Hammurabi," as we have seen, was not really a code. Such texts placed no constraint on a judge: he can of course take inspiration from them as masterworks of his profession, but he is not held to apply them in the cases brought before him, and the texts draw their authority from the power of the king who enacts them. In contrast, the Torah is taken to be the Book of the Law, which explains definitively what must be done and has no need of any authority but its own.

The Bible avoids representing the king as legislator.[21] The one lawgiver is God. That idea was an unparalleled novelty in the ancient Middle East, where only the king made laws. The Torah has no real parallel in those ancient civilizations. The God of Israel replaces the Oriental king in the role of lawgiver. Hence the predicates attributed to the pharaoh in Egypt are reserved for God alone in Israel.[22]

In Israel the Torah replaces the king. It replaces the word endowed with authority of the Oriental king, the king whose word has force of law. To repeat a felicitous expression of Aleida Assmann, we see here an "excarnation" of the law.[23] In the ancient East the word of the king was traditionally considered to be the divine word. In Israel the divinity of the word is transmitted to the Law. A fairly obscure verse in Moses' blessings of the Israelites, speaking of the Lord, reads variously "there was [a] king" or "he was king in Yeshurun" (Deut. 33:5). It is unclear whether the statement should be read as impersonal ("there was a king") or whether the subject is previously given. Who or what was this king who reigned over Israel, designated here by an archaic term? Rashi, Nahmanides, Sforno, and contemporary exegetes see a reference to YHWH himself; Ibn Ezra sees Moses as the reference. The most profound comment perhaps comes from Jehuda Halevi, cited by Ibn Ezra: "King" is an allusion to the Torah. Halevi interprets "There was no king in Israel" in a similar sense: The Law is the true king of Israel, replacing the flesh and blood king.[24]

The Idea of Election

In a parallel development, the idea of election changes in important ways. Its origin is political. In Egypt election is a privilege of the king, who is elected by god or the gods. To be sure, similar formulas can be found in Israel: YHWH chooses a priest, chooses a place for his temple, and chooses the king himself in a text we have already examined (Deut. 17:15). Still, a modification of capital importance arises: in Israel it is the people as a whole that is elect (Deut. 7:6; 14:2), or else it is Jacob, the eponymous ancestor of Israel (Isa. 41:8).[25] We note, interestingly, that the choosing of the king avoids the difficulty mentioned above because he is taken from among the chosen people. The king of Israel is replaced by YHWH in his function as legislator, but he is also replaced by the people as the subject of history. The covenant with David is transferred to the people of Israel as a whole (Isa. 55:3), which appears as an undifferentiated totality, without consideration of its political articulation. The laws of the Old Testament suppose a preexistent order that is not that of a state and that Martin Noth sees as the pre-state federation that he reconstructs.[26] Conversely, one can see it as a projection to the past of a purely ideal situation.

This shift to the idea of election from the particular prince to the entire people returns us to the problem of the origin of the human community. The Greeks resolved this problem in various ways. The dominant tradition relies on the idea of nature: there is something like a natural sociability of man. Aristotle formulates the notion as "man is by nature a political animal" (zōon physei politikon); the Stoics supposed man's spontaneous good will toward his fellow man.[27]

The Bible resolves this problem by means of the historical fact of election. The problem first arose in the context of an explanation of the origin of all the "nations" at a time when populations everywhere were becoming sedentary; in this context, the idea of a people led by a god from a former place of residence to their definitive homeland is not exclusive to the Bible.[28] Thus Chemosh, the god of the Ammonites, is supposed to have given them their land in the same way that YHWH gave his people the Promised Land.[29] In the Bible, the people originate from the will of God, who goes to seek them and make them his people: "You alone have I favored, more than all the families of the earth" (Amos 3:2). The idea is balanced by being generalized: Israel, at base, has received no more than other peoples: "Are you not like the Ethiopians to me, O men of Israel, says the LORD? Did I not bring the Israelites from the land of Egypt as I brought the Philistines from Caphtor and the Arameans from Kir?" (Amos 9:7).

The Pentateuch goes a step further: Exodus speaks of Israel as the "special possession" (*segullah*) of its god and as a "kingdom of priests" (19:4–6). The notion is well represented in Deuteronomy, where it appears three times (4:34; 7:6; 14:2).

The idea of wisdom evolves as well. In Egypt, that idea was incarnate in the figure of the king. In the ancient East, it was usually the authorities, the scribes, and the literate who held a monopoly of it. Traces of this perspective remain in the Bible, for example, in the connection between "the wise" and judges (Deut. 16:19). But Israel generalizes wisdom: it thinks of itself as being, collectively, "truly a wise and intelligent people," and its wisdom is that of the Torah (Deut. 4:6). The same expression is used regarding Solomon. The wisdom that the people are supposed to contain derives from the precise competence of the scribe or the priest. A "kingdom of priests" (Exod. 19:6) is synonymous with "a wise . . . people" (Deut. 4:6). In Israel the people as a whole appropriate "wisdom," or the power of decision. A later exegetic tradition interprets all such sayings about wisdom as referring to the Torah,[30] a tendency that follows the ideas of Deuteronomy but is barely sketched out there.

In later times, the wisdom of the king was drawn into a movement that estranged it from the king and made it circle around the Law. It became a useless addition to the wisdom of the people as a whole, which was supposed to take responsibility for the law and even, in extreme cases, to do without a king.

The Law of Moses and the King's Law

The law that the authors of Deuteronomy dreamed of as enjoying an exclusive reign coexisted in reality with the power of the kings, coming together only exceptionally, as in the case of Josiah. History, ironically, took them at their word. The connection between the political and the religious in Israel, paradoxically, came from outside. The religion of Deuteronomy was imposed by a political power, "Persian bayonets," that lent it force of law.[31] The Persian Empire took a tolerant position where religion was concerned; moreover, the God of Israel had a certain affinity with the Persian "god of heaven" (which encouraged the euphemism designating God as "Heaven"). A more general line of reasoning determined Persian politics, however. Foreign domination always leaves the dominated population in a contradictory situation: without the rulers' wanting to do so, it sets society in movement, even though conscious policy is, to the contrary, to fix society in place by appealing to its ancient traditions.[32] Similarly, the Persian Empire wanted the peoples under its domination to be governed by their own laws. Thus it sought out the oldest version of those laws. The Persians attempted a similar move in Egypt, which remained under their control after the conquest of the land by Cambyses II in 525 BCE: the new rulers installed a commission charged with collecting the laws in force up to the forty-fourth year of the reign of Ahmose II, a few years before the Persian victory. The Persians also imposed observance of the Jewish holy days on the military colony at Elephantine.[33] The same solution pertained after the Ptolemies had replaced the Great King. Their power recognized Jews' right to follow their own law. For that to occur, the text of that law had to be accessible to the functionaries charged with applying and translating it. This is why the Torah was translated into Greek, and under the title of "Law."[34]

It is within this more general framework that Ezra's mission is to be understood. Although it is difficult to date his activities precisely (between 458 and 398 BCE), we can at least reconstruct them within the overall context of the end of the Exile with the edict of Cyrus, which allowed the Israelites to resettle in Palestine in 538. The reconstruction of the Temple was begun almost simultaneously, but it was interrupted by the resistance of the "Samaritans" and was completed only in 515 BCE.[35] Because the Samaritans also opposed the reconstruction of the ramparts of Jerusalem, Ezra went there with the mission of imposing the law of Moses as the king's law. Nehemiah, "cupbearer" to King Artaxerxes I, was charged with the reconstruction of the city walls.

Ezra is called "the priest-scribe, the scribe of the text of the LORD's commandments and statutes for Israel" (Ezra 7:11). These are technical terms of the Persian administration: Ezra was a state commissioner charged with enforcing "a law of the God of heaven"—the latter being the official name of YHWH for the Persians.[36] He read the law and provided a solemn translation of it, which was equivalent to promulgating it (Neh., chap. 8). The decisive phrase equating the two is "the law [*dath*] of your God and the law of the king" (Ezra 7:26). Every word counts here: the law is that of *your* god; it is not the law *of the god* of the king, but the law of the king; the king puts his power to the service of a god who is not his own. The word in old Persian, *dath* (law), takes on in Hebrew the sense of "religion," a meaning that it has kept down to our own time.[37]

What ensued was a total redefinition of the relationship between the juridical and the political. Usually, a particular regime issues its laws and enforces them. The laws in that case are an emanation of the state and they reflect its orientation. Here Jewish Law was imposed by a third party; a regime for which it was not law. This means that the law *signifies* political power but does not *resemble* it. It is the sign of that power, not its image. The connection between power and the law that it imposes is arbitrary. In such a case, the law can survive longer than that power. In return, the relationship of representation, from image to model, is liberated from an association with the political and can apply to a totally different, religious instance.

The People of the Law

This situation also implies an original and novel way of defining what constituted Israel as a people. Unlike most of the peoples of antiquity, Israel was not defined by a territory, by allegiance to a king, or—as was often the case—by both of these at once. It was defined by "religion," and by religion alone. There are two aspects to that religion. The first is the cult at the Temple of Jerusalem, whose claim to a complete monopoly was finally realized; the second is adherence to the precepts of the law.

The people of Israel now had an exclusively religious definition. It was supposed to be made up of "all . . . who have separated themselves from the peoples of the lands in favor of the law of God" (Neh. 10:29). There is a paradox here: returning from exile to their land of origin—a concrete process of reappropriating territory—had in fact led, on the symbolic level, to a disappropriation in relation to that land. Finding oneself among one's compatriots does not lead to reinsertion among them, but rather to a separation off from them. As a result, the exiles are never more exiled than they are since their return "home." The Diaspora is never more intense than in the Holy Land. Exile from one's land of origin can henceforth end up being a generalized exile. A recurrent image gives the measure of this fact: Israel forms a "holy seed" (*zera*) (Ezra 9:2; Neh. 9:2). The word *zera* is often translated as "race." Although not incorrect, that translation supposes a zoological representation and even suggests a certain "racism," both of which are anachronistic. Moreover, it offers the more serious drawback of glossing over the underlying image: grain is planted in the soil, but it does not originate from it.

This "floating," mobile people stands in opposition to the "people(s) of the land(s)" (ʿam ha-aretz), a phrase that may originally have designated landowners but that takes on a special meaning in the books of Ezra and Nehemiah.[38] We can read there an amazing formula, which might look contradictory: The Israelites who had taken "as wives *foreign women of the peoples of the land*" are urged to separate themselves from those "peoples of the land" by dismissing their "foreign wives and the children born of them."[39] Foreignness is defined by its opposite: belonging to the land. The formula "peoples of the land" remained in latter parlance, where it designates the ignorant—not those who lack general knowledge, but, precisely, those unaware of the law of Moses.

Those who live according to the precepts of that law acquire an identity that they are ready to defend. "Zeal for the law," a quality often attached to the biblical figure of Phinehas and that later gave the Zealots their name, stems from such an identity.[40] This led the people of the law to enter into new ties of sociability, as suggested by the name by which rabbis were designated: *haverim*, associates, or companions. Between the rabbis and the "peoples of the land" who did not know the law (ʿam ha-aretz) there reigned a hatred and a scorn that was at times given violent expression: Rabbi Akiba, who had himself been ʿam ha-aretz before becoming a Talmudic scholar somewhat late in life, says that in his past he would have liked to bite the rabbis with all the force of an ass.[41]

The Divine Space of the Law

It is paradoxical that this law detached from the land had originally been understood as the law of a land, and even as a law whose divinity was tied to one geographical area.

It has often been remarked that the connection established by the prophets of Israel between the ethical and the religious represented a novelty in the Middle East, where "religion" and "morality" were separated, as were "cult" and "customs." The prophets tirelessly recall that sacrifices alone serve no purpose and that justice is indispensable. This connection between the religious and the moral can also be placed in a spatial context. It seems in fact to come from a desire for ritual purity. The religious may in fact come before the moral: it is the care taken not to defile a holy space that invites respect of a certain conduct.[42]

Rules

Thus the law appears as the teaching of a way to live that applies within a specific spatial area—that is, as a *rule*. This situates it beyond the distinction that is habitually made between law and custom. In concrete terms, it is possible that the rule in question was "posted" at the entrance to a sacred space. Such places are fraught with danger: one does not enter them without taking precautions, and a certain state of purity is required, for it is always foolhardy to settle in a land without knowing how to come to terms with the local god.[43] Not just anyone can enter into a sanctuary: the blind and the lame are excluded (1 Sam. 5:8). Since physical integrity is accompanied by moral integrity, one must confess innocence at the entrance (Deut. 26:13–14). This task is facilitated by lists of sins, like those cited by the prophets (Ezek. 18:5–9). We have analogous lists from Egypt, litanies of sworn declarations, promises of abstention ("I will not do . . .") and denials ("I have not done . . .") to be recited by the priests. The *Book of the Dead* enumerates forty-two sins that the dead, at their appearance before the judgment of the gods, must deny having committed. These are ritual taboos, but also moral failings. Certain negative confessions are inscribed at temple entrances.[44] The same occurs in Asia Minor: the gods who inhabit the holy space are supposed not to tolerate those who transgress certain rules.[45]

It is possible that certain texts contain traces of that literary genre. Psalm 15, for example, also situates moral demands within the framework of access to a sacred space.[46] This psalm might be interpreted as a liturgy that sets up a dialogue between the people and the priests who live within the temple grounds. The people comes to "demand the *torah*" of the priests. They pose a question, from outside of the sanctuary: "Oh LORD: who shall sojourn in your tent? Who shall dwell on your holy mountain?" The priests answer, from inside the temple walls, by enumerating moral rules. This is why the door to the temple is "the gate of justice," through which "the just shall enter" (Ps. 118:19–20; see also Isa. 26:2). The approved forms of conduct are social rules. These are first presented globally, then backed up by specific negative examples of behavior: the blameless man "slanders not with his tongue" (Ps. 15:3); "lends not his money at usury" (Ps. 15:5; Lev. 25:37); "accepts no bribes against the innocent" (Ps. 15:5; see also Exod. 23:8; Deut. 16:19). These rules are also found in the Torah; they are based on tribal solidarity and on having the same friends and the same enemies as the group (Ps. 15:4). Still, one must think the truth "in his heart" (Ps. 15:2). He who respects all these rules "shall never be disturbed" (Ps. 15:5). That expression has a precise meaning: he will cling to the "eternal Rock" of Isaiah 26:2–4, thus entering into communion with God.

In a similar context, Micah recalls that the rules have already been laid down: "You have been told, O man, what is good, and what the LORD requires of you: Only to do the right and to love goodness, and to walk humbly with your God" (Mic. 6:8). Thus it is not the moral demands of the prophets that have influenced the cult: to the contrary, those demands arose from the cult itself. The idea of Israel as a people of priests (Exod. 19:6) means, among other things, that Israel is obliged to observe, at all times, the code of conduct that pertains to priests and to behave as if within the sanctuary.

According to one intriguing hypothesis, the Decalogue (Exod. 20:2–17) was the list of rules for entrance to the sanctuary of the Tribe of Dan, whose priests claimed to descend from Moses. This would explain the fact that the Decalogue has been attributed to them.[47]

Law and Land

The link between moral conduct and physical space was a generalization of the connection between the Temple and the Land, so that the idea that a certain level of conduct was required by life within a certain area was applied to the relations between the Law and the land of Israel. Thus Ezekiel asks the people how it thinks it can at the same time sin and keep possession of the land (Ezek. 33:25). The whole of Deuteronomy supposes an idea of the sort. The entire law is repeated there, but it is placed within a specific setting: no longer the desert or Sinai, but the spot that they occupy before entering into the Promised Land. By implication, that land is compared to a temple, with the law recapitulated at its entrance. The laws are to be *applied in the land*, as Deuteronomy repeatedly insists (Deut. 4:5, 14; 6:1; 12:1).

In the latter passage, the law appears in a highly interesting context, that of regulations regarding cult sites that must be destroyed so that sacrifices would be offered in one place only. That place is presented as still to be indicated by God, but it is clear that it is the Temple in Jerusalem: "You shall not do as we are now doing; here, everyone does what seems right to himself, since you have not yet reached your resting place, the heritage which the LORD, your God, will give you" (Deut. 12:8–9). The immediate historical context is that of the concentration of the cult in the Temple in Jerusalem, the monopolization of the priesthood by the family of the Aaronites, and the prohibition of cult images. More precisely, it speaks to the shift from a pre-state situation to the state.

A passage in Judges provides an interesting parallel to the one in Deuteronomy. Judges states: "There was no king in Israel" (18:1). The absence of a king and the pre-state anarchy are evoked here precisely regarding the story of a private sanctuary, served by a private priest, and in which the god of Israel is represented by "a carved idol overlaid with silver" (18:14). It was the royal power that had allowed these three transgressions to be prohibited by a law. With the short reign of Josiah (when Deuteronomy is supposed to have been rediscovered), ancient Israel underwent something like an alliance of the throne (of David) and the altar (of Aaron).

The Code of Free Men

The Decalogue is to be understood with this as its background. Its contents contain nothing extraordinary. Its only merit is to have formulated and regrouped the fundamental conditions of human society. The rules that it formulates can be found stated, more or less explicitly, in a number of other places. It has even been remarked that the Qur'an contains a passage that lists analogous commandments. The same is true of the clauses of the pact concluded at Aqabah between Muhammad and his allies in Medina.[48] To be sure, that text lacks mention of the Sabbath as a day of rest, an absence that was to have profound consequences.[49] It might be pointed out that the Sabbath ruling applied only to the Jews. The most important absence is that of the first words of the Decalogue, "I, the LORD, am your God"—which are not a commandment properly speaking but rather the identification of the speaker through a recall of his liberating act. The phrase places the entire Decalogue in a new light.

Here I shall permit myself a somewhat prosaic analogy to compare the Decalogue and the rules for an office building or apartment house. Those first words give the name of the proprietor before the code of proper conduct in his building is spelled out. Hence, the first words are: "I am the LORD." Moreover, the bearer of this name is identified as responsible for bringing the Jews out of captivity in Egypt and their imminent entry into a new land. This Magna Carta of sorts begins with an identity card. It recalls the circumstances in which the reader was placed at the threshold of what he is about to enter into.

The rules that follow are not a series of dictates. On entering into someone's house, you learn what sort of person lives there. If the rules of a building prohibit smoking, for example, it is because the proprietor does not like tobacco; if they ask people to wipe their feet on entering, it is because he likes cleanliness, and so on. Similarly, on entering God's domain, one learns something about him. To be sure, all of this occurs purely by analogy: we learn that God is the sort of "person" who, if he were a man, would not kill, would not steal, and so forth. This is the sense in which the law is, quite literally, a teaching (torah). The law liberates, and at the same time it teaches. If I may once more use colloquial terms, I might say that it cuts you in on the deal. Furthermore, in regulations for a building, what is forbidden to the tenants is also something that the proprietor forbids himself. The law is at this point linked with a pact, covenant, or mutual engagement. The aim of the commandments is not to impose obedience but to provide an entry into the divine mores. Entering into the land of God is also, by that token, entering into the intimacy of the One who lives there.

The overall framework, with its opening note of an experience of liberation, gives meaning to the commandments. Only men who have first been liberated can live according to them. Their aim is not to reduce men to slavery, to make them the slaves of God. To the contrary, it is to concretize their liberty in a conduct worthy of free men—people who, precisely because they are "gentlemen," and because *noblesse oblige,* will not permit themselves bad behavior.[50]

The Covenant

Thus the deepest meaning of the law is no less than life with the divinity. Its basic rule is the idea of pact or covenant (*berith*), as orchestrated in Deuteronomy. The source of that idea lies in both private law and international law. In private law there can be covenants between equals (Gen. 14:13; 21:27; 26:28; 31:44; 1 Kings 5:26; 15:19), between brothers (Amos 1:9), between friends (1 Sam. 23:18), between spouses (Mal. 2:14), and between vassal and lord (1 Sam. 11:1; 2 Sam. 3:12ff.). In international law there have been treaties ever since the one drawn up between Egypt and the Hittites in 1280 BCE, the first to have left a historical trace. It was what Joshua thought he was drawing up with the Gibeonites (Josh. 9:11–15). Usually, such agreements enumerate clauses that both parties swear to respect and maledictions that will ensue should these not be respected. Bloody rites visualized the dreadful fate awaiting the transgressor: a sacrificed animal is split in two (probably the origin of the technical term for "cutting" an alliance, *karath berith*) and the contracting parties pass between the two halves (Jer. 34:18).[51] The same elements appear in the Bible in Abraham's covenant with God (Gen. 15:9, 17).

The novelty of Israel, however, is to have effected something like a shift of the divine. Before the Bible, the gods were invoked when a treaty was drawn up, hence a treaty between nations supposed something like mutual recognition of the gods of the other contracting party. To draw up a pact with someone was thus also to make a covenant with his gods (Exod. 23:32). The contracting people took its own god for granted; he was, so to speak, part of the furniture, at times literally so, as with the portable god of certain nomad groups.[52] With the Bible, however, the idea of an alliance of a people *with* a god first appears, as is the case in Exodus 19–20. This means that *the god who had been the guarantee of the alliance became a partner in it.*

This change had highly important consequences. The first of these regards the representation of the divine. The god enters into a contract with a people who becomes his people; he becomes a party to the contract. The divine no longer hovers far above human history; it enters into it. Moreover, the juridical, in the strict sense, is affected by its entry into the domain of the religious, which communicates to him something like a new dimension. The clauses of the treaty no longer hold any validity in themselves; they are the conditions—the necessary conditions, to be sure—of a more essential phenomenon, which is the entry into contact with the god, the communion with the divine.

The covenant is at first without conditions. God engages himself unilaterally, without demanding anything in exchange. Later on, conditions are formulated. These are gathered in a book (Exod. 24:7; Deut. 4:13). Respect of the clauses is a condition of the covenant (Deut. 7:12).

The covenant is given a sumptuous staging at the end of the book of Joshua, in the narrative of the gathering of the tribes of Israel at Shechem (Josh. 24:1–28). The people are invited to "put away the strange gods that are among you" (24:23)—specifically, the fetishes from "the region beyond the River" (24:3). The choice before the people is threefold: they can continue to serve "the gods your fathers served beyond the River"; they can worship the local gods, here the gods of the Amorites; or they could serve YHWH (24:15). The god of Israel is not the god of the land of Canaan, and that land is not the land of the god in the sense that the god is "part of the landscape" as the Greek gods are "the gods of Greece," as Schiller put it. YHWH is a "floating" god who settles in a territory with his people.[53]

A Book of Divine Law

It is within this context that the expression that comes closest to the Greek idea of divine law appears in Israel and in biblical Hebrew—a language extremely poor in adjectives that, in particular, does not include the adjective "divine." The conclusion of the covenant at Shechem (Josh. 24:26) implies the redaction of its clauses. The "words" of that covenant are "statutes" and "ordinances," which Joshua "recorded in a book of god's law" (*sefer torat elohim*), an expression not found anywhere else in the Bible. The word *elohim* has no article here: the god who intervenes in this instance is not the Lord of Israel, usually invoked by name or—precisely—singularized by the definite article. The generic term that designates any divine being is used here in one of the relations of annexation (or "constructed state") that Hebrew uses to replace an adjective.

We might note that the law is termed divine at the very moment that it is recorded in a book, and in a formula that implies that the literary genre of "book of god's law" was something well known. This takes us as far as possible from Greece: there, as we have seen, if a law was divine it could not be, nor should it be, written.

5

The Legislation of the Sacred Books

We can now turn toward the content of the books presented as containing divine laws. My subject made it obligatory to speak at length of the first of these, the writings of the Old Testament, focusing more on the contexts of these texts than on their juridical content. Here I intend to offer only a few remarks on the content and the form of the rules stated in the Pentateuch.

I shall have more to say about the two later works, the New Testament and the Qur'an. For one thing, they make their first appearance on my stage here. For another, they had a decisive influence on Christianity and Islam—that is, on the two religions that, during the age that interests me here, either took on a political dimension or possessed one from the start. In each case I shall need to pay special attention to the moral and political teachings presented in these texts. We have already reviewed the teachings of the Pentateuch in chapter 4.

The Old Testament

The Old Testament is not simply a list of commandments—far from it. The literary genres it contains vary widely, from chronicle to poetry and from a quasi-philosophical meditation to edifying narration, and its composition stretched over an entire millennium. Even the Torah (the Pentateuch) is not limited to the law of Moses. The entire first book of the Old Testament, Genesis, narrates events that occurred before the gift of the law.

The Commandments in Context

Some have wondered why the Pentateuch does not begin with the first commandment given to Moses, which institutes the feast of Passover (Exod. 12:2). The question is attributed to Rabbi Isaac, a sage of the period of the redaction of the Mishnah, in technical terms a Palestinian Amora of the third generation (the late second century CE).[1] A bit earlier, a work attributed to a Tanna of the second generation who died in 135 poses an analogous question: Why did the Torah not begin with the Ten Commandments?[2] It is interesting to note that the question was formulated just as the period of the redaction of the Mishnah, the first collection of commandments, was coming to an end. In the eleventh century, Rashi, rabbi of Troyes, led off his commentary on the Bible, which was to become classic, with a response: the history preceding the gift of the Law must be narrated in order to legitimate Israel's possession of the land that was its own.[3] Thus the rabbis testify to an awareness that the law implied a history, real or imaginary, and a place within which the law pertained.[4]

Aside from the historical narratives and the hymns that it contains and that no one would mistake for legislative dispositions, the Bible has a wealth of wisdom literature to accompany those texts and nourish them.[5] The sapiential books do not command; they advise. They are never placed on the same plane as the Law, but they communicate with it. This is also true of their redaction: King Hezekiah's collection of sayings of the sages (Prov. 25:1) may spring from the same movement as the contemporary compilation of juridical traditions of the Northern Kingdom in what would later be the book of Deuteronomy.[6] Moreover, the contents of the two collections are convergent: the sages recommend obedience to the law (Prov. 6:23; 28:4, 7, 9), and the law is presented as the culmination of wisdom (Deut. 4:6), to the point that later texts identify the two without further formalities (Baruch 4:1; Ecclesiasticus [Sirach] 24).

The Style and Categories of the Commandments

The fact remains that what is particular about the Jewish Law is the presence within it of commandments announced in what Albrecht Alt calls the "apodictic style." Commandments and prohibitions are not presented along with consequences or sanctions, but in the absolute: "Thou shalt not"; "Thou shalt." This is true of certain of the "Ten Commandments" brought together in the two decalogues, but it is not exclusive to them. The absence of sanctions would prevent modern jurists from applying their own concept of the law to them, and perhaps to reject them as *lex imperfecta* or even regard them as simple counsel.[7]

With the exception of the book of Genesis, the Pentateuch contains commandments that can be regrouped in several series dating from different epochs and situated within different milieus of origin. I have no intention of enumerating these various documents here.[8] The commandments contained in these texts have bearing on a number of domains of moral, social, and/or religious life: purity and cleanliness (leprosy, menstruation), but also on sacrifices and many other topics. Parallels, close and less close, can be found in what we know of the juridical systems of nearby peoples.[9]

We can distinguish several types of precepts, for example *mishpatim* and *huqqim*, which would later be called moral laws and ceremonial laws.[10] A certain number of commandments seem so obvious that it seems hardly necessary to formulate them; the reason for others is so unclear that one might even call them bizarre. Examples of the latter that are often cited include the prohibitions against mixing threads of different sorts in one woven piece and against sowing different types of grain in the same field (Deut. 22:9–11). At a later date this led to the problem of the "meaning of the commandments" (*ta'amey ham-mitzvot*) and to various attempts to elucidate them on the part of philosophers and kabbalists at times against the strong opposition of the more liberally minded.[11]

The Talmud

Chronologically speaking, the Talmud belongs after the New Testament. In fact, the final redaction of the oldest layer of the Talmud, the Mishnah, took place toward the end of the second century CE, and that of the Gemara, which completes it, can be situated around the end of the fifth century for the Babylon Talmud and only a bit earlier for the Jerusalem Talmud. That timing—around 500 CE—is significant. The idea of a complete collection of laws was in the air, and only a few decades later Emperor Justinian pursued the same endeavor for a Roman Empire that had become Christian. The fact remains, however, that the Talmud was a prolongation and consolidation of an evolving movement that had begun well before the Christian era.

The Talmud deepened discussions that had already found a preliminary crystallization in the Mishnah. It was not intended to contain any new commandment not present in the Bible. Anyone claiming to do so would be guilty of the most terrible sacrilege, that of modifying divine law, an act against which Deuteronomy had already threatened malediction (Deut. 4:2; 13:1). And indeed, the Talmud only claims to render the commandments of the Torah more explicit. Thus it seeks to eliminate all risk of ambiguity by explicating the least (and apparently redundant) details in their formulation and by making the conditions of their concrete application as precise as possible. That did not prevent the rabbis from declaring new commandments or, conversely, from "uprooting" some of the divine commandments.[12]

The Talmud's teachings are not original, let alone revolutionary, and they do not focus on the political.[13] The rabbis' view of human nature was somewhat disillusioned: without an authority, men would devour one another raw.[14] Consequently, they recommend the greatest respect for authority: all persons endowed with authority were supposed to have been designated by God, down to functionaries as low on the scale as the French *garde-champêtre*, such as the man who supervises the allocations of water for irrigation. The least must be shown the same respect as the greatest.[15] Terrestrial kingship is a reflection of divine kingship, hence any lack of respect to the king is an offense to God.[16] Still, the ultimate authority comes from the people, as it is the people who name the king. No magistrate can be named without consulting the community.[17] The legislative body, the Sanhedrin, is more important than the king, and the rabbi's word trumps the Sanhedrin's, as reported in an anecdote related in a number of texts.[18]

An awareness of a separation between political power and spiritual power is already present in the Talmud: "From Moses to Rabbi, teaching (*torah*) and [political] greatness have not coincided."[19] The fact that the Jews were not anchored to a territory made them take a further step: the political power is not Jewish, but rather that of the land in which the Jews live. The Jews respected the civil law of the land where they cannot live by their own laws, following the Talmudic injunction: "The civil law of the kingdom has force of law (*dina de-malkutha dina*)."[20] In the Middle Ages a distinction was drawn between the law of the kingdom, which was traditional and obligatory, and the law of the king, which was new and thus arbitrary. By that fact, this regulation is "just as much a principle of disobedience as of obedience."[21]

Finally, the Talmud is not restricted to reflecting the Jewish condition as it relates to the law. It places that condition within the context of a theory, to be sure not extensively developed, of the condition of all humankind, in contrast to which the privilege of Israel stands out. The rabbis understood that what makes a human being—and thus is characteristic of all men, Jews and non-Jews alike—is a relationship to a law. They thought of this relationship on the model of Israel, but generally applied. The essence of man was not to be open to the *logos,* to be a citizen, or to be free, but to be subject to a law. That law is not natural, but in spite of being situated within a history, it is what is closest to it. It is the law received by Noah, from whom all humankind is descended. The rabbis recognize seven commandments given to Noah as he emerged from the ark, commandments subsequently valid for the whole of the humanity issued from him. Only one of these commandments—to establish tribunals—is positive. The six others prohibit idolatry, blasphemy, murder, rape, incest, and the consumption of any part of a living animal.[22] They define something approaching minimal requirements for being human in a list that anthropology finds highly interesting, including as it does rules ranging from the prohibition of incest to culinary advice. The idea of a law given to Noah permits a resolution of the problem posed by the presence of elementary moral rules among pagans who had not received the law. Moreover, it does so without having recourse to an idea such as that of nature or of a reason spontaneously attuned to hear the law of nature because it is consubstantial with it.[23]

Consequently, it is with the Old Testament that a new manner of experiencing the divinity of the law enters onto the scene: the law is essentially a gift, and because of that fact it is situated within a history. Such a law is not hidden deep within things, whose profound structures it expresses. It is something that has not always existed but has come to pass. In this, the law is parallel to the way in which Israel conceives of the world into which it made its entry, not as a nature reposing on itself, but as a *creation*. That perspective remains in the background of the later sacred books.

The New Testament

The writings grouped together in the New Testament represent a selection from among a larger literature arising out of the events tied to the life and the teaching of Jesus of Nazareth. The criterion by which certain texts were chosen as canonical and others rejected as "apocryphal" is conformity to an orthodoxy that came to be constituted gradually during the first century of the common era. I shall limit my remarks to respect that selection, because only those texts were received during the Middle Ages as having official value. They contain quite different literary genres: narrations that seem to be biographies or chronicles, letters, and an apocalypse; within these there are hymns, arguments in the form of conversations ("diatribes"), and administrative memoranda. Interestingly enough for my purposes here, one of the few literary genres that has only scarce representation in it is the law.

Christian Politics?

The preaching of Jesus, although situated within a political framework, cannot be reduced to the political. Jesus had few tender thoughts for the authorities, and he had little reason to have any: Herod had ordered the death of John the Baptist, and Jesus refers to him as a "fox" (Luke 13:31–32). Jesus' disciples included men of various tendencies: Pharisees (Luke 7:40–44)—a group that later was portrayed, retrospectively, as the very type of his adversaries—and even one Zealot, Simon (Matt. 10:4; Luke 6:15; Acts 1:13). But Jesus did not permit himself to be attached to, and even less to be reduced to, one party. It seems that, following John the Baptist (Matt. 3:2; 4:17), he announced the approach of the direct reign of God and called on his listeners to convert, stressing the urgent need to put their lives and thoughts in order. The kingdom of God is described with the aid of parables and in the style of eschatological pronouncement. Political action would be redundant when God is about to intervene directly. This is why Jesus kept aloof from the Zealot movement.[24]

The relationship with the political is orchestrated by means of powerful symbols when it comes to the account of the Passion, but all of those symbols are inverted, as they are in the mockeries of the Roman soldiers, who salute Jesus as king and load him with signs of kingship, including the crown of thorns (Matt. 17:28–29; John 19:2). The royal title is inscribed on the cross (Matt. 27:37). The New Testament takes this mockery literally and sees it, implicitly, as an anticipated acknowledgment of a real kingship. The Fourth Gospel adds to this account the dialogue of the Jews with Pontius Pilate (John 19:19–22). It relates the discussion between Jesus and Pilate and quotes Jesus as saying, "My kingdom does not belong to this world" (John 18:36). The paradox of a crucified king is stressed by the Fathers of the Church: John Chrysostom, for example, states, "I call him king because he is crucified."[25]

The Christian message nevertheless appeared as political, even as subversive: the Jews accused the Christians of wanting to revolutionize the world and to have another king—Jesus—than Caesar (Acts 17:6–7). The scene related by John, which ends with a declaration of loyalty put into the mouth of the Jews, "We have no king but Caesar" (John 19:12–15), may perhaps be an allusion to this.

Christianity did indeed have a political effect to the extent that it created a new type of social organization, the church. With the church there arose, for the first time, a purely religious form of social organization with no national dimension. A society is usually founded on such natural ties as kinship, shared territory, or allegiance to a common sovereign. Here a community appeared in which the unifying principle was not political. Judaism had already founded membership in the community on respect for the law. With Christianity, the community was founded on faith.

Christianity rendered such natural ties as those of the family relative. It reasserted the duty to assist one's parents that is implied in the Decalogue (Matt. 15:4), but flesh and blood kinship cedes to a new type of family

(Matt.10:35–37; 12:48). As has been remarked, this was a revolutionary message. Paul tells the Christian that he is neither Jew nor Greek, neither free man nor slave, neither man nor woman (Gal. 3:28). The point is not to eliminate or deny these differences but to refuse them definitive pertinence.

Christianity has not had any direct influence on slavery. It has not, as Monsieur Homais declares in Flaubert's *Madame Bovary*, "freed the slaves," or "introduced into the world a moral code."[26] It has been content with making slavery increasingly difficult, without demanding its immediate abolition. The Bible, like the Qur'an at a later date, accepted the inequality between masters and slaves as a social fact admitted throughout the ancient world. I might recall that slaves engaged in a revolt—Spartacus in Roman antiquity or the Blacks (Zanj) in ninth-century Iraq—themselves owned slaves.[27]

For Paul, the true state (*politeuma*) was in heaven (Phil. 3:20); Christians, having no permanent city here below, are strangers on this earth (Heb. 13:14; 11:14). The conduct of the Christian is expressed in the vocabulary of participation in the affairs of a city. "You are strangers and aliens (*paroikos*) no longer. No, you are fellow citizens of the saints and members of the household of God" (Eph. 2:19). The true city is the heavenly Jerusalem (Heb. 12:22; Rev. 21:2, 10). Its laws should, in the final analysis, render those of the state inoperative: Paul expresses dismay that a Christian could bring a case against another Christian to be adjudicated before a pagan court (1 Cor. 6:1–8); thus he puts into place the idea of an alternative jurisdiction, a move that would have weighty consequences.[28]

In contrast, Christianity made no political demands, strictly speaking. This is because it was not a community of a political sort. But there are also reasons of principle: the Christian is urged to pray for the head of the state, who in Paul's day was Nero, an emperor who persecuted Christians (1 Pet. 2:13–17; 1 Tim. 2:1–2; Titus 3:1). These somewhat conventional exhortations sound decidedly conservative to our ears. They do, in fact, sketch out a political theory: all authority comes from God, hence it seeks the common good. As a result, resisting authority can only be the affair of wrongdoers (Rom. 13:1–7).

This recognition of the state might seem a meek resignation or a comfortable installation within the temporal. It is in reality just the opposite, for it is deduced from the status of Christians as foreigners, which Peter begins by recalling (1 Pet. 2:11). It is an eschatological attitude: by living as if the end of the world were nigh, the Christian cannot settle down in that world.[29] Moreover, there are moral reasons for submission to the state. It internalizes obedience: one must obey out of conscience, not simply out of fear (Rom. 13:5). By the same token, obedience no longer refers directly to the state; its first object is God and God alone. The state receives all that it demands in order to function as a state, but it is opposed by a radical refusal when it asks to be taken as the object of a cult. Idolatry of the state is excluded.

One aspect of the New Testament puts Christianity into a direct relation with the notion of the law: the enemy *par excellence,* the enigmatic figure of the Antichrist, is called "mystery of iniquity" (*anomia*). He or it is opposed to the ambiguous figure, inflected alternately in the masculine and the neutral, of the person or thing that "restrains" him or "holds him back"(2 Thess. 2:6–7).[30]

New Laws?

As compared to the Old Testament, the New has almost no juridical texts. Ibn Khaldun even expresses astonishment at the absence of "juridical qualifications" (*ahkām*), and he remarks that, for the most part, the Gospels contain narrations and moral exhortations. Qirqisānī, a Karaite Jew, comments that Paul imposes no obligation on anyone and reduces religion to humility alone.[31] At the center of these narrations there is that of the life of Jesus, in particular of his final days, and the message of his resurrection. It has been said that the Gospels are accounts of the Passion with long prefaces. They mention Jesus' explicit refusal to act as judge or arbiter in a question of inheritance (Luke 12:13–15).[32]

The commandments are not rejected, but, quite to the contrary, maintained with total rigor. The Gospel according to Matthew tells us (5:17–19) that Jesus stated that he had not come to abolish the law but to fulfill it (*plerōsai*).[33] This verse probably originated in a conservative Judeo-Christian milieu in response to groups of enthusiastic followers of "false" prophets, if not directly in response to Paul, as Rudolf Bultmann thought.[34] The Jesus presented in Matthew goes even further than the rabbis of the Talmud concerning the intangibility of the law by adding the prophets as similarly untouchable.[35] Not only does Jesus recall the commandments; he reinforces them. The height that the evangelists choose as the setting for the Sermon on the Mount alludes to the gift of the law on Mount Sinai. Jesus gives certain commandments a more radical form, introducing them by the recurrent formula: "You have heard the commandment imposed on your forefathers. . . . What I say to you is . . ." (Matt. 5:21–22, 27–28, 31–32, 38–39, 43–44). Overall, what matters is that external actions be completed by the inner attitudes that are their source. Thus the commandments shift from the socio-political sphere to that of morality, carrying through the thrust of the Decalogue, which ends with the prohibition of envy.[36]

For Jesus, fulfilling the law means interpreting it according to God's original intention. His attitude toward the law is characterized by a demand for authority that sets him off from the scribes (Mark 1:22). It contests much more than the order of the law, bearing instead on all structures of constraint. Certain commandments—those that concern the Sabbath or dietary purity, for example—become less stringent (Mark 2:27; 7:15).[37] Others reinterpret the connection between the law and wisdom (Matt. 7:24–25; Mark 13:33–34; Luke 12:35; 16:1–2).

Only once is Jesus presented as dictating a law, and he does so consciously: "I give you a new commandment" (John 13:34), which he later states is "his" commandment (15:12). The claim is shocking, if not blasphemous, but what is new about it is not the content: "You shall love your neighbor as yourself" appears in the Old Testament (Lev. 19:18), and the Greek of the New Testament mirrors unswervingly the Hebrew turn of phrase that expresses reciprocity. Admittedly, in Leviticus the phrase is drowned within a large body of apparently unrelated dispositions, and emphasizing it is already a significant gesture. Jesus was not the first to do so, however: a century before him, Hillel had already reduced the Torah to that commandment alone.[38] Moreover, it had been true for some time that one's "neighbor" no longer referred only to members of the tribe, but had taken on the universal sense of "all men."

Jesus' only real addition is a reference to a specific history, when he immediately follows "love one another" with "as I have loved you." The comparison implies the whole of the life of Jesus, up to and including his death on the cross, which is interpreted as a death for love: "There is no greater love than this: to lay down one's life for one's friends" (John 15:13); "It is precisely in this that God proves his love for us: that while we were still sinners, Christ died for us" (Rom. 5:8). In the Old Covenant, the commandments were linked to a historical event, the exodus from Egypt, the liberation of the people of Israel, and its installation in the Promised Land. The historical fact here is the Passion: it is interesting that at the moment of the Transfiguration, the Passion is referred to as a passage (*exodus*) (Luke 9:31).

The Christian reinterpretation of the commandments affects their context, not their content. What changes is not the practice that God demands of men, but rather the context of practice within the action that God deploys in favor of mankind. *The passage from the Old to the New Covenant is a change from one exodus to another one.*

Commandments and Counsels

A distinction was thus set up between "commandments" and "counsels" that was to become classic throughout later Christianity. The differentiation was implied in the Old Testament, where the wisdom literature recommends, but does not order, prudent comportment.[39] Such advice does not form a "Christian morality" different from other moral systems, in particular, different from the "Jewish morality" out of which it emerged historically.[40] To tell the truth, counsels do not form a moral code at all. This is clear in the episode of the "rich young man" (Matt. 19:16–22). Jesus reminds him of the commandments and tells him to keep them "if you wish to enter into life." Then, as the young man seems discontented with the answer, Jesus adds that there are more radical demands to be met "if you seek perfection (*teleios*)." The two statements are hypothetical imperatives. Those who are dissatisfied with the indispensable minimum are at liberty to seek more.

The Christian vocabulary of counsel is rooted in the parable of the "Good Samaritan." After the Samaritan has cared for the wounded man, he entrusts him to the care of the innkeeper, promising the latter that he will reimburse him, on his return, for "any further expense." The Vulgate translates: *quodcumque supererogaveris* (Luke 10:35). This is the source of the term "supererogation."[41]

The writings of St. Paul contain many injunctions that Paul delivers regarding concrete cases that had been put to him. This limits their application. They contain another distinction to be added to this first one, between what Paul says as advice or counsel (*suggnōme*) and what he delivers as a commandment (*epitage*) (1 Cor. 7:6). Paul also distinguishes between what the Lord says and what he says in his own name. He states, for example, "To those now married, however, I give his command (*paraggeōl, praecipio*) (though it is not mine; it is the Lord's): a wife must not separate from her husband" (7:10), and he cites a teaching of Jesus (Matt. 9:3–9). He adds immediately afterward: "With respect to virgins, I have not received any commandment from the Lord, but I give my opinion as one who is trustworthy" (7:25). This distinction leaves room for interpretation: how to do good in a particular case is entrusted to the imagination of those who feel themselves called to do so.

New Testament writings thus contain nothing "political" and, in the final analysis, hardly any "morality" either. In compensation, they contain the seeds of a transformation of the entire domain of the practical.

The Qur'an

We are much less well informed about the real origin of the Qur'an than Muslim tradition would have us think.[42] Tradition tells us the fine tale of a message that was first oral, then noted in fragmentary fashion on a number of material supports. When divergences in the recitations became highly apparent, these were supposedly collected together to form the Qur'an and "published" by the caliph Uthman (644–55), who reportedly ordered the destruction by fire of all other versions but his. The philologists are somewhat dubious, and their conclusions tend to diverge widely: for some, the Qur'an is a later text, made of bits and pieces, that attained its definitive form only with the caliph 'Abd al-Malik (685); others go Muslim tradition one better and trace the composition of certain portions of the text to the Prophet himself.[43]

The oldest datable manuscripts of the Qur'an were thought to come from the late eighth century and the ninth century until the discovery made in the Great Mosque of Sanaa, in Yemen, in 1972, which permitted the identification of some texts as dating from slightly earlier than 750.[44] The oldest passages that can be dated securely, however, are the inscriptions on the Dome of the Rock (called the Mosque of 'Umar) in Jerusalem, built in 691. These inscriptions are more in the Qur'anic style than they are Qur'anic, strictly speaking, since they do not coincide perfectly with the text we possess.

Literary Genre and Origin

In the form in which we have it today, the Qur'an begins—if we start with the final surahs, which are the shortest but probably also the oldest—with menaces in an apocalyptical style, accompanied by descriptions of the end of the world. These warnings are based on comparisons with treatments of fate in other, earlier prophets, either biblical or from Arabic legend.

The Qur'an does not contain arguments, strictly speaking, that draw a conclusion from general premises. Rather, it proceeds by analogy on the basis of signs. In this it prefigures one of the most striking traits of the type of reasoning by analogy (qiyās) that dominates later Muslim thought.

Neither does it contain narratives, in the strict sense of the term. No history is recounted from beginning to end except that of Joseph, which is introduced as "the most beautiful of stories." Moreover, logical order is often turned upside down. No plot line is original, and none claims to be. Everything comes from elsewhere and can be found elsewhere, in the earlier holy books, but also in the Midrash or the apocryphal books of the New Testament. The Qur'an is presented as the confirmation (tasdīq) of such earlier texts. Thus it contains what I prefer to call paranarratives, variations on themes supposed to be known, in which force of conviction resides more in the style than in working out the content of the narrative.[45]

In theory, the Qur'an sets itself apart from purely human writings and narrations. The text that has come down to us uses the term kitāb on a number of occasions. In classical Arabic, the word means "book." As it is used in the Qur'an, it seems to communicate not so much the idea of a physical support covered with signs than the general notion of a text fixed in advance, and that proclamation simply delivers.[46]

Unlike the books of the Bible, both Hebrew and Christian, which are inspired texts, the Qur'an is dictated. Muhammad explicitly denies being its author. A messenger (rasūl) has transmitted it to him, causing the text to descend into the heart of the Prophet.[47] That messenger is sometimes called the Spirit of Holiness, sometimes the Spirit of Faith and Truth, and, on one occasion, Gabriel.[48] A rather obscure passage alludes to the specific circumstances of that revelation.[49]

In Christianity, the idea of inspiration does not apply to the result of the activity of proclamation or writing, but rather to the person carrying out that activity: the prophet who, preaching or writing, receives the inspiration that prompts him to proclaim or redact the message. This process does not short-circuit human initiative; rather, that initiative is illuminated from the inside. This is uniquely the case concerning the message to be transmitted. The vehicle of that transmission can be weak, but his message remains true concerning its teaching about God and about what conduct to follow, even if it also conveys a vision of an outdated world. For Islam, in contrast, the Prophet is in no sense the author of the Qur'an. He is merely its passive receiver. Thus he must be described as being as free as possible from any influence.

A large part of the traditional biography of Muhammad was composed with that need in mind. Thus the scene of the beginnings of his revelation is to be placed within an extremely ancient series of narratives in which an unauthorized speaker—not a "professional," not inscribed in the guild of singers or prophets—wins legitimacy by invoking a supernatural authority. Hesiod, in the Greek tradition, and Amos, in Israel, use analogous strategies at roughly the same epoch in narrations structured in similar ways, admitting their amateur status before mentioning the Muses, in the first case, and YHWH, in the second.[50] Tradition relates a dialogue between Muhammad and the angel Gabriel in which the former claims himself incapable of "proclaiming" until he is constrained to do so. A somewhat troubling parallel can be found in the experience of the Anglo-Saxon poet Caedmon, the author of poetic paraphrases of Scripture, as told by the Venerable Bede (d. 735).[51] Moreover, the surname that Muhammad received, al-Amīn, means, literally, "he who returns what has been left on deposit with him as he received it." An adjective that probably designates the Prophet as of the pagan nations (ummī) is traditionally interpreted as meaning "unlettered."[52] Just as Mary had to be a virgin in order for the Incarnation to take place, so the

Prophet had to be intact, innocent of all writing, in order for his "inlettera-
tion" to be possible.[53]

Status

A first consequence is that the Qur'an is supposed to be inimitable. A repeated challenge, always following the same schema, states: Let anyone
who may bring one surah or ten or a narration (hadith) that even resembles
what Muhammad has just recited; let them invoke another than Allah, if
they are sincere! This challenge leads to a positive affirmation: neither men
nor jinni could do anything of the sort, even if they combined forces.[54] These
verses provide the basis for the doctrine, elaborated later, of the inimitability
of the Qur'an, or, more precisely, of the idea that Allah makes men incapable
(i'jāz) of equaling it.[55] A "theologian" of the late tenth century, Baqillanī,
compares the masterpieces of Arabic literature and the Qur'an; while Occi-
dentals find the former far superior, he shows the contrary to be true.[56] There
are even texts in which freethinkers are reported to have tried to take up the
challenge by writing parodies (mu'ārada) of the Qur'an, with the obvious result of a resounding failure.[57] The inimitable perfection of the Qur'an is the
greatest—indeed the only—miracle claimed by Islamic dogma. It is a permanent miracle, perpetually accessible to anyone who will acknowledge it.[58]

A second consequence is that interpreting the Qur'an becomes a problematic enterprise. Although it was common practice in the early days, interpretation (tafsīr) becomes suspect by the end of Islam's first century. It is
acceptable only on the basis of an attested tradition, as was the case with
juridical traditions. When interrogated about the meaning of a passage, a
Companion is reported as answering simply: "God has well said what he
wanted" (qad asāba 'LLahu bihi alladhī arāda).[59]

A final consequence is that everything in the Qur'an must be true. The
precepts that it contains come from Allah and from Allah alone. They can
only be interpreted in light of the circumstances of their application. It is
out of the question to subject them, as in a judgment in equity, to a reasoning that appeals from the letter of the law to the intention of the legislator.
This gives Qur'anic precepts a totally different weight from biblical ones, in
spite of a content that is at times identical.

The female veil provides a typical example. It appears in both the Qur'an
and the New Testament, as has often been remarked. In the Qur'an it is Allah who is speaking and who commands believing women to "draw their
veils over their bosoms" and "cast their outer garments over their persons."[60]
In the New Testament there is a fairly long and fairly obscure passage in

which Paul, too, tells women to be veiled when they pray (1 Cor. 11:3–16). The two recommendations are thus quite close in their content, but the text of the epistle is not a command from God but counsel from Paul. We can interpret Paul's intention as a desire for women to be decently dressed, advice that can be adapted according to the criteria in force in a given place and time. If, on the contrary, Allah in person is the author of the injunctions in the Qur'an, it is hard to see how any interpretation could go beyond an explication of the length or opacity of the veil or an examination of words: exactly what parts of the body and what sort of "garments" are involved? To claim to return from the letter to the unsoundable intention of God the legislator is unthinkable. Generally speaking, when Muslim law does use interpretation, it does not consider it to be the source of law.[61]

Legislation

The Qur'an insists on the necessity of obeying divine injunctions; it recalls the unhappy fate of those who disobeyed in the past and that still awaits the adversaries of the Prophet. The content of these injunctions appears only quite discreetly, however.

The Qur'an does not seem to be presented, as a whole, as a "law." The idea of law is not clear in it. What is at times translated as "law" is *furqān*, which probably signifies "salvation" and, taken in the sense of "discrimination," later designated the Qur'an as a whole.[62] Still, according to a tradition that goes back to the Abbasid period, the Qur'anic message was perceived from the outset as "law." The "monotheist" (*hanīf*) Waraqa ibn Nawfal is supposed to have equated the first revelations to Muhammad with the great *nāmūs* (from the Greek, *nomos*, "law") handed down to Moses. The expression may have originated in the Eucharistic liturgy of the Eastern churches, which draws a parallel between "called by the Law" (*dia nomou*) and "trained/educated by the prophets," thus suggesting that Nomos could be a proper name. In any event, the Greek word was later taken to be an Arabic expression designating the angel Gabriel.[63] One of the earliest mentions of Islam in Christian chronicles speaks of the "unity of the law" brought by Muhammad, who is often characterized as a legislator in the oldest non-Muslim accounts of his biography.[64]

The Qur'anic message implies a new deal, politically and socially; it brings a redefinition of ties among men. The Last Judgment, which the initial preaching of Muhammad said was imminent, was to dissolve all social ties: no one could intercede for another person, for example, the patron for the client.[65] Conversely, universal judgment presupposes criteria common to all, according to which every individual will be judged impartially.[66]

The constitution of a group of believers who have accepted the prophetic announcement changes the situation: radical isolation operated eschatologically for the Last Judgment; it is transposed in the daily life of the political. Instead of facing God, who judges, the individual faces Muhammad, who recruits. Brothers and kin can become enemies; hence adhesion to the group of believers must have priority over ties of filiation or affiliation. Jesus had already weakened the importance of family ties. Islam, too, results in a redistribution of social allegiances. The isolation of believers is here stronger than in Judaism or Christianity.[67] The social magma, made fluid more deeply than in the former two religions, might crystallize differently.

The rules of judgment, which were at first only implicit in the pronouncements made in Mecca, were made explicit at Medina. Muhammad's aim in his preaching was not to lay the foundations for legislation. Genuine Islamic law was derived from it later and was only partially dependent on it. Verses regarding legislation are, admittedly, few in number, but the passages are long, and they lack the repetitions that abound elsewhere. A few precepts, however, do have legislative value.[68] The Qur'an calls these "commandments" or "laws (hudūd) of God." These are primarily dispositions concerning rites and the cult.[69] The juridical is represented above all by regulations of civil law: rulings regarding inheritance, debts (to which the longest verse of the entire Qur'an is dedicated), and prohibiting fermented beverages and certain games. There are also detailed dispositions regarding marriage, the repudiation of a wife, and women's garments, including the veil.[70]

Even the regulations pronounced at Medina responded to specific cases. The commentators connect them with strictly specific circumstances in the life of Muhammad, for example, with the story of ʿĀʾishah, the Prophet's youngest and favorite wife, when she was accused of adultery. The verses protesting her innocence serve as a base for legislation: one hundred lashes to the woman or man guilty of adultery, but only if there are four witnesses, which renders conviction extremely difficult.[71]

There are problems inherent in all of these points, however. In spite of the formal interdiction to Muslim women against marrying an infidel, Ibn Masʿūd, one of Muhammad's Companions, implores his sister not to do so, but he does not invoke the Qur'an. This suggests that the text we read today did not exist at the time.[72] Similarly, according to a hadith, Muhammad boasts of maintaining the biblical stoning of adulterous women in its full rigor, at a time when the Jews had long abandoned the practice. The Qur'an, as we have it, speaks only of whipping. Thus a verse regarding stoning had to be invented, a purely virtual passage that somehow missed being included in the written collection of revelations.[73]

Redefinition of Social Ties?

At this point we can return to the relations that, according to Aristotle, make the "household" the nucleus of the polis—relations, that is, of man and wife, the father and his children, and the master and his slaves.[74]

Relations between man and wife are clearly unequal: "Men are the protectors and maintainers of women, because Allah has given the one more [strength] than the other."[75] There is nothing exceptional about this inequality according to the accepted morality of the ancient world, as expressed, for example, by St. Paul (1 Tim. 2:11–12). Contrary to what is often affirmed, however, the position stated in the Qur'an represents a step backward from the way things were before Islam. Thus the way in which Khadījah took the initiative by proposing marriage to Muhammad indicates a freedom of mores of which revelation disapproved. Medieval Muslims were at times aware of this restriction, for example, when the writer Jāhiz, in the ninth century, remarks that men and women could converse freely before the Prophet imposed the veil on his wives.[76] A stupid legend, still too widespread, attributes to the Qur'an the injunction to beat one's wife periodically: the verse cited above limits its advice to recommending the beating of wives suspected of infidelity. A woman can inherit only one-half of a man's share, and her testimony is worth only one-half of a man's in law cases.[77]

It has often been remarked that the Qur'an protests female infanticide and burying female children alive. Such practices are not unheard of among very poor peoples, and in China as well. We have no idea how widespread they were in pre-Islamic Arabia, nor even whether they existed. One passage is often understood as speaking of a baby girl buried alive (*al-maw'ūida*), but it may refer to the result of a miscarriage. What is prohibited is infanticide in general, of both male and female babies. Allah promises to "provide sustenance," thus warding off the poverty that is behind such an act.[78] And in fact the practice declined, thanks to a revolution that was a good deal less moral than economic: the Arab conquerors took the places of the previous elites and, like their predecessors, lived on the peasantry of their subject lands. At that point they could give up drastic means of birth control.[79]

The Qur'anic message has often been credited with a concern for "social justice." It accepts the inequality between masters and slaves as a social fact. Does it recommend modifying that situation? The Qur'an is ambiguous: "Allah has bestowed His gifts of sustenance more freely on some of you than on others: those more favored are not going to throw back their gifts to those whom their right hands possess [their slaves], so as to be equal in that respect. Will they then deny the favors of Allah?" This can be understood as an injunction: not to keep his gifts would be to deny the liberality of Allah.

The passage could also be seen as expressing a regret, however: to deny Allah's favors would be to fail to imitate his liberality by repeating it. It is simpler to see the passage as a bare and morally neutral statement. A parallel suggests this interpretation: just as the rich do not distribute their goods to the poor, so Allah does not abandon his dignity to the false gods.[80]

Could Muhammad have had in mind a redistribution of goods in favor of the poor? His earliest partisans seem to have been young and poor: today we might call them the down and out or the marginalized. This is in any event what we can deduce indirectly from the fact that Noah's disciples are reported to have been caricatured by their adversaries as "the meanest among us." St. Paul describes the early Christians in hardly more flattering terms. Sociology find this quite plausible: revolutions find their perpetrators among those who have nothing to lose.[81]

It could also very well be said that the Prophet took the part of the notables of Mecca when he decided to Islamize the pilgrimage that was a source of revenue for that city, even playing into the hands of the Quraysh by eliminating all religious and commercial competition and by centralizing the cult, somewhat as the kings of Israel had done by allying themselves with the priests of Jerusalem. It even seems that Muhammad's agreement with his compatriots disappointed certain of his poorer partisans, who then fled to the shores of the Red Sea to live on brigandage. They declared themselves Muslims, but until the taking of Mecca without recognizing the authority of Muhammad. All things considered, Muhammad did little to change the structure of Meccan society.[82] The great upheavals were more the consequence of the conquests.

The Birth of a State

The political dimension of the Qur'an springs from precepts that seem at first sight to have more to do with morality alone. As examples of this one might point to the many verses regarding alms (sadaqa). In general, they say to give what is "superfluous" or "beyond your needs," but they also specify a percentage: one-fifth of the "booty."[83] Those who are to receive alms are listed repeatedly: close kin, orphans, the needy, "the wayfarer," beggars ("those who ask"), and perhaps captives ("ransom for slaves"); "parents and kindred," orphans, "those in want," "wayfarers" and beggars (again, perhaps captives); parents, kinsfolk, orphans, those in need, near neighbors or neighbors who are strangers (not members of the tribe), "the Companion by your side," the wayfarer, and slaves ("what your right hands possess"); Allah, "the Messenger" (the Prophet) and those close to him, orphans, the needy, and "the wayfarer."[84] It is difficult to see how Allah could benefit directly from alms, but in any event, the Prophet's upkeep was a responsibility of the community.

The most detailed list serves as a basis for later legislation. According to this verse, alms "are for the poor and the needy, and those employed to administer the (funds); for those whose hearts have been (recently) reconciled (to Truth); for those in bondage and in debt; in the cause of Allah, and for the wayfarer." Those wayfarers, or "sons of the road," are understood by the commentators as being travelers, but the "road" in question is Allah's— that is, the "road" on which Muslims combat their enemies.[85] Succor offered to a group of emigres on their arrival in Medina is a sort of revolutionary tax; in the context of an established Muslim city, alms would have the function of a redistribution of wealth. The city is already a presence, however, and the lists of who should receive alms reads like an outline for an apparatus of state.[86] To translate almsgiving in bald but anachronistic terms: the taxes go to the leaders, to the functionaries of the financial arm, to propaganda, to social security, and to the army.

A Political Theology and a Political Anthropology

If the message that the Qur'an attributes to God contains political aspects, the presence of the political is even stronger, and more influential, in the very manner in which the text imagines God. The God of the Qur'an is intrinsically "political." In the early 1900s Julius Wellhausen gave striking expression to this notion: Allah is "the personification of the sovereignty of the state."[87] Thus state revenues are called "goods of Allah" as early as Muhammad's time, an expression that prefigures the audacity of Hobbes when he defined "holy" as the religious equivalent of what kingdoms call "public."[88]

One particular attribute of Allah—his omnipotence—is emphasized.[89] The idea of course appears in the Old Testament (Gen. 18:14) and the New Testament (Matt. 19:26; Luke 1:37), and it made its way into the *Credo* by which Christians confess "the all-powerful Father" (*pantokratōr; omnipotens*). But in Christianity—precisely—omnipotence is a modality of paternity. It is as Father that the Christian God is all-powerful, and that all-powerfulness has no other aim but the affirmation of his fatherhood. God is, in effect, capable of proposing to all beings, without exception, to enter into a relation of filiation with Him. Moreover, God is able to deploy an entire economy of salvation such that all creatures can recognize that they will benefit by accepting that filiation. In Islam, on the other hand, Allah is not father, and his omnipotence stands alone. It, and not the beauty of the Creator, is what creation reveals. That power is more likely to be manifested in a capacity for destruction than for construction.[90]

In the Qur'an, Allah's omnipotence is explicitly situated "on earth": to resist it is to want to "reduce [Allah] to powerlessness on the earth." The will of Allah must be done, "on earth as it is in heaven," as in the "Our Father." In Christianity, however, the fulfillment of the will of God is left to his divine initiative, and the "Thy will be done" really means "Do Thy will." The Qur'an, in contrast, conceives that fulfillment as the installation of the terrestrial reign of that will, thanks to the obedience that is due the Prophet. This is why refusing him obedience, "frustrating" him, is claimed to reduce Allah to powerlessness.[91] Divine omnipotence is thus realized through a terrestrial reign that legitimates the use of force. The famous Qur'anic formula "no compulsion in religion" is by no means an interdiction, but rather the resigned acknowledgment of a fact. Moreover, it applies to entering into Islam, not to leaving it.[92]

The notion of "tyranny" (*zulm*) is applied to wicked leaders, but not to criticize or correct their attitude toward their subordinates, as is true in the Bible, where God intervenes to liberate his people. It is toward Allah, not toward Israel or toward his own people, that Pharaoh is "tyrannical."[93]

It has been said that Muslim anthropology derives from the domain of the law.[94] The anthropology of the Qur'an is "political" from the start, in that it conceives of the relation between man and the other creatures as one of dominator to dominated. It does not depart from the biblical vision of man where the content of that domination is concerned, but rather by its modality: for the Bible, subjecting the rest of creation is a task that God gives humankind, and it is couched in the imperative; for the Qur'an, that submission is a given, because it has already been realized by Allah: "Don't you see that Allah has made subject to you [men] all that is on the earth?" Similarly, Genesis represents God as learning from Adam the names of the animals that He presents to him, but in the Qur'an these names as dictated by Allah.[95]

There have been a number of glosses on the title "caliph" as attributed to man, but it is probably appropriate to moderate speculation. In fact, where the term appears, it is used absolutely, without a noun complement, and the formula "caliph of Allah" never appears. Given that the word originally applied to a person who succeeds a previous occupant of an abandoned territory, not a representative or a delegate, it seems that man was conceived of as being the successor . . . of the angels.[96]

The Function of Legitimation

With the general theory of authority as a background, there is one concrete authority that Allah himself legitimates: that of Muhammad. The Qur'an, speaking through Muhammad, demands obedience to Allah and to the Prophet himself. There are eight reiterations of the injunction, "Obey Allah and His Messenger!"[97] The prophet of Islam is simply reiterating and applying to himself an attitude that he considers typical of all prophecy: "So fear Allah and obey me" is an echo of Noah and the prophets Hud, Salih, Lot, and Shuʿayb.[98] Muhammad appears to have used the formula elsewhere than in the Qurʾan, speaking in his own name in some of his letters that have come down to us addressed to various groups of Arabs who made their submission to him—providing that the letters are authentic. No authority can be more vast in its scope, because disobedience prompts immediate and definitive punishment: obedience to Allah and his Prophet makes a believer worthy of paradise; disobedience condemns him to hell.[99] A hadith founds this rigor on the notion that to resist Muhammad is to resist God himself: "Whoever is a rebel to Muhammad is a rebel to God."[100]

Authority must be transmitted to those who are not prophets, however. The Qurʾan permits this. The clearest statement of this is a passage that has been called the "verse of the leaders [emirs]": "O you who believe! Obey Allah, and obey the Messenger, and those charged with authority among you."[101] The problem is, of course, to know to whom this vague expression applies. To generals, of course, and to scholars, with each of the two milieus making special demands that vary from one age to another, according to the influence each group wields at the time.[102]

The content of that obedience is not always specified, but the divine power is concretely present in the messengers: "Allah gives power to His Messengers over any He pleases."[103] The Qurʾan also sketches out something resembling a penal code. The punishment for unbelievers is not only *post mortem*: the Qurʾan describes hell with a wealth of details, some of which even Muslims found shocking, such as the idea that the skin of the damned, once "roasted through," regrows, to be burned anew, like Prometheus' liver.[104] Even during this life, the Qurʾan lists a number of specific punishments: "The punishment of those who wage war against Allah and His Messenger, and strive with might and main for mischief through the land is: execution, or crucifixion, or the cutting off of hands and feet from opposite sides, or exile from the land."[105] By their unbelief, unbelievers place themselves outside of common humanity; they are "the worst of beasts."[106]

But the Qurʾan presents *something like an empty, or open, legitimacy, waiting for a content to come and fill it*. The question of the devolution of power is not resolved, nor is that of its exercise. It is nearly impossible to draw from the Qurʾan any indication of the type of regime—monarchy, aristocracy, or democracy—that Allah might desire. What we do find is the idea of a political power exercised by Allah himself. The question of the earthly agent of that power is not even posed in the Qurʾan. This is because there is no need to do so, given that Muhammad is present and exercises authority over his community directly. His death thus represented a serious difficulty. We can understand that it was hard to permit the announcement of his death, and we are told that ʿUmar and Uthman were ready to spread the rumor that Muhammad, like the Jesus of the Qurʾan, had been whisked away to Allah, or, according to a model that flourished later in Shiism, had "entered into occultation."[107] Only the intervention of Abū Bakr, Muhammad's father-in-law and later the first caliph, forced them to accept an ineluctable truth. We can also guess why Islam, which celebrates the birth of the Prophet with growing pomp in the course of its history, does not remember his death, while Buddhism celebrates the definitive extinction of its founder and the Christian calendar is focused on the death (to be sure, followed by the resurrection) of Christ.[108]

The central political problem of Islam—a problem that returns in new forms throughout the history of Muslim civilizations—was thus to know how to make use of the overabundance of legitimacy that it made available, to decide who was to be the beneficiary of that legitimacy, and where that massive, terrifying, but floating power should be invested.

Sacred Books and the Legitimation of Power

Other sacred books provide passages similar to the ones we have just examined. The Old Testament contains narratives of bloody conquests in which God orders that the vanquished be massacred to the last man. The Bible relates cruel punishments, commanded by God, in which the divine desires go well beyond the exigencies of the political. The king of the Amalekites is executed by Samuel's own hand, in spite of some shilly-shallying on the part of King Saul; thus God uses his prophet to disavow the magnanimous conduct of that king (1 Sam. 15).[109] This is history, however, or at least a reconstructed account of imaginary events of the past. The true kingdom is to come, relegated to an eschatological future. Nothing indicates that any divine legitimation can be credited to a present power. Far from receiving sanction from religion, such powers are rendered relative by it.

The Qurʾan, in contrast, gives eschatological hope a new and concrete existence. The only biblical passage quoted in the Qurʾan and cited with a specific reference performs just this task. It is the shortened version of a verse from the Psalms: "My servants, the righteous, shall inherit the earth. / The just shall possess the land and dwell in it forever."[110] The eschatological promise is replaced within the context of an actual conquest.

In the New Testament the writings of St. John contain several statements in which Christ asserts that what is done unto him affects the Father. Other passages apply the same exchange to the disciples. Several of these speak of "hearing my word," where "hearing" should probably be read in the biblical meaning of "obeying." In still others the analogy is quite explicit: "He who accepts anyone I send accepts me, and in accepting me accepts him who sent me."[111] Is this a prefiguration of the statement in the Qur'an that demands obedience to God *and to his messenger*? Only to a certain extent. In the New Testament, no punishment on this earth is mentioned. Moreover, the example of the leader is totally contrary to a victorious political chief. Jesus does indeed promise his disciples a sort of rule: they will sit on thrones and "judge": that is, they will lead the twelve tribes of Israel (Matt. 19:28). Even here, however, the New Testament goes no further than the apocalyptical dreams of the epoch, or than the Qumran group, who imagined and even described in full detail in the Dead Sea scrolls a war between the "sons of light" and the sons of darkness. The promised kingdom is uniquely eschatological. Its arrival is felt to be closer or more distant according to the epoch and, in any case, is left to God's will.

Before the coming of that kingdom, the New Testament recommends obedience to the authorities in terms that are, as we have seen, quite close to those of the Qur'an.[112] Still, there is an essential detail to be stressed that, although it draws a parallel between the Qur'anic injunction and certain passages of the Old Testament, radically distinguishes the Qur'an from the New Testament. In the Pentateuch, the obedience due to God and to the prophet is transferred to the leaders only if they are taken from among the community, just as the king and the prophet of Israel must be taken from among the people (Deut. 17:15; 18:15). The New Testament preaches obedience to rulers who are not necessarily Christians and who even persecuted Christians.

✧

A comparison among the three religions shows a profound difference in how each one articulates the connection between religion and the political structure:

> Judaic messianism, quite apart from being Judaic, was inherently a religious legitimation of a climatic event, not of an ongoing authority. Equally, the Christian empire . . . was a mere adjunction of two distinct conceptual orders which provided no intrinsically religious rationale for imperial rule. What neither the Christians nor the Jews could contrive was an intrinsically religious legitimation of an ongoing authority.[113]

Furnishing the principle of that legitimation was precisely what Islam did.

PART III

Succession through Time

6

Mother Religions and Daughter Religions

Up to now I have presented the three medieval religions in the chronological order of their entry onto the stage of history, which is, quite naturally, also the order of the emergence of their fundamental ideas. That order offers more than an exterior framework. For these religions, succession through time was also a fact that was to become the object of explicit reflection.

The Problem of Posteriority

Later religions (or "daughter religions") all face the same problem: they have to position themselves in relation to the mother religion—or mother religions, if there were several. This problem had its effect on the sacred texts. Each text or group of texts refers back to a prehistory.

The Old Testament provides a model. It is itself pregnant, thick with its own prehistory. It refers to earlier documents and rewrites them. This is the phenomenon that has been called "deuterosis."[1] The Book of Deuteronomy—"Repetition of the Teaching" (*mishneh torah*)—is the prime example. But for Judaism the problem of the attitude to take toward an earlier religion is simply never posed: there are no other holy scriptures earlier than its own. If such did exist, they would be the documents of an "idolatry" with which one must break all ties, and which was all the more dangerous when its object was the *logos* of the philosophers that is, in itself, a sort of law. This was why the rabbis forbid reading such texts.[2] Moreover, Judaism in the strict sense, that is, according to the closing of the canon after the year 70, chooses to accentuate the Torah as well as to include or exclude certain texts.

Christianity and Islam, in contrast, arise when the Jewish Scriptures already exist. Thus both have to face the same problem. They are born in very different circumstances, however: Christianity *arises out of* Judaism, in the two senses that Judaism is its source and that Christianity departs from it—by both expulsion and secession. Christianity concerns Jews, beginning with Jesus and Paul. Islam, on the other hand, is born outside of the Jewish people, far from the land of Israel, and it boasts of a prophet who is explicitly *ummī*—which probably means belonging to the nations; a "gentile."[3]

Regarding the sacred texts, the two later religions found themselves faced with a symmetrical problem: in a word, the first Christians had *too many* sacred texts, while the first Muslims *did not have enough*. One might say they suffered from a complex of being without a book, hence ignorant (*jāhil*) in comparison to the Jews and the Christians, who had one.

Christianity: Revolution

Christianity was born in a Jewish milieu: Jesus, his disciples, Paul, and later on the first to be designated as Christians were all faithful Jews. All of them, either as pious laymen or, in the case of Paul, as a professional, had a profound knowledge of Scripture and of the oral traditions that commented on Scripture and that began to put its teachings into systematic order.

The New Testament as a Pesher of the Old

Christianity is a particular interpretation of the religion of Israel on the basis of an event that it considers to be central and that, according to the evangelical tradition, makes it obligatory to reread all of the experience of the Jewish people in a new light and a new hermeneutic key. Judaism has a technical term to designate the exegetic style in which a passage of Scripture is understood and re-actualized on the basis of an event: it is *pesher*. Thus the Qumran texts contain a *pesher* of the prophet Habakkuk aimed at showing how that prophet's predictions are realized in current events. There is an example of this procedure in the New Testament itself in the Gospel of Luke, when Jesus speaks in the synagogue in Capernaum, commenting on a passage from Isaiah. After reading the scroll, he states: "Today this Scripture passage is fulfilled in your hearing" (Luke 4:21). A comment of the sort is in itself in no way extraordinary, and must even have been banal at the time. Its novelty lies in the claim that the accomplishment of prophecy is tied to the person speaking.

Where content is concerned, certain passages of Scripture must have been scrutinized with particular attention, such as the famous "Songs of the

Servant of the Lord" in Second Isaiah, which seemed to prefigure Christ's Passion. All of the New Testament, however, rests on a rereading of the Old Testament on the basis of the events in Galilee and Jerusalem. The account of the pilgrims at Emmaus furnishes the canonical formula: the risen Jesus, "beginning . . . with Moses and all the prophets," "interpreted for them every passage of Scripture which referred to him" (Luke 24:27).

In any event, that procedure implies that the old Scriptures are conserved in their full legitimacy—indeed, it demands that they be, and even that they cannot be replaced by others. In point of fact, though, the Scriptures mentioned in the New Testament are not the New Testament itself: when St. Paul, in a passage that was to be used with a normative value, declares that "all Scripture is inspired by God and is useful for teaching" (2 Tim. 3:16), he is thinking exclusively of the writings of the Old Testament.

Paul: "Christ Is the End of the Law"

The problem that Christianity came second, chronologically, is at the center of Paul's teaching, because it was at the center of his own personal experience. It is Paul who has reflected the most intensely on the law. His meditation rethinks the concept from top to bottom and establishes the background for all of the thought of the Christian Middle Ages. In the Christian and post-Christian world, thought about the law was established on the terrain that he conquered.[4]

Paul's theory of the law is not systematic, nor perhaps even coherent, but it responds—in what has been preserved of his epistles—to precise problems.[5] It is only comprehensible as an entire set of effects produced by a new fact of colossal importance that, like a powerful magnetic field, reshapes everything that approaches it. That new fact is nothing less than the coming of the Messiah of Israel—and of a paradoxical messiah, a crucified messiah.

Converted in the year 34, Paul threw himself (after 43) into missionary voyages that bore good fruit. Communities of converts were formed. What he announces to them is what was transmitted to him (1 Cor. 15:3): the saving significance of the crucifixion of Jesus, manifested by his resurrection. The message was received by Jews and by pagans, and above all by "the God-fearing" (*phohoumenoi, metuentes*), sympathetic to Judaism, who had not adopted all Jewish practices, circumcision in particular. The question soon arose of whether all of the commandments should be imposed on the newcomers. Paul represents the negative response in that controversy.

For Paul, the presence of the Law is what distinguishes the Jewish people: it separates Jews from the others like a dividing wall that now must fall (Eph. 2:14).[6] Nowhere does Paul say that Christians of Jewish origin can dispense with practicing the commandments. Rather, the question is to know if such practice should be obligatory for pagan converts. Given that for Jews, they alone have access to God, the Law that separates Jews from the others becomes for pagans a law that bars their way to God. Such a law can be compared with cosmic regularities: subjecting oneself to the celebration of predetermined dates is to be once more enslaved by "cosmic forces" (Gal. 4:9–10; Col. 2:16, 20). It suggests the idea of a "law of the world" parallel to the law of Moses.

How are we to understand Paul's lapidary statement, "Christ is the end (*telos*) of the Law" (Rom. 10:4)? He does not speak of an abrogation of the law, to be replaced by another and more perfect law. That concept is Islamic rather than Christian. Some have suggested that certain rabbis of the time held the idea of the abolition of the Torah in the messianic age. If that were the case, Paul would have done little more than acknowledge the paradoxical coming of the Messiah and draw its consequences for the Law. It seems, however, that this is a mistaken interpretation of passages in which the rabbis are actually speaking of a renewed teaching (also *torah*) of the injunctions handed down at Sinai. The only liberation from the Law that the rabbis admit is the one brought by death and entry into a beyond quite distinct from any messianic age.[7]

If salvation is accomplished by the intervention of God, who resuscitates Jesus, the law can no longer have more than a merely instrumental value. The one and only goal, once attained through the law, is henceforth attained by grace. This supposes that one can trace the law to its "end," in relation to which it is merely a means, and even one means among others. Hence Paul launches into an interpretation of the law, not concerning one detail or another, but as a whole.

Conscience

Knowledge of the law thus ceases to be the exclusive prerogative of the Jews. Pagans must also have access to norms. Paul does not hesitate to adapt a body of ideas of Greek origin.[8] In particular, he returns to the Stoic notion of conscience, of the "holy spirit [that] indwells within us, one who marks our good and bad deeds and is our guardian."[9]

In order to will, rather than simply desire, one has to "know what one wants." Willing the good implies knowledge of the good. Paul shifts the problem. It is no longer that of knowing the law: in principle, we already know it. More or less clearly, more or less willingly, we accept letting it shine within us of its own brilliance, but in all cases we have the means of knowing it within ourselves. This is true for all humankind. Jews know the divine will through the law of Moses; pagans know it in another manner. "When Gentiles who do not have the law keep it as by instinct (*phusei*), these men although without the law serve as a law for themselves. They show that the demands of the law are written in their hearts. Their conscience (*syneidesis*) bears witness together with that law, and their thoughts will accuse or defend them" (Rom. 2:14–15). Our conscience enlightens us about what we should do.

That idea is not found elsewhere among Jews. The notion of a knowledge of the law through the force of the conscience alone is foreign to the rabbis. Moreover, Judaism is ill at ease with the idea of conscience: according to Yeshayahu Leibowitz, it is a pagan idea that has no place in Judaism.[10] The idea of conscience can be found in the apocalyptical literature, but presented in a negative light—the impious had the means of knowing what to do, but they failed to profit from the fact: "Each of the inhabitants of the earth committed evil knowingly; it is out of pride that they ignored my Law."[11]

The Qur'an supposes that no one can know how to act well without a revealed Book. Muhammad's adversaries make excuses for their misconduct by offering the pretext that, unlike Jews and Christians, they have received no Book.[12] Significantly, Muhammad does not answer them by appealing to an innate sense of good and evil, but rather by stressing that henceforth, now that a Book is in the process of descending in him, this excuse is no longer valid (which implies that it was valid up to then). Still, after that time the idea of conscience comes to the surface from time to time, for example in apologetics (*kalām*): certain representatives of the so-called "Mutazilite" tendency speak of the angel that God sends to every intelligent man and who speaks to him in a silent language.[13]

Autonomy

Another idea, that of *autonomy*, appears in Paul (Rom. 2:14). The idea is primarily political: the word belongs to the technical vocabulary of international law, and it designates the way in which a political community governs itself, even when it lacks complete authority. Unlike the word used for "liberty" (*eleutheria*), which springs from the most ancient sources of the Greek language and is found as early as Cretan documents written in linear B, the word for "autonomy" is recent, first attested only in 445 BCE. What is more, it does not derive from *nomos*, but rather from the verb *nemō*, "to share": thus one who has his own share is "autonomous." This is the meaning that Sophocles gives to the term when Antigone, condemned to be buried alive, is called *autonomos* because she does not die of sickness or by the sword.[14] Aristotle, as we have seen, speaks of people who are a law unto themselves, but what he means, in the particular context of this passage, is that exceptional beings are *for others* a model to imitate, rather than that there is a rule of some sort that applies only to them. Once, however, Aristotle uses the expression in the same sense as Paul: referring to the citizen and the outstandingly virtuous man, he declares that "such men . . . are themselves a law" (*nomos . . . heautō*).[15] Paul transposes the idea into the realm of individual conduct: certain men spontaneously conform to a rule. In doing so, he reflects a basic tendency of his age. The expression that Paul uses—"the law written on the heart"—comes from the prophets, but he has the audacity to apply it not only to Jews but also to pagans.[16]

A law that can be supposed to be known, and known to all men, must be comprehensible. Thus its content will coincide with the elementary rules that permit the coexistence of individuals and the permanence of the species, what C. S. Lewis called "the Tao."[17] The legal dispositions in question derive from commandments, the reasons for which are intelligible, which are moral in nature, and which are what was later called *mishpatim*. St. Paul pays little attention to the laws known as "ceremonial," unless perhaps to offer an allegorical explanation—for example, of the prohibition on muzzling an ox who is threshing grain.[18] Finally, all of this implies that a special revelation of the law is not necessary. God does indeed appear as the origin of the Law, but not as a lawgiver, strictly speaking.[19] The scene of the gift of the law to Moses loses something of its impact: in the allegorical interpretation that Paul proposes, Hagar, Abraham's concubine "slave girl," stands for the covenant of Mount Sinai, not Sarah, his "freeborn" legitimate wife and mother of the patriarchs (Gal. 4:24–25).

The Ambivalence of the Law

Paul prolongs and radicalizes the process of interiorizing norms that Jesus had already initiated when he identified envy as their adversary.[20] The commandment, which had stated "Thou shalt [do]" becomes "Thou shalt will to."[21] Henceforth the law is the object of the will. In parallel fashion, Paul discovers the central phenomenon of our powerlessness to do good: "The desire to do good is there [in my flesh: *parakeitai*, literally, 'next to me; available'] but not the power." It is all the more painful to acknowledge this fact because we not only fail to do what we want to do, but we do what we do not want to do. Paul says as much just before and just after the above phrase: "I do not do what I want to do but what I hate"; "I do, not the good I will to do, but the evil I do not intend" (Rom. 7:18, 15, 19). The idea seems to have been in the air at the time: the same realization, disillusioned or scandalized, occurs among the Romans, in Ovid's famous "I see the better and approve it, but I follow the worse" (*video meliora proboque, deteriora sequor*), among the Greeks in Epictetus, and, in Judaism, among the Essenes of Qumran.[22]

Thus we might say: We know the law, and only too well—the point is to love it. However, we find it impossible to love the law. By its very existence, the law enables us to know sin (Rom. 3:20; 7:7). Differences become acute, in the sense of the French verb *accuser*, as in a light that heightens the shadows. Where there is no law, there cannot be transgression (Rom. 4:15); sin is not immediately imputed, not charged against the person committing it, perhaps as if in an entry in heaven's books. That only happens the moment that there is law (Rom. 5:13). This precept supposes the same notion as the one forged at a later date: "No crime nor punishment without law" (*nullum crimen, nulla poena sine lege*).[23]

The law, taken in this sense, merely indicates the limit between good and evil. But human covetousness turns it to its own profit: henceforth one can act badly and be fully aware. This is where the paradox lies: the law has two sides to it. On the one hand, the law is holy, just, and good. Evil is illegality (*anomia*) (Rom. 7:12; 6:19). The culmination of evil is even called the "secret force or lawlessness" (2 Thess. 2:7), a phrase that the King James Bible, among others, renders as "the mystery of iniquity." On the other hand, "the law came in order to increase offenses" (Rom. 5:20). It even encourages envy: "I should never have known what evil desire was unless the law had said, 'You shall not covet.'" (Rom. 7:7).[24] Hence "The sting of death is sin, and sin gets its power from the law" (1 Cor. 15:56).

"Everything Would Be Lawful"

The phrase that Dostoevsky puts into the mouth of Ivan Karamazov, where it is a consequence of atheism,[25] is drawn from First Corinthians. It is given there in the context of a discussion of dietary restrictions, and it may have been something like a slogan that came from Paul himself. Paul does not attempt to do away with those rules; rather, he stresses that seeking to know whether an action is permitted or not is beside the point. The criterion is what is "advantageous"—that is, beneficial or constructive—more than the more banal "edifying." If an act is forbidden it is because it is in itself dangerous for the person committing the act, as when one "forbids" a child to play with fire. The texts goes on to say: "'All things are lawful,' but not all are advantageous. 'All things are lawful'—which does not mean that everything is constructive" (1 Cor. 10:23). This statement implies a decision of capital importance: the commandments are not to be heeded to do the will of a god who might find some advantage for himself in the act, but because they are aimed at the good of those on whom they are imposed.

Paul uses a play on words to explain his thought more explicitly: "'Everything is lawful for me (*exesti*)'—but I will not let myself be enslaved (*exousiasthesomai*) by anything [or anyone?]" (1 Cor. 6:12). One might express the same thought, perhaps awkwardly, as "Everything is authorized, but as for myself, I am not subject to any authority," or "Everything is of my domain, but I am not dominated by anything." This means that the good that is the goal of the commandments seems to be liberty. What "edifies" is what liberates. Here this is the description of a state, but it implies an entire program of liberation—which is an infinite task.

Nonetheless, Paul is able to retain the notion of law in what he announces. There is a "law of Christ," and Paul declares himself subject to it (*ennomos Christou*) (1 Cor. 9:21). Only on one occasion does the rabbinic literature use the expression "law of the Messiah" in a phrase that refers to a new interpretation of the law of Moses, not a replacement for it.[26] Paul suggests a content for this notion: "Help carry one another's burdens; in that way you will fulfill the law of Christ" (Gal. 6:2). Elsewhere he speaks of the "law of faith," which he opposes to the law of works (Rom. 3:27). That "law" is less a collection of commandments and prohibitions than a *different regime of salvation.*

The Law and Love

The law is accomplished by love (Gal. 5:14). Here Paul reiterates a statement made by Jesus himself (Matt. 22:40), or by Hillel, who summarized the Law as "you will love your neighbor as yourself," everything else being simply commentary.[27] The commandment to love God is added to the Decalogue beginning with the oldest summaries of the Law, such as the Nash papyrus (ca. 150).[28] That "love" has no resemblance to a "sentiment" that might be opposed to respect for others or obedience to the Law.[29] Paul enumerates as examples of commandments fulfilled by love of one's neighbor the three prohibitions of committing adultery, murder, and theft, which are the seventh, sixth, and eighth in the Decalogue, then jumps to the tenth, "you shall not covet" (Rom. 13:8–10). The point is to prohibit the desire to do wrong, not just the action.

In a famous phrase, St. Augustine summarized Paul's thoughts: "Love and do what you want" (*dilige et quod vis fac*).[30] The statement is highly ironic. On one level, the irony lies in the demand to love, which poses an impossible condition, then immediately supposes it to be realized. To love is precisely what we do not know how to do. But the second part of the statement is just as hard to fulfill as the first, for nothing is more difficult for "me" than to do what *I* want. Most of the time, I want what *they* want me to want, and whether "they" are social or psycho-physiological entities or something else changes nothing. The command to "love" is what makes possible the "do what you want." The necessity for love is thus not the dream of an exalted leap outside the moral domain; to the contrary, it implies an entire program of work for the human subject, turned back to his own responsibility.

Islam: Restoration

Islam arose among a people without a holy book who, as a consequence, felt itself to be "ignorant." In Arabia there were Jewish or Christian tribes, and certain of these seem to have known their own Scriptures quite well. But the Arabs had nothing. They received their holy book by the intermediary of Muhammad. How can we conceive of the relationship of this new Book and those that preceded it? Islam chose to mount a dual strategy of borrowing accompanied by denial of that borrowing.[31]

Confirmation

The Qur'an asserts on several occasions that it confirms (saddaqa) the earlier books, a notion which the Qur'an is probably alluding to when it speaks of confirming "the revelation which is with you" or "what went before."[32] It returns to the figures of the previous Scriptures, with their names and titles: along with certain prophets who appear only there, such as Salih or Hud, the Qur'an presents the great series of biblical ancestors: Adam, Noah, Abraham, Moses, and Jesus.

The Qur'an does not always make much of these personages. Nothing in the Qur'an informs us about the chronological order in which the figures who people this gallery of ancestors should be ranged. This leads to some confusion, such as the famous example of confusing Mary the mother of Jesus with Mary the sister of Moses and Aaron.[33] The history of salvation is replaced by a series of edifying stories. All personages are placed on the same plane in the Qur'an: all are precursors of Muhammad, and all show how God punished those who disobeyed him. Thus Jesus is indeed called "the Messiah."[34] But the title of Messiah is no longer understood as deeply rooted in the history and the hopes of Israel.

Rather than borrowing, we might speak of appropriation. Jacqueline Chabbi observes:

> The elements that we are pleased to think "borrowed" are as if emptied of
> their substance. . . . The borrower takes what he wants. He does not feel
> obliged to refer to anyone, except to himself, in constructing his own legiti-

> mation. . . . The operation of appropriation . . . is conducted in the name
> of a myth of loyalty to a past to which the other lays claim, but of which he
> finds himself totally dispossessed. Wherever he turns, "the other" has no
> other choice than betrayal. He betrays himself by renouncing what he is.
> He betrays the faith placed in him by not wanting to recognize himself in
> the gaze focused on him through his deconstructed past.[35]

Past history is recounted, not like a river bearing the narrator along, but as
something that he captures and fixes.

Falsification

The texts that the Qur'an confirms are not the real texts that we can read in
the Bible, Jewish or Christian, but rather—and exclusively—virtual texts,
to be found nowhere. In fact, according to Islam, the texts of the earlier
Scriptures were tampered with by those who passed them on. This is the
theory of "falsification" (tahrīf).[36] Texts that had been disfigured in that
fashion do not merit belief, should not even be read, and even less associated with the Qur'an. The same argument appears among Christians against
Jews, and even among Jews in polemics against Christians.[37] Among the Fathers of the Church, the idea of a falsification is primarily the consequence
of the absence of a unified text on which agreement can be founded. The
Greek of the Septuagint does not always correspond with the Hebrew text,
and Christians themselves have several versions of any given text. Thus
Justin reproaches the Jews for having deleted all passages announcing the
Christ from their copies. Origen, who was well aware of the philological
problems involved, nonetheless echoes that idea, while other Fathers—Augustine and Bede—reject it.[38] These two tendencies alternated throughout
the Middle Ages. One of the factors that pushed Christians to give up this
claim around the twelfth century seems to have been the need to respond
to the accusation that Islam had launched against the two predecessor religions. The accusation gained ground again in the thirteenth century, however, and beginning with the *Pugio Fidei* of the Dominican Ramón Martí
(1284), it found corroboration in the presence of scribal corrections in the
Hebrew text.[39]

As for Islam, the doctrine of falsification is founded on the passages in
the Qur'an that accuse certain groups, in particular among the Jews, of having changed the received word, of having replaced certain words with others, of having hidden parts of the word, or simply of having forgotten it or
passed it over.[40] It is hard to tell exactly which Jews are accused in this manner, or whether they are Muhammad's contemporaries or people who lived

somewhere between Moses and Muhammad. Nor is it easy to see exactly what they stand accused of: whether it is of having modified the text by addition or subtraction, having replaced some words by others; or simply of misinterpretation. Some verses from the Meccan period suppose the legitimacy of the Torah.[41] The same is true of some Medinan verses, despite their context of polemics against both Jews and Christians.[42] The very logic of the argument demands such a recognition of authenticity, since the Jews are reproached with not conforming to the prescriptions of their own holy book.

The hadiths are not unanimous on the question, even within one line of transmission. Thus of the two narrations transmitted under the name of Ibn Abbas—supposing them to be reliable—one suggests that verbal alteration has occurred, while another speaks of erroneous interpretation.[43]

Certain later authors widen the accusation of falsification to the "peoples of the book," both Christians and Jews, and interpret the "distortion" as removing all authenticity from the books that preceded the Qur'an. The Andalusian Ibn Hazm (d. 1063), a man whose temperament ran to excesses, represents an extreme position here. He rejects all the biblical writings, which he ridicules by exposing their contradictions and absurdities. His attitude toward allegory is remarkable: he accuses the Old Testament of containing rank anthropomorphisms, such as "YHWH is a devouring fire," but he energetically rejects rejoinders that cite statements in the Qur'an such as "Allah is the Light of the heavens and the earth."[44]

The first author to have put into place a systematic exposé of the doctrine of alteration of the letter of the sacred text is perhaps al-Qarafī (al-Sinhājī, d. 1282).[45] He resolves the difficulty arising from the Qur'anic declarations, stating that they "confirm" preceding Scriptures by offering a distinction: what this assertion confirms is the former state of those texts, before they became distorted, not the texts that Jews and Christians use currently. He offers one highly revealing argument: the passages regarding the Christ (including the crucifixion of Jesus, which the Qur'an rejects) cannot be part of the Gospel; the authentic Gospel is the one that was announced by Christ.[46] This supposes that such a Gospel must, *a priori*, be similar to the Qur'an. That Gospel is thus unique and does not coincide with the other four Gospels. As for the Torah, it was lost with the death of the last descendant of Aaron: what we have today under that title is the work of Ezra. Analogous arguments can be found in the polemical writings of 'Abdallāh al-Taryūmān (the former Franciscan friar Anselmo Turmeda) against his former religion, in which he notes contradictions and absurdities in the Gospels in a manner recalling Ibn Hazm.[47]

In their discussion of the content of the sacred books affected by such distortions, the authors often mention changes of a legislative sort. Thus they reproach the Jews for having replaced the stoning of adulterers with whipping, and the talion ("an eye for an eye") with a monetary compensation. Their prime complaint, however, is that the earlier texts concealed announcements of the coming of Muhammad. One author even bases his demonstration that the Gospels were falsified on the fact that they make no mention of Muhammad.[48] There is little agreement among such writers regarding the extent of the deformations that the holy books have suffered, but they all agree on the unassailable principle that Islam grants itself the right to hold up its own holy book as the standard for measuring the material authenticity of the earlier books. That fact alone is enough to strip the latter of any normative value.

Islam and the Other Books

It is in this sense that non-Muslims understood the position of Islam in the Middle Ages. Maimonides, as favorable to Islam and critical of Christianity as he was, nonetheless recognized that the latter had the merit of never accusing the Jews of having manipulated the Scriptures. On the Christian side, the great scholastics, beginning with St. Thomas Aquinas, note that, unlike Judaism and Christianity, Islam shares no scriptural base with the religions that preceded it.[49]

In actual practice, Muslims only rarely read the earlier books. Anecdotes relate that the caliph ʿUmar punished one Muslim whom he surprised reading such a work.[50] On the other hand, Muslims often read collections of stories about the earlier prophets, Jesus included, that Muslim authors compiled on the basis of various sources, both biblical and apocryphal.[51] As for the establishment of juridical norms, it became less and less acceptable to invoke the legal dispositions contained in the earlier texts to settle questions not discussed in the Muslim sources.[52]

The legislative dispositions of the earlier books were abrogated. Muslims show that a law can be rescinded by another by arguing that the Mosaic Law was abrogated by that of Jesus. In doing so, they make no distinction between abrogation and fulfillment: fulfillment effects a passage to another sort of law; abrogation replaces a law with something more perfect, but of the same sort.[53]

Why shouldn't that process be repeated? Why shouldn't Islam itself be subject to it? In point of fact, both of the post-Judaic religions were paid back in their own coin: several religious groups have claimed to "fulfill" Christianity (Theosophy, for example), even by bringing a new book to it (as with the Mormons); other groups have claimed to abrogate the Qurʾan (Bahaʾism). Orthodox Islam furnishes a response that is highly revealing about the question of the articulation of the religious and the political: If Jews and Christians allowed the message with which they were charged to be adulterated, it is because they lost (or never possessed) political power. The Muslims' possession of power, in contrast, guarantees the integrity of the Qur'an. Thus political power is directly legitimized by the duty to respect divine revelation.[54]

Two Strategies of Affiliation

Nor does the novelty of the two religions, Christianity and Islam, in relation to what went before them spring from the same source. *Christianity presents no new texts; it simply presents a new fact:* the life of Jesus, culminating in his death and his resurrection, provides a new Exodus.[55] But in itself that event represents a form of text in that it produces meaning by polarizing around itself the preceding texts. The text of the New Testament is the anamorphosis produced by the new event on the text of the Old Testament.

Islam presents no new fact, but it does present a new text, which is the Qur'an. The prophetic mission is too complex to be adequately described by the concept of an event.[56] If one can speak in such terms, it is the coming of a new text that is the event, a textual event. The only "good news" that Islam announces is that prophecy, thought to be interrupted, is revived.[57] Moreover, it is the sudden appearance of a new text that prompts reflection about its status.

Allegory or Replacement

The New Testament differs from the Qur'an in the relationship that each of these maintains with the writings of the preceding holy books. I have called the Qur'an accounts "paranarratives": one might call those of the New Testament "metanarratives," or, if Jewish exegetic terminology is more acceptable, one might say that the New Testament is a *pesher* of the Old and the Qur'an is a *midrash* of the Bible.[58] The New Testament imitates the texts of the Old: in this manner, the Magnificat (Luke 1:46–55) returns to Hannah's canticle (1 Sam. 2:1–10). The New Testament also takes inspiration from the narrations of the Old Testament in its relation of events. In this manner its central theme, the Passion of Christ, is perceived through the suffering of the Servant of YHWH (Isa. 42:1–9; 49:1–6; 50:4–11; 52:13–53:12).

The Qur'an also includes a number of metanarratives, above all in the many passages in which it presents resistance to Muhammad on the model of the opposition to earlier prophets, including some instances mentioned in the Bible. On one occasion the Qur'an presents Muhammad as the realization of a prediction in the Old Testament.[59] Most of the time, however, it embroiders on older themes, adding new details often borrowed from Jewish or Christian *midrashim* that already circulated (at least orally) in the milieus in which the Qur'an was redacted. Examples that might be cited include details on the background of Joseph, on Moses' mission to Pharaoh, or on the childhood of Jesus.

Two strategies were applied to adjust and downplay the earlier texts. Christianity chose allegory or adaptation; Islam chose replacement. The aim was only partially the same. Neither the texts of the Old Testament nor those of the New were redacted or brought together to serve as the holy book of a community. Once the community had formed, it chose the book after the fact. The Qur'an, on the other hand, was produced *in order* to be used as a holy book. This fact distinguishes it from the Bible, and it makes it more comparable to the writings of Manes (Manichaeus) or, in nineteenth-century America, to the Book of Mormon or to "Oahspe" or, in the Middle East, the writings of Bahaullah.[60] The announcement of the Paraclete promised in the Gospel of John supposedly refers to Muhammad, but he does not seem to have proclaimed himself the Paraclete, as had Manes and Montanus.[61] Muhammad places himself within an overall vision of the maturing of humanity: Islam is the religion of the maturity of the human species, whereas the Old Testament was proper for its infancy and the New for its adolescence.[62]

Concerning legislative texts, the two later books make closely related changes in the Old Testament in instances in which both Christianity and Islam declare certain legislative dispositions outdated. With a difference, however: whereas Christianity does not seek to extract directives from the holy texts, Islam places itself on the same terrain as the Old Testament. This means that Islam cannot simply *annul* the biblical dispositions, but must *replace* them with others.

Changing History

The most profound difference between those two tactics lies in the problem posed by history. Christianity places itself in the same historical pattern as the Old Testament, as a prolongation of it; Islam moves toward another history. This can be seen in genealogy. The Hebrew word for genealogy, *toledōt*, has even taken on the meaning of "history." It is by means of genealogy that each religion connects with the patriarchs: Islam changes genealogy; Christianity keeps genealogy but allegorizes it.[63] This is the context within which the allegorical method makes its appearance in the New Testament. St. Paul explains that the pagans who have rallied to the church are legitimate descendants of Abraham by his wife Sarah (Gal. 4:21–31). For the first (and only) time, we see here the verb *allegorein* (Gal. 4:24).

Islam lays claim to the other ascendance, the one that the Bible attributes to Hagar, who is, incidentally, never named in the Qur'an. At most there may perhaps be a trace of her in the narrative about Mary and the miracle of the palm tree, which also contains a clearer reference to an apocryphal gospel.[64] The Qur'an credits Abraham and Ishmael with being the builders of a temple that later tradition identified as the shrine of the Ka'bah. It seems that the Qur'an has substituted Ishmael for Isaac in the story of Abraham's sacrifice. At least one can suppose this by reading the surah in which the promise of Isaac is made *after* the narration of the sacrifice of "a boy ready to suffer and forbear," who seems to be Ishmael.[65] Certain authors present Hagar in a better light than Sarah.[66]

Self-Reference in the Qur'an

The Qur'an stands out from the other two earlier sacred books by its massive self-reference. The Old Testament hardly ever speaks of itself; in the New Testament, on one occasion Peter recommends Paul (2 Pet. 3:15ff.). Unlike the Bible, then, the Qur'an speaks a lot about itself, beginning with the very first surah (if we except the Al-Fatiha, the prayer with which the book opens). We learn from such mentions that this book possesses an entire list of properties: it is in Arabic, it is clear, it is a warning, and it indicates a direction.[67]

The self-referential status of the Qur'an becomes complicated when it applies to its own text the same method of abrogation that it applies to the earlier books. Recourse to abrogation results from a practical problem, that of contradictions within the Qur'an, a problem posed at least as early as the exegete Muqātil.[68] There is nothing surprising in the presence of these contradictions: according to the accepted history, Muhammad preached for some twenty years and in very different conditions: at first, as an isolated messenger who announced the imminent coming of the Last Judgment to his city of birth; at the end of his career, as the leader of a victorious community to which he dictated his laws. Between these two moments, he was obliged to engage in polemics with pagans, Jews, and Christians, but also to negotiate with them and establish tactical alliances with one or more of them against the others.

According to the theologians, there *can be* no contradictions in the Qur'an. The solution to this problem was the theory of abrogation (*naskh*), a theory founded on a passage in the Qur'an in which God promises not to delete or permit to be forgotten so much as a verse of the text without furnishing something similar or even better.[69] When two verses contradict one another, the earlier one is replaced by the later one. To be sure, only exceptionally, as with the famous "satanic verses" supposed to have been inspired by the devil, is the abrogated verse no longer recited.[70] An abrogated verse is still recited; yet, if it contains legal dispositions, they are abrogated to the profit of those contained in the later verse.

The self-referential status of the Qur'an has as its consequence another phenomenon by which it can be distinguished from Christianity. As early as the New Testament, and even more with the Fathers of the Church, Christianity systematically applies the allegorical method to the Old Testament. In this manner it seeks to show how what was latent in the Old Covenant becomes patent in the New. In contrast, Christianity does not apply allegory to the New Testament, or, in any event, not in any fundamental sense. Its only allegorization applies to what had always conceived as bearing a hidden sense—namely, the parables. Narrations are almost never allegorized.

Islam turns the allegorical method back to the text itself, applying it to its own holy book. It is within the Qur'an that the distance between the literal sense and the figurative sense deepens. That distance is without danger in certain verses that quite obviously require an interpretation, as for example the famous "verse of light" that has often been the focus of commentary, among others, by Avicenna and Ghazali.[71] However, it fed a recurrent temptation to relativize what is presented as a commandment beyond reasonable measure. I shall return to the topic below.

7

The Law as Enforced

I have just discussed the ways in which the medieval religions were positioned in relation to one another, and how the later religions negotiated their relationship with the preceding one or ones. Now we need to turn to a more global phenomenon: the three medieval religions, taken together, suppose divine law to be a reality, whereas the Greek world, which had first formulated the concept, saw divine law as merely virtual. Moreover, those three religions also had to resolve the problem of their relationship with that "Greek" conception of the law that either preceded them (in the case of Christianity and Islam) or had developed independently (in the case of Israel).

Thus the first topic to examine here is how thinkers of Greek culture viewed the Jewish phenomenon of divine law. Next I shall turn to the thinkers within medieval cultures who prolonged antiquity's thoughts about law and examine how they reflected on the transition from the classical model to the medieval model of divine law. Finally, I shall discuss the elements that those medieval thinkers selected from ancient writers to construct their own syntheses.

The Greek Echo of the Monotheistic "Divine Law"

Certain Greek authors of the Hellenistic age knew Judaism and sought to understand it within the framework of their own concepts. Given that the idea of "divine law" was present in both traditions, there was a strong temptation to equate Mosaic law with a phenomenon that the Greeks considered characteristic of "barbarians" in general, and to view that global phenomenon in the light of Greek categories. Which they did. The Hellenistic thinkers did not attempt a direct comparison of legislative systems; instead, they preferred to examine the human type of the legislator. They hesitated to place the sacred laws in the same category as the Greek idea of "divine law," choosing instead to integrate Moses as legislator into their gallery of soothsayers and oracles or the kings that had been inspired by them.

Pagan Historians and Geographers

This is true of the oldest Greek witness to the Jewish religion, Hecataeus of Abdera (ca. 300 BCE).[1] The narrative describes the foundation of a colony, discussing successively the colonists' reasons for leaving their original homes, the choice of a place at which to settle, the foundation of a temple, the political system, and wars with their neighbors. Political power is in the hands of priests, and, according to Hecataeus, Israel never had kings.[2] He summarizes Hebraic law, which stresses military training of the young, the inalienable nature of landed property, and the prohibition against exposing infants. On two occasions Hecataeus notes that the Hebrews take pains to make sure that their customs run counter to those of other nations. He does not state explicitly the relationship between these laws and the divine, however. The priests are described as messengers of the decrees of God. Moses is presented as a political leader and legislator (*nomothetes*); he is placed above his fellow men by his intelligence and his courage, but his piety is not mentioned, and even less his status as prophet. Hecateaus notes that written Hebraic laws conclude with the phrase "Moses, having heard it from God, said this to the Jews," which is a fairly accurate account of the final words of Leviticus and Numbers.

Diodorus Siculus (first century BCE) places his account of the Jews within a history of the writing of the laws, inaugurated in Egypt by Mneves,[3] who is supposed to have claimed that the laws of that land came from Hermes (Theuth). Similarly, in Greece, Minos, king of Crete, attributed the laws to Zeus, and in Sparta, Lycurgus attributed them to Apollo. When he turns to the "barbarian" legislative systems, Diodorus mentions the laws of Moses, which he attributes to the god Iao, as analogous to Zoroaster's laws in Iran and to those of Zalmoxis among the Getae, which were also attributed to divinities. Attributing the laws of city states to gods is a common practice. Diodorus proposes two hypothetical explanations: either people thought that an idea of such utility was miraculous and fully divine (*thaumastè kai holōs theia*), or else the masses were deemed to be more docile if their eyes were turned toward the superiority and power of those said to have invented the laws. This means that Diodorus does not take the attribution of the laws to gods very seriously. The divinity of the laws resides in their intrinsic qualities or in those of their human legislator. To claim that their origin is divine is a useful manner of speaking. We note here a theme that flourished much later among the authors of the radical Enlightenment: religion is a hoax that allows leaders to deceive a naive people.[4] In Diodorus the theme takes a positive turn: it is for their own good that the common people are deceived.

The geographer Strabo (64 BCE–23 CE) returns to Hecataeus' scenario.[5] But where Hecataeus presents the Jews as a group of foreigners in Egypt under the leadership of Moses, Strabo supposes that the Jews were Egyptians and Moses a priest,[6] and that defection was caused by a religious disagreement involving Moses' disapproval of zoomorphism. Moses' original teaching contained little more than equating God with Heaven, and only later was superstition added to that celestial religion, and with it dietary prohibitions, circumcision, and then tyranny, which led to external conquests. Attaching legislation to the divinity is for Strabo a natural tendency that, like that of community life, requires a common rule. That rule can be human or divine, but the peoples of the ancient world were more inclined to obey what was supposed to come from the gods, as is shown by the use of oracles, for example, by the legislator-king Minos. Moses was thus a divine or seer, like many other men, ancient or modern. The law is of divine origin because it is an oracle—or was held to be such, for Strabo gives us to understand that he does not subscribe to that idea.[7]

Alexandrian Judaism and Philo

It is somewhat surprising that Jewish authors of Greek culture, although attentive to defending their law, should have repeated the same explicative schemas. Thus the Alexandrian author of the "Letter of Aristeas to Philocrates" (ca. 130–100 BCE) says of Jewish Law that it is a "divine legislation." Nothing in it was left to chance, nothing follows the inspiration of the moment or appears under a mythic form. But what, the author asks, is the source of the excellence of the law? His affirmation of its divine origin is somewhat weak: it is "august and born of the action of a god" (dia theou). The wisdom of the legislator seems to be more important. To be sure, the law derives from the fact that God made that legislator capable of knowing all, but it is to all the legislators that God gives the ideas that permit them to make human life secure.[8]

Philo of Alexandria (b. ca. 15 BCE) has a conception of the divinity of the law that is just as "Greek" as it is "Jewish."[9] Although he mentions that, according to some (as it happens, the Essenes), no human soul could have conceived of the ancestral laws without "divine possession," he also recalls that, for the Jews, the laws are oracles from God, not human inventions. It is in order to inculcate that conviction to the people that they had to be led to the

desert and shown so many miracles. Moses is the intermediary of those oracles.[10] Philo takes over the idea with little enthusiasm, however. His central formula is highly ambiguous: "The oracles . . . are both words of God
and laws given by men whom God loves" (*nomoi . . . anthrōpōn theophilōn*).
Are we to understand by that, with Harry Austryn Wolfson, that God revealed
the laws to those men out of his love for them? Or rather, as seems more
likely, that they are the work of men whom God loves?[11]

For Philo, divine law is above all natural law and unwritten. Thus Abraham
fulfilled all the commandments, which he had not learned by reading them,
but under the influence of his own "unwritten nature": not only was he acting in conformity with the law, but he himself was a law and an unwritten
decree. That law contains the most general principles of morality, beginning with the principle of all principles, the finest law, which orders respect
of morality for its own sake. It is his law that punishes misdeeds: the guilty
are pursued, either by God, by the Word, or by a divine law. It is this law that
enjoins us to respect the natural equality between master and slave: "In the
law of God the standard of justice is adjusted to nature and not to fortune."[12]

Philo applies the adjective "divine" to Mosaic Law as well. The divinity
of that Law resides less in its origin or the fact that it "comes from the Heavens" than in its intrinsic worth: given that Moses was an incomparable
legislator, his laws are excellent and truly divine. This is shown, on the
one hand, by the lasting power of his law through the vicissitudes of the
history of the Jewish people, as if it were marked with the seal of nature itself, and, on the other hand, by the admiration of other nations toward its
wise dispositions.[13]

Philo leaves open the question of the legislator's identity, however: was
Moses himself this legislator, or was he merely the interpreter of God the
legislator? On occasion, Philo calls Moses "the Lawgiver" and even attributes to him the narrations or the legal dispositions of the Bible.[14] To be
sure, he also says that God is lawgiver, and even that he is the "original and
perfect Lawgiver." But is the law of which God is the author more than the
law of the universe as the Stoics defined it? The laws of the other nations
also come from the divine: "He Himself is the lawgiver and the foundation
of laws, and on him depend all particular lawgivers."[15] Moreover, Philo does
not attribute to God any particular article of Mosaic Law.

Flavius Josephus

In order to defend Judaism against Apion, an Egyptian, Flavius Josephus
(37–100?) wrote an apology of the law that turns into a praise of the legislator. He places the superiority of Jewish Law within a much larger context,

using as his principal arguments its permanence and coherence. Thus, whereas the Greeks have a literature that is abundant but riddled with contradictions, the Jews have only twenty-two sacred books, but they are in perfect agreement with one another, thus forming what we would call a canon. No one has even permitted himself to add or remove anything from their precepts.[16] Similarly, the Greeks used ill-defined maxims to guide their actions and obeyed the orders of the kings; they followed unwritten customs, which they modified according to circumstance. Moses, on the other hand, defined everything and left nothing to chance.[17]

There are several reasons for the superiority of the Mosaic Law. It is the most ancient of all laws, older even than the most venerable Greek laws. It is universal: whereas the Greek philosophers addressed only the elite among their own contemporaries, Moses addresses the masses in all generations. Moreover, where the other legislators taught either by precept or by example, Moses used both conjointly.[18] Moses' superiority lies in his genius. The virtue of the legislator is to see what is best and persuade those who will make use of his law. The excellence of the law does not come from the fact that God knows man and reveals to him the precepts that are best for him; it comes, to the contrary, from the fact that the legislator knows the nature of God and deduces his law from it. For Flavius Josephus, the error of the Greek legislators is not to have been able to grasp God's nature, and not to have regulated their legislation on what they knew of it.[19]

When he comes to the divine character of the law, Flavius limits himself to a somewhat vague report of Jewish belief: the Jews have a "conviction that the original institution of the Law was in accordance with the will of a god." Instead of an argument, he provides an awkward repetition of Hellenistic clichés, even putting Moses and Minos on the same plane, since both attributed their laws to a divinity. He goes so far as to suggest that Moses used the divine to legitimate his own mission as the founder of a political community: Moses rightly believes that he has God to guide and advise him; he persuades himself, first among others, that everything he does and conceives of is according to the will of God.[20] In this manner, Josephus anticipates the theory of law that was later developed by the Aristotelians of the Middle Ages, and even later by liberal Protestants.[21] As Arnaldo Momigliano has quite rightly written, "For Flavius, it is not God who imposes the Law on Israel through Moses; it is Moses who imposes God on Israel through the Law."[22]

The Rule of Divine Law

The Middle Ages stands out from the period that preceded it by the status granted to divine law. The dream (for some, the nightmare) of the Hellenistic thinkers whom we have just discussed comes true, at least in its major features: divine law was no longer just a notion or an abstract program, nor was it a rule valid for only one isolated people. It became an effective reality, operating within history and affecting the masses.

An All-Embracing Law

In principle, such a law must (at least in the dreams of the jurists charged with administering it) govern the whole of human life. This is why it is important to summarize—and as exhaustively as possible—all of its stipulations. Catalogues were drawn up by Maimonides within Judaism, but also, and before him, within Islam.[23]

Such catalogues admittedly give examples of trivial acts—twiddling one's thumbs or scratching one's beard—but they operate on the principle that nothing is totally unimportant. Large domains of daily life are subjected to rules, beginning with the care of infants and what games children should play. A philosopher, and not the least among them—Plato—had already laid down laws for nurses, although not without encountering sarcasm from fellow philosophers.[24] In the Middle Ages, Ghazali forbade certain children's games.[25] Even in our own day, the last official declaration of the late Lubavitcher Rebbe banished from babies' cribs plush animals belonging to species the consumption of which is banned by Jewish Law.

This exactitude was applied to the humblest activities. May the gestures accompanying prayer be performed in the latrine? Maimonides raises the question: if a man has inadvertently kept on his phylacteries on entering the latrine, at exactly which stage must he interrupt doing what he went there for to take them off? A Muslim author discusses when breaking wind does or does not render prayer inoperative. Another asks in what measure touching one's penis (involuntarily, of course) makes one impure. One sublime mystic considers which hand to use to wipe oneself, and Ghazali discusses the right method for doing so at some length.[26] As for Joseph Karo, the author of a great sixteenth-century codification of Jewish Law: "Foolishness to the Greeks and a scandal to later liberal Judaism, he told man to love God, how to tie his boot-laces, and what kind of misspellings rendered a bill of divorce invalid."[27]

It is hardly surprising that the enemies of the collectors of hadiths called these writers "traditionists" and ridiculed them for their desire to regulate everything. According to such critics, the pagans who were Muhammad's contemporaries flung such insults as "Your companion teaches you how to sh—" at his disciples.[28] Nonetheless, one can see in this maniacal desire to leave no detail uncovered a reflection of a noble idea that everything is holy: since God is present everywhere, he must be worshipped in all things.

The Fundamental Law

The reign of the law was so far-reaching in the Middle Ages that the word "law" was used to designate what we prefer to call "religions." Latin Christianity used the work *lex* in this sense. For example, Thomas Aquinas speaks of the "law" of the Moors or the Saracens, by which he means Islam.[29] The usage passed into the vernacular, especially to compare the beliefs of different communities. Thus Ramon Llull relates in 1311 that he had been asked, "What is the law (*lei*) that is false and in error: that of the Christians or that of the Moors?"[30] In the *Decameron* Boccaccio (d. 1375) has Saladin say to the Jew Melchizedek, "I should like to know from you which of the three Laws (*leggi*) you believe to be the true one: the Jewish, the Saracen, or the Christian."[31] Melchizedek's response contains the oldest version of the parable of the three rings that cannot be told apart, which Lessing later took up in *Nathan the Wise*. Jorge Manrique, a Castilian of the later fifteenth century (d. 1479), writes in a poetic epitaph to his father that the latter died "after having risked his life for his law (*ley*) a thousand times."[32] And in his *Canterbury Tales* Chaucer (d. 1400) praises a pagan king: "As for the secte of which he was born, he kepte his lay [law] to which that he was sworn."[33] The usage is attested in French beginning with the *Chanson de Roland*, and it survived long into modern times.[34]

Nevertheless, the received translation of *lex* as "law" that I have just taken up is less evident than it may seem at first sight. That some Christians should call the Jewish or Muslim religion a "law" is hardly surprising, given the importance of juridical regulations that these two traditions bring to bear, each in its own way. But isn't it a step backward, with respect to St. Paul, for Christians to speak of their own religion—and the New Testament that is its basic document—as a "law"? We can understand the Protestant polemic against the medieval church, which they accused of having betrayed St. Paul's message, understood by Protestantism as a farewell to the law.

This means that we need to return to the idea contained in the French word *loi* or the English "law" and trace it back to the notion of which these are merely particular cases, as in the Latin *lex*. What since the start of modern times has been called "religion" was perceived in the Middle Ages as an apparatus established by God within human history to serve as the framework for his encounter with humankind, which was to permit humans to accomplish what the divine design expected of them. A device of this sort can take several forms. For example, it can be a system of positive and negative prescriptions telling man what actions he should and should not take. This is what we see in Judaism with the *halakhah* or in Islam with the *sharia*. Or, as in Christianity, it can consist in an economy of salvation taking place through time to form a whole that comprises history. Each of these variant paths to salvation can be called a *lex*. But this should be understood less as a system of legislation than as a particular form of smooth operating conditions for access to salvation. It is in this sense that the term *lex* can be used to cover both the "law" of the Old Testament and the "grace" of the New, and that it becomes possible to speak paradoxically of a "law of grace."[35]

The New Era of the Law

The translation of these "laws" in history produced what is usually referred to as the Middle Ages. The expression is both pejorative and anachronistic: at the start of that age, no one could foretell what kind of novelties it had to offer, and even less—as the historiography of the Modern Age implies—that the period would be reduced to an intermediary stage, a time of latency between two supposed summits.

Coming Awareness?

Late pagan thinkers suggested that they had at least a vague idea of the external circumstances that were to lead to the emergence of a "Middle Ages." Proclus seems even to have grasped the implications of Christianity's coming to power, but he always concealed his disapproval of the new faith and its practical consequences under the veil of allusion. Although pagan authors were certainly quite aware of what was coming to pass, they may have had no idea that a new age was opening up: they thought that Christianity's takeover of power was not going to last. Thus, the philosophers of the School of Athens, who had been obliged to close shop when Justinian confiscated their landholdings, did not destroy the statues of their gods when they left for Persia: they simply hid them in a well, probably because they thought they would soon return.[36]

Traces of a similar reaction can be found in the authors of early Islam, for example in Ibn al-Muqaffa'; a character in his work, the Persian physician Burzoe, remarks that "the Ancients never went too far when they praised their own religion or blamed the confessions that did not agree with it."[37]

No one expressed the coming to power of these divine "laws" as an irreversible fact better than Maimonides. He writes, in what may have been his first work:

The sages of the peoples of antiquity made rules and regulations, according to their various degrees of perfection, for the government of their subjects. These are called *nomoi*; and by them, the peoples were governed. On all these matters, the philosophers have many books which have been translated into Arabic. Perhaps those that have not been translated, are even more numerous. But in these times we do not need all these laws and *nomoi; for divine laws govern human conduct.*[38]

At a later date Nasīr ad-Dīn Tūsī distinguishes between the terminology of the Ancients, who spoke of the divine law (*nāmūs*) and of the king, and that of the Moderns, who speak of *sharia* and the *imām*.[39]

This is true for the Jews, but not only for them. One might say the same of the three religious communities that claim Abraham as their founder. For Maimonides, these constituted the majority of humanity, considering that Muslims and Christians contributed, whether they wanted to or not, to the diffusion of monotheism. That opinion was predominant at the time, although it did not remain uncontested.[40]

For Muslim thinkers and the Jewish thinkers who followed in their wake, the divine commandments were the novelty. For Christians, on the other hand, it was the Incarnation that introduced a new fact into human history. Pagan philosophers—including Aristotle, who was the first among them to have considered the political as an autonomous discipline and to treat it systematically as the topic of a particular work—had neither foreseen nor been capable of foreseeing that God would be made man.[41]

The Testimony of the Medieval Philosophers

We can find traces of an awareness of a rupture brought about by divine law among the medieval Aristotelians who spoke and wrote in Arabic.

It seems that the first of these, Alfarabi (d. 950), conceived of his task as an effort to revive philosophy after it had disappeared from the public scene. At the end of his treatise on how to attain happiness he writes, "The philosophy that answers to this description was handed down to us [literally, 'transported'] by the Greeks from Plato and Aristotle only. Both have given us an account of philosophy, but not without giving us also an account of the ways to it and of the ways to reestablish it when it becomes confused or extinct."[42]

Elsewhere Alfarabi suggests that the opinions on which the community in which he lives was founded, far from being genuinely evident, merely pass for true because of habit—among other "passions" that lead us astray from the road of truth. Moreover, he notes, opinions are affected by upbringing and routine: a good teacher, even if he follows Aristotle, must choose new examples better adapted to his public. Aristotle himself would have done as much, for "it did not escape him that many [of those things] would change in the *future with a change of regime.*"[43] What is important to note here is that a change of regime can bring new opinions. The decisive element in received opinions is thus political in nature. Dialectics is grounded in the political.

A few lines higher, Alfarabi had given several indications regarding the way in which certain opinions take control of a nation. They can be imposed by a leader or a reformer. Indeed:

> The opinions of the common people have already changed during the [course] of time, not only concerning practical [affairs], but in speculative matters as well. This is the case if [the man] who reigned over them was of the opinion that the most appropriate [thing] for them at a [given] time was to have him impart to them one sort of knowledge and opinion, and if the traditions and the models that he had imposed on them had made necessary a certain sort of opinion regarding speculative affairs, and if the opinions of that sort have become those that were well known among them.[44]

The same sensitivity can be found in Maimonides, the greatest of Alfarabi's Jewish disciples. As a diagnosis of the contemporary age, Maimonides cites a passage in which Alexander of Aphrodisias enumerates three causes of discord among men, which are a desire for domination and love of strife, subtlety and obscurity of the object of apprehension, and the intellectual weakness of those who attempt to grasp that object. Maimonides adds: "In our times, there is a fourth cause that he did not mention because it did not exist among them. It is habit and upbringing. For man has in his nature a love of, and an inclination for, that to which he is habituated." He offers Bedouins, "the people of the desert," as an example: indifferent to urban pleasures, they prefer the disorder and hardships to which they are accustomed. Similarly, man prefers the opinions with which he has been brought up. This is why he is quick to admit the corporeality of God: "All this is due to people being habituated to, and brought up on, texts that it is an established usage to think highly of and to regard as true and whose external meaning is indicative of the corporeality of God and of other imaginings with no truth in them, for these have been set forth as parables and riddles."[45] Commentators did not hesitate to propose an interpretation of what Maimonides alludes to here. Moses of Narbonne writes of this passage: "They [the Ancients] did not have religious Law, but only a legal religion."[46]

The medieval philosophers in Islamic lands thus found themselves torn between two loyalties: a social, cultural, and spiritual loyalty binding them to their religion, and a fidelity that reached over the centuries to attach them to their patron saints. The first made them feel responsible for the well-being of the communities in which they lived; the second made them aware of the fact that the ideal city in which philosophy had flourished lived according to laws that had little in common with those of their own actual communities.

"Laws": From Customs to Religions

The same awareness of a change in the intellectual atmosphere connected with the appearance of religious laws can be observed by following the medieval reception of a passage from Aristotle. At the beginning of his *Metaphysics*, he mentions the power of habit. In the second book of this work (which was the first for the Arab world) he states: "The powerful effect of familiarity is clearly shown by the laws (*nomoi*), in which the fanciful and puerile survivals prevail [over knowledge of things], through force of habit."[47]

Many writers have commented on this passage, beginning with Alexander of Aphrodisias, surnamed "the Exegete," because he explained the entire *Metaphysics* and because portions of his commentary had been translated into Arabic.[48] He states:

> The legislators who established as laws many legendary things, because it was useful that people believed that this was the case, persuaded the people, who respected that law because they had grown up with these affirmations— for example, that certain persons are autochthonous and grew up out of the ground, that others sprang up from teeth sown in the ground, and that, for that reason, one must fight for the ground as for a mother, or because the gods fought about it, for its value is such that one must have a care for it.[49]

Several medieval authors after Alexander commented on the same passage. One of these was the ninth-century Christian translator and philosopher, Abū Bishr Mattā b. Yūnus:

> The extent and magnitude of the force of habit are made clear by (considering) the laws. . . . For we are habituated from our childhood to parables and tales (*khurāfāt*). . . . The enigmas occurring are, if considered from the point of view of demonstration [knowledge: *burhān*], similar to (idle) tales [*khurāfāt*]. For not they, but (the theses) opposed to them can be demonstrated. If, however, they are considered from the point of view of the purposes of their promulgators, they will be found to be noble and of great utility. For supposing that they were abolished, what a fight of beasts of prey would come about—for they (the beasts of prey) constitute the majority (of

the people) of the world, or rather all of them except but for some rare exceptions—and in consequence civil life (al-harth wa'l-nasl) would perish. If it behooves us to be grateful to the father who engendered us, how much more must we be grateful to those who established the enigmas by means of which the continuance of our lives and the preservation of our intellects [are assured] together with the existence of the cause conserving us.[50]

We possess a commentary on the same passage from Aristotle by another Christian philosopher who lived somewhat later, Yahyā b. Adī, a pupil of Alfarabi's. He states:

One can know how powerful habit is if we look at the laws, for one finds there that it is clear that what is said there derives from the genre of enigmas or of arguments that do not clearly explain the ideas that are presented there. In fact, they only allude to them by means of comparisons and things that resemble fables. And Aristotle compares the expressions used in the laws to fables, because they advance by means of comparisons and similitudes, not by means of true things that designate the desired ideas with total clarity. Similarly, fables simply present ideas, and the expressions they use do little to reveal their truth, because, for the soul, what is familiar in them is greater and more powerful than their teachings of truth.[51]

Finally, the same passage was the object of a commentary by Averroes toward the end of the twelfth century:

[Aristotle's] intention . . . is to show the things that keep us from becoming aware of the truth in human knowledge. The most powerful of those things is to have been brought up from infancy in conformity with a certain opinion, and even, it is the thing that can the most sovereignly lead gifted minds away from knowing the truth of things, and in particular that of the things that that science [metaphysics] contains. For the greater part of the opinions that such a science contains are opinions that spring out of a law (arā'nāmūsiyya), which are established so that people will seek virtue, not in order to have them know the truth, and in these opinions there are enigmas taken from the truth. The reason for all of this is that the existence of people does not attain its perfection without their coming together [in a society]. Now, that coming together is not possible without virtue, so that urging people to practice the virtues is something necessary for them all, whereas urging them to know the truth of things is not, for it is not true that all are capable of doing so.[52]

As we can see, the passage from Aristotle, which in itself is fairly anodyne and speaks above all about bizarre customs, becomes a burning topic when it receives connotations taken on through the Arabic translation of the Greek work for "custom": *nomos*. When this happens, the passage can be read as an almost subversive challenge to the truth of religions.

Socrates as a Figure of Philosophical Existence

The medieval philosophers also reflected on their own status within a political community ruled by divine laws. They often did so by meditating on Socrates' fate. His destiny remained exemplary, and his memory kept alive an awareness of danger. Christians saw in Socrates a sort of prophet or precursor persecuted for his monotheism, and the theme of a "Christian Socrates" had a long life. Muslims echoed the idea until a rather late date.[53] Alfarabi and Averroes recall that Socrates preferred to die rather than live in a corrupt regime.[54]

The fact remains that the "primitive scene" of medieval religions is different. Christ died on the cross. Muhammad died in his bed, a victor; there are declarations attributed to him that suggest that he was aware of that difference from the prophets who had preceded him.[55] Consequently, and in parallel fashion, Islam understands the martyr as a combatant who falls while killing, not as a victim who accepts being put to death. Defeat is not conceived as concealing a deeper victory, reserved for resurrection. Thus it seems that an authentic philosopher, in the Islamic context, must be in power. Since being at the head of Plato's ideal city is impossible, he would be the vizier of the actual sovereign. To repeat a lapidary saying: "Socrates was judged; Maimonides and Averroes were judges." They might even have considered it their duty to condemn those who, in their own times, might have been equivalent to Socrates.[56]

Plato's ideal philosopher exercises power in the good city that he has founded. In comparison with him, Socrates can even seem clumsy. Alfarabi reproaches him with having viewed things unilaterally: he had addressed the common people in a style more proper for the elite; his method should therefore be completed by that of Thrasymachus.[57] The combination of the two produces the Platonic art of writing. It permitted remaining a loyal subject of the laws one is born under and to which one owes the possibility of living and living well, at the same time transmitting the truth to those who are worthy of it. I might remark in this connection that Plato's famous prosopopoeia of the laws in the *Crito* that posed the problem of the philosopher's relationship with the laws, has, curiously, left no clear trace in Arabic.[58]

Certain authors—Alfarabi and Avicenna, for example—attribute the presentation of Christianity by their adversary John Philoponus to a desire to deceive the religious authorities of his time, suggesting also that he had not forgotten Socrates' fate. Averroes hints, in his response to Ghazali's attack on the philosophers, that the latter had concealed his profound sympathy for them in order to appear in a good light to the regime.[59] We have every right to suspect that the medieval philosophers themselves operated with a prudence equal to that of their earlier brothers.

The Common Sources of Medieval Thought Regarding the Law

The Greeks who came after Socrates were also the people who had contributed the intellectual instruments that enabled philosophers to think about the political community and the law, a fundamental dimension of the polis. But not all of the text in which that reflection was set down reached the medieval worlds in the same manner.

Plato or Aristotle?

Nothing is more foreign to the Middle Ages of Arabic culture—and in its wake, to the Jewish world of the same epoch—than the fondness for the "divine Plato" of the Neoplatonists of a waning antiquity or of the Florentine Renaissance. Nor is there any trace of literary enthusiasm for dialectical fencing matches or high-flying myths. For an Arabic cultural world largely dominated by Aristotelianism, Plato is quite simply a poor writer who says just about the same thing as Aristotle, but says it less well. Maimonides saw little need for reading Plato and expresses this opinion brutally: "The writings [literally: words] of Aristotle's teacher Plato are in parables and hard to understand; *one can dispense with them*, for the writings of Aristotle suffice, and we need not occupy [our attention] with the writings of earlier philosophers."[60] Similarly, Thomas Aquinas writes soberly, "Plato's method of teaching was faulty; he constantly used figures of speech."[61] This is just an indication of a more general tendency. There were exceptions: for example, the physician and freethinker Razi (Rhazes), took a stand against Aristotle and with Plato, who was for him "the prince of philosophers and the greatest among them."[62] But the philosophers of the dominant current (Avicenna and Maimonides) had a low opinion of Razi. Moreover, he probably had never read a single line of the dialogues.

Thus Aristotle by far dominated Plato. Averroes holds him to be the absolute summit of the intellectual possibilities of the human species. He covers him with fulsome praise on several occasions: Aristotle is a gift of God to humanity; the most perfect man; "a norm in nature, a model that nature found in order to show the supreme perfection of man."[63] This sort of praise could seem shocking, to the point that Malebranche saw it as a typical example of the "prejudice of commentators."[64] Averroes is not alone, however. Dante's famous phrase "the master sage of those who know" is more a rule than an exception.[65] For al-Kindī, Aristotle is the most distinguished of the Greeks in philosophy. For Alfarabi, he represents the supreme and final stage in scientific knowledge.[66] Maimonides, Averroes' contemporary, writes: "The works of Aristotle are the roots and foundations of all works on the sciences. . . . Aristotle's intellect [represents] the extreme of human intellect, if we except those who have received divine inspiration."[67]

Where Hellenism, either late or renascent, spoke of the "divine Plato," Averroes baldly states that the ancients spoke rather of the "divine Aristotle."[68]

An Absence: Aristotle's Politics

Nonetheless, a surprise awaits us here: Aristotle's Politics represents a special case in the incident-filled history of the transmission of the Aristotelian corpus to the West. The destiny of that treatise differs from that of the other works of the Philosopher: it is in fact the opposite of theirs. The Politics did not pass through the Arab world, but went directly from the language and the intellectual universe of the Greeks to the Latin domain, when William of Moerbeke made a translation of it, based on a manuscript now lost, on which St. Thomas immediately wrote a commentary. Nor was the Politics translated into Hebrew.[69]

There is an opinion of fairly long standing that Aristotle's Politics was never translated into Arabic.[70] We have no text of such a translation, nor, for even better reason, of any commentary on it such as those that Alfarabi or Averroes composed on the translations that they read.

Still, the Arabs know of the existence of a work of Aristotle called Politics that is clearly the one that we know. A certain number of texts, cited by several orientalists, make this clear.[71]

The only mention of a Politics among the works of Aristotle is on a list composed by Ptolemy and transmitted to us by al-Qiftī.[72] The mention of the Politics in al-Kindī is unclear: "As for his goal in the second among those [works on ethics and politics], namely, the one that is called Bulitiqa, or the political, which he wrote for one of his brothers, it is similar to what he says in the first: he speaks in it more about the political regime; and certain of its books [are] identical to the books of the first."[73] After a brief introduction on political science, Alfarabi notes that the topic can be found "in the book Bulītīqā, which is [in another reading: which is in] the book of 'government' of Aristotle, and also in the books of 'government' of Plato and in the books of Plato and others." But Alfarabi's systematic presentation of the philosophy of Aristotle does not breathe a word of the *Politics*, and a passage of his *Book of Letters,* which some have thought drawn from the *Politics,* can be explained in a more economical way without that hypothesis.[74] The polymath al-Amīrī (d. 992) has passages quite obviously inspired by Aristotle's *Politics.*[75] At the end of his Middle Commentary on the *Ethics,* Averroes admits that he was unable to locate the text and supposes that it could be found in the East; at the beginning of his explication of Plato's *Republic,* he again admits that he was unable to consult a text.[76]

In any event, even if it were established that the *Politics* was never translated into Arabic, that fact would send us back—more than ever—to the question of why there is no Arabic version of the work. Did this happen by more or less conscious decision within the early Muslim world? Or, to the contrary, should we consider the lack of a translation to be simply a result of the little interest the work aroused within the Hellenistic world itself as it was first Romanized, then Christianized?

Thus, given the lack of a translation in the language that was at the time the cultural *koine* of the East, Aristotle's *Politics* appears to have been unknown in that part of the world. This was an absence that had one important consequence: Islam founded its political philosophy, not on Aristotle, but on Plato, whose political reflections—the only ones available—thus replaced Aristotle's, to play the role in the East that the latter filled in the Christian West. If there was a deliberate decision not to translate Aristotle's *Politics,* it is not impossible that this was because the work was judged less appropriate than Plato's dialogues on the ideal regime for use in connection with the Muslim community in search of a theory of its own, and therefore that in Muslim lands such theory was deliberately founded on principles that were more Platonic than Aristotelian.[77]

That decision—supposing that there was one—was not unanimous, or at least the fact (which we shall admit for the moment) that the *Politics* was not to be found in the libraries of the Muslim world left some with regrets. To be sure, Aristotle's other works contain passages that touch on politics (such as the sections on justice and friendship in the *Nichomachean Ethics*), and the *Rhetoric* contains a chapter on various regimes, but this is not enough to render the *Politics* forgettable. Some sought the work, and in a certain sense found it, under the deceptive guise of an apocryphal work, the *Secret of Secrets,* which sometimes bears the title *The Politics of Aristotle,*[78] or as *The Letter of Aristotle to Alexander on the Politics of Cities.*[79]

Some authors went so far as to have Aristotle say things he never said, even giving a reference. For example, while speaking of the idea of divine law, the Persian moralist Miskawayh imagines that he is citing a source when he states: "Aristotle said that money is just law (*nāmūs*). Law in his language denotes administration, management, and the like. In his work known as *Nicomachea*, he said: The highest law is from God (blessed and exalted is He!), the ruler is a second law on His behalf, and money is a third law. The law of God (exalted is He!), i.e., the [Religious] Law [*sharia*], is the model for all the other laws. The ruler, who is second, imitates it and money is a third imitator."[80]

Plato, in Spite of Everything

The Platonism of the great dialogues on the polis was not passed on to the Middle Ages, or only in fragments in such writers as al-Amīrī or al-Bīrūnī. The dialogues may have been known through Galen's summaries, which Al-farabi probably used in his own summary of the *Laws* and Averroes used in his compendium on the *Republic*.[81] These gaps were compensated for by apocryphal writings treating the topic of politics in whole or in part, such as the so-called *Laws of Plato*.[82]

As has been said, in spite of the weight of Aristotle, Islam had an affinity for Plato. One contemporary historian has also compared the Muslim political community with the organization of Plato's ideal city.[83] One author whom one might not expect to meet in this context—Nietzsche—saw this similarity with an astonishing clarity. For Nietzsche, Muhammad is a Plato who succeeded. If the philosopher, necessarily a critic of the mores of the society in which he lives, does not manage to become the legislator of new mores, he leaves behind him the image of a dangerous dreamer. This was the case with Plato. But in his Syracusan adventure, Nietzsche continues, Plato "thought he could do for all the Greeks what Muhammad did later for his Arabs . . . viz. establishing both minor and more important customs, and especially regulating the daily life of every man. His ideas were quite practicable, just as certainly as those of Muhammed were practicable. . . . A few hazards less and a few hazards more—and the world would have witnessed the Platonization of Southern Europe."[84] The philosophers of Islam seem to have seen in Muhammad the philosopher king that Plato had postulated, and to have seen the Muslim community as the realization of Plato's city.[85] Did they sincerely believe this? Their practice shows, in any event, that they felt an affinity between Plato's political works and Islam.

They found Plato's *Laws* fascinating because the work seemed an exception in Greek thought. As we have seen, the idea of a divine law that might also be the law of a polis (or, in other terms, that the law or the laws of a human community might be divine) is scarcely ever met with in the ancient world—except in Plato's *Laws*.[86] It was a text that could not help but attract the attention of Muslims. One who noted it was Abū Sulayman al-Sijistānī (d. ca. 985). According to him, those who want to harmonize philosophy and the law claim that "Plato composed *The Book of Laws* so that we might know what to profess, what to investigate, and to what we should give precedence." Similarly, al-Amīrī cites the famous passage in the *Republic* in which Plato says that even if the ideal city is not realized, it remains a model for action in heaven, but he reads the word for "heaven" (*samā'*) as "law" (*sunna*). Avicenna found Plato interesting; according to him, Plato was the author of the exemplary treatise on prophecy and on the *sharia*: "What touches on prophecy and religious Law is contained in the books of these two philosophers [Plato and Aristotle]."[87] It is unclear, however, whether he was referring to Plato's dialogue and not to the apocryphal work mentioned above.

As for Plato's authentic work, the philosophers were particularly attracted by a passage in Book 10 of the *Laws* on the classification of three forms of atheism. Several Muslim or Jewish writers cite or summarize the book.[88] Al-Bīrūnī reproduces specific passages from the first four books of the *Laws* in his work on India. In particular, he borrows Plato's doctrine of cataclysms, the idea that men are descended from the gods, and the praise of wine and festivities.[89] A passage from the chapter on legislation gives three citations from Book 1, in particular the very first line of the dialogue, the question about the divine or human origin of the laws, although the word "god" is replaced by "angel." Al-Bīrūnī quotes Plato as saying, "It is the duty of the legislator, if he comes from God, to make the acquisition of the greatest virtues and of the highest justice the object of his legislation." In this way, the legislator becomes closer to the Islamic idea of a messenger of God. He goes on to praise the laws of Crete, describing them as "rendering perfect the happiness of those who make the proper use of them, because by them they acquire all the human good, which is dependent upon the divine good."[90]

The Sources Peculiar to a Tradition

Unlike what had occurred in the Muslim and Jewish worlds, Christendom had the benefit of a continuous transmission of certain texts. Here we need to distinguish between Byzantine and Latin Christianity.

Byzantium conserved the political writings of Plato and Aristotle, but it paid little attention to the *Politics*. Two facts bear witness to this lack of interest, and I cite them only to recall them to mind. On the one hand, we possess hardly any Greek commentaries on the work, with the exception of Proclus' refutation of the criticisms addressed by Aristotle to Plato's *Repub-*

lic and of the scholia of Michael of Ephesus.[91] On the other hand, we possess only a small number of Byzantine manuscripts of the work, which are late in date (fourteenth–fifteenth centuries), with the exception of one fragmentary palimpsest of the tenth century.[92] It is not hard to guess why the work was neglected: in the Middle Ages people tended not to have the curiosity regarding the historical past that is characteristic of the modern age, and they read only what they really needed to.[93] For the most part, the *Politics* speaks of regimes that had long since ceased to represent a viable option. It was as if the work offered instructions on how to operate an outdated machine.

Byzantium had only a limited acquaintance with the political texts of Latin authors, and that familiarity diminished as knowledge of the Latin language declined.[94] It did, however, have some knowledge of the Oriental "Mirrors for Princes" through texts such as *Barlaam and Josaphat*, a distant avatar of the life of Buddha, or the *Stephanitēs and Ichnēlatēs*, a Greek adaptation of the fables of the *Kalila wa-Dimna*. The first of these works spread to the West and adaptations of it appeared in the languages of Latin Europe.

Although Latin Christianity had no difficulty retaining possession of the writings of the authors who wrote in its own language, it had to recuperate the Greek heritage by the intermediary of translations. It only had access to Aristotle's *Politics*, as we have seen, through William of Moerbeke's translation. As for Plato's dialogues, the two that had been translated in the thirteenth century by Henricus Aristippus, the *Meno* and the *Phaedo*, contain little mention of the political. Western Europe had to wait for the end of the fifteenth century and Marsilio Ficino to read a Latin version of the great dialogues on political regimes or on laws.

Cicero's political dialogues, whose titles echo Plato's, were known above all in the Latin West. In these works Cicero develops a political outlook of Stoic inspiration, but adapted to Roman tradition. He insists on the rational nature of the city: reason (*ratio*) and speech (*oratio*) are the common bonds of society.[95] He develops the Peripatetic (and Stoic) argument of the natural sociability of humankind: we will indicate the right road to a stranger who has lost his way and will pick him up if he falls.[96] The beehive as a model for human kingship can be found in Virgil and Seneca.[97]

The Fathers of the Latin Church then transmitted these themes. Lactantius introduced into Christianity Cicero's views on divine law. St. Ambrose wrote a *De officiis* in which he gave a Christian version of Cicero's work of the same title.[98] The influence of these works in part explains the importance in the Middle Ages of the idea of nature, which Ovid and Claudian saw as an intermediary between God and man.[99] John of Salisbury synthesized these same ideas and passed them on to high scholasticism.[100]

Whereas Islam was unacquainted with the Latin classics, it was able to draw from sources to which Christianity could have no access. Iranian thought had a sweeping influence on Islam, especially in the Abbasid period, beginning in the eighth century, which witnessed a vast reorientation of Islam toward the model of the Sassanid dynasty. This was especially true in the political domain. It is hardly surprising, then, that certain maxims regarding government passed from Iran to the court of the caliphs. One of these is the formula attributed to the Sassanid king Ardashīr: politics and religion are inseparable twins; one cannot reach perfection without the other.[101]

❖

This somewhat lengthy examination has enabled us to take a glance at the medieval thinkers' toolbox. Such men set themselves the task of understanding what were these laws that were thought universally valid and that shaped the cultures in which they lived. In order to do so, they made use of intellectual tools that, for the most part, came from traditions going back to classical antiquity and that were reflected in different ways in the cultures that had assured their transmission. Making a fairly detailed inventory of these was a must.

More often than not, those instruments were inappropriate for working the raw material at hand: they had been forged to account for laws that had a different relation to culture than was true in the Middle Ages, and of laws whose "divine" character was conceived otherwise than by medieval thinkers. Medieval thought about the law bears the mark of these heritages, of those inadequate legacies, and of those unsuitable tools, that were made to make the best of what was available.

PART IV

Laws and Cities in the Middle Ages

The next thing I would like to do is to fill in, with broad strokes, the background of medieval thinking about the law. The picture will be historical, but it will be history as it relates to my topic. I shall review the religions present on the medieval scene in the order of their appearance. Each time, my theme will be the articulation of the religious onto the political, but viewed from the perspective of the idea of divine law.

I shall begin with Judaism, by which I understand not the entire religious heritage of the Old Testament, but the specific configuration of that heritage once it had been re-focused around the Law—the idea that is my theme. In its medieval period, Judaism had no real political dimension, which means that it furnishes an interesting counterexample.

Next I shall examine the two religions that appealed to the experience of the Old Testament for their authority, Christianity and Islam. Despite their many differences, the two religions share one aspect that concerns the object of my inquiry: they both coincided with an empire, Christianity because it inherited one, and Islam because it gained one by conquest. This gave the problem of the coexistence of the political and the religious a concrete, even a quotidian, importance for them both. Moreover, this was not an abstract clash, played out uniquely in the heaven of ideas; it was a combat between real forces.

I shall insist on these differences, and I shall do so in spite of the misunderstandings in the minds of medieval thinkers of all confessions, who tended to confuse—for example—the functions of the caliph and those of the pope.[1]

8]⸘

Judaism: A Law without a State

Medieval Judaism represents a particularly interesting body of evidence for the question of divine law. In conditions of virtually chemical purity, divine law permeated both communal life and intellectual reflection. Indeed, for one thing, medieval Judaism has no political expression; for another, it was based in a religion in which the law is the foundation of all the other dimensions of religious life.

Events

Concerning the three superimposed levels that make up the domain of practical philosophy, medieval Judaism had a long-established disinvestment in the highest level, that of the state. Social support came entirely from the two underlying levels of the social structure—that of the family, within which its transmission continued to take place, and civil society. In society the Jews' role as economic agents is far from negligible, especially in international trade. In the Latin West, where Jews could not own landed property or become members of a guild or corporation, they turned to commerce. For a long time they had a near-monopoly on money trading. That favorable situation led them to feel that their fate was better than others', thus that they continued to benefit from the attentions of divine providence.[2]

An Apolitical Status

The Jews were dispersed, however; without a state, they lacked political power. Judaism was a "despised faith," a phrase that appears in the title of Jehuda Halevi's *Kuzari*, a masterwork of Jewish apologetics, but one that Saadia Gaon had already used.[3] The Jews formed something like a state only in exceptional cases, geographically on the margins and only for brief periods. One example is the kingdom of the Judaized Arab Yūsuf Asʾar Yaʾthar, called Dhū Nuwās ("the man with the side locks"), in sixth-century Yemen.[4] A better-known example is the kingdom of the Khazars (or Kuzari) around Crimea from the sixth century to the eleventh century. The Khazar elite converted to Judaism around 740, an event that provided the plot and the most commonly used title for the work by Jehuda Halevi just mentioned. The Khazars' Judaism seems to have been fairly superficial, however. In particular, their law system was more Turkish than rabbinic.[5] In any event, their culture had only a few centuries in which to develop, whereas the two other monotheistic religions had the benefit of a good deal more time to become ingrained in the peoples who had adopted them. A possible third example, if the controversial thesis can be confirmed, is that of the Narbonne region in the Carolingian era under Pippin the Short, from 768 to the late ninth century.[6]

Elsewhere the Jews exercised political power only on an individual basis, as representatives of their community or as the counselors of princes of other religions. In particular, that happened in Islamic lands, where Jews had "protected" status (*dhimmi*). Certain individuals even held quite high positions, for example, Samuel "al-Nagid" Ibn Nagrila became the vizier of a minor king of Grenada in the early eleventh century; he is best known for the inordinately violent attacks on him on the part of his Muslim compatriot, Ibn Hazm.[7]

Autonomy

In Muslim lands, the Jewish communities were governed by an exilarch who represented them before the Muslim authorities. This function had arisen in Babylonia, and in the tenth century it was transported to Egypt under the Fatimid caliphs, though not necessarily at the caliphs' instigation.[8] The post was a purely civil one and had no strictly political component; the Muslim authors who speak of it stress that succession from one exilarch to another had nothing in common with the dynasty of the kings of Israel.[9] The question was far from simply academic: for the Jews it confirmed (or, for the Muslims, vitiated) realization of the prophecy that promised perpetual rule to the descendants of David.

The function of exilarch did not imply any spiritual authority, however. This led to conflicts between exilarchs and rabbis that recall, although on another scale, those between popes and emperors in the Latin West. The life of Maimonides provides an example of this sort of conflict when he insists, *ad hominem,* on the danger of uniting in one person the functions of exilarch and rabbi: "If the affairs [of religion] are attached to the function of chief, piety disappears."[10]

In Christian lands the Jews administered their own communities, holding synods that enabled them to adjudicate in internal matters, levy a tithe to cover community expenses, and, in extreme cases, to apply the punishment of the *herem* (excommunication). Some legislative activity in the field of civil law occurred in the form of regulations (*taqqanot*), including those drawn up by Rabban Gershom, which have remained famous. Contact between the Jewish communities and the Christian authorities was effected through representatives who were sometimes referred to as "the bishops of the Jews."[11]

That relative autonomy had a paradoxical consequence: within the limits assigned to them by the rules of the *dhimma,* the Jews could—and had to—administer themselves. This assured them an apprenticeship in political life that the Muslim masses, who were governed autocratically, lacked.[12] This is one of the explanations for the European Jews' rapid adaptation to the modern state, much as Christians played a role out of proportion to their numbers in the modern Arab world.

Dreams

The apolitical situation that was forced upon the Jews did not prevent them from developing a political reflection that goes well beyond a pure and simple utopia, retrospective or prospective. The concrete conditions under which the Jews were obliged to live led them to meditate on the nature of kingship and monarchic government. They even managed to profit from their position as a people without a country to hazard a comparison of the various political regimes they were acquainted with.[13]

When the Jews reflected on their own religion, they based their thoughts on biblical revelation, which is expressed in concepts (for example, "people," or "covenant") that also have an inherently political dimension. Above all, Judaism presents itself more as a law than as a faith: the Torah is designed to regulate the life of a people in a land in which, during the Persian era, it seems to have thrived for some time. Medieval Judaism remained conscious of the political dimension of the Torah, especially of Deuteronomy. The latter differs from the earlier books of the Pentateuch in that it also includes political laws, and not just the stipulations that had also pertained when Israel was in exile.[14]

Nor did Judaism give up the idea that the Torah might on occasion return to political relevance. The "Day of YHWH" that the prophets of the Old Testament had awaited was also a form of revolution. This was how Dāwud al-Muqammas interpreted that idea as soon as Judaism began to develop a theology, borrowing the methods of the Kalām: divine intervention was to bring on the ideal political regime (al-dawla al-mahmūda).[15]

As Maimonides reread the history of Israel, he stripped the great figures—King Solomon, for one—of any political dimension.[16] Nonetheless, he may possibly have redacted his code to serve as a future constitution for a Jewish state that would make possible the coming of the Messiah.[17] Did Maimonides seriously believe in the calculations regarding the date of the messianic age that he puts forth? Or is he suggesting them to bolster the courage of his co-religionaries in face of persecution, as he credits Saadia Gaon with doing several centuries earlier?[18] When he assembled in the *Mishneh Torah* all the legal dispositions regulating Jewish life, Maimonides took pains to include rulings concerning all the situations in which Judaism might find itself, not just those relevant to its current state of exile. Thus we also find laws concerning the messianic period, as it was supposed to reestablish the initial situation of the people, returned to their own land, around a reconstructed Temple in which sacrifices would be offered by legitimate priests. Maimonides also includes in the last book of the *Mishneh Torah* norms that regard the "kings"—that is, the governors.[19] In the age of Saladin, the idea of a return to the Holy Land was not unthinkable.

In the mid-thirteenth century, Judah ben Shelomo Ibn Matqah declared that he was persuaded of the necessity of reestablishing the kingdom of Israel, not thanks to divine intervention, but to a doctrine of the cyclical nature of history. In the early fourteenth century, Joseph Ibn Caspi still examined the probability of that event. There is also a well-known passage in Spinoza on the probability of seeing the Jews—given their gifts—one day reestablishing their kingdom. Even if that passage in Spinoza is of a totally different style from the former two, it would thus be the end result of a long tradition.[20]

❖

Thus the situation of medieval Judaism was such that the law of Moses could not possibly be the law of a state. That law did not have political force to back it up; instead, it had to limit itself to regulating daily life on the level of families and communities. In compensation, and perhaps also because of that restriction, which made it the sole factor of the identity of the people, the law takes on capital importance in Jewish life. As we shall see, it was also to be the object of intense and subtle reflection on the part of Jewish thinkers.

9

Christianity: A Conflict of Laws

Here we need to return to a topic we set aside earlier: the history of Christianity. I shall begin by setting the context and indicating some long-term trends.

The Historical Framework

The final centuries of the Roman Empire and the Middle Ages to the eleventh century were a period of population movement: perhaps because they were pushed by Chinese expansion, the peoples of Asia jostled one another toward the west, where they entered into the regions of Christian and Muslim culture. After a while, these populations converted to the form of monotheism that they encountered in their new lands: Turks to Islam, Bulgars to Orthodox Christianity, and Hungarians to Roman Catholicism.

Conversion to Christianity stretched over a period of almost a thousand years, from the Franks (in 496) to the Lithuanians (in 1386). The Roman world's conversion to Christianity took place within civil society. Once the state passed over to Christianity, its enemies became the enemies of the empire. Missionary pressure toward the north and the east was not always peaceful: the case of the Saxons, forcibly converted by Charlemagne, is there to remind us, and it represents more the exception than the rule.[1] Adopting the dominant religion implied also entering into peaceful relations—at least in principle—with the other nations who were part of the same world, thus setting off a slow process of access to civilization.

In the Middle Ages, the typical political regime was monarchy in the overwhelming majority of cases. Once Augustus had instituted the Principate, democracy was little more than a memory; in Byzantium the word was even pejorative. It was with the emperors, and later with kings, that the church had to negotiate. Yet on the outer limits of the empire, in Italy and in Switzerland as early as the ninth century, some more or less aristocratic democracies began to appear, gradually emancipating themselves from the central power. Finally, far from everything, Iceland offered its rare visitors the bewildering spectacle of a land that gave concrete proof that a society could live without a king, that is, with a law alone, or with no other king than the law.[2]

The Ambiguity of the "Constantinian Turning Point"

We left off the history of Christianity at the point at which it was making progress within Roman societies, in spite of state persecution. Constantine eventually understood that the time had come when Christianity could not be ignored, and even that he could make use of its dynamism to give the Roman Empire a second wind.[3]

Temptations

Only with the "Constantinian turning point" did Christianity begin to become Christendom. At a later date, when Protestantism, seeking historical legitimacy, needed to pinpoint when the decadence of the church had begun, a tenacious legend saw that moment as a rupture with the heroic church of the early centuries. In fact, "the peace of Constantine had not completely anaesthetized Christianity."[4] Even less had it delivered it over to the discretion of the civil power. To the contrary, conflicts between princes and clerics were continuous. Constantine had sought to meddle in theological matters, calling himself "the bishop of those from outside," that is, the pagans. He called the Council of Nicaea in 325, which defined the orthodox position on christology. The bishops resisted the solution that the emperor favored, however, and Constantine exiled Athanasius, the prime champion of orthodoxy. On his deathbed the emperor received baptism from an Arian bishop.

Nontrinitarian monotheism was well suited to the empire, which saw itself as the terrestrial image of divine monarchy. The Arian doctrine, which saw Christ as a sort of representative of a First God—the Caesar of a celestial Augustus—shifted the structure of Roman power to God. Eusebius of Caesarea became the theoretician of that view, completing it with a theology of history in which the victories of the Roman Empire and the progress of Christianity went hand in hand. Many gave in to this temptation.[5]

Toward a Counter-Power

In contrast, over a long span of time, institutions were set in place that later—at times centuries later—were to permit the constitution of a counter-power. The primitive church had little need to assert its difference from a civil power that persecuted it. With Constantine, the risk of confusion arose. It was within this context and in the early stages of the collaboration between the Roman Empire and Christianity that we encounter, in Bishop Ossius of Cordova, the first application of the adage "Give unto Caesar . . ." to the limitation of imperial power.[6] Something like a transparent membrane was formed to render the church distinct from the civil power and prevent the one from absorbing the other.

This first occurred on the juridical level. The privileges accorded to the bishops and the emergence of a canon law prepared the constitution of the church as a society endowed with its own rules; in particular, the church became capable of controlling its conditions of access (through the catechumenate) and internal promotion (by setting up degrees among the clergy). The temptation was strong to model the structure of the church on that of the empire and to transpose civil functions into religious responsibilities. There are examples of Roman functionaries named as bishops by those under their administration, who did not fuss too much about whether or not the new bishop was a Christian. Synesius of Cyrene (d. after 413) had a career of the sort. Establishing a clear system of recruitment cut down the number of abuses.

None of this could have been accomplished without strong social support. The monastic movement provided just that. The first anchorites appeared in Egypt with Anthony (d. 356), who was soon followed by the first cenobites with Pachomius (d. 346). The rise of monachism represented an institutionalization of evangelical and Pauline "counsels."[7] Monastic life offers the interesting paradox of drawing up rules on the basis of what is different from rules. Monachism displays a protest against the "world" as a whole and against compromise with the world.[8] It may even have seen itself as an attempt to rediscover voluntarily the precarious situation that persecution had imposed on the earliest communities, hence seen itself as a substitute for martyrdom. The early Christian martyrs were put to death by the political authorities; the monk's mortification perpetuated martyrdom, once the civil authorities had passed over to Christianity. The division between laity and clergy is concrete sign that eschatological matters were reserved for the latter. Celibacy, long a mark of the functionary of the temporal state, came to indicate membership in another, nontemporal, kingdom.[9]

Although medieval Christianity had defined a space for itself—that is, Christendom—the latter nonetheless remained split between the temporal and the spiritual. Relations between the bishops and the emperors, even when the latter had become Christians, were conflicted from the start, as with the clashes—which incidentally were somewhat disturbing for their anti-Jewish aspect—between St. Ambrose and the emperors, first Gratian, then Theodosius.[10] It was Pope Gelasius (d. 496) who first offered an explicit formulation of the separation of the church and the empire.[11] That same division was realized in different ways in the two halves of the empire. I shall treat the "Byzantine" East first, then the West.

Byzantium

There is a cliché regarding the West's view of the Byzantine world that presents the latter as a theocracy in which the political and the religious are merged in a situation of "caesaropapism." This is a caricature that cries out for correction. The tendency to equate the church and the Roman Empire, which appeared under (and with) Constantine, was exorcised in Byzantium as it was in the Latin half of the empire. Although one can speak of an "interdependence" or of a "permanent and freely consented solidarity" between the two in Byzantium, and one can say that "the emperor and the patriarch are condemned . . . to collaborate," the fact remains that "the separation of the Empire and the priesthood is a fact established by Byzantine law and respected by the interested parties, despite their mutual attempts to nibble at the prerogatives of the opposing party."[12]

The emperor at Constantinople, the second Rome, was the direct heir of the pagan, then the Christian, Roman emperors. This made him a totally secular personage: in spite of his ordination as a deacon (never as a priest), he was simply first among the laity. The temporal sovereign was first acclaimed by the army, then crowned by the church in a rite that showed that the separation was maintained with care. The honors rendered to the emperor developed with time, giving rise to a ceremonial that Charlemagne pretended to be shocked by. The sacrality of the Byzantine emperor was founded more on the Old Testament than on the New: "In Byzantium, the Old Testament had a constitutional value; it had the same normative role in the political sphere as the New Testament had in the moral sphere."[13]

The idea that God alone gives power undoubtedly contributed to conferring incontestable legitimacy on the emperor, but it also resulted, paradoxically, in rendering the royal power more fragile. Indeed, if God gives royal power, he guarantees its duration only if that power is exercised according to his views, which are impenetrable. Moreover, when dignitaries owe their positions to God alone, it is out of the question that they take the emperor as the object of a fidelity that only God deserves: "[The] constant implication of the divine will in all that concerns . . . the government of the world justifies, in the final analysis, successful revolts against the emperor, who is then considered to be unsatisfactory and unworthy of the divine confidence, hence as having to be replaced by someone whose virtues make him worthy of being Christ's chosen representative."[14]

In theory, the spiritual and the temporal are distinct, although they are conceived of as forming a harmonious accord (symphonia).[15] In reality, there were plenty of conflicts, but they were not situated on one and the same plane: the political power of the emperors was not defined in relation to the papacy, which could play the sovereigns of the West against one another, but in relation to the patriarch whom the emperor named and who, what is more, lived in the same capital city. The patriarch could rely only on the purely spiritual backing of the monks, who were also keeping a watch on him and whom he needed to handle with care. The laity, however, intervened in spiritual affairs more frequently than in the West and let its feelings be known about what it thought to be in conformity with Christianity.

The national character of the office of patriarch of Constantinople, and the fact that it was located in the capital city, near the emperor, made impossible any autonomous evolution of canon law comparable to what was occurring in the West. Tension between emperors and patriarchs was situated on the juridical level, where the imperial law, with its focus on giving expression to reasons of state, contradicted the ecclesiastical canons. For example, how could one give Christian soldiers, whom the church refused to consider martyrs, any hope of a paradise as appealing as the one that Muhammad promised his warriors? How could the need to defend a territory threatened by Turkish incursions be reconciled with the prohibition for the clergy to bear arms, not to mention the punishment of refusing the sacraments to anyone, even a soldier, who had killed someone? One amusing case was that of Themel, a priest who had been suspended by his superiors for having defended his parish by force of arms, who then passed over to Islam and participated in Turkish raids.[16]

The Byzantine Empire collapsed in 1453, so it experienced the transition to the modern period only indirectly, through its more or less authentic heirs in the Balkans and in Russia. Since my principal interest is the genesis of the modern world in Western Europe, I feel that it is legitimate to mention it only superficially, reserving my lengthier comments for the Middle Ages in Latin Europe.

Popes and Emperors

In late antiquity in the West, the problem was posed differently. The "barbarian" invasions had produced an upheaval in civil exchanges and solidarities, paralyzing the system installed by the Roman state. The religious network, centered on the bishops, had resisted better. When civil society was reconstituted, it crystallized around the ecclesiastical. This meant that for the time being, the church had to assume responsibility for the common good, which included the connected tasks of education, public health, and assistance. The bishop became a temporal sovereign.

The Rise of Papal Power

The bishop of Rome occupied a special place among the bishops. Even very early, the see of Rome had received a certain primacy of authority, linked to the memory of the presence and the martyrdom of the apostles Peter and Paul, which is probably historical fact (ca. 64–67).[17] Several passages in the writings of the Fathers of the Church attest to that primacy.[18] The question of precisely what weight to attribute to these attestations is of course a matter of controversy. In any event, the prestige of the see of Peter grew with time, because in the era of the great dogmatic quarrels "it escaped the Constantinian seductions better than others."[19] This remained true until the martyrdom of Pope Martin (655), who had refused to support a compromise in matters of christology that the emperor had proposed. When the papacy held firm in questions of dogma it gave credibility to the promises that Christ had given to Peter that he would "strengthen his brothers" (Luke 22:32).[20]

The popes themselves began to claim some primacy for Rome: this is perhaps true of Victor (d. ca. 198), more certainly of Stephen I (d. 257). Calixtus (d. 222) defended the idea of the special authority of the bishop of Rome against Tertullian and Origen. Around 375, Damasus used the term "apostolic see." Emperor Theodosius recognized the bishop of Rome as the guarantor of orthodoxy. In 385 Siricius began redacting *decretalia* on the model of those of the emperor in which he equated the pope with Peter. In 444, Leo the Great formulated the doctrine of papal primacy.[21] The following year the emperor, Valentinian III, confirmed the primacy of the bishop of Rome over the West. At that time the popes were considered "vicars of Christ." In 451, Pope Leo protested against canon 28 of the Council of Chalcedon, which put Rome and Constantinople on the same plane. Under the papacy of Symmachus (d. 514) the principle that the pope was subject to the judgment of no one was established. Gregory the Great (d. 604) was the first pope to be a monk. He became sovereign of the city of Rome and his administration formed the nucleus of the States of the Church.

The pope was also a temporal sovereign: he was head of a state until 1870, and after that date, with the Lateran Pact of 1929, he was granted sovereignty over the extremely small territory of the Vatican. Where did that sovereignty come from? Emperor Constantine is supposed to have made a donation to the pope of what was to become the Papal States. The document that attests this donation is of course a forgery, as the humanist Lorenzo Valla proved in 1440. The forgery is far from being worthless, however, because the fact that it was produced points to the interests that were at stake: those who had forged the document were less intent on exalting papal power than on weakening the local episcopacy. The denunciation of the document is equally worthy of note, given that it occurred in the context of a quarrel between Pope Eugenius IV and Valla's patron, Alfonso of Aragon, who was contesting the pope's legitimacy as pope.[22]

The temporal power of the popes really resulted from a change of direction in the eighth century. The popes had been connected to Byzantium since Justinian, in the early sixth century, but Pope Stephen II, disappointed by the emperor's weakness when the latter was slow to come to his aid, asked help from the Franks of Pippin the Short against the Lombards (754). Pippin defeated the Lombards and returned to the pope some twenty towns and cities in central Italy, which became the Papal States. Thanks to this move, the papacy and the sovereigns of the West became direct partners for the first time, short-circuiting the official Roman Empire, the capital of which was Constantinople, the former Byzantium.

Half a century later, the "bargain" struck between Charlemagne and the pope was a consequence of this direct partnership. Charlemagne protected Pope Leo III against the suspicions of his own clergy, although at the price of a humiliating inquiry. In return, the pope accepted that Charles be crowned emperor of the West in Rome at Christmas in the year 800, arranging matters so that he himself crowned the new emperor, thus putting less emphasis on popular acclamation, hitherto an essential part of the process of the legitimation of a sovereign.

Otto I launched a similar operation when he reestablished the Roman Empire, which had expired in 924, receiving his crown from the hands of John XII in Rome in 962. By this move, Otto distanced the pope from the influence of the Roman nobility and the Italian minor sovereigns and placed him under direct imperial protection, and in fact the papacy remained under imperial influence for more than a century. After then, the mode of election of the popes began to change, accentuating their independence from the great families of the Roman nobility and from the emperor. Leo IX (d. 1054) surrounded himself with aides from Lorraine who formed the nucleus of the college of cardinals. The papal court became the *curia*. At the Lateran Synod of 1059, Nicholas II gave the cardinals a central role in papal elections. Around 1100 the college of cardinals was created, and in 1179 Alexander III limited the right to vote in papal elections to that body.

The presence of the papacy and its increased power imposed some constraints particular to the West. Three forces contended for control: the pope; local ecclesiastical institutions, divided into the secular clergy (the bishops) and the regular clergy (the monastic orders); and the temporal power, where there were also divisions among local sovereigns and between the latter and the emperor. This opened the way to a many-sided conflict in which the various forces formed alliances with one another. The pope was able to resist the emperor thanks to the pan-European network of the monastic orders, Cluny in particular. On another plane, the rise of the universities in the twelfth century was made possible by the establishment of a direct connection between those institutions and the pope, bypassing the bishops and their cathedral schools.

The Church and the Empire

Through all of these shifting relations, the political and the religious remained separate. Curiously, however, that separation hinged on two ways of interpreting the same thing: popes and emperors both claimed to be the heirs to the city of Rome. Rome itself underwent something like a "recycling": one French canonist, Gilles de Bellemère, wrote around 1400: "As for the thing itself in its true state, the Roman empire (*imperium*) is today in the hands of the Roman Church. But as for the way in which people commonly speak of it, it still remains in the hands of the Emperor."[23]

European Christendom might have coincided with the Western Empire. Charlemagne had only sketched out that political structure, and he himself may not have understood that he was creating an entity destined to last. In any event, the empire was re-created by Otto I in 962. Soon after the year 1000, Pope Sylvester II (Gerbert d'Aurillac) introduced a new era. He did so quite deliberately by choosing a papal name other than his baptismal name—an exception that became the rule. Moreover, the name he chose was highly significant, given that the first Sylvester was pope at the time of the conversion of Constantine.[24] He set a precedent: from 1000 to 1145, one pope out of every two bore the number "II," and at the end of that period, after 1088, all eight of the following popes were number twos.

With the support of Otto III, Sylvester II was able to accept the baptism of the young nations of central Europe without imposing Germanization and membership in the Holy Roman Empire as a condition of their conversion. He crowned Stephen king of Hungary (1001), and Boleslaw, "the Brave," had to wait until 1025 to be crowned king of Poland. Sylvester created independent dioceses that were directly attached to Rome, hence were no longer branches of sees of the Holy Roman Empire. This was true of the archdiocese of Gniezno in Poland (1000) and Gran (Esztergom) in Hungary (1001). In this manner, Sylvester II permitted the peoples of central Europe to become Christian nations and, at the same time, independent states, thus detaching in quite a concrete way the domain of the state from that of religion.

There was constant conflict between the popes and the emperors. It came to a head, as is known, with the Gregorian reform, which in turn brought on the quarrel over lay investitures, later dubbed a "papal revolution."[25] The controversy began in 1075, when Pope Gregory VII (formerly Hildebrand, a Tuscan Benedictine) issued a manifesto of twenty-seven theses, the *dictatus papae*.[26] In this document he claimed papal sovereignty (*plenitudo potestatis*), given concrete form by a universal right of appeal. The conflict focused in particular on investitures, or the nomination of bishops. It lasted until 1122, when Pope Calixtus II accepted the Concordat of Worms. What was at stake in this conflict was the constitution of the ecclesiastical hierarchy as a body independent of political society. The bishops had become the ecclesiastical version of the nobility and had often been chosen from among the younger sons of the sovereigns. The practice was henceforth declared comparable to the sin of simony, or buying sacred things, so named for Simon Magus (Acts 8:18ff.).

The popes' decision to extend the rule of celibacy was based on the same logic. A movement of protest against the marriage of priests (stigmatized as "Nicolaitanism") was launched with the support of the regular clergy. Until that time celibacy was particular to the bishops, who were recruited from among monastics, as is still the case in the Eastern Church. The rule of celibacy set Western priests at a distance from society by detaching them from family and patrimonial networks.

The "papal revolution," much like other revolutions that dot the history of the West, was carried on in the name of liberty. Popes and emperors both defended *libertas*. But the emperor defended the *libertas ecclesiarum* (in the plural), or the status of the local churches that had been granted by the temporal sovereigns, whereas the pope was defending the *libertas Ecclesiae* (in the singular), by which he understood the status accorded by Christ to a unified church entrusted to papal direction.[27] From that time on, the church conceived of itself as an autonomous institution, entrusted uniquely with the care of souls.

Before discussing the relations between the papacy and the empire as a conflict involving the church and the state, it is important to realize that the existence of those two institutions is in no way to be taken for granted, either in general or in the Middle Ages. Nor should we seek the state where we might be tempted to. In fact, the church of the Gregorian Reform is the first institution in history that willed and understood itself to be a state: "The réal State of the Middle Ages in the modern sense—if the words are not a paradox—is the Church."[28] The word *status* appears in the sense of "state"—even long before Machiavelli—in ecclesiastical authors of the thirteenth century.[29] "If the concept of State could be employed at all in the Middle Ages," Walter Ullmann writes, "it could only be applied to the pope himself: He alone was *superior*, was, in the modern terminology, a sovereign because he stood *above* the society of the faithful, his subjects, and was no member of the Church."[30] The idea of sovereignty arose to express the power of the pope before it prompted, in response, an extension to the power of kings.[31]

There is more, however: it was the church that forced the state to constitute itself, in parallel fashion, as an autonomous institution. The church assigned to the state its task of the proper operation of the temporal community summarized in the word "justice." "As paradoxical as it may be," Jeannine Quillet notes, "one might say . . . that it is the action of the popes that tended, beginning in the eleventh century, to 'laicize' the political power by removing from it all initiative in spiritual matters." In other words, "The institutional concept of secularized society is an effect of Christianity in its rivalry with the Empire."[32]

In the Middle Ages, unlike what has seemed totally obvious from modern times to today, the game was not played between the church and the state. Instead, Christianity was stretched between two poles that both—first the papacy, then the empire, following in its traces—attempted to crystallize into a state. That movement ended up forming the church as we know it today and, in reaction to it, the first incarnations of the modern state. This combat took place on the level of the law, which each of the two adversaries sought to articulate around the divine to its own advantage.

Two Laws

It was in order to impede the claims of the papacy that the kings of the West sought a transcendent instance of legitimization. In doing so, they were simply paying back the popes in their own coin. There remained a large difference, however: the pope mobilized transcendence only in order to attach a spiritual power to it, and his demand to set the rules for all temporal power could only be quite indirect, and then only in the best of cases. The kings, on the other hand, sought to make sure that the divine weighed, with its full weight, on a system of constraint that was totally direct. Thus what distinguishes the two adversaries is not so much the origin of the legitimacy that they claimed as the nature of what was attached to a transcendent authority. As is known since Stalin's quip about the pope, whether or not one has armored divisions available can make a great difference.

In the juridical domain that is my primary interest here, the conflict between the two powers was expressed in and realized through the distinction between two laws. The law was the focus point, the point of arrival and point of re-departure, for two movements that crisscrossed, which were the desacralization of kingship and the sovereigns' claim to sacred status.[33]

The Divine Right of Kings

Contrary to a tenacious legend, the idea of a divine right of kings is not medieval. In the Middle Ages the king considered himself subject to the laws and in no way above them. This was stated incessantly, beginning with Cicero and Plutarch. The fact that the king was no longer pagan but Christian and even a reflection of Christ, far from elevating him above the laws, subjected him to them in an even more radical manner. John of Salisbury first, then Henry de Bracton, drew magnificent comparisons between the situation of the king and that of the King of kings who, although sovereign, had opted to be "born under the law" (Gal. 4:4) in order to bring salvation to humankind.[34]

The idea of a divine right of kings developed as a response to abuses of the right of resistance. It transformed the moral duty of patience imposed on the Christian subject into a right of the sovereign to be obeyed without reservation. It gave material form to the consecration of the king, turning it into a taboo that rendered the sovereign inviolable and an almost priestly person. It removed the king from the authority and the jurisdiction of the priests and set up an opposition between the king and his subjects in which he seemed a god present on this earth in bodily form, against whom revolt would be a blasphemy.[35] In the Middle Ages the idea of the divine right of kings stood opposed to that of popular sovereignty, which may have been formulated for the first time around 1080 by the Alsatian monk Manegold von Lautenbach, a supporter of the pope.[36] Manegold suggested the idea of a contract between the prince and the people. The idea of popular consent was a familiar one in the Middle Ages, and it was also present in Judaism, either as an explicit avowal or a tacitly accepted notion, for example, regarding the coinage of a given prince.[37] It was only when the medieval vision of the world was receding that the idea of divine right remained in play alone, without the counterweight of the idea of popular consent.

The idea of divine right in its most complete form supposes that the authority of kings is sovereign. This notion, typical of the modern age, goes back to the sixteenth and seventeenth centuries. Its opponents missed no opportunity to point out how recent it was.[38] It reflected the rise to power of monarchies that prefigured the modern state, and it sought to legitimize their absolutism. Its proponents were kings' functionaries.

Given that the idea of the divine right of kings emerged out of the conflict between kings and the papacy, it is hardly surprising that the theologians, who took the pope's side, deliberately attacked it.[39] They gave St. Paul's statement that all authority comes from God (Rom. 13:1) a deeper interpretation: it meant that God created humankind as having to live in a civil society, which requires organization, hence the need for authority comes from God. On the way to choose the person who holds that authority, they say little, however. Bonaventure went so far as to mock succession in order of primogeniture.[40] "The emperor is from the people, but the empire is called divine from God" was the central idea of these theologians.[41] The emperor might be designated by acclamation, for instance in the case of a general proclaimed emperor by his army. This did not mean, however, that one could not proceed by majority vote, as was the case in the councils. That was also how the superiors of the religious orders were chosen, not to mention the pope himself. The proverb *vox populi, vox Dei* was evoked in this context.[42] Nicholas of Cusa went so far as to define divine authority by the very fact that decision comes from subjects collectively reaching an agreement: "All legitimate authority arises from elective concordance and free submission. There is in the people a divine seed by virtue of their common birth and the equal natural right of all men so that all authority—which comes from God as does man himself—is recognized as divine when it arises from the common consent of the subjects."[43] This shows that the model for modern democracy and its electoral procedures was not so much Athens, where choices depended on drawing lots, but the medieval church.

The commonly accepted fable that the state in the modern age arose out of a process of secularization ignores the fact, as one contemporary author puts it, of "the strictly theological determination of that new figure of the absolute state: arriving at absolutism . . . necessarily and as a priority occurs by means of a resacralization of the State."[44] There was no demand for "laicization" on the part of the temporal power. Quite to the contrary, that demand was suggested to the state by the church as something pertaining to the state's domain, where it can fulfill its task of maintaining the "peace." In fact, when the imperial or royal function was forced to act by the claims of the papacy, far from spontaneously occupying the terrain of the profane, it was constantly tempted to claim a right to a direct and independent access to sacrality, as we shall soon see.

The two elements brought together in the expression "divine right" thus formed an interplay of reciprocal interaction. The sacred that was put into operation—and put into play—resisted being reduced to archaic affects of more or less ambiguous sorts. It was not the epithet "divine" qualifying the right that pushed the juridical back toward primitive taboos; it was just as decisively the substantive "right" that did so by subjecting the sacrality that qualified such a "right" to political rationality, thus profoundly and forcibly transforming it.

The Demand for Sacrality

The emperors developed a strategy that made them demand sacrality. "Holiness" figures in the Credo among the words that describe the church: "one, *holy*, Catholic, and apostolic." Sacrality was demanded by the emperors of what henceforth was to be called the "Holy" Roman Empire. Remarkably, the first to make such a claim, Frederick Barbarossa, appealed to juridical principles: the Roman power (*imperium*) is sacred because the jurist Ulpian called the *law* of the state a sacred law.[45] The emperors put forward the idea that the law itself was a gift of God.[46] An analogous idea served as an argument against the Holy See: to claim that there is no human law that is not founded on divine law, as John Wycliffe did in the fourteenth century, to pick one example, is to support the claims of the temporal sovereigns, because, if human law can be deduced *immediately* from divine law, there is no need to go through the pope as a supreme interpreter.[47]

The emperors also sought to slip directly into occupying an eschatological place in the history of salvation. St. Paul had alluded to a mysterious power capable of restraining or holding back (*katechon*) the manifestation of the Antichrist at the end of time. Tertullian had applied the idea to the Roman Empire. The Christian emperors, placing themselves within the quite real continuity of the state, sometimes understood their role in similar terms. That role was ambiguous: it held off the Antichrist and thus warded off the catastrophes that were to follow his reign, but it also delayed Christ's glorious return.[48]

Rites of legitimation borrowed from the Old Testament were reinterpreted, resulting in the ceremonial of coronation. The principal rite in this connection was anointment, although it simply manifested the legitimacy of the king's rule rather than conferring that legitimacy.[49] The custom is attested as early as 672 in Spain and 787 in England. As for France, in 848 Hincmar of Reims launched the legend of the "Holy Ampulla," and around 1130 Reims replaced Sens as the place for the coronation of kings. Reference to the baptism of Clovis, which took place at Reims, was thus reinterpreted as the first coronation, and the anointment that Clovis received there (in the same way as every new Christian) became a sign of election. The royalty that all converts received through baptism, when they became integrated into the new people of God, a "people of kings," was understood in the sense of the wholly terrestrial royalty of a unique individual. The holy chrism that marks the forehead of all who are baptized or confirmed was invested with a magical value, conserved in the Holy Ampulla that serves only to anoint the forehead of kings. Analogous legends can be found in England from the fourteenth century. England pushed assimilation of Old Testament customs to the point of adopting circumcision of the king as the sovereign of a new Israel.[50] In contrast, the church sought to minimize the sacred aspects of coronation, excluding it from a list of sacraments that was being drawn up.[51]

The medieval king was not just the receptacle of the holy; he was saturated with holiness to the point of radiating it. This could be seen in his ability to perform miracles: once crowned, the king of France went immediately to the sanctuary of St. Marcoul (Marculfus) at Corbeny to touch people afflicted with scrofula, the "king's evil," a rite attested as early as 1124, in Guibert of Nogent.[52] According to a tradition noted toward the end of the thirteenth century, the king of England also possessed the power of the king's touch and could even transmit his curative power to rings that he had blessed, which were supposed to cure epilepsy.[53]

All of these elements gave concrete form to a process of sacralization of the temporal power. When that process had reached its end—that is, with the modern age—conflicts of a new type appeared between the papacy and the temporal sovereigns. In the Middle Ages the conflict was a vertical one between two superimposed instances that attempted to define themselves in relation to one another. Henceforth, the two powers struggled for the same prerogatives, which brought an end to the possibility of regulating conflict by subordination.[54]

The idea of the divine right of kings was based, as the term indicates, on juridical principles. It was also on a juridical foundation that the church became constituted as an independent entity, endowed with rules of its own that formed canon law.

Canon Law

It is within the framework of the "papal revolution" of the late eleventh century that canon law was first systematized. Up to then, it had formed by gradual sedimentation around a nucleus of norms in effect in the primitive church. Certain of these had been drawn from the New Testament, for example, those relating to marriage (Mark 10:2–12; 1 Cor. 7:10). Others came from the *Didache,* or teachings of the apostles. Still others were rules ("canons," whence the term) decided by church councils. The principal additions to these were taken from the legislative texts ("decretals") of successive popes. There were also penitentials listing the penances for the various sins. Until the eleventh century, a number of collections of these rules existed, but there was no manual that attempted to group them all together. Moreover, no code had any authority broader than local.[55]

The very existence of a discipline like canon law is at once the cause and the consequence of the church's constitution as an autonomous juridical system. Canon law is in fact conceived of as distinct from the law in general, which was also taking on concrete form. This was a necessity, as the Justinian Code, brought together in 533–34, was no longer applied in the Byzantine Empire. It was even replaced in 740 by a short collection of precepts known as *Ecloga tōn nomon* ("Choice of Laws") condensing Justinian's compilation into 144 chapters. Justinian's entire compilation entered into the West by the intermediary of the works of the Bologna jurist Irnerius.[56]

The constitution of canon law as an autonomous entity and as a pendant to, and a counterpart to, civil law was a necessity of the papal revolution. Its basic synthesis is known as the *Decretum Gratiani* (Decretum of Gratian), which was probably elaborated in Bologna shortly before 1140.[57] As indicated by the actual title of this work, "Concordance of Discordant Canons," it represents an attempt to harmonize earlier precepts by deducing them on the basis of principles. For the first time, law was taught as a distinct and systematic corpus of knowledge.[58] Reducing the law to a system coincided with a social fact: the emergence of a class of jurists. Some people of the time perceived the importance of this novelty: one chronicler, while recapitulating the events that had occurred under the emperor Lothair, couples Gratian's work with what Irnerius had accomplished in civil law and with the achievements of the great religious reformers, St. Bernard of Clairvaux and St. Norbert.[59]

Canon law both supposes and encourages the existence of a sphere of specifically religious activities, distinct from the behaviors by which men seek goods that were henceforth considered to be "temporal." It legislates the activities of Christians insofar as they are Christians, not as they seek to regulate their relations in domains in which salvation is not at stake. Canon law regulates the faithful's access to the sacraments and to the ministrations of those who provide those sacraments. In contrast, it has nothing to do with the distribution of property (in commercial transactions or in inheritance) or with punishing secular crimes. The proper domain of canon law is humankind as it makes its way toward life eternal.[60] The order that it introduces into human life is its marching orders.

That orientation toward a goal situated beyond earthly life is not without influence on the content of juridical dispositions, however. Even in late antiquity, Christian emperors—Theodosius and Justinian—had inserted into the *Corpus juris civilis* dispositions of Christian origin that not only had a bearing on conduct to be followed (giving alms, liturgy), but that affected convictions as well (in the condemnation of certain heresies). The problem of distinguishing between the domains of the profane and the religious had thus already been posed.

The Dispute between Laws

That distinction between the sacred and the profane was not easily made. In theory, of course, all one had to do was to apply the principle expressed very early on by Gelasius. As Accursius put it: "Neither the pope in secular matters nor the emperor in spiritual matters has any authority."[61] In practice, however, the division between the domain of the church and that of the temporal power was far from reflecting peaceful respect for the other's realm of competence, and it soon became grounds for conflict.

Fault

The care to avoid sin and what leads to sin made canon law diverge from Roman law in certain points that seem, from the profane point of view, simply details. Their implications for salvation are vast, however. For example, unlike what occurs in Roman law, canon law requires good faith (*bona fides*)—not only initial but ongoing—in cases of the acquisition of property by prescription. In a Christian context, the word *fides* had taken on a good deal more weight than it had for pagan jurists: it had become the keyword of salvation; everything that departed from it is sin (Rom. 14:23). The demand for *bona fides* thus permitted the canonists to reject the notion that the law is content to consider exterior behavior alone.[62]

The way in which the canonists introduced the notion of sin gave rise to all manner of difficulties. By the decretal *Novit ille* (1204) Pope Innocent III, citing the need to avoid sin (*ratio peccati*), arrogated to himself the right to judge questions of feudal law, thus claiming a right to intervene at the very heart of the feudal system. And he had to determine where sin had occurred. The pope was thus claiming competence for deciding on competence. The jurists were quick to point out that such a move permitted the church, and the pope in particular, to intervene in domains that might pertain to the profane authorities alone.[63]

In the Middle Ages the borderline between the sacred and the profane, which is always fluid, did not follow the same traces as today. At the time canon law regulated entire segments of life that no one in our own day would dream of considering to be religious. This was true of teaching and aid to the needy, at the time the province of the church. It was especially true in matters relating to private life, through such rules about marriage as the prohibition of consanguinity. The struggle between the church and social mores regarding marriage continued for centuries. Society tended to view marriage as an alliance between two families, an attitude that privileged parental consent. The church sought, to the contrary, to found the marriage of couples of a proper age on consent alone; the priest was authorized to marry them not only without the consent of their parents but even against the family's wishes. In the very long term, this discrepancy resulted—in a consequence that we still feel today—in the rise of the isolated individual, cut off from family and social allegiances. In this sense, canon law, a medieval construction, forged the individual who later became the subject of the modern state.[64]

Although canon law did its utmost to set itself off from civil law, it nonetheless exerted an influence on it. For example, canon law served civil law as a model in defining the "trial," and, in the realm of the nature of proof, by replacing oaths and ordeals by material evidence, concordant witness, and the statements of the accused. The greatest influence of canon law, however, may have consisted in imposing the very existence of a duality of law systems. That duality is reflected in a similar duality in social logic, where only the law was capable of deciding which pertained. In this manner, it created an atmosphere favorable to the reign of law.[65]

The case of the ordeal, or single combat, is particularly interesting for our concerns, because it opposes two conceptions of the law, and even two conceptions of the divinity of the law. The French term for a solemn oath, *serment*, shows its sacred origin in its etymology, which makes it a doublet of "sacrament." Moreover, the ordeal was presented as a "judgment of God." It was thus the locus *par excellence* where the divine was supposed to intervene in the juridical domain. Historians have examined the social logic that presided at the ordeal and even lent it a certain rationality.[66] Still, in the long run it was excluded from the realm of jurisprudence. Doubts about its validity appeared for the first time in a text that dates from 731: "We are in incertitude as to the judgment of God, and we have heard speak of many people who have lost their cause unjustly after a combat."[67] Eventually, clerics were prohibited from attending trials by combat in a ruling formulated at the Fourth Lateran Council (1215), which, "by making the law of the text prevail over the law of the body," brought about a "de-corporalization" of the law.[68]

It is not enough to show how canon law differed from the other regulatory systems in force in the West during the Middle Ages. We need to leave Christendom and see how canon law differs from the other similar systems within Judaism and Islam. Internal differences, within the Christian world, and external differences, between that world and the exterior, overlap, however: what distinguishes Christian canon law from those analogous juridical systems resides, precisely, in the specific way in which it traced its own limits.

Heterogeneity in Religious Law Systems

Even though those borderlines are often difficult to situate, everyone was persuaded that they exist. Canon law does not aim to regulate the whole of human life. To the contrary, one might almost say that its proper function is to trace the frontier that surrounds specifically religious activities. That is where the essential difference between canon law and the juridico-religious systems of Judaism and Islam lies.

Jewish and Muslim juridical scholarship, although considerable in both quantity and quality, does not seem to have influenced medieval European law. The Christian glossators of the Bologna school and the Jews who annotated the Talmud (and who were known as "Tosaphists"), although contemporaries, do not seems to have had left any trace on one another. The same is true regarding the rabbis of Judaism and the Muslim doctors of law (the ʿulamāʾ).[69] On the other hand, it is possible that Boniface VIII, in his encyclical Unam sanctam (1304), the most extreme expression of the claims of the Holy See, formed his conception of the role of the pope by taking inspiration from the theory of the caliph developed by Avicenna.[70]

It is thus clear that the translation, encountered now and then, of the Arabic sharia by "canon law" is profoundly and irremediably wrong.[71] It is equally erroneous to put on the same plane Christian canon law and the Jewish and Islamic laws. This is true even when the canonists designate the law that they are administering as "divine law," in particular in contexts in which they are attempting to stress the primacy of that law over the purely human civil law (in which case the adjective "divine" attached to the former simply signifies that the canon law regards divine objects).[72]

From the historical point of view, canon law became an autonomous discipline, independent of exegesis. That new independence resulted in setting it at a distance, this time from theology. This was the contribution of the school of Saint-Victor. Canon law tends to use Holy Scripture in the form of citations, as illustration and extrinsic legitimization, but no longer as a source of law.[73] That does not mean that the Bible was simply forgotten. As one canonist recalls, "Canonical decisions derive, nonetheless, initially from the authoritative texts of the New and the Old Testament."[74] To be sure, few biblical laws were utilized directly. The fact remains, however, that a large portion of the canon law is informed indirectly by the Bible, which provides it with a nurturing milieu.[75]

The difference between the canon law and the two other systems of law can be observed on several levels. On the one hand, the canon law does not claim to embrace the whole of human behavior; it leaves aside the entire domain of morality. On the other hand, it is not founded on the religion's fundamental sources—that is, its sacred texts, primary (the Pentateuch, the Qur'an) or secondary (the Talmud, the Hadith). Consequently, it does not put into operation an exegetic method comparable to those of Judaism and Islam. Islamic "theocracy," as the direct power of the legislator-God, always runs the risk of short-circuiting human mediation. Conversely, Christian "hierocracy," which delivers legislation over to the priest, makes the intermediary of a human law necessary.[76]

10]﴾··

Islam: Law Rules

Islam, in the form of the Arabs' submission to Muhammad, preceded Islamic law: "Islam was in existence before the Koran."[1] The
"Constitution of Medina (or Madīnah)," by which the émigrés
from Mecca and their "aides" in Medina accepted Muhammad as
their chief, predates the Qur'an, or at least the definitive form of
the Qur'an.[2]

The Historical Problem

In the reality of daily practice, political power was fairly rapidly separated from religious authority. If we can believe the traditional histories, the unity of the Arab nation lasted for less than a generation,
under the first four caliphs, whom tradition celebrates as the "rightly
guided" (*rāshidūn*), that is, from the death of Muhammad in 632 to
661. After then the nation divided, with the appearance of Kharid-
jism and Shiism, which in turn further split into branches. The dynasty of the Umayyads was overturned in 750 by a revolution that
put the Abbassids in power, except in Andalusia, where a dynasty
claiming Umayyad ancestry remained in power.

Once Islam had become a state, it set itself up as a legislative system. Solutions had to be found for a good many problems not covered in the Qur'an. One solution would have been to turn to codes
that already existed in the Syro-Mesopotamian area. That did not occur. In fact, Islam had appeared on the scene of history as the religion of the Arab conquerors. It was that situation that prohibited
Islam from doing what Christianity did when it borrowed juridical
norms covering everything situated outside the religious domain
from the conquered "pagan" state, introducing only a few minimal

amendments. Islam, on the other hand, had to replace one state with another. For the moment, it could of course begin by slipping into the more technical structures of domination (post communications, tax collecting), even leaving in place the families of the functionaries who had served Byzantium, such as that of St. John Damascene (d. 749). This is exactly what occurred with the first Umayyad caliphs of the Sufyanid dynasty.

That system functioned until a brusque change of direction occurred under the caliphate of ʿAbd al-Malik, the first of the Marwanids (685). The Marwanid army was recruited by voluntary service alone, thus effacing the last vestiges of the tribes. But Islam could not act in the same manner on the juridical level without putting itself in danger: conforming to the legal practices of the state that it had just overturned would have meant relaxing its hold. For the new governing class that emerged from the conquest, this would have endangered their legitimacy and even, over the long term, have risked their melting into the conquered populations and losing power. The greatest problem was thus to create an elite impermeable to the mores of the conquered.[3] In order to do so, that elite must conform to a law totally of its own, and to that law only.

The Prophet as Law

Thus Islam had to draw the whole of its legislation out of its own sources. This was hardly possible, first, because, as a general rule, "codes are not made; they make themselves," but even more so in the special case in which a minority of conquerors had become masters of populations that were a good deal more evolved and had more broadly differentiated social systems.

Islam thus adopted a strategy that allowed it to "mask" the content of that legislation and, instead of having to acknowledge the need of borrowing it from elsewhere, to pass it off as having coming from within. This is why it had to attribute to Muhammad all that was needed to legitimate the many practices that it hoped to promote. Moreover, primitive Islam as a whole presented itself as a takeover of preexistent authorities, which it invested with new meaning by connecting them to a new source of legitimacy.[4]

The Function of the Hadith

The Hadith collections had precisely that function: lending legitimacy to a preexistent state of affairs.[5] The current practices that people abided by— the administrative regulations of the Umayyads, popular customs, the reasoning of the earliest jurists—were projected back in time and attached to the prophetic source "by a fiction perhaps unequaled in the history of human thought."[6] Authors disagree on the extent of this recuperation. In any event, we can cite Patricia Crone's paradox: "It is the lawyers who determined what the Prophet said, not the other way round."[7]

The principle that the jurists chose was imitation of Muhammad, who was taken as an example on the basis of a verse of the Qur'an: "You have indeed in the Messenger of Allah a beautiful pattern [of conduct]" (*uswa hasana*). It is difficult to ascertain the precise meaning of this stereotype, used only here and in a passage referring to Abraham.[8] Be that as it may, the jurists consulted the accounts (*hadīth*) that relate the declarations and acts of Muhammad. Citations were not collected for historiographic purposes, to be used as evidence for a biography, but as authorized sources of law. Their power of legitimation explains the extreme care given to assuring their authenticity. Thus the Hadith bring together all the usages in effect at the time of Muhammad and in the conquered lands. Some of these may be of Roman origin.[9] Others were filtered through Jewish Law. What is essential is that any such origin outside of revelation was denied, and that Islamic law was supposed to be wholly of prophetic origin.

As a consequence, there was a long-term tendency to accord greater authority to the Hadith. Some commentators even placed them explicitly on the same plane as the Qur'an, or even considered them capable of abrogating legislative dispositions in the Qur'an. Among Muslim authors there existed a fiction analogous to the Jewish fiction that stated that at Sinai God gave Moses not only the written Torah but also all of the most minute dispositions of oral law. A hadith has Muhammad saying, "What is in agreement with the Qur'an is from me, whether I really said it or not."[10] Ibn Qutayba (d. 889) states: "If it is admissible that the Qur'an be abrogated by the Qur'an, it is just as admissible that the Qur'an be abrogated by the Sunna, for *the Sunna was brought to the Prophet by Gabriel, sent from God.* Thus the Word of God that is Qur'an can be abrogated by the revelation of God that is not Qur'an. It is in this sense that the Prophet said: 'The Qur'an was brought to me, along with other similar things,' that is, the Sunna." A parallel passage specifies: "Gabriel transmitted the normative traditions [to Muhammad] just as he transmitted the Qur'an to him."[11]

The Two Extremes

The personal power of Muhammad over his partisans, which was followed, after his military and political successes, by power over the Muslim community as a whole, preceded the organization of the latter as a civil society. Thanks to the principle of imitation of the Prophet, Muhammad's authority, which already took advantage of a legendary aura, also acquired a logical anteriority. That concentration of legitimacy in one original focus was bound to raise the problem of *transmission*. Two radical solutions to the problem seemed possible: either an extreme personalization of power, or an extreme depersonalization of the law.

First of all, the personal authority of the Prophet could be transmitted to those of his successors who marched at the head of the community and on whom the community was to pattern its behavior—the *imām*. But which successors? There was discord from the very start, and it was soon followed by assassinations and civil wars, with the first caliphs being chosen by commissions whose legitimacy was fragile. Shiism first practiced, then theorized, that first solution: it constructed a theory according to which the prophetic charisma was transmitted from the Prophet to his descendants, supposed to be "preserved" from sin and to be infallible.

With the Abbasid revolution in 750, it became possible to oppose the reigning caliph by invoking the true Islam against him, but it was not yet possible to imagine an *umma* (a community) without a caliph. Opposition to the reigning caliph came, in fact, in the name of another branch of the Prophet's family, that of 'Ali. After 750 the Abbasid caliphs laid claim to the family identity, which meant that the partisans of 'Ali had to develop a specifically religious identity, then forge for themselves a competing vision of the world patched together on the basis of the popular Neoplatonism of the time. Shiism offered no more than the old solution, however.

Another solution consisted in making the instance of the law bear all the weight of legitimacy by relating it to the unique and irreplaceable person of Muhammad, but also totally detaching it from the person of the governors to reside in an impersonal class of "scholars." This led to the emergence of a religious authority that was not dependent on the effective authority of the caliph, but resided in the class of men of religion.[12] It was these scholars who gradually monopolized everything that pertained to religion, rather than politics, in Islam. This meant that the political power had to function in accordance with its own logic.

The Birth of the Sunna

It was the "traditionists" or the "people of the Hadith" who proposed a solution to the problem of the transmission of power in opposition to that of the Shiites. The intellectual tool that enabled them to resolve the question to their satisfaction was the notion of *sunnah,* more precisely, the new significance that they gave to that ancient word. The term originally designated the spontaneous sense, widespread among the population, of what is just and appropriate. It eventually designated a rule of law guaranteed by the authority of the Prophet, which at times had little in common with the law of the caliph.

The jurist al-Shāfiʿī (d. 820) played a decisive role in this connection, even though his influence did not become preponderant until more than a century after his death.[13] He made a condensation of his principles in a fairly brief treatise: the judgment of the Prophet was that of God himself; the *sunnah* was to be identified with the Wisdom that the Qurʾan connected to "the Book"; analogy serves only in cases of necessity, to palliate the absence of a tradition.[14] Shāfiʿī's position can be summarized thus: "To every act performed by a believer with which the Law is concerned there corresponds a statute deriving from revealed Law. That legal statute is either given as such in the scriptural sources (the Qurʾan and the Sunna), which Shāfiʿī calls 'the foundation,' or else it is possible, by means of analogous reasoning, to infer it from the foundation, which is the bearer of a latent 'intelligible content.'" As for the Sunna, one must "strictly equate it with the sayings, the acts, and the approbations of the Prophet alone, as reported in solidly established traditions; it is . . . no longer possible to think naively that the different living local traditions faithfully reflect the practice of the Prophet." All analogy must "imperatively rest on a legal proof . . . certainly at times difficult for the jurist to locate, but whose existence, by postulate, is certain."[15] In this manner, Shāfiʿī defended a law whose origin was held to be exclusively divine because it was exclusively prophetic.[16]

One of the perverse effects of that method was paradoxical: the stress put on the need to found law on sources that surely went back to the Prophet made it all the more profitable to put controversial hadiths into circulation. Forgers took the precaution of creating irreproachable chains of transmission. Historical criticism draws from this a somewhat disillusioned rule of thumb: the older the authority invoked, the later the tradition; the more perfect the chain of origins, the more the hadith is likely to be forged.[17]

Given that there is no situation for which the Qurʾan and the Sunna cannot furnish a rule, there can be no appeal to any sort of personal judgment, even that of a supremely authorized person, the caliph, for example. The Sunna is efficacious without there being any need of a sovereign. Those who control it are not the sovereigns but the scholars.[18] Shāfiʿī was thus the first to reduce the *sunnah* to the status of a thing and to make it a dominant instance capable of overruling the caliph himself.

The Superfluous Caliph

Initially, the caliphs concentrated religious authority and political power in their own persons. The idea of separating the two did not enter anyone's mind. They were God's representatives, and if that title was taken seriously, it implied that there was no room left for religious personnel. The caliphs acted as judges, and their judgments counted as sacred law. The law was given by God, and it was formulated by the caliphs, who were also gifts of God.[19] In contrast, once the law became independent of the person of the Prophet's successor, the caliph in time became useless.

The Failure of Codification

The first to understand that dialectic seems to have been Ibn al-Muqaffa', a Persian convert from Manicheism. Some years after the Abbasid revolution, he saw that the only way to maintain both the caliphate and the law was for the caliph to reserve to himself juridical authority for its interpretation.[20] The problem on which he had put his finger arose out of the existence of contradictory juridical practices. One way to harmonize these would have been to create a supreme magistracy charged with deciding between them, a role that Ibn al-Muqaffa' reserved to the caliph. In 754 he addressed a memoir to the caliph al-Mansur, the second of the Abbasids, stating his ideas for reform. Among other measures, he proposed two legislative tasks. The first was the redaction of a "short but complete catechism" containing the principal articles of faith obligatory for army service, a concise public rule "clearly defining the beliefs to be held by the officers and men of the imperial army."[21] Second, the caliph should order the redaction of "a collection of the divergent decisions and customs, accompanied by proofs that each group draws from practice (sunnah) or from analogy." With this in hand, the caliph will give "the opinion (ra'y) that God will have inspired in him" and he will impose it, prohibiting the judges from varying from it. He will then write "a complete book"—what we would call a code of laws.[22] The point was to take control of both religion and the law (if these can be considered distinct from one another). The caliph must present his inspired opinion persuasively—a condition that supposes a theory of religious law that sees the law as not including the totality of life and that leaves room for free decision. But that decision, far from being entrusted to individual conscience, is reserved for those who hold authority.[23] Baldly stated: everything for which the Qur'an and the oral tradition provided no explicit solution must be left to the discretion of the caliph.

The caliph did not listen to Ibn al-Muqaffa', who in fact was executed two years later, perhaps not without having his political audacity give credence to the religious accusation of crypto-Manicheism that was the official pretext for the sentence. For that reason, religion won what the state lost in becoming weaker. The place that Ibn al-Muqaffa' had wanted to reserve to "opinion" was occupied by the consensus (*ijmāʾ*) of the community, an idea that increased in strength and was rooted in the Stoic and Epicurean idea of a "common notion" (*koine ennoia*). The failure of the reform attempted by Ibn al-Muqaffaʾ represents the first divorce between the state and the law.[24]

The Mutazilite Crisis

The Mutazilite crisis, which occurred almost a century later, can be interpreted as a final attempt on the part of the caliph to reserve to himself the role of supreme arbiter of the law, against the traditionists. The context of this crisis was at first political: it lay in the consequences of the civil war for the caliphate between al-Amīn and his brother al-Maʾmūn, who emerged the victor in 813.[25] The insecurity that gripped Baghdad gave rise to a movement of self-defense. The duty of "commanding the good and prohibiting the bad" that had until then been the role of the caliph and his functionaries was henceforth claimed by all Muslims. The religious and communitarian interests of Islam were represented by a group that stood opposed to the caliph, who was thus no longer accepted as the incarnation of the community. Maʾmūn responded by reasserting the authority of the caliphate, enhanced by an extended religious role borrowed from the Shiite model.

The combat focused on the question of the status of the Qurʾan: was it created or uncreated? The question probably reflects two branches of an earlier doctrine according to which the Qurʾan was indeed created but preexisted the creation of the rest of the world, an idea that can be found in Judaism regarding the Torah.[26] This was more than a metaphysical question, however. Indeed, the ontological status accorded to the Qurʾan implies a practice of the text that varies according to the answer given to this question. In a word, a created Qurʾan can be *interpreted;* an uncreated Qurʾan can only be *applied.* The dogma of a created Qurʾan proposed by the Mutazilites authorized interpretation, in the juridical sense of that term. A Qurʾan of the sort would require the existence of an authority charged with what Christianity calls the "discerning of spirits." That authority should of course reside in the caliph. On the other hand, an uncreated Qurʾan is only susceptible to grammatical explication (*tafsīr*) and mystical elucidation (*taʾwīl*). Neither of these two methods compromises or mitigates the demand for absolute application of the Qurʾan; neither personal application, reliant on the behavior of the believer, that springs from the heart, on the one hand, nor, on the other, juridical application by the sovereignty of a law that, in principle, embraces all conduct. An uncreated Qurʾan was an object for both mystics and jurists.

The caliph attempted to use force to impose the Mutazilite doctrine of the created Qurʾan, persecuting those opposed to that belief between 833 and 847. A coalition began to form against him, bringing together the circles that had offered resistance in the streets of Baghdad twenty years earlier and the "traditionists," the people of the Hadith, for whom Ibn Hanbal provided a figurehead. For Ibn Hanbal, maintaining the law was the duty of all Muslims, not just the caliph. Hanbalism introduced the potential of militant opposition to the caliphate at the very core of Sunni Islam. The caliphate ceased to be the one symbol of Muslim identity and the sole organizational institution. With the end of the persecution, decreed by al-Mutawakkil in 848, the caliph renounced the function of his juridical guidance.[27]

The Law Becomes Autonomous

At that point, it was not long before the caliphs became purely symbolic. Friday sermons were delivered and coins minted in their name, but power passed to the military leaders, at first the Buyid emirs, who were Persian (936), then Seljuk Turk sultans (1038), not to mention the fact that their crumbling power descended to local dynasties in armed competition with one another. As this was occurring, the caliphs, hesitating at first (as can well be imagined) before a doctrine that condemned them to a purely secondary role, ended up officially rallying to the Sunni interpretation of the law. This was the case of the caliph al-Qādir in a letter of 1018 that represents something like an official catechism.[28]

By that time, the caliphate served little other purpose than to legitimize usurpers who had risen to power by force of arms and were subsequently presented as having been delegated to hold that power.[29] The theory of the caliphate of al-Mawardi (d. 1058) took into account the "emirate of conquest," thus ratifying a practice that had already been in existence for over a century.[30] The criterion of legitimacy of the governing power tended to become its orthodoxy—that is, the willingness of the ruler to apply the law.[31]

The law became increasingly disembodied, or at least the authority that had responsibility for it was obviously crumbling and tended to become collective rather than individual. "A law that regarded itself as based, even in its details, on revelation, either actually or virtually, had to be independent from the state."[32] What the state, with the caliph at its head, should have done was instead done by the class of the doctors of the law ('ulamā'). Divine law developed, becoming the sharia, which was administered by these doctors of law.

Power, which had initially been tied to concrete persons—Muhammad, then the caliphs—split into two. The 'ulamā' won the battle for religious authority, but they had to accept the secular power of the de facto leaders.[33] To one side there was a political power, in theory exercised in the name of religious values, but in reality regulating its actions toward maintenance of public order, without truly respecting the law, as everyone was perfectly aware.[34] The prince was nonetheless implicitly obliged to display piety by honoring the men of religion and by going through the motions of consulting them.[35] To the other side there was a religious authority that weighed on the conscience alone and seldom acted except to mobilize popular approval or indignation. Consensus (*ijmā'*), which supposedly guaranteed the nation against error, appeared in the form of social pressure; in a reciprocal move, that pressure on mores put into circulation practices with which the scholars had to compromise.

Juridical Ossification?

Historians sometimes evoke a decadence of Islam, which they suppose to have occurred, to a varying extent according to region, beginning in the eleventh century. Rather than an absolute decline, they tend to speak of a relative stagnation in relation to other cultures, in particular to Latin Christendom in Europe. To be sure, the lands under Islam continued to expand, both in Africa and in Asia. Islam had become the military Islam with the Arab conquest; Christianity had become Christendom by a peaceful penetration into Roman society. At a later date the situation reversed: the Christian Empire, without ceasing to preach the faith, reached out to the north and to the east in a way that was just as political and warlike; the world of Islam, without giving up war (we need only recall the invasion of the Punjab by Mahmūd of Ghazna in 1020) spread by means of a mission that was also commercial and spiritual.

In spite of that expansion, the cultural creativity of the Islamic world, with a thousand variations according to period and place, seems to have been marching in place. Historians seek the causes for this slowdown in various domains, but without reaching any agreement.[36]

Open or Closed?

One of the domains in which people seek, if not the cause, at least the principal focus of that stagnation refers us directly to the problem that occupies me here—that of the relation between divinity and legislation—because that was exactly what Muslim "religious law" was all about. Some think they have located a juridical ankylosis, customarily referred to not much earlier than the eighteenth century as the "closing of the gate of *ijtidād* (personal effort)."[37]

To be sure, the jurists' activity did not cease, or even diminish. It is quite possible that, on the level of reality, new solutions were discreetly proposed, but on the conscious level, we encounter the idea that a personal search for original juridical solutions is a thing of the past, all possible problems having already been resolved, in principle, by one or another of the recognized schools (or "rites"). This state of affairs needs to be placed within an evolution of broader intellectual scope. In the eleventh century, Sunnism seems to have begun to believe that Islam had arrived at its maturity, and that any further development would represent a decline, a fear that can be perceived throughout the eleventh century.[38]

If we suppose that the ankylosis in question had been juridical in origin, the phenomenon would be all the more interesting, because it would be roughly contemporary with the juridical revolution that occurred in Latin Europe in the wake of the "papal revolution." In a fascinating change of roles, Latin Christianity was evolving in the opposite direction from Islam. Until that time, it had placed salvation in flight from a world thought to be on the point of disappearing. After the "papal revolution," attempts to institute reforms in the temporal world began to appear, thus providing a parallel in the juridical domain to the change in direction in the economic realm during the same period.[39]

Mysticism and Politics: A Two-Way Road

Whatever the validity of these hypotheses, an important change took place: the political was no longer an element of salvation. Religion retired from the field of the political. Governing the state, for the Sunni, no longer meant guiding the community toward paradise, but rather reigning over a people to whom paradise was already promised.[40] Concrete evidence of that promise lay in other practices than participation in public life, such as private devotion. It became exemplary even for the political: a "Mirror for Princes" that figures among Ghazali's reputed works goes so far as to propose to the head of state that he take as a model the totally nonpolitical life of a wandering dervish.[41]

During the same period, mysticism was even working to re-create, in compensation, a new form of social organization, independent of the state and drawn from foundations of its own: the Sufi "brotherhoods" (turuq) expanded enormously in the twelfth century, when they deployed an intensive missionary campaign. Although it might seem surprising, not only the fabric of society but even entire portions of the state apparatus could be reconstituted on the basis of the sociable network of the Sufi confraternities. This is true to the point that the nucleus of a good many Muslim states of the modern age was in a confraternity. This is the case of the Almoravids, who emerged from the Senegalese ribat (some sort of convent-fortress) that lent them its name, who took power in Andalusia in the late eleventh century. Another case in point is that of the Safavid dynasty of Iran in the early sixteenth century, which also owes its name to a Sufi *tariqah*. One could cite other examples from the African continent.

❖

The history of Islam as a civilization displays a rich diversity. The history of Islam as a religion, from the viewpoint that interests me here, can also be understood as tending toward an ever purer formulation of the dream of a *kingdom of the Law*—what Louis Gardet called a "nomocracy."[42] The embodiment, in a political body, of a law whose principles were directly derived from revelation was to remain a pious hope. Thus Islam retraced, in its own manner, the itinerary of "excarnation" that had been typical of ancient Israel. Contrary to a legend tenacious in the West, Islam thus experienced a separation of the political and the religious. But this separation was gradually attained thanks to circumstances; it was inscribed in facts, not in ideas. In Islam, nothing corresponds to the separation—which was theorized elsewhere—of the temporal and the spiritual.[43]

❖

The historical period that the West rather oddly calls the "Middle Ages" was a watershed moment in many areas. As for the problem that occupies me here, the apogee of divine law was reached in the Middle Ages. This is primarily true of the law that was considered as a juridical, and even a political, reality.

Judaism and Islam, in quite different contexts—necessarily apolitical for the first and decidedly political for the second—elaborated systems of religious law in styles that were just as different. Thanks to these systems of religious law, every human act was considered subject, in principle and through a number of human mediations, to a God-given norm. Christianity's point of departure was a break with two systems of law: it was subjected to the law of the Roman Empire, but without adhering to the religious aspects of that law, such as the cult of the emperor; it eliminated everything in Jewish Law that went beyond "natural" moral rules. The medieval period saw a repetition of the conflict between law systems, but in a world that had become Christian. The empire witnessed the constitution of the church as an autonomous entity that would have been unable to find a structure if it had not been able to draw on a law of its own.

The Middle Ages were equally decisive for the question of divine law as an idea offered to the thinkers of the time. Their reflections will form the object of the next part of this work.

Divine Law in Medieval Thought

What I would like to present now are the different ways in which divine law was conceptualized. I shall examine successively the situation in Islam, in Judaism, and in Christianity in this regard, accentuating three central witnesses: Ghazali, Maimonides, and St. Thomas Aquinas. The order in which these three figures are presented calls for a justification. Although it corresponds to chronological order among the three thinkers, it seems to upset the chronology of the three religions related to them: Judaism, which up to now has been presented first, figures here between the two other religions, which—each in its own way—appealed to Judaism as an authority.

In reality, my guiding thread remains chronological. But my chronology is no longer that of events but rather of their reflection in medieval thought and, above all, in the philosophical style elaborated by that thought. As it happens, it was in Islam that the central concepts of a body of thought regarding divine law were first expressed and applied. To be sure, well before Muhammad, Judaism had set up an all-embracing and fully detailed juridical system. But the Jewish thinkers borrowed from the thinkers of Islam—first from the *Kalām*, then from Muslim Aristotelianism—the intellectual tools that permitted them to think about their practice.

As for the medieval period of Christianity, its thought regarding the law culminates in the synthesis of St. Thomas Aquinas. Nonetheless, he made large use of the previous efforts of Muslims and Jews: Avicenna and Averroes, and Maimonides.

Finally, one more reason leads me to place Christianity third: the claim to have definitively left the Middle Ages behind arose—or arose *first*—in Christian lands. Christian Europe was the stage on which modern times reinterpreted the idea of divine law. This reinterpretation was achieved in reaction—conscious or unconscious—to how divine law had been conceived in the Middle Ages, which means that if we are to understand modern attacks on divine law (and, by that same token, the essence of the modern project), we need to have a clear grasp of the medieval definition of divine law.

11

The Aims of the Law: Islam

Political thought as it really existed in Islamic lands was not, either immediately or exclusively, based on divine law. The caliphs at first attempted to conceive of their role as a simple technique of government. To that effect, they borrowed from the political wisdom of Persia of the Sassanid dynasty, a wisdom centered on the idea of justice rather than on that of knowledge or of religious orthodoxy.[1] Two formulaic expressions condense that wisdom: one, constantly repeated, is attributed to the Sassanid king Ardashir: "Religion and royalty are twin sisters";[2] the other is an image: "The king is the shadow of God on Earth."[3] Another dictum stresses the pragmatic and scarcely edifying nature of the power that it defends: "A government can subsist with impiety, but it cannot last with oppression and tyranny."[4]

An entire literary genre—that of the "Mirror for Princes"—gives an evolving vision of the relationship between the prince and religion.[5] Ibn al-Muqaffaʾ, whose sources are primarily Persian, recognized a system of royal government taking religion as its foundation, but "religion" meant little more than purely formal duty. It was only gradually that Arabic elements were introduced into the literature of the Mirrors for Princes and that Muhammad also became a model of the perfect sovereign.[6] The law scarcely appears in this literature. One text of this sort, attributed to Ghazali, mentions the law (shar ʾ) only once, and then in a fairly neutral context.[7] Later, this relationship was reversed, and the law absorbed wisdom all the more easily because the Qurʾan had already integrated the wisdom of Luqmān.[8]

The Law, Omnipresent and Invisible

In the two religions in which the law gained a central place—Judaism and Islam—it is presented in a particular light. In Islam, the law is already the central content of revelation.

A Non-Natural Law

Islam in fact thinks of the relation of God to man, and indeed to all creatures, as regulated by prophecy, and it understands the latter as culminating in the gift of a law.[9] Classically, it distinguishes several levels of prophecy. Certain men receive a message that is addressed to them either personally or, by their mediation, to a community that they must inform. Others—and they are few—are "messengers" (rasūl), the bearers of a book that dictates right conduct in terms of system of law.[10] Muhammad is the last representative of these. The Qur'an has him designated by God as the "Seal of the Prophets," a somewhat obscure formula, especially given its context, that may have been inherited from Manes, and which commentators have interpreted as signifying both the one who confirms and the one who completes.[11]

Consequently, the basic religious attitude is a relation to the law—that is, obedience. Every virtuous act is an act of obedience; conversely, evil in all its forms is disobedience, infraction of the law. To be more precise, what God imposes is less a "law" strictly speaking (sharia) than a process by which he assigns to human life a moral quality and a moral responsibility (shar'). The object of obedience is thus not the law, but God. It is only subsequently that the law became a thing, hence what must be applied.[12] Such a law cannot be the invention of men. The veritable legislator (hākim) can only be God.[13] One nineteenth-century author could still state: "No one who professes Islam would be so brazen as to regard the human reason as lawgiver."[14] This excludes all temptation to associate anything else—nature, for example, or reason—with the Unique.

In general, Islam does not easily accept the idea according to which things have a "nature." And nature, even if conceived as created, is not a valid source of law. This means that the idea of natural law has no place in Islam. In any event, that idea is present only extremely discreetly in the ancient sources that reached the Muslim world, among which the Stoics—and, for even greater reason, Cicero—do not figure. Aristotle was familiar with the idea of what was "just" by nature. When Muslim thinkers found that idea in his works, they had difficulty knowing what to do with it. Alfarabi, for example, distinguishes clearly between the laws proper to a nation or an epoch (do not eat pork; do not slit an animal's throat) and common laws valid for any community and all times (do not return evil for good; do good to your parents; do to others what you would want them to do to you; honor your friends and your kin), but he does not insert the idea of nature in them.[15] Similarly, when Averroes encounters the idea in the text of Aristotle that he is to comment on, he paraphrases the text well, but he pays no particular attention to the notion. It is even interesting that he substitutes for the distinction Aristotle draws between "natural justice" and "legal justice" a distinction that puts the legal as a common factor between what was "just by nature" from the legal standpoint and "merely legal justice."[16]

Reason has no bearing on the content of law and cannot be its foundation; it is radically powerless to discover by itself what would permit a harmonious human life, and must limit itself to recognizing the revealed nature of the Law.[17] Questions on the foundation of the authority of the state and on the source of its laws, a matter of prime importance for the Greeks, were thus hardly even posed for Islam: the Law precedes the state, which exists with the sole aim of maintaining and applying the Law. The question of legislation and of legislative power thus simply does not arise.[18] The presence of a law of divine origin, hence removed from the vicissitudes of human interests, is perceived as the basis for the superiority of Islam over the paganism that preceded it, as well as over Christianity and the communities that it rules over. In the Christian nations, as the Muslims saw them, rules of conduct fluctuated according to circumstances and rulers.[19]

Still, the real importance of the law, which is immense, does not have as an automatic consequence its being the central object of the reflection of Muslim thinkers. Quite to the contrary, it is the very evidence of the law and its omnipresence that made it difficult to reduce it to direct thematic analysis. These two qualities affected the law both before and after the fact, hence the notion of law is as if in a vise, held tight between its origin and its realization.

Indeed, on the one hand, what the Islamic thinkers must show as divine is not directly the content of the law; rather, they have to go back to its very origin, to the fact that it had been conveyed through the mediation of a prophet. The question of the divinity of the law is thus secondary in relation to that of the divine authenticity of Muhammad's mission: once that is established, the rest follows easily.[20] On the other hand, working forward from that fact, Islam is presented as an effective system of regulation, as an objective morality (*Sittlichkeit*) more than a subjective one (*Moralität*). Its object of reflection is a real social community, not a law. This is why the philosophers of Islam reflect more about the political community than about the law. On this point, Islam differs from Judaism, which, if it is also a religion of the Law, is the religion of a law that does not draw its effectiveness from a political system.

A Native Law

The law is in a certain sense something manifest, however. A paradox arises here. I have just recalled that the idea of nature, and for even greater reason, that of natural law, had no place in Islam. Yet Islamic law appears as quasi natural, or in any event, as *native*. If it cannot be called "natural" in strict terms, it might be said to be "quite natural." This paradoxical status of the law is one aspect of the general paradox of Islam, which Alain Besançon expresses in a profound formula: "Islam is the natural religion of the revealed God."[21]

Islam supposes that all humans are born Muslim. The European, marked by Christianity, thinks spontaneously, with Descartes, that "we were born men before we became Christians."[22] One could almost say that the contrary was true for Islam. A passage of the Qur'an relates that the entire human species was miraculously drawn from the loins of Adam, and when God asks, "Am I not your Lord?" humanity responds unanimously, "Yes! We do testify!"[23] The Qur'anic pact (*mīthāq*) is analogous in its content to the way in which Israel chooses YHWH as its partner in the Covenant; moreover, by its context, it resembles the benediction of all humanity, to whom God "has bestowed . . . every spiritual blessing in the heavens . . . before the world began," that Paul speaks of in the Epistle to the Ephesians (1:3–4).

All these examples reflect attempts to create a memory of things past, to found an irrevocable engagement. But there is an important difference between the passage in the Qur'an and the two biblical texts. In the Old Testament, God's choice is situated within history. In Israel, the event of the alliance is not set within the immemorial time of what is situated in "pre-eternity" (*azal*); the event is perhaps mythical, but those who write of sacred matters present it as situated within the time of human history. As for Christianity, the project of salvation is simply proposed to man. It does indeed embrace "all things," which are to be recapitulated in Christ. But if the gift of God is anterior to historical time, man's response to it is not. It is given within history. In a sense, that response coincides with the very history of what is made possible by the promise of what is proposed "in the heavens." Man remains free to respond. A positive response is of course expected, but it is not given immediately. There is something like a hope on the part of God that precedes that of humankind.

The Qur'an speaks of a religious duty to be fulfilled according to the nature that God has given men in creating them. According to a hadith explaining the Qur'anic passage, "no new-born is born if not according to the natural (*fitra*). Then his two parents make of him a Jew, a Christian, or a Zoroastrian." He does not need to have his parents make him Muslim: he is born Muslim; it is his parents who turn him into an adept of another religion. In this manner, according to Islamic law, in the absence of contrary evidence, a foundling is reputed to be Muslim.[24] One important consequence of this fact is that any other religious position than Islam is not only an error, but, objectively, an apostasy. By that token, the non-Muslim—in the measure in which he does not use reason, which should lead him to know God and make him understand the interest that he has in submitting to him—is basically undistinguishable from the animals.[25]

It is precisely this "naturally" Muslim man to whom the prophets spoke. The message that has been confided to them is always identical, and it was given to each one of them in turn, beginning with Adam. In fact it simply ratifies an alliance situated before history, in pre-eternity. The idea of a history of salvation is absent, even impossible.[26]

Moreover, a confirmation of the quasi-natural character of the Islamic Law comes from the fact that, unlike the Jewish Law, it contains few commandments whose justification would require particular efforts. To be sure, not everything in it derives from the demands of life in society, and the "pillars" of Islam—prayer, fasting, and pilgrimage—require explication.[27] But Islamic Law does not contain bizarre commandments, the reasons for which are impenetrable. Muslim polemics with Judaism unfailingly stress Islam's advantage over Mosaic law, for example, regarding the mysterious biblical rite of the ashes of the red heifer that enter into the formula for lustral water.[28]

As a consequence, Islam has little that might be comparable to the literary genre of the "reasons for the commandments" and to the vast development that sort of literature took within Judaism. Authors who attempted to give a rational foundation to the cult are said to have been condemned. Al-Qaffāl (d. 976), in particular, composed an "almost Maimonidian" work on "The Virtues of the Law" as a "justification of the ways of God to man."[29] But al-Qaffāl and others like him remained marginal and exceptional and had few followers.

Jurists and Mutakallimūn

Beginning in the eighth century, Muslim thinkers began to construct an apologetics in the Arabic language to show, through dialectical arguments, that their own religion was plausible and the others were absurd. This discipline received the name *kalām*. The "book of charges" consisted less in showing the intrinsic value of the law than in establishing the authenticity of the prophetic mission that had brought it into being. The quality of the law, briefly recalled, could nonetheless be invoked as a proof of the superiority of the Qur'an over the other holy books.[30] A typical treatise of *kalām* begins by establishing the necessity of prophecy. It then shows its reality by comparing the claims of various prophets, and it ends by insisting on the definitiveness of the message of Muhammad. The first step was to establish the need for prophecy in face of adversaries for whom human intellect was enough. That thesis is commonly attributed to persons whom the Muslim apologists (*mutakallimūn*) call *Barāhima*, a term easily recognized as a stylized version of Brahman Indians.[31] The religions of India represent a challenge for Islam, given that their laws do not claim to originate in revelation.

The response was a tendency to trace prophecy back to the very origin of the human species and place it at the origin of all human knowledge, including the secular arts and crafts. The Greek theme of the first inventor of a technique is thus transposed into a theory of prophecy. Al-Jāhiz, in the ninth century, was perhaps the first to present the need for revelation in a systematic manner. In the early eleventh century, the Andalusian Ibn Hazm took another step and, like Louis de Bonald at a later date, attributed the origin of language to a primitive revelation. At the end of the same century and at the other end of the Islamic world, Ghazali made the existence of arts such as medicine and astronomy a proof of the existence of prophecy.[32]

The style of Muslim Law made inevitable a conflict that has remained classic. That law introduced a set of duties, to the point that Islamic law (*fiqh*) has been characterized as primarily a *deontology*. A law of the sort, Christiaan Snouck Hurgronje writes, "cannot be divided into religion, morality, and law. It treats only external duties, controllable by a human authority." He adds, however, "But these duties are, without exception, duties toward God and founded on the unsoundable will of God himself."[33] This means that controversy arose over the question of knowing whether the good is commanded by God because it has something like a nature that made it intrinsically worthy of having God command it, or whether, to the contrary, it is the divine commandment that makes a practice good when it would otherwise be indifferent. Two tendencies came to grips with each other over this question.[34]

The Polemic about Reason

This confrontation centered on a word—*'aql*—which can mean intelligence and, for the philosophers, intellect, as a translation of the Greek *nous*. No one in Islam attacked the idea, and all praised it. Still, even appreciation can contain diametrically opposed notions. Everything depends on whether "intelligence" has an active role or involves mere reception. Is intelligence a legislating organ, capable of finding the good rule to follow? Is it simply the capacity to obey? Mawardi establishes a distinction, but he immediately brings the question back to one principle: either the commandments are what reason demands, in which case they are confirmed by the law, or else they are what reason admits as possible, in which case the law renders them obligatory. Reason is thus, in both cases, the pillar on which everything rests.[35]

Certain of the Mutazilites came near to the idea of a natural law independent of revelation and the will of God. They find another basis for the commandments than divine will. There is, in fact, another criterion of good and evil, the one used by Aristotle, which states that certain actions are generally praised, whereas others attract unanimous condemnation.[36]

Finally, some authors draw a distinction between two sorts of commandments, the revealed and the rational. The Jewish thinkers of the time, while recognizing its Islamic origin, made extensive use of this distinction (as did Christians of a later date).[37] According to al-Nazzām, certain prohibitions are rational and derive from natural law. For Amr ibn Ubayd, revelation completes and modifies natural law; limiting certain prohibitions: for example, the taboo regarding the killing of animals does not apply to sacrifices and ritual slaughter.[38]

Conversely, when a mystic like Muhāsibī focuses his reflections on the idea of "intelligence," he means by that the ability to understand that it is in one's interest to follow the regulations already decreed by God. The *mutakallim* Juwaynī defines that faculty as what permits subjection (*taklīf*) to the obligations of dogma, just as we speak of a child reaching the "age of reason." The eleventh century "marks the reduction of the status of reason to the instrumental level. It could no longer be a legislative instance, nor even a regulatory one."[39]

❖

The general trend of Muslim thought was unfavorable to the Mutazilites. The more time passed, the more the rival school of al-Ash'arī gained ground, dominating the scene from the eleventh century on. The Ash'arites are more faithful to the "most fundamental principle of Sunni jurisprudence, which is that God decides in all things, and that the human mind is totally incompetent where it is a question of functioning as a judge of any human action."[40] Their school could hardly conceive of the idea of a system of law or a law that would be natural, or even of the very idea of nature, to which they set up a deliberate and staunch rejection. For al-Ash'arī, the revealed

Law is thus the one foundation of good and evil: the good is what God commands, and evil is what he prohibits, and that is that. If in extraordinary circumstances he should command one to lie, it must be done. Al-Māturidī represents a more moderate version of the same stance: norms are certainly put in place by God alone, but his wisdom disposes them in such a way that they form a stable and intelligible system.[41]

Juwaynī, Ghazali's teacher, formulated the Ash'arite doctrine with an implacable rigor:

> The intellect does not indicate either that a thing is noble or that it is vile in a judgment that obliges (*hukm al-taklīf*). It is informed about what it must consider as noble and as vile only by the resources of the law (*shar'*) and by what tradition renders necessary. The principle of what must be said [on the subject] is that a thing is not noble by itself, by its genre, or by an attribute that belongs to it. It is possible that something may be noble for the law, while something similar to it and equivalent to it is vile according to all judgments of attributes of the soul.

The characteristics of good and bad, purely exterior to actions, come only from the judgment that the law brings to bear on them. "The nobility or the vileness [of an action] signifies nothing other than the simple fact that a commandment or a prohibition has come down [to us about them]." Juwaynī recognizes that he considers only what is noble according to the judgment of God.[42] "Obligation is not an attribute of what is obligatory. That a thing is obligatory signifies that it is said of it: 'Do it!'"[43]

Certain Ash'arites even stated that the commandments have no other aim than to reduce humankind to obedience. Their doctrine of the ends of the law is founded on a more general vision of the ends of creation. Unlike the Christian view of it, the goal of creation is not the entry of a creature into the divine life by adoption. Its goal is the submission of creatures to God. The aim of the commandments of the law is uniquely to realize the "enslavement" (*ta'abbud*) of man to God.[44] In a general manner, God can in fact assert himself only by limiting man's power and already, as early as the moment of the creative act, giving him limited capacities.[45] To fulfill that purpose, incomprehensible commandments are more efficacious. Al-Hillī (d. 1325) credits prophecy with the fact that the prophet installs rules that are inaccessible to the intellect. Some authors even specify that "enslavement" formally excludes the search for the reasons behind the commandments (*ta'līl*).[46]

It is impossible to trace dispositions of the law back to a knowledge of the character of God. By that same token, the fact that a commandment is ordained by God has only an extrinsic relationship to its utility for man. One can of course lend an intention and a utility to a number of laws, but intention and utility are not the *reason* for which God imposed them on his creatures, and they are never the *goal* of divine action. God does not have man's advantage in mind.[47] For Juwaynī, an object about which something is said does not acquire an intrinsic property by that fact. Consequently, the prohibition of wine does not mean that the wine would be bad. It is possible that the law effectively contains rational aims, but they are secondary and may not even have been willed by the divine Legislator. No one has the right to suppose that God always aims at the good of creatures. What the law demands of man may very easily be indifferent, or even harmful, to him.[48]

On this plane, the Ash'arites simply prolonged a tendency also represented among the adversaries of the Kalām. The caliph al-Qādir declares that "everything that [a man] accomplishes purely for the pleasure of God in legal observances" is a matter of faith and will be counted in his favor. The jurist Shāfi'ī goes even further: he who judges by himself creates his law; in doing so, he associates another source of law with the divine Legislator. He is thus, objectively, a polytheist.[49]

This way of viewing the question dominated the greater part of juridical theory until the nineteenth century, with only a few exceptions. The thinkers who escaped this tendency and who, for that reason, are today invoked by reform-minded Muslims, attempted to formulated the juridical system on the basis of the idea of common interest (*maslaha*) and the intention of the legislator.[50]

The Philosophers

Setting philosophers as a category apart is artificial. In Islamic culture, philosophy was never institutionalized, remaining instead a private activity. Moreover, at times philosophers had political responsibilities, like Avicenna, or politico-juridical ones, like Averroes. The scrupulous application of the law is for them a duty linked to one's social status and role that takes priority over all other considerations.[51]

The expression "divine law" is found occasionally in the writings of the Muslim philosophers. This time, it designates revealed codes—that is, precisely, a law of divine origin but which is at the same time the law of a specific human community. The term can be found, for example, in the encyclopedia of popular philosophy of the "Brethren of Purity," which speaks of the "divine laws" (*nawāmis*). To cite another example, Averroes uses the expression in his *Fasl el-maqāl,* but less frequently than Léon Gauthier suggests when he translates the word *shar'* by "loi divine." Gauthier's translation of the same word fluctuates, however, between "loi divine" and "loi religieuse," and elsewhere he renders *sharia* as "loi religeuse." The *sharia* is one of the things taught by the *shar'*—more precisely, one of the forms of knowledge that the latter teaches, in contrast to practices. The adjective "divine" is applied only to the *sharia*, and then only on two other occasions and in the same fixed formula: "that divine law that is ours."[52] The meaning of the word does not seem to go beyond that of a stereotyped meliorative, and Averroes, in this text at least, is not reflecting on what makes up the divinity of the law.

I shall begin by studying a certain number of themes common to the philosophers, after which I shall see how certain of these writers introduce their own variations on these themes.

The City and the Law as a Need

Man is "by nature a political animal." The idea comes from Aristotle, of course, but everyone repeated it. Alfarabi attaches the notion to an innate trait (*fitra*) specific to humans, tied to one another in the actions they want to accomplish, and who, as a consequence, need to live with others in relations of proximity and association in order to reach perfection in living. Man is by nature such that he has a penchant for association and sociability.[53] Once again, the notion of man as a social animal is Greek and, more precisely, Stoic.

The city is rendered necessary by the need for a division of labor. One man alone would never be born, or, supposing that he exists, could never survive. The idea comes from Aristotle. The existence of an absolutely isolated man is admissible only as a thought experiment. The most famous example of this (not the only one, however) is the philosophical novel of Ibn Tufayl, *Hayy ben Yaqdhān*.[54]

The theme of the division of labor comes from Plato and his ideal genesis of the city on the basis of need. According to Avicenna, there are physiological reasons for this: the human stomach cannot digest raw plants, and even less raw meat. Other authors stress more the greater ease that arises from cooperation. The theme is frequently treated, and by a great variety of authors.[55]

It is perhaps Avicenna who dug deepest into this idea, in a passage of his treatise on psychology in which he suggests a deduction of the faculties in which he seems to have discerned that the higher functions of man have a social foundation, thus sketching out a sociology of knowledge or a social psychology.[56] The text figures in the treatise on the soul in his great encyclopedia of the philosophical sciences. Part Five treats the higher functions of the soul. From the start, Avicenna, before giving a systematic description of the intellect, inserts a section in which he speaks of the various particularities of man in contrast to the animals.[57] He bases these particularities on man's need to prepare his food, hence on the division of labor that process entails. For that reason, man needs to communicate with his fellows. At the beginning, the need for a division of labor leads to a need for social life. Next come language and feelings of wonder and sadness, sensing the vulgar and the noble, and experiencing shame and fear—a sentiment that supposes an understanding of the future. In this way, Avicenna composes an ordered image of man that gives articulated form to the different features of what is proper to humankind. To be sure, these had been signaled in passing by Aristotle, but nowhere did Aristotle present them as leading from one to the other and forming a system.

Still, the most interesting aspect of this passage is where it appears. A discussion of the division of labor is usually found in treatises on political science that explain the extent to which social life is founded on natural needs. But our text is inserted just before a presentation of the higher faculties of the soul, which are the exclusive privilege of humans. Those higher faculties are rooted in the desire to communicate, which in turn is founded on the body's felt need for prepared food. What is more essential to the "I" is its social dimension. It seems, however, that Avicenna retreated before the logic of his own explanations. He writes that the need for signs and for language appeared "as a result of these causes and as a result of other causes that are more hidden and firmer than these."[58] He tells us no more about these other higher causes, however.

Did this text influence later thinkers? A passage from Maimonides may contain a distant echo of it. In his *De anima,* Albertus Magnus does not make use of the passage. St. Thomas alludes to it when he speaks of the division of labor.[59] I do not know if it left any traces in Duns Scotus.

Natural diversity is great among men. An authority is needed to draw them into a stable order. Certain authors suppose a natural malice in man that makes something that can curb him (*wāziʾ*) necessary. The philosophers do not conceive that the human species can subsist without virtues, justice first among them. That justice is brought by the laws, and the laws are brought by prophets.[60] This leads to a highly important thesis: the continued existence of the human species is made possible by prophecy; without prophecy, there would simply be no humankind. This thesis is at times quite explicit, as in Avicenna.[61]

The text that expresses these ideas the most clearly is perhaps a passage at the end of Avicenna's *Metaphysics.* The first chapter begins with an overall vision of the world: among the sublunary beings, the best is man, and the most excellent of men is the prophet. The second chapter establishes that men cannot live in isolation but need a division of labor. If human association is to be harmonious, it requires law and justice. Thus a prophet is necessary to the survival of the human species. Divine Providence gives the living species whatever will assure their permanence, which is a proof of the existence of God. Thus Providence gives the human species prophets. Divine wisdom even demands that they be sent.[62]

The idea of the political need for prophecy and laws permits the establishment of a strong connection between the political and religion. Conversely, however, it introduces the suspicion that religious law has a merely political function. The idea that religion is the instrument of something like the domestication of human savagery is extremely ancient. In the Middle Ages, it received new support from the legal character of religions.[63] Thus one can pass from necessity to a reality capable of satisfying the aspirations of man, to a fully human life within the framework of a community, a "city."

The Virtuous City: Ideal or Reality?

Man, by nature a social and political animal, must live in community. Mutual aid can concern only basic needs (as in the case of the "necessary city"). It can also pertain to illusory benefits. Thus one obtains the iniquitous cities of which Alfarabi draws up a detailed typology, each one of which corresponds to a false or incomplete good: the ignorant city, with its six subspecies: the cities of basic needs, of exchange, of degradation, of honors, of power, and of extravagance (aimed, respectively, at the satisfaction of elementary needs, money, pleasure, praise, victory, and freedom). There are also the immoral city, the versatile city, and the lost city. But mutual aid can also aim at genuine beatitude, in which case one would have the "virtuous (fādila) city."[64]

Avicenna distinguishes more clearly than Alfarabi between the public and the private. The political does not suffice to produce human excellence. It is content to establish a minimum of justice. The aim is thus no longer the "virtuous city" but the "just (ādila) city."[65] The city no longer has the objective of assuring a few elect the full play of their potential, but to create, along with social stability, the basic conditions of that fulfillment. The rest is entrusted to individual effort. The importance of the political thus retreats before that of individual ethics. Government is assured by men who have no need for the exceptional intellectual capacities that Alfarabi demands: all they need is practical wisdom. This means that the ruler will be more strictly subject to the laws than in Alfarabi, for whom the wise man remained above the laws. The purpose of the city is to permit the satisfaction of essentially material needs, not intellectual ones. The sovereign good is attained by contemplation and morality, not by contemplation and the political.

The philosophers live in real communities, where Islam is the religion of the governing class. When they describe the virtuous city, one might wonder what exactly they are aiming at. At times we have the impression of reading an *a priori* deduction of the Muslim city, but we are also struck by the pedantic way in which they avoid naming it too explicitly. Alfarabi is the master of ambiguity in this domain. On reading his great treatise on the *Virtuous City*, we note that the first principle, whose attributes he describes at length, only much later receives the name of Allah, and that the word appears for the first time as the object of the imagination.[66]

Similarly, Avicenna takes two entire chapters to describe a city that he calls, successively, "virtuous," "just," and "of good conduct."[67] His description can be read as a deduction of the dispositions of Muslim law. Avicenna enters into fairly precise detail, all the while pretending to proceed *a priori*, a quality that anticipates certain caricatures of the idealism of Fichte. He goes so far as to justify the prohibition on gambling, women's veils, the procedures for naming a new caliph, and the poll-tax imposed on "protected" religions. But this also includes, like a superimposed image, details that recall Plato's *Republic*, such as the division of citizens into three classes and the regulation of marriages. In any event, Avicenna seems to take a wicked pleasure in avoiding technical terms that would permit the reader to identify too easily what he claims to deduce and what he takes from the juridical dispositions in force in Islam in his day. One wonders whether he is imagining a utopia or describing a real society.

The Audacities of Averroes

Averroes (d. 1198) raised this question to a general level. He is vague about whether the virtuous city is the best choice among the various models for a political regime, the Muslim city being the ideal. He severely criticizes the concrete realizations of the Muslim city, pointing, for example, at the Almoravids, who started off with good principles but degenerated as time went by. It should be added, however, that Averroes was a loyal servant of their conquerors and successors of the Almohad dynasty.[68] As for practices, he has particularly severe words to offer on the lot of women. Seizing the occasion of Platonic egalitarianism, he condemns the practice of confining women to the role of reproduction or, at best, to spinning and weaving. Such a useless existence doubles the male burden and, consequently, weakens the political community.[69]

When he turns to the origins of Muslim domination, Averroes gives a somewhat unorthodox version of the victory over Persia at the start of Islamic expansion: the caliph ʿUmar, the leader of a poor and greedy people, attacked a rich country sunken into a peaceful slumber, "as it happened for the king of the Arabs with the king of Persia."[70] Elsewhere, he proposes his own version of the idea of *jihād*. According to him, this is a real war, and by no means a purely metaphorical "spiritual combat," but what it accomplishes is less the submission (*islām*) of recalcitrant peoples as bringing them wisdom.[71]

Finally, Averroes risks a discreet but very audacious phrase concerning the nucleus of the Islamic faith: whereas the fiction that attributes to the Prophet the qualities of a philosopher were essential to the doctrine of the Aristotelian Arabs (*falāsifa*), Averroes leaves open the question of whether it is necessary that the legislator be a prophet. "This is a matter for intensive investigation," he observes, "and we shall seek it in the first part of this science, if God wills it so."[72] Averroes does not propose a psychological and gnoseological explanation of prophecy, as was the case with Alfarabi and Avicenna. He apparently rejects the explanation of prophecy as an emanation of the intellect acting on the imagination.[73]

The passage concerning the "government of the Arabs of the earliest times" is ambiguous. There, Muhammad and the first four "rightly guided" caliphs are not distinguished from one another. Averroes states: "You may understand what Plato says concerning the transformation of the ideal constitution into the timocratic constitution [that is, founded on the sentiment of honor], and that of the excellent into the timocratic man, from the case of the government of the Arabs in the earliest period. For they used to imitate the ideal constitution, and then were transformed in the days of Muʿāwiya into timocratic men."[74] The underlying historical schema is classic: the Umayyads succeeded the "rightly guided" caliphs. But are we to understand that those first caliphs "imitated" the virtuous government, hence were but pale copies of it? In that case, the ideal city would never have been realized, not even at the very start of Islam. Or, to the contrary, did they "resemble" the virtuous government in the same way that the citizen resembles the regime in which he lives? In the latter case, Averroes can be supposed to have chosen the fiction according to which Muhammad and his immediate successors were philosophers. The question turns in part on a certain linguistic ambiguity for which, in the absence of the original, we have to rely on the uncertain ground of the Hebrew translation.[75]

In his *Paraphrase of the "Republic,"* Averroes uses the expression "divine law" only once. But the context is extremely interesting, because he seems to hold that the divine law must be measured by the standard of "human laws" (*tōrōt enoshiyyōt*) that he evokes immediately afterward and later on, and which seem to be the ones that philosophy deduces from its own knowledge of nature and of human needs.[76] Thus Averroes represents—at least in this work—the extreme limit of Aristotelian philosophy's ambiguous flirtation with Islamic Law.

The Philosopher in the City

If we suppose that the good city is unrealized, how are we to live? According to what laws is the philosopher to regulate his conduct? The distinction between mass and elite is a commonplace of medieval Muslim thought. The philosophers give a version of it that implies a "graded" participation of men in humanity. Here, too, Greek thought furnished points of departure: Aristotle placed men whose behavior is bestial lower than common humanity, and he also indicated, in passing, the possibility that some men might be of a superhuman, heroic, virtue.[77]

For the philosophers, real kings, who are "kings of the common people," are themselves part of the common people, and the "elite," strictly speaking, has only one member, the philosopher. After him come the dialectician and the sophist, and only then the legislators. The philosopher has no need of the virtuous city in order to exist. He remains a king, but his "realm" is not immediately political, given that he may govern over "citizens" scattered geographically and even through time.[78] His reign is not reliant on rhetoric, a discipline that is certainly necessary in all "cities." Alfarabi repeats the Platonic allegory of the cave as an image of the city (*Republic* 7), and he compares it with the ascending series of the arts of discourse treated by Aristotle in the *Organon*, to which the commentators had added the *Rhetoric* and the *Politics*. Thus leaving the cave corresponds to the solitary climb toward apodictic reasoning, the object of the *Posterior Analytics*; the return of the philosopher, liberated from his chains in the cave, corresponds to the descent back toward dialectics, rhetoric, and eventually poetics.[79]

Does the city need philosophy? The philosophers respond that the king who governs according to a preexistent law has no need for them. The philosopher is a man, and because he is a man, he needs the city. But does he need it as a philosopher? He cannot be perfect without the ability to make the virtues exist in the cities. Socrates had preferred death to life in a corrupt regime.[80] The philosopher would do well to take inspiration from Plato instead, and from his attempts to bring to pass a better regime. But the absence of a city that recognizes his royal art does not strip him of it.[81] The possession of the royal art is enough to make him king. An anecdote presents Alfarabi before Sayf ad-Dawla, who reigned over Syria at the time. He invites the philosopher to be seated, and the latter asks, "At my place?" When the prince says yes, Alfarabi pushes him from his throne and sits there himself. This tale, which is highly unlikely to be true, illustrates an idea of Plato's: the true king is he who possesses the royal art, whether he wields power or not.[82] Alfarabi seems to have held firm in this wholly speculative attitude, never joining any specific politico-religious party, which means, for instance, that some scholars' attempts to place him within the Shiite movement are unsustainable.[83]

For Alfarabi, the philosopher nonetheless feels himself responsible toward the mass of men:

> From the fact that we [the elite, or the philosophers] are political by nature, and by that token it is our duty to be tied to the mass (*jumhur*), to love it, and to prefer to do that which profits it, and [to make sure that] our acts result in an amelioration of its situation, as is its duty toward us, we share with it the good whose realization has been entrusted to us, just as it shares with us the goods whose realization has been entrusted to it: we make it see the truth in the opinions that are its in its religion, and, because it shares the truth with us, it may share with the philosophers the beatitude of philosophy, in the measure of its capacity, and that we remove from it what we see, in its arguments, opinions, and laws, to be incorrect.

The philosopher will express himself in a style that is not strictly demonstrative, but rather dialectical, so as to make himself accessible. "Thus when he communicates with the mass, he takes pains not to be so unbearably abstruse that they reject his orders."[84]

Virtuous men in the imperfect cities are as if outsiders or "strangers." Alfarabi returns to the image that Plato's Socrates uses to explain that, up to the present, philosophers spring up, against the will of the cities, like weeds (*nawābit*). They appear more often in the cities that aim at satisfying only elementary needs or in democratic cities.[85] Should the virtuous city come into existence, their duty would be to emigrate there.[86] And if the good city is not realized, the philosopher must at least live according to its laws. Here, too, the idea is Platonic: whether the good city is realized or not, the philosopher can adopt the good regime here and now.[87] In such a case, this would be a "regimen of the solitary," a title that Ibn Bājja gave to a work in which he outlined his political thought. Maimonides, who had taken lessons from a pupil of Ibn Bājja's, took up the idea, but without stating it explicitly.[88]

Who Is the Legislator?

The philosophers can interpret the law of the good city as given by a prophet, the prophet of Islam. What remains to be seen is whether the role of the supreme leader, analogous to the Philosopher King of Plato's *Republic* and postulated by all of the Falāsifa, is filled by Muhammad—who is supposed to have been a philosopher—or whether it remains an empty description of a function. Avicenna is a good example of this ambiguity: in his description of the founder of the just city, certain traits evoke Muhammad, but they might also refer to the ideal philosopher. One of Avicenna's disciples saw his teacher's description as a self-portrait.[89]

In any event, if the Prophet of Islam communicated a philosophical message, he had to transmit it to a rough-hewn people far detached from any philosophy.[90] Any prophet must be content with providing simple teachings, thus avoiding having the citizens worry about investigations that might prove too absorbing and generate doubts. Without stating that he is keeping a hidden truth to himself, he will speak in symbols that will awaken those capable of carrying on speculative investigations. Knowing himself mortal, he will prescribe attempts to keep his memory alive: those rites will recall God to the mass and awaken elite individuals to the purification of their souls. The Prophet must therefore have spoken the language of his audience. The Falāsifa draw a parallel between the various types of discourse that Aristotle enumerates (apodictic, dialectic, sophistic, rhetorical, poetic) and the intellectual levels (elite/mass).[91] The Prophet addressed the mass in an imagistic language that was rhetorical and poetic, but his message contains matter capable of capturing the attention of the elite and pushing it to demonstrative reasoning.

Still, simple people have to be taught certain rudiments of speculative things.[92] This is done by means of the imagination, as used by religion, which is the "science of legislation." By that very fact, religion is an imitation of philosophy, and subjected to philosophy. There can be several virtuous cities, hence several excellent religions and several possible images to express the highest verities. Such images must above all be efficacious, something that depends less on their fidelity to their original than on their capacity to serve as a model for imitation. Thus laws will be like medical regimens: they will depend on the temperament of the community that is to be set on its way toward the good.[93]

It is in Alfarabi's works that the expression "political philosophy" can first be seen in Arabic. It constitutes one of the species of practical philosophy, defined primarily by the perspective of human happiness or unhappiness.[94]

Beatitude is the goal of human existence, but what sort of beatitude? Can it be reduced to contemplative perfection, through a "conjunction" with the agent intellect, a process that implies a nonmaterial existence for the soul? Or does it involve a practical dimension, too? At times Alfarabi reserves beatitude to a future life.[95] But his lost commentary on the *Nichomachaean Ethics*, to the contrary, may have denied the possibility of such a conjunction, thus implying that the only real beatitude is political.[96]

The virtuous city has a "first leader" as its founder. A divine man, too noble to serve, is the true king, a king by nature. The judgment of the superior ruler, as in Plato's *Statesman*, prevails over the written laws. He can change those laws as circumstances require. Nothing opposes this, for the laws are basically just as conventional as language. A regime with codified laws is incompatible with the rule of supreme heads of state.[97] The rule of the law is only a second best.

To read the philosophers, it is thus difficult to say precisely what the legislator brings, for whom he brings it, and even just who he is.

Where Does the Law Come From?

Some texts call "divine" the law necessary to establish order in communities because it is transmitted through a prophet. Alfarabi was probably the first to propose a philosophical theory of prophetism as it existed in the monotheistic religions, perhaps continuing older doctrines elaborated in the Hellenistic world to account for the phenomenon of divination. Alfarabi makes prophecy comprehensible within the framework of a hierarchical vision of the world, which itself results from a cosmological transposition of the doctrine of the intellect sketched out by Aristotle and developed by his commentators. The nine spheres fitted within one another of the astronomy of the age correspond to as many souls, the one emanating from the other and each one including an intellect. A tenth and lowest soul corresponds to the sphere of the Moon, and its intellect is the agent-intellect that rules the sublunary world. The emanation from that intellect to the human soul produces prophecy, which in turn constitutes the highest degree of the imagination.[98]

Following Alfarabi's example, Avicenna presents a detailed psychology of prophetic inspiration, which he credits to the "holy intellect." Another of Alfarabi's disciples, Maimonides, although Jewish, borrows the notion of an association of the human intellect with the agent-intellect, from which a "noble emanation" flows on it. Ibn Khaldun develops a detailed cosmology within which to lodge prophecy.[99]

The philosophers see revelation as a natural phenomenon. Avicenna de-

duces prophecy from a constant of nature: the most perfect beings command those who are less perfect; above all, the prophet must command the
rest of humanity. Alfarabi develops at some length an analogy between the
structure of the city, the cosmos, and the human body: the "first leader" is
to the city as God is to the universe, or the heart to the animal. He must
therefore know speculative philosophy in order to be able to imitate the way
in which God governs the world. And the citizens must be in agreement on
some principles of metaphysics and cosmology.[100]

❖

Thus the "philosophers" of medieval Islam, faced with the central question
of divine law, chose a solution of their own. It was an extremely radical solution that, for that reason, is expressed only with caution. It consists in
seeking out the origin of the law within nature. The idea of divine law is retained, but it passes from historical becoming to cosmological permanence.
Prophecy, which makes possible communication between the domains of
the divine and the human, and which thus constitutes the origin of the law,
is consistently interpreted as an emanation. The prophet's knowledge is at
base cosmological as well; its object is the structure of the universe. Homo-
geneous with its origin, it is a faithful image of that of which it is itself the
purest expression, and thus it simply transmits what has constituted it.

The Falāsifa were able to effect this reinterpretation all the more easily
because they lived in Islamic lands. In fact, as we have seen, Islam furnished
them with a model of revelation that could easily be reshaped according to
their own schemas.[101] Prophecy also changed. It was no longer a warning
about what was to come, but a teaching about what is. As a consequence,
salvation became beatitude.

By that very fact, the divine itself entered into the pale of the city. The
philosophers called "divine" what allowed the city to develop according to
its essence—what possessed the characteristics that the city needed. Aristotle points out that it is not because the laws of the city regulate the cult in
the temples that laws have any influence over the divine.[102] In contrast, his
medieval disciples in Islamic lands did not hesitate to define God in terms
of the needs of civil life. This is why the philosophers' adversaries repeatedly
accused them of reducing the prophetic function to the organization of the
terrestrial city.[103] It was as if metaphysics were conceived in terms of the political and the conception of God was measured by the city's needs.[104] The
clearest instance of this general attitude can probably be read in Alfarabi: in
a brief treatise, he calmly states that he is about to speak of "the thing that
it is convenient to put forward as god in the virtuous religious community."[105] In substance, God is some sort of elected president.

All this could not help causing a scandal. We have an idea of its extent thanks to an anecdote related by Ibn Arabi, who took umbrage. The first thing that his eyes fell upon as he opened a book (the title of which, *The Virtuous City,* he gives us, but without mentioning the author) was the sentence: "In this chapter, I would like us to consider how we will institute a god (*ilah*) in the world." Ibn Arabi remarks that the author does not even use the proper noun "Allah." It is hardly surprising that the Andalusian mystic immediately returned the book to the friend who had lent it to him.[106]

Mysticism between Anomism and Legalism

The Muslim philosophers who placed themselves in the line of the Greek thinkers thus proposed an overall theory that threw light on the relationship between law and divinity. That theory was accepted at the time and in the circles in which philosophy of the Aristotelian tradition was itself authoritative. As it happens, in Islamic lands philosophy remained a pastime for amateurs, who may well have been men of genius, but who had no institutional outlet for assuring the diffusion of their thought within society. It was a graft that was rejected after a few centuries, except where philosophy was absorbed in a highly attenuated form into a vaguely defined "wisdom" in which it had to come to terms with apologetics and mysticism. The harmony of religion and philosophy was a theme that the philosophers treated again and again, but the idea caught on only partially and for only a short time.[107] In the long run, the Muslim public mind was more strongly marked by the mystical currents. This is why I need to say a few words now about Islamic mysticism as it relates to the idea of divine law.

Temptation

Mysticism above all had to overcome the temptation of thinking that it had passed beyond the need for the law. It is a recurrent temptation wherever there is morality—that is, wherever the human is defined by positing a distinction between right conduct and transgression. Even Pauline Christianity, which is certainly not a religion of the law, includes the idea, given that St. Paul calls the Antichrist "mystery of iniquity" (*anomia*) (2 Thess. 2:7, KJV). The tendency to believe oneself above moral norms is a predictable consequence of all claims to a privileged and direct access to the divine, as suggested by a certain interpretation of the mystical experience. In Christianity this was a temptation that always had to be conjured away: one example is Jan van Ruysbroeck's attacks against the Beghards in fourteenth-century Flanders; another is the philosophy of religion of Kant, in which everything that exceeds religion as morality is rejected as "enthusiasm" (*Schwärmerei*).[108]

For the religions in which good and evil are determined by a reliance on law, a weakened morality takes on the image of anomie. Two levels can be distinguished here: on the one hand, there is factual transgression, which does not deny the pertinence of the rule but declares itself exempt; on the other hand, there is the position of principle that refuses all validity to the rule. The second position, because it is systematic, could be called *anomism*. In the eyes of the defenders of the law, it is infinitely graver than simple omission. Sins of omission are excusable and can easily be blamed on the weakness of man, a toy of his passions. Anomism, in contrast, is the positive and deliberate act of a perverse will.

In Islam that anomism was called by various names, among them "licence" (*ibāha*) or "abandon of works" (*isqāt al-aʾmāl* or *tark al-harakāt*). Islam's polemic against anomism attacks an ideal type, a model attitude, present in anyone who believes he has attained the goal of the commandments and can thus reject them as the ladder up which he has climbed.[109] It is easier to conceive of the possibility of it than it is to prove its reality by specific, localized, and dated examples. Anomist attitudes are pointed to fairly early on.[110] But, as it often happens in heresiography, the heresy is more a possibility than the doctrine of an actual school; many deviations are constructions by which the heresiographs have given form to their nightmares rather than being historically attested facts.[111] As for a possible historical reality, the communist community of the Qarmatians of Bahrain (894–977) was subjected to utopian (or, more accurately, dystopian) reports rather than more trustworthy ones. Nasir-i Khusraw, who had visited the Qarmatians but was himself affiliated with the rival sect of the Fatimids, reports that the inhabitants of Lahssa, their capital, never drank wine, but they failed to say the canonical prayers and did not observe the commandment to fast.[112]

Anomism as a theory is well attested in the extremist tendencies of Shiism, for which the messianic personage (Mahdi) who is expected—more accurately, who has arrived—abolishes the *sharia*. In contrast, moderate Shiites, like the Fatimid dynasty who ruled over Egypt between 969 and 1171, promised a new law, which was to be founded on the "true meaning" of the texts, but that law failed to materialize, and they retained the established jurisprudence in their practice.[113]

Other groups were much more radical. On 8 August 1164, Hasan-e Sabbah—called the "Old Man of the Mountain," an Ismāʾīlī leader of the Nizārī (called "Assassins") in the fortress of Alamūt—celebrated a deliberate transgression of the fast of Ramadan as a way to symbolize the raising of Muslim

law. That lasted until 1210, when Hassan b. Muhammad reestablished that
Muslim law. The former event was presented as a "resurrection." The abolition of the law indicated that it had been short-circuited in favor of a clearer
manifestation of the divine, henceforth physically present in the person of
the imām (although the Ismāʿīlīs rejected the idea of incarnation).[114] Thus
the law was not really abolished but rather generalized: prayer at specific
moments had to give way to incessant prayer; determined direction (*qibla*)
ceded to an omnipresence of the divine. The law moved on to a messianic
way of being. Even if the law had been done away with, obligation did not
cease, because non-transgression itself was now punished: everything was
transposed to the imperative.[115]

Something resembling the Christian operation of the fulfillment of the
law was on the march. For the Ismāʿīlīs, the law of the past was historicized
in a style that recalls St. Paul: formerly it had been necessary to humankind;
but if it was insufficient from the start, it had become perverse. Ismāʿīlīsm
was aware of Jesus' alleged abolition of the law, but it relegated the definitive manifestation of the Truth to a future that never arrived.[116]

When heterodoxy took the form of a rejection of the law, orthodoxy
needed to be defended by both arms and arguments, but above all by setting
up a plausible model of a relation to the law also capable of satisfying the
spiritual needs of believers.

The Response

The supporters of orthodox Islam fought against moral license, which they
claimed led to a rejection of religious law. Throughout the history of Islam,
many major thinkers wrote to oppose the specter of license,[117] including such
representatives of a moderate Sufism as Qushayrī or Ghazali. The first of
these published a treatise in 1046 in which he presented the Sufi masters as
paragons of obedience to the commandments of the law. Both men cited declarations in which various Sufi authorities defended the permanent value of
religious practices. To no one's surprise, the authors they invoked included
Junayd, the teacher of al-Hallāj, who had been reproached, among other
things, for excessive liberty relating to the rulings of the law.[118] Qushayrī even
solemnly condemns laxity: "If someone thinks that man can without harm
lay down the harness of servitude toward God and turn away his gaze from
what determines commandment and prohibition, while, within the house of
obligation, he is capable of discernment, that man, by that fact, detaches himself from religion."[119] True liberty is to free oneself from all that is not God.
Qushayrī thus repeats a traditional formula: to be free is to submit to God.[120]

Law and mysticism learned to get along together beginning in the eleventh century. Still, it is important to grasp the logic behind the facts that made them both possible. In a word, legalism calls for mysticism as its compensation. In fact, the law does little to make access to the divine possible. Mysticism permits having an experience of just that. Far from standing opposed to the law, or even to being an antidote to some form of legalism, mysticism attaches to the law and is a part of it to the extent that it constitutes its experiential dimension. Mysticism in Islam is all the more necessary because the law cannot be interpreted by a search for equity in the Greek sense of *epieikeia*. Sufism represents something like a search in that direction. Sufism responds to the question of how to return to the intention of the Legislator by permitting a direct grasp of the divine source. The only exegetical method is allegory (*ta'wīl*). Acceptance of the law is compensated for by Sufi internalization.[121]

There is more, however: that internalization facilitates acceptance of the law. The commandments must not be broken, and obedience to them is a weighty task if one fails to grasp their hidden meaning. That is what moderate Shiites such as Sijistanī (d. after 971) propose: Intelligence must comprehend its identity with the divine Imperative. "That identification is such," Sijistanī writes, "that you understand its truth when you observe with care the laws of the prophets and you put a part of it into practice by an agreement that does not reason. The soul feels repulsion for that: it feels that it is an absurd game and a vexation. But when [the soul] comes to know [the laws'] spiritual exegesis and esoteric meaning, its repulsion comes to an end."[122]

In practice, a mysticism apparently indifferent to the external forms of the cult can coincide quite easily with a totally punctilious application of the rules of the *sharia* according to their strictest interpretation. Thus, at the beginning of the thirteenth century, Ibn Arabi writes in lines that everybody repeated that it matters little if one goes in pilgrimage to Mecca or to Jerusalem: all that counts is love. But when he gives his opinions as a jurist, he demands the severest application of the dispositions aimed at humiliating tribute-paying Jews and Christians (*dhimmis*). Islam has no lack of representatives whose tastes seem to us contradictory: one of the most inflexible accusers of the mystic al-Hallāj, executed in 922, was Ibn Daoud, the famous author of a treatise on courtly love.[123]

Law and lived piety are thus not necessarily opposed. They can even be united in one person.

Ghazali

The finest example of that union is probably Ghazali (d. 1111), by profession a teacher of law, who worked deliberately to combine legalism and mysticism, thus providing Islam with a stable model of a solution to the problem posed by the existence of divine law. His works probably represent the summit of Muslim thought about and practice of the law. Ghazali, a Persian who spoke and wrote in Arabic, was at once a jurist of the Shāfiʿite school, a mystic, and a champion of Sunni orthodoxy against all those whom he considered adversaries of that orthodoxy, the philosophers among them. Everything indicates that he considered himself one of the "renewers" that one tradition promised Islam for each century. In any event, he remains a guide (hence his title of "Imām") not only for the generations that came after him, but up to the present day.[124]

The Political Context

Ghazali's work is part of a specific historical context, a fact of which he himself seems to have been acutely aware. This context was primarily political. Ghazali proposes something like a bargain to the governing powers, which, once the caliphate was reduced to a purely symbolic role, had no real legitimacy. Their de facto power had to be recognized, however: it was better to obey them than risk a civil war.[125] Moreover, the sacred legislation (shar') was little known, in particular among country people—Bedouins, Kurds, and Turcomans. Hence the appeal for a mission toward such groups and for a reinforcement of religious education.[126] This implies an entire program to survey and control the various populations that could not be carried out without a political dimension. The scholar is responsible for the ignorance of those around him, whom it is his duty to enlighten; the governing class has the duty to name a "scholar" or "wise man" in each locality. As a result, scholars figure at the head of the list of those to be subsidized by the public treasury.[127]

An even more serious reproach is not stopping at ignorance of the law, but being unwilling to know it, placing oneself above the law by "libertine living" (ibāha). Ghazali imagines that there exists a school (madhab) of libertines (which seems quite spectral). In any event, he levels this accusation against all whom he intends to discredit—the Philosophers, the Sufis, and the Shiites, who claimed that the texts have an inner meaning that can only be deciphered by the hidden (batibiyya) imām.[128] Ghazali devotes an entire short treatise to criticism of these supposed libertines, but in spite of his accusation of sexual promiscuity, which is always recurrent in such cases, the "libertines" are not so much debauched as they are extremist Sufis inebriated by asceticism.[129] Their principal fault consists in imagining that they have attained such a high degree of perfection that they are dispensed from the practice of concrete commandments. For them, "he who still holds himself under the sway of the law has not yet attained the level of freedom." They also state: "We have arrived at the goal. The cult of God and the renunciation of sin were necessary only to attain it; now that we have arrived, sin and neglect of prayer do us no harm."[130] Not only does Ghazali promise the "libertines" hell later on, he demands immediate and tangible punishments for them: death and—to begin with—obligatory divorce.[131] His polemical text attacking the allegorists ("batinites") and in support of the caliph al-Mustazhir concentrates on countering the purely speculative idea that an infallible imām would make individual judgments unnecessary, but he also includes the reproach of specific libertine behaviors concerning religious prohibitions.[132]

The Conception of the Law

Ghazali's conception of the law follows that of his master Juwaynī. The law has and can only have one origin: strictly speaking, there can be no human legislator. The unique legislator is God: he alone is *hākim*, capable of determining the value (*hukm*) of an action.[133] Other persons who hold authority can only give orders that derive from those given by God. The highest form of the political act is thus that of the prophets, who transmit the rules of human action on the basis of their divine source: "They make known the rules of the Law that permit maintaining justice among men, the rules of politics that make it possible to tame them, and the criteria that permit an evaluation of the imāmate and the sultanate on the basis of religious law, thus guiding them toward temporal success, without forgetting that they direct them toward religious success."[134]

Nothing escapes legislation, Ghazali observes. What is neither commanded nor prohibited but is permitted is not for all that left out of the law, but is defined on the basis of the law, which decides by a positive act to leave it to its original indifference. The law is the sole and unique foundation of obligation. It is only by the law (*shar'*) that one can know whether a thing is good or bad. It alone allows us to distinguish between justice and violence.[135]

Before the "descent" (or the revelation of divine will), men were in a state of legal non-subjection. Reason is unable to act as a foundation for obligation. The most it can do is to show after the fact the advantages of one or another commandment. Reason is "brought back to *istishāb*, that is, to the principle of presumption of continuity in the absence of a cause motivating the rupture of that continuity." Reason "limits itself to assuring formal coherence to the law."[136] In themselves, God's designs are not knowable. Any imposition of a legal value probably comports a deeper meaning, which is the good (*maslaha*) resulting from that valuation, but that good is not necessarily known.[137] Moreover, there exist practices—pilgrimage, for example—whose only purpose is the "pure subjection" of man, on whom they force awareness of his condition as a slave and a servant.[138]

Knowledge of the reasons behind the commandments is not within the capabilities of human nature. It is possible that the laws have still other meanings that remain hidden to us, but for which God imposed them on us. Ghazali illustrates this idea by a parable, giving as an example a practice whose properties are unknowable—a magic square supposed to facilitate childbirth.[139]

Interiorization

Ghazali belongs within a long-term trend toward the interiorization of religion. This same trend can be seen in contemporary Judaism with Bahya Ibn Paquda (who, moreover, shared Sufi sources with Ghazali), and again, a half-century later, in Christianity with Abelard, who situates the moral value of an action uniquely in the intention with which is performed.[140] One commentator reconstitutes Ghazali's central argument in these terms: "What God loves above all, is his Law (*sharia*). God's love, far from dispensing men from obeying the prescriptions of His Law, puts them in a position to observe these even more scrupulously and more profoundly."[141]

One can interpret in this light the project that Ghazali outlined, at the turn of the eleventh to the twelfth century, in a monumental work, *The Revival of the Religious Sciences.* As the title indicates, Ghazali had already perceived a risk of sclerosis in Islamic law. He had noted a tendency to neglect the religious sciences to the profit of an exclusive interest in systematic law. The law, he points out, remains basically a branch of knowledge that concerns this world here below; even if it indicates the path to the beyond, it remains a means, not an end. Moreover, many doctors of law succumb to the temptation of power and allow themselves to be corrupted by the sovereigns, whom they in turn corrupt.[142]

In this work Ghazali attempts a synthesis of legalism and mysticism, a task for which a more moderate Sufism was indispensable. In particular, Sufism could no longer be suspected of relativizing the practice of the commandments of the *sharia* to the profit of an allegorism that extenuated its content. This is why Ghazali attacks the allegorists as well. He injects into a scrupulous practice the highest possible dose of Sufi spirituality. This operation has a literary component: as has long been remarked, entire passages of his great work are copied from spiritual authors of the epoch.

The adepts of a "deeper meaning" (*bātin*) emphasize the need for interiority. For Ghazali as well, what makes the value of a practice is to be sought in its profundity, but from then on, that profundity is one of intention (*niyya*). That word originally designated a fully rendered oral declaration that accompanied a religious gesture made with the explicit aim of worshiping God. It came to designate an inward orientation.

The Orientation of the Heart

That inward orientation is that of the "heart" of the believer. Ghazali, who devotes an entire book to developing this basic theme, defines the "heart" as "the secret that derives from the world of the commandment" (*sirr min ʾālam al-amr*)—that is, as the presence within man, plunged deep within the world of the flesh, of what opens him up to the world of the Creator.[143] According to a hadith that he cites often, "sin is a trouble of the heart."[144] The juridical sciences only regulate external actions, and the heart is outside the competence of the doctors of law. They do not even pay any attention to what is within, whereas the most important knowledge of all is that of the qualities of the heart.[145]

The man who aspires to a delicate probity (*waraʾ*) must keep his heart safe from the two opposed dangers of indifference and scrupulosity.[146] The heart must be consulted; one has to know in what direction it is leaning.[147] "In similar cases, the one who decides [literally, the mufti!] is the heart; the heart is attuned to slight indications for which the reasoning of reason (*nutq*) is too narrow."[148] This does not mean that the heart is infallible, and the importance accorded to it does not threaten the primacy of the law where the law is unequivocal, nor even the primacy of the holder of the law: "One must take into consideration only the heart of the scholar [that is, the jurist] who succeeds in detecting the slightest details of cases." Moreover, the heart's role in juridical matters is purely negative: when a doctor of law prohibits a practice, the pious man will abstain from it; it is only when the jurist declares the practice licit that the pious man consults his heart to know whether a more exigent piety would not prohibit it.[149]

Guiding the heart toward God enables one to give cult practices a depth that totally removes them from the routine of a simple ritualism. This means that one must distinguish between the duties of the parts of the body and the duties of hearts. The commandments of the law must be understood on the basis of their profound (*sirr*) meaning and their authentic goal (*maʾnā*).[150] From this point of view, the believer will not be content with conforming to the commandments; he will seek a more demanding spiritual life, one not satisfied with duties but that instead aims at merits.[151]

The aim of religion is beatitude through an encounter with God. The reason behind cult practices is thus not—as it is in all forms of magic—to exert an influence on their object (in this case, a divine object). It is rather a matter of acting upon their subject. External practices—those of the body—seek to change the "heart" by modifying its characteristics.[152]

❖

With Ghazali we are in the presence of one of the possible solutions to the problem that occupies me here, that of the articulation of the legal on the divine. Ghazali's works can be seen as an attempt to give a divine dimension back to the law. The point no longer is to found the law on its prophetic origin, which is of course by no means denied but which is considered as a basic given that is so evident that there is no need for in-depth examination of its meaning. Rather than offering a meditation on the divine nature of the law, Ghazali remains on the level of practice, of "experience," so as to breathe something of the divine into the law. He does so on the basis of an orientation to God that must dominate the heart of those who fulfill his commandments. The compromise that Ghazali represents permitted—or in any event, demonstrated the possibility of—the flowering of a rich and (as far as we can ascertain) very authentic spirituality. He did so on the very terrain of the relationship with a God who is defined, above all, as Legislator.

12]⅏··

The Law as an End: Judaism

The People of Israel had experienced centuries of turbulence. Their country had fallen into foreign hands—Babylonian, Persian, Greek, and finally Roman. They had lost the lineage of the Davidic dynasty (or what remained of it). They swarmed throughout the Mediterranean Basin, cutting ties with the homeland and often forgetting their language of origin. And above all, the second Temple had been destroyed, and with the end of sacrifices the last link between Israel—and the God of Israel—with a specific place was broken. The Law became the Jews' only means for apprehending something of the divine and the only nucleus around which the people could construct their identity.

Refocusing on the Torah

After the failure of a large-scale Jewish revolt against Rome, and beginning with the formation of the Academy at Yavneh (ca. 70 CE), the rabbis worked to recenter the whole experience of Israel on the Torah. The Torah had to be transmitted, and in order to protect it from possible distortions, it required the construction of a "fence" of rules for the determination of its precise application.[1]

From the Start

At that point, Judaism developed a piety of the law, which, incidentally, had solid biblical roots, especially in the long Psalm 119. According to a custom that became established in the second century,[2] Judaism celebrated the gift of the Torah with the Feast of Weeks (*chavū'ōt*), on 6 Sivan, fifty days after Passover. The joy of the Torah (*simchat Torah*) was celebrated on the 23rd day of the month of Tishri, which began the Hebrew year, after the Feast of Booths (*sukkōt,* or Succoth), which was celebrated from the 15th to the 21st. That feast, originally probably related to the harvest, was reinterpreted as a commemoration of the sojourn in the desert after the Israelites' escape from Egypt.

It is on the basis of the law that Judaism reinterpreted the series of events that made up the history of Israel and of the biblical texts that captured the memory of those events. The Covenant with God was brought down to the Law: "There is no covenant outside of the Torah."[3] That process of reinterpretation goes back to the very beginning of human history: the Torah was supposed to preexist the world, which was created for it. In order to demonstrate this, the exegetes compared three verses of the Bible and identified the "principle" by which the heavens and the earth were created with wisdom, the first of the works of God, and that wisdom with the Torah, which was claimed to be the wisdom of Israel in the eyes of the nations. In doing so, they arrived at the idea that the world was created in view of the Torah.[4] The rabbis reinterpreted the nature of prophecy, seeing it as simply a reiteration of the law of Moses, which they took as given, as invariable. But this postulate demanded exegetic virtuosity, for example, regarding the final chapters of Ezekiel (40–48), which appear to propose a new law competing with the one given to Moses.

The law of Moses derives its unique validity from its divine origin, which is for the majority of rabbinic Judaism overwhelmingly self-evident. Still, it leaves open the question of what the people heard directly from the mouth of God and what they heard from Moses.[5] The Torah was redacted by Moses, but he is in no way its author, Philo to the contrary. Very few passages suggest any intervention on the part of Moses in the composition of the book. To the contrary, certain narratives show Moses constrained by God to write down things that Moses himself disapproved of. That idea is sanctioned by a rule that states that anyone who attributed as much as one word of the Torah to anyone but God will have no share in the afterlife. The ideal type of the miscreant who doubts the divine origin of the Torah is the impious king Manasseh, reported to have mocked some apparently trifling details in it.[6]

As for the rules regarding practice, Talmudic Judaism had to draw a complete system, the *halakhah,* out of the Torah.[7] It managed to do so at the price of exegetical acrobatics that can at times seem forced. Here and there an awareness of the fragility of the resulting deductions cannot help but show through. If the solidity of the scriptural foundation of the groups of rules that the rabbis picked out vary, that does not mean that the rules themselves would be either more or less obligatory. Certain dispositions—for instance, those regarding vows—came be said to "float" on air, and others—

such as those regarding the Sabbath or the feast days—are "mountains suspended by a thread." The rest of the legislation, which makes up the body of the Torah, has a solid base. The Torah forms an unassailable block. No one thing is more important in it than another. For example, the Decalogue is deemphasized by worship in the synagogue, in reaction to the way that Christianity and certain currents of Judaism took it as absolute.[8]

The rabbis redistributed the role of the human and divine elements in the legislative contents of the Torah, thus introducing a certain secularism. The Mishnah remarks that the "judgment of God" (or trial by ordeal) has fallen into disuse. Oracles and prophecy are replaced by oaths. The "god" before whom litigation is to be brought is interpreted as referring to human judges. Conversely, some institutions of human justice were transferred to the domain of the divine in order to avoid the application of a disposition perceived as overly severe. In this way, it is God who is supposed to punish certain homicides committed through negligence, rather than human tribunals.[9]

The Future in the Beginning

The rabbis simultaneously put forward two extreme theses regarding the status of the Torah as a system of law. On the one hand, they insist on the impossibility of a new revelation: the Torah is given definitively and is irrevocable. It is no longer to be sought in heaven, with God, but here below, in the discussion of the sages. Even the most spectacular miracles, even the voice of God, cannot prevail against what the majority of the sages deem to be the law.[10]

On the other hand, the rabbis remove from the gift of the law at Sinai its nature as a historical event, which would set it back in the past. They maintain the fiction of a legislation given in its entirety and in its least detail: not only the written Law (of course), but also, and to just as great an extent, orally transmitted teachings are of direct Mosaic origin. Talmudic Judaism is aware that this theory is legendary, as an amusing anecdote about Rabbi Akiba shows: The rabbi is giving his course on the law. Moses in person, miraculously brought back to life, is seated at the back of the amphitheater. The discussion becomes so subtle that he understands not a blessed word of it. Akiba's disciples, who are themselves astonished, ask their master where on earth he could have found all that. He answers calmly: It was given to Moses on Sinai. At this Moses, still lost, feels reassured.[11]

According to the same fiction, the scribes' discussions were also revealed on Sinai, along with their most minute exegeses, and even including innovations still to come. In other words, God himself is still talking through the mouth of the sages. To be sure, the prophetic spirit no longer hovers over

Israel after its loss of a homeland; nonetheless, the gift of prophecy was never taken away from the sages. All prophets received prophecy from Sinai, and the sages who have arisen in each generation received their teaching there as well.[12] Thus they must be obeyed, even if they should say that right is left and left is right.[13]

That fiction also authorizes the integration of later developments of Jewish Law into the revealed whole. There is an obvious danger that human decisions will be attributed to the will of God and the work of men be taken to be divine. In our own day Yeshayahu Leibowitz, who approves of this procedure, describes it with stupefying precision (and in a positive sense) by returning to the biblical definition of idolatry: claiming divinity for the work of one's own hands.[14]

Thus the question of the divinity of the law receives an implicit response: the law derives its divine character from its origin in God, which at times is understood in spatial terms. According to the rabbis, the law has literally descended from the heavens; it was awaiting Moses there, and he rose up to the heavens to enable the law to descend.[15]

The Jewish Kalām

With the Arab conquest, the Jewish communities in southern areas of the Mediterranean and the Middle East, where the intellectual centers of Judaism were concentrated, passed under Muslim domination. As a consequence, Judaism itself came under the intellectual influence of Christian and Muslim thinkers.

Judaism thus received a particular way of formulating its intellectual program and of responding to the questions that figured in that program. The result was the constitution of a Jewish apologetics influenced by the methods of Islamic apologetics, the Kalām, first developed by Christians and Muslims.

The Task at Hand

More than ever, Jewish identity was based in the rule of life proposed by the law of Moses. Although political questions remained academic when deprived of any concrete application, the legitimation of Jewish Law became a burning necessity.

Faced with the other religion of the Law, Judaism had to distinguish more carefully between the prophecy of Moses and that of the other prophets. Islam conceived of Muhammad as the last of the prophets. His chronological position is an objective fact that suffices to make his mission unique, and it invites a consideration of that mission as a synthesis that crowns all previous prophetic activity. Moreover, the content of the Islamic revelation is not radically different from the other prophetic messages; it represents the stable form of those others, a mature form that was assured of not undergoing the same distortions that previous messages had suffered, thanks to the fact that the political power exercised by the Muslims guarantees them that their Book does not risk falsification. For Islam, proving that Muhammad is distinct from the other prophets is thus not a primordial task. Judaism, in contrast, must justify its survival after the appearance of Christianity and Islam. Its prophet was in the past; it had to show that he was not obsolete.

The strictly theological differences between Judaism and Islam are not of prime importance: in both religions, God is conceived of as an absolute unity, and there is no incarnation to bridge the abyss that separates him from the created.[16] Thus nothing stops Judaism from borrowing many aids to self-definition from Islam.

This can be seen regarding one point of capital importance: God's revelation in the Bible is conceived of on the same model as in the Qur'an, that is, as a supernatural dictate entirely from the mouth of God. It is the Egyptian Saadia Gaon (d. 942) who expressed this idea most clearly. He presents two theses: first, the Bible is wholly dictated by God, even in passages that contain dialogue between individuals, such as the book of Job; second, everything in the Bible can be brought back to commandments, positive and negative, even texts—such as the Psalms—that seem to be prayers.[17] Bahya Ibn Paquda goes so far as to call the Torah "the Book of God," which Muslims call the Qur'an, while speaking of the rest of the Bible as "the books of the prophets." The Jews use the word *sharia* to speak of the Torah, but also to refer to rabbinical decisions.[18]

The divinity of the law thus refers less to its origin than to its perfection. The law cannot be rendered relative, as the Christians assert, nor can it be replaced by another, better, law, as the Muslims believe.

Saadia Gaon

If Saadia Gaon is not the first Jew to have followed the method of the Kalām, he is the one whose work has had the most influence.[19] Al-Muqammas, a Jew who converted to Christianity and then returned to Judaism, preceded Saadia Gaon, but his works have come down to us in a highly incomplete form. Moreover, certain of the fragments that we do possess discuss the qualities that make up the authentic prophet and the conditions that guarantee the veracity of the traditions reported regarding him, but they give few details about the content of the law.[20] At most, we learn why certain practices are prohibited and others are obligatory: the only actions that are commanded are good ones (*mahāsin*), which are identified with the virtues (*fadāʾil*), or the equilibrium between the faculties of the soul.[21] There are thus actions that are good in themselves: the intellect—as defined by the Greeks and by the Jews—cannot but approve of them, and the law is based on them. This is why al-Muqammas adopts a Mutazilite position on the question of the relation between divine will and the moral value of actions.[22]

Saadia Gaon returns to the doctrine of the Talmud that excludes from the "world to come" those who deny that the Torah comes from heaven. He explains this dogma, however, by speaking of revelation—literally, of the "descent of the Law"—and by adding faith in the "veracity of the transmitters." He borrows the Islamic idea that a tradition is worthy of belief when it rests on an uninterrupted chain of morally irreproachable transmitters.

Worship of God consists in obedience to the commandments. Just conduct will be determined by wisdom and religious law (*sharia*).[23]

Saadia Gaon studies the content of the Torah in a portion of his work that treats commandment and prohibition. He divides laws into "intellectual laws" and "traditional laws" (literally, "heard laws"). Saadia is the first Jew to make this distinction, which he does by drawing on the Kalām thinkers, whose method he follows.[24]

The Law was first given by prophets. The miracles they performed led the children of Israel who witnessed them to immediate and sincere belief in their mission. Only with opportunity for reflection do we see that these first prophets were imposing laws on us. In fact, the intellect demands, on the one hand, that man be grateful to his Creator and honor him. It also demands, on the other hand, that God's creatures not harm one another and reward one another at a just price for services rendered. All the laws of the Torah had be grouped under these four headings. Regarding these rules as a whole, "it is implanted in our intellects that we approve them."[25]

The second category of laws, the traditional ones, cover practices for which the intellect has no inclination but feels no repugnance, and that God commands us to follow to augment our merit, hence our reward. To the extent to which we obey them with the aim of glorifying God, they depend indirectly from the rational laws that form the first category; what is more, if we think about it, in their details the traditional laws also contain certain advantages, so that up to a point we can find reasons for them.[26]

The commandments of the first category are rational in that they derive from the wisdom of God. Consequently they do not depend uniquely on his will. This is what makes Saadia Gaon, like al-Muqammas, opt for the Mutazilite solution to the question. Saadia Gaon uses various arguments to show the rationality of these commandments. The most striking of these is probably his argument for the prohibition against stealing, which recalls Kant's: stealing is contradictory, because to authorize it would be to abolish property, which would render theft impossible. The commandments of the second group are indifferent to the intellect. Although their main force lies in the fact that they are commanded by God and they bring us supplementary merit, most of them contain at least partially valid reasons.[27]

Saadia Gaon's ultimate aim is not to propose a theory of law but rather to justify prophecy, above all, of course, Moses' status as a prophet. In order to do so, he must first show that humanity needs prophets in general. They are needed to proclaim not only the traditional commandments but the rational commandments as well. Furthermore, since the latter contain only very general indications, the prophets also have the task of discerning the details that permit their application. Thus reason commands us to pray, and the prophet tells us how many times a day; reason prohibits stealing, and the prophet determines commercial law; reason requires that punishment exist, and the prophet sets sentences.[28] This means that Saadia Gaon must discuss the signs that establish the authenticity of a prophet's message. It should hardly surprise us that such signs paint a portrait of Moses or, conversely, that the types of prophet that they reject irresistibly evoke Jesus and Muhammad.

In all of this argumentation, the question of the divine nature of the law is never directly posed. The authenticity of the prophet who transmits the law suffices to establish its permanence and, at the same time, to establish the identity of the Jewish people, who share in the eternity of the law. Since the nation subsists uniquely by its laws, and given that God promised the nation that it would last as long as the heavens and the earth, its laws are promised the same eternity.[29] Saadia sought above all to defend the validity and the perpetual existence of Jewish Law. It was only after him that people began to ask what, within its content, makes it divine.

The Andalusians

In southern Spain, which lay under Islamic domination at the time, Jewish thought flourished from the eleventh century to the expulsion of the Jewish elites by the Almohads in 1148. There are four important authors whose portraits need to be sketched.

In his famous *Duties of the Heart* (ca. 1085), Bahya Ibn Paquda introduces into Jewish spirituality the distinction between "our physical duties" (or, to follow through on the metaphor, "duties of the bodily members") and our "duties of the heart." The first designate the ritual gestures to be fulfilled; the second, the attitude that should animate those gestures from within. Bahya stresses the intellectual origin of rules. Among the three gates that God opens to knowledge of his religion and his law—along with the Holy Book and traditions—he counts "a healthy mind." A good half of one's external duties are "those *mitzvot* that common sense would suggest even if they were not ordained by the Torah." As for the duties of the heart, they are "all rooted in common sense." There is a surrender to God that comes from an "instinct implanted in the intellect and set deep within the natural of man"; indeed, a surrender "that comes from an instinct of the intellect and from a method of argumentation that is closer to God and receives his contentment and his favor more" than the submission that comes from the Law.[30]

Jehuda Halevi (d. 1141) defines the "divine laws" by distinguishing them from rational laws. Here I am using the same word, "law," to translate two different terms in Arabic: "rational law" is *nāmūs,* which is simply the Greek *nomos;* "divine law" is *sharia.* "The rational laws," Halevi writes, "are the preparation and the principle of the divine law; they precede it by nature and in time, and are indispensable in the government of any human community." A bit further on, the word *sharia* is used for both types of law: "Divine law does not become perfect except after the end of the rational law pertaining to government." Finally, the same word—*nāmūs*—seems to be used for both types of law: "Governmental actions and rational laws are the ones that we know. As for the divine [laws] that are added to those, so that they will arrive in the community of the living God who governs it, they are not known until they come from Him explained and spelled out in detail."[31] Halevi takes as examples of rational commandments that of loving God and respecting justice, and he takes as examples of "divine laws" circumcision, keeping the Sabbath, and respecting feasts. Adapting traditional categories, he distinguishes divine laws from the two other sorts, the social laws that command justice, and the laws of the soul that concern the relationship with God.[32] Divine law draws its "divinity" from what it contains that is unknowable, inaccessible to the human intellect, which is powerless to recognize it by its own forces, and even less to penetrate its reasons. The characterization of the law as divine is more than just a laudatory but somewhat vague epithet. It sometimes implies the precise indication of its origin: the destiny of the Jewish people is the proof that "God has a Law on Earth." According to Halevi, "The Law that draws its origin from God" emerges just as suddenly as creation does. "The lowest of the adepts of the divine Law is of a more noble rank than the noblest of the pagans, for the Law that comes from God accords to the soul the comportment and the dispositions of the angels, which cannot be attained by study. . . . The Law of God permits it to have an angelic comportment and raises it up to the level of the angels." The divinity of the law resides in its origin, to be sure, but it is also attested by its result. The law is also divine because it brings man closer to the divine. The law that permits access to the level at which the soul becomes divine "is the Law of which one can be certain that it assures the survival of souls after the annihilation of bodies."[33]

A generation after Halevi, Abraham Ibn Ezra (d. 1167)—a grammarian, an exegete, and a great traveler—developed a theory of commandments in his biblical commentaries and in particular in his *Foundation of the Fear of God* (*Yesod Mora*), written toward the end of his life, when he was in London. In it he classifies the commandments according to several criteria: some are principles, while others include restrictions; some are specified according to group, place, or time; those that are not so specified are thrust deep into the heart of all men even before the gift of the law to Moses; some serve to recall other, more important commandments; some are given in the Pentateuch, while others are traditional; some are positive, while others are negative; some are given with their justification and others without, which does not make them any less obligatory.[34] The Torah is divine in that it permits man, who was created for that purpose, to know God. To serve God is to know his actions, and the Torah consists in knowing the Creator.[35] God gives two witnesses to himself: creation and the Torah. Thus the Torah can deploy its full meaning only for the intelligent.[36] The deeper meaning (*sōd*) of the commandments is inscrutable, but the purpose of all commandments is correction of the heart.[37]

Some years after Ibn Ezra, Abraham Ibn Daoud (d. ca. 1180) began to introduce Aristotle's ideas into Judaism. For Ibn Daoud, the law is to be understood within the framework of a practical philosophy, in the Aristotelian sense of the term. The aim of that philosophy is happiness, which is obtained through ethics, economics, and politics; regulations concerning those three disciplines can be found in the Torah in their most perfect form.[38] What gives divine law an advantage over the laws made by man is the presence in it of religious commandments that form ceremonial law. Such commandments must be obeyed in order to prove one's obedience to God.[39]

In their thinking about the law, the Andalusians thus achieved a double interiorization: first, regarding the subject, or "heart," who fulfills the law and whose right attitude they stress; and, second, regarding the content of the law, the intrinsic, rational value of which they stress. Their reflection on what makes the divinity of a law nonetheless remains sketchy. In a movement contrary to their tendency to stress inwardness, they seek it in what makes the commandments radically external to the subject who fulfills them—that is, in the historical nature of their proclamation and in their solicitation of pure obedience on the part of those who receive them.

Maimonides

Maimonides, who was also Andalusian, was born in Cordova in 1138, but he lived much of his life in Egypt, where he died in 1204. He deserves special consideration, first because of his considerable influence on later Judaism, but also because he is the person who treated the question of the divinity of the law in the most focused and most systematic fashion. The law was for him a professional activity. In fact, whereas Alfarabi, his principal inspiration, was not a *qadi* (Muslim judge), Maimonides' professional career was as a rabbinical judge and as a judge who devoted the better part of his time to the study and application of the Jewish Law.[40] The texts that have made him famous are, above all, his commentary on the Mishnah and the *Mishneh Torah*, in which he codifies all the rules contained in the Talmud. It was only the reputation that he earned from his juridical writings and as an authority above suspicion in questions of *halakhah* that created an atmosphere in which the *Guide for the Perplexed* was favorably received—a work that the generation following Maimonides felt came dangerously close to philosophy.

Thanks to his status and role in society, Maimonides had an obligation to defend the law that he practiced. But he was also a philosopher. Thus he had to make philosophy serve in the defense of the Jewish Law, all the while showing that the Jewish Law can include philosophy, agrees with philosophy, and even recommends the study of philosophy.

Political Philosophy

This man, generally acknowledged as the greatest philosopher of medieval Judaism, is also its greatest political thinker. He personally fulfilled responsibilities within the community, and even if he did not produce a treatise on the subject, he quite surely had a political philosophy. That philosophy—like that of his predecessors—is strongly influenced by Islam, this time not by the Kalām but rather by a Hellenizing, Aristotelian philosophy focused on logic and physics, with strong Platonic echoes in its ethics and politics, represented at the time by the philosophy of Alfarabi.

Maimonides defines "political science" as early as his first work:

> The government of a city is a science imparting to its masters a knowledge of true happiness, showing them the way to obtain it, and a knowledge of true evil, showing them the way to avoid it. It shows them how to use their habits in abandoning illusory happiness so that they will not desire it nor delight in it; and it explains to them what is illusory evil so that it will cause

them no pain or grief. It also lays down laws of righteousness for the best ordering of the groups.[41]

The primary aim of political science, according to Maimonides, was thus not power, but rather—as in Alfarabi—true happiness. To obtain it is for man to reach the ultimate goal that nature sets for him. The political is thus founded on an anthropology. It is by nature that man is a political animal. He requires a political community, first to satisfy his needs, but also in order to conceal the extreme natural diversity of humans under the mask of convention.[42]

One important aspect of religion thus pertains to life in society. This is true not only for Judaism: idolatry also betrays a political motivation. It is in this connection that Maimonides returns to older critiques of religion in the context of an attack on astrology:

> It is necessity that has made all of these things. In fact, in past times, the cities came together because of them, and [their inhabitants] made the masses of the common people believe in them. They were told that the salvation of their country and of their situation [depended] on those forms [the idols], on their assembling in their temples and doing honor to the ancient ones who knew their secrets. Power thrived, and people believed that there was something true in it.[43]

Idolatry also had political consequences. Maimonides reformulates the traditional explanation of the Babylonian Exile (which placed the blame on the sins of Israel, idolatry in particular) in a more naturalistic vein: absorbed by astrological studies, Israel neglected the art of war and domination.[44]

If the basic political problem is that of the diversity among humankind, that diversity reaches a peak in the tension between the mass of men and the elite, which creates the fundamental division in society. Maimonides uses extreme terms to describe the abyss separating the two groups: "The vulgar were created to serve superior people. . . . The purpose of this world and all that is contained therein is [to help make] a wise and good-natured man."[45] This is why the practical part of philosophy, the elite science, consists in first knowing how to adapt one's discourse to one's public. This is also God's policy, that is, the way he operates when he adapts his commandments to what the people are capable of accepting, just as he has the people of Israel travel from Egypt to Canaan by a long route so as to inure them to hardship.[46] It is also the policy of Maimonides himself in his responsibilities within the community: he recognizes Saadia Gaon's purpose in saying that the Messiah would come soon was to encourage people not to lose heart, and he proposes a near date himself. He understands that one can tolerate the common people's application of the commandments out of hope of reward and fear of punishment.[47]

Prophecy

Maimonides also provides a theory of prophecy, which he rethinks on the basis of Alfarabi's and Ibn Bajjah's notions of the virtuous city. What is more, he does so in the "Letter on Persecution," a work written in his youth (1162) on the occasion of the Almohad persecution. Here he advises giving lip service to a confession of Muslim faith rather than seeking martyrdom, and to escape to exile at the earliest opportunity. He takes advantage of the opportunity to remark that the obligation to change residence would apply in Israel as well: if one lives in a city that fails to apply the commandments scrupulously and there is another, stricter, city, it is imperative to move to the latter: "It is a duty for him who fears YHWH to leave that city whose actions are not good and [to leave] for that good city." Maimonides expresses himself here in the language of Alfarabi, and he alludes to the latter's "Virtuous City" in order to transpose into Judaism the duty of emigration formulated by Alfarabi.[48] The same thing is true of similar passages in later works. In the *Mishneh Torah,* the same advice to settle in a city in which mores are good is repeated, but with this addition: "And if all the cities that one knows or has heard of conduct themselves in a fashion that is not good, as in our own day . . . , one will live apart, as a hermit." His negative opinion of contemporary cities he has seen or heard about combines wording from Alfarabi and Ibn Bajjah, and it leads to the same sad necessity professed by the latter: the solitary life.[49]

Maimonides is the first figure within Judaism to see the prophet as one who realizes the perfect city, governed by the perfect Law that he himself gives to it. The prophet is a man whose intellectual and moral perfection puts him into contact with the agent intellect, which suffuses him with its emanation. Whereas the philosopher—"the class of men of science engaged in speculation"—has a "rational faculty" filled by "the intellectual overflow," his defective "imaginative faculty" makes him unable to translate his ideas for the crowd, and while "those who govern cities" have an efficacious imagination but a deficient intellect, the prophet combines the two faculties to perfection and can translate speculative verities into a language of imagination.[50]

Only Moses, the greatest of all the prophets, can provide an exact translation of received revelation, whether he makes no use of his imagination or retains entire mastery of it. With him, prophecy, which had been uniquely private and focused only on the perfection of the individual, becomes a legislative activity that commands and prohibits. Its perfect law will be immutable, although adaptable according to circumstance. It contains both true beliefs and necessary beliefs—that is, beliefs necessary for the good order of the city. Certain commandments will be demonstrable in an apodictic manner; others, without being so, will nonetheless have a rationale. For Maimonides, one cannot follow Saadia and those contaminated by the Kalām and distinguish between "rational commandments" and others that are not rational.[51]

But the essence of man, according to Maimonides, is not exhausted in his political dimension: the true man is the elite individual, not the mass. All people must therefore be regarded "according to their various states with respect to which they are indubitably either like domestic animals or like beasts of prey." This means that "if the perfect man who lives in solitude thinks of them at all, he does so only with a view of saving himself from the harm that may be caused by those among them who are harmful if he happens to associate with them, or to obtaining an advantage . . . from them if he is forced to it by some of his needs."[52] For that elite individual, the supreme perfection is contemplative in nature; practice and morality, which bring order within perfection, are secondary.[53] Indeed, intelligible concepts (true and false) should not be equated with moral values (noble or shameful); values are no more than commonly admitted opinions that our natural sentiment of justice urges us to admit.[54]

It follows that the political is not limited to "politics": to be sure, the political aims at the imitation of God and of his government of the world by founding a harmonious city, but it is also, according to the title of a work by Ibn Bajjah, the "conduct of the solitary." All law is general, as is nature, and neglects the details.[55] Thus what is needed is to find a society that renders justice to elite individuals by also permitting them access to the contemplative life, which is radically non-political. The perfect law will assure the two perfections, that of the body as well as that of the soul. The first of these, which is inferior, must come first; the second, supreme, is prepared for by the good of the body that assures a healthy political regime. The perfect law, by assuring peace to the mass, on the one hand, creates the social framework for the search for truth and treats moral questions in detail; on the other hand, although it contains only the general principles of the theoretical questions, it awakens the attention of the elite by scattered allusions that incite that elite to seek solutions to such questions. The law that permits the perfection of the political, and that also permits going beyond the political, is once again that of Moses. Mosaic law in fact contains an external meaning that permits the betterment of human societies and an internal meaning that leads to the true.[56]

The Divinity of the Law

Maimonides is far from being the first to have constructed a philosophic defense of the divine law of Judaism, but he is perhaps the first to raise the
question of what makes up its divinity. As early as his "Epistle to Yemen"
(1172), Maimonides furnished the criterion for distinguishing divine law
from a simply human law or from the Christian and Islamic laws that simply
plagiarized divine law: they imitate external features, and their inner core
(*bātin*) bears no resemblance to that of the Jewish Law. Human laws merely
regulate the actions of the body; the purpose of all commandments and
prohibitions in Jewish Law is to encourage man to strive for the two perfections of the body and the spirit.[57]

Some twenty years later, the *Guide for the Perplexed* expressed the same
criterion with greater precision and solemnity:

> If . . . you find a Law (*sharia*) all of whose ordinances are due to attention
> being paid . . . to the soundness of the circumstances pertaining to the body
> and also to the soundness of belief—a Law that takes pains to inculcate cor-
> rect opinions with regard to God, may He be exalted in the first place, and
> with regard to the angels, and that desires to make man wise, to give him
> understanding, and to awaken his attention, so that he should know the
> whole of that which exists in its true form—you must know that this guid-
> ance comes from Him, may He be exalted, and that this Law is divine.[58]

The first goal, concerning the body, is itself subordinate to the second, which
concerns opinions: man must be permitted to worship God in peace. The divinity of the law derives from the fact that it opens the way to a total knowledge of nature: the science of nature is thus legitimized by "religion" itself.

On the other hand, if the political begins with nature, it ends there as
well: the perfect law leads to the perfection of a life according to nature. Nature is not a starting point but a goal. Because it permits that perfect life, religion, without being natural, participates in some way in nature.[59] *The law
is perfect because it is "perfecting,"* because it leads to perfection as a maximal
equilibrium. That perfection consists, for the mass of men, in the best political constitution and, for the elite, in the philosophic life. There is perhaps more, however: the commandments assure the unity of Being with its
ultimate form, which is God; they constitute the human means for realiz-
ing a metaphysical law that is universal, but that man alone realizes consciously. They are not given to man for the sole purpose of his attaining perfection; rather, they derive from the very nature of being.[60]

Maimonides conceives of the law as being wholly rational. Before him, thinkers explained what appeared difficult to justify in the law as a pure test of obedience. After him, the search for the reasons behind the commandments was not just a possibility; it was a duty. Thus Maimonides returned to the way in which the Bible linked commandment and counsel (*'etsa*).[61]

Expelling History

Maimonides justifies the apparently bizarre commandments contained in the Bible by seeking historical reasons within them, but reasons that might be called those of a "negative historicity." As for origins, the history of salvation that renders the gift of the law intelligible is transposed to the metaphorical plane and replaced by a cosmology. The historicity that remains is expelled in two directions, to the past of idolatry and to the messianic future. I shall review these two operations of expulsion and transposition one after the other.

The historical past is one of idolatry. Maimonides illuminates the difficult commandments by the use of a theory that was to have a durable and extremely varied reception.[62] He constructs the fiction of a primitive universal religion, which he calls "Sabianism," and which he describes on the basis of a number of treatises on magic.[63] According to him, Abraham was raised in this religion and rebelled against it. The law of Moses was intended to eradicate it by systematically opposing it, point by point. Mosaic law thus commands what idolatry prohibited and prohibits what it commanded. The animals proper for sacrifice will be precisely those that the idolatry considered taboo. Maimonides echoes ideas already present in certain Fathers of the Church, but also among the Jewish thinkers who preceded him.[64] In this manner, commandments that seem not to make sense are rendered intelligible: garments made of cloth that combines animal and plant fibers are prohibited because the idolatrous priests wore such garments for their ceremonies, and so on. The reason for such commandments is therefore purely negative. They permit one human group to distinguish itself from others, and nothing more. Interestingly enough, we find similar justifications within Islam: certain hadiths present Muhammad recommending to Muslims to let their beards grow so as to avoid doing what idolaters do, and to dye their hair because the Jews and the Christians do not do so. Ignaz Goldziher explains the phobia regarding dogs that a hadith attributes to Muhammad (and about which the ancient sources say not a word) by the desire of the Arab conquerors of Iran to set themselves apart from Zoroastrians, for whom the dog was a sacred animal.[65]

The future is that of the messianic era. Maimonides eliminates the rabbinic distinction between a military Messiah, the son of Joseph, and a religious Messiah, the son of David. The Messiah is merely a political leader whose military victory delivers Israel. Not so that it can dominate the nations, but to assure it, along with peace, the conditions that will make it easy to achieve full observation of the law, hence, the realization of the ideal city.[66] All concrete political action, Maimonides writes, is governed by some section of the law. The authority of the king cannot contradict a disposition of the Torah, even though he does have the right, in response to the needs of the hour, to increase its rigor, just as he can declare taxes that the Law did not foresee. But the tension between the *halakhah* and the political will be truly resolved only with the coming of the king-messiah.[67] In a similar spirit, later thinkers were to explain that the nations cannot enjoy peace because of the defective nature of their laws, and will only know peace when they are subject to the Torah.[68]

"The Law Comes from Heaven"

As for the origin of the law, Maimonides admits, by implication, the natural character of prophecy and invokes divine intervention only in a negative way: God can prevent someone capable of doing so from prophesying.[69] He is proposing here something equivalent to the way in which certain Muslim theologians explained the impossibility (*i'jāz*) of composing a text comparable to the Qur'an.

The *origin* of the law remains an open question. The supreme principle is "the Law comes from heaven" (*tōrah min ha-shamayim*). Judaism attributes great importance to that principle, and, in that basically nondogmatic religion, it functions as a quasi dogma. It represents a fundamental presupposition to action. Whoever denies it will have no part in the "world to come"; he is a heretic and, as such, does not belong to the community of Israel. Maimonides heavily insists on this principle. He understands it as the definitive character of the law.[70] In this way, he responds to Christianity and to Islam, for whom the law of Moses can be replaced by another and subsequent law. He shows that Mosaic law is definitive in relation to the later prophets, genuine or self-proclaimed, and even that it alone retrospectively renders obligatory the commandments given to the previous prophets, Noah and Abraham.[71]

But precisely what does "to come from heaven" mean? Originally, "heaven" was of course a euphemism for God. What does Maimonides mean by "coming from" (*min*) in the expression "from heaven"? It seems as if Maimonides had kept the formula but invested it with a new meaning, replacing the "heaven" that stands for God with the concrete contents of the cosmic architecture. He prolongs and, by that token, adapts the doctrine of the Falāsifa, Alfarabi first among them. Thus the Law comes indeed from heaven, and very literally so.

The parallel between law and nature is constant in Maimonides' thought. According to him, the law imitates nature.[72] Maimonides attributes to nature what, for the Bible, is historical. When he comments on the commandment to love God, he gives the traditional explanation that the commandments must be studied in depth, but he adds that "works" must also be studied, and he understands these not as the mighty deeds of God within history but as the admirable structure of the physical world.[73]

The culmination point in Maimonides' cosmological reinterpretation of the history of salvation probably lies in the concept of covenant, the keystone of the history of Israel. In the *Guide*, the Hebrew word for "covenant," *berith*, appears only rarely—at my count, only twice. Once it designates the covenant of Abraham, which is circumcision. The second occurrence is in a biblical text, Psalm 25:10, which states: "All the paths of the LORD are kindness and constancy toward those who keep his covenant (*berith*) and his decrees." Maimonides explains: "Those who keep to the nature of that which exists, keep the commandments of the Law, and know the ends of both, apprehend clearly the excellency and the true reality of the whole."[74] To be sure, equating "covenant" and "the nature of being" in this context is not totally arbitrary: God's covenant with Noah (Gen. 9:9–17) concerns the whole of what we would call nature. The fact remains, however, that the equation is as violent as it is revealing: the entire history of salvation that was concentrated in the idea of a pact between God and his people is discreetly, but nonetheless brutally, pared down into a purely intellectual and nontemporal contact between man and a Creator who is barely distinguishable from his creature.

✧

Thus Maimonides drew inspiration from the Muslim Aristotelians to construct a theory of prophecy and of the law that prophecy brings that is powerful, coherent, and capable of explaining how the law can be called "divine." But in rethinking the law, he also recasts the idea of the divinity of the law and, at base, the idea of divinity, period. The law draws its divine character from its origin "in heaven" and from the perfection that it assures to the man who observes it. On both sides, however, the divine looks dangerously much like nature: the heavens also designate the hierarchical structure of the universe; human perfection also consists in knowing the truth regarding God *and*—in what should perhaps be understood as "*that is to say*"—regarding his creation.

Philosophers After Maimonides

After Maimonides, the intellectual centers of Judaism moved northward, encountering the scholastic spheres of influence. The task of the Jewish thinkers was modified in the process: henceforth they also had to defend the Law against the legislative systems of Christian Europe, with which it was compared. The first to do so, and evidently to the advantage of his new religion, was the apostate Abner of Burgos, in his *Moreh Tsedeq*, written around 1340.[75] Choosing among many possible authors, I shall present briefly five examples of thought regarding the Law.

The Avignon philosopher and astronomer Gersonides (d. 1344) can be placed in the lineage of Maimonides, as he justifies the need for a revealed law by the difficulty of extracting from the intractable raw material of human diversity and human liberty an order capable of leading man to his perfection. He, too, compares the law to nature, but he admits for both of them the possibility of temporary exceptions. The law is an art that sets nature on its way to its perfection. Since it is perfect, the Torah is definitive. As it is as inexhaustible as nature, interpreting the symbols that it contains cannot lead to an abandonment of their practice. Gersonides explicates the commandments of the Torah in the same fashion as Maimonides, but he generalizes the procedure by bringing in astrology, medicine, and zoology. He also attempts to provide a general theory founded in metaphysics: the commandments all serve to detach man from matter, the source of all evil, and to orient him toward form.[76]

Nissim ben Reuben Gerondi (d. 1375) breaks the connection between law and nature and understands the divinity of the law in a more literal fashion than Maimonides. The commandments serve to liberate men from the domination of nature. The law is the instrument that permits the divine influence to rest over Israel. Thus he views the divinity of the law in sacral terms, through the idea of divine influence (*inyan elohi*), which he borrows from Jehuda Halevi. Nissim distinguishes between the law of the Torah and the law of the king. It is possible that the Torah is less able to correct the political system than are the laws and statutes of the nations. But he supposes the defects of the Torah to be compensated by the measures taken by the king. Above all, the laws that the Torah contains permit divine influence to flow over Israel.[77]

The Catalan Hasdaï Crescas (d. 1412) devotes a chapter of his philosophical work to the eternity of the Torah.[78] He states immediately that the law of Moses is "divine." It can only be modified by provisional adaptations (*hōraʾat shaʾa*). It is eternal because it is perfect. To change it for another equally perfect law is useless, and for one less perfect, stupid. It is perfect because it expresses God's beneficent designs, which are to lead man to salvation by the perfection of his mores, knowledge, and affectivity. It is not enough to say that the law is perfect because it comes from a perfect being such as God. In fact, one might object that those who receive it can progress toward perfection, hence can receive a law that is better than that of Moses, as the Christians classically argue.[79] Thus one must show that the law is perfect in itself, both for perfect beings—for it leads to the perfection of wisdom—as for the less perfect, to whom it brings perfection of mores and of piety. As Crescas had shown previously in detail, the authentic goal of the law is to bring about the four perfections: those of mores, conceptions (deōt), and the salvation of the body and of the soul, which is precisely what Jewish Law does.[80]

Joseph Albo (d. 1444) introduces into Judaism (which had not known it previously) the idea of a conventional and independent law sufficient to regulate human affairs.[81] This means that he abandons the central idea of the Muslim thinkers about the law in whose orbit the Jews had evolved up to that time. According to them, man cannot set up a viable social organization without the aid of a law dictated by God. Albo, for his part, enters into the sphere of influence of Christian thought about the law. His political outlook also takes a Christian perspective as its point of departure: the city is not an institution charged with setting man on his way to salvation. It has a purely negative function: it must be correctly organized in order for man to be able to attend tranquilly to the business of pursuing perfect beatitude. The divine law guides political association toward perfection by clarifying it or by motivating it. Albo uses the word dath to designate divine law, thus bringing it back to its Persian etymology. He defines it from two points of view.[82] The origin of divine law is given by a prophet or by an envoy: Adam, Noah, or Abraham and Moses. Its end is double: it teaches what is true beatitude, and it indicates the right methods of the political. The law of Moses is not the only law that is divine. God is one, admittedly, but those who receive the law vary according to climate and temperament. Divine laws can thus change, not in their fundamental principles, but in their details. They can succeed one another; what is more, there can be two of them at the same time, as with the law of Moses and the law of Noah. Change is also possible within a law—there, too, on the part of the person receiving it. As with a doctor who changes his patient's regimen when his health improves, God can add to the law of Moses by prohibiting what that law permits or by permitting what it prohibits, if the reason for the prohibition has disappeared.[83]

Isaac Abravanel (d. 1509) is known best for his critique of the monarchical regime, which makes him an exception among medieval thinkers. The

overall framework of his political thought is even more decisive.[84] He min-
imizes the role of the city, observing that it is not indispensable to man. It
is a result of the sin by which man turned away from the simple and contemplative life that he led before the Flood, when he enjoyed the unmediated guidance of God. There is no need for divine intervention through the
prophets to organize the city. Similarly, he separates prophecy from the political and relegates it to the domain of contemplation: far from taking any
interest in the vile realities of the city, it occupies itself with speculation
alone. Moses is not his own master in the political realm, but borrows from
the pagan Jethro.[85] In this way, Abravanel draws prophecy out of the political domain, stripping the altar of sacrality in the process. This was only a
few decades before the state came to be constituted on an entirely "natural"
basis, as in Machiavelli, who also proposed—in contrast to Abravanel—an
interpretation of prophecy in purely political terms.

❖

In spite of the praise they heap on "the Master," philosophers after Maimonides often distance themselves from him, and this is particularly true
of their reflections on the law. For the three centuries that led up to the
modern age, the gap grew larger and larger in relation to the model (Islamic
in origin) from which Maimonides began: the idea of a law, given by God to
a prophet, that realizes the perfect city of the philosophers' dreams. Henceforth the political belonged to a less heady vision. In compensation, a tendency arose to seek the divinity of the law among the more mystical ideas
by which philosophy—sometimes in one and the same person—appears
side by side with the Kabbalah. Thus, according to the Catalan Abraham
Shalom (d. 1492), who was nonetheless a defender of Maimonides, the eternal law that brings immortality is divine because it emanates from the eternal force of God.[86]

The Kabbalah

Medieval Jewish thought was not dominated by philosophy alone. The Kabbalah challenged its primacy and grew in influence over time. I speak of it
only after having discussed Maimonides because of chronology, but also for
more basic reasons. In fact, even though Jewish mysticism has roots that
reach further back in the history of Judaism, it reached its classic crystallization in the Zohar ("Book of Splendor"), citations from which can be found
beginning in 1280. The Sefer ha-zohar is probably the work of Moses de León
(d. 1305), with the exception of the portion entitled Ra'ya' meheimna' ("The
Faithful Shepherd"), written by an anonymous author of the early four-

teenth century, which interests me particularly because it includes an explication of the commandments.

The overall intention of the Kabbalah was to refute what was judged to be the excessive rationalism of the Aristotelian philosophers, Maimonides first among them. That effort led first to reinforcing the value of the Torah over the secular sciences, which the Torah was supposed to contain.[87] Consequently, those sciences could not possibly rival the work that contained them. At that point, Jewish mysticism concentrated on a commentary of the Torah in which the legislative portions of that work receive no more privileged treatment than did the narrations, prophetic pronouncements, or hymns that it contains.[88] In fact, for the kabbalists, the Torah is patterned on divinity in a much more intrinsic fashion than a simple relationship of sender to the message sent. It corresponds to the very structure and dimensions of the divine; it constitutes its name (or names).[89] It is entirely spoken by the mouth of God.[90] Everything within it exists on the same plane: contrary to the philosophers, who fail to resist the temptation to distinguish the essential from the secondary, the kabbalists stress that no passages in the Torah are more important than others.[91] In so stating, the Kabbalah reinterprets the rabbinic refusal to privilege any one part of the Torah over another.

For the *Zohar*, the Torah constitutes something like a body with its various members: it is an archetype of the human body. It even represents the form of God. At the limit, with Menahem Recanati, it is one with God.[92] Meir ibn Gabbai explains that the Torah is divine because it is the name of God. For Joseph Gikatilla, "The Torah of YHWH" does not mean the Torah given by YHWH but rather the teaching of the name of YHWH.[93] Thus, Moshe Idel writes, "The status of the Torah as an independent entity standing between man and God and separate from both—such as we find in the talmudic midrashic literature—vanishes."[94]

One of the reasons for the crystallization of Jewish mysticism in the Kabbalah lies precisely in dissatisfaction with Maimonides' solution to the problem of the reasons underlying the commandments. The historical explanation proposed by Maimonides had the same drawback as allegorism: it implied that once the goal of the law—that is, the elimination of idolatry—was attained, the practice of certain of the commandments became optional.[95] Another way had to be found to explain why practice should be obligatory, and for the most serious reasons. Thus the kabbalists opposed the allegorical hermeneutics of the philosophers, which eliminated the literal meaning, by offering a symbolical hermeneutics that kept the literal meaning but made it the vehicle of superior realities. The Kabbalah's explication, which might be called "theurgic," has precisely the merit of showing how the symbol takes on meaning only by the effective fulfillment of the commandment.[96] That fulfillment is supposed to permit the descent to earth of the divine presence, and even to reestablish an equilibrium in heaven between the various attributes of the inaccessible divinity. By that very act, the pious man rescues creation from being lost in chaos. It is thus out of the question to relegate to the domain of the optional a practice that would set such grave consequences into motion.

Concerning the question of what makes up the divinity of the law, we are faced with a paradox: basically, the solution of the Kabbalah is patterned after that of Maimonides, which it attempted to combat. With one difference in transposition, however. The idea that "the Law comes from the heavens" is reiterated, but "the heavens" has changed meaning. The kabbalists no longer understand the term as a metaphorical heaven, a euphemism for God, nor as the physical heavens of the Aristotelian cosmology, but rather as the celestial world and the internal life of the divinity.

Moreover, Judaism, in its historical realization, displays the same union of the kabbalist and the jurist in one person as in Islam, for example, in Joseph Karo, who was both a mystic and the author of the most widely utilized code of *halakhah*.[97] The idea of a Torah that might be presented under different aspects from one era to another might lead to viewing the law as relative, as is the case today, to the advantage of its eschatological status, fomenting a certain antinomianism. In the Middle Ages, that temptation was held at a distance. It passed into action only with the movement connected with Sabbatai Tzevi and his abortive messianism: for some of his partisans, the suppression of the Torah represented its very fulfillment.[98] In any event, we will have to wait until the seventeenth century for that development.

⬧

The Kabbalah thus endowed the law with an incomparable value and permitted an in-depth appropriation of it without running the risk of compromising the definitiveness of its obligation. The connection between divinity and the law tightened: at first simply a way to describe the one by the other, the linked terms came to stand for one entity. The question was thus resolved, but somewhat expeditiously: in fact, once the two poles were absorbed into one another, it was no longer relevant.

13]&··

The End of the Law: Christianity

Nascent Christianity faced the need to define itself in relation to Judaism, from which it had emerged. As it happens, Judaism, as we have just seen, was in the process of refocusing around the notion of law. The problem of the relation of primitive Christianity to Judaism is thus posed in terms of the relationship to a *law* that preceded it.

The Early Fathers

One simple and radical way to resolve that problem was for Christianity to break with the Jewish Law, following an extremist interpretation of the thought of St. Paul. This was the choice of the Gnostics, in particular Marcion (d. ca. 160) and Valentinus (d. ca. 165). For them, the law of Moses is, at least in part, the work of the evil demiurge that the Gnostics saw as the creator of the world rather than of the good God, who transcends the world. The God of the Law is *just*, to be sure, but he is not *good*.[1] Where the law was concerned, the Fathers of the Church were leagued against the Gnostics, however.

Christ and the Law

The Gnostic temptation was exorcised by writers of the second generation of the Fathers of the Church, Irenaeus of Lyon (d. ca. 190), for example, and Tertullian (d. 220), both of whom wrote works against Gnosticism, and the latter against Marcion in particular.

Another solution to the problem consisted in presenting what came after the Jewish Law as a new species of a genus that remained the same, hence as also constituting a law. In the New Testament,

St. Paul—as we have seen—was already talking about the law of Christ.[2] What was in Paul an isolated turn of phrase grew to become a consistent theme. The expression is already a commonplace in St. Ignatius of Antioch. Cyprian speaks of the law of the Lord and of the law of the Gospel or evangelical law.[3] Christianity came to think of itself as a law brought by Christ in the same way that Judaism is a law brought by Moses. The Fathers even speak of a "new law" (something that the New Testament never does).[4] Origen speaks of the Christ as a lawgiver to the Christians who brought a divine (*entheos*) legislation. For him, the Gospel is the true Deuteronomy, the veritable "second Law."[5] Tertullian distinguishes between the earlier law and the law of the Christians, which is the Gospel.[6]

These doctrines received artistic representation in images such as that of a lawgiver Christ giving St. Peter the scroll of the Law in a mosaic in the church of Santa Costanza in Rome, on the sarcophagus of Probus in Rome, or in the basilica of St. Ambrose in Milan.[7] This scene is adapted from the pagan model of the investiture of a high functionary by the emperor. After Constantine, the ideology of the Christian Empire utilized the notion of a unique law.[8] This iconographic theme is present from the fourth century to the sixth, when it was replaced by another image in which the Christ gives Peter not the Law but rather the Keys to the Kingdom.

The Fathers also passed on the idea that the Christ is not a legislator but rather the Law itself. The *Shepherd of Hermas* (*Hermae Pastor*) draws a parallel between "the law of God given to the entire world" and "the Son of God announced to the ends of the earth." The philosopher and martyr Justin (d. ca. 165) speaks of the Christ as being himself the eternal Law and the new Covenant.[9] The expression that the Stoics used to designate governments, the "living law," returned to use. After Philo, it can be found among the Greek Fathers, beginning with Clement of Alexandria.[10] It occurs among the Latin Fathers as well: Lactantius (d. 325), for instance, uses both formulas interchangeably. "Since there was no justice on earth," he writes, God "sent his teacher like a living law, to establish his name and found a new temple, and to sow true and pious worship throughout the earth by word and by example." He also writes that God sent from heaven "his deputy and messenger," a "master and commander of us all" who would give his new worshipers a new law "in him or by him," and not, as before, through a human mediator.[11]

Finally, and this is perhaps the most profound interpretation, the new law is at times identified with the act of salvation *par excellence*, the death and resurrection of Christ, as those events are symbolized by the cross: "The Law of the Christians is the holy Cross of the Son of the living God."[12] Equating the law with the cross seems to betray what Paul had conquered.

This is by no means true, for, in fact, in this sort of statement, the term "law" can no longer designate a set of commandments, but rather what Christ's sacrifice has made uniquely possible, which is *a new regime of salvation*. It was in meditating on that new regime that medieval thinkers—as we shall see—produced their works of greatest genius.

The Articulation of the Laws

The Fathers of the Church reflected on the coexistence of these different laws. Supposing that the new law was henceforth the only one in effect, how, then, should one understand the old law? Was it simply abrogated? What meaning had it? Christ's declaration that he had come to fulfill (*plerōsai*) the law, not to abolish it (Matt. 5:17), could be interpreted in at least two ways: either as an addition, a complementary law that rendered the old one more stringent, or as an overcoming that surpassed the old one. The Fathers had to fight on two fronts. On the one hand, they had to respond to the Jews and to such "Judaisers" as the Judeo-Christian groups who saw Jesus primarily as a new Moses and who continued to observe the Mosaic laws.[13] On the other hand, as we have seen, they had to resist the Marcionite temptation of a rupture, pure and simple, with the Old Covenant. Both positions can be found in their writings. For Irenaeus, for instance, the Decalogue had been and enlarged and deepened rather than abolished.[14]

The most efficacious weapon that the Fathers had to combat Judaism was, paradoxically, borrowed from the Jews: it is the idea of the allegorical value of the dispositions of the law. They drew totally new consequences from this old device, however. For the Jews, the dietary laws, for example, took their meaning from the moral teaching that they contained: abstaining from eating the flesh of an animal is equivalent to avoiding contamination by the vices observable in that animal's behavior.[15] Philo devotes an entire text to this method. No one before St. Paul, however, had concluded that one could dispense with practical observance of the law: allegory added to the practice of the laws, giving it added legitimacy, but not replacing it. Allegory was used more as symbol than as strict allegory, and in all epochs of Judaism the dangers of allegorizing were stressed.[16]

Beginning with the *Epistle of Barnabas*, however, the Fathers asserted that the allegorical interpretation permitted the faithful to dispense with observation of the laws or, in any event, of certain laws.[17] They distinguished between permanent commandments and others that were provisional and due to historical or moral circumstances, such as God's pedagogical interests or men's hardness of heart. For the permanent commandments, some Fathers began to appeal to the idea of nature: "Those who are obliged to obey the Law of Moses will find in it . . . precepts . . . that in themselves [*naturally*] are good, holy, and just."[18] For Origen, the portion of Mosaic law that redemption had not rendered vain was the portion that coincided with natural law.[19]

Gradually a theory began to take shape that aimed at the articulation of the various laws. By the Fathers' count, there were three: natural law, the law of Moses, and the law of Christ. This three-part division occurs among such writers of the early fifth century as Pseudo-Cyril and Theodoret of Cyrrhus. The Fathers called the Mosaic law "divine," as they did moral law, but each of the three laws that they distinguished might be called "divine."[20] But what does it mean for a law to be divine? According to what criteria can one judge one law to be divine and another not? Is each of these laws divine in the same way? The Fathers barely scratched the surface of these questions.

The distinction between commandments and counsel, which the New Testament applied without thinking twice, was fully discussed. St. Ambrose (d. 397) draws this distinction: "A commandment is issued to those subject, counsel is given to friends. Where there is commandment, there is law; where counsel, there is grace. A commandment is given to enforce what is according to nature, a counsel to incite us to follow grace."[21]

For its part, the idea of natural law came to be conceived with the aid of the Stoic system of "common notions" inscribed in the "directive faculty" (*hegimonikon*).[22] Lactantius, for example, introduces into Latin Christianity a meditation on the law, and on the divinity of the law, that borrows from Stoic theories. He refers to a long passage from the lost book of Cicero's *De Republica*, commenting that Christianity can be seen as the realization of a divine law that had remained in a virtual state among the pagans. He introduces an important nuance into his paraphrase of Cicero's text: Cicero spoke of the law as something that *is* like the master and the commander of all things. Lactantius transposes: the law is *transmitted* by "that one God who is master and commander of us all."[23] Ambrose recycles Cicero's idea to the profit of Christianity by rewriting *De officiis*: the "law of nature" that demands that each person consider himself as part of one body with the others is also the "law of the Lord."[24]

❖

Thus the Fathers of the still undivided Church—that is, before the schism between Eastern and Western Christendom—put into place a way of thinking about the law or, rather, about the laws in their differentiation. Within this framework, the quality of divinity attached to the law tended to take on another meaning; as it left the orbit of Judaism to enter into that of Greek philosophy, it moved out of the sphere of history and into that of nature. Divine law was just as much the Torah given to Moses as it was the natural law that governed the cosmic city of the Stoics. How could those two faces of divinity be reconciled? That question received little response. It was, in any event, on that still rudimentary theory that medieval thought about the law was to be constructed. The various strands to that thought developed out of a divergence between the two halves of the Roman Empire that was already taking form at the end of antiquity. I shall examine the situation in the East very rapidly, and consider more at length the West, whose direct heirs we are.

Byzantium

In the Byzantine world, a political literature developed on the basis of themes already present among certain of the Fathers of the Church, such as John Chrysostom (d. 407).[25] It seldom rose above the level of the "Mirrors for Princes," eulogies, or collections of aphorisms, works that contain less theory than moral advice.[26] There is hardly any reflection on the fundamental requirements of the city in this literature, although it might have drawn on Aristotle's *Politics*, a work that remained largely unexploited, even though we possess the rudiments of a commentary on it. The rare exceptions to this rule include the idea that the city developed out of a need for a division of labor, as the Aristotelian philosophers of Islam had suggested.[27]

The central problem is that of the articulation between the spiritual powers and the temporal powers. No one doubted that a connection between them is essential: in the eleventh century, Theophylactus of Ochrida recalls that piety is the basis of kingship.[28] A few years before the fall of Constantinople, the patriarch Antonius reminded Vasili I, the grand prince of Russia, that it is impossible to have a church without an empire.[29] But how should their respective roles be divided? In the late tenth century, Emperor John I Tzimisces expressed his conception of the relationship between the emperor and the patriarch in these terms: "In the life and circuit of things here on earth I know two things, the power of the priesthood and that of the kingship, the one entrusted by the Creator with the cure of souls and the other with the government of bodies." Theodore Balsamon, at the end of the thirteenth century, reformulated that classical division of responsibilities, but stretched the line between the two in an unexpected way: the emperor's task is to enlighten and reinforce the body *and the soul;* the patriarch's responsibilities are confined to the service of the soul alone.[30]

It was within the juridical question that the two powers clashed and constantly renegotiated their relations. As early as Constantine's reign, Eusebius of Caesarea (d. 340) had theorized that the emperor is the depositary of the royal law, which originates in God.[31] The idea of the emperor as living law entered into jurisprudence with Justinian's Novel of 536 on the consuls. In practical terms, that idea is expressed in the principle that the emperor is not bound by the laws but rather is above them.[32] A separation between the monarchy and ecclesiastical law found expression in John Damascene (d. 749), who refuses the emperors the right to pass laws regarding ecclesiastical matters, citing the biblical "render unto Caesar," and also in Theodore Studites (d. 826), who insists that control over "dogmas divine and celestial" should be reserved to the apostles and their successors.[33]

Theoretical reflection on the division between the two laws also separates an immutable sacred law (*hieron diatagma*) from civil laws, which change often.[34] In the theological domain, Maximus the Confessor (d. 662) draws connections among three laws: natural law, written law, and spiritual law. Nestorian or Jacobite theologians writing in Arabic propose various other three-part divisions, and even six categories of law.[35] One Nestorian theologian of the late tenth century, Ibn Zur'a, takes an original position distinguishing between natural, rational, and positive laws. The first of these is simply the animal instinct to dominate, while the last is revealed by the Creator. Rational law is not an awareness of good and evil, but is rather a morality of the happy medium, a notion of philosophical origin. In these ideas Ibn Zur'a's thought resembles that of Islamic doctrines of his time or those of another Christian, Mattā Ibn Yūnus.[36]

St. Augustine

In the western half of the Roman world, the tone was set in the fifth century by St. Augustine, the most philosophical of the Fathers of the Latin Church, and a man whose thought had an immense influence on all of European Christendom. He rarely presents his doctrine of the laws thematically, and his terminology is far from consistent. Augustine seldom uses the expressions "divine law" or "law of God." When he does use the latter term, it does not suggest that God is subject to any law: it is men who are subject to a law given by God. Augustine distinguishes the law of God from the natural law of reciprocity summarized by the "golden rule": do not do to others what you are unwilling to have them do to you. The law of God is given during the course of history—to Moses, for example—and it comes to establish, augment, or reassert natural law.[37]

If Augustine speaks rarely of the "law of God," he speaks fairly often of the "eternal law" (*lex aeterna*), an expression that he borrows from Stoicism but bases on the personal will and wisdom of God rather than on an impersonal principle. He defines it in terms borrowed from Cicero: the eternal law is the supreme reason that must always be obeyed and by which the good merit happiness and the wicked, unhappiness; it is on the basis of eternal law that one can evaluate the justice or injustice of temporal laws.[38] Temporal laws are indispensable to remind sinful men of natural law when their awareness of it has become clouded. What is more, natural law can only be actualized as human laws. In compensation, it is from the eternal law that the lawgivers of the temporal cities can take counsel. The eternal law is what permits judgment, and, by that token, it is not itself subject to judgment. More precisely, the eternal law coincides with divine reason—or the divine will—that commands men to respect natural order and prohibits them from troubling it.[39] It is "that law in virtue of which it is just that all things exist in perfect order."[40] That order thus possesses an inherent consistency, by which it belongs to the natural. The eternal law does not create that order; it acknowledges its existence inasmuch as it is reason, and it enjoins us to conform to it inasmuch as it is will—that is, desire ruled by reason. To the extent that the divine law coincides with nature, it imposes sanctions against what is opposed to nature. Crimes against nature, even if they were admissible everywhere, nonetheless would be punishable according to divine law.[41]

Because it is natural, divine law must be knowable by all men: "God has written the natural law in the hearts of men"—or, more precisely—he has copied it in the heart of the sages.[42] The locus of its original version is God himself, or divine Wisdom. We can even equate law with that wisdom.[43] The law thus does not derive from the will of God, but from his Wisdom, a wisdom in which creation participates, and in the first rank of creation, man, for whom that participation is conscious. Thus "divine Law" designates both the order of the universe and legislation adapted within history to a specific state of humanity.

Divine law does not belong to the political domain, however. The idea of a divine law that rules a city appears in Augustine's writings only in connection with the laws of the pagan gods, which shape the conduct of the gods' votaries and urge them to imitate the behavior (unedifying though it may be) of those gods.[44] Augustine even sketches out a theory of Christian indifference to the political and juridical systems designed to maintain the peace of the terrestrial city: the church gathers together citizens that it calls from within all the nations; it pays no attention to diversity of mores, laws, and institutions; it neither restricts nor abolishes those mores but instead conserves them and conforms to them; it asks of human institutions only that they not thwart the religion that teaches men to worship the one supreme and true God.[45] This is visibly the origin of a tradition of thought that appears elsewhere in the Middle Ages and that we might call (at the risk of anachronism) "liberal": the tradition that renounces the Platonic dream of a social order in which the supreme power assigns to each individual a place and a trade in favor of a conception of providence that gives the individual the inclination to follow a certain profession, thus doing away with the need for the ideal city.[46]

According to Augustine, the written law—that of the Bible—came into history not because there was no law written in people's hearts but rather because they refused to read it there. Thus man, exiled from his own inner being, had to be sought where he was, that is, within the exteriority of the letter of the law.[47] Respect for external law helps to return to internal law, and thus to move from the state of one who is *under* the law (*sub lege*) to that of one who is *in* the law (*in lege*). The first *is acted upon* according to the law; the second *acts* according to the law. The first is a slave; the second is free.[48] Augustine returns here to the distinction made by St. Paul between the letter and the spirit of the law. The letter kills without the spirit. The spirit, Paul explains in an untranslatable play on words, does not assure that one hears (*audiendo*) the law but assures that one obeys it (*obediendo*); it does not make one read (*lectione*) the law, but rather makes one love it (*dilectione*).[49]

Augustine reinterprets ancient thought regarding the law by detaching it from its context within the Roman state and making it the instrument of an unmediated relation to God situated within the moral and spiritual domain, while at the same time detaching it from its political role.

The Jurists

The idea of the law remains very much a part of thought in the Latin world after Augustine. The point of departure in the early Middle Ages, as is true of many other questions, is given in the *Etymologiae* (or *Book of Definitions*) of Isidore of Seville (d. 636), a work that assured the survival of the essence of ancient and patristic thought. According to Isidore, all law is either human or divine. The divine laws receive their stability from nature; human laws, from mores. Isidore distinguishes between *fas* and *jus*: only the former merits the name of divine (*fas lex divina est, jus lex humana*).[50]

St. Anselm (d. 1109) seems to avoid the idea of divine law: he is aware of the term, as his correspondence shows, but he does not use it once in his own treatises. In its stead he uses the notion of the will of God, and when he does mention "the law of God," he immediately explains that he means God's will. What is more, he distinguishes two categories within the divine institution—that is, the will of God—the precepts of Holy Scripture and natural law. The latter can be summarized in the golden rule, as it is formulated in the Book of Tobit: do not do to others what you would not wish to undergo yourself. Both the precepts of Scripture and the observations of the church can be called the will of God,[51] but Anselm seems to avoid calling them the "law of God."

The reason for the limitations in the thought of these two men may be the result of the historical circumstances that surrounded them. Anselm lived during the upheavals of the eleventh century, while Isidore lived well before then. Their thought about the law did not have to confront more than what the Fathers of the Church had already elaborated in that domain. The major intellectual event that returned the idea of law to the center of Christian thought in the Middle Ages was the elaboration of a coherent system of canon law, beginning with the "papal revolution" of the late eleventh century.

Law, Nature, God

Those upheavals led the jurists to reflect on the very notion of law, divine law in particular. This they did in constant dialogue with the professors of the liberal arts, theology, and philosophy, three disciplines that were often embodied in one person.[52]

The jurists of the time did not maintain that the law derives its divinity from its origin in a revelation, but rather held that it derives it from its natural character. Divine law and natural law tended to be considered one and the same. "The divine law," the jurist Étienne de Tournay (Stephanus Tornacencis) writes in the twelfth century, "is also called natural, because the supreme nature (*summa natura*), that is, God, has educated us by the law and by the prophets, and has given us the Gospel."[53] It seems that Plato's *Timaeus* played the role of a decisive intermediary here: the distinction between the natural and the positive is rooted in a tradition of commentaries on this dialogue that began with Calcidius in the fourth century. William of Conches (d. after 1154) speaks of "natural justice" that results from a divine construction of the world on the part of the Demiurge, whom Christian commentators see as superimposed on the Creator of Genesis.[54] Other authors who reflect on that combination remark that *Deus* signifies *natura* in this connection. Thus they anticipate Spinoza's famous formula, but within a context that gives it a meaning totally detached from the pantheism that has at times been attributed to him.[55]

The "nature" in question here is not "Nature" as defined by the Moderns, a nature flattened into one whole in order to be set against artifice, which is erected on the base of nature but also rejects it. Rather, it is a nature understood in a formal sense, as the nature *of* each thing. It has gradations according to the level of being occupied by the entity of which it is the nature.

Every being (including inanimate beings and plants) thus has a right (*jus*) that consists in doing what is in conformity with its nature. This anticipates Spinoza's definition of right: "Whatever each man does from the laws of his own nature, he does by the sovereign right of Nature."[56] As for man, he is nature in all the dimensions of his being, as those dimensions are expressed by his definition as a rational animal: man's nature concerns both the genus ("animal") that he shares with the other animals and also the specific difference ("rational") that distinguishes him from them. As a consequence, what nature demands of man inasmuch as he is an animal and what it recommends to him as a rational being must be differentiated. The centrally important example of marriage demonstrates this. Coupling with more than one female is not against animal nature, since females seek to perpetuate the species. But polygamy goes against rational nature, in that nature "invites man to an equality of alliance, obligation, and conjugal amity towards woman, and even to an indivision of life [with her], . . . all things that a man cannot maintain with several [partners]."[57]

The introduction of the concept of nature provides the basis for understanding the origin of Christianity as introducing no new commandments. It also permits the acknowledgment of a basic agreement between Christianity and those for whom the idea of nature is central—that is, the philosophers. For the theologians, the philosophers' morality is irreproachable in its content. Hence nothing prevents its integration into a moral theology. Even as strong an adversary of philosophy as Manegold von Lautenbach remarks, toward the end of the eleventh century, that philosophical arguments agree with the Catholic faith, in particular in its description of the virtues. A half-century later, Abelard notes that the precepts in the Bible constitute a recasting (*reformatio*) of natural law, and William of Auxerre stresses that divine law and natural law differ only in their form and not in their content. Thomas Aquinas can thus integrate Aristotle's morality into his treatise on the virtues, and Roger Bacon, in his *Moralis philosophia*, can copy extensive passages from Seneca.[58]

Such thinkers fully developed an idea, already to be found in Augustine, that equated the God of truth with supreme justice: God is not to be found outside the law; law exists within him. For St. Bernard, God himself lives by a law, which is charity: "The unspotted law of the Lord is charity. . . . It is called the law of the Lord . . . because He Himself lives by (*ex*) it. . . . Nor let it seem absurd that I said that even God lives by law; since I said, by no other law save charity. . . . This is the eternal law, that creates and rules the universe."[59]

The mystic and the jurists were speaking the same language. Thus we can read: "Equity is no other than God." Or, in the prologue to a work on

German law, the *Sachsenspiegel*: "God is himself law, which is why what is law is dear to him."[60] As the idea passed into the thought of the great scholastics, they developed a major consequence: the laws assure a continuity between the Creator and the creature. The laws are not the expression of a will, but rather of the very nature of God. St. Bonaventure says this magnificently: the three laws—the law of nature, the law of Scripture, and the law of grace—"come from God [and] live with God, who lives from them. Indeed, no law emanates from Him and is reproduced in the creature without His living by it first, and He lives by the very laws by which He governs the world."[61]

Law, Reason, Grace

If the law is not external to God, man's relationship with the law puts him into contact with God, a contact that is not solely obedience, but participation in the divine. This is implied in the role that the thinkers of the period attribute to reason. Thus Gratian, in the canonic synthesis that appeared around 1140, brought innovation to earlier theories of the law when he introduced, between the concepts of divine and human law, the idea of a natural law that provides a criterion for distinguishing between good customs and bad ones. In itself this was a revolutionary act and one that led to all manner of further revolutions, because it led to the notion that custom could no longer represent a final authority: all custom was in principle subject to nature, and with nature, to the faculty that enables us to grasp nature—that is, to reason.[62]

John of Salisbury (d. 1180) borrowed his conception of divine law from Stoicism. For him, nature is the source of the law to the extent that it provides man with the reason that makes him capable of constructing a rational social order. Thus the *lex* (natural law and reason) is a gift of God.[63] God does not dictate the law, giving it directly or ready-made; the law is the indirect result of a divine gift, in the sense that it is reason, God's gift to man, that discovers it.

The *Summa theologica* attributed the Franciscan Alexander of Hales (d. 1245) divides natural law into three: *nativum, humanum*, and *divinum*. The first of these applies to what every living being receives at its birth, that is, the various instincts that permit it to survive and perpetuate its species; the second is human reason. The third concerns human actions in their relationship with divine grace: this sort of natural law represents "that by which the rational creature is disposed to grace." In this sense, the commandments of the law of Moses that pertain to mores (the Decalogue, for example) emanate from natural law: "In the measure in which the natural law is ordered according to the divine law, it is ordered according to grace, and one then speaks of natural law. . . . It orders us according to grace in two ways: either by ordering us in accordance to God or to our neighbor."[64]

Thus according to the authors of this period, the law finds its organizing principle in reason and is raised up within the divine. The divine intervenes as a supreme law of charity, above all civil or even ecclesiastical laws. According to an oft-cited play on words that originates with Augustine, the law of the forum (*jus fori*) must cede to the law of heaven (*jus poli*).[65] Yves, bishop of Chartres (d. 1116), cites another famous dictum of Augustine's, "Love, and do as you will," at the head of the prologue to his code, a purely juridical work, though. To summarize: the divine element in the law appears under the species of nature (created) or of grace, and in some cases as the principles of mercy and equity, but never to describe a commandment or mark the origin of a commandment.[66]

We shall now see how these elements find a place in the synthesis of Thomas Aquinas.

St. Thomas Aquinas

The works of Thomas Aquinas represent perhaps the most profound reflection that medieval scholasticism has passed on to us regarding the notion of law in general and divine law in particular.[67] The better part of his thought on the topic is elaborated in two places, Book 3 of his *Summa contra Gentiles* (ca. 1264) and a treatise on laws that figures in the *Summa theologica* (ca. 1270). Thomas's teaching regarding laws has often been studied, especially in connection with its influence on the philosophy of the law. Here I shall concentrate on what pertains to the problematic of the present work.[68] In my discussion I shall follow the order of the *Summa contra Gentiles*, but freely.

The Four Laws

Thomas lists four types of law: eternal law, natural law, human law, and divine law, the last of which he divides into ancient and new law. These categories have corresponding questions, which he develops in some cases more fully than in others.[69] Although the idea of natural law is traditional (and Stoic), placing eternal law into a category that is not synonymous with it, but distinct and anterior, seems to constitute an innovation. The formula occurs in Augustine, to whom Thomas refers constantly, and it enabled Yves of Chartres to separate immutable precepts, indispensable for salvation, from provisional measures that smooth out the path to salvation.[70]

Thomas does not *constate* eternal law, however: he *deduces* it as a condition of possibility for the other forms of law. He also draws from it something new: the idea of eternal law makes it possible to think that there is a law common to God and his creatures, and that God, in a certain manner, submits himself to a law: "For God to will anything except what is held in the exemplar of his wisdom is out of the question. It is here that the law of justice lies whereby his will is right and fair. . . . God is a law unto Himself."[71] Consequently, the law cannot be reduced to a commandment that would merely be the imposition of a will. The law is rational and, at least within itself, intelligible.

If there is a common law, there can be a society that reunites God and man. Thomas asserts this, but in full awareness of what separates him from Aristotle on the question, citing (not without a pinch of provocation) Aristotle's statement that the gods are not virtuous. For Thomas, "The divine law directs us by its precepts in spiritual life, according to which we enter into society not only with man, but with God."[72] There cannot be full reciprocity between man and God, however, which means that the divine law derives not from the *jus* but from the *fas*.[73]

As we have seen, there are two versions of the idea of divine law. The first is apolitical, being instead theological or cosmic—or, if it must be called political, it is cosmo-political. The other version designates a code of conduct, which can indeed provide the basic rules of a political community and be established by divine revelation, but which either replaces the rational laws or comes to be added to those laws in an extrinsic fashion. Thomas Aquinas attempts to integrate those two dimensions. He uses the adjective "divine" to characterize two types of laws. On the one hand, it applies specifically to the fourth type of law; on the other hand, it also describes the eternal law.[74]

The Providential Function of the Law

Thomas discusses the law in general at a specific location within the overall argument of the *Summa contra Gentiles*, Book 3, which examines the entire question of how creatures order themselves according to God as toward their end, and where the development on the laws follows his treatise on providence.[75] The term "providence" is used in a very general sense here: it is the way in which God governs the created species, not the particular providence by which God "keeps an eye on" the single individuals whom he directs within history. Placing the law within this divine government, rather than within the economy of salvation alone, Thomas shows that he considers salvation a particular case of divine providence.

Indeed, providence acts most effectively upon rational creatures, who are free and who also seek the final end of all that exists directly and not mediately through their interactions with other created beings. Divine governance operates differently according to the various levels occupied by the beings to which it applies, in particular according to their intelligence. Thus Thomas returns to a general principle of Maimonides that individual providence "follows the intellect and adheres to it" (although Thomas generalizes Maimonides and probably modifies the underlying intention of his statement). We can say, *grosso modo*, that for Thomas the higher a being's rank on the ontological scale, the more God delegates his providence to him, up to the point that his providence coincides with prudence, a word that, in the history of language, is a doublet of "providence," since both are derivations of the Latin *providentia*.[76]

Providence attends to rational creatures for their own sakes, not because of some other thing whose instruments they might be. Rational creatures constitute ends in themselves, not means. God cares for them for themselves (*propter se procuratae*). Providence pertains to man, not only as a species, but as an individual, an idea that Thomas may have borrowed from Maimonides. One might wonder, however, whether, for the latter, separate individuals still subsist where man is truly man, that is to say, at the level of the intellect. Individuation seems to disappear, which is why the idea of individual providence, which Maimonides nonetheless claims to defend, remains highly problematic.[77]

For Thomas, on the other hand, the personal nature of man represents a fundamental value: the intellect operates in the singular, activated by one individual or another. There is no Man, no "humanity," but a plurality of persons, all of whom are irreplaceable. Providence must thus reach people where they are, which is to say in their variety, a variety so great that the instinct common to the species does not suffice to regulate it. It pertains to individuals within the diversity of circumstances in which they must act, the complexity of which they themselves are able to grasp. The rational creature can grasp the reason of providence. He or she is thus capable of taking onto himself or herself the exercise of such a providence. The rational creature has a share in providence not only as object, but also as subject.[78]

We see here the fruition of a principle formulated elsewhere: God's goodness goes so far as to transmit to what he creates his own creative powers. The confidence that God displays toward his creatures derives, Thomas states, from "the immensity (*immensitas*) of His goodness, whereby He has willed to communicate His likeness to things, not only so that they might exist, but also that they might be the cause for other things."[79]

Thomas envisages the law on the basis of the way in which God gives it, which is why the treatise on the laws is structured to follow the treatise on providence. It is not the first time—far from it—that the gift of the law was understood as an effect of divine providence: the Arabic Aristotelians had done so many years earlier.[80] Thomas gives the idea a new turn, however: he sees in the law one of the means by which the external principle that makes us act properly—that is, God—influences us (the other means being grace). Through the law, God "instructs" (*instruit*) humankind, although that seeming cognate is a mistranslation of the Latin word. Rather, he "equips" us. It is a question not of teaching man what he must do, but rather of putting in his hands the instruments that permit him to do it.[81]

Thomas considers the law to be a gift of God to a rational and free creature. Law is the form that providence takes in relation to a free being; the law is to the rational creature what instinct is to the irrational one. Thomas defines law as the way we act when in full possession of our freedom. Nothing seems more difficult than to act in this way, however. The difficulty divides into a general one and one that is specific to Christianity. In general, it is possible to have power over a free being by taking hold of it where it is not free, for example, in the body, which can be bound and imprisoned; but, by doing so, one does not have power over freedom *itself*. The problem this poses is thus to know how to make sure that a subject is acting of his own free will. For Christianity in particular, the problem becomes even knottier. It is not to know whether God will pardon sins, because he always does so. The problem is to know whether a person wants that pardon; whether he accepts being freed from the chains of sin. That acceptance can only be manifested by an act of freedom—of that same freedom that sin has made us lose. It is thus not enough to assert that God is clement and merciful, a banal notion that has been taken for granted since the Old Covenant. What is needed is to construct a mechanism capable of freeing freedom itself, and of producing the effect that man can accept forgiveness of his sins. It is this mechanism—in technical terms, the economy of salvation—that Thomas has in mind, even when he speaks only of the gift of the law.

As a consequence, the economy of providence, which aims at the good of all creatures, is deployed as both nature and history. As nature, its goal is conservation; as history, it seeks salvation. The eternal law is refracted in the rational nature of man in the form of the natural law made accessible to consciousness. It finds a concrete realization in the historical adventure of man, where it takes form as a series of human legislative codes by which various societies adapt natural law. It lies within the historical destiny of man, where it constitutes the economy of salvation. The divinity of the law appears redoubled where it takes on (so to speak) the figure of a supererogatory work on the part of God, proposing to man what lies beyond his capabilities.[82] The economy of salvation is structured as a series of covenants:

the New Law succeeds the Old Law, and the New Law coincides with grace: "The New Law is chiefly the grace itself of the Holy Spirit." Equating the law with grace, as one commentator has written, is "the most daring equation that has ever been set up in the history of humanity for the ethical domain." The new law is law of faith, law of liberty. Christ does not give that new law, for example, by dictating it in the Sermon on the Mount; rather, by making the grace of the Spirit overflow on the believers who form his mystical body, as communicated by the sacraments and in the faith.[83]

It remains to be seen how the divine law can enter into human history.

The Divinity of the Law

In what follows in the text that I am commenting on here, Thomas explains the expression "divine law" (*lex divina*) as "law . . . divinely given to man" (*lex divinitus data*).[84] This substitution is not without importance, as it shows that the adjective "divine" is not metaphorical but rather designates the origin, not the end, of the law, and even its sole internal perfection. With this indication of the origin of the law, we enter into the domain of the law as revealed, as historical. Thomas does not explain clearly the articulation between the eternal law and the law that is communicated at a certain date within historical becoming. Everything suggests that the implicit response to that question is contained in a preceding question: the law concerns individuals as individuals, and they live within the irreversible time of history, where the law must reach them

Moreover, for the first time in the text that we are following, Thomas says what he means by law, or, more precisely, by the type of law that he is studying, which is "a rational plan of divine providence, in its governing capacity, proposed to the rational creature." The definition is pagan, in fact Stoic, in origin. The adjective "divine" does not refer directly to the God of Revelation. Similar expressions can be found regarding the God-nature of the Stoics and the government of the cosmic city.[85] There are two things worthy of note in this definition. First, the law is a *ratio* and not, for example, a will or an arbitrary decree. Of course, *ratio* in Latin does not mean uniquely what we understand as "reason." Its Latin meaning is broader (like that of the Greek *logos*), and it includes the notions of "order" and of "the way to operate." But within the full extension of this term, one idea remains constant: that of a capacity to make something one's own, to appropriate what is given. One can become part of an order and not simply submit to it; one can understand a manner of acting and not merely imitate it in servile fashion. Second, that *ratio*, Thomas tells us, is *proposita* to the rational creature.

That word can be translated as "proposed," but only on the condition that is understood etymologically as "placed before," not imposed from above.

That law given by God has an aim: "The end for the human creature is to cling to God, for his felicity consists in this."[86] Thomas's use of the idea of adhesion implies a further important point: the difference between the law and the person subject to the law is not intended to be definitive. It is abolished in the long run: "The law has, according to the intention of God as lawgiver, the task of rendering itself superfluous," not, of course, in its content, but in its positive form, which makes it external to the person who conforms to it.[87] We hear echoes of the New Testament in Thomas, for example, of St. Paul when he speaks of men as "God's co-workers" (1 Cor. 3:9), or St. John, who quotes Jesus as saying, "I no longer speak of you as slaves, for a slave does not know what his master is about. Instead I call you friends, since I have made known to you all that I heard from my father" (John 15:15). What makes the law divine cannot thus consist in the fact that it is inaccessible to human knowledge, hence "mysterious." Or rather, the Christian concept of "mystery"—which exists uniquely as revealed—designates not an inability to understand but rather the boundless intelligibility inherent to what is given, inasmuch as it is given.[88]

Love as the End of Law

Humankind is accorded the capacity for receiving that gift and clinging to it. For Thomas, adhering to God is accomplished by *amor*. What exactly does that Latin word mean? Is it more akin to desire or to charity? Thomas limits himself to saying that the end of the divine law is *amor*, which is the "love of the highest good." The end of the law is thus the good of man, not, for example, the interest of God (if that expression were not in itself ridiculous). All of providence has the aim, not of adding something to the goodness of God, but to arrange things so that "the likeness of this goodness, as much as possible, is impressed on things." A bit further on, Thomas recalls this notion with a magnificent formula: "We do not offend God except by doing something contrary to our own good."[89] The only way in which we can offend God is to do harm to his creature and, in particular (since we are perhaps his most worthy creature and certainly the only creature on which we can act from the inside), to harm ourselves.

This notion avoids a naive representation of a "zero-sum game" in which one cannot give to God without taking away from God's creatures, and vice versa. It also avoids a supposed "Prometheanism" that attempts to pay God with his own coin by taking away from him the goods of which he is supposed to have deprived man. Thomas solemnly asserts the contrary somewhat earlier in the text, returning to Maimonides' quarrel with the Kalām theologians: "To remove anything from the perfection of the creatures is to remove something of the perfection of the divine power."[90]

The good of man is not only a good turn that might be done to him but also a good that he becomes capable of doing. When man is conceived of in these terms, he enters the scene as a subject, not just as object. At that point we penetrate the domain of morality, as a theory of the good as it is doable by man, who makes that good his own in human excellence, or virtue. In fact, the intention of the lawgiver is to make men good—that is, Thomas explains, virtuosi, which I would like to render as "virtuosi" as well as "virtuous" to emphasize that the good is appropriated, assimilated by the subject to the point of becoming a competence that he possesses on his own.[91]

The law allows us to love one another. Amor becomes specific in friendship, as Aristotle's philia is expressed as social concord. Thomas, from this point on, echoes Maimonides and his doctrine of divine law. Thomas adds that "divine law is offered to man as an aid to natural law." In saying that mutual love is inscribed in the nature of man ("it is natural to all men to love each other") and responds to some sort of natural instinct, Thomas is also returning to the Stoic idea of the natural sociability of human beings.[92]

Divine law makes it possible for us to have a "right faith" in God. Here is where Thomas reinterprets the second goal of divine law according to Maimonides. The latter spoke of conviction, but also of healthy opinions, whereas Thomas speaks of faith. This is because the Christian God is presented in such a way that implies that the instrument permitting adequate access to him is faith and faith alone. Moreover, Thomas neglects the other objects of knowledge that Maimonides enumerated when he associated the angels and even "the totality of what is" with God. In any event, the object of faith is truth. Thomas states this explicitly. He recalls the notion in a lapidary formula: "He who believes something false does not believe in God."[93]

The law is thus crowned by faith, which is itself conceived of as access to truth. We are now as far as possible away from the conception of the law as representing nothing more than a conventional order with no relation to the truth of things.

Divine Law and the City of Men

Thomas Aquinas does not limit his meditation on the law to the theological domain: he also reaches out to investigate the consequences for the way in which men govern their conduct and rule their communities. For Thomas, the divine law has the aim of establishing order in man, and in such a way that everything in man is subjected to reason. There is no question of "humbling proud reason" but, to the contrary, of liberating reason and permitting it to be itself. The divine law leads man to respect the order of reason in all the things he might make use of, and first and foremost with other men. Hence each individual will occupy his proper place and rank.[94] The order that is to be respected is that of reason, not just an "established" order. There is no rejection of social mobility in the name of a "tradition" here; rather, we recognize the Platonic ideal according to which each person does—in the deepest sense of the word—what he must do, which is the ideal of peace through concord and justice.

This is shown in a passage from the *De regimine principum*, the only political treatise that Thomas Aquinas composed (more accurately, that he began), and which contains the only occurrence in this work of the expression "divine law":

> From divine law we know the way (*via*) that leads to true beatitude and the things that are impediments to it, the teaching of which pertains to the office of priests. . . . In Deuteronomy the Lord orders: "After the king sits on the throne of his kingdom, he will copy this law of Deuteronomy into a volume, taking the copy from a priest of the Levitical tribe, and he will keep it with him and read it all the days of his life, so that he might learn to fear the Lord his God and guard his works and ceremonies, which were ordered in the law." Therefore, instructed by this divine law, he ought especially to be zealous to attend to how the subject multitude might live well. This zealousness has three parts: first, to institute a good life among the subject multitude; second, to preserve that which was instituted; and third, to move from what has been preserved to something better.[95]

Thomas is attempting here to define the way in which the divine law operates within the city of men, as it is represented by its leader. Thomas, who has just argued in favor of monarchy, calls that leader a "king" here. This does not prevent us from generalizing, for the selection of the person who governs is beside the point, and whether this happens by primogeniture or election is not in question. In any event, nothing in Thomas recalls any "divine right of kings"—a doctrine that is in no way medieval, as we have seen, but exclusively modern.[96] What is more, the passage alludes to the role of the priests as guardians of the law, and it is fairly easy to see that Thomas is seeking here to situate the temporal power and the spiritual power in relation to one another. But the divine law, as the concept has just been discussed, does not constitute a principle of organization of the city. For Thomas, the divine law belongs wholly within the ethical domain. It does not indicate conduct to follow in the concrete organization of life in society. "Applying" it is not in question. Its influence is not that of an external norm but rather that of an internal principle. It designates the goal to be reached and it liberates reason, so that reason will be able to see clearly the goal in question and seek with certainty the means for arriving at that goal.

❖

The thought of the three authors to whom I have devoted particular attention—Ghazali, Maimonides, and Thomas Aquinas—by no means exhausts reflection on divine law in the Middle Ages in Islam, Judaism, and Latin Christianity. Although their authority has been and remains very great, none of the three was received, immediately and without reservations, by his coreligionists. To the contrary, their works elicited quarrels and critiques. Ghazali became the target of Averroes' counterattack, but also of the doctors of the law who were enemies of the Kalām; Maimonides was posthumously at the center of two quarrels about the legitimacy of philosophical studies. Certain of the theses of Thomas Aquinas were condemned only a few years after his death. All three of these men had to face competition from thinkers who either occupied the same terrain as they did or defended rival approaches. It is only long after their death that they came to be considered authoritative. Ghazali now passes for a spiritual master and is commonly hailed with the laudatory epithet of "Imām"; Maimonides is cited as one of the highest authorities concerning *halakhah,* even though his philosophical works fall outside of orthodox Judaism; Thomas Aquinas has received from the Magisterium of the Catholic Church the stature of an official theologian, with the title of Doctor of the Church.

Be that as it may, it seems to me that these three thinkers have given the most telling formulation of how their religions considered the divinity of the law. With them, conceptual decisions that had been taken many centuries earlier, even that had been implied in the inaugural acts of the traditions they rely upon, come to full flowering. This is precisely why I have singled them out for special attention here. I am by no means claiming that they represent such summits that all earlier thought was merely so many preparations for them and later thought a simple decline after the miracles that they represent. What I do claim, however, is that for their successors they represented obligatory points of reference, and that those successors situated their own thought about divine law within the terrain that these three men had conquered.

This is why it seems to me permissible, in order to narrate the rest of this history, to change the style of my investigation and, above all, to accelerate its pace to give an overview of the post-medieval intellectual world.

PART VI

Sans Foi ni Loi:
Neither Faith nor Law?

Was ist aber unsinniger,
eine loi athée, ein Gesetz,
welches keinen Gott hat,
oder ein Dieu-loi,
ein Gott, der nur ein Gesetz ist?

—Heinrich Heine

14]ɞ··

The Modern Age:
Destruction of the Idea of Divine Law

Need I remark that this survey of the post-medieval intellectual landscape makes no pretense of presenting the entire evolution of practical philosophy—ethical, economic, political, and juridical— in the modern period? I shall permit myself to be highly schematic about modernity, given that one of my basic theses is, precisely, that in this case as perhaps elsewhere, the modern age did little but draw the consequences of decisions that had been taken long before. I shall limit my remarks to stressing certain key concepts that, as we have already seen, took form in the ancient world and peaked in the Middle Ages. My guiding thread will be, once again, the idea of divine law. I shall show how that concept underwent reinterpretation, to the point of losing its original meaning, at times of disappearing entirely.

First, the modern idea of divine law needs to be placed within the context of modernity in general.

Restructuring the Field of the Normative

We can observe, in fact, that modern times brought about a long-term tendency to redefine the entire area of what appears to have normative value. That redefinition affects the way in which modern thinkers rethought the articulation of the divine and the law. It is a change that merits a brief description.

Law and Counsel

I have recalled above the distinction between commandment and counsel; between what an authorized will imposes and what wisdom recommends, a distinction that is rooted in the Old and the New Testaments and was then passed on to the Fathers of the Church and to the medieval world as a whole.[1] Premodern times thrived on a dialectic between the two: the law bathed in counsel as in a nourishing environment. Counsel preceded the law that was based upon it, but it also surpassed the law by adding a further stage to it. On the one hand, the law was what had to be observed in order to assure the full deployment of a nature that, by that fact, realized what counsel wanted. On the other hand, counsel, in the form of evangelical advice, led to reaching beyond the minimal demands stated in the law and to striving for perfection.

The law was perceived as the accomplishment of a nature. The law as external commandment was not unfamiliar with the law as the internal rule of a being. Something resembling "autonomy" was there from the beginning, even before modernity, following Kant, raised it to the level of a supreme principle of morality. That "autonomy," however, was not a determination on the part of the subject, because it did not consist in a way for the subject to arrive at self-mastery—and because it did not in any manner derive from the dimension of mastery. That "autonomy" signified coincidence with the rule that constitutes all things as they are, not submission to the rule that a subject gives himself.

At a lower level and prior to the law, counsel needed to make its way to the law without hindering it, much like a preamble. This is why authors before the modern age demonstrate that paying attention to one's own benefit leads seamlessly to an attention to the good in general. For example, in antiquity the Stoic theory of *oikeiōsis* (in Latin, *commendatio*) expresses this viewpoint quite explicitly: the virtues elaborate and refine basic tendencies present from the beginning in all living creatures. Similarly, in the Middle Ages, Maimonides relates the parable of the child who begins to learn so that people will give him sweets, then gradually takes a liking to study, to the point of devoting himself to learning in a disinterested manner. Bernard of Clairvaux shows how the four degrees of charity emerge smoothly one from another, eventually reaching the surprising fourth degree, where "a man love[s] himself only for the sake of God."[2]

Moreover, its proximity to the law gave counsel something that raised it above itself. Because it perfected the law, it supposed a perfect and scrupulous fulfillment of the law as an indispensable preliminary requirement. This is why spiritual authors all insist on the necessity of not moving to a higher plane until one is fully compliant with the commandments: one should not enter into the "Garden" without a stomach weighted down with a detailed knowledge of the commandments. One should even be ready at any moment to return from the highest mystical experience to fulfill the humblest duty; leaving the "third heaven" to give a slice of bread to a poor man, for example.[3]

With the modern age, the two poles of law and counsel separated, each going its own way in a pursuit of extremes.

Counsel underwent a dual evolution. On the one hand, the lower level of counsel, left to its own devices in regard to the law, no longer constituted a pedagogical preparation for the plenitude of the law. Egoism, or *philautia*, lost its pejorative meaning at the cost of a change of name, becoming "interest."[4] Counsels of prudence concentrated on advising people to seek their interest—a remarkable bit of advice, given that its content is the very essence of counsel. It is true that in antiquity, Aristotle placed the essence of "prudence" (*phronesis*) in seeking the good for oneself;[5] but this prudence was insufficient for determining the good. With the modern age, to the contrary, it was as if the use of the concept of interest consisted in rendering superfluous that determination of the good by replacing it with pure care for oneself. Liberal thought moved unanimously in that direction. Montesquieu, among the moderates, states in his praise of commerce that it places men in a situation in which, "though their passions inspire in them the thought of being wicked, they nevertheless have an interest in not being so."[6] It was probably the English and the Scottish thinkers, from Bernard Mandeville to David Hume and Adam Smith, who moved most radically in this direction, going to far as to show that virtue can be superfluous or even counterproductive.

The higher level of counsel, on the other hand, which came after the law, became detached from obedience to the law. This can go so far as to reverse the relationship between the obligatory and the optional. For example, for the revolutionary, counsel is obligatory and the commandments are optional and subject to an evaluation of their tactical value. The revolutionary must live in chastity, poverty, and obedience, but he has the right to kill, steal, and lie if it advances the cause.[7]

The law, for its part, extricated itself from the counsels that formed a protective gangue around it, now showing forth in its full might as commandment. This was the result of a long-term evolution that had begun within scholasticism. In part following Ockhamist theology, the law was defined more and more explicitly on the basis of an exclusion of the idea of counsel to the advantage of the idea of sanctioned obligation. Francisco Suárez arrived at his concept of the law as *praeceptum* by seeking a definition capable to excluding all traces of counsel.[8] For the moderns, that reduction became an axiom. For example, Jean Bodin (d. 1596) distinguishes between *droit* (right) and *loi* (law), defining the latter as "nothing but the commandment of the sovereign, using his power." Consequently, everything that might claim to be a law without presenting itself as a commandment is relegated to the realm of metaphor.[9]

If it were to distance itself strongly from counsel, the law had to avoid pulling in the same direction. Thus the law manifests itself in its full purity when it takes the opposite course from counsel. It can even come to the point of seeming to be pure repression of the natural. It is perhaps in Montesquieu that it can first be seen in that guise.[10] It was probably Kant, however, who gave this position its most impressive presentation: for him the law must be purely formal, repressing anything that derives from affect, desires, and tastes—all of which he calls "pathological."

A similar evolution appeared in the human type taken as the exemplification of goodness. The virtuous man or the saint, even the Stoic sage in his harmony with the cosmos, were beautiful: Goethe could still admire St. Philip Neri. In the modern age, the altruistic moral hero (Dickens's Sidney Carton, Tolstoy's Platon Karatayev) is sublime. We thus can observe in the ethical domain the same evolution from the beautiful to the sublime that occurred in the cosmological realm.[11]

The Laws of Nature

Still, the upheaval in the economy of the notion of law remains incomprehensible unless one takes into account the sudden arrival of a new player in a game that had, up to that point, defined varieties of law in relation to one another, and in particular, divine law within the entire set of laws. This was the idea of the "laws of nature" by which modern mathematical physics understands its object.[12] To be sure, ancient thought spoke from time to time of "laws of nature," if that is indeed the meaning that should be given to the Greek *nomos*.[13] It was only with Descartes, however, that the modern notion of a law of nature was most fully thought through.[14] The meaning of the term "law of nature" is obviously dependent on the meaning of "nature," and the way in which nature was perceived underwent a decisive change at the dawn of the modern period. The laws involved are essentially the laws of motion, and it was precisely the conception of the motion that changed with regard to the premodern model, the essence of which came from Aristotle. Moreover, that change brought the very idea of nature, with motion as its basic trait, to a turning point.

The premodern concept of law was in fact based on a concept of nature that was also premodern. That concept of law remained for the most part implicit, but it was stated explicitly when it was threatened by the concept of scientific law. We can see this at the end of the sixteenth century in Richard Hooker's examination of the sort of motion that is neither violent nor accidental (that is to say, that is natural). He writes: "That which doth assigne unto each thing the kinde, that which doth moderate the force and power, that which doth appoint the forme and measure of working, the same we tearme a *Lawe*."[15] The same concept appears again in the early eighteenth century in A. M. Ramsay, who declares, taking his inspiration from Fénelon, "The law in general is nothing else than the Rule which each Being ought to follow, in order to act according to his Nature."[16]

The idea of a divine law subsists in this context, but at the price of a profound change of meaning. In fact, in order for the modern concept of law of nature to make sense, a God is needed, and a God characterized by the fundamental trait of all-powerfulness: "The lawgiver of nature is freed from His own laws."[17] Descartes asserts: "It is God who has established the laws of nature [eternal mathematical truths], as a King establishes laws in his Kingdom." Such laws, Descartes continues, are innate, "*inborn in our minds, as a king would establish his laws in the heart of his subjects, if he had power enough to do so.*"[18] In the modern concept of law, the fundamental distinction between the descriptive and the normative—between the laws of nature and the laws of the political community—must pass through a normative moment, and even pass through an intensification of the norm's imperative dimension. In fact, the laws that an all-powerful God imposes on his creatures cannot be other than the laws that nature follows absolutely. In the case of an absolute imperative, the normative and the descriptive coincide. Spinoza understood this well, and he criticizes the use of the term "laws of nature," which he views as purely metaphorical: God is such that his laws are obeyed in all circumstances, and hence they coincide with the totality of events.[19]

The law of God is identified with the laws of nature, and it, too, moves to the plural. Thus Hobbes writes that "the laws of nature [are] divine," and that "the laws of God . . . are none but the laws of nature."[20] The idea of a law of nature existed before this revolution, but in the singular. Its shift to the plural implies the disappearance of the idea of a global order, replaced by a collection of constant and observable relations. Science after Galileo even reflects on what is implied by the idea of laws of nature; it gives up the search for causes. Science in the modern age, as Auguste Comte writes, has quite deliberately substituted for "the inaccessible determination of causes . . . a simple search for laws—that is, for the constant relations that exist between observable phenomena."[21] With positivism, however, the indistinct figure of the clockmaker God invoked by the Deists of the eighteenth century became superfluous: there was no longer any need to claim to found observable regularities in nature on the divine; soon, what is more—beginning in the nineteenth century—thinkers preferred not to speak of "laws" at all, instead simply writing the equations that were a condensation of such laws or speaking vaguely of "formulas" or "principles."

Between Description and Norm

A break within the notion of law threatened its unity, indeed, if not reducing that unity to pure equivocality. "Law" has in fact a descriptive meaning and a normative meaning; the same word, in an ambiguity that is perhaps not totally accidental,[22] designates both a constant relation among phenomena and an arbitrary commandment. There was no lack of attempts to envision these two dimensions of the law as a unified whole, as is the case in Malebranche's works. Pushing the Cartesian revolution to an extreme, Malebranche reduces the notion of nature to that of law: "What is called *nature* is nothing other than the general laws which God has established to construct or to preserve his work by very simple means, by an action which is uniform, constant, perfectly worthy of an infinite wisdom and of a universal cause."[23] Malebranche founds his ethics on the idea of Order, which he calls, indifferently, "Divine Law" and "law of God": "It is the obedience we render to Order, our submission to the Divine Law, which is virtue in the complete sense."[24]

The dominant tendency in modernity is to separate the two notions, however. Once separated, each forced the other to move to a more extreme position. Kant formulated his position on moral law in its absolute purity in reaction to the way that Galilean and Newtonian science formulated physical laws. Moreover, for Kant, the presence of the moral law within us is precisely what proves our freedom from the natural laws.

As we have just seen, the discovery of the law as a constant relationship among phenomena, hence as simple description, was possible only by an indirect route in which the notion of law takes on absolute normativity. The laws of nature are the laws that God imposed on his creatures, and the absoluteness of the power of God has as an effect that the orders that he gives cannot help but be followed. What some read as the pure will of the Creator can also be read as nothing but the result of a divine commandment. As it happens, the fact that divine law should appear as being simply a commandment supposes an entire prehistory: the presence of the Creator within the created must first be reduced to that of a pure imperative. A reduction of the sort can be seen in the late Middle Ages. In the early Middle Ages, Augustine still saw in the law *either* reason *or* the will of God—a will distinguishable from simple caprice by the presence of reason within it. The modern conception of the law was prepared by a long-term shift to the primacy of the will.[25] The law eventually came to be reduced to the divine will: the Swiss reformer Zwingli states, for example, "The law is none else than the eternal will of God."[26] This voluntarist conception of the law found expression in Duns Scotus (d. 1308), then in William of Ockham (d. 1349), for whom all law, divine or human, is positive.[27] That conception fits within an overall movement that shifts the center of gravity of the divine attributes from wisdom toward power, a shift that was perceived fairly early on.[28] Omnipotence became independent and general, splitting off from the paternity that it originally qualified, as expressed in the *Credo,* which confesses "the Almighty *Father (patrem omnipotentem)."* It was henceforth considered as the general regime of the relationship of God to the created; it designated the immediate, therefore irresistible, character of divine intervention in nature. In making this shift, Christian theology echoed motifs that recall and were perhaps indirectly derived from the Muslim Kalām.[29]

Consequently, the divine law was understood above all as the expression of the will of God imposed on things already created, and no longer as the impression of divine wisdom on the very nature of the created. It became difficult to conceive of a law that would not be positive—that is, the result of a willed decision. Thus Marsilius of Padua (d. 1324), for example, crushes natural law between the two positive laws, human and divine.[30] The evolution of the way in which God was represented ran parallel to a similar shift in the representation of man and of man's expected response to God. Before, what was stressed was man's acceptance of entering into a filial relation with God, an acceptance freely exercised, before freeing liberty itself to higher flights. Now the relationship of God's creatures to God consisted in a simple obedience in which the created bows before the divine commands.

With these shifts, the notion of law escapes from the human sphere. As natural law—in the sense of the physical laws—it governs nature, henceforth conceived of as that which has nothing in common with man, to the point that man is incapable of understanding it. As moral law, it dictates to the rational being conduct to be followed in general—and there is nothing that tells us whether that rational being is a man or, let us say, an angel.[31] To call a law of this sort "divine" is simply pasting a traditional adjective on this radical alterity.

Faced with a law that contained nothing of the human, there arose, in reaction, a law that was nothing but human.

The Anthropological Reduction

The birth of a wholly human law was at first a consequence of the modification of the notion of the law of nature. When the latter became a metaphor for natural regularities, it rebounded back to the meaning that the notion of law itself received in its original domain of practice and practical norms.

Man as the Sole Lawgiver

The "law of nature" was a metaphor. In compensation, law in the strict sense was conceived of as what *cannot* be natural. Even the human comes to be conceived of as not natural, as what tears itself away from nature. The law, because it is not natural, must therefore be something purely human. We can see this in Spinoza, who supposes the law, by definition, to be of human origin. A law is "a prescribed rule of conduct (*ratio vivendi*) that man prescribes for himself or that he prescribes for others with some aim in mind." If there is a divine law, it is inscribed in the human mind. The divinity of a law thus has nothing to do with its origin, but rather with the nature of the goal at which it aims. In this Spinoza is returning to a criterion expressed by Maimonides; he states: "By human law I mean a rule of living which serves no other purpose than to preserve life and the state"; divine law is "one whose sole object is the supreme good, that is, true knowledge and love of God."[32]

The reduction of the idea of law to a purely human phenomenon is clearly visible in Montesquieu, whose *Esprit des lois* probably represents the broadest synthesis regarding the law that the eighteenth century produced. Montesquieu seems unaware of medieval thought regarding the law. Like most of the authors of his age, he speaks of scholasticism only with scorn. He never mentions Suárez. He cites Thomas Aquinas only once, in a response to the Faculty of Theology, in which he refers to a short treatise on usury. Montesquieu uses the expression "divine law," as opposed to "purely philosophical ideas" derived from Aristotle, in connection with arguments drawn from the Bible and the Fathers of the Church.[33] Finally, in his central work, which is far from brief, Montesquieu uses the expression "divine laws"—in the plural—only in the title of a chapter that distinguishes between divine and human laws.[34]

The *Esprit des lois*, Montesquieu's principal work, opens with a definition: "Laws, taken in the broadest meaning, are the necessary relations deriving from the nature of things."[35] It is remarkable to begin with a plural: at this level, we will never know what is *the* law. Montesquieu goes on to state: "the divinity has its laws." The formula presents nothing new. As we have seen, it is frequent in medieval texts.[36] What is original is Montesquieu's explanation of it: "God is related to the universe, as creator and preserver; the laws according to which he created are those according to which he preserves; he acts according to these rules because he knows them; he knows them because he made them; he made them because they are related to his wisdom and power."[37] God knows what he does and knows because it is he who has done it.[38] Thus laws are a creation; they come to be added to things once those things are created; they are not the very structure of created things.

Shortly after this passage, Montesquieu gives a second definition of law, this time in the singular: "Law in general is human reason insofar as it governs all the peoples of the earth."[39] It is interesting to note that Montesquieu speaks specifically of *human* reason. Elsewhere he quotes and translates the Stoic definition of the "true and primal" law given by Cicero as *divine* reason or the "right reason of supreme Jupiter" (*ratio est recta summi Iovis*).[40] He may even have thought of using this classical formula as an epigraph to the *Esprit des lois*. He omitted it from the published version, however, thus showing that in his more mature thought he no longer embraced it as his own. This omission is a discreet but revealing sign of a desire to break with tradition.

The Pressure of Society on Itself

Our contemporary societies consider themselves to be democratic. That adjective has taken on a different meaning from the one it had in ancient Greece: the subject who holds force (*kratos*) now tends to be the people as a whole, rather than a clubby group of non-slave males. On a deeper level, the force exerted has changed nature. The people has inherited the sovereignty that the popes claimed as theirs in the Middle Ages and kings as theirs at the dawn of modern times. The people gave a universal extension to that sovereignty: as the sole source of political legitimacy, it tends to become the source of all ethical value as well. The law is reduced to being simply the convention of a society as it organizes itself. The term "autonomy" takes on a totally new meaning to describe this situation.

On the theoretical level, the relations between the descriptive and the normative are presented in a new light: the distinction between being ("is," *Sein*) and the should-be ("ought," *Sollen*), which has become the first lesson of moral philosophy, appeared only in the late eighteenth century, the effect of a hatchet blow delivered in Scotland by David Hume and in Prussia by Immanuel Kant.[41] In practice, however, and perhaps in compensation for the first phenomenon, modern societies exist as if exerting a pressure on themselves that tends to identify what is with what should be. That seemingly gentle pressure may turn out in fact to be more tyrannical than ever.[42] The new focus on the notion of normality bears witness to this. The norm as a rule of law, and before that, according to the etymology of the word (*norma*), as the rectilineal, becomes the "normal," a term that combines description and valorization. Society defends that norm by deploying a system of discipline with which it merges.[43]

Instrumentalization of the Divine

If all political law is human, the divine laws must also be, in the final analysis, a product of the wiliness of certain particularly clever men. Thus Machiavelli presents recourse to God as a wise move on the part of those who want to establish laws that go beyond what is commonly accepted (*ordinare . . . leggi straordinarie*). The clever man knows what is good, but others do not find those goods obvious enough to be persuasive.[44] Thus it is to the extent that it is civil that the law requires an appeal—of pure imagination, to be sure— to the divine authority. For Machiavelli, who reconnects here with the Hellenistic and medieval thinkers, the founders of religions are lawgivers, Moses just as well as Lycurgus or Solon. The first laws—the ones that are truly "extraordinary" in that they precede all order and lay the foundations for order—are those that institute a religion, and hence that cannot be based on that religion. Religion introduces something more to be feared than the laws, which is God.[45] In a similar spirit, Montesquieu states in an essay written around 1725: "Any law, without which [society] could not exist, becomes by that token a divine law." This idea should perhaps be connected to the notion that the first concern of providence is the health of the state.[46] *It is where it is not divine, indeed, it is because it is not divine, that law has need of the divine.*

This is why the Enlightenment thinkers, in spite of their stated desire to break with what later became known as the ancien régime, returned to the vocabulary of the sacrality of the law. Rousseau, within a critique of Christianity, sketched out the idea of a "Civil Religion." Among the articles comprising the very simple dogmas of that religion, he mentions the "sanctity of . . . the Laws."[47] Later, the legislators of the French Revolution declared certain rights "inviolable and sacred." First among these was the right of ownership.[48] Incidentally, it is amusing to note that, in practice, recourse to the notion of the sacred served above all to guarantee the rights of those acquiring goods that were declared "national"—that is, goods that resulted from the despoilation of the church. Thus sacralization serves here to cover up a secularization and, if I may be permitted the play on words, to consecrate a desacralization. The contemporary ideology of the "rights of man" makes use of an analogous operation: the more it appeals to a sacralizing rhetoric, the more it avoids evoking to what source "man" owes the humanity that renders him capable of having rights.

In the period that followed the French Revolution, the idea of divine law did not totally disappear. Occurrences of it can be found in the nineteenth century, but its treatment empties it of all content, which is perhaps worse than simply being forgotten.

Austin

One example of that tactic is the English jurist John Austin (1790–1859), a disciple of Bentham and one of the last authors to maintain the idea of divine law within the framework of a general theory of legislation. He asserts in his lectures *The Province of Jurisprudence Determined,* published in 1832, that "the divine law is the measure or test of positive law and morality."[49] Austin defines God as "the intelligent and rational Nature which is the soul and the guide of the universe," and as "the Author of man's nature." God's law is either revealed or not revealed: Austin does not develop the former sort very much, and he makes only vague allusions to prophecy and the sacred texts.[50]

When the law is not revealed and the commandment remains tacit, by what means, what indications, do we recognize it? Not by a supposed moral sense, and even less by any practical reason, but rather by the principle of general utility, which is in turn deduced from the wisdom and the benevolence of God.[51] Here Austin reflects a current of thought present in another utilitarian philosopher, John Stuart Mill, and even in their common target, William Blackstone.[52] Austin defines positive law as "fashioned on the law of God as conjectured by the light of utility." For him, the divine law is "known through" or construed by "the principle of utility." What the common good demands becomes what God demands.[53]

For Austin, a law consists essentially in a commandment, which relegates the laws of physics and biology to the realm of metaphor.[54] The commandment can be distinguished by the threat of a sanction. God thus appears as one who can inflict punishments by making people suffer. Austin does not mention the symmetrical idea of rewards, and as a Unitarian thinker he seems unaware of the notion of a divine plan of salvation. Nor is there any question of representing God as himself subject to a law. Austin can thus speak of the law of God *or* of Nature.[55]

Why, then, should Austin choose to designate that law as "divine"? Because, he responds, the "divine law" represents "the only natural law about which it is possible to speak without a metaphor," hence because it permits, precisely, avoiding the "ambiguous and misleading" appellation "Law of Nature."[56] In this manner, invoking God allows Austin to win two games at once. On the one hand, that discreet God presents the advantage of founding a law that is sufficiently natural to permit man to rearrange its content to suit himself. On the other hand, the presence of God prohibits hypostatizing a Nature to which man would have little choice but to subject himself.

Religious Space

It is not merely by chance that a thinker like Austin can conceive, somewhat summarily, of a God who is lawgiver in that he exercises an authority that takes on concrete form in his capacity to punish. Along with many others, Austin places himself in a line of thought that had opened up long before him and that tended to reduce the religious to the legislative, or at least to think of the religious in terms of legislation. This was a reduction that took place within the religious domain.

Paradoxically, the Reformation represents an important stage in that reduction. Luther initially set off the Reformation by returning to St. Paul's polemic regarding faith alone, against law. Luther redirected that polemic, however, aiming it at the very thing that, for the medieval church, was supposed to replace the law. To be sure, he accords a central position to the notion of grace, but he separates grace from its concrete form within an economy that uses the sacraments as a means of salvation. In reality, Luther's ultra-Pauline position turned out, rather oddly, to be a renewed valorization of the Old Testament, as is manifest in the cultures influenced by the Reformation. For thinkers after Luther, the question of the validity of the biblical laws regarding social organization (called "judiciary" laws) was posed anew, and if Luther himself rejected them, others (Zwingli, for one) accepted them.[57]

A certain trend in apologetics set out to justify Christianity by explaining that it constituted the religion closest to natural law. Among the authors of utopias, the imaginary peoples that these authors describe have a religion that represents the closest possible approximation to Christianity, which they would adopt if they knew it. This is the case, for example, in both Thomas More and Tommaso Campanella.[58] Whatever the intentions of these quite different authors may have been, they both risked the retort that man might well be content with that natural law and do without the concretions added by Christianity, or in fact do without any religion at all.

Within the thought that emerged from Christianity or turned against it, Christianity came to be perceived in terms of juridical categories. The formula that called Jesus "Lawgiver of the Christians" had appeared in certain Fathers of the Church, and it had not totally disappeared during the Middle Ages. It returned in the eighteenth century, both among the critics of Christianity and among its defenders.[59] The formula came to be seen as a catchword of "Enlightened" rhetoric, which means that the adversaries of the Enlightenment treated it with derision. This is true of Chateaubriand (who uses the phrase, however) and later of Baudelaire.[60] The phrase presents the drawback of suggesting the existence of a "Christian morality" whose "laws" differ from the laws that invite all men to be true to their own humanity.

Kant

The tendency to place the notion of the law at the center of religion found a rigorous culmination in the work of Kant, who rethought the entire field of moral reflection on the basis of the notion of commandment. The moral law that commands me, with no hope of appeal, has no need of a source, and even less so if the law must draw its legitimacy from that source. God is in no way the foundation of moral obligation, and especially not if we are to imagine him making use of his omnipotence to take revenge on offenses against his desire for glory and domination.[61] Moral law rests on no religious foundation; to the contrary, religion is defined on the basis of moral law. Kant states that religion is

> the recognition of all duties as divine commands, not as sanctions, i.e., arbitrary and contingent ordinances of a foreign will, but as essential laws of any free will as such. Even as such, they must be regarded as commands of the Supreme Being, because we can hope for the highest good (to strive for which is made our duty by the moral law) only from a morally perfect (holy and beneficent) and omnipotent will; and, therefore, we can hope to attain it only through harmony with this will.[62]

It is our duty to seek the sovereign good—that is, the agreement of virtue and happiness. Its realization postulates not only the liberty of man but also the existence of an all-powerful God and the immortality of the human soul.

Kant conceives of God as the lawgiver of the moral world. When he speaks of divine law, it is in order to stress the necessity that it appear, at the same time, as a law of nature. He joins the ancient quarrel on the origin of values, insisting on their objectivity: evil is not what it is because God is supposed to have prohibited it; to the contrary, God prohibits it because evil is wicked in itself. To back up his point, he distinguishes between the legislator and the author of the laws. The two roles are not necessarily identical: one cannot say of the prince who prohibits theft in his land that he is the author of the prohibition against stealing: "The law that is within us we call conscience."[63]

The book in which Kant provides a systematic exposition of his philosophy of religion devotes a paragraph to the divine commandments in which

he reduces them to simple moral commandments.[64] Man's obligations toward his fellow man are simultaneously and from the start divine commandments. He groups together all of the commandments contained in books
that claim to be revealed under the term "statutory (*statutarisch*) commandments." Whereas the moral commandments are dictated by the conscience,
a revelation addressed to a particular group is needed to clarify to the conscience the way in which it should worship God. As a result, Kant concludes,
"the one true religion comprises nothing but laws" rather than "statutes,
i.e., ordinances held to be divine, which are arbitrary and contingent as
viewed by our pure moral judgment."[65]

Romanticism and Restoration

Accompanying the tendency that makes religion a simple appendix to morality, a second trend sees a specific reality in religion. Kant tipped the legislative
to the moral side. The Protestant theologian Friedrich Schleiermacher went
further, not only stripping the religious experience of all legislative dimension, but even prohibiting it. A religion, in his opinion, can have no claim
to pass laws: religion, he writes, "has no right to utilize the universe in order to deduce duties; it does not have the right to contain a code of laws."[66]

The notion of divine law persisted into the nineteenth century, but the
French Revolution created a new situation that affected it in two ways. On
the one hand, the partisans of the new order reinterpreted the idea of divine
law, giving it a metaphorical sense. This is the case with Chateaubriand in
his later days, for whom Christianity "contains the three great laws of the
universe, divine law, moral law, political law: the divine law, unity of God in
three Persons; the moral law, *charity;* and the political law, that is, liberty,
equality, fraternity."[67] Equating divine law with the Trinity does more honor
to the writer than to the theologian.

On the other hand, the partisans of the Restoration of Louis XVIII in
1814 understood the idea of the divine law in relation to a backward-looking
dream of a unification of the political and the religious. For example, the
German Friedrich von Gentz (d. 1832) writes that it would be a good thing
"to reestablish religion—not only as *faith,* but as *law.* . . . Never will religion
be reestablished as *faith* if it is not first restored as *law.*"[68] When Joseph de
Maistre speaks of divine law, it is at times in order to proclaim a general law
of history, and at other times to name an absolute point of reference as the
sole standard by which to measure the justice of human laws.[69] His doctrine
regarding the origin of norms is medieval, however: "Laws come from God
in the sense that he wills that there should be laws and that they should be
obeyed: yet those laws come also from men in that they are made by men."[70]

The most lucid defenders of the idea of progress retained a sometimes nostalgic awareness of the losses that are the price of all progress and of the need to find ways to compensate for them. Auguste Comte describes historical evolution as moving from the theological age to arrive at the positive age, but he chooses to retain the medieval idea of a spiritual power.[71] After Comte, those who practiced the science for which he had coined a name, sociology, occasionally insisted on the need of religion for the social existence of man.

The Historicization of Divine Law

A generation later, Western thought had become historical, and it returned to the connection between the law and the divine. The historicization of the idea of divine law was in fact a highly honorable burial. Historical study of the law arose within the context of the Restoration in France. Its aim was to counter the attempt, born of the French Revolution, to fabricate juridical rules out of nothing (criticized, for example, by Edmund Burke) by emphasizing the fact that systematic law develops by organic growth. It is within this context that the German jurist Friedrich Carl von Savigny (d. 1861) saluted the awakening of the "historical sense," an expression that he invented.[72] Fifty years later the perspective had changed, however, and historians were more interested in setting a distance between themselves and the past rather than in placing themselves in its trajectory.

I would like to offer here a brief presentation of three examples of that historical viewpoint regarding divine law: in the early 1860s, almost simultaneously, Henry Sumner Maine in England, Johann Jakob Bachofen in German Switzerland, and Numa Denis Fustel de Coulanges in France investigated the sacral roots of the law. Their overall perspective was the idea of progress (a legacy from the Enlightenment), complicated by the idea of biological evolution, which was already in the air when Charles Darwin endowed it with an experimental base in 1859. From then on, the divine was reduced to the idea of a sacrality supposed to be primitive and perceived as a foil to the reestablishment of a purely rational legislation that seemed to constitute the program of an enlightened West.

Maine

In 1861, the English jurist Henry Sumner Maine took on the task of applying to the study of the law the historical method that had given good results in other domains from geology to philology—a method accompanied by a belief in the moral progress of humanity. Maine's book purported to show the superiority of a method that offered the advantage of doing away with such fictions of the modern age as the state of nature and, along with it, the social contract that was supposed to have brought that state to an end.[73] As with Montesquieu before him, that method annihilates the idea of a law of nature, its great opponent. Better, it shows the essentially historical character of anything that claims to hover over becoming.[74] For Maine, the idea of a natural law originated in the need to find principles to use in the integration of foreigners who had no legal status in ancient Rome. The rules for foreigners, called *jus gentium*, were later combined with the Greek idea of a law of nature.[75]

As for the original state of societies, Maine considers the basic social unit not to be the individual but the group and above all the family. He does not base kinship on a collective cult, however. He remarks that at a very early period, the respect for rites and ceremonies was decisive for the juridical value of transactions.[76] Maine never treats religion as a theme: it appears under its own name only in a very general manner in his work, merged with the law or immobilizing the law. At the most, Maine notes the influence of the church on institutions and that of the canon law on the evolution of Western law in general.[77]

Maine was aware of the idea that certain prescriptions are of divine origin, but his overall view of history sees the individual moving to free himself from the group: human relations pass from statute to contract. As a corollary, the law leaves the religious sphere. For Maine, it was in Roman law—which stands in extreme contrast to Hindu law—that the law had broken its primitive attachment to religion.[78]

Bachofen

In 1861, the same year that Maine published his *Ancient Law*, a jurist in Basle, Johann Jakob Bachofen, who had been a pupil of Savigny, published a voluminous work in which he set himself the task of establishing the existence of a primitive matriarchate. His overall viewpoint was historical distance: the domain that he was studying, he explains, was the one in which "the absolute antithesis between our present-day thinking and that of antiquity is nowhere so startlingly disclosed as in the field upon which we are entering."[79]

Bachofen saw history as advancing from the maternal principle to the paternal one, both of which he depicts with their various harmonic overtones: "The destination of the human species consists in surpassing, more and more, the law of matter and raising itself up above that material side of man's nature according to which he resembles the rest of the animal world, toward a higher and more pure human existence." Moreover, "One great law governs the juridical development of man. It advances from the material to the immaterial, from the physical to the metaphysical, from tellurism to spirituality. . . . What begins materially must end immaterially."[80]

Initially, "justice forms a part of religion," and the various levels of family law are dependent on a number of corresponding religious ideas, in particular, that of Mother Earth.[81] This is why "the principle that stands at the summit of material creation must also be the source and foundation of a justice concerned solely with the material life of man." The idea of justice is simply the consequence of the initial freedom and equality of the children of one mother, the earth: the physical concept of earth broadens to become a juridical concept, and the maternal quality of matter gives birth to the idea of justice. This is why the law is a priestly activity—that of the priests of Aphrodite.[82] It follows that "the ancient *jus naturale* is thus not, like what is called by the same name today, a pure philosophical speculation. It is a historical event, a stage in civilization, older than the purely positive law of States, an expression of the most primitive religious idea, a monument to lived human relations, as historical as the maternal Law, which is itself a part of that event."[83]

Fustel de Coulanges

In 1864, Numa-Denis Fustel de Coulanges, who had probably not read his two predecessors' works, attempted a global description of the ancient city. He proposed to show by that description the extent to which the liberty of the moderns could not point to that of the ancients as an example. In this, Fustel returned to the accusations of Hobbes, who viewed classical studies as a source of sedition. Fustel's prime target, however, was Rousseau and his revolutionary posterity, who were obsessed with the Roman example.[84]

The basic reality governing the ancient city, and from which it would gradually emancipate itself, is religious in nature. That religion was familial before being civic. Fustel treats ancient law in a separate chapter in which he states his central thesis: "Law was first a part of religion." Regarding those laws, he adds, "No man invented them." Laws "presented themselves without being sought. They were the direct and necessary consequence of the belief; they were religion itself applied to the relations of men among themselves. . . . The veritable legislator among the ancients was not a man, but the religious belief which men entertained."[85] This explains a good many characteristics of ancient law: the laws are never abrogated; they include no explanations for a law and no judges' reasons for their decisions; originally they were unwritten, learned by heart, and chanted; their wording was held secret; they were valid only for citizens. "Ancient law," Fustel concludes, "was not the work of a legislator; it was, on the contrary, imposed upon the legislator."[86]

Fustel expresses his own judgment on the limitations of ancient law. He quite clearly does not share the vision of reality of the ancient world. The ancients' belief was sincere and in no way an imposture, but it was false; an alienation: "A belief is the work of our mind, but we are not on that account free to modify it at will. It is our own creation, but we do not know it. It is human, and we believe it is a god. It is the effect of our power, and it is stronger than we are. . . . Those gods, so powerful and so beneficent, were nothing but the beliefs of men." As for the content of the law: "The ancient law, because it conformed itself to religion, misunderstood nature."[87] This system thus came undone (in a process to which Fustel devotes an entire chapter), with the result that "the principle of the law, henceforth, is the interest of men."[88] That evolution in fact began so early that we can already see it taking place in the earliest documents we possess. Hence a purely religious law exists more as the result of a reconstruction of the prehistorical than as the object of an exploration of the givens of history.

The three authors whom I have just presented opened the way to a sociological study of religious phenomena. That study has developed from Durkheim and Max Weber until our own day, and it has produced a number of masterpieces. Faithful to its methodological postulates, sociology sets aside all claims to validity of the objects that it studies. It reduces the notion of divine law, in particular, to the content of an opinion that has left traces in the history of societies and produced effects within that history, but sociology has nothing to say about its truth.

15

Judaism and Islam in the Modern Age

To treat Judaism and Islam, I will need to place them after Christianity, reversing the order in which the three religions have appeared thus far. In the modern age, it was in fact a world permeated by Christianity that prompted the movements that modified the two other religions: events that had their epicenter in the Christian world produced upheavals in Muslim societies and Jewish communities, and thinkers who were Christian in origin furnished the conceptual framework within which Judaism and Islam had to reformulate their thinking about the law. Moreover, when Jewish and Muslim thinkers returned to the problem of the connection between the political and the religious, they tended to view that connection from an "Euromorphic" perspective—that is, with the aid of concepts that have little meaning outside of a Christian context. For example, they apply the distinction between church and state to human groups that, although they certainly have a religious dimension, cannot in themselves be understood in the same terms as the Christian church. Thus Moses Mendelssohn speaks of "the Synagogue," even of "the Mosque," to speak, not of buildings, but rather of all Jewish or Muslim believers. Or, turning the image around, Rashīd Rida speaks of the "separation of Church and State" in connection with Atatürk's abolition of the caliphate.[1]

I shall discuss Judaism first, given that it entered into the sphere of influence of modern European thought before Islam.

Judaism

Overall Tendencies

The entry of Judaism into modern times can be dated by the defeat of the last messianic movement, symbolized by Sabbatai Tzevi (1666). Two changes were taking place in the Jewish world. On the one hand, it divided into tendencies, one of which, Reformed Judaism, abandoned some of the ceremonial commandments. On the other hand, political emancipation, which began in central Europe and was later furthered by France, allowed the Jews to evolve within the same world as the other European groups and, in particular, to speak freely in the same languages that they spoke.

Beginning in the nineteenth century, Jewish thinkers offered a critique of Christianity, one theme in which is, precisely, the Law as a value, where they accuse Christianity of "anomism." One of the first to express this criticism, Joseph Salvador (in a book published in 1838), created the neologism *légicide* to parallel the *déicide* perpetrated by the Romans against Christ and the Romans' *populicide* of the Jewish people.[2] Judaism reacted to Christianity's reproach to it of "legalism" (following the tradition of St. Paul) by moving to a broader concept of the Torah, even going beyond the received meaning of the term "torah" as "law" to an interpretation more faithful to its original meaning as "teaching."[3]

An observable tendency within modern Judaism reduces the biblical history to a message and, within that message, to the *halakhah*, thus making the *haggadah* optional—a tendency that has its source in Spinoza.[4] Even among religious thinkers, the law takes on a sort of independence from the divine. Far from deriving its validity from its divine origin, the law gives a content to the idea of divinity. This can lead to somewhat risky formulations such as, in Emmanuel Lévinas, "loving the Torah more than God."[5]

Finally, and paradoxically, the idea of the law survived both secularization and loss of belief in its divine origin. It remained a recurrent theme among thinkers of Jewish origin, even among those who had abandoned the idea of God in favor of an impersonal structure that governs all things human, be their field sociology or cybernetics, including structural anthropology.[6]

Views of the Law

Judaism in the modern period saw a number of attempts to rethink its essence and its historical mission and, in particular, to provide a theory of the Law, which the Middle Ages had viewed as divine, that would express its singularity. Since full examination of all of these attempts is out of the question, I shall summarize four of them here. Three are from German Judaism, from one end of its historical career to the other; the fourth offers an example of thought after the extermination of European Judaism.

Moses Mendelssohn (d. 1786), who lived in the age of the Enlightenment, refocused Judaism on the idea of divine law. Against the rationalist conception of revelation as the communication of indisputable verities, he stressed that "Judaism knows nothing of a *revealed religion.* . . . The Israelites possess a *divine legislation.*" The eternal verities have no need to be revealed or, for even better reason, to be commanded: a Jew does not receive an order to believe, but to act.[7] What God commands him to do is of a purely moral character. Mendelssohn draws a distinction between religion as individual conviction and the Torah as fidelity to traditional usages. He sees in the laws that he calls "ceremonial," according to a translation from the Hebrew *huqqim* that has become classic even within Judaism, a perpetual commentary on the moral commandments.[8]

Hermann Cohen (d. 1918) presented Judaism as a "religion of reason," in the spirit of Kant. For Cohen, the notion of law is present from the beginning; it is inherent in reason, which is the "organ of the laws." Religion is added to morality to prevent it from being uniquely law and norm.[9] God appears less as the source of the law or a quality of the law than as the Law itself: God coincides with a certain legality that guarantees "the agreement between theoretical causality and ethical teleology."[10] Thus Cohen remains within the boundaries of Kant's thought: God is one of the postulates that permit the realization of the sovereign good by assuring that happiness can not only be merited, but obtained.

Franz Rosenzweig (d. 1929) went back from the idea of law to that of commandment. The commandment is to the law as the name is to the object and as revelation is to creation.[11] At the center is the commandment by which God demands love. That commandment is situated in the instant, unlike the law, which introduces the notion of time. Since the commandment to love is the only one that is nothing but a commandment, it is the supreme commandment. Loving one's neighbor is the content of all the commandments: it is the presence of that love that saves commandments from having the fixity of laws and makes them living commandments.[12] One effect of the law is that the present world can no longer be distinguished from the world to come. Rosenzweig reinvests the explications of the Talmud, and even of the Kabbalah, with meaning regarding the reason for fulfilling the law, not out of personal interest, not to obtain terrestrial satisfactions, but in order to "unite God and the *shekhinah*" (the divine presence in the world).[13] Rosenzweig says this, in part, in response to Martin Buber, who, according to Rosenzweig, shrinks the law, when he speaks of it, to fit the way in which nineteenth-century orthodoxy viewed it. That law is not valid uniquely because it was given on Mount Sinai, but also because it preexists the world and includes elements still waiting to be deduced from it. The law must once more become a commandment, and a commandment that is translated into act in the very instant that it is perceived.[14] Rosenzweig expresses no doubt that the law is the "law of God," but the question of what makes up the divinity of the law is not central to his thought.[15]

Closer to our own day, Emmanuel Lévinas (d. 1995) sought the origin of commandment in the strictly inter-human phenomenon of the face: "There is a commandment in the appearance of the face, as if a master spoke to me." The exteriority said to be in the face is "wholly commandment and authority." Moreover, "To see a face is already to hear, 'You shall not kill.'"[16] The Law is not the highest entity, however: ethics "leads us to the law." There is a "responsibility prior to the law," and "it is from that responsibility that the law itself flows." What one must do is "to be responsible beyond all limit fixed by an objective law."[17] For Lévinas, the law is an "essential harshness" that offends, "within the will, a dignity other than that which attaches to respect for human laws. The dignity of goodness itself!" The law puts an end to the dream of a humanity capable of managing by itself: "To recognize the necessity of a law it to recognize that humanity cannot save itself by denying its condition, immediately, magically." The existence of the law is diametrically opposed to autonomy. This is why the idea of heteronomy is rehabilitated as a positive dimension of ethics: Lévinas speaks of a "justice whose laws are revealed only in their form as pure commandment, and which consequently demand an obedience of pure heteronomy" and also of an "obedience which answers to a totally exterior will where man does not even discover the formal universality of Kant's categorical imperative."[18] Thus a place is reserved for commandments that apparently make no sense (huqqim). One might even wonder if creating a place for these might not even be the principal goal of such a doctrine.

❀

The object of Jewish fidelity remains the Torah, which is more and more clearly envisioned as reaching beyond a narrow "legalism." In contrast, the tendency to focus Judaism on ethics brings out an unexpected proximity between the Torah, the purpose of which is to singularize Israel in relation to the other nations, and a moral law with a universal vocation.

Islam

In the modern period Islam was obliged to change after the Ottoman Empire suffered a series of defeats dealt to it by the European powers at Lepanto (1571) and Vienna (1683), then by the Russian Empire, and even more sharply with the shock of the Napoleonic expedition into Egypt of 1798. Once much of the territory of Islam had passed under the control of non-Muslim powers, the inhabitants of the Islamic world were exposed to the modern ideas and practices brought by those powers.

Modernization

Islam had to borrow juridical elements from European systems. To speak only of the states that had remained independent of the colonial powers, this was the case in the Ottoman Empire after the reforms of 1839, then of Iran with the constitution of 1906. Basically, this movement differed from previous practice only in degree. The actual governments in Islamic lands had never taken their operational rules from religious sources alone. Still, the modern epoch stands out from those that preceded it on several points. First, in some cases, more and more massive borrowings of a legislative nature came to form a systematic corpus. Second, such borrowings did not come from an older culture but from a contemporary civilization. Finally, and most importantly, the fact that these were borrowings (something that until that moment had been systematically denied) was now increasingly admitted.

In the face of Western knowledge and in response to it, the religious domain developed an interest in systematic concordance, as other religions that had entered into contact with the West had done. To read certain apologists of an inexhaustible fecundity, the Qur'an already contains the seeds of all the latest scientific advances, from atoms to molecular biology, as they came along.[19]

Similarly, the Kalām was modernized by borrowings from the West. Thus the old reproach to Jews and Christians that they falsified scripture was returned to service, but with a new method that used the biblical criticism practiced by Christians of the modern age, Protestants in particular, for the purposes of Muslim apologetics, to the point of demonstrating that biblical texts were dubious. The first to apply this technique was probably the Indian scholar al-Hindī, in a work written around 1854. Of course, al-Hindī and his emulators rejected the reverse procedure just as decidedly as Ibn Hazm had done in his day: it is out of the question for anyone to apply to the Qur'an the same historical-critical method that was applied to the Bible.[20]

Religion, Politics, Law

When the thinkers of modern Islam returned to the past of their own culture and to the "legacy" they had received from it, they did not always demand the separation of the spiritual and the temporal, much vaunted in Christendom. In the eyes of Rashīd Ridā (d. 1935), such a separation was foreign to the teachings of Islam. This did not prevent him, in practice, from preaching a division of functions that was equivalent to a genuine separation.[21] Some people, far from chiming in with the Christian theme of "God and Caesar," were shocked by the very thought, interpreting the phrase to imply an abandonment to Caesar of a power that was legitimately held by God alone. Others made use of it, however, among them Ali Abderraziq in his famous book about (and against) the caliphate (1925), the last trace of which had just been abolished by Atatürk.[22] In this work Abderraziq attempts to show that the mission Muhammad had received was purely religious, not political. The Prophet's authority surpassed that of kings, but because it transcended kingly power. The caliphs, in contrast, saw to the organization of the city. The caliphate has no religious basis. Thus nothing prevents the task of administration of the city from being entrusted to human reason.[23]

As for the divine law, a new apologetic strategy was gradually set in place. In particular, it aimed at showing that Islamic law, either considering it as an intangible whole or as residing exclusively in its sources (given that human elaborations are open to revision), furnishes an answer to all of man's problems, and especially to the challenges of modernity. Islamic law allegedly constitutes the richest and the most perfect of all juridical systems, even containing in embryo answers to all the difficulties that Western legislation failed to resolve.[24] A nuance of capital importance appears here, however, regarding the ways in which this strategy justifies the concrete dispositions of the law. Here invoking divine will no longer suffice: this apologetics based such dispositions on nature, the object of supposedly scientific observations (for example, in the field of medicine).[25]

It is at that point, and perhaps only at that point, that the idea of the *sharia*—itself a relative newcomer—was enhanced by the addition of a legend in three acts that constitutes the basis of "Islamist" or "fundamentalist" history. The legend is this: long ago the *sharia* regulated all of Muslim life; it was then thrust aside (for unspecified reasons) to the advantage of juridical dispositions of foreign origin, thus bringing on the decadence of Islamic civilization; it must be finally reestablished in a utopian future whose coming must been hastened.[26]

Certain reformers began to put forth the idea that Islam is a purely religious phenomenon with no connection with the political. Most of the time, however, the religious dimension of Islam continues to be perceived—also by these reformers—as achieving concrete form in a law, with Muhammad playing the role of imposing that law. Even Abderraziq states this.[27]

In Judaism as well as in Islam, the idea of law thus remains central and continues to constitute one of the points on which those two religions, each in its own way, differ from Christianity.

Conclusion

The moment has come, at the end of this road, to summarize, gather up some loose ends, and suggest some conclusions.

❖

Beyond the theologico-political problem, and providing a horizon for it, lies the underlying question of the need for a divine nature or origin for the norms that govern the entire field of human conduct, a question that I have called "theio-practical." The term "divine law" presents this problem in a concentrated form.

The idea appears quite early, as soon as Greece and Israel said farewell to the river civilizations of Egypt and Mesopotamia. This break was made in two styles, Greek and Jewish. In the first case, the divinity of the law expressed its "natural" character, thus its accessibility as a matter of principle. In the second case, it expressed instead the historical character of the law and, as a consequence, the necessity that it be revealed. In Greece the divine appears as a neutral domain of being that may crystallize in specific divine figures. In Israel the divine is, to the contrary, no more than the characteristic of a personal God. Hence Greece provides a *theio-practical* model, and Israel illustrates the *theo-practical* model.

In Israel's experience of the divine, divine law became concrete in rules that were actually promulgated and gathered together in a written code. It is in that form that the law was presented to a nascent Christianity and to Islam as it arose. Islam, which appeared independently from the history of the Jewish people, replaced its legislation by another, modified, legislation. Christianity, which issued from within Israel, moved away from the Jewish Law when the revolution launched by St. Paul invoked "grace" as another source of

256

salvation than the law. Following Paul's lead, the church captured that source in a sacramental economy, leaving the government of men to common ethics, with its juridical elaborations, and leaving the administration of political communities to preexistent authorities.

Thus the history that I am narrating here has the same overall rhythm as the one that I related in *Wisdom of the World*: there I was interested in the articulation of human practices with the cosmic; here, with the divine. The system of norms that claims to regulate human practice thus began in association with another principle, cosmological in the earlier book, and theological here, only to dissociate itself subsequently.

❖

The separation of the ethical and the cosmological occurred in modern times. Examination of the connection between the divine and the normative obliges us to distinguish between cultures. In Christianity, that separation was present, in nascent form, as early as the High Middle Ages; more importantly, it constituted the basis on which what we call medieval Europe was later constructed. The Western Middle Ages is when the conceptual distinction between the political and the religious and their mutual alienation took concrete form in two separate, and even competing, institutions. In Islam, it was during the same period that the political and the religious, at first merged into one, grew apart in practice.

Today there is constant talk about the distinction between the political and the religious. Some boast of living in a culture in which such a distinction has occurred, and they advocate carrying it through to the point of eliminating all influence of the religious in public life. Others congratulate themselves for living in a culture in which that same distinction is not always irreversible, or else they dream of mending the tear threatening the fine wholeness of the community. Both camps invoke this distinction to reproach the other for having abandoned (or for not having abandoned) what they both suppose to be a primeval indistinction. This mirror symmetry creates distortions in the way that cultures view one another: Europe perceives that separation as progress; Islam, as a sign of decadence.[1]

One might well wonder, however, whether that separation, which has received so much praise, and its concrete translation in the "separation of church and state," ever actually took place. Moreover, that pat phrase is deceptive. For one thing, it suggests the existence of an initial union; for another, it supposes that the state and the church are institutions that have always existed. Neither hypothesis has much of a foundation. We would do better to speak of the parallel development of two institutions that never formed a unit. The political and the religious are two independent sources of authority; they have crossed one another's paths more than once, but they never have merged, in spite of attempts to fit them together, sometimes to the advantage of one, sometimes to that of the other. Although there has been cooperation between the two, there has never been confusion about which is which.

Judaism was only constituted as Judaism—that is, on the base of the religion of ancient Israel—after it lost all political power. The Law had already become crystallized outside of the apparatus of state, but it retained the same sphere of influence claimed for the state authority: the Jewish people and only the Jewish people. Henceforth the Law could be deployed only in the private domain; its political dimension remained virtual, reserved for the eschatological time of the Messiah.

⟡

One widespread view of Islam insists on the impossibility of separating the political and the religious. Even within Islam, however, the tendencies that present it as both "religion and regime" (dīn wa-dawla), which are attested almost from the start, became dominant only at a fairly recent date.[2] The Islamic world has hardly ever experienced that unity except as a retrospective dream intended to compensate for a reality that was drifting further and further away from that ideal. May I be permitted one more paradox: Islam is the culture within which a separation in the exact sense of the Latin word has occurred—that is, a disjoining of what was originally one. That separation was achieved within the concrete evolution of Islamic societies that I have sketched above.

Still, the idea of divine law persisted: it was even part of the same whole as the separation that we have just seen, since the one counterbalanced the other. Judaism and Islam made a symmetrical connection between the emergence of the divine law and theologico-political separation: what was for the first a consequence was for the second a cause. Indeed, in Judaism, it is the initial loss of the political dimension that led to a renewed concentration of all Jewish life on the Torah: the pressure to which Israel subjected the Torah brought forth an entire halakhah. In Islam, to the contrary, the development of a more and more precise sharia that demanded more and more clearly a direct connection to the origins and became more and more incarnate in a class of jurists ended up rendering superfluous a caliph who claimed to unite in his person the political authority of the head of state and the religious authority of the successor to the Prophet.

We can thus see the importance of the distinction suggested at the beginning of the present work between the genus of the practical and the political that is simply one species of it. In Islamic lands, the end of a liaison between the political and the religious permitted the religious to demand, with increased virulence, not just the domain of the political, but the entire field of the practical. Conversely, in Christianity, separating the entire genus of the practical from the divine made it possible for the three species of that genus—the ethical, the economic, and the political—to declare their independence.

The problem of Islam, in the dual sense of the problem that modern societies pose for it and the problem that it poses for those societies, cannot be reduced to the separation or nonseparation of the political and the religious. The two have reached a de facto separation—if not a necessary one—in the realm of ideas. Nonetheless, although in Islam the political species of the practical has fallen out of step with the divine, the genus as a whole (including the two other species, the ethical and the economic) remains subject to divine law.

❖

What has been said of the political domain applies to that of ethics as well. There is no theological morality, nor is there any long-term historical movement that might lead morality to emancipate itself from theology. It is even more false to make an emancipation of that sort begin with modern times.

One might even wonder, more generally, whether a noun such as "morality" can take on any singularizing epithet, and this in spite of the fact that contemporary chatter constantly proposes juxtapositions such as "traditional" or "bourgeois," usually with pejorative overtones. In particular, there is no Jewish morality, no Christian morality, no Muslim morality. Nor is there a "secular morality." There is a common morality capable of Christian, Jewish, Islamic, "secular," or other *interpretations*.

If there is no religious morality, the reasons for that absence vary from one religion to another, even to the point of direct opposition. In Islam and Judaism, ethics is an integral part of the religious law. According to certain interpretations of Judaism, in particular, it even constitutes its only content.[3] Admittedly, Islam used Greek and Persian sources to develop a literary genre of treatises on "the correction of conduct" that later became traditional. In these treatises morality goes hand in hand with practical suggestions for living well, and any religious reference is secondary. But where the law claims to determine, at least in principle, the whole sphere of human action, it finds it difficult to dispense with an autonomous ethics. Such an ethics pertains above all to inner tendencies that give rise to acts, but it supposes as known and admitted the moral evaluation of actions practiced by the science of the law.[4]

Christianity had no other morality than common morality. During the course of its history, it adopted various formulations of that morality, to the point of adopting into its own thought the philosophers' exhortations and even their theories. Christianity may have emphasized one virtue or another, according to the needs of the state of the civilization in which it was operating, at some times inviting the faithful to generosity, at other times to economy, or placing chastity first or last among the virtues. All of these variations remain within an invariable system of goods, however, in which one cannot isolate one "value" from the others so as to render it absolute without corrupting it.[5] To speak of a Christian morality is either to confuse commandments and counsels—the obligatory and the optional—or else the content of precepts with the weight that they receive from the religious context in which they are formulated.[6]

Benjamin Constant speaks to the point here. "There is," he writes, "a common morality, based on calculation, interest, and surety, which can, I think, at a pinch, do without religion." I myself take the expression "common morality," to which Constant gives a pejorative tone, in a neutral, if not a laudatory, sense. Thus I cannot agree with his cry: "But woe betide the people who have only this common morality!" If religion seems to him "desirable," it is for "the creation of a more elevated morality." I would subscribe more willingly to the role that he would like to see religion play: not to add to morality, but rather to provide it with the nourishing environment in which finer versions of the practices dictated by common virtue might crystallize, and thus—to use his words—"ennoble all the virtues."[7]

❖

Hellenism and Judaism have in common the idea of divine law, as we have seen. Perhaps we can add, with Schelling, that they both find themselves "under the law."[8] That phrase does not mean that Christianity—which Schelling, following St. Paul, sets against both—is without law; rather, it means that for Christianity the relationship to the law is not one of "being under" it; it is not a subordination. Above all, the Christian figure of the divine does not present God as lawgiver. Rousseau understood this in his fashion. Within the context of a critique of Christianity, which he holds responsible for a cleavage between man and the citizen, and to which he opposes the idea of a "civil religion," he states that Christianity, "since it has no particular relation to the body politic, *leaves the laws with only the force they derive from themselves* without adding any other force to them."[9] Fustel de Coulanges notes, in a somewhat more generous tone, "Christianity is the first religion that did not claim to be the source of the law."[10]

Very early on, Christianity's image of itself was as a "new way" (Acts 9:2; 19:9). On occasion it called itself, more specifically, "the way of justice," an expression that, taken literally, recalls the Jewish *halakhah* or the Muslim *sharia*.[11] In fact, the "way" that the text speaks of is not a *sharia* and cannot become one. Christianity does not propose a "way": it supposes "the way" to have been known for a long time, perhaps even forever. It is the way of common morality. What Christianity proposes is only the means for following it. God enters into the domain of practice as a source of aid and pardon. For Christianity, grace is not opposed to the law; rather, it gives what enables one to fulfill the law. In a much-quoted phrase, St. Augustine first asks God to give him the means for accomplishing what He commands, and only then does he ask God to command him as He wishes (*da quod jubes et jube quod vis*).[12]

In Christianity, the economy of salvation is the mechanism by which God proposes to equip man for the way. It finds its permanent actualization in the system of the sacraments. We do not reflect enough on the fact that the central sacrament of Christianity, the Eucharist, is a meal. To be sure, Christianity insists that the nourishment shared in that sacrament is not just any food, but indeed the resuscitated body of Christ, present under a new mode, and in its Roman Catholic version, Christianity also understands that sacrament as an actualization of the sacrifice of Jesus. The fact remains, however, that this sacrificed body is made accessible as nourishment, and a nourishment that does not dictate to the person ingesting it what he or she must do, but gives the strength to do it.

This becomes clear if we meditate on the word *viaticum*, from the Latin *via*, road or way, a word that derives from the same system of metaphors as *halakhah* or *sharia*. That term has traditionally taken on (especially in Latin) the meaning of the last communion of those on point of death, something supposed to bring them provisions for their final voyage. However, the Greek equivalent, *ephodion*, which also derives from a word for "way" (*hodos*), designates the Eucharist in general, and even other sacraments.[13] Every form of the Eucharist, and with it all sacraments, provides an aid to a "way." *Christianity replaces the* sharia *by the* viaticum.

In Christianity, the divine immediately ceased being an entity that determined the content of the practical domain by saying *what* should be done. With the New Testament, the relationship with the divine no longer appeared as a relationship to a law. In contrast, in Judaism and in Islam, the separation between the religious and the political, which each realizes in very different ways, leaves untouched the way in which the divine determines practice. That determination takes on the figure of a law. At that point, the content of revelation is not a person, but God's will, as delivered in commandments. The *logos* of revelation is not the one by which God presents himself as God—that is, as the unfathomable mystery of a personality. It is the dictation of a rule to be followed. As a result, there can be no theology as an unfolding of the *logos* by which God states *himself*, but only an explication of what he dictates.

Lichtenberg, in a passage that I have cited in the preface, thought that he observed a shift from theology to what he called "theonomy."[14] Giving those words the meaning that I have explained above, I should like to sketch the contrary movement, in the hope of moving once and for all from a theonomy to a theology: that is, to replace the idea of a God giving his law to men by that of a God who speaks. We have become accustomed to understand by "theology" a discipline by which we apply to the divine the tools of reason (*logos*). The term also designates, in classic fashion, the fact that God includes within himself a "Word" that was in the "Beginning," and that, when he speaks to men, he "shows himself fully."

In the Bible and in Christianity, in fact, the presence of the divine does not comport an immediate demand for obedience. A space opens up in which God manifests himself, thus offering Himself to a gaze that might risk something like a description. The divine shows itself, or rather, gives itself, before asking anything of us and *instead of* asking. Not only is it true that "God owes us nothing" (Leszek Kolakowski),[15] but he does not *ask* anything of us. Although God does indeed *expect* something of his creatures (that we develop according to our own logic), he does not, in fact, *demand* anything, or rather, he asks nothing more than his gift already asks, thanks to the simple fact that it is given: to be received. In the case of man, that reception does not require anything but humanity. As magnificently stated by a somewhat unexpected author, "God wants nothing from us but ourselves."[16] That claim is addressed to all aspects of the human, the intelligence among others. Anselm's formula, *fides quaerens intellectum,* before being the program for the human knowledge of God, is thus the rule for the gift of God to man. In the latter case, one might translate Anselm's dictum as "what God entrusts to man demands human intelligence."

The principal break in my narrative comes at the beginning of the Middle Ages, not on the threshold of the historical period that claims to succeed the medieval and that uses that claim as the principal argument for its legitimacy. The modern age, as we have seen, was the theater in which profound upheavals in the domain of the normative took place. These included the shift that placed the law under the domination of the will alone, the sudden appearance of the idea of (scientific) laws of nature, and a redistribution of relations between commandment and counsel. As for the relationship between law and divinity, the modern age did little more than store up results of conquests that began several centuries earlier. In particular, the state and the church had been in place for a long time, and were well established as clearly distinct institutions, when they renegotiated their relations. What is more, it is the new conception of the divine law that distinguished those two institutions.

If we consider our societies today, they are societies of a law without any divine dimension: "It has become incongruous or grotesque," Marcel Gauchet writes, "to mix the idea of God with the norm of the society of men."[17] Our societies like to imagine the history that led up to their own days as one of a separation from sacrality, a separation viewed as an emancipation. Contemporary societies are tempted by unlimited power, much more than was true, in the premodern age, even of the king most jealous of his absolute sovereignty. Jean Bodin hammered at that notion as self-evident while he defined (for the first time, as he thought) the concept of sovereignty: even the prince who thought himself the most "freed from laws" (*legibus solutus*) was nonetheless subject to "divine law, the law of nature, and the common law of all people."[18] Removing those restrictions, which were still taken for granted at the beginning of the modern period, was part of what Stephen Toulmin has called the "hidden agenda" of our modernity.[19]

Our societies, with their agenda of a law with no divine component, are in fact made possible, in the final analysis, by the Christian experience of a divine without law. Even atheism as "unbelief" supposes the primacy of faith in the definition of the religious. It is possible that the theologico-political problem is a serious problem in appearance only. All it does is to cash in, on the level of the species (politics), on a separation that had been acquired some time ago on the level of the genus (practice). The supposed combatants for the "secularization" of institutions fly to the aid of a victory that was assured centuries ago, and which is, what is more, the victory of Christianity itself in its most official form, that of the church, establishing the borderline that separates it from the secular domain.

❖

Even when the presence of the divine is no longer conceived of and experienced as the presence of a law, the problem of the articulation of the divine and the practical remains. There is nothing to prove that the Western conception of the political is secure, or even viable in the long run.[20] Whether human action can unfold freely, with no reference to the divine, rather than losing its way in suicidal dialectics, remains to be seen. It is possible, moreover, that parting ways with the divine law is precisely what liberates that question, and even what brings out its more burning aspects.

If this is the case, we will have to contest the now-habitual opposition between autonomy and heteronomy, and from two angles. On the one hand, from that of the prefixes, because that opposition separates the *autos* from the *heteros*, the "oneself" from the "other," with a hatchet blow.[21] But also from that of the root of those terms and the substantive that they share. It is not to be taken for granted that the question of the *nomos*, the law, is a first question; to ask whether one gives himself the law or whether it is received from elsewhere goes to the bottom of things even less.

The idea of divine law is *one* model of the articulation of the theio-practical. It does not exhaust the question, however: the idea of norm is not the only way in which the divine can enter into a relation with practice. It can do so according to all the modalities of causality, for example, as a model that attracts, as a light that guides, or as an aid to advancement. Becoming conscious of the manner in which the divine appears at times as a norm for action permits us to investigate other possibilities and grasp their pertinence. Perhaps it is even when one ceases to believe that the normative modality of the relation to the divine is the only possible one that such a relation to the divine in general has a chance of appearing as necessary to the full deployment of human action.

Notes]℘··

Preface

1. Brague, *La Sagesse du monde*, 178; 2d ed., 224; *The Wisdom of the World*, 153.

2. See *HWPh*, s.v., vol. 10 (1998), cols. 1113–16 (Ernst Reil). Lichtenberg viewed theology as becoming theonomy just as astronomy replaced astrology: see *Sudelbücher I*, Book I, no. 184, in *Schriften und Briefe*, ed. Wolfgang Promies (Munich: Hanser, 1973), 877. Paul Tillich used the word in senses that evolved with his thought, but began by making a distinction between "theonomy" and "autonomy." See Tillich, *Das System der Wissenschaften nach Gegenständen und Methoden* (1923), in his *Gesammelte Werke*, vol. 1: *Frühe Hauptwerke*, (Stuttgart: Evangelisches Verlagswerk, 1959), 227, in English translation as *The System of the Sciences According to Objects and Methods*, trans., with an introduction, by Paul Wiebe (Lewisburg, Penn.: Bucknell University Press, 1981). Most of the time, however, he treated the first as a deeper meaning of the second. The word also appears in book titles: see F. W. Graf, *Theonomie: Fallstudien zum Integrationsanspruch neuzeitlicher Theologie* (Gütersloh: Mohn, 1987), and Barone, *Teo-nomie*.

Introduction

1. On the history of this problem, see the synthesis of Heinrich Meier, "Was ist Politische Theologie?," in J. Assmann, *Politische Theologie zwischen Ägypten und Israel*, 7–19, and the illuminating summary in Manent, *Histoire intellectuelle du libéralisme*, 17–30.

2. See, for example, E. Rosenthal, *Political Thought in Medieval Islam*, and especially Butterworth, *Philosophy, Ethics and Virtuous Rule*, and idem, "Political Islam"; Galston, *Politics and Excellence*; Kreisel, *Maimonides' Political Thought*; and Mahdi, *La Cité vertueuse d'Alfarabi*; Eng. trans., *Alfarabi and the Foundation of Islamic Political Philosophy*.

3. See Brague, *Eccentric Culture*, 165; *Europe, la voie romaine*, 208.

4. Johann Gottlieb Fichte, *Anweisung zum seligen Leben* (Berlin, 1806), 6th lecture; Michel Henry, *C'est moi la vérité: Pour une philosophie du christianisme* (Paris: Éditions du Seuil, 1996), in English translation by Susan Emanuel as *I am the Truth: Toward a Philosophy of Christianity* (Stanford: Stanford University Press, 2003).

5. Niccolò Machiavelli, *Il Principe*, 6 and 26, in *Tutte le opere*, 1:18, 94; *Discorsi*

1.1, 1.9, 2.8, 3.30 in ibid., 1:94, 120, 253, 409. See also Machiavelli's summary of two sermons of Savonarola in his letter to Ricciardo Becchi of 9 March 1498, in Machiavelli, *Opere*, ed. Franco Gaeta (Turin: UTET, 1984), vol. 3, *Lettere*, 67–70.

6. See Franck, *Nietzsche et l'ombre de Dieu*.

7. Machiavelli, *Discorsi*, 3.30, in *Tutte le opere*, 1:409; *Discourses on Livy*, trans. Harvey C. Mansfield and Nathan Tarcov (Chicago: University of Chicago Press, 1996), 280.

8. Max Weber, *Wirtschaft und Gesellschaft: Grundriss der verstehenden Soziologie* (1922), 5th ed., rev., ed. J. Winckelmann, 2 vols. (Tübingen: Mohr, 1976), 2:387–513. The quotations can be found in II, vii, "Rechtssoziologie," no. 8, p. 504. See also *Economy and Society: An Outline of Interpretive Sociology*, ed. Guenther Roth and Claus Wittich, trans. Ephraim Fishoff et al., 2 vols. (Berkeley and Los Angeles: University of California Press, 1978), 647–48, 656, 657. For a perspective on Weber of a specialist in Islamic law, see Johansen, *Contingency in a Sacred Law*, 46–48.

9. See Martin Heidegger, *Nietzsche*, 2 vols. (Pfullingen: Neske, 1961), 2:146. For an overview of the German problematic of secularization, see Monod, *La Querelle de la sécularisation*.

10. See H. Maier, *Kritik der politischen Theologie*, and Meier, *Das Theologisch-politische Problem*.

11. Anselm *Cur Deus Homo* 1.1, PL 158:362b; SC 91:212; G. W. F. Hegel, *Enzyklopädie der philosophischen Wissenschaften*, ed. Hermann Glockner (Stuttgart: Fromanns, 1956), 8:183, par. 77 n.

12. See, for example, al-Kindī, in F. Rosenthal, "From Arabic Books and Manuscripts," 27b and n. 6; Maimonides, *Traité de Logique*, trans. Brague, chap. 14, p. 99; idem, *Maimonides' Treatise on Logic*, trans. Efros, 63; Thomas Aquinas, *S. Thomae Aquinatis in decem libros Ethicorum Aristotelis ad Nicomachum expositio*, ed. Raimondo Spiazzi (Turin: Marietti, 1949), 1.1.6, p. 4a; Nasīr ad-Dīn Tūsī, *The Nasirean Ethics*, Preamble, pp. 25, 28. Medieval authors sometimes call the government of the individual *monostica*: see Claude Lafleur, *Quatre introductions à la philosophie au XIIIe siècle: Textes critiques et étude historique* (Montreal and Paris: Vrin, 1988), 335.

13. To avoid mentioning living authors, I shall refer only to Bloch, *Les Rois thaumaturges*; English trans., *The Royal Touch*, and Kantorowicz, *The King's Two Bodies*.

14. Flavius Josephus *Contre Apion* 2.16, no. 165, p. 86; English trans., *The Life; Against Apion*, vol. 1 of *Josephus*, LCL. The term is suggested, but not yet formulated, in Plato *Laws* 4, 713a.

Chapter 1

1. See Gagnér, *Studien zur Ideengeschichte der Gesetzgebung*, 57–60.

2. As Émile Durkheim remarks in *De La Division du travail social* (Paris, 1893), chap. 4, 2, pp. 108–109, in English translation by W. D. Halls as *The Division of Labor in Society* (New York: Free Press, 1984). For the Chinese example, see Bodde and Morris, *Law in Imperial China*, 11–12.

3. Here and below, see Rudolf Otto, *Das Heilige: Über das Irrationale in der Idee des Göttlischen und sein Verhältniss zum Rationalen* (Breslau, 1917), 27–30, in English translation by John W. Harvey as *The Idea of the Holy* (New York and London: Oxford University Press, 1958).

4. Bodde and Morris, *Law in Imperial China*, 10.

5. See Wolfgang Helck, *Zur Verwaltung des mittleren und neuen Reichs* (Leiden: Brill, 1958). On this distinction, see also Henri Cazelles, "Royauté sacrale et désacralisation de l'État dans l'Ancien Testament," *Dictionnaire de la Bible: Supplément*, vol. 10 (1984), col. 1062.

6. E. Otto, "Prolegomena zur Frage der Gesetzgebung und Rechtssprechung in Ägypten," 152; Boochs, "Zur Bedeutung der *hpw*," 89.

7. Lorton, "The Treatment of Criminals in Ancient Egypt," 59; idem, "The King and the Law," 57.

8. Papyrus Cairo 58092 = Bulaq, 10, in Schafik Allam, *Hieratische Ostraka und Papyri aus der Ramessidenzeit*, 2 vols. (Tübingen, 1973), no. 268, p. 290; for commentary, see Théodoridès, "À propos de la loi dans l'Égypte pharaonique," 116, 123–24.

9. See Théodoridès, 139. For a similar notion in medieval Europe, see Bellomo, *L'Europa del diritto comune*, 54; English trans., *The Common Legal Past of Europe*, 43–44.

10. See Lorton, "Treatment of Criminals," 60; "The King and the Law," 53.

11. *LA*, 2:571a. For a summary of this controversy, which reaches no clear conclusion, however, see Allam, "La problématique des quarante rouleaux de loi."

12. See J. Assmann, *Stein und Zeit*, 24–27.

13. See Brunner-Traut, *Frühformen der Erkenntnis*, 94–98.

14. See Otto, "Prolegomena zur Frage," 151; Griffiths, *The Divine Verdict*, 176–78; Wilson, *The Burden of Egypt*, 49–50; and Posener, *De la divinité du pharaon*, 58.

15. In this connection, see the summary in J. Assmann, *Ma'at*. See also Lorton, "The King and the Law," 58.

16. J. Assmann, *Ma'at*, 137, who cites Siegfried Morenz.

17. "The Protests of the Eloquent Peasant," 8th protest, B1, *ANET*, 407b–410b, esp. 410a, l. 304. See the translation by Friedrich Vogelsang, *Kommentar zu den Klagen des Bauern* (Leipzig, 1913), 210 (and discussion on p. 87); Seidl, *Einführung in die ägyptische Rechtsgeschichte bis zum Ende des neuen Reiches*, 1:42; Miriam Lichtheim, *Ancient Egyptian Literature: A Book of Readings*, 1:181; *Textes sacrés et textes profanes de l'Ancienne Égypte*, vol. 1, *Des Pharaons et des hommes*, trans. Claire Lalouette (Paris: Gallimard, 1984), 209; *Altägyptische Dichtung*, ed. and trans. Erik Hornung (Stuttgart: Philipp Reclam, 1996), 24. Seidl interprets this formula as an approach to the idea of natural law.

18. See Bottéro, *Mésopotamie*, 191–223; *RAVA*, s.v. Gesetze, 3:256a (H. Petschow).

19. See Kramer, "Ur-Nammu Law Code," 46.

20. *ANET*, 164a, "The Code of Hammurabi," trans. Theophile J. Meek.

21. *RAVA*, s.v. Gesetze, 244a, 246a (J. Klima).

22. See below, pp. 61, 62, 63–64.

23. See Kojève, *Esquisse d'une phénoménologie du droit*, 35–39 and 207–14, but especially 210.

24. Strauss, *The Rebirth of Classical Political Rationalism*, 248; see also idem, *Gesammelte Schriften*, 2:126.

Chapter 2

1. Vernant, *Les Origines de la pensée grecque*, 2, 4, 47, 63, 84, 102; quotation from the English translation, *The Origins of Greek Thought*, 107. This work represents a type of account of the transition from myth to *logos*, or of the birth of reason, that comes close to being a literary genre.

2. See Benveniste, *Le vocabulaire des institutions indo-européennes*, 2:99–105.

3. Plato *Laws* 7, 793a, Bury trans. See also 8, 841b3–4.

4. See, for example, Plato *Minos* 317d, 321bc.

5. Flavius Josephus *Contre Apion* 2.15, no. 155, p. 84. The argument is often repeated, for example in Jean Bodin, *Les Six Livres de la République de I. Bodon angevin* (Paris: Jacques du Puis, 1583; Aalen: Scientia, 1961) 6.6, pp. 1021–22, or in Pascal, *Pensées*, ed. Léon Brunschvicg (Paris: Garnier Flammarion, 1976), par. 619.

6. Exodus 26:30; 2 Kings 1:7; Judges 13:12.

7. Hesiod *Works and Days* 276, quoted from *Hesiod: The Homeric Hymns and Homerica*, trans. Hugh G. Evelyn-White, LCL. See also Propertius 3.5.25 (*naturae mores*). On the meaning of *nomos*, see Heinimann, *Nomos und Physis*, 61–63; Ostwald, *Nomos and the Beginnings of the Athenian Democracy*, 21–22; Neschke-Hentschke, *Platonisme politique et théorie du droit naturel*, 1:36; Strauss, *Natural Right and History*, 82, and *Rebirth of Classical Political Rationalism*, 253–54; Brague, *La Sagesse du monde*, 133 and n.32, *Wisdom of the World*, 112. Hesiod's idea is inverted in Philemon, frag. 96, in *Poetae Comici Graeci*, ed. Rudolf Kassel and Colin Austin, 8 vols. (Berlin: de Gruyter, 1983–89), 7:279.

8. Hesiod *Works and Days* 9–10; Netschke-Hentschke, *Platonisme politique*, 1:33.

9. Xenophon *Memorabilia* 1.2.42, trans. Marchant, LCL; Hirzel, *Themis, Dike und Verwandtes*, 376–80; Ostwald, *Nomos and the Beginnings of the Athenian Democracy*, 55, and idem, "Was there a Concept *agraphos nomos* in Classical Greece?" (1973), 84, 96.

10. Hirzel, *Themis, Dike und Verwandtes*, 1–18, 138–56.

11. Homer *Iliad* 2.206, 9.99, trans. Benveniste, LCL.

12. Aeschylus *Eumenides* 391–93, trans. Herbert Weir Smith, LCL.

13. Xenophon *Cyropaedia* 1.6.6., trans. Miller, LCL.

14. Solon 3 (4).33, in *Anthologia Lyrica Graeca*, ed. Ernst Diehl, BT, 1936, 1:32. See also Jaeger, "Solons Eunomie," 334.

15. Demosthenes "Antiphon" 1.3.27; Xenophon *Memorabilia* 4.4.19; Isocrates *Panathenaicus* 169; Lysias, Oration 6, "Against Impiety," par. 10, Lamb trans., LCL; Plato *Laws* 8, 838b. See also Ostwald, "Concept *agraphos nomos* in Classical Greece?," 103; Demosthenes "Against Aristogeiton I" 25, 16.774, quoted here from *Demosthenes*, vol.3, *Against Meidas, Androtion, Aristocrates, Timocrates, Aristogeiton*, trans. J. H. Vince., LCL, 524, 545. The saying is quoted in *Digest* 1.3 (*Corpus Iuris Civilis*, 2:112), which simply changes the word "god" from the plural to the singular. Henri Weil sees in this an extremely ancient interpolation.

16. Sophocles *Antigone* 457, quoted from *The Complete Greek Tragedies*, ed. David Grene and Richmond Lattimore (Chicago and London: University of Chicago Press, 1992), *Antigone*, trans. David Grene, ll. 498–501.

17. Sophocles *Oedipus Rex* 863–71, quoted from *The Complete Greek Tragedies*, vol. 2, *Sophocles, Oedipus the King*, trans. David Grene, 864–71.

18. See J. Assmann, *Moses der Ägypter*, 261.

19. *Odyssey* 1.282–83; 2.216–17; Hesiod *Works and Days* 763–64, trans. Evelyn-White The Latin proverb is attested for the first time in the early ninth century in Alcuin, *Epistolae*, no. 166, 9, *PL* 101:438.

20. Pindar "Isthmian Odes" 5, opening line.

21. See Heinemann, "Die Lehre vom ungeschriebenen Gesetz im jüdischen Schrifttum," 149–50.

22. Sophocles *Antigone* 454–55, Grene trans., l. 499.

23. Euripides *Ion* 442–43, quoted from *Trojan Women; Iphigenia among the Taurians; Ion*, ed. David Kovacs, LCL, 373; de Romilly, *La Loi dans la pensée grecque des origines à Aristote*, 169–70. See also Aeschylus *The Suppliant Maidens* 673ff.

24. Plutarch "The Oracles at Delphi," trans. Frank Cole Babbitt, vol. 5 of *Plutarch's Moralia*, LCL, 7; Rahman, *Prophecy in Islam*, 73 n. 32.

25. Latte, *Heileges Recht*.

26. *Odyssey* 1.39; Aristotle *Eudemian Ethics* 129b13–14, quoted from *Aristotle's Eudemian Ethics, Books I, II, and VIII*, trans. Michael Woods (Oxford: Clarendon Press, 1982), 45–46.

27. See Ellul, "Loi et sacré, droit et divin,"

28. Galen, in Walzer, *Galen on Jews and Christians*, 10–11, 18–23, 87–88. See Kühneweg, *Das neue Gesetz*, 195–200; Alexander of Aphrodisias *In Aristoteles Topicorum libros octo commentaria . . .* , ed. Maximilian Wallies, *CAG*, p. 84, nos. 26–30 (= *SVF*, 3, par. 711). For comparison, see the examples given below, pp. 23–24.

29. Heraclitus, DK 22B114, quoted from Mourelatos, "Heraclitus, fr. 114" (1965), 258. See also Heinimann, *Nomos und Physis*, 65–67; Blass, *Gott und die Gesetze*, 31 and *passim*; Fränkel, *Dichtung und Philosophie des frühen Griechentums*, 445–46; Gigante, *ΝΟΜΟΣ ΒΑΣΙΛΕΥΣ* [Nomos basileus], 50–55, proves disappointing.

30. Plato *Phaedrus* 249c6–7.

31. Plato *Laws* 12, 957c6–7. See also Plato *Republic* 589d1; Neschke-Hentschke, *Platonisme politique*, 1:97.

32. Aristotle *Politics* 3.16, 1287a 28–29, 3.13, 1284a10–14, Rackham trans.; *Rhetoric* 1.13, 1373b18.

33. Epictetus *Entretiens*, ed. J. Souilhé, CUF, 2.16.28, p. 66; 3.24, 42; English translation by W. A. Oldfather as *The Discourses as Reported by Arrian*, LCL, 1:321.

34. *SVF*, 3, par. 337; 1, par. 162, (on which, see Schofield, *The Stoic Idea of the City*, 110); 3, par. 4.

35. *SVF*, 3, par. 334 (on which, see Schofield, *Stoic Idea*, 62).

36. See Schofield, *Stoic Idea*, 69, 103, 138; Villey, *La Formation de la pensée juridique moderne*, 396.

37. Cicero *De legibus* 1.6.18; 1.7; Keyes trans., LCL, 317, 383. See also Arius Didymus in Eusebius *Préparation évangélique* (*De evangelica praeparatione*), SC 14:15 (on which see Schofield, *Stoic Idea*, 66); and also *De legibus* 2.4, 3.1. See also Cicero *Philippics* 11.11, 28; and Neschke-Hentschke, *Platonisme politique*, 197, 199.

38. Musonius Rufus, in Stobaeus *Anthologium*, ed. Curtius Wachsmuth and Otto Hense, 5 vols. (Berlin: Weidmann, 1884–1912), 4.7, par. 67, vol. 2, p. 283; Xenophon *Cyropaedia* 8.1.22; Aeschylus *Suppliant Maidens* 430–32; Aristotle *Pol.* 3.13, 1284a14, 3.17, 1288a2. On the notion in general, see Steinwenter, "Νομος έψνος: Zur Geschichte einer politischen Theorie."

39. Diotogenes, in Stobaeus *Anthologium* 4.7, par. 61, pp. 263, 265; Sthenidas, in ibid., 4.7, par. 63, p. 270. See also Dvornik, *Early Christian and Byzantine Political Philosophy*, 1:543.

40. Pseudo-Archytas, in Stobaeus *Anthologium* 4.1, par. 135, p. 82; Plutarch, "To an Uneducated Ruler," in *Plutarch's Moralia*, trans. Harold North Fowler, LCL, 780c. See also Dvornik, *Early Christian and Byzantine Political Philosophy*, 1:518.

41. Cicero *De legibus* 3.1.2, p. 338; *De re publica* 1.34.52, p. 56; Ulpian, in *Digesta* 1.4.1, on which, see Dvornik, *Early Christian and Byzantine Political Philosophy*, 1:518.

42. Plotinus *Enneads* 4.3 [27], 24, 10; in *Enneads IV.1–9*, trans. A. H. Armstrong, LCL.

43. Hierocles, "Commentary on the Golden Words" of Pythagoras, 13,52–53, in *FPhG*, 1:468b; in English translation from the French translation of André Dacier by N. Rowe as *Commentary of Hierocles on the Golden Verses of Pythagoras* (Wheaton, Ill.: Theosophical Pubishing, 1971). For the general context, see Brague, *La Sagesse du monde*, 111; *Wisdom of the World*, 92.

44. Porphyry, *Lettre à Marcella*, ed. E. Des Places, CUF, par. 26, pp. 120–21; quoted from *Porphyry's Letter to His Wife Marcella*, trans. Alice Zimmerman (Grand Rapids, Mich.: Phanes Press, 1986), 34.

45. *Tragicorum Graecorum Fragmenta*, ed. August Nauck, Frag. Adespota, no. 471, p. 932; Plato "Letter VIII" in *Epistles* 354e5–355 A1; Hierocles, in Stobaeus *Anthologium*, 3.39, 36, p. 733, 10–11. See also Gigante, *ΝΟΜΟΣ ΒΑΣΙΛΕΥΣ*, 266.

46. Plutarch *À un prince ignorant*, ed. M. Cuvigny (1984), 4.2 [2.781b], p. 42; quoted from "To an Uneducated Ruler," trans. Harold North Fowler, *Plutarch's Moralia*, LCL, 10:61.

47. Themistius *Paraphrase de la Métaphysique d'Aristote* (book Lambda), trans. from the Hebrew and the Arabic with introduction, notes, and index by Rémi Brague (Paris: Vrin, 1999), 7, par. 10, p. 86; par. 29, p. 94.

48. See below, pp. 114–19, 173–74.

49. Plato *Meno* 99a–100a; *Rep.* 6, 486a, 500b; 10, 611e; 9, 592b; 2, 383c; 6, 500c; 7, 540c; 9, 589cd, and 590ab. See also Gundert, "ΘΕΙΟΣ im politischen Denken Platons."

50. Plato *Laws* 1, 624a1–2; 7, 803c–804b; 4, 716c4–5; 5, 726a, 728b; and 12, 966e.

51. Plato *Laws* 4, 715c–d (on which, see also Gundert, "ΘΕΙΟΣ," 102); 4, 709a1–3 and b7–8. See also Montesquieu, *De l'esprit des Lois*, 14.10 and 14.4, in *Oeuvres complètes*, pp. 616b, 641b; Welton, "Divine Inspiration and the Origins of the Laws in Plato's *Laws*."

52. Plato *Laws*, 1, 634e1–2, 2, 662c7; *Minos* 318c1–3; Strauss, *Natural Right and History*, 84 and n. 4.

53. Plato *Laws* 12, 957c and 965c; Edmond, *Le Philosophe roi*; Fustel de Coulanges, *La cité antique*, 3.11, p. 223; Posidonius, in Seneca, *Letters to Lucilius* (= *Epistles*), trans. Richard M. Gummere, LCL, 94, 38.

54. Plato *Laws* 9, 875c3–d5. The expression quoted is from Edmond, *Le Philosophe roi*, 160 (see also 172). See also Plato *Laws* 3, 691d.

55. Plato *Laws* 4, 714a1–2, Bury trans.

56. Plato *Statesman* 271d–e; *Laws* 7, 713c–e. See Rosen, *Plato's "Statesman": The Web of Politics*, 158; Castoriadis, *Sur le "Politique" de Platon*.

57. See Laks, "L'utopie législative de Platon."

58. Plato *Laws* 10, 889a, 892a–b.

59. Plato *Statesman* 290d–e.

60. Neschke-Hentschke, *Platonisme politique*, 1:307; Pierre Bayle, *Pensées diverses sur la comète* (1683), par. 161: "If one wants to know my conjecture concerning what a society of atheists would be like in regard to morals and civil actions, it would be very much like a society of pagans." *Various Thoughts on the Occasion of a Comet*, trans., with notes and an interpretive essay, by Robert C. Bartlett (Albany: State University of New York Press, 2000), no. 161, p. 200.

61. Plato *Laws* 10, 889e4.

62. Aristotle *Physics* 2.8, 199a16, trans. Philip H. Wicksteed and Francis Cornford, LCL, 173.

63. Montesquieu, *De l'esprit des Lois*, 25.7, quoted from *The Spirit of the Laws*, ed. and trans. Cohler et al., 486.

64. Plato *Laws* 885b7–9; *Gorgias*, DK 82B3.

65. On the history of this word and its reprise today, see J. Assmann, *Moses der Ägypter*, 208–9.

Chapter 3

1. See Alt, "Die Staatenbildung der Israeliten in Palästina"; Buccellatti, "Da Saul a Davide."

2. Judges 21:25. The phrase occurs earlier, in 17:6; see also 18:1 and 19:1; Deut. 12:8.

3. See Noth, *Das System der zwölf Stämme Israels*. On the uncertainty of these reconstructions, see Levin, "Das vorstaatliche Israel."

4. See Lohfink, "Der Begriff des Gottesreichs," 42; Maddox, *Religion and the Rise of Democracy*, 23. On the word *hofshi*, see Albright, *From the Stone Age to Christianity*, 285.

5. Ezekiel 16:3–4 does not mention the Egyptian episode; Hosea 2:17 speaks of the flight from Egypt ("when she came up from the land of Egypt") but without mentioning Moses; Jeremiah 2:6 ("Where is the Lᴏʀᴅ who brought us up from the land of Egypt, Who led us through the desert, through a land of wastes and gullies, Through a land of drought and darkness, through a land which no one crosses, where no man dwells?") links it to the trek through the desert.

6. The expression is from Maddox, *Religion and Rise of Democracy*, 50. Spinoza stresses the private nature of primitive Christianity: *Tractatus theologico-politicus*, 19, in Spinoza, *Opera*, ed. Van Vloten and Land (1914), 2:303. On the humble origin of the first Christians, see 1 Cor. 1:26–27; Celsius, in Origen *Contra Celsum* 2.55, SC 136:128–29.

7. See Hadas-Lebel, *Hillel*, 117.

8. See Acts 7:57ff.; Hegesippus, quoted in Eusebius *Ecclesiastical History*, ed. Theodor Mommsen (Leipzig, 1903), 166–70, in English translation as *Eusebius' Ecclesiastical History*, trans. C. F. Cruse, reprint ed. (Peabody. Mass.: Hendrickson, 1998), 59–60. There is a rapid allusion to the topic in Flavius Josephus *Jewish Antiquities* 20.200.

9. Pliny the Younger, "Letter to The Emperor Trajan," *Letters and Panegyricus* 10.96, trans. Betty Rice, LCL, 285–91; Tacitus *The Annals* 15.44, trans. John Jackson, LCL, 4:282; Suetonius, "Life of Claudius," *Suetonius*, trans. J. C. Rolfe, LCL, 2:51.

10. See the thoughts on method in Crone, *Slaves on Horses*, 3–17. See also Humphreys, *Islamic History*, and Calder, *Studies in Early Muslim Jurisprudence*, 151–52, 214.

11. See Décobert, *Le Mendiant et le combattant*, 57; Donner, *The Early Islamic Conquests*, 267–71; Morabia, *Le Gihād dans l'Islam médiéval*, 126, 142; Djaït, *La Grande Discorde*. On the biography of the Prophet by Ibn Hisham-Ibn Ishāq, see Sellheim, "Prophet, Chalif und Geschichte" (1967).

12. There are hints of a missionary call in Qur'an 9:33, 61:9, and 48:28. See also Paret, "Toleranz und Intoleranz in Islam," 355.

13. For the discourse on the question of caliph Abū Bakr, see Abū Bakr Ahmad al-Hatib, *Tarīkh Baghdād* (Cairo, 1931), 11:149, 14–17; Al-Amiri, *al-I'ām fī manāqib il-Islām*, ed. A. A. Ghurab (Ryad: Dar Assala, 1988), 173, 17–20, cited in Nagel, *Staat und Glaubensgemein-schaft im Islam*, 1:19, 57–58; Crone and Hinds, *God's Caliph*, 105. See also the text published in Sourdel, "Un pamphlet musulman anonyme d'époque 'abbāside contre les chrétiens." For the notion of a religion that pays dividends, see Hergé, *Tintin en Amérique* (Paris: Casterman, 1947), 44.

14. Al-Ghazali, *Ihyā' 'ulūm id-Dīn* (Revival of the religious sciences), 37, "Will or Intention," 2.4, vol. 4, p. 406.

15. *Papyrus Erzherzog Rainer: Führer durch die Ausstellung*, notes by Josef von Karabacek, Jacob Krall, and Carl Wessely (Vienna, 1894), no. 558, p. 139, or Adolf Grohmann, *From the World of Arabic Papyri* (Cairo: Al-Maaref Press, 1952), 113–15. See also Crone and Cook, *Hagarism*, 157 n. 39; Hoyland, *Seeing Islam As Others Saw It*, 688.

16. See Wolf, "The Social Organization of Mecca and the Origins of Islam."

17. This expression of Muhammad ibn Maslama is quoted in Rodinson, *Mahomet* (1961), 225.

18. See Fattal, *Le Statut légal des non-musulmans en pays d'Islam*, 18–26.

19. Djaït, *La Grande Discorde*, 41. For other, similarly energetic expressions, see ibid., 39, 43, 47, 59, 65–66, 68, 80, 377. Ali Abderraziq speaks of colonization and exploitation: see his *L'Islam et les fondements du pouvoir*, 3.8.3, p. 145. We are far from the rosy vision of the conquest in Muhammad 'Abduh, *Rissalat al Tawhid*, 123–32.

20. 'Ali is quoted in Morabia, *Le Gihād dans l'Islam médiéval*, 270. 'Umar's letter is mentioned in Abū Yūsuf Ya'qūb, *Livre de l'impôt foncier [Kitāb al-Kharād]*, 218: see Calder, *Studies*

in *Early Muslim Jurisprudence,* 193–94, and the texts cited in Fattal, *Le Statut légal des non-musulmans,* 91.

21. Ibn Taymiyya, *Le Traité de droit public d'Ibn Taimīya: Traduction annotée de la Siyāsa shar῾īya,* 35–36, cited, with other authors, in Morabia, *Le Gihād,* 237–38, 246. One might add the philosopher Avicenna, *Al-Shifā, al-Ilāhiyyāt (Metaphysics),* 10.5, p. 453, 2–5.

22. See Rodinson, *Mahomet* (1994), 193–94; Morabia, *Le Gihād,* 85. Djaït sees such motivations as the main thrust of the conquest: Djaït, *La Grande Discorde,* 39, 47, 59.

23. See Nevo, "Towards a Prehistory of Islam," 110.

24. "Brethren of Purity," *Rasa̓il Ihwan as-Safa̓,* 4.1; vol. 3, pp. 493–97; Marquet, *La Philosophie des Ihwan al-Safa̓,* 56. Abderraziq, who rejects this combined role, notes that it is traditional: *L'Islam et les fondements du pouvoir,* 2.6.1, p. 115.

25. Qur̓an 2:30. See al-Qadi, "The Term 'Khalīfa' in Early Exegetical Literature," summarized in Brague, *La Sagesse du monde,* 74; *Wisdom of the World,* 60.

26. Ibn Khaldūn, *Prolégomènes [Muqaddimah]* 3. 29 (first lines), vol. 1, p. 393.

Chapter 4

1. See Schmidt, *Königtum Gottes in Ugarit und Israel,* 21–22, 47, 71; Jeremias, *Das Königtum Gottes in den Psalmen,* 12, 43.

2. See Mowinckel, *Psalmenstudien,* 1:44–145, 189–209.

3. See Jeremias, *Das Königtum Gottes,* 17, 27, 39.

4. See J. Assmann, *Herrschaft und Heil,* 48.

5. Xenophon *Cyropaedia* 5.1.24; see also *Economics* 8.32; Plato *Statesman* 301e1; Virgil *Georgics* 6.210–18; and—although it lacks the beehive image—Aristotle *Pol.* 14, 1332b16ff. I am here following Brague, "Du prince au peuple," 7–23.

6. See, for example, Xenophon *Cyropaedia* 1.6.

7. See Gauchet, *Le Désenchantement du monde,* x; English trans., *The Disenchantement of the World,* 9.

8. See Crüsemann, *Der Widerstand gegen das Königstum.*

9. See Balthasar, *Herrlichkeit,* vol. 3, pt. 2: *Theologie,* pt. 1: *Alter Bund,*105.

10. See, for example, Heinrich Heine, "König David," *Romanzero,* 1: Historien, no. 13, in Heine, *Werke,* ed. Stuart Atkins, 2 vols. (Munich: Beck, 1977), 2:736, which embroiders on 1 Kings 2:5–6.

11. Herodotus 3.8.2–5.

12. See J. Assmann, *Herrschaft und Heil,* 47. For the general context, see J. Assmann, *Das kulturelle Gedächtnis,* chap. 5, "Israel und die Erfindung der Religion," 196–228.

13. See also, for example, Ibn al-Muqaffa̓, *Le Livre de Kalila et Dimna,* trans. André Miquel (Paris: Klincksieck, 1957), pars. 411–12, pp. 163–64; La Fontaine, "The Frogs Who Wanted a King," in his *Fables.*

14. On the meaning of this word, see Driver, *Notes on the Hebrew Text and the Topography of the Books of Samuel,*69, who refers to 2 Kings 15:20; Ruth 2:1.

15. See Maddox, *Religion and the Rise of Democracy,* 1, 28, 94.

16. Hosea 13:11; Rabbi Nehemia (some editions spell Nehoray), in b*Sanhedrin* 11.20b; Flavius Josephus *Jewish Antiquities* 1.269, par. 223; Tosafot on *Sanhedrin* 19a, s.v. *aval;* Gersonides, *Commentary on 1 Samuel 8:6,* MG, p. 93b; Abravanel, *Commentary on 1 Samuel 9,* in *Peyrūsh,* pp. 105b–206b. See also Urbach, "Die Staatsauffassung des Don Isaak Abravanel," 260–67; Pines, *La Liberté de philosopher,* 442–44. Maimonides, in contrast, includes having a king among the commandments: Maimonides, *Livre des commandements,* Positifs, no. 173, pp. 146–47. On Maimonides see Blidstein, *Political Concepts in Maimonidean Halakha* (in

Hebrew), 19–23. For Christianity, see Buc, *L'Ambiguïté du livre*. I recall that Christianity had a theory of legitimate tyrannicide as early as John of Salisbury *Policraticus* 8.20, vol. 2, pp. 372–79.

17. For the reception of this requirement, see, for example, John of Salisbury *Policraticus* 4.4–7, vol. 1, pp. 244–61; Thomas Aquinas, *De regimine principum*, in *Opuscula Philosophica*, 1.16, par. 824, p. 276a.

18. Aristotle *Constitution of Athens* 41, 2d ed. Thalheim, BT, 1909, p. 58.

19. b*Makkot* 23b.

20. See, for example, Maimonides, *Guide des égarés*, 1.66, pp. 110–11/293–96; English trans., *The Guide of the Perplexed*. See also Heschel, *Theology of Ancient Judaism* (in Hebrew), 2:353–56.

21. Noth, *Das Gesetze im Pentateuch*, in *Gesammelte Studien zum Alten Testament*, 25; Jackson, "The Concept of Religious Law in Judaism," 39 n. 28.

22. See J. Assmann, *Herrschaft und Heil*, 68; and Brunner-Traut, *Frühformen der Erkenntnis*, 104.

23. A. Assmann, "Exkarnation," 135–55.

24. Ibn Ezra on Deut. 33:5 in MG, p. 105a. I cannot confirm that Jehuda Halevi expresses this idea; it is not to be found in the *Kuzari*. For modern exegesis, see Crüsemann, *Der Widerstand gegen das Königstum*, 81–82.

25. See J. Assmann, *Herrschaft und Heil*, 48.

26. See Noth, *Das Gesetze im Pentateuch*, 42–43.

27. Aristotle *Pol.* 1.2, 1253a2–3, Rackham trans.; SVF 3, pars. 340–48.

28. See the translation of the Hittite text in *ANET*, 395; see also Albrektson, *History and the Gods*, 40.

29. Deut. 2:10–11; Judg. 11:24, on which, see John Locke, *Second Treatise of Government*, 151–52; Jean-Jacques Rousseau, *Du contrat social*, vol. 3 of *Oeuvres complètes*, 4.8, p. 461.

30. See below, p. 61.

31. See the histories of Israel for the historical context, for example, Noth, *The History of Israel*; French trans., *Histoire d'Israël* (1970), pars. 25–26, pp. 309–35. The ironic anachronism on bayonets is from Jacob Taubes, quoted in J. Assmann, *Das kulturelle Gedächtnis*, 208.

32. For the example of Octave Houdas imposing classical Arabic on the Algerian *medersas*, who wanted to write in dialect, see von Grunebaum, *L'identité culturelle de l'Islam*, 162.

33. "Demotic Chronicle," col.c, 8–14, in Spiegelberg, ed. and trans., *Die sogenannte Demotische Chronik des Papyrus 215 der Bibliothèque Nationale zu Paris*, 31; see J. Assmann, *Das kulturelle Gedächtnis*, 207. On Elephantine, see *ANET*, 491a; Noth, *Das Gesetze im Pentateuch*, 101.

34. See Mélèze Modrzejewski, "La Septante comme *nomos*," 147–48.

35. The origin of the "Samaritans" is explained, with obvious bias, in 2 Kings 17:24–41, where the coexistence of cults is interpreted retrospectively as syncretic.

36. See Noth, *History of Israel*, 329.

37. David Kimhi, *Dictionarium Hebraicum*, 76; Joseph Albo, *Book of Principles*, ed. and trans. Isaak Husik (Philadelphia: The Jewish Publication Society, 1920), 1.7, vol. 1, pp. 78–79, in Lorberbaum, *Politics and the Limits of Law*, 72–73.

38. Ezra 3:3, 4:4, 9:2, 10:2; Neh. 9:30, 10:29. On this expression, see Voegelin, *Order and History*, vol. 1: *Israel and Revelation*, 167.

39. Ezra 10:2–3. See also 10:11.

40. Num. 25:11–13, and Hengel, *Die Zeloten*, 154–81.

41. See Urbach, *The Sages*, 2:584–88, 632–39.

42. See Fustel de Coulanges, *La cité antique*, 2.9, p. 105. In a lighter vein, see G. K. Chesterton, *Orthodoxy* (1908) (San Francisco: Ignatius Press, 1995), chap. 5, p. 73.

43. Ps. 119:18; 2 Kings 17:24–28; see Bornkamm, "Wandelungen im alt- und neutestamentlichen Gesetzesverständnis," 81.

44. *Book of the Dead*, chap. 125: see J. Assmann, *Ma'at*, 140–49, and *Das kulturelle Gedächtnis*, 185ff.

45. Inscription no. 20, Philadelphia, "Prescriptions for the participants in a private cult," first century BCE, lines 31–35, in Franciszek Sokolowski, *Lois sacrées de l'Asie Mineure* (Paris: De Boccard, 1955), 54.

46. See also Ps. 24:3–4; Koch, "Tempeleinlassliturgien und Dekaloge." On Psalm 15, see García de la Fuente, "Liturgias de entrada, normas de asilo o exhortaciones proféticas?"; Beyerlin, *Weisheitlich-kultische Heilsordnung*; Beauchamp, *Création et séparation*, 51–53.

47. Judg. 18:30. Here, most interestingly, the scribes change the name of Moses into that of the impious king Manasseh by inserting a letter above the line: see Mowinckel, *Le Décalogue*, 141–57, and Cazelles, "Dix paroles: Les origines du décalogue."

48. Qur'an 17:22–39; see Antes, *Ethik und Politik im Islam*, 44–46.

49. See Brague, *La Sagesse du monde*, 71; *Wisdom of the World*, 57.

50. See Aristotle *Met.* 1075a19–21, and Bertie Wooster's description of Roderick Spode as "a *pukka sahib* who plays the game and does not do things that are not done": P. G. Wodehouse, *The Code of the Woosters* (London: Penguin, 1953), chap. 5, p. 102. See also Beauchamp, *D'une montagne à l'autre*, 32–33.

51. This term should be compared with the Greek *orkia temnein:* see Fustel de Coulanges, *La cité antique*, 15, p. 245; *The Ancient City*, 200–202.

52. Fustel de Coulanges, *La cité antique*, 3.6, p. 175; 7, no. 4, p. 191; 15, p. 242. On the idea of a covenant between gods, see ibid., 3.15, p. 247.

53. See Beauchamp, *Création et séparation*, 172–86 for an interpretation of the word *merahephet* in Gen. 1:2c.

Chapter 5

1. *Midrasch Tanchuma*, ed. Salomon Buber (Wilna: Wittwe & Gebrüder Romm, 1885), on Genesis 11, and *Yalqut Shim'oni*, Exodus, remez 187 [*non vidi*]. I owe these references to the amiable courtesy of Gad Freudenthal. My thanks to José Costa for pointing out an error in the first French edition of the present work, which I am correcting here.

2. *Mekhilta de-R. Ishmael*, Ba-Hodesh, V, ed. H. S. Horovitz and I. A. Rabin (Frankfurt, 1931), 219 [*non vidi*], cited and translated into English in Urbach, *The Sages*, 316–17.

3. See Rashi on Genesis 1:1; see also Baron, *A Social and Religious History of the Jews*, vol. 6: *Laws, Homilies, and the Bible*, 51. For a probable source, see *Genesis Rabbah: Midrash Bereshit Rabba* 1.2, vol. 1, pp. 4–5.

4. For this generalization, see Carmichael, *The Spirit of Biblical Law*, which summarizes several earlier works.

5. Bornkamm, "Wandelungen im alt- und neutestamentlichen Gesetzesverständnis," in *Gesammelte Aufzätze*, 4:84–85.

6. *Dictionnaire de la Bible: Supplément*, s.v. "Loi israélite," vol. 5 (1957), col. 518 (H. Cazelles).

7. See Alt, "Die Ursprünge des israelitischen Rechts" (1934), in *Kleine Schriften*, 2:278–332, and Jackson, "Concept of Religious Law in Judaism," 43.

8. For a rapid catalogue, see *Dictionnaire de la Bible: Supplément*, s.v. "Loi Isréalite," vol. 5, 503–5.

9. See *ANET*, the entire section II: Legal Texts, 159–223.

10. b*Yoma* 67b.

11. See Heinemann, *La Loi dans la pensée juive*; Heschel, *Theology of Ancient Judaism*, 1:232–37; Urvoy, *Les Penseurs libres dans l'Islam médiéval*, 139 and (for what follows) 89, 90, 108, 109, 112–19, 302, 304.

12. b*Shabbat*, 23a; b*Yebamot*, 89a–90b.

13. See Goitein, *Studies in Islamic History and Institutions*, 202.

14. Mishnah, *Pirke Avot*, 3.2: see also Xenophon *Hellenics* 3.3.6. The notion appears in many texts: see, for example, Bahya Ibn Paquda, *Al-Hidāja'ilā Farā'id al-Qulūb* 2.5., p. 120; English trans., *The Duties of the Heart*; Nissim, in Ravitzky, *Religion and State in Jewish Philosophy* (in Hebrew), 68. The proverb of big fish eating little ones appears in Joseph Hayyun, *Milley de-Avot* (Venice, 1470), 24b; see Ravitsky, 132.

15. b*Baba Bathra* 91b; b*Rosh ha-Shana* 25b.

16. b*Berakot* 58a; *Genesis Rabbah*, chap. 94, p. 1183.

17. b*Berakot* 55a.

18. Lorberbaum, *Politics and the Limits of Law*, 7; b*Sanhedrin* 19ab, and, quoting other names, Flavius Josephus *Jewish Antiquities* 14.9.

19. b*Sanhedrin* [IV] 36a. Here "Rabbi" designates Jehuda ha-Nasi, Tanna of the first generation (late second century). Rashi *ad locum* explains "grandeur" by "royalty" in the case of Moses and by "dignity of head of the community" (*nesi'uth*) in the case of Rabbi.

20. See *TE*, s.v. "Dina de-malkutha dina," 7 (1968), cols. 295–308 (S. Shilo). I have been unable to consult Shmuel Shilo's long monograph of the same title (Jerusalem: Academic Press, 1974).

21. Funkenstein, *Perceptions of Jewish History*, 157. On this distinction, see Ravitzky, *History and Faith*, 63–64, and idem, *Religion and State in Jewish Philosophy*, 79–80.

22. b*Sanhedrin* 56a; Maimonides, *MT*, Sanhedrin 11.1. See Baron, *Social and Religious History of the Jews*, 6:5, 144–45; Urbach, *The Sages*, 317ff.; Leben, "La question du droit naturel dans le judaïsme," 1113–15.

23. See Faur, "La doctrina de la ley natural en el pensamiento judio del medioevo"; idem, "The Source of the Obligatory Character of the Commandments in the Thought of Maimonides" (in Hebrew), 43–47; Rosenthal, *Studia Semitica*, 1:321.

24. See Hengel, *Was Jesus a Revolutionist?*

25. The expression is attributed to St. John Chrysostom, but I have been unable to locate it.

26. Gustave Flaubert, *Madame Bovary: Moeurs de province*, pt. 3, chap. 9, quoted from *Madame Bovary*, trans. Francis Steegmuller (New York: Random House, 1957), 375. See also, for example, Jaime Balmes, *El protestantismo comparado con el catolicismo . . .* , chaps. 15–19, in Balmes, *Obras*, ed. Ignacio Casanovas (Madrid: Biblioteca de autores cristianos, 1967), 4:134–93.

27. See von Grunebaum, *Medieval Islam*, 210.

28. On the importance of this notion, see Prodi, *Una storia della giustizia*, 27; Villey, *La Formation de la pensée juridique moderne*, 136.

29. See Schlier, *Der Zeit der Kirche*; French trans., *Le Temps de l'Église*, 20.

30. The idea of "Mystery of Iniquity" is unknown in the German tradition because Luther translates this passage differently. In contrast, it appears in the King James Bible and has had a long career in the Anglo-Saxon imaginary: see, for example, Claggart in Herman Melville, *Billy Budd*, chaps. 12 and 22.

31. Ibn Khaldūn, *Prolégomènes* [*Muqaddimah*] 3.31, vol. 1, pp. 415, 3–18: see Brague,

"Trois regards musulmans sur la cité chrétienne," 20–26; Qirqisānī, *Kitāb al-Anwār*, ed. Leon Nemoy, 5 vols. (New York: Alexander Kohut Memorial Foundation, 1939–43), 1:43.

32. See Brague, *Europe, la voie romaine*, 201–2; *Eccentric Culture*, 58.

33. Rather than a thousand Christian citations in this connection, let me offer one Muslim one: Nasīr ad-Dīn Tūsī, *The Nasirean Ethics*, 3.3, p. 215.

34. See Bornkamm, "Wandelungen im alt- und neutestamentlichen Gesetzesverständnis," 75; Lambrecht, *"Eh bien! Moi je vous dis,"* 82; Rudolf Bultmann, *Theologie des Neuen Testaments*, 2d ed. (Tübingen, Mohr, 1954), 56; English trans., *Theology of the New Testament*, 2 vols. (New York: Scribner, 1951–55).

35. See Urbach, *The Sages*, 293–94. Jacob Emden (d. 1776), the first rabbi to have had positive things to say about Jesus, credits him with this attitude: see Hadas-Lebel, *Hillel*, 86–87.

36. See Lambrecht, *"Eh bien! Moi je vous dis"*; Beauchamp, *D'une montagne à l'autre*, 47, 116.

37. See Bornkamm, "Wandelungen," 100, 102; Lambrecht, *"Eh bien!,"* 81; Beauchamp, *D'une montagne à l'autre*, 119.

38. bShabbat 31a. The idea is omnipresent in later Judaism: see, for example, Abraham Ibn Ezra on Exodus 31:18 in *Reader: Annotated Texts with Introductions and Commentaries* (in Hebrew), 181; Nahmanides, *Torat Hashem temimah*, in *Kitvey Rabbenu Mosheh B. Nahman*, 1:141–75, at 152; Crescas, *Light of the Lord* (in Hebrew), 2.6.1, p. 230. Franz Rosenzweig notes the agreement between Jews and Christians on the topic: *Der Stern der Erlösung*, 2.3, p. 229.

39. See p. 62 above. The distinction is developed as a theme in the Talmud: see Heschel, *Theology of Ancient Judaism*, 1:v.

40. I am thinking here in particular of Elia Benamozegh, *Morale juive et morale chrétienne*; English trans., *Jewish and Christian Ethics, With a Criticism on Mahomedism*. On a possible origin of this idea, see Villey, *La Formation de la pensée juridique moderne*, 310.

41. See Thomas Aquinas, *Sententiarum* 4, d. 15, q. 3, a. 1d, ra. 2, in *S. Thomae Aquinatis Opera Omnia*, ed. Roberto Busa, 7 vols. (Stuttgart: Frommann-Holzboog, 1980), vol. 1, *In quattuor libros sententiarum*, 512a.

42. Among recent publications, see Prémare, *Les Fondations de l'Islam*, and idem, *Aux origines du Coran*, and also a revolutionary work, Luxenberg, *Die syro-aramäische Lesart des Koran*.

43. See Wansbrough, *Quranic Studies*; for the contrary view, see Burton, *The Collection of the Qu'rān*.

44. See Puin, "Observations on Early Qur'an Manuscripts in San'a."

45. Qur'an 12:3. For an explication, see Rippin, "Interpreting the Bible through the Qur'ān," 250–51.

46. See Chabbi, *Le Seigneur des Tribus*, 74–75, 252–53.

47. Qur'an 81:18, 19; see also 2:97; 26:193–94.

48. Respectively: Qur'an 16:102; 26:193; 2:97–98.

49. Qur'an 53:4–18.

50. Amos 8:14–15; Hesiod *Theogony* 22–34.

51. Ibn Hishām, *Al-Sirat al-Nabawiyyah li Ibn Hisham*, 1:273/106 [152]; English trans. by Alfred Guillaume as *The Life of Muhammad*. Alfred Guillaume translates "What shall I read?" rather than "I cannot read." See also The Venerable Bede, *Ecclesiastical History of the English People*, in French translation by Philippe Delaveau as *Histoire ecclésiastique du peuple anglais* (Paris: Gallimard, 1995), 4.24, p. 283. If the thesis stated in Luxenberg, *Die syro-aramäische Lesart des Koran*, that the Qur'an was at first a lectionary, should prove accurate, the parallel would be even more striking.

52. Qur'an 2:78; 7:157. The interpretation "belonging to a people not having received

writing" is noted in the commentator Baydāwī (d. 1286) regarding Qur'an 30:1: see Gardet, *Dieu et la destinée de l'homme*, 227 n. 2; Di Matteo, "Il 'tarîf' od alterazione della Bibbia secondo i musulmani," 90 n. 1.

53. See Schimmel, *Und Muhammad ist sein Prophet*, 55. On the descent of the book replacing the Incarnation, see Rosenzweig, *Der Stern der Erlösung*, 2.2, par. 147, p. 186.

54. Qur'an 2:23; 10:38; 11:13; 52:34.

55. Qur'an 17:88: see *EI*, s.v. I'jāz, 3.1044a–1046b (G. E. von Grünebaum).

56. See Jeffery, *The Qur'ān as Scripture*, 5; Urvoy, *Les Penseurs libres*, 112, 125.

57. See S. Stroumsa, "Écritures alternatives?," 284–89; Urvoy, *Les Penseurs*, 55–58; one example in van Ess, "Some Fragments of the Mu'āradat al-Qur'ān Attributed to Ibn al-Muqaffa'," 154–60. See also al-Qasim Ibn Ibrahim, *La lotta tra l'islam e il manicheismo*, trans. Guidi.

58. See, for example, Averroes, *Tahafot at-Tahafot: L'incohérence de l'incohérence*, "Questions of Physics," Introduction, 515.

59. Shakik b. Salama Abū Wā'il, in Ibn Sa'd, *Biographien Muhammeds, seiner Gefährten und der späteren Träger des Islams bis zum Jahre 230 der Flucht*, 9 vols. (Leyden: Brill, 1904–40), vol. 6, *Biographien der Kufier*, ed. K. V. Zetterstéen (1909), 67, 22–23, cited in Goldziher, *Die Richtungen der islamischen Koranauslegung*, 56. See also Birkeland, *Old Muslim Opposition against Interpretation of the Koran*.

60. Qur'an 24:31; 33:59: see Masson, *Monothéisme coranique et monothéisme biblique*, 610.

61. See d'Emilia, "Il diritto musulmano comparato con il bizantino dal punto di vista della tipologia del diritto," 68.

62. Qur'an 2:185; 25:1; *Le Coran*, trans. Denise Masson, p. 303. On this word, see Jeffery, *Foreign Vocabulary of the Qur'ān*, 225–29.

63. See Baumstark, "Das Problem eines vorislamischen christlich-kirchlichen Schrifttums in arabisher Sprache," 565–66; Ibn Hishām, *Al-Sirat al-Nabawiyyah*, 1:275/104 [153]; Bukhari, SB, vol. 1, p. 4 and n. 1.

64. Sebeos (after 661), *History of Heraclius*, chaps. 30–31, in Cahen, "Note sur l'acceuil des chrétiens d'Orient à l'islam," 53; Crone and Cook, *Hagarism*, 7. I have been unable to locate the passage in Hoyland, *Seeing Islam As Others Saw It*, 124–32, 414 n. 87.

65. Qur'an 31:33; 44:41. The same thought occurs in a text in Old High German of the early ninth century: *Muspilli*, l. 57; see Alfred Jolivet and Fernand Mossé, *Manuel de l'allemand du Moyen Âge, des origines au XIVe siècle* (Paris: Aubier, 1947), 297.

66. See Nagel, *Staat und Glaubensgemeinschaft im Islam*, 1:60.

67. Qur'an 9:23. Compare with the discussion above, pp. 63–65, 66. See also Donner, *Early Islamic Conquests*, 57.

68. See Calder, *Early Muslim Jurisprudence*, 218–19; Schacht, *An Introduction to Islamic Law*; French trans., *Introduction au droit musulman*, 21–23.

69. Qur'an 2:187, 229–30; 4:13; 58:4; 65:1. In these passages the word translated as "limits" does not have the later sense of "legal punishments": see Ibn Taymiyya, *Le Traité de droit public*, 121. On commandments regarding the cult, see Rivlin, *Gesetz im Koran*.

70. Qur'an: on inheritance, 4:11; on loans and similar obligations, 2:282–83; on wine and gambling, 2:219; on marrying unbeliever women, 2:221; on divorce, 2:232; on female modesty, 24:31.

71. Qur'an 24:2–4. On the story of 'Ā'isha, see Rodinson, *Mahomet*, 1975 ed., 232–38.

72. Qur'an 60:10: see Crone and Cook, *Hagarism*, 180 n. 17.

73. Bukhari, SB, 86 (on criminal sentences), no. 24, pp. 386–87, and no. 37, 2, pp. 397–98. See also Di Matteo, "Il 'tarîf' od alterazione della Bibbia secondo i musulmani," 82; Vajda, "Juifs et musulmans selon le hadith," 93–99; Wansbrough, *Quranic Studies*, 198.

74. Aristotle *Pol.* 1.3, 1253b6–7.

75. Qur'an 4:34.

76. Jāhiz, *Kitāb al-Qiyān*, no. 14 in *Rasā'il al-Jāhiz*, ed. A. M. Harūn (Cairo, n.d.), 149, cited in Bürgel, *Allmacht und Mächtigkeit*, 286. The exclusion of women from public and social life was achieved in the age of Harun al-Rashid: see von Grunebaum, *Medieval Islam*, 175.

77. Qur'an 2:282 and 4:11. The same proportion applies for the indemnity due in case of accidental wounds: see Abū Yūsuf Ya'qūb, *Livre de l'impôt foncier*, 245.

78. Qur'an 81:8: see Gräf, "De Koran, Uit het Arbisch vertaalt door J. H. Kramers," 366–67; Antes, *Ethik und Politik im Islam*, 60. See also Qur'an 6:151; 17:31.

79. See Rodinson, *Mahomet*, 262; Morabia, *Le Gihād*, 91.

80. Qur'an 16:71: see Rudi Paret, *Der Koran: Kommentar und Konkordanz* (Stuttgart: Kohlhammer, 1971), 191. For this injunction, see Denise Masson, *Essai d'interprétation du Coran inimitable* (Beirut: Dar al-kitab allubnani, 1967), 355. For the parallel of the rich, see Qur'an 30:28.

81. See Rodinson, *Mahomet*, 128–30. For a nuanced interpretation, see Ammann, *Die Geburt des Islam*, 48–49; Qur'an 11:27. This attitude appears in the "Brethren of Purity," *Rasa'il Ihwan as-Safa'*, 4.1 [42], par. 15: vol. 3, pp. 429–32. See above, p. 33.

82. See Nagel, *Staat und Glaubensgemeinschaft im Islam,* 69; Bürgel, *Allmacht und Mächtigkeit,* 22, 74, 351; Antes, *Ethik und Politik im Islam,* 28; Djaït, *La Grande Discorde,* 42, 227; Muranyi, *Die Prophetengenossen in der frühislamischen Geschichte,* 165–76; Chabbi, *Le Seigneur des Tribus,* 118, 494 n. 140.

83. Qur'an 2:219 (see Paret, *Der Koran,* 46); 8:41. On the word *sadaqa,* see Jeffery, *Foreign Vocabulary,* 194.

84. Respectively, Qur'an 2:177, 215; 4:36; 8:41; 59:7.

85. Qur'an 9:60. See, for example, Ibn Taymiyya, *Le Traité de droit public,* 33–34; see also Paret, *Der Koran,* 38.

86. Abderraziq, seeking to demonstrated the non-state character of the primitive community, does little more than show the rudimentary nature of institutions, which nobody denies: see Abderraziq, *L'Islam et les fondements du pouvoir,* 2.5.12, p. 107.

87. Wellhausen, *Das arabische Reich und sein Sturz,* 5.

88. See Nagel, *Staat und Glaubensgemeinschaft,* 97; Lambton, *State and Government in Medieval Islam,* 13; Hobbes, *Leviathan,* ed. Oakeshott, 3.35, p. 270; and, in the Bible, Zach. 14:20–21. On the connection between the sacred and the public, see Kantorowicz, *The King's Two Bodies* (1957), 168, 187–88.

89. See Gimaret, *Les Noms divins en Islam,* 235–51.

90. See Bürgel, *Allmacht und Mächtigkeit,* 107, 222–23; Massignon, *La Passion d'al-Husayn Ibn Mansūr al-Hallāj,* 3:135 n. 3.

91. Qur'an 11:20; 7:12; 42:31; 46:32.

92. Qur'an 2:256. The passage is explained by Qur'an 10:99–100: see Paret, "Toleranz und Intoleranz in Islam," 346.

93. See Chabbi, *Le Seigneur des Tribus,* 537 n. 300; 573 n. 405.

94. Antes, *Ethik und Politik im Islam,* 37.

95. Qur'an 22:65; Gen. 2:19; and Qur'an 2:31. See also Brague, *Europe, la voie romaine,* 152–53; *Eccentric Culture,* 119.

96. Qur'an 2:30; 38:26. See also Goldziher, *Sur l'Islam,* 284–85; Paret, "Halifat Allah—Vicarius Dei."

97. Qur'an 3:32; for the hadith, see Abū Yūsuf Ya'qūb, *Livre de l'impôt foncier,* 14, cited in Lambton, *State and Government,* 57.

98. Qur'an 26:108, 110, 126, 131, 144, 150, 163, 179.

99. See Nagel, *Die Festung des Glaubens*, 70–71, 288.

100. *CTM*, 4.252; Bukhari, SB, 93, "Sentences," 1, 1, vol. 4, p. 497, and 94, "Traditions," 2, 6, vol. 4, p. 547.

101. Qur'an 4:59. The phrase is cited widely: see, for example, al-Māwardī, *Al-Ahkām al-sultānīyah wa-'l-walāyāt al-dīniyya*, 5; ed. and trans. into French by Edmond Fagnan as *Les Statuts gouvernementaux*, 6; Nizām al-Mulk, *Siasset Namèh: Traité de gouvernement* 3, p. 18. Charles Butterworth compares it with Rom. 13:1–7, without remarking, however, that St. Paul recommended obeying non-Christian rulers: Butterworth, "Political Islam."

102. See Nagel, *Staat und Glaubensgemeinschaft*, 1:238; Lewis, *The Political Language of Islam;* French trans., *Le Langage politique de l'islam*, 138. Ibn Taymiyya, himself a doctor of law, obviously includes such men among the "holders of authority": see Ibn Taymiyya, *Le Traité de droit public*, in *Power in Islamic Political Thought*, 415. A "modernist" like Rashīd Rida believes that the phrase applies to the community, but the community represented by the "sages": Rida, *Le Califat dans la doctrine de Rasīd Ridā*, a translation by Henri Laoust of *Al-Hilāfa au al-Imāma al ʿuzmā*, 47, 98, 157. The Shiites, of course, see these leaders as the imāms, such as Ibn Babūyā: see Lambton, *State and Government*, 21, 232. Others see them as the military: Shāfiʿī, *Islamic Jurisprudence: Shāfiʿī's Risāla*, chap. 5, par. 88, p. 122; for Ghazali and Ibn Jamāʿa, see Lambton, 121, 232.

103. Qur'an 59:6.

104. Qur'an 4:59. Criticism of this notion is implied in the "Brethren of Purity," *Rasaʾil Ihwan as-Safaʾ*, 4.1 [42], par. 51, vol. 3, p. 527.

105. Qur'an 5:33. See also Montesquieu, *Mes pensées*, 23, par. 1945, p. 1048b. For the application of such punishments, see Nizām al-Mulk, *Siasset Namèh*, 11, p. 101; 39, pp. 178–79, and the examples cited in Tyan, *Institutions de droit public musulman*, 1:463–65, or Kraemer, "Apostates, Rebels and Brigands."

106. Qur'an 8:22. On this topic, see Brague, "Le déni de l'humanité: Sur le jugement: 'ces gens ne sont pas des hommes' dans quelques textes antiques et médiévaux," *Lignes*, vol. 12, *Penser le racisme* (1990): 213–72. The Shiite Ibn Babūyā divided creation into three classes: 1. prophets, messengers, and imāms; 2. believers; and 3. unbelievers and animals: see Lambton, *State and Government*, 229. See also the remark of a Turk (whom he describes as "fanatical") recorded by Ignaz Goldhizer in the journal of his trip to the Orient under the date of 23 September 1873, in Raphael Patai, *Ignaz Goldziher and His Oriental Diary: A Translation and Psychological Portrait* (Detroit: Wayne State University Press, 1987), 89, 92.

107. See Ibn Hishām, *Al-Sirat al-Nabawiyyah*, vol. 4, pp. 312–13/682–83 [1012].

108. See the suggestive remarks of Youssef Seddik in his *Dits du Prophète* (Paris: Sindbad; Arles: Actes Sud, 1997), 117–20.

109. See Strauss, *Rebirth of Classical Political Rationalism*, 249.

110. Qur'an 21:105, citing Psalm 37:29.

111. Respectively, John 5:23; 12:48; 15:23; 1 John 2:23, and Matt. 10:40; Luke 10:16; Mark 9:37, Luke 9:48, and John 13:20 (quoted). See also Masson, *Monothéisme coranique et monothéisme biblique*, 306–7.

112. See Masson, *Monothéisme*, 602–3.

113. Crone and Cook, *Hagarism*, 26, emphasis mine.

Chapter 6

1. The term is from Beauchamp, *L'un et l'Autre Testament;* see also Fishbane, *Biblical Interpretation in Ancient Israel*.

2. Maimonides, *Mishneh Torah, The Book of Knowledge*, "Idolatry," 2.2, p. 67b; the Talmu-

dic source, b*Shabbat* 149a, is distant. On philosophy as law, see Lachterman, "Torah and Logos," 6, and Voegelin, *Order and History,* 1:131.

3. See above, chap. 5, n. 52.

4. See Strauss, *Gesammelte Schriften,* 2:428.

5. See Sanders, *Paul, the Law and the Jewish People,* 144–48; Räisänen, *Paul and the Law,* 199–202.

6. The image of the dividing wall or barrier is in *Lettre d'Aristée à Philocrate,* SC, no. 89, par. 139, p. 170, as well as in Flavius Josephus *History of the Jewish Wars* 2.18.488; Flavius Josephus *Jewish Antiquities* 1.192.

7. b*Shabbat* 151b and b*Nidda* 61b: see Schäfer, "Die Torah der messianischen Zeit."

8. See Bornkamm, "Gesetz und Natur," 101–2. On the sort of law that Paul attacks, see Taubes, *Die Politische Theologie des Paulus,* 36.

9. Seneca *Letters to Lucilius* 41.2, quoted from Seneca, *Epistles,* trans. Richard M. Gummere, LCL, 273.

10. Oral declaration cited by Falk, *Law and Religion,* 66; see also Yeshayahu Leibowitz himself, cited in van Ess, *Theologie und Gesellschaft,* 4:574.

11. *Apocalypse de Baruch,* introduction, translation from the Syriac, and commentary by Pierre Bogaert, SC nos. 144–45, 2 vols. (Paris: Éditions du Cerf, 1969), 1:496.

12. Qur'an 6:156–57; see also 35:40, and 37:167–69.

13. See Juwaynī, *El-Irchad,* chap. 20, pars. 2–1, p. 156, 7/243; al-Ghazali, *Ihyā''ulūm id-Dīn,* 4:425, in Laoust, *La Politique de Ghazali,* 216.

14. *HWPh,* 1, cols. 701–19 (R. Pohlman), which does not mention St. Paul; Bickerman, "Autonomia," 432–51; Sophocles *Antigone* 821 (chorus); Hirzel, *Agraphos Nomos,* 54 n. 3.

15. Aristotle *Pol.* 3.13, 1284a3–14, trans. Rackham. The idea also appears in Hasidism: see Nachman of Bratslav, "The just (*tsaddiq*) is in itself precepts and commandments," quoted in Heinemann, "Die Lehre vom ungeschriebenen Gesetz im jüdischen Schrifttum," 171; see also Aristotle *Nic. Ethics* 4.18, 1128a52.

16. Jer. 31:32, in the Greek of the Septuagint. See also Arnold Ehrhardt, *Politische Metaphysik von Solon bis Augustin* (1959–69), 2:35–39.

17. C. S. Lewis, *The Abolition of Man* (1943); see also the ideas cited and criticized by Ibn Hazm, *Al-Fisal fī al-Milal wa-l'ahwā'wa-l-nihal,* 3:304, in Urvoy, *Les Penseurs libres,* 154.

18. 1 Cor. 9:9, and 1 Tim. 5:18, citing Deut. 25:4.

19. Contrary to Legendre, *Le Désir politique de Dieu,* 29–30, 132, 155, 213, 262.

20. See above, pp. 68–69, and Beauchamp, *D'une montagne à l'autre,* 213–15, 222–27.

21. See Arendt, *The Life of the Mind,* vol. 2: *Willing,* 68.

22. Ovid *Metamorphoses* 7.20ff., trans. Frank Justus Miller, rev. G. P. Gould, LCL, 343. See also Seneca, *Letters to Lucilius* 21.1; Epictetus, *Epicteti Dissertationes ab Arriano digestae,* ed. Heinrich Schenkl (Leipzig: Teubner, 1916), 2.26.4, p. 203, English trans. by W. A. Oldfather as *The Discourses as Reported by Arrian,* LCL; *Book of Mysteries* (1Q 27), 8–12, in Fiorentino García Martínez and Eibert J. C. Tigchelaar, *The Dead Sea Scrolls Study Edition,* 2 vols. (Leiden and New York, Brill, 1997–98), 1:66–68.

23. "Non . . . consisteret peccatum, si interdictio non fuisset," Peter Lombard *Sententiarum* 2, d. 35; *PL,* 191–92, 734 [d], after Augustine *Contra Faustum Manichaeum* 22.27; *PL* 42:418c. The complete formula, which I cite in the text, may have had to wait for the Bavarian jurist Paul Johann Anselm Feuerbach, and it entered into the Bavarian Code in 1813.

24. See also Ovid *Amores* 3.4.17: *nitimur in vetitum;* Nasir ad-Dīn Tūsī, *Nasirean Ethics,* 2.4, p. 168.

25. Fyodor Dostoevsky, *The Brothers Karamazov*, 1.2.6, trans. Constance Garnett, revised, with an introduction, by Avram Yarmolinsky (New York: Heritage Press, 1949), 69.

26. *Qohelet Rabba* 11, 8 (52a), in Hermann L. Strack and Paul Billerbeck, *Kommentar zum Neuen Testament aus Talmud und Midrasch*, 6 vols. (Munich: Beck, 1978–82), 3:577.

27. See above, chap. 5, n. 38.

28. See Beauchamp, *D'une montagne à l'autre*, 29.

29. See, for example, Benamozegh, *Morale juive et morale chrétienne*, 2:34.

30. Augustine *In Epistulam Joannis ad Parthos tractatus decem* 7.8, SC, no. 75, p. 328.

31. I have attempted elsewhere to show how that strategy had repercussions in other domains than the religious, and that it even structured the entire Islamic model of the relationship with culture: see Brague, *Europe, la voie romaine*, 135–41.

32. Qur'an 2:41; 2:97.

33. Qur'an 19:28.

34. Qur'an 3:45 and *passim*. On the word "messiah," see Jeffery, *Foreign Vocabulary*, 265–66.

35. Chabbi, *Le Seigneur des Tribus*, 60–61.

36. See Goldziher, "Über muhammedanische Polemik gegen Ahl al-Kitāb," in *Gesammelte Schriften*, 2:1–47; Di Matteo, "Il 'tarîf' od alterazione della Bibbia secondo i musulmani"; Gandeul and Caspar, "Textes de la tradition musulmane concernant le *tahrīf* (falsification) des Écritures"; Lazarus-Yafeh, *Intertwined Worlds*; Adang, *Muslim Writers on Judaism and the Hebrew Bible*, 223–48. This highly important element is often neglected: see, for example, Djaït, *La Grande Discorde*, 35–36.

37. See Adler, "The Jews as Falsifier"; Resnick, "The Falsification of Scripture and Medieval Christian and Jewish Polemics," 353ff. For the Jewish examples—Qimhi among others—see Resnick, 366–67.

38. Justin Martyr *Dialogue avec Tryphon* 72–73, 2:346–52; Origen *Homiliae in Jeremiam* 16.10, *PG*, 13, 451; Origen *Epistola ad Africanum* 9, *PG* 11:65b. For those who reject the notion, see Augustine *De civitate Dei* 15, 13.1, *La Cité de Dieu*, 3:86; Augustine, Letter 82.5, 34, *PL* 33:290d; The Venerable Bede, Epistola 3, "Ad Plegwinum," 3, *PL* 94:671c.

39. See Resnick, "Falsification of Scripture," 369–71, 374.

40. Qur'an 2:75; 4:46; 5:41; 7:162; 5:15; 6:91; 5:13.

41. Qur'an 28:43–54; 46:10; 6:159. See also Di Matteo, "Il 'tarîf,'" 77–80.

42. Qur'an 5:48; 2:79, 41; 5:15; 4:46. See also Di Matteo, 80–97.

43. Bukhari, SB, 52, "Shahādāt," no. 29, 1, vol. 2, p. 229, and 94, "Reliance on the Book," 25, 3, vol. 4, pp. 574–75; in the opposite sense, Bukhari, SB, 97, "Unity of God," 55, vol. 4, p. 648 (explanatory introductory note by Bukhari).

44. Ibn Hazm, adaptation in Castilian by Miguel Asín Palacios, *Abenházam de Córdoba y su Historia crítica de las ideas religiosas*, 5 vols. (Madrid: Revista de Archivos, 1927–32; reprint ed. Madrid: Turner, 1984), vol. 2, chap. 15, pp. 238–392 (on the Torah and the Gospels), and vol. 3, chaps. 18–19, pp. 21–118 (on the Gospels and other Christian texts). See also Deut. 4:24, and Qur'an 24:35, in Ibn Hazm, *Al-Fisal*, 1:185, 1, chap. 15, par. 43; Asín Palacios, *Abenházam*, 2:301–2.

45. Ahmad b. Idris al-Qarafī [al-Sinhājī], *al-Ajwiba al-fahira 'an al-aswila al-fajira* (Cairo, 1986). For a summary of the as-yet unpublished manuscript, see Di Matteo, "Il 'tarîf,'" 236–38.

46. For parallels, see Di Matteo, "Il 'tarîf,'" 244 n. 3, 251.

47. Miguel de Epalza, *La Tuhfa, autobiografía y polémica islámica contra el Cristianismo de*

ʾAbdallāh al-Taryūmān *(fray Anselmo Turmeda)* (Rome: Accademia Nazionale dei Lincei, 1971), 192–495.

48. Saʿīd b. Hasan of Alexandria: summary in Di Matteo, "Il 'tarîf,'" 239.

49. Maimonides, *Responsa,* ed. Joshua Blau, 4 vols. (Jerusalem: Mas, 1986), Responsum no. 149, 1:285. On Maimonides' positive attitude toward Islam, which he exonerates from suspicion of idolatry, see Maimonides, "Letter to the Convert Ovadia," in ibid., no. 448, 2:726. See also Thomas Aquinas *Summa contra Gentiles* 1.2; Bonaventura *Collationes in Hexaëmeron,* ed. Vivès, 19, 14, d., vol. 9, p. 124a (disputation between St. Francis and the Sultan); John Duns Scotus *Prologue de l'Ordinatio,* trans. Gérard Sondag (Paris: PUF, 1999), par. 99, pp. 136–37.

50. See Crone, *Slaves on Horses,* 18 and n. 110; Mosche J. Kister, "Haddithu ʿan bani israʾila wa-la haraja: A Study of an Early Tradition" (1972), in his *Studies in Jāhiliyya and Early Islam* (London: Variorum, 1980).

51. See *EI,* s.v. *kisās al-anbiyya,* vol. 5 (1986), cols. 180a–181a (T. Nagel).

52. See Reinhart, *Before Revelation,* 11.

53. See Gardet, *Dieu et la destinée de l'homme,* 216 and n. 7.

54. A trace of this idea can be found in a text of Ibn Khaldun, who does not accept the idea of an alteration of Scripture by Jews and Christians: see Urvoy, "Ibn Haldūn et la notion d'altération des textes bibliques," 171. My thanks to Dominique Urvoy for providing me with this information. It seems to me that I read it expressed more explicitly somewhere, but I have lost track of where.

55. See above, p. 68.

56. See Weiss, "Covenant and Law in Islam," 58.

57. See 1 Macc. 9:27; Ps. 74:9; Lam. 2:9; Flavius Josephus *Contre Apion* 1.8.41, p. 10; Jeffery, *Qurʾān as Scripture,* 41 n. 56.

58. On these terms, see above, pp. 86–87.

59. Qurʾan 21:105, citing Ps. 37:29: see above, chap. 5, final section.

60. See Jeffery, *Qurʾān as Scripture,* 6–7.

61. John 15:26; Qurʾan 61:6. For Ubayy's interpretation of the question, see Prémare, *Aux origines du Coran,* 89. For the Muslim interpretation, see, for example, Ibn Hishām, *Al-Sirat al-Nabawiyyah,* 1:267–70/103–4 [149–50], or Ibn Hazm, *Al-Fisal,* 1:133–34. On Manes and Montanus, see Augustine *Contra Felicem* 9, and Eusebius, *Ecclesiastical History,* ed. Theodor Mommsen (Leipzig, 1903), 5.14, p. 458. See Jeffery, *Qurʾān as Scripture,* 41 and n. 54, for a comparison.

62. Tertullian *De virginibus velandis* 1; Gregory of Nazianzus *Oratio* 12.11.

63. Crone and Cook, *Hagarism,* 224 and n. 8.

64. Qurʾan 19:16–20; Gen. 21:16, and *Gospel of Pseudo-Matthew,* in *Los Evangelios Apocrifos,* ed. Aurelio de Santos Otero (Madrid: Biblioteca di Autores Cristianos, 1988), chap. 20, pp. 212–13.

65. Qurʾan 2:125–27; 37:101–13, esp. 101 and 112.

66. See Di Matteo, "Il 'tarîf,'" 242.

67. Qurʾan 12:2ff., where the terms "Qurʾan" or "the Book" appear thirteen times in all; or 5:115ff., where they appear nine times.

68. See Wansbrough, *Quranic Studies,* 163–66.

69. Qurʾan 2:106. For a recent synthesis regarding this theory, see Powers, "The Exegetical Genre nāsikh al-Qurʾān wa mansūkhuhu," 117–38.

70. Qurʾan 53:20ff. For the parallel with Manes, see Jeffery, *Qurʾān as Scripture,* 55.

71. Qurʾan 24:35; Qurʾanic exegesis and Sufi terminology in Avicenna, *Al-Tafsīr al-quʾānī*

wa-l-lughat al-sufiyya fī falsafat Ibn Sīnā, ed. Hasan ʿAsi (Beirut: M. J., 1983), 86–88; Ghazali, *The Niche of Lights*, ed. and trans., with notes, by David Buchman (Provo, Utah: Brigham Young University Press, 1998).

Chapter 7

1. Hecataeus is known through Diodorus of Siculus *Bibliotheca historica* 15,3.5–6; in Stern, *Greek and Latin Authors on Jews and Judaism* (1974), no. 11, 1:26–27.

2. The absence of kings can also be found in Tacitus *Histories* 5.8.

3. Diodorus Siculus *Bibliotheca historica* 1.94, 1–2; in Stern, *Greek and Latin Authors*, no. 58, 1:171. Well into the ninth century Photius was still using this work: see Dagron, *Empereur et prêtre*, 234.

4. See, for example, *Critias*, DK 88B25; Abū Bishr Mattā b. Yūnus, cited below, pp. 111–12 and n. 50; Machiavelli, *Discorsi*, 1.11–15, in Machiavelli, *Tutte le opere*, 1:125–26; Gabriel Naudé, "Apologie pour tous les grands personnages qui ont été faussement soupçonnés de magie," in Jacques Prévot et al., eds., *Libertins du XVIIe siècle*, 2 vols. (Paris: Gallimard, 1998), 1:164.

5. Strabo *Geographica* 16, 760Cff. in Stern, *Authors*, no. 115, 1:295–96. For a comparison between the two texts, see Reinhardt, "Poseidonios über Ursprung und Entartung," 412–13.

6. Strabo *Geographica* 2.2, par. 35; in Stern, *Authors*, Greek, 1:294, English trans, 299–300. The idea appears in the text of Manetho cited in Flavius Josephus *Contre Apion* 1.26, par. 250, p. 47—if this was not an anti-Jewish addition.

7. Strabo *Geographica* pars. 37–39; in Stern, *Authors*, Greek, 1:295–96, English trans. 300–301.

8. *Lettre d'Aristée à Philocrate*, SC, no. 89, pars. 31, p. 120; 161, p. 180; 168, p. 182; 313, p. 234; 139, p. 170, and 240, p. 208.

9. See Heinemann, *Philons griechische und jüdische Bildung*, 475–78.

10. Philo of Alexandria *Quod omnis probus liber sit* 80, in *Philonis Judaei Opera*, ed. Thomas Mangey, 2 vols. (London, 1742), henceforth abbreviated as "M," 458, ed. Madeleine Petit (Paris: Éditions du Cerf, 1974), 202; *De Decalogo*, M, 155, ed. Valentin Nikiprowetzky (Paris: Éditions du Cerf, 1965), 46. See also Philo *Legato ad Gaium* 210, ed. André Pelletier (Paris: Éditions du Cerf, 1972), 216; *De vita Mosis* 2.188, M, 163, ed. Roger Arnaldez et al. (Paris: Éditions du Cerf, 1967), 274.

11. Philo of Alexandria *Quod deterius potiori insidiari soleat* 13, M, 194, ed. Irène Feuer (Paris: Éditions du Cerf, 1965), 30 and note 1, quoted from "The Worse Attacks the Better," trans. F. H. Colson and G. H. Whitaker in *Philo*, 2:211, LCL. See Wolfson, *Philo*, and, against Wolfson, Amir, "Mose as Verfasser der Tora bei Philon," 92.

12. Philo of Alexandria *De Abrahamo* 275–76, M, 40, ed. Jean Gorez (Paris: Éditions du Cerf, 1966), 132–33. The text comments on Gen. 26:5. See also Philo, *Commentaire allégorique des saintes lois d'après l'oeuvre des six jours*, 3.58, ed. Émile Bréhier (Paris: Picard, 1909), 258; *De Iosepho* 174, M, 66, ed. Jean Laporte (Paris: Éditions du Cerf, 1964), 112; on which, see Goodenough, *The Politics of Philo Judaeus*, 58. See also Philo *De specialibus legibus* 3.137, M, 322, ed. André Mosès (Paris: Éditions du Cerf, 1970), 146, quoted from "On the Special Laws," trans. F. H. Colson, *Philo*, 7:563, LCL.

13. Philo of Alexandria *De vita Mosis* 2.12, M, 136, ed. Arnaldez, 198.

14. Philo of Alexandria *Quod Deus sit immutabilis* 52, M, 280; ed. André Mosès (Paris: Éditions du Cerf, 1963), 88; *De vita Mosis* 2.11, M, 136, ed. Arnaldez, 196–97; *De specialibus legibus* 2.104, M, 289, ed. Suzanne Daniel (Paris: Éditions du Cerf, 1975), 294–95, on which, see Amir, "Mose as Verfasser der Tora."

15. Philo of Alexandria *De fuga et Inventione*, ed. Esther Starobinski-Safran (Paris: Édi-

tions du Cerf, 1970), 99; p. 131, and 66, p. 124; quoted from "On Flight and Finding," trans. F. H. Colson and G. H. Whitaker, *Philo*, 5:65, LCL; *De vita Mosis* 2, ed. Arnaldez, 213; *De sacrificiis* 131, M, 189, ed. Anita Méasson (Paris: Éditions du Cerf, 1966), 180, quoted from "The Sacrifices of Abel and Cain," trans. Colson and Whitaker, *Philo*, 2:189, LCL.

16. Flavius Josephus *Contre Apion* 1.8, par. 38, p. 10; par. 42, p. 10.

17. Ibid., 2.15, par. 155, p. 84; 16, par. 171, p. 88. There is a comparison between the laws of the "Romans" and of Islam in Averroes, *Commentaire moyen à la Rhétorique d'Aristote*, 69, 20–70, 3: see Brague, "Trois regards musulmans sur la cité chrétienne," 19–20.

18. Flavius Josephus *Contre Apion* 2.15, par. 154, p. 84. See also ibid., 1.2, par. 7, p. 4 (on which, see above, chap. 2, "The Word *Nomos*" section, and n. 5); 2.16, par. 169, p. 87; par. 172, p. 88.

19. Ibid., 2.15, par. 153, p. 84; 2.35, par. 250, p. 103.

20. Ibid., 2.21, par. 184, p. 91; 16, par. 161–62, p. 86; par. 160, p. 85, quoted from Josephus, *The Life; Against Apion*, trans. H. St. J. Thackeray, LCL, 367.

21. See Jehuda Halevi *Kuzari* 1.87, p. 24, 5–6/22; in French translation as *Le Kuzari: Apologie de la religion méprisée*, trans. Charles Touati (Louvain and Paris: Peeters, 1994); Nissim of Marseilles, in Sirat, "The Political Ideas of Nissim ben Moses of Marseille" (in Hebrew),2:68; Friedrich Schleiermacher, *Über die Religion*, 3, p. 67.

22. Momigliano, "Un'apologia del giudaismo," 66; quoted from the English trans., "An Apology of Judaism," 61.

23. Maimonides, *Sefer Hamitzvot: Book of Commandments.* On the *Lex Dei* from the end of the reign of Diocletian, see Barone Adesi, *L'età della Lex Dei*, 192; on the Islamic catalogs, see Goldziher, *Sur l'Islam*, 274–75.

24. Plato *Laws* 7, 789e. For sarcastic comments, see G. W. F. Hegel, *Grundlinien der Philosophie des Rechts*, ed. Bernhard Lakebrink (Stuttgart: Reclam, 1970), Preface, 57; in English trans., by T. M. Knox, as *Philosophy of Rights* (London and New York: Oxford University Press, 1973).

25. Laoust, *La Politique de Ghazali*, 306, which refers to al-Ghazali, *Ihyā' 'ulūm id-Dīn*, 2:60. I have been unable to locate the passage, which may refer to *Ihyā'*, "Exercise," 10, 3:79.

26. Maimonides, *Mishneh Torah*, "Prayer," 4.12, in *The Book of Adoration*, trans. Moses Hyamson (Jerusalem and New York: Feldheim, 1981), 102a; "Phylacteries," 4.16–20, pp. 125b–126a (Hyamson does not translate paragraphs 20 and 21, for understandable reasons). For Muslim authors on breaking wind, see Nagel, *Die Festung des Glaubens*, 187; for "penis," see Calder, *Studies in Early Muslim Jurisprudence*, 58–60; for "left hand," see Umar as-Suhrawardī, *'Awarif al-ma'arif*, chap. 33, in German translation by Richard Gramlich as *Die Gaben der Erkenntnisse des 'Umar as-Suhrwardi* (Wiesbaden, 1978), 257, cited in Antes, *Ethik und Politik im Islam*, 52. For "the art of wiping oneself," see al-Ghazali, *Ihyā'*, 3, "Purity," 2, vol. 1, p. 157. To be compared with Augustine *De ordine* 8.22; *BA* 4:336.

27. Werblowsky, *Joseph Karo*, 7.

28. In Goldziher, *Muhammedanische Studien*, 2:135. This calls to mind the title of a book that Rabelais (*Pantagruel*, 7) places in the catalogue of the library of St. Victor: *Tartaretus, De modo cacandi* (in the Jacques Le Clercq translation, p. 186, *A Treatise on Crapping*), or the German slang term *Klugscheisser*.

29. Thomas Aquinas *Summa contra Gentiles* 1.23, p. 25b; 3.69, p. 303a and 97, p. 346a. For an example of the use of *lex divina* to speak of the New Testament, see Abelard *Dialogus inter philosophum, Judaeum et Christianum, PL*, 178, 1656c–d.

30. Ramon Llull *Vida coetània* par. 37, in Llull, *Obres essencials*, 2 vols. (Barcelona: Selecta, 1957), 1:51a.

31. Boccaccio *Decameron*, ed. Vittore Branca (Turin: Einaudi, 1991), 1.3, p. 80, quoted

from *The Decameron,* selected, trans. and ed. Mark Musa and Peter Bondanella (New York: Norton, 1977), 32.

32. Jorge Manrique, *Coplas sobre la muerte de su padre,* poem no. 33, ll. 1–3.

33. Chaucer, "The Squire's Tale," *The Canterbury Tales,* ed. Jill Man (London: Penguin, 2005), 382.

34. *La Chanson de Roland* 2, v. 38, "lei de christïens"; 6, v. 85, "la chrestiëne lei"; 10, v. 126, "lei de salvetét," in the edition by T. Atkinson Jenkins (Boston: D. C. Heath, 1924), 8, 12,16. For the modern age, see, for example, Malebranche, *Traité de morale,* 2.8.6, in Malebranche, *Oeuvres,* 2:595; Montesquieu, *De l'esprit des Lois,* 4, p. 706b: "la principale branche de la loi chrétienne."

35. See below, pp. 224–25, 260–61. On the notion of "law" among Christian Arabian theologians, see Pines, "La loi naturelle et la société," *Studies in the History of Arabic Philosophy,* 162, 177–78.

36. See Saffrey, "Allusions antichrétiennes chez Proclus le diadoque platonicien"; Frantz, "Pagan Philosophers in Christian Athens," 36–37. On an oracle announcing the brief duration of Christianity, see Augustine *De civitate Dei* 18.53.2; *La Cité de Dieu,* 3:678–80.

37. Ibn al-Muqaffaʾ, *Kalila wa-Dimna,* French trans. André Miquel (Paris: Klincksieck, 1957), Miquel preface, 35–36 (see Urvoy, *Les Penseurs libres,* 39); available in English translation as *Kalila wa Dimna: Fables from a Fourteenth-Century Arabic Manuscript,* ed. Esin Atil (Washington D.C.: Smithsonian Press, 1981).

38. Maimonides, *Traité de Logique,* trans. Brague, chap. 14, p. 33, 10–16; quoted from *Maimonides' Treatise on Logic,* trans. Efros, 64, my emphasis. On this passage, see Strauss, *What Is Political Philosophy?,* 155–69, corrected by L. Berman, "A Re-examination of Maimonides' Statement on Political Science." See Nasir ad-Dīn Tūsī, *Nasirean Ethics,* Preamble, p. 29.

39. Nasir ad-Dīn Tūsī, *Nasirean Ethics,* 3.1, p. 191.

40. Maimonides *Guide for the Perplexed* 3.29, p. 375, 17–23/221–222, ed. Joël; Halevi *Kuzari* 4.23, p. 172, 15ff.; Gersonides, *Mihamot ha-shem* (The wars of the lord), 6.15, p. 58d. For the opposite opinion, see Ibn Khaldūn, *Prolégomènes [Muqaddimah],* 1, pp. 72–73. See also Thomas Aquinas, Commentary on Psalm 48:1, in Gauthier, *Somme contre les gentils: Introduction,* 112.

41. Marsilius of Padua *Der Verteidiger des Friedens (Defensor Pacis)* 1.1.3 and 19.3–4, pp. 5, 127.

42. Alfarabi *Tahsīl as-Saʾada* par. 65, in *The Philosophical Works,* 196; English trans. as "The Attainment of Happiness," par. 63, in Alfarabi, *Alfarabi's Philosophy of Plato and Aristotle,* 49–50.

43. Alfarabi *Sharaʾit al-yaqīn,* in *Al-Mantīq ʾinda al-Farabi* 4:101, 3; Alfarabi *Jadal* 1, in ibid., 3:19, 20–22, both translated in Vajda, "Autour de la théorie de la connaissance chez Saadia [II]: Al-Farabi sur la valeur de la connaissance dialectique," *Revue des Études Juives* 126 (1967: 375–97, esp. 394, 381, reprinted in Vajda, *Mélanges Georges Vajda,* 127–49; Alfarabi *Burhān,* chap. 5, in *Al-Mantīq ʾinda al-Farabi* 3:85, 22–86, 22, and *Al-Mantiqiyyat li-al-Farabi,* ed. Mohammed Taqī Daneshpajuh, 3 vols. (Qum, b. 1410), 336–37. My emphasis in the text.

44. Alfarabi *Burhān,* in *Al-Mantīq ʾinda al-Farabi,* p. 85, 11–17; ed. Daneshpajuh, 336.

45. Maimonides *Guide* 1.31, p. 44, 29–45, 16/107–109, quoted from *Guide of the Perplexed,* trans. Pines, 66–67. See also Strauss, *Gesammelte Schriften,* 2:455–56.

46. Moses of Narbonne, *Commentary to "The Guide of the Perplexed" / Der Commentar des Rabbi Moses Narbonensis, Philosophen aus dem XIV. Jahrhundert zu dem Werke More Nebuchim des Maimonides,* ed. J. Goldenthal (Vienna: 1852; Vienna: Aus der K. K. Hof- und

Staatsdruckerei, 1952), 4b; Shem Tov, *Sefer Mōreh Nevukhim le-ha-rav ha-elohī rabbeynū Mosheh b. Maïmon* (Warsaw, 1872; reprint, Jerusalem, 1960). See Maimonides, *Guide*, 1:49b.

47. Aristotle *Met.* 995a3–4, trans. Tredennick, LCL.

48. See Steinschneider, *Die arabischen Übersetzungen aus dem griechischen*, 104–5.

49. Alexander of Aphrodisias, *Alexandri aphrodisiensis in Aristotelis Metaphysica commentaria*, ed. Michael Hayduck (Berlin:De Gruyter, 2002), p. 167, 15–20. See also Asclepius, *ad loc.*, CAG, 6.2 (1888), p. 135, 4–8. It is not certain that this commentary existed in Arabic, hence whether it was available to medieval thinkers.

50. Cited in the book of magic, *Picatrix*. For the Arabic original, see Pseudo-Magrītī, *Das Ziel des Weisen*, ed. Helmut Ritter (Leipzig and Berlin: Teubner, 1933), 283–84, quoted in part from the English translation in Pines, "Yahyā ibn 'Adi's Refutation of the Doctrine of Acquisition (*Iktisāb*)," in *Studies in the History of Arabic Philosophy*, 110–55. On the meaning of the world *khurāfāt / hurāfāt*, see S. Stroumsa, "'Ravings': Maimonides' Concept of Pseudo-Science."

51. In Badawi, *Traités philosophiques*, 198.

52. Averroes, *Tafsīr mā ba 'da al-tabī 'ah: Grand commentaire de la Métaphyique d'Aristote*, C 14, pp. 43–44.

53. See, of course, Guez de Balzac, *Socrate chrétien* (1652) and, before him, Justin *Second Apology* 10.8; Origen *Contra Celsum* 2.41, SC no. 132, p. 380. On Islam, see Alon, *Socrates in Mediaeval Arabic Literature*; Berman and Alon, "Socrates on Law and Philosophy."

54. Alfarabi *Philosophy of Plato* 5, par. 30; Alfarabi, *Alfarabi's Philosophy of Plato and Aristotle*, 64; Averroes, *Long Commentary on the Physics of Aristotle*, Proemium, in S. Harvey, "The Hebrew Translation of Averroes' Prooemium," 66 (for the Hebrew) and 75 (for the English).

55. Cited in Ibn Taymiyya, *Le Traité de droit public*, 28.

56. W. Harvey, "On Averroes, Maimonides, and the Ideal State" (in Hebrew), 21. See also Urvoy, *Avveroès*, 145–46.

57. Alfarabi *Philosophy of Plato* 10, par. 36; Alfarabi, *Alfarabi's Philosophy of Plato and Aristotle*, 66.

58. The passage from the *Crito* 50a–54d, appears, summarized to an extreme, in al-Qiftī, *Ihbār al-'ulamā' bi-abhār al-hukamā*, in Badawi, *Aflatun fi al-Islam*, 138–39.

59. Alfarabi *Against John the Grammarian* 4.8; see Muhsin Mahdi, "Alfarabi Against Philoponus," 257; Avicenna, *Correspondence with al-Biruni*, 2d question, par. 16; Averroes *Tahafot at-Tahafot* 1, par. 52., p. 30, 5–9; and par. 199, p. 108, 1–7.

60. Maimonides, *Letter to Samuel ibn Tibbon*, quoted from Shlomo Pines, Introduction to his translation of the *Guide of the Perplexed*, lix, my emphasis. Original in Marx, "Texts by and about Maimonides," 380a–b.

61. Thomas Aquinas *Commentary on De anima* 1.8, par. 107, p. 42a, quoted from *Aristotle's De Anima in the Version of William of Moerbeke and the Commentary of St. Thomas Aquinas*, trans. Kenelm Foster and Sylvester Humphries (New Haven: Yale University Press, 1951), 107.

62. Razi, *La Médecine spirituelle*, chap. 2, p. 72: see my introduction to this work, 16–20.

63. Respectively, Averroes *Commentary on the Generation of the Animals* 1, at the end, Juntine edition, VI–2, p. 64b, and Averroes, *Long Commentary on the Treatise of the Soul / Averrois Cordubensis Commentarium magnum in Aristotelis de anima libros*, ed. F. Stuart Crawford (Cambridge, Mass.: Harvard University Press, 1953), 3, par. 14, p. 433. See also Averroes *Tahafot at-Tahafot* 3, par. 83, p. 187, 10; Averroes, *Averroes' Commentary on Plato's Republic*, 1.12.3, p. 46, 20–21.

64. Malebranche, *Recherche de la vérité*, 2.2.6, in Malebranche, *Oeuvres*, 1:224–25,

quoted from Malebranche, *The Search After Truth,* trans. and ed. Thomas M. Lennon and Paul J. Olscamp (Cambridge and New York: Cambridge University Press, 1997), 147.

65. Dante *Inferno* 4.131, quoted from *The Divine Comedy,* vol. I, *Inferno,* trans. Mark Musa (Harmondsworth: Penguin, 1984), 101. For the same expression applied to Moses, see Maimonides *Guide* 1.54, p. 83, 21/216; 3.12, p. 323, 15/82; 3.54, p. 470, 24/465.

66. Al-Kindī, "On the First Philosophy,"in *Rasā'il . . . falsafiyah,* vol. 1, p. 103; Alfarabi, *Alfarabi's Book of Letters (Kitāb Al-Hurūf),* par. 143, pp. 151–52.

67. Maimonides, *Letter to Samuel ibn Tibbon,* quoted from Pines, Introduction to his translation of the *Guide,* lix. See also Marx, "Texts by and about Maimonides," 379b and 380b.

68. See S. Harvey, "Hebrew Translation of Averroes' Proemium," 70, 22 (Hebrew), 83 (English).

69. See Zonta, *La filosofia antica nel Medioevo ebraico,* 157, and Melamed, "Aristotle's Politics in Medieval and Renaissance Jewish Thought" (in Hebrew).

70. See Steinschneider, *Die hebräischen Übersetzungen des Mittelalters und die Juden als Dolmetscher,* par. 116, pp. 219–20; for a more recent example, see Walzer, "Early Islamic Philosophy," 649. See the question posed by Abderraziq, *L'Islam et les fondements du pouvoir,* 1.3.6, p. 74.

71. See Rosenthal, *The Muslim Concept of Freedom,* 31–32 n. 74; Arkoun, *Contribution à l'étude de l'humanisme arabe au IVe/Xe siècle,* 232; and Pines, *Studies in Arabic Versions of Greek Texts and in Medieval Science* (from whom I have borrowed the greater part of my documentation).

72. Al-Qiftī, *Kitāb ta'rīkh al-hukamā,* ed. August Müller and Julius Lippert (Leipzig: Dieterich'sche Verlagsbuchhandlung, 1903), p. 44, 15, in French in Moraux, *Les Listes anciennes des ouvrages d'Aristote,* 291, and in English in Düring, *Aristotle in the Ancient Biographical Tradition,* 225.

73. Al-Kindī, *On the Quantity of Books of Aristotle,* in al-Kindī, *Rasā'il,* 1:384, ll. 16–18. Some of the information given about the *Politics* seems to apply just as well to Aristotle's *Eudemian Ethics,* which al-Kindī knew (see ibid., p. 369, 10–11).

74. Alfarabi, *Catálogo de las ciencias,* ed. and trans. Angel González Palencía, 2d ed. (Madrid and Granada: CSIC, 1955), text on p. 96, medieval Latin translation, p. 170; translation in Castilian, p. 70. See Alfarabi, *Alfarabi's Philosophy of Plato and Aristotle,* 71–130; Brague, "Note sur la traduction arabe de la *Politique* d'Aristote."

75. See Kraemer, *Humanism in the Renaissance of Islam,* 233–41 (for a summary, with bibliography). See also Al-Amīrī, *Assa'āda wa-'l-is'ād / On Seeking and Causing Happiness,* ed. Mojtaba.Minovi (Wiesbaden, 1957–58), p. 150, 11–13; p. 187, 12–188. These passages recall Aristotle *Pol.* 1.2, 1253a27–29, and 1.5, 1254a28–31. There is a summary of the work in Arberry, "An Arabic Treatise on Politics."

76. Averroes *Commentary on "Nicomachean Ethics"* 10, toward the end, in *Aristoteles Opera* (Venice: Juntas, 1550), vol. 3, fol. 79a, col. 1, 1, 36–38; and Averroes, *Averroes' Middle Commentary on Aristotle's Nicomachean Ethics in the Hebrew Version of Samuel ben Judah,* p. 354, 11. See also Averroes, *Averroes' Commentary on Plato's Republic,* p. 22 b3–5, p. 112.

77. This is suggested in Strauss, *Maïmonide,* 146–47; it is explicit in Strauss, *Gesammelte Schriften,* vol. 2: *Philosophie und Gesetz,* 197.

78. For example, see *Les générations des médecins et des sages* of Abū Dāwūd Sulaïman ibn Hassān ibn Jujul al-Andalūsī, ed. Fu'ad al-Sayyid (Cairo: Institut Français d'Archéologie Orientale, 1955): "There is a letter [of Artisotle's] in eight chapters on the government of [Alexander's] reign and the whole of what conditions it and appertains to it, and it is the book on politics on the government of power, which is known [under the name of] *Secret of Secrets*" (p. 26, 9–10). On the *Sirr all-Asrār (Secretum secretorum)* and for a bibliography and

a summary of scholarship on the question, see Ryan and Schmitt, *Pseudo-Aristotle, The Secret of Secrets.*

79. *Lettre d'Aristote à Alexandre sur la politique envers les cités,* ed. and French trans. Józef Bielawski and Marian Plezia (Warsaw: Academy of Sciences of Poland, 1970).

80. Miskawayh *Tahdhīb al-Akhlāq wa Tathīr al-A'rāq* 4, p. 110; French trans. as *Traité d'éthique,* 181; quotation from the English trans. by Constantine K. Zurayk as *The Refinement of Character,* 103. For the following, see Nasir ad-Dīn Tusī, *Nasirean Ethics,* 1.7, pp. 97–98; 2.2, p. 157; 3.1, p. 191. The source, traceable through a number of mistranslations, is, as the context indicates, Aristotle's treatise on justice in *Nic. Ethics* 5.5, 1133a30: see the Arabic translation, *Aristūtlīs, al-Akhlāq,* ed. A. Badawi (Kuwait: Wakālat al-matbūʿāt, 1979), 3.1, p. 187.

81. Alfarabi, "Le sommaire du livre des 'Lois' de Platon"; Strauss, "Farabi's Plato," and idem, *What Is Political Philosophy?,* 134–54; Gutas, "Galen's Synopsis of Plato's Laws and Fārābī's Talkhīs," 101–19; Averroes, *Averroes' Commentary on Plato's Republic,* 1.22.2, p. 46; 26.8, p. 56; 3.20.11, p. 105.

82. In Badawi, *Aflatun fi al-Islam,* 197–234.

83. See Goitein, *Studies in Islamic History and Institutions,* 149–50 and n. 1.

84. Nietzsche, *Morgenröte,* 5, par. 496, in *Kritische Studienausgabe in 15 Bänden,* ed. Giorgio Colli and Mazzino Montinari, 15 vols. (Munich: Deutscher Taschenbuch; Berlin and New York: De Gruyter, 1980), 3:291–92, quoted from *The Dawn of Day,* trans. J. M. Kennedy, vol. 9 of *The Complete Works of Friedrich Nietzsche,* ed. Oscar Levy (New York: Gordon, 1974), 346–47. The allusion to Plato refers to Letter VII, 325bl, el. These lines, published in late 1881, probably date from the summer of 1880 (see 4 [286], *Kritische Studienausgabe,* 9:170–71). It is hard to know whether Nietzsche's ideas have a source. In any event, he does not seem to have read the works of Julius Wellhausen on Islam before November 1887. See Nietzsche, reading notes, in 11 [287–93], *Kritische Studienausgabe,* 13:112–13, and the two long fragments that follow, which are reflections based on that reading.

85. On the theme of the philosopher king at Byzantium as a *topos* in praising a governor, see Agapetus to Justinian, chap. 17, and Georgius Acropolites, "A Funereal Oration on John III Ducas Vatatzes delivered in A.D. 1254," in *SPTB,* 56–57, 160.

86. See above, pp. 26–29.

87. Sijistani in Tawhīdī, *Kitab al-imtā 'wa-al-muanasah* (n.d.), 2:20, 20–21, quoted from Kraemer, *Philosophy in the Renaissance of Islam,* 237–38; al-Amirī in Kraemer, "The Jihād of the Falāsifa," 288 (Plato *Rep.* 9, 592ab); Avicenna, *On the Division of the Rational Sciences,* in Avicenna, *Tis'rasā'il fi al-hikmah wa-al-tabī'iyāt* (Cairo: Dar al-Arab, n.d.), 73–74. The discovery of this phrase represented a decisive turning point in the intellectual development of Leo Strauss: see Strauss, "A Giving of Accounts," *The College* 22 (1970):3b.

88. On the text of the *Laws,* see above, pp. 117–18 in this chapter.

89. These citations to the *Laws* are conveniently gathered together in Badawi, *Aflatun fi al-Islam,* 133–35 (al-Bīrūnī) and 162–68 (al-Amirī). See also al- Bīrūnī, *Tahīq mā li-'l-Hind min maqūla maqbū fī 'l-'aql aw mardūhla;* extracts in French trans. as *Le livre de l'Inde,* chap. 11, p. 86, 9–14 (French translation, 132); chap. 43, p. 287, 13–288, 4 (French translation, 234); p. 292, 8–14 (not in the French translation); English trans. as *Alberuni's India* (1964).

90. Al- Bīrūnī, *Tahīq mā li-'l-Hind,* chap. 10, p. 744, 10–75, 1, quoted from *Alberuni's India,* 106. The corresponding passages in Plato are very probably *Laws* 624a1–2, 3–5; 630e1–3; 631b3–8.

91. Proclus, *In Platonis Rem publicam commentarii,* ed. Wilhelm Kroll, BT, vol. 2 (1901), pp. 360–68; Michael of Ephesus, "Commentary on the *Politics* of Aristotle," in *SPTB,* 136–41.

92. On the reception of Aristotle's Politics, see Aristotle, *Politique,* ed. Jean Aubonnet,

2d ed., 3 vols. in 5 pts. (Paris: Les Belles Lettres, 1960–89), vol. 1 (1968), cxx–cxcvi, esp. p. cxlvii n. 1

93. See Brague, *Europe, la voie romaine*, 93–99.

94. One exception to this rule is the mention of Cicero in the anonymous "A Byzantine Dialogue De Scientia Politica," *SPTB*, 63–75; see also ibid., 81–84,141–45.

95. Cicero *De officiis* 1.16.

96. See Aristotle *Nicomachean Ethics* 7.1, 1155a 21; Cicero *Off.* 1.16.52; Seneca *De vita beata* 1.2; Seneca *De beneficiis* 4.24.1; Seneca *Letters to Lucilius* 95.51, pp. 394–95; Juvenal 14.103; Arius Didymus in Stobaeus, *Eclogarum physicarum et ethicarum*, ed. Curtis Wachsmuth and Otto Hense, 5 vols. (Berlin: Weidmann, 1884–1912), 120–21, or in *Fragmenta philosophorum, graecorum*, ed. Friedrich Wilhelm August Mullach, 3 vols. (Paris: Didot, 1881–83), 2:87b–88a. It is very probably to this argument that Carneades would later oppose the apology of the two shipwrecked men fighting over a floating plank: see Cicero *Republic* 3.20; *Off.* 3.23.89.

97. Virgil *Georgics* 4.210–218; Seneca *De clementia* 1.19.2–4; Ambrose *Hexaemeron* 21, 5.21.67–68, in *PL* 14:248–49. See also Dvornik, *Early Christian and Byzantine Political Philosophy*, 2:528, 675.

98. Lactantius *Divinae Institutiones* 6.10, in his *Opera omnia*, ed. Samuel Brandt, CSEL, no. 19; Ambrose *De officiis ministrorum*, in *PL* 16:25a–194b. For an analysis of these texts, see Flückiger, *Geschichte des Naturrechts*, 364–77.

99. See Curtius, *Europäische Literatur und lateinisches Mittelalter*, chap. 6, pp. 116–37.

100. John of Salisbury *Policraticus* 4.2, vol. 1, p. 237.

101. See, for example, "Brethren of Purity," *Rasa'il Ihwan as-Safa'*, 2.8 [22], vol. 2, p. 368; 4.1 [42], vol. 3, p. 495; Miskawayh, *Tahdhīb al-Akhlāq wa Tathīr al-A'rāq*, 5, p. 129; *Traité d'éthique*, 220; al-Ghazali, *Ihyā'*, 14, "On the Licit and the Illicit," 5, vol. 2, p. 153; Nasir ad-Dīn Tūsī, *Nasirean Ethics*, 3.3, p. 215.

Chapter 8

1. For medieval examples, see Arnold, *The Caliphate*, 167–70; Monneret de Villard, *Lo studio dell'islâm in Europa*, 61–62 (esp. n. 2); Gagnér, "Boniface VIII and Avicenna," 278. For a modern example, see Rida, *Le Califat*, 109, 175, despite the warning from his teacher, 'Abduh, quoted, p. 213.

2. See Bahya ibn Paquda, *Al-Hidāja'ilā Farā'id al-Qulūb*, 2.5, p. 119, 4–8.

3. Saadia Gaon, *Book of Beliefs and Opinions* (in Hebrew), 3.10, p. 148.

4. *EJ*, s.v. "Yūsuf 'As'ar Ya'thar Dhū Nuwās," vol. 16, cols. 897–900 (H. Z. Hirschberg).

5. See Dunlop, *The History of the Jewish Khazars*, 92 n. 15, 115.

6. See Zuckerman, *A Jewish Princedom in Feudal France*.

7. For a summary of the Ibn Nagrila–Ibn Hazm controversy, see García Gomez, "Polémica religiosa entre Ibn Hazm y Ibn al-Nagrila," or Arnaldez, *Aspects de la pensée musulmane*, 175–82.

8. See Cohen, *Jewish Self-Government in Medieval Egypt*.

9. Al-Birūnī, *Chronologie orientalischer Völker*, 17; Ibn Hazm, *Fisal* (Cairo, 1317 AH), 1:152–53.

10. Maimonides, "Letter to Joseph," in Maimonides, *Igrot ha-Rambam Epistles*, ed. D. H. Baneth (Jerusalem: Magnes, 1985), par. 15, p. 63.

11. See Finkelstein, *Jewish Self-Government in the Middle Ages*, and "Gemeinde, jüdische," *LM*, 4:1211–12 (M. Illian); "Juden, -tum," III, "Gemeindeorganisation," *LM*, 5:782–83 (M. Toch).

12. See Goitein, *Studies in Islamic History and Institutions*, 200.

13. Ravitzky, *Religion and State in Jewish Philosophy*, 8, 16–17; see also Funkenstein, *Perceptions of Jewish History*, 167; Lorberbaum, *Politics and the Limits of Law*, xii.

14. Abraham bar Hiyya, *Hegyōn ha-Nefesh ha-ʾatsūvah*, pt. 4, p. 140; *Meditation of the Sad Soul*, 136–37.

15. Al-Muqammas, *Dāwūd ibn Marwān al-Muqammis's Twenty Chapters*, 15, par. 30, pp. 290–91 and n. 39. The editor of this work indicates in a note that the literal meaning of what she translates as "ideal polity" is "the praiseworthy revolution."

16. See Klein-Braslavy, *King Solomon and Philosophical Esotericism in the Thought of Maimonides* (in Hebrew), 112 and n. 26.

17. This is the hypothesis of Zeitlin, *Maimonides: A Biography*, 83–88.

18. Maimonides, "Letter to Yemen," in *Igrot: Letters*, 48, 41–42.; see "The Epistle to Yemen," trans. Joel L. Kraemer, in *Maimonides' Empire of Light: Popular Enlightenment in an Age of Belief*, ed. Ralph Lerner (Chicago: University of Chicago Press, 2000), 99–132, at 124–25, 119–20.

19. Maimonides *Mishneh Torah* 14; see also Twersky, *Introduction to the Code of Maimonides*, 207.

20. See Gad Freudenthal, "Providence, Astrology, and Celestial Influences on the Sublunar World in Shem-Tov Ibn Falaquera's *De 'ot ha-Filosofim*," in *Medieval Hebrew Encyclopedias of Science and Philosophy*, ed. Steven Harvey (Amsterdam: Kluwer, 2000), 335–70, reprinted in Freudenthal, *Science in the Medieval Hebrew and Arabic Traditions* (Aldershot: Ashgate, 2005), Essay 16. See also Pines, *Studies in the History of Jewish Philosophy* (in Hebrew), 277–305; Spinoza, *Tractatus theologico-politicus*, 3.2, in *Opera*, 1:133.

Chapter 9

1. Einhard *De vita et gestis Karoli Magni* 7. For an English translation, see *Charlemagne's Courtier: The Complete Einhard*, ed. and trans. Paul Edward Dutton (Peterborough, Ont.: Broadview Press, 1998).

2. On the pejorative sense of the term "democracy" in Byzantium, see Ahrweiler, *L'Idéologie politique de l'Empire byzantin*, 58–59. On Iceland, see Adam von Bremen *Gesta Hammaburgensis Ecclesiae pontificum* 4.36 (35), par. 244, in *PL* 146:654a, scholium 150, "apud illos non est rex, nisi [sed, v.l.] tantum lex." Available in English as *History of the Archbishops of Hamburg-Bremen*, trans., with an introduction and notes, Francis J. Tschan (New York: Columbia University Press, 1959).

3. See above, pp. 33–34.

4. This idea seems to have found its first expression in Gottfried Arnold. It was then picked up by Voltaire, then by Jakob Burckhardt and by Ernst Bloch: see Piétri, "Mythe et réalité de l'Église constantinienne," 24–25, whom I have quoted.

5. See Erik Peterson, "Monotheismus als politisches Problem" (1935), in Peterson, *Theologische Traktate*, 45–147. The subject is treated briefly in Brague, "Le sérieux de l'incarnation," and in greater detail in Eslin, *Dieu et le pouvoir*, 69–71.

6. See Bori, "'Date a Cesare quel che è di Cesare' . . . (Mt 22, 21)"; Kantorowicz, *King's Two Bodies*, 53 and n. 24 (after Marsilius of Padua), according to Butterworth, "Political Islam," 27b.

7. See above, pp. 69–70.

8. See Piétri, "Mythe et réalité," 34–38.

9. See above, pp. 44–45.

10. See Eslin, *Dieu et le pouvoir*, 79–82.

11. Gelasius *De anathematis vinculo*, PL 59:102c–110c, cols. 108–109; cf. Justinian, preface to the *Novellae* 6, *SPTB*, 75–76.

12. Ahrweiler, *L'Idéologie politique de l'Empire byzantin*, 129–31.

13. Dagron, *Empereur et prêtre*, 70, quoted from *Emperor and Priest*, 50. See also *Empereur et prêtre*, 20, 68, 321.

14. Ahrweiler, *L'Idéologie politique*, 145. See also Dagron, *Empereur et prêtre*, and Guilland, "Le droit divin à Byzance," 208–209.

15. Justinian *Novellae* 6 (on the ordination of bishops and other clerics), Preface, *SPTB*, 36; Basil I, *Epanagoge*, p. 885; Ducellier, *Les Byzantins*, 38.

16. Beck, *Nomos, Kanon und Staatsraison in Byzanz*, 15, 37.

17. Clement I *First Epistle to the Corinthians* 5.3–7, Biblioteca de autores cristianos, p. 182; Tertullian *De praescriptione haereticorum* 36.1–3.

18. Irenaeus *Adversus Haereses* 3.3.2, SC 34:102; available in English as *St. Irenaeus of Lyons Against the Heresies*, trans. and annotated by Dominic J. Unger, rev. John J. Dillon (New York: Paulist Press, 1992); Cyprian *De unitate ecclesiae* 4, PL 4:498, available with English translation by E. H. Blakeney, with introduction and notes (London: SPCK; New York and Toronto: Macmillan, 1928); Maximus the Confessor, extract from a letter from Rome, *PG* 91:144ac.

19. Piétri, "Mythe et réalité," 36.

20. See Pelikan, *The Christian Tradition*, 2:159–69.

21. Leo the Great, Sermon 95, SC 200:266–72, in English translation by Jane Patricia Freeland and Agnes Josephine Conway as "On the Beatitudes," in Leo the Great, *Sermons* (Washington, D.C.: Catholic University of America Press, 1996), 394–400.

22. See Rials, "*Veritas juris*: La vérité du droit écrit," 107–30. On the Byzantine utilization of forgeries, see Ahrweiler, *L'Idéologie politique*, 49–50.

23. The phrase is taken from Legendre, *Le Désir politique de Dieu*, 236, but see also ibid., 112, 152. On the same statement, see Rials, "*Veritas juris*," 127–28.

24. See Rosenstock-Huessy, *Die europäischen Revolutionen und der Charakter der Nationen*, 106.

25. For recent syntheses of these events, see Blumenthal, *Der Investiturstreit*; Laudage, *Gregorianische Reform und Investiturstreit*; and Gaudemet, *Église et cité*, 283–373. Harold J. Berman's *Law and Revolution* (1983) prompted a good deal of discussion, on which see Bellini, "Il riformismo gregoriano." I owe thanks to Philippe Nemo for introducing me to the Berman book several years before it was translated into French. The idea according to which the Gregorian Reform constituted the first of a long series of revolutions in European history is due to Rosenstock-Huessy, *Die europäischen Revolutionen*, a view repeated, notably in Legendre, *Le Crime du caporal Lortie*, 52.

26. The text of the *dictatus papae* can be found in *Quellen zum Investiturstreit*, vol. 1: *Ausgewählte Briefe Papst Gregors VII*, trans. Franz-Josef Schmale (Darmstadt: Wissenschaftliche Buchgesellschaft, 1978), no. 47, pp. 148–51.

27. See Tellenbach, *Libertas*; Szabó-Bechstein, *Libertas ecclesiae*, 224.

28. Figgis, *Political Thought from Gerson to Grotius*, 19. See also H. Berman, *Law and Revolution*, 276; Prodi, *Una storia della giustizia*, 111–12. The idea can already be found as early as Nietzsche, in a fragment dating from the spring or summer of 1883: 7 [242], *Kritische Studienausgabe* 10:318, cited in Franck, *Nietzsche et l'ombre de Dieu*, 240.

29. See Augustinus Triumphus *Summa* 88.1, p. 439, in Wilks, *The Problem of Sovereignty in the Later Middle Ages*, 158; Legendre, *Le Désir politique de Dieu*, 237.

30. Ullmann, *Principles of Government and Politics in the Middle Ages*, 87.

31. See Bodin, *Les Six Livres de la République,* 1.8, 132, for the implications of this parallel.

32. Quillet, *Les Clefs du pouvoir au Moyen Âge,* 44. See also Legendre, *Le Désir politique de Dieu,* 262, 257; Kantorowicz, *King's Two Bodies,* 320–21; H. Berman, *Law and Revolution,* 115, and Gauchet, *Le Désenchantement du monde,* 118.

33. See Kantorowicz, *King's Two Bodies,* 95, 192

34. This notion is hinted at in John of Salisbury *Policraticus* 4.6, 1:252; it is more clearly expressed in Henry de Bracton *De legibus et consuetudinibus Angliae* 1.8.5; ed. Sir Travers Twiss (1878); 6 vols. (London: Longman, 1878–83; Kraus reprint, 1964), 4:38–40. See also Kantorowicz, *King's Two Bodies,* 105; Kern, *Gottesgnadentum und Widerstandsrecht im früheren Mittelalter,* 264.

35. My translation, summarizing Kern, *Gottesgnadentum,* 243–44; see also ibid., 202–3.

36. Manegold von Lautenbach *Liber ad Gebehardum* par. 30 (Monumenta Germanica Literaria, 1:365), par. 47 (pp. 391–92), par. 48 (p. 392), in Kern, *Gottesgnadentum,* 216 n. 470; see also ibid., Appendix 16, no. 294, pp. 311–14.

37. Maimonides *Mishneh Torah,* "Theft and Lost Objects," 5.18; Blidstein, *Political Concepts in Maimonidean Halakha* (in Hebrew), 154–60; Lorberbaum, *Politics and the Limits of Law,* 65–67.

38. See, for example, Locke, *Second Treatise of Government,* 8.2, p. 58; among the historians, see Maine, *Ancient Law,* chap. 9, p. 203.

39. See Figgis, *The Divine Right of Kings,* 14, 51, 59, 257.

40. Bonaventure *Collationes in Hexamaëron* 5; (Paris: Vivès, 1864–71), vol. 9, p. 58a.

41. Kantorowicz, *King's Two Bodies,* 297; Villey, *La Formation de la pensée juridique moderne,* 334, 364.

42. See above, pp. 21–22.

43. Nicholas of Cusa *De concordantia catholica* (1432) 3.4, par. 331, ed. Gerhard Callen, in Nicholas of Cusa, *Opera omnia,* 22 vols.(Hamburg: Meiner, 1932–), vol. 19 (1963), p. 348, in English translation by Paul E. Sigmund as *The Catholic Concordance* (Cambridge and New York: Cambridge University Press, 1991), 230. See also Maddox, *Religion and the Rise of Democracy,* 98.

44. Courtine, *Nature et empire de la loi,* 19.

45. See Kantorowicz *King's Two Bodies,* 197, 207; Post, *Studies in Medieval Legal Thought,* 535.

46. Post and May, "The Medieval Heritage of a Humanistic Ideal," 197–210; John VIII in Gratian *Decretum* IIa pars, causa 16, q. 3, c. 17, p. 796, cited in Legendre, *L'Empire de la vérité,* 138.

47. John Wycliffe, *Tractatus de officio regis,* ed. Alfred W. Pollard and Charles Sayle (London: published for the Wyclif Society by Trübner and Co, 1997), 73, cited in Figgis, *Divine Right,* 67.

48. See above, p. 68; Tertullian *Apologeticum* 32.1. On this idea in general, see the dossier gathered by Walter Seitter, *Katechonten: Den Untergang aufhalten;* Tumult: Schriften zur Verkehrswissenschaft, no. 25 ((2001). On the use of this idea by Carl Schmitt, see Meier, *Die Lehre Carl Schmitts,* 243–46.

49. See Figgis, *Divine Right,* 8–10.

50. Legendre, *Dieu au miroir,* 287; for another example, see Voegelin, *Order and History,* vol. 1: *Israel and Revelation,* 28.

51. See Kantorowicz, *King's Two Bodies,* 319.

52. See Bloch, *Les Rois thaumaturges;* Guibert of Nogent *De sanctis et eorum pigneribus* 1, *PL* 156:616a, or Guibert of Nogent *Dei gesta per Francos et cinq autres textes,* ed. R. B. C.

Huygens, CCCM, 127 (Turnhout: Brepols, 1993), p. 90. On the ancient example of Vespasian in Alexandria, see Suetonius *Divus Vespasianus* 7; Tacitus *Histories* 4.81; Dio Cassius *Historiae Romanae* 66.8.1. This custom was known in the Middle Ages: see, for example, John of Salisbury *Policraticus* 2.10, vol. 1, pp. 83–84. It had no parallel in Egypt: see Posener, *De la divinité du pharaon*, 63–70.

53. Peter of Blois, Letter 150, *PL* 207:440d, in Bloch, *Les Rois thaumaturges*, 41, 159–83.

54. Courtine, *Nature et empire de la loi*, 11.

55. For an inventory of these collections, see Gaudemet, *Les Sources du droit de l'Église en Occident du IIe au VIIe siècle* and *Les Sources du droit canonique, VIIIe–XXe siècle*, 13–101; Padovani, *Perché chiedi il mio nome?*, 17–88. On the beginnings of canon law, see Buisson, "Die Entstehung des Kirchenrechts."

56. See Bellomo, *L'Europa del diritto comune*, 50, 72–75, *Common Legal Past*, 39, 72–75; Legendre, *L'Empire de la vérité*, 138.

57. Gratian *Decretum*: Gaudemet, *Les Sources du droit canonique*, 108–19.

58. H. Berman, *Law and Revolution*, 120 and 143.

59. *Die Chronik des Propstes Burchard von Ursberg*, ed. Oswald Holder-Egger and Bernhard von Simson, Scriptores rerum Germanicarum in usum scholarum, ex Monumentis Germaniae Historicis, no. 16; 2d ed. (Hanover and Leipzig: Hahnsche, 1916), 15–16.

60. See Grossi, *L'ordine giuridico medievale*, 119; Helmholz, *The Spirit of Classical Canon Law*, 395. On Gratian's values, see Chodorow, *Christian Political Theory and Church Politics*, 113, 123.

61. Accursius, gloss, *conferens generi*, Auth. *Coll.*, 1.6, fol. 11va, cited in Bellomo, *L'Europa del diritto comune*, 87, quoted from *Common Legal Past*, 75 and n. 25. See above, pp. 130–31.

62. See Nörr, "Recht und Religion," 6–7; Helmholz, *Spirit of Classical Canon Law*, 188–89; Maine, *Ancient Law*, chap. 8, 168–69; Prodi, *Una storia della giustizia*, 140.

63. Odofredus *Lectura in cod.* 1.1.4, *de Summa Trinitate*, 1: *nemo clericus*, no. 3 (Lugduni, 1552), fol. 6rb; and Cynus of Pistoia, *Lectura in* Auth. *Clericus post* C. 1.3.32(33), *de episcopis et clericis*. 1. *omnes qui*, no. 2 (Francofurti ad moenum 1578; anastatic reprint, Turin, 1964), fol. 18vb. These two texts are cited in Bellomo, *L'Europa del diritto comune*, 88, *Common Legal Past*, 76, nn. 26, 27.

64. On marriage, see, for instance, Rabelais, *Tiers Livre*, chap. 48, which pleads in favor of paternal consent. On the genesis of the modern individual, see Prodi, *Una storia della giustizia*, 170.

65. See Donahue, "The Interaction of Law and Religion in the Middle Ages," 474–75.

66. See Brown, "Society and the Supernatural," and, in his day, Montesquieu, *De l'esprit des Lois*, 38.16–17, pp. 730b–31b.

67. Liutprand, *Edicta*, ed. Friedrich Bluhme, in Monumenta Germaniae Historica, *Leges*, 4 (Hanover, 1868), par. 118, p. 156, quoted in Bellomo, *L'Europa del diritto comune*, 61, n. 8, *Common Legal Past*, p. 50 n 8.

68. Legendre, *L'Empire de la vérité*, 202–6; idem, *Le Désir politique de Dieu*, 320.

69. See Baron, *Social and Religious History of the Jews*, 6:54; H. Berman, *Law and Revolution*, 160–61; Calder, *Studies in Early Muslim Jurisprudence*, 234.

70. See Gagnér, "Boniface VIII and Avicenna," 277–78.

71. See, for example, Rashīd Rida (or his translator, Laoust), *Le Califat*, 102, 118, 151; Chehata, *Études de droit musulman*, 1:11–12; Lorberbaum, *Politics and the Limits of Law*, xi.

72. For examples, see Cortese, *Il diritto nella storia medievale*, 1:387; 2:84–93; Weigand, "Das göttliche Recht," 118–19.

73. See Kantorowicz, *King's Two Bodies*, 117; Foreville, "Le recours aux sources scriptuaires," 50.

74. Hostiensis *Lectura* ad. X 1.1.1., n. 15: see Helmholz, *Spirit of Classical Canon Law,* 404 and n.44.

75. See Helmholz, *Spirit of Classical Canon Law,* 20–22.

76. See Donahue, "Malchus' Ear," 116–17; Cortese, *Il diritto nella storia medievale,* 2:92.

Chapter 10

1. Wellhausen, *Das arabische Reich und sein Sturz,* 6, quoted from *The Arab Kingdom and Its Fall,* 9.

2. For a translation of the Constitution of Medina in Italian, with commentary, see Caetani, *Annali dell'islām,* 1:395–402; for an English version, see Serjeant, "The *sunna jāi'ah,* Pacts with the Yathrib Jews, and the *tahrîm* of Yathrib."

3. See Crone, *Slaves on Horses,* 37–38, 49–50; Weiss, *The Spirit of Islamic Law,* 3.

4. See the example of Abu Bakr, analyzed in Décobert, *Le Mendiant et le combattant,* 127–32.

5. See Goldziher, *Muhammedanische Studien,* 2:84–85. Critical study of the *fiqh* originated with Schacht, *The Origins of Muhammadan Jurisprudence;* see also Chehata, *Études de droit musulman,* 1:16. For the history of studies on the question, see the summaries in Motzki, *Die Anfänge der islamischen Jurisprudenz,* 7–49; Burton, *An Introduction to the Hadith,* ix–xxvi.

6. Schacht, "Classicisme, traditionalisme et ankylose dans la loi religieuse de l'islam," 142; see also Schacht, "Zur soziologischen Betrachtung des islamischen Rechts," 216; Crone and Hinds, *God's Caliph,* 91, 93; Morabia, *Le Gihād,* 180. For a philosopher's viewpoint, see Rosenzweig, *Der Stern der Erlösung,* 2.3, par. 202, pp. 241–42.

7. Crone, *Roman, Provincial and Islamic Law,* 33. Among those who tend to minimize this divergence, see Motzki, *Die Anfänge der islamischen Jurisprudenz,* 262–64.

8. Qur'an 33:21; see also 40:4 and 6.

9. See the consideration of Goldziher's works in Crone, *Roman, Provincial and Islamic Law,* 14; Calder, *Early Muslim Jurisprudence,* 209–17.

10. von Grunebaum, *Medieval Islam,* 111 n. 9; compare with Seneca *Letters to Lucilius* 16.7. For a comparison with the Talmud, see Baron, *Social and Religious History of the Jews,* 6:8.

11. Gérard Lecomte, *Le Traité des divergences du hadīt d'Ibn Qutayba (mort en 276/889),* translation with notes, of *Kitāb ta'wīl muhtalif al-hadīt* (Damascus: Institut Français de Damas, 1962), 46, par. 216a, p. 217; 34, par. 192, p. 184; Lambton, *State and Government in Medieval Islam,* 7. For a contrary view, see Shāfi'ī, *Islamic Jurisprudence: Shāfi'ī's Risāla* 6, par. 101, pp. 123–24.

12. See Lapidus, "The Separation of State and Religion," 367–68.

13. See Hallaq, "Was al-Shāfi'ī the Master Architect of Islamic Jurisprudence?"; Calder, *Early Muslim Jurisprudence,* 67; Reinhart, *Before Revelation,*14.

14. Shāfi'ī, *Risāla* 5, par. 90, p. 116; par. 98, p. 121; 15, par. 823, p. 351.

15. *EI,* s.v. Shāfi'ī, vol. 9, p. 189b (E. Chaumont): Hallaq, "Was al- Shāfi'ī the Master Architect?" 1993, 18, mentions a precursor, al-Shaybānī.

16. See Hallaq, *A History of Islamic Legal Theories,* 29.

17. See Crone, *Roman, Provincial and Islamic Law,* 29.

18. See Nagel, *Staat und Glaubensgemeinschaft im Islam,* 1:299–305.

19. See Crone and Hinds, *God's Caliph,* 5, 21, 44–45, 50.

20. See Goitein, *Studies in Islamic History and Institutions,* 149–67; Nagel, *Staat und Glaubensgemeinschaft im Islam,* 1:159–70.

21. Ibn al-Muqaffa', *Conseilleur du Calife,* par. 11, p. 25; quoted from Goitein, *Studies,* 157.

22. Ibn al-Muqaffaʾ, *Conseilleur du Calife*, par. 36, p. 43; see Goitein, *Studies*, 163.

23. Ibn al-Muqaffaʾ, *Conseilleur du Calife*, pars. 19–20, p. 31.

24. See Goitein, *Studies*, 154, 166, 157; von Grunebaum, *Medieval Islam*, 152 and n. 23; Lambton, *State and Government*, 54.

25. See Crone, *Slaves on Horses*, 77; Crone and Hinds, *God's Caliph*; Lapidus, "Separation of State and Religion," 370–77.

26. See Wolfson, *The Philosophy of the Kalām*, 241.

27. See Lapidus, "Separation of State and Religion," 382–83; Crone and Hinds, *God's Caliph*, 97.

28. The letter is given in Arabic in Ibn al-Djawzi, *Muntazam*, ed. Fritz Krenkow (Hyderabad, 1938–40), vol. 8, pp. 109–11, and in French translation in Makdisi, *Ibn ʾAqīl et la résurgence de l'Islam traditionaliste*, 304–8. See Nagel, *Die Festung des Glaubens*, 56, 109.

29. See Nagel, *Staat und Glaubensgemeinschaft*, 181.

30. See al-Māwardī, *Al-Ahkām al-sultānīyah*, 39 = *Les Statuts gouvernementaux*, 66–67; and Nagel, *Staat und Glaubensgemeinschaft*, 1:350–55.

31. See Lambton, *State and Government in Medieval Islam*, 107 (for Ghazali), 181, 187, 309.

32. Schacht, "Classicisme, traditionalisme et ankylose," 144.

33. See Crone and Hinds, *God's Caliph*, 88.

34. See, for example, al-Ghazali, *Ihyāʾ ʾulūm id-Dīn*, 14 "Licit and Illicit," 5, vol. 2, p. 152; Ibn Kammuna, *Saʾd b. Mansūr ibn Kammūna's Examination of the Inquiries into the Three Faiths*, chap. 4, pp. 102–48.

35. See, for example, Nizām al-Mulk, *Siasset Namèh* 8, p. 82.

36. See the essays in Brunschvig and von Grunebaum, *Classicisme et déclin culturel dans l'histoire de l'Islam*.

37. See Hallaq, "Was the Gate of Ijtihad Closed?"

38. See Nagel, *Die Festung des Glaubens*, 13, 203.

39. See Rosenstock-Huessy, *Die europäischen Revolutionen*, 115, 148. See also H. Berman, *Law and Revolution*, 83, 118; on economic history, see Lombard, *L'Islam dans sa première grandeur*, 259 and *passim*.

40. See Nagel, *Die Festung des Glaubens*, 17.

41. Pseudo-Ghazali, *Sirr al-ʾAlamayn wa-kashf mā fī d-dārayn*, MS. Berlin Landberg 281, fol. 10a, cited in Richter, *Studien zur Geschichte der älteren arabischen Fürstenspiegel*, 88.

42. See Gardet, *La Cité musulmane*, 28 and note; 111 n. 2, 119, 134, 167, 175. The term "nomocracy" is repeated in Morabia, *Le Gihād*, 112, and Wansbrough, *The Sectarian Milieu*, 148. For another use of the word by the Italian historian Pietro de Francisci, see Villey, *La Formation de la pensée juridique moderne*, 61.

43. Lambton, *State and Government*, xvi. Tyan, *Institutions de droit public musulman*, 2:244–51, gives a critique of the expression "separation of the temporal and the spiritual."

Chapter 11

1. See, for example, Nizām al-Mulk, *Siasset Namèh* 6, p. 56; see also Lambton, *State and Government in Medieval Islam*, xvii. On sacred kingship in Persia, see Widengren, "The Sacral Kingship of Iran."

2. "Brethren of Purity," *Rasaʾil Ihwan as-Safaʾ*, vol. 3, p. 495, in Lambton, *State and Government*, 294; Nizām al-Mulk, *Siasset Namèh* 8, p. 83; Ghazali in Laoust, *La Politique de Ghazali*, 197, 237; Richter, *Studien zur Geschichte der älteren arabischen Fürstenspiegel*, 67; Goldziher, *Gesammelte Schriften*, 5:136 and n. 1; von Grunebaum, *L'identité culturelle de l'Islam*, 26 and n. 36; Dakhlia, *Le Divan des rois*, 73. There are Jewish echoes in Joseph Hayyun,

Miley de-Avot (Venice, 1470), 24b, in Ravitzky, *Religion and State in Jewish Philosophy,* 132. For application of the relationship of the Law to Wisdom in Shem Tov Ibn Falaqera, *'Iggeret Ha-Viqquah,* p. 1, see Jospe, *Torah and Sophia,* 79.

3. See Goldziher, *Sur l'Islam,* 280–83; Lambton, *State and Government,* 309.

4. See, for example, Nizām al-Mulk, *Siasset Namèh* 2, p. 10.

5. See Gutas, "Ethische Schriften im Islam," 355–62 and bibliography, 364–65.

6. See Richter, *Studien zur Geschichte der älteren arabischen Fürstenspiegel,* 6, 71–72, 81.

7. Ghazali's *Book of Counsel for Kings* (*Nasīhat al-Mulūk*), English translation by F. R. C. Bagley (London and New York: Oxford University Press, 1964), 1, 31. For a negative opinion of the authenticity of this work, see Crone, "Did al-Ghazālī Write 'A Mirror for Princes'?"; see also Pseudo-Jahīz, *Livre de la couronne,* French translation by Charles Pellat (Paris: Les Belles Lettres, 1954), preface, p. 30; chap. 3, pp. 74, 80, 83.

8. Qur'an 31:11–19. See also Gutas, "Ethische Schriften im Islam," 348.

9. See Gardet, *Dieu et la destinée de l'homme,* 168–69; for an example in Razi, *La Médecine spirituelle,* see my introduction to that work, 33–34.

10. See, for example, Jurjānī, *Definitiones* (in Arabic), ed. Gustav Flügel (Leipzig, 1845), 258–59; Miskawayh, *Le Petit Livre du Salut* 3:8, pp. 139–41/88–90.

11. Qur'an 33:40. For the source in Manes (or Mani), see al-Bīrūnī, *Chronologie orientalischer Völker,* p. 207, 19; Jeffery, *Qur'ān as Scripture,* 79; G. Stroumsa, *Savoir et salut,* 275–88.

12. See Nwyia, *Exégèse coranique et langage mystique,* 304; Smith, "The Concept of Shari'a" 585–89, 593.

13. Ghazali, *Al-Mustafa min 'ilm al-usūl* 1.83, in Laoust, *La Politique de Ghazali,* 153. For a modern example, see Nagel, *Das islamische Recht,* 64. For a modern attempt to attribute a legislative power to the community, see Rida, *Le Califat,* 156.

14. 'Abd al-'Alī Muhammad al Ansarī, in Muhibb Allah al-Bihārī, *Musallam al Thubūt* (Bulaq, 1913–14), vol. 1, p. 25 (*non vidi*), in Weiss, *Spirit of Islamic Law,* 36.

15. Alfarabi, *Didascalia in Rethoricam [sic] Aristotelis,* part. 5, ed. M. Grignaschi (Beirut: Dār al-Mashreq, 1971), 159.

16. Aristotle *Nic. Ethics* 1134b18–19, in Arabic translation, *Aristūtlīs, al-Akhlāq,* ed. A. Badawi (Kuwait: Wakālat al-matbū'āt, 1979), 192, commented in Averroes, *Averroes' Middle Commentary on Aristotle's Nicomachean Ethics* 1.326, p. 189. See Strauss, *Persecution and the Art of Writing,* 97 n. 5.

17. This idea has persisted up to contemporary times, for example, in 'Abduh, *Rissalat al Tawhid,* 54; see also Frank, "Reason and Revealed Law," 137; Pines, *Studies in the History of Arabic Philosophy,* 165–71, 187n76.

18. See Lambton, *State and Government,* xiv–xv, 1.

19. See, for example, al-Bīrūnī, *Chronologie,* chap. 15, p. 291, *The Chronology,* 287; Averroes, *Commentaire moyen à la Rhétorique d'Aristote,* 1.8.8, p. 70. I examine these texts in Brague, "Trois regards musulmans sur la cité chrétienne." See also al-Sijistānī, in Tawhīdī, *Kitab al-imtā 'wa-al-muanasah,* vol. 2, p. 22, in English in Kraemer, *Philosophy in the Renaissance of Islam,* 238–39.

20. See Weiss, "Covenant and Law in Islam," 63; on the signs of prophecy, see G. Stroumsa, *Barbarian Philosophy,* 21–36.

21. Besançon, *Trois tentations dans l'Église,* 167.

22. Descartes, *Notae in programma quoddam . . . ,* AT, VIII–2, p. 353, quoted from "Notes Directed Against A Certain Programme Published in Belgium at the End of the Year 1647 . . . ," in *The Philosophical Works of Descartes,* trans. Elizabeth S. Haldane and G. R. T. Ross, 2 vols. (Cambridge: Cambridge University Press, 1978), 1:439.

23. Qur'an 7:172. For examples of the utilization of this notion, see Brague, *La Sagesse du monde*, 114–15; *Wisdom of the World*, 95–96.

24. Qur'an 30:30; hadith, in *CTM*, 5:179b–180b; *Fiqh akbar II*, par. 6, in Wensinck, *The Muslim Creed*, 191. The two are given together, for example by Averroes, *Kashfa 'an manāhij al-adilla fī 'aqā'id al-milla* 5.4, p. 130: see Morabia, *Le Gihādl*, 163–64; B. Lewis, *Political Language of Islam*, 143. On foundlings, see Fattal, *Le Statut légal des non-musulmans en pays d'Islam*, 169.

25. See above, p. 80; on reason distinguishing humans from animals in Judaism, Nahminides, *Torat Hashem temimah*, 143.

26. Qur'an 4:163. See Shahrastānī, *Kitāb al-Milal wa-l-Nihal*, ed. William Cureton, 233. The order (*amr*) is unique; the expression varies according to language: see Falaturi, "Das Fehlen einer Heilsgeschichte im Islam."

27. See van Ess, *Theologie und Gesellschaft*, 1:451; Urvoy, *Les Penseurs libres*, 111 (al-Warraq), 207–8 (Ibn Kammuna), and 218.

28. Numbers 19; al-Samau'al al-Maghribi, *Ifhām al-Yahūd*, 36.

29. The author in question is al-Hakīm al-Tirmidī (ninth-tenth centuries) and his *'Ilal al-'Ubūdīya* (also known as *al-Sharī'a*): see Sezgin, *GAS*, 1:654. Despite its title, Ibn Bābūya al-Qummī al-Sadūq, *'Ilal al-Sharā'i' wa-'l-ashāb* does not seem to contain anything of the sort: see Sezgin, *GAS*, 1:547. On al-Qaffāl, see Sezgin, *GAS*, 1:497–98 and Reinhart, *Before Revelation*, 18, from whom the quotations are taken. Why Reinhart uses the Miltonian formula that I have quoted is not explained, and the comparison with Maimonides is not elaborated.

30. See, for example, Averroes, *Kashfa 'an manāhij al-adilla fī 'aqā'id al-milla* 5.2, p. 118.

31. See S. Stroumsa, "The Barahima in Early Kalām." The oldest mention is in al-Muqammas, *Twenty Chapters* (*'Ishrūn Maqāla*) 13, par. 1, pp. 254–55: see Norman Calder, "The Barāhima"; S. Stroumsa, *Freethinkers in Medieval Islam*, 145–62.

32. Jāhiz, in Lambton, *State and Government*, 56. On Ibn Hazm, see Asín Palacios, "La tesis de la necesidad de la revelación," 352–55, and idem, "El origen del lenguaje"; Ghazali, *Al-Munqid min adalal* (*Erreur et délivrance*), pp. 42/105; Ghazali, *Streitschrift des Gazālī gegen die Batinijja-Sekte*, pp. 20/34; Averroes, *Tahafot at-Tahafot* 3, par. 123, p. 208.

33. Snouck Hurgronje, "Sur la nature du 'Droit' musulman"; Becker, *Vom Werden und Wesen der islamischen Welt*, 1:44; Lambton, *State and Government*, 2. On the history of this representation, reprised by Ignaz Goldziher, see Johansen, *Contingency in a Sacred Law*, 42–54.

34. See al-Iji, *al-Mawāqif fī ilm al-Kalām* (Cairo: 1875), 8, 181–207, summarized in Stieglecker, *Die Glaubenslehren des Islam*, 127–44.

35. Māwardī, *Adab ad-Dunyā wa-al-Dīn*, p. 3, in Nagel, *Staat und Glaubensgemeinschaft*, 1:376.

36. See van Ess, *Theologie und Gesellschaft*, 4:573.

37. Saadia Gaon, *Book of Beliefs and Opinions* 3.3, pp. 122–23; Rosenblatt translation, 145–46; Thomas Aquinas, *Summa Theologica*, IaIIae, q. 99, a. 2, ad 2m; see van Ess, *Theologie und Gesellschaft*, 4:576; Maimonides, *Traité d'Éthique*, chap. 6, p. 22, 5–7, *Eight Chapters*, 88.

38. See Wansbrough, *Sectarian Milieu*, 110–12; van Ess, *Theologie und Gesellschaft*, 2:301–2.

39. Urvoy, *Les Penseurs libres*, 181. On Muhāsibī, see de Crussol, *Le Rôle de la raison*; Juwaynī, *El-Irchad*, chap. 2, par. 4, p. 9, 7/26.

40. Hallaq, *Islamic Legal Theories*, 135. On the overall evolution of this dispute, see van Ess, *Theologie und Gesellschaft*, 4:576.

41. Ash'arī, *Kitāb al-Luma'* in R. J. McCarthy, *The Theology of al-Ash'ari* (Beirut: Imprimerie Catholique, 1963), no. 171; see Gimaret, *La Doctrine d'Al-Ash'ar'*, 444–46; Antes, *Ethik und Politik im Islam*, 42. On the rejection of the idea of nature, see Richard M. Frank,

"The Science of Kalam," *Arabic Sciences and Philosophy* 2 (1992): 7–37. On al-Māturīdī, see Rudolph, *Al-Māturīdī und die sunnitische Theologie in Samarkand*, 332.

42. Juwaynī, *El-Irchad*, chap. 20, par. 3, p. 148, 11–15/233–234; p. 150, 11–12/236; p. 153, 7/239. See also ibid., chap. 22, par. 9, p. 205, 20–21/305. The translations are mine.

43. Ibid., chap. 22, par. 3, p. 197, 18–19/295; see also ibid., par. 7, p. 204, 14–303.

44. Ibid., chap. 19, par. 20, p. 145, 2–5/229: see Nagel, *Die Festung des Glaubens*, 183; the contemporary text cited in Nagel, *Das islamische Recht*, 335. Note the use of ta'abbada in al-Māwardī, *ADD*, p. 3, Nagel, *Staat und Glaubensgemeinschaft*, 1:375. On another usage, see Calder, *Early Muslim Jurisprudence*, 81.

45. Al-Māwardī, *Adab ad-Dunyā wa-al-Dīn*, p. 116, in Nagel, *Staat und Glaubensgemeinschaft*, 1:379.

46. Al-Hillī, in *EI*, s.v. "Shari'a," vol. 9 (1988), col. 331a (N. Calder); and Taftazanī, in Goldziher, *Die Zahiriten*, 12 n.1.

47. See Nagel, *Die Festung des Glaubens*, 158, 267, 345, 355; Gimaret, *La Doctrine d'Al-Ash'ar'*, 499–51.

48. See Nagel, *Die Festung des Glaubens*, 225, 191, 297

49. Al-Qadir in Makdisi, *Ibn 'Aqīl et la résurgence de l'Islam traditionaliste*, 306; Shāfi'ī in Nagel, *Die Festung des Glaubens*, 198.

50. See Hallaq, *Islamic Legal Theories*, 136, 151 (on Tufi), 162–206, esp. pp. 168, 180 (on Shatibi), 214 (on the utilitarianism of the school of Manār), 224 (on al-Fasī).

51. See Keddie, "Symbol and Sincerity in Islam"; Jadaane, "Les conditions socio-culturelles de la philosophie islamique."

52. "Brethren of Purity," *Rasa'il Ihwan as-Safa'*, 4.1 [42], vol. 3, pp. 422, 455; Miskawayh, *Tahdhīb al-Akhlāq wa Tathīr al-A'rāq* 3, p. 101/159; Averroes, *Traité décisif (Façl el-maqāl) sur l'accord de la religion et de la philosophie*, pp. 100; 8, 11, 17, 20ff.; 24–25, 27, 30; 22, 13ff.; 7, 14; 8, 5.

53. Aristotle *Nic. Ethics* 1.7, 1097b11; see also Marsilius of Padua, *Der Verteidiger des Friedens (Defensor Pacis)* 1.4.3, p. 18; Alfarabi, *Tahsīl as-Sa'ada*, par. 16, in Alfarabi, *Philosophical Works*, pp. 139–40, and in *Alfarabi's Philosophy of Plato and Aristotle*, par. 18, p. 23; Miskawayh, in Kraemer, *Humanism in the Renaissance of Islam*, 232; Fakhr ad-Dīn Razī, in Lambton, *State and Government*, 132; Nasir ad-Dīn Tusī, *The Nasirean Ethics* 3.1, p. 190. On sociability, see, for example, Ibn Abī al-Rabī', *The Political Philosophy of Ibn Abī al-Rabī* (in Arabic), chap. 4, p. 175.

54. Ibn Tufayl, *Hayy ben Yaqdhān*. Aristotle *Pol.* 1, 1253a27–29; Ibn Khaldūn, *Prolégomènes* 5, pp. 289–90, *The Muqaddimah*, 329. On Ibn Tufayl, see Brague, "Cosmological Mysticism"; for other examples on the same theme, see Vajda, "D'une attestation peu connue du thème du Philosophe autodidacte,"

55. Plato *Rep.* 2, 369a; Aristotle *Pol.* 1.2, 1253a7–18. Given that the latter work was never translated into Arabic, we have to surmise that there were summaries of it or quotations from it. On this thesis, see Razi, *La Médecine spirituelle*, chap. 17, pp. 161–62; Alfarabi, *Idées des habitants de la Cité vertueuse*, chap. 26, p. 101 (in Arabic) / 85 (in French); "Brethren of Purity," *Rasa'il Ihwan as-Safa'*, 2.2 [2], vol. 1, pp. 99–100; Māwardī, *Adab ad-Dunyā wa-al-Dīn*, p. 119, 1–6; Avicenna, *Al-Shifā, al-Ilāhiyyāt (Metaphysics)* 10,2, pp. 441–42; Ghazali, *Ihyā' 'ulūm al-Dīn* 26, "World," 3:239–40; Averroes, *Commentary on Plato's Republic* 1.2.3–4, pp. 22, 22–30 (in Hebrew); p. 113 (in English); Maimonides, *Guide* 3.27, p. 372, 4–5; Ibn Khaldūn, *Prolégomènes [Muqaddimah]* 1:69, 3–16; 2:234–35; see Mahdi, *Ibn Khaldūn's Philosophy of History*, 188–89 and n.4.

56. Avicenna, *Avicenna's De Anima*. 5.1, p. 202, 1–203, 9. This passage seems not to have attracted attention. See Avicenna, *Psychologie d'Ibn Sina (Avicenne) d'après son oeuvre as-*

Sifa', ed. and French translation by Ján Bakos (Prague: Académie tchécoslovaque des Sciences, 1956), translation, pp.143–48, where the passage is not mentioned in the notes on p. 227. In his preface to *Avicenna Latinus, Liber de anima: Seu Sextus Naturalibus*, ed. Simone van Riet (Louvain: Éditions orientalistes; Leiden: Brill, 1968), 13–20, Gérard Verbeke, among many highly pertinent remarks, neglects what seems to me essential., which is the place of the text.

57. Avicenna, *Avicenna's De Anima* 1.4, p. 37, 16–17.

58. Ibid., p. 203, 5.

59. Maimonides, *Guide* 1.72, p. 132/370; Thomas Aquinas, *Contra impugnantes Dei cultum et religionem* (1256), chap. 4, 1, ll. 453–59, vol. 41, Leonine edition (1970), 41:A90b.

60. Maimonides, *Guide* 2.40, p. 270, 7–22/306–7; Ibn Khaldūn, *Prolégomènes* [*Muqaddimah*] 1:63, 13; 67, 4; 252, 13; Alexander of Aphrodisias, *Alexandri Aphrodisiensis praeter commentaria scripta minore "De anima" liber cum mantissa*, ed. Ivo Bruns (Berlin: Reimer, 1887), 156–59; Ibn Taymiyya, *Refutation of the Logicians*, ed. Rafik el-'Aham, 2 vols. (Beirut: Dār al-fikr al-lubnānī, n.d.), 2:171, in English translation by Wael B. Hallaq as *Against the Greek Logicians* (Oxford: Oxford University Press, 1993).

61. Avicenna, *Al-Shifā, al-Ilāhiyyāt* 10 (at the end) = Avicenna, *Najāt*, ed. Muhyi al-Din Sabri Kurdi (Misr: Matba'at al-Sa'adah, 1912), pp. 303–8; Avicenna, *al-Hidāya*, ed. M. Abduh (Cairo, 1965), pars. 188–89, pp. 298–99.

62. Avicenna, *Al-Shifā, al-Ilāhiyyāt* 10.2–5, pp. 441–55; French translation by Georges Anawati, pp. 175–89 (which is not very helpful, however). Chapters 2 and 3 of this work are copied in their entirety in Avicenna, *Najat*, pp. 338–43; for details, see, respectively, chap. 2, p. 441, 12 and 442, 6; chap. 4, p. 448, 15; chap. 3, p. 446, 10.

63. See, for example, *Critias*, DK 88B25; Mishnah, *Pirke Avot*, 3.2; Bahya ibn Paquda, *Al-Hidāja'ilā Farā'id al-Qulūb* (Duties of the heart) 3.4, p. 146.

64. Alfarabi, *Idées des habitants de la Cité vertueuse*, chap. 29, pp. 115–16/97; Alfarabi, *Al-Siyāsah al-Madaniyah*, pp. 87–88; then Alfarabi, *Cité vertueuse*, chap. 26, p. 102/85–86; Alfarabi, *Fusūl Muntaza'ah*, par. 28, p. 45, 1–5.

65. See Galston, "Realism and Idealism in Avicenna's Political Philosophy."

66. Alfarabi, *Cité vertueuse*, chap. 25, p. 99/83.

67. Avicenna, *Al-Shifā, al-Ilāhiyyāt* 10.4 and 5. On these terms, see ibid., chap. 5, p. 453, 4.7.13.

68. Averroes, *Commentary on Plato's Republic* 3.11.5, p. 92, 4–8. On Averroes' fidelity to the Almohads, see Urvoy, *Avveroès*, 57–58.

69. Ibid., 1.25.9–10, p. 54.

70. Ibid., 1.21.2, p. 44, 19. It is possible that the expression "king of the Arabs" comes from the Hebrew translator.

71. Ibid., 1.7.10, p. 26, 14–15. See also Averroes, *Averroes on Plato's Republic*, p. xviii; Brague, "Der Dschihad der Philosophen," 87.

72. Averroes, *Commentary on Plato's Republic* 2.1.7, p. 61, 17–18; see Pines, *Studies in the History of Jewish Philosophy*, 86.

73. Averroes, *Tahafot at-Tahafot*, "Physics," 10, p. 516—if we can believe Teicher, "Averroès, 'Paraphrase de la République de Platon,'" 190.

74. Averroes, *Commentary on Plato's Republic* 3.9.13, p. 223.

75. Ibid., 3.9.7, p. 88, 22 (*domeh*) and 3.9.5, p. 92, 5 (a man resembles [*mehakkeh*] a regime), and 8 (a historical regime imitates [*domeh*] a type of regime).

76. Ibid., 1.7, p. 26, 16–17; II, III, p. 63. On this contrast, see Pines, *Studies in the History of Jewish Philosophy*, 91.

77. Aristotle *Nic. Ethics* 7.1, 1145a18–30; Arabic translation, *Aristūtlīs, al-Akhlāq,* p. 233 (see n. 16 above). Averroes does not comment on this passage: see Averroes, *Middle Commentary on Aristotle's Nicomachean Ethics,* 225.

78. Alfarabi, *Alfarabi's Book of Letters,* 2, par. 139, p. 149, 18–21; see Najjar, "Farabi's Political Philosophy and Shī'ism"; Alfarabi, *Book of Letters,* 2, par. 113, p. 133, 14–15; p. 134, 12–13; Alfarabi, *Al-Siyāsah al-Madaniyah,* p. 80, 5–9.

79. Alfarabi, *Didascalia in Rethoricam [sic] Aristotelis,* par. 31, p. 201, 17–18; par. 38, pp. 213–14.

80. Alfarabi, "Enumeration of the Sciences" (Ihsāʾ al-ʿulūm), in Alfarabi, *Kitāb al-Millah wa-nusūs ukkrá* (Alfarabi's book of religion and related texts), p. 74, 5–6; Aristotle *Nic. Ethics* 10.9, 1178b33; Alfarabi, *Tahsīl as-Saʿada,* par. 63, in Alfarabi, *Philosophical Works,* 193; in Alfarabi, *Alfarabi's Philosophy of Plato and Aristotle,* par. 61, p. 48. For another interpretation, see Daiber, "The Ruler as Philosopher"; see also above, pp. 113–14.

81. Alfarabi, *Tahsūīl as-Saʿada,* par. 64, in Alfarabi, *Philosophical Works,* 195–96; Alfarabi, *Alfarabi's Philosophy of Plato and Aristotle,* par. 62, p. 49. This recalls the incredible elitism of Friedrich Gundolf, *Shakespeare und der deutsche Geist* (Berlin: Bondi, 1914), 279–84.

82. Ibn Khallikān, *Wafayāt al-Aʾyan,* in Alfarabi, *Cité vertueuse,* preface (in Arabic), p. 5. See also Plato *Statesman* 259b and 292e; Alfarabi, *Al-Siyāsah al-Madaniyah,* p. 96, 18–97, 9; Alfarabi, *Fusūl Muntazaʾah,* par. 32, p. 49, 3–6.

83. For a demonstration of this point, see Mahdi, "Alfarabi's Imperfect State," 705–13.

84. Alfarabi, *Jadal,* in Alfarabi, *Al-Mantīq ʾinda al-Farabi,* 3:36, 16–37, 2; 37, 9–11. On this idea, see al-Māwardī, *Adab ad-Dunyā wa-al-Dīn,* in Nagel, *Staat und Glaubensgemeinschaft,* 1:377.

85. Alfarabi, *Al-Siyāsah al-Madaniyah,* p. 101, 2–3; p. 102, 3–4; Plato *Rep.* 7, 250b2. See also Alon, "Farabi's Funny Flora."

86. Alfarabi, *Kitāb al-Millah,* p. 56; Alfarabi, *Fusūl Muntazaʾah,* par. 93, p. 95, 10–13.

87. Plato *Rep.* 9, 592a–b.

88. Ibn Bājja, *El Régimen del solitario;* see Leaman, "Ibn Bājja on Society and Philosophy"; and Lerner, "Maimonides' Governance of the Solitary."

89. Bahmanyār, *Kitāb al-Tahsīl,* ed. Murtazá Mutahhari (Terehan: Dāneshgah, 1970), 90, 816–17, in Morris, "The Philosopher-Prophet in Avicenna's Political Philosophy," 185–86.

90. See, for example, Avicenna, *Epistola sulla vita futura,* ed. Francesca Lucchetta (Padua: Antenore, 1969), 3.1, pp. 43, 57–58, 73, 85–86, 93.

91. Avicenna, *Al-Shifā, al-Ilāhiyyāt,* p. 442, 20; p. 443, 2–4 and 11; chap. 3, p. 445, 10–11; Alfarabi, *Book of Letters,* 2 par. 143, p. 152, 2–5; Averroes, *Traité décisif (Fasl el-maqāl),* pp. 8, 17, 26.

92. See Avicenna, *Al-Shifā, al-Ilāhiyyāt* 10.2, p. 443, 11–12; Alfarabi, *Al-Siyāsah al-Madaniyah,* p. 85, 12.

93. Alfarabi, *Book of Letters,* 2, par. 111, p. 132, 12–13, and par. 144, p. 152, 9–10; Alfarabi, *Tahsīl as-Saʿada,* par. 56, p. 90, 15, in *Philosophical Works,* 185; Alfarabi, *Alfarabi's Philosophy of Plato and Aristotle,* par. 55, p. 44; Alfarabi, *Kitāb al-Millah,* pp. 46–47; Alfarabi, *Fusūl Muntazaʾah,* par. 93, p. 94, 2; Alfarabi, *Cité vertueuse,* chap 23, p. 128/110; Alfarabi, *Al-Siyāsah al-Madaniyah,* p. 85, 18–86, 1; p. 86, 17–87, 4; Alfarabi, *Kitāb al-Millah,* p. 45, 20–24. On the medical image, see Marquet, *La Philosophie des Ihwan al-Safaʾ,* 48–49.

94. Alfarabi, *Jadal,* in Alfarabi, *Al-Mantīq ʾinda al-Farabi,* 3:70, 4, Alfarabi, *Tanbih fī sabil,* par. 17, in Alfarabi, *Philosophical Works,* 76; Alfarabi, "Ihsāʾ al-ʿulūm," in *Kitāb al-Millah,* p. 71; Alfarabi, *Jadal,* in Alfarabi, *Al-Mantīq ʾinda al-Farabi,* 3:69, 17–18; Alfarabi, *Kitāb al-Millah,* p. 52, 10.

95. Alfarabi, *Fusūl Muntazaʾah,* par. 48, p. 81, 5–6; Alfarabi, *Cité vertueuse,* chap. 27,

p. 110/92; Alfarabi, *Al-Siyāsah al-Madaniyah,* p. 55, 9–10; Alfarabi, *Cité vertueuse,* chap. 23, p. 93/77; Alfarabi, *Kitāb al-Millah,* p. 52, 14–15.

96. Alfarabi, *Cité vertueuse,* chap. 23, p. 93/77. See also Ibn Bājjah, *Philosophical Writings,* 197. The thesis in Pines, *Studies in the History of Jewish Thought,* 404–46, has recently been severely criticized by Philippe Vallat, *Al-Farabi et l'École d'Alexandrie: Des prémisses de la connaissance à la philosophie politique* (Paris: Vrin, 2004).

97. Alfarabi, *Fusūl Muntaza'ah,* par. 12, p. 33, 10–12; Alfarabi, "The Attainment of Happiness" *(Tahsīl as-Sa'ada)* in Alfarabi, *Philosophical Works,* par. 43, p. 77, 12–13; Alfarabi, *Kitāb al-Millah,* p. 49, 10–14; Alfarabi, *Al-Siyāsah al-Madaniyah* 80.15–81.2; *Alfarabi's Commentary on Aristotle's Peri hermeneias (De Interpretatione),* ed., Wilhelm Kutsch and Stanley Marrow, 2d ed., rev. and corr. (Beirut: Dār al-Mashreq, 1971), p. 27, 15–18. See also Macy, "The Rule of Law and the Rule of Wisdom," 208–10; Galston, *Politics and Excellence,* 97 n. 5, 107.

98. Alfarabi, respectively: *Cité vertueuse,* 2.3.9–10, p. 104; ibid., 4.13, p. 202; French translation, p. 90/74; *Al-Siyāsah al-Madaniyah,* p. 79, 17–80, 3; *Cité vertueuse,* 4.14.9, p. 224; French translation, p. 100/84.

99. Avicenna, *Avicenna's De Anima* 5.6, p. 248, 9–250, 4; Maimonides, *Commentary on the Mishnah* (in Arabic), Heleq, 8, 6th principle, p. 371; Maimonides, *Guide,* 2.36, p. 260, 20–21/281; Ibn Khaldūn, *Prolégomènes [Muqaddimah]* 1, 1:173–81.

100. Avicenna, *Ithbāt al-Nubuwwāt (Proof of Prophecies),* par. 14, pp. 46–47; Alfarabi, *Kitāb al-Millah,* par. 27, p. 66; Alfarabi, *Fusūl Muntaza'ah,* par. 61, pp. 70–71; Alfarabi, *Al-Siyāsah al-Madaniyah,* p. 84, 17–18.

101. See above, pp. 162–63.

102. Aristotle *Nic. Ethics* 6.13, 1145a10–11.

103. See, for example, Mu'ayyad fī d-Dīn al-Shirāzī and Abū Ya'qub as-Sijistānī, in Nagel, *Staat und Glaubensgemeinschaft,* 1:252, 254.

104. For an extreme presentation of this thesis, see Parens, *Metaphysics as Rhetoric.*

105. Alfarabi, *Alfarabi's Book of Religion and Related Texts,* chapters on the "Opinions of the People of the Virtuous City," p. 79; Badawi, *Rasa' il falsafiyah,* 33, 4.

106. Ibn Arabi, *Futuhāt al-Makkiyyah,* 4 vols.(Beirut: Dar Sadir, 1968?), 3:178, par. 344, 11–14, in F. Rosenthal, "Ibn 'Arabi between 'Philosophy' and 'Mysticism,'" 19; Bürgel, *Allmacht und Mächtigkeit,* 126. I remember a similar statement in Louis de Bonald, but have not been able to retrieve it.

107. Those who were in favor of such harmony include: Miskawayh, *Tahdhīb al-Akhlāq wa Tathīr al-A'rāq* 4, p. 117/195; Averroes, *Kashf 'an manāhij al-adilla fī 'aqā' id al-milla,* p. 90 (more clearly so than in the *Fasl al-maqāl* itself); Against: al-Sijistānī, in *Tawhīdī, Kitab al-imtā 'wa-al-muanasah,* vol. 2, p. 18, 21, in English in Kraemer, *Philosophy in the Renaissance of Islam,* 235, 238.

108. See Zaehner, *Mysticism, Sacred and Profane,* chap. 11; Kant, *Die Religion innerhalb der Grenzen der blossen Vernunft,* 4.2, pars. 1–2, in Kant, *Werke,* 4:839–47.

109. See *EI,* s.v. "Ibāha," vol. 3 (1975), II, 683a–b (W. Madelung), and III, 683b–684b (M. G. S. Hodgson). The image of the ladder is in Halevi, *Kuzari* 3.65, p. 141, 1–2; *Le Kuzari,* 140.

110. For examples, see Nizām al-Mulk, *Siasset Namèh* 10, p. 91; Ghazali, *Streitschrift des Gazālī gegen die Batinijja-Sekte,* pp. 4–5.

111. See Montesquieu, *De l'esprit des Lois,* unpublished fragments, p. 796a; Montesquieu, *Pensées,* par. 292, p. 883b. See also Anatole France, *Crainquebille,* 2: for a policeman, "any insult necessarily takes on the traditional, regular, consecrated, ritual, one might even say liturgical, form of 'Mort aux vaches!'"

112. See *EI, s.v.* "Karmati," vol. 4 (1978), 687a–692a (W. Madelung); al-Bīrūnī, *Chronologie*, p. 213, 2–6; *Sefer Nameh: Relation du voyage de Nassiri Khosrau* . . . , trans. Charles Schefer (Paris: Leroux, 1881), 226–28.

113. Ghazali, *Streitschrift des Gazālī gegen die Batinijja-Sekte*, 23–24 and n.4; Marquet, *La Philosophie des Ihwan al-Safa'*, 211; Jambet, *La Grande Résurrection d'Alamût*, 88.

114. See Buckley, "The Nizari Isma'ilites Abolishment of the Shari'a," 137; Jambet, *La Grande Résurrection*, 97, 144, 309 and (on the rejection of incarnation) 297, 321.

115. See Jambet, *La Grande Résurrection*, 100, 103, 109, 111.

116. Ibid., 71, 118, 123, 330–31.

117. See Schimmel, *Mystische Dimensionen des Islam*, 132, 158.

118. Qushayrī, *Al-Risāla al-Qushayriyya fi 'ilm al-atsawwuf*, chap. 1, no. 23 (Junayd), pp. 66–67 = chap. 47 (Knowledge of God), no. 8, p. 433 (with indication of parallels); IV, 65, p. 430 = II, 40, p. 314. See also Ghazali, *Al-Munqid min adalal* (*Erreur et délivrance*), pp. 47/111.

119. Qushayrī, *Al-Risāla*, p. 219; chap. 31 (Liberty), no. 3, Gramlich translation, p. 311.

120. See Seneca *De vita beata* 15.7: Augustine *De libero arbitrio* 2.13.37, *BA*, 6:286; Augustine *De vera religione* 46.87.245; Proclus *De providentia* 24.9–10. For the Middle Ages, see Halevi, *Kuzari*, 5.25, p. 229, 2; *Le Kuzari*, 236.

121. See Jambet, *La Grande Résurrection*, 334; Weiss, *Spirit of Islamic Law*, 18. For a different point of view on the relationship between legalism and Sufism, see Benkheira, *L'Amour de la Loi*, 180–81.

122. Abū Ya'qūb al-Sijistānī, *Kashf al-mahjūb* (*Le Dévoilement des choses cachées*), trans. Henry Corbin (Lagrasse: Verdier, 1988), 54, in Jambet, *La Grande Résurrection*, 198.

123. Ibn Arabi, *The Interpretation of Longing*, no. 11, vv. 13–15, quoted in Schimmel, *Mystische Dimensionen des Islam*, 384; *Mystical Dimensions*, 264; Ibn Arabi, *Futuhāt al-Makkiyyah*, 4:547. On the complex personality of Ibn Daoud, see Massignon, *La Passion d'al-Husayn Ibn Mansūr al-Hallāj*, 1975 ed., 1:386–416.

124. See Lazarus-Yafeh, *Studies in Al-Ghazzālī*, chap. 6, "Place of the Religious Commandments in the Philosophy of al-Ghazali," 412–36.

125. Ghazali, *Ihyā'* 14 "Licit and Illicit," 5, 2:154.

126. Ibid., 19, "Commanding Good," 3, 2:370; Laoust, *La Politique de Ghazali*, 131, speaks of "indoctrination": see Nizām al-Mulk, *Siasset Namèh* 47, p. 273.

127. Ghazali, *Ihyā'* 31, "Conversion," 4, 4:53; 14, "Licit and Illicit," 5, 2:153.

128. Ibid., 2, "Marriage," 2, 2:41; Ghazali, *Tahāfut*, p. 5, in Laoust, *La Politique de Ghazali*, 70; Ghazali, *Al-Munqid min adalal* 5, p. 47/111, in Laoust, *La Politique de Ghazali*, 140, 139, 356.

129. Nizām al-Mulk, *Siasset Namèh* 45, p. 248 (Mazdak); 47, pp. 288–89, 291, 198 (Batinites); Ghazali, *Die Streitschrift des Gazālī gegen die Ibāhīja im persichen Text*, p. 21, 26; Ghazali, *Streitschrift des Gazālī gegen die Batinijja-Sekte*, pp. 37.

130. Ghazali, *Die Streitschrift des Gazālī gegen die Ibāhīja im persichen Text*, p. 26, 33; see also ibid., p. 37. Since I do not know Persian, I am translating from the German of Otto Pretzl. On "licence," see also Ghazali, *Ihyā'* 1, "Science," 3, 1:48; 30, "Illusion," 2, 3:427.

131. Ghazali, *Die Streitschrift des Gazālī gegen die Ibāhīja im persichen Text*, pp. 49–50.

132. Ghazali, *Streitschrift des Gazālī gegen die Batinijja-Sekte*, pp. 47–48/10–11.

133. Ghazali, *Al-Mustafa min 'ilm al-usūl* 1:222–23; Laoust, *La Politique de Ghazali*, 153–55, 365, 368.

134. Ghazali, *Ihyā'* 1, "Science," 1, 1:24; 32, "Gratitude," 2, 4:125.

135. Ghazali, *Al-Mustafa min 'ilm al-usūl* 1:192; see Laoust, *La Politique de Ghazali*, 87, 89;

Ghazali, *Ihyā'* 37, "Intention," 1, 4, 4:388; Ghazali, *Streitschrift des Gazālī gegen die Batinijja-Sekte*, p. 94 and n.1.

136. Laoust, *La Politique de Ghazali*, 154, 87, and 161.

137. Ghazali, *Al-Mustafa min 'ilm al-usūl* 2:406.

138. Ghazali, *Ihyā'* 5, "Tithing," 2, 1:251. On "enslavement," see above p. 166.

139. Ghazali, *Die Streitschrift des Gazālī gegen die Ibāhīja im persichen Text*, pp. 38–41.

140. Abelard *Ethica* 3, in *PL* 178, 644a; Bernard of Clairvaux *De praecepto et dispensatione* 11.26, in his *Opera*, 3:272. See also my introduction to Maimonides, *Traité d'Éthique*, 18–19.

141. Laoust, *La Politique de Ghazali*, 329, citing Ghazali, *Ihyā'* 36, "Love," 11, 4:350. I have been unable to find either the idea or the word *sharia* in this passage. See also the translation of this work by Richard Gramlich, *Muhammad al-Gazzālīs Lehre von den Stufen zur Gottesliebe* (Wiesbaden: Steiner, 1984), 702.

142. Ghazali, *Streitschrift des Gazālī gegen die Batinijja-Sekte*, p. 14; Ghazali, *Ihyā'* 1, "Science," 2, 1:28–29; 96, "Retreat," 2, 2:259.

143. Ghazali, *Ihyā'* 31, "Conversion," 2, 2, 4:27. The definition given at the beginning of this work in 31, "Mysteries of the Heart," 1, 3:4, is more prosaic. See also ibid., 18, "Music," 2, 2:317.

144. Ibid., 14, "Licit and Illicit," 2, 2:116, 126, 131; 3, 2:133.

145. Ibid., 1, "Science," 2, 1:2, and 3, 1:51; 4, "Prayer," 3, 1:190.

146. Ibid., 14, "Licit and Illicit," 2, 2:131.

147. Ibid., 3, 2:134.

148. Ibid., 3, 2:138. There is an amazing resemblance here to Pascal's "The heart has its reasons which reason does not know": see his *Pensées*, no. 277.

149. Ghazali, *Ihyā'* 14, "Licit and Illicit," 2, 2:131.

150. Ghazali, *Streitschrift des Gazālī gegen die Batinijja-Sekte*, p. 109; Ghazali, *Ihyā'*, cited in Ghazali, *Streitschrift des Gazālī gegen die Batinijja-Sekte*, p. 106. For equivalents in Judaism, see Heschel, *Theology of Ancient Judaism* (in Hebrew), 1:168–69. The distinction between the duties of the body and those of the heart, inherited from a Sufi who lived a bit before Ghazali, has given its title to a central work of medieval Jewish spirituality, the *Duties of the Heart* (*Al-Hidāja'ilā Farā'id al-Qulūb*) of Bahya Ibn Paquda.

151. Ghazali, *Ihyā'* 31, "Conversion," 1, 4, 4:12.

152. Ibid., 37, "Intention," 1, 3, 4:387.

Chapter 12

1. *Pirke Avot* 1.1.

2. See de Vaux, *Les Institutions de l'Ancien Testament*, 2:397.

3. *Mekhilta de-R. Ishmael*, ed. H. S. Horowitz and I. A. Rabin (Frankfurt, 1931), pp. 31, 16–17 (on Exod. 12:6). See also Bornkamm, "Wandelungen im alt- und neutestamentlichen Gesetzesverständnis," 83.

4. Gen. 1:1; Prov. 8:22–23; Deut. 4:6; *Genesis Rabbah: Midrash Bereshit Rabba* 1.6, p. 9. See also Rashi on Genesis 1:1: Heschel, *Theology of Ancient Judaism* (in Hebrew), 2:8–12.

5. See Heschel, *Theology*, 1:31.

6. b*Makkot* 24a; b*Temura* 16a; *Shemot Rabba* 16.22. On Philo, see Amir, "Mose as Verfasser der Tora bei Philon." In the mouth of heretics: b*Sanhedrin* 99b; b*Menahot* 65a. See also Greenberg, "Jewish Conceptions of the Human Factor in Biblical Prophecy"; *Genesis Rabbah* 8.8, p. 61; b*Sanhedrin* 99a.

7. See Touati, *Prophètes, talmudistes, philosophes*, 11–18.

8. Mishnah *Hagigah* 1.8.10a; Heschel, *Theology*, 1:5; J. Maier, "'Gesetz' und 'Gnade,'" 78 and n.18.

9. This entire paragraph follows Jackson, "Concept of Religious Law in Judaism," 44–51. See also Mishnah *Sotah* 9.

10. b*Baba Metsia* 59b.

11. b*Menahot* 29b; see Carmichael, *Spirit of Biblical Law*, 12–13. For a Muslim parallel, see Baron, *Social and Religious History of the Jews*, 6:8.

12. Respectively: b*Megillah* [2.13] 19b; b*Hagigah* [2.1] 15b; b*Baba Bathra* [1.6] 12b; and *Exodus Rabba* 28.6, in Jeffery, *Qurʾān as Scripture*, 81 n. 23. See also Heschel, *Theology*, 2:234–38; Scholem, *Über einige Grundbegriffe des Judentums*, 96–101; Urbach, *The Sages*, 304 and n. 59. In Islam, there is a hadith according to which the scholars are the heirs of the prophets: cited by Ghazali, in Laoust, *La Politique de Ghazali*, 271 and n.1.

13. Simon Qayyara, in Baron, *Social and Religious History of the Jews*, 6:78; Rabbi Isaiah Horowitz, *Shney luchot habrit: On the Written Torah* trans., with notes by Eliyahu/Max Munk, 2d ed. rev., 3 vols. (Jerusalem and New York: Lambda, 1999), in Ravitzky, *Religion and State in Jewish Philosophy*, 83. Compare with Ignatius of Loyola, *Ejercicios espirituales*, in *Obras completas de san Ignacio de Loyola*, ed. Ignacio Iparraguire (Madrid: Biblioteca de Autores Cristianos, 1963), 13th rule, par. 365.

14. See Yeshayahu Leibowitz, *Israël et judaïsme: Ma part de vérité; Suivi de Job et Antigone: Entretiens avec Michaël Shasher*, French trans. Gérard Haddad (Paris: Desclée de Brouwer, 1996), 168–69.

15. *Midrash sur les Proverbes*, ed. Solomon Buber, 8, 9, p. 30a, in Heschel, *Theology*, 2:6–7.

16. See, for example, Maimonides, "Letter on Persecution," 4, in Maimonides, *Igrot*, 118.

17. Saadia Gaon, *Sefer Yetsirah: Kitab almabadi: Commentary on the Psalms* (in Arabic), ed. Joseph Qāfih (Jerusalem: n.p., 1973), 35 and 53 [*non vidi*]; in English translation in Mosche Sokolow, "Saadiah Gaon's Prolegomena to Psalms," *Proceedings of the American Academy for Jewish Research* 15 (1984): 166–68; 143, 146.

18. Bahya Ibn Paquda, *Al-Hidāja ʾilā Farāʾid al-Qulūb* (Duties of the heart), Introduction, 15. See also Klein-Braslavi, *King Solomon and Philosophical Esotericism in the Thought of Maimonides* (in Hebrew), 41 n. 10; 58 n. 61.

19. On Saadia's doctrine concerning the Law, see Altmann, "Saadya's Conception of the Law."

20. Al-Muqammas, *Twenty Chapters* (ʾIshrūn Maqāla) 13, pp. 254–55, and 14, pp. 262–63.

21. Ibid., 15, par. 23, pp. 286–87; see also ibid., 14, par. 13, pp. 268–69.

22. Ibid., 15, par. 9, pp. 276–77. See above, pp. 152–53.

23. Saadia Gaon, *Book of Beliefs and Opinions* (in Hebrew) 10.4, p. 270/335; 10.15, p. 316/396; 10.17, p. 319/399.

24. Ibid., 3.2–3, pp. 119ff. The same distinction can be found in Saadia Gaon, *Sefer Yetsirah*, Preface, p. 11. See also Faur, "Origin of the Classification of Rational and Divine Commandments."

25. Saadia Gaon, *Beliefs and Opinions* 3.1, p. 117/138; p. 118/140.

26. Ibid., 3.1, pp. 118–19/140–41.

27. Ibid., 3.2, p. 119/141–42 (on which, see Kant, *Kritik der praktischen Vernunft*, 3.3.1, par. 4, in Kant, *Werke*, 4:136); Saadia Gaon, ibid., p. 120 (where "optional" is slightly inexact); p. 121/143.

28. Ibid., 3.3.

29. Ibid., 3.7, p. 132/158.

30. Bahya Ibn Paquda, *Al-Hidāja ʾilā Farāʾid al-Qulūb*, Introduction, 5, 11; 5, 16–17; 6, 2;

then ibid., 3.3, p. 133, 6–7 and 9–10, quoted from *The Duties of the Heart*, xxix. On the law in Bahya, see Golinski, *Das Wesen des Religionsgesetzes in der Philosophie des Bachja ibn Pakuda.*

31. Halevi, *Kuzari* 48, p. 68, 13–15 and p. 69, 2–3 (*Le Kuzari*, p. 67); 3.7; p. 95, 16–17 (*Le Kuzari*, p. 95). On the undifferentiated use of "*sharia*" to render revealed laws and human customs, see Kraemer, "Namus and Shari'a in Maimonides' Doctrine"(in Hebrew), 185–88, also in idem, "Naturalism and Universalism in Maimonides' Political and Religious Thought," 47–52.

32. Halevi, *Kuzari*, 3.11, p. 97, 11 (*Le Kuzari*, p. 97); p. 98, 3–9 (*Le Kuzari*, p. 98).

33. Ibid., 1.10, p. 9, 19 (*Le Kuzari*, p. 9); 1.81, p. 22, 1 (*Le Kuzari*, p. 20); 5.20, p. 223, 19–224, 2 (*Le Kuzari*, p. 230); 1.103, p. 35, 13 (*Le Kuzari*, p. 34).

34. Abraham Ibn Ezra, *Yesod Mora* 8.1, in Abraham Ibn Ezra, *Reader*, 335. On Exod. 20:1, see *MG*, 821.

35. Abraham Ibn Ezra, on Hosea 6:3, and *Yesod Mora* 1.9 and 7.12, in Abraham Ibn Ezra, *Reader*, 237, 320, 332; on Deut. 6:7, on Psalm 1:3, pp. 214 and 252.

36. Abraham Ibn Ezra on Psalm 19:8, in *Reader*, 236; *Yesod Mora* V 7.12, in ibid., 333; Prologue to the commentary of the Torah, 3, in *MG*, unpaginated [1d]; on Exod. 20:1, in *MG*, 82a.

37. Abraham Ibn Ezra on Exod. 31:18 in *Reader*, 181; *Yesod Mora* 7.8, in ibid., 331.

38. Ibn Daoud, *The Exalted Faith* 3.1, pp. 303–299/259–66; E. Rosenthal *Studia Semitica*, 1:313.

39. Ibn Daoud, *Exalted Faith* 3.1, p. 299b/265b.

40. On the influence of Alfarabi on Maimonides, see H. Davidson, "Maimonides' Shemonah Peraqim and Alfarabi's Fusūl al-Madani"; L. Berman, "Maimonides, the Disciple of Alfarabi"; Kraemer, "Alfarabi's *Opinions of the Virtuous City* and Maimonides' *Foundations of the Law*."

41. Maimonides, *Traité de Logique*, chap. 14, pp. 4–10/101, quoted from *Maimonides' Treatise on Logic*, 64. The passage in Maimonides immediately following this one is quoted above, p. 109.

42. Maimonides, *Guide* 2.40, p. 270, 5/306; 3.27, p. 372, 6/212.

43. Maimonides, *Commentary on the Mishnah* (in Arabic), Avoda Zara, 4.7, p. 27, 4–11, ed. J. Wiener (Berlin, 1895); ed. Qāfih, p. 358.

44. Maimonides, *Letter on Astrology*, edited by Alexander Marx (in Hebrew) in "The Correspondence Between the Rabbis of Southern France and Maimonides about Astrology," *Hebrew Union College Annual* 3 (1926): 311–58, esp. 350/24–25; in English translation by Ralph Lerner as "Letter on Astrology," in Lerner, *Maimonides' Empire of Light: Popular Enlightenment in an Age of Belief* (Chicago: University of Chicago Press, 2000), 178–87.

45. Maimonides, *Treatise on Resurrection*, par. 32, p. 22, 10; *Igrot*, p. 87; *Commentary on the Mishnah*, Introduction, p. 356, 6 and 11–12, quoted (in part) from *Maimonides' Introduction to His Commentary on the Mishnah*, trans. and annotated by Fred Rosner (Northvale NJ and London: Jason Aronson, 1995), 98.

46. Maimonides, *Commentary on the Mishnah*, Helek, 3, p. 364, 13; Maimonides, *Guide* 3.32, p. 386, 4–7/253; Maimonides, *Treatise on Resurrection*, par. 47, p. 32, 16; Maimonides, *Igrot*, p. 96.

47. Maimonides, *Igeret Teman/Epistle to Yemen*, Arabic original and the three Hebrew versions, ed. Abraham S. Halkin; English trans. Boaz Cohen (New York: American Academy for Jewish Research, 1952), 20.1109, p. 64; 8; 27, p. 84, 4; Maimonides, *Commentary on the Mishnah*, Helek, 2, p. 363, 6–7.

48. Maimonides, "Letter on Persecution," 4, in Maimonides, *Igrot*, p. 119; Alfarabi, *Kitāb al-Millah*, p. 56; Alfarabi, *Fusūl Muntaza'ah*, par. 93, p. 95, 10–13.

49. Maimonides, *Mishneh Torah, The Book of Knowledge*, "Mores," 6.1, p. 54b (*Livre de Connaissance*, p. 150). The passage may reflect traces of the influence of Alfarabi, for example, that of Alfarabi, *Kitāb al-Millah*, par. 14a, p. 56, 6–7. See also Ibn Bājjah, *El Régimen del solitario* 1, p. 43.

50. Maimonides, *Mishneh Torah, The Book of Knowledge*, "Foundations of the Law," 7.1, p. 42b; Maimonides, *Commentary on the Mishnah*, Helek, 8, 6th principle, p. 371, 9; Maimonides, *Guide* 2.36, p. 260, 20–21/281; 2.37, p. 264, 17–18/291, quoted from *Guide of the Perplexed*, 369, 374. See also Galston, "Philosopher-King v. Prophet."

51. Maimonides, *Guide* 1.63, p. 105, 27–28/281; 2.39, p. 268/301; 3.41, p. 412, 14–413, 1/324–25;28, p. 373, 12 and p. 374, 15–18/214, 216–17; Maimonides, *Traité d'Éthique*, chap. 6, p. 22, 5–6/88–89; see Kasher, "Maimonides' Philosophical Division of the Laws" (in Hebrew).

52. Maimonides, *Guide* 1.54, p. 85, 2; 86, 1–2; 87, 7/219, 221, 224; 2.36, p. 262, 22–27/286, quoted from *Guide of the Perplexed*, 372. The medieval commentators saw clearly the proximity to Ibn Bājjah: see Shem Tov on Maimonides, *Guide* 3.27, 54, last portion; Lerner, "Maimonides' Governance of the Solitary."

53. Maimonides, *Guide*, Introduction, p. 11, 4/25. See also Maimonides, *Treatise on Resurrection*, par. 26, p. 18, 18; Maimonides, *Igrot*, p. 84; Maimonides, *Guide* 3.27, p. 372, 9–10/212.

54. Maimonides, *Guide* 1.2, p. 16, 17–18/39; 3.17, p. 339, 23/127.

55. Ibid., 3.34, p. 391, 3; 10–11, 17–18/265–68.

56. Ibid., 3.28, p. 373, 7–8; p. 214; and Introduction, p. 3, 20–21; p. 10: see Strauss, *Persecution and the Art of Writing*, 38–94. For a summary, see Klein-Braslavi, *Solomon and Philosophical Esotericism*. See also Maimonides, *Guide* Introduction, p. 8, 1/19; p. 5, 2/13.

57. Maimonides, "Epistle to Yemen," 1, in Maimonides, *Igrot*, p. 24. On the dialectic nature of this demonstration, see Kraemer, "Namus and Shari'a in Maimonides' Doctrine," 197, 201, repeated in Kraemer, "Naturalism and Universalism in Maimonides' Political and Religious Thought," 78–80; Lerner, *Maimonides' Empire of Light*, 19.

58. Maimonides, *Guide* 2.40, p. 271, 24–29, quoted from *Guide of the Perplexed*, 384–85: see W. Z. Harvey, "Between Political Philosophy and Halakhah in the Teachings of Maimonides" (in Hebrew), 205–8. The idea was broadly accepted: see, for example, the text of Nissim of Marseille quoted in Sirat, "Political Ideas of Nissim ben Moses" (in Hebrew), 61.

59. Maimonides, *Traité d'Éthique*, chap. 4, p. 11, 21–24/60–61; Maimonides, *Guide* 2.40, p. 270, 22–23/308: see Brague, "La porte de la nature."

60. Maimonides, *Traité d'Éthique*, chap. 4, p. 11, 21/60 and n. 48: see Faur, "The Source of the Obligatory Character of the Commandments in the Thought of Maimonides" (in Hebrew), 48; Kraemer, "Namus and Shari'a," 200–201; Ben-Sasson, "On the Doctrine of the Reasons for the Commandments in the *Guide for the Perplexed*" (in Hebrew), 280–81. The idea of a law that is perfect because it induces perfection has often been reiterated: see, for example, Abraham Shalom, quoted in Tirosh-Rothschild, "The Political Philosophy of Rabbi Abraham Shalom" (in Hebrew), 433, or the Yemenite midrashim such as the anonymous fourteenth-century *Sefer ha-amitiyut; The Book of Truth*, ed. Joseph Qāfih (Tel-Aviv: Afikim, 5758/1997), par. 8 p. 35.

61. Maimonides, *Mishneh Torah*, Temura, 14, 13, vol. 9, p. 306: see Twersky, *Introduction to the Code of Maimonides*, 416–17.

62. Maimonides, *Guide* 3.32 and 46. On reactions to this theory, see Heschel, *Theology*, 1:52–53. Among the Jews, reaction ranged from the enthusiasm of certain allegorists to the criticism of Nahmanides: see Nahmanides, *Torat Hashem temimah*, p.171; Nahmanides, *Perush ha-Torah* (*Commentary on the Pentateuch*), ed. Charles B. Chavel, 2 vols. (Jerusalem: Mosad Rav Kook, 1960), 2:11–13 (on Lev. 1:9), where he states that the explication of sacrifices as a remedy for idolatry cannot explain the sacrifices of Abel and Noah, which oc-

curred before idolatry. On Gersonides, see Touati, *La pensée philosophique et théologique de Gersonide*, 503. The notion was well received by the scholastics, William of Auvergne among them: see Rothschild, "Philosophie (gréco-arabe), 'philosophie' de la Loi," 497. In the seventeenth century, Maimonides' theory of a primitive religion was an obligatory reference for the founders of the comparative history of religions: see G. Stroumsa, "John Spencer and the Roots of Idolatry."

63. See S. Stroumsa, "Entre Harrān et al-Maghreb."

64. Among Christian writers, see the anonymous *Les Trophées de Damas: Controverse judéo-chrétienne du VIIe siècle*, Greek text ed. and trans. Gustave Bardy (Paris: Firmin-Didot, 1920), 3.6.6; *Patrologia Orientalis*, no. 15, 248; Theodoret of Cyrrhus, *Graecorum affectionum curatio* 7, in *PG* 83:996c–997a; Pseudo-Athanasius the Sinaite, *Dialogus parvus ad Judaeos* in *PG* 89:1271d–1274c. Among Jewish writers, see Saadia Gaon, *Beliefs and Opinions* 3.2, p. 121 (English trans., *Book of Beliefs and Opinions*, 144). The idea is accepted by certain modern exegetes, for example Noth, *Das Gesetze im Pentateuch* (1940), 76–80, who does not mention Maimonides by name, perhaps because of the time at which he was writing: see Leben, "L'interprétation du culte sacrificiel chez Maïmonide."

65. Bukhari, SB 77 (Clothing), 64, 3, and 67, 4:122–23. I owe these references to M. J. Bosshard. On dogs, see Goldziher, *Sur l'Islam*, 129–32; for a modern application, see Antes, *Ethik und Politik im Islam*, 15. On beards, see Calder, *Early Muslim Jurisprudence*, 217 and n. 47.

66. Maimonides, *Mishneh Torah, The Book of Knowledge*, Conversion, 9.2, p. 92a; Maimonides, *Mishneh Torah*, Kings, 9, par. 4, in English translation, ed. Raymond L. Weiss with Charles Butterworth as *Ethical Writings of Maimonides* (New York: Dover, 1975), 176; see also Ravitsky, *Religion and State in Jewish Philosophy*, 24.

67. Maimonides, *Mishneh Torah*, Kings, 3.9; 4.1; Lorberbaum, *Politics and the Limits of Law*, 54, 77.

68. Isaac Arama, *Aqedat Ishaq* (The binding of Isaac), par. 46, fol. 133b, in Ravitsky, *History and Faith*, 37, 41–43. Ravitsky, *Religion and State in Jewish Philosophy*, 117, refers to Abravanel, "Commentary on Isaiah 2:2–3," p. 26a–b, where the idea seems to me somewhat unclear.

69. Maimonides, *Guide* 2.32, p. 254/262.

70. b*Sanhedrin* [X 1] 90a; Maimonides, *Commentary on the Mishnah*, Helek, 8, 8th principle, pp. 372–73: see Bland, "Moses and the Law According to Maimonides," 64–66; Galston, "The Purpose of the Law according to Maimonides," 31; Lorberbaum, *Politics and the Limits of Law*, 31; Ravitsky, *Religion and State*, 22.

71. Maimonides, "Letter to Joseph b. Jābir," in Maimonides, *Igrot ha-Rambam* (*Correspondence*), ed. Isaac Shailat, 2 vols. (Jerusalem: Birkat Moshe, 1987), 1:411, 8.

72. Maimonides, *Guide* 3.34, p. 391, 7–9/266; 49, p. 444, 28–445, 11; 3.43, p. 418, 13–14/341: see L. Berman, "Political Interpretation of the Maxim," 58.

73. Maimonides, *Livre des commandements*, P 3, pp. 59, 71: see W. Harvey, "On Averroes, Maimonides, and the Ideal State" (in Hebrew), 29.

74. Maimonides, *Guide* 3.49, p. 448, 13/419; 3.12, p. 322, 6–7/77, quoted from *Guide of the Perplexed*, 446.

75. Abner of Burgos, *Moreh Tsedeq*, final chapter, MS. Paris, fols. 292–93, in Baer, *A History of the Jews in Christian Spain*, 1:349–50.

76. Gersonides, *Mihamot ha-Shem* 6.2, 1, p. 69a; 6.15, p. 59a. This paragraph reflects Touati, *La pensée philosophique et théologique de Gersonide*, 478–85 and 492–505.

77. Nissim ben Reuben Gerondi, Sermon 11, in his *Derashot ha-Ran*, ed. L. A. Feldman (Jerusalem: Mekhon Shalem, 1973), 191, quoted in Ravitsky, *Religion and State*, 70: see also Lorberbaum, *Politics and the Limits of Law*, 126, 139.

78. Hasdai Crescas, *Light of the Lord* 3.2.4, 5, chaps. 1–2, pp. 251–56.

79. See, for example, Thomas Aquinas *Summa Theologica* IaIIae, q. 107, a. 1, ad2m.

80. Crescas, *Light of the Lord* 2.6.4, 5, chap. 1, beginning, pp. 226–31. On the four perfections, see Maimonides, *Guide* 3.54, pp. 468–69, 459–62.

81. Joseph Albo, *Book of Principles* 1.10; 1:96: see Lerner, "Natural Law in Albo's Book of Roots."

82. Albo, *Book of Principles* 1.7; 1:78–80. On the etymology of *dath,* see above, p. 53.

83. Ibid., 1.25, pp. 196–97; 3.14, p. 127; 16, pp. 147–48.

84. See Urbach, "Die Staatsauffassung des Don Isaak Abravanel"; Strauss, *Gesammelte Schriften,* 2:195–231; for a summary of Abravanel's thought, see Goetschel, *Isaac Abravanel,* 115–43.

85. Isaac Abravanel, *Peyrūsh,* commentaries on Gen. 11:1–9; 1 Kings 3:6, p. 490; Exod. 18:13–27.

86. Abraham Shalom, *Sefer Neveh Shalom (The Dwelling of Peace)* (Farnborough, Hants: Gregg International, 1969) (reprint of Venice, 1574), 136b–137a; in Tirosch-Rothschild, "Political Philosophy of Rabbi Abraham Shalom," 2:432–33.

87. Jacob ben Sheshet Gerondi, *Sefer Meshiv devarim nekhohim,* ed. Georges Vajda (Jerusalem: Israel Academy of Sciences and Humanities, 1968), chap. 3, p. 79: see Vajda, *Recherches sur la philosophie et la Kabbale,* 340–50, esp. 340–41 and 349.

88. For a synthesis regarding the Torah in the Kabbalah, see Scholem, *Kabbalah,* 168–74.

89. On "name," see Nahmanides, *Perush ha-Torah: Commentary on the Torah,* trans., with notes, by Charles B. Chavel, 5 vols. (New York: Shilo, 1971–76), Introduction, 1:6; on "names," see Nahmanides, *Torat Hashem temimah,* pp. 167–68: see Idel, "The Concept of the Torah in Heikhalot Literature and Its Metamorphoses in Kabbalah" (in Hebrew), 49, 52–53, 57.

90. In Azriel of Gerona (Pseudo-Nahmanides), *Commentary on the Song of Songs.*

91. Azriel of Gerona, *Perush ha-agadot: Commentary on Talmudic aggadoth,* ed. Israel Tishby (Jerusalem: Magnes, 1943), 37–38, in Idel, "Concept of the Torah in Heikhalot Literature," 51. For the contrary view, see Ibn Daoud, *Exalted Faith* 3.1, p. 300/263, cited much later, with praise, in Cohen, *Religion der Vernunft aus dem Quellen des Judentums,* 16, p. 409.

92. See Idel, "Concept of the Torah," 58, 65, 68; Scholem, "Der Sinn der Tora in der jüdischen Mystik," 64; Idel, "Infinities of Torah in Kabbalah," 144.

93. See Idel, "Concept of the Torah," 74; Scholem, "Der Sinn der Tora," 61.

94. See Idel, "Infinities of Torah in Kabbalah," 152.

95. Maimonides, *Guide* 3.49, 450, 12/423. On Gersonides, see Touati, *La pensée philosophique et théologique de Gersonide,* 501.

96. See Idel, *Maïmonide et la mystique juive,* 27, 30; J. Maier, "'Gesetz' und 'Gnade,'" 110; Scholem, "Der Sinn der Tora," 75.

97. See Werblowsky, *Joseph Karo,* 127 and *passim.* For Islam, see above, p. 181.

98. See Scholem, "Der Sinn der Tora," 109, 114.

Chapter 13

1. Ptolemy the Gnostic, *Lettre à Flora,* ed. and trans., with an introduction, by Gilles Quispel, SC no. 24, p. 50: see Fassò, "Dio e la natura presso i decretisti ed i glossatori," 7; Kühneweg, *Das neue Gesetz,* 88–95; G. Stroumsa, *Barbarian Philosophy,* 246–57. On Marcion, see the classic synthesis of Harnack, *Marcion.*

2. See above, p. 92.

3. Ignatius of Antioch, "Epistle to the Magnesians" 2, SC no. 10, p. 80; for other refer-

ences, see *PGL*, s.v. "*nomos*," p. 922a; Cyprian *Epistulae* 27.4, ed. G. F. Dierks, CCSL, vol. 3b, p. 132; 36.1.3, p. 174; 36.2.3, p. 175.

4. *Epistle of Barnabas* 2.6, *PA*, p. 773: see Kühneweg, *Das neue Gesetz*, 40–46; Justin Martyr *Dialogue avec Tryphon* 11.4, 1:54.

5. Origen *Contra Celsum* 3.8, SC no. 136, pp. 26–28; Origen, *Vier Bücher von den Prinzipien (De principiis)*, ed. Herwig Görgemanns and Heinrich Karpp (Darmstadt: Wissenschaftliche Buchgesellschaft, 1992), 4.3.13, p. 770.

6. Tertullian *De monogamia* 8, *PL* 2:9739ff.

7. See André Grabar, *Le Premier Art chrétien (200–395)* (Paris: Gallimard, 1966), no. 207, p. 192; nos. 283–85, p. 255–57; no. 290, p. 261; no. 293, p. 263. See also Kollwitz, "Christus als Lehrer und die Gesetzesübergabe an Petrus in der konstantinischen Kunst Roms"; Congar, "Le thème du 'don de la Loi' dans l'art paléochrétien."

8. See Peterson, *Theologische Traktate*, 81 and n. 115; 89–91.

9. *Hermae Pastor*, Parable 8, 3, 2, in *PA*, p. 1037; Justin *Dialogue avec Tryphon* 11.2, 1:52, and 43.1, p. 190. For other references, see *PGL*, s.v. "*nomos*," p. 922a.

10. For these references, see *PGL*, s.v. "*nomos*," p. 922a; Dvornik, *Early Christian and Byzantine Political Philosophy*, 2:590, 598, 601; Goodenough, *The Politics of Philo Judaeus*, 107–10.

11. Lactantius *Divinae institutiones* 4.25.2, in *Institutions divines*, ed. Pierre Monat, SC no. 377, 4:204, (on which, see Kantorowicz, *King's Two Bodies*, 128); ibid., 4.13.1, SC no. 377, p. 110; Dvornik, *Early Christian and Byzantine Political Philosophy*, 2:614. Lactantius is quoted here from *Divine Institutes*, trans., with an introduction and notes, by Anthony Bowen and Peter Garnsey (Liverpool: Liverpool University Press, 2003), 268, 346.

12. Anonymous, *De montibus Sina et Sion* 9, in CSEL 3, pt. 3, p. 115, in Congar, "Le thème du 'don de la Loi,'" 930.

13. See Schoeps, *Theologie und Geschichte des Judenchristentums*, 88, 117–218.

14. Irenaeus *Adversus Haereses* 4.16.4, in SC, no. 100, p. 570.

15. *Lettre d'Aristée à Philocrate*, par. 147, p. 174; Nahmanides *Torat Hashem temimah*, p. 166.

16. See Philo *De migratione Abrami*, ed. Jacques Cazeaux (Paris: Éditions du Cerf, 1965), vol. 14 of Philo, *Oeuvres*, pars. 89–94; Scholem, "Der Sinn der Tora in der jüdischen Mystik," 268 and n. 44. For Gersonides, see Touati, *La pensée philosophique et théologique de Gersonide*, 483.

17. *Epistle of Barnabas* 3,6, *PA* 775. For other references, see *PGL*, s.v. "*nomos*," p. 921b. Among Latin authors, see Tertullian *Adversus Judaeos* 3.8, CCSL 2:1346.

18. Justin *Dialogue avec Tryphon* 45.3, 1:200, *Dialogue with Trypho*, 68. For references, see *PGL*, s.v. "*nomos*," 920a–b.

19. Origen *Commentaria in Evangelium secundum Matthaeum* 2:9 and 6:12, in *PG* 13:829–1600, esp. 892, 1097.

20. See *PGL*, s.v. "*nomos*," 921a; 920a. See in particular Pseudo-Cyril *Collectio dictorum Veteris Testamenti* (on 2 Kings 21:1), *PG* 77:1253b; Theodoret of Cyrrhus, Commentary on Psalm 18, *Interpretatio in Psalmos*, *PG* 80:989c–991a.

21. Ambrose *De viduis*, 12.72, *PL* 16:269c, quoted from *Some of the Principal Works of St. Ambrose*, trans. H. De Romestin, E. De Romestin, and H. T F. Duckworth (Grand Rapids: William B. Eerdmans, 1955), 403.

22. Justin *Dialogue avec Tryphon* 93.1, 2:94–96; Origen, "Commentary of Origen on the Epistle to the Romans" (on Romans 7:7), ed. A. Ramsbotham, *Journal of Theological Studies* 14 (1913): 10–22, esp. 11–12; Tertullian *Adversus Judaeos* 2.7, CCSL 2:1342.

23. Lactantius *Divinae institutiones*, ed. Samuel Brandt, in Lactantius, *Opera omnia*,

CSEL, no. 19, 2 vols. in 3 pts. (Leipzig: Freytag, 1890–97), 6.8.6, 1:508–9, quoted from *Divine Institutes*, 346. On the passage from Cicero, *De republica*, see *De re publica librorum sex quae manserunt*, ed. Konrat Ziegler, 7th ed. (Leipzig: Teubner, 1969), 3.22.33, p. 17.

24. Ambrose *De officiis ministrorum* 3.3.20, *PL* 16:159a–b: see Flückiger, *Geschichte des Naturrechts*, 364–77.

25. See Dvornik, *Early Christian and Byzantine Political Philosophy*, The relative texts can be found in *SPTB*.

26. I am paraphrasing Dagron, *Empereur et prêtre*, 37, here.

27. Manuel Moschopoulos, "Letter 5" to Emperor Andronicus II Paleologus, in Levi, "Cinque lettere inedite di Emanuele Moscopulo," 64–65.

28. Theophylactus of Ochrida *Institio regia* 12, *PG* 126:273d; *SPTB*, 147.

29. Letter of the patriarch Antonius to Vasili I, grand prince of Russia, in *SPTB*, 194–96.

30. John I Tzimisces in Leo Diaconus *History* 6.7, quoted from *SPTB*, 96. See also Ahrweiler, *L'Idéologie politique de l'Empire byzantin*, 132. Theodore Balsamon *Meditata* (*Meletai*), *PG* 138:1017d; *SPTB*, 106.

31. Eusebius of Caesarea *Oratio Eusebii de laudibus Constantini* 3 [6], *PG* 20:1332a.

32. Beck, *Nomos, Kanon und Staatsraison in Byzanz*, 13 and n. 20.

33. John Damascene *De Imaginibus Oratio II* 12, *PG* 94:129c and 1297a–b; *SPTB*, "On the Divine Images," 86–87; Theodore Studites (Theodore of Studion), "Epistle 129," *PG* 99:1417bc; *SPTB*, 88.

34. See d'Emilia, "Il diritto musulmano," 67.

35. Maximus the Confessor *Quaestiones ad Thalassium de Scriptura sacra* 64, *PG* 90:724c, on which, see von Balthasar, *Kosmische Liturgie*, 288–312; Pines, *Studies in the History of Arabic Philosophy*, 163–64.

36. See Pines, *Studies in the History of Arabic Philosophy*, 173, 181–83, and the text of Abū Bishr Mattā Ibn Yūnus cited above, pp. 111–12.

37. Augustine *De civitate Dei* 22.2.1; *La Cité de Dieu*, 5:530; Augustine "Letter 157" 3.15, *PL* 33:681 [a]; Augustine *De ordine*, in *Dialogues philosophique: De Ordine* (*L'Ordre*), ed. and trans., with notes, by Jean Poignon, BA, no. 4, 2 (Paris: Institut d'Études Augustiniennes, 1997), 2.8.25, 4:406; Augustine *Enarrationes in Psalmos* 118.4, 3:1750. On the theory of law in Augustine, see the syntheses in Schubert, *Augustins "lex-aeterna"-Lehre*, and Chroust, "The Philosophy of Law of St. Augustine," and "The Fundamental Ideas of St. Augustine's Philosophy of Law."

38. Augustine *De libero arbitrio* (*Du libre arbitre*) 1.6.14, BA 6:158–60. See Chroust, "The Philosophy of Law from St. Augustine to St. Thomas Aquinas," 26.

39. Augustine *De vera religione* 31.58, *PL* 34:148 [bc]; Augustine *Contra Faustum Manichaeum* 22.27, *PL* 42:418 [bc].

40. Augustine *De libero arbitrio* (*Du libre arbitre*) 1.6.15, BA 6:162, quoted from *The Teacher; The Free Choice of the Will; Grace and Free Will*, trans. Robert P. Russell (Washington, D.C.: Catholic University of America Press, 1968), 85. See also Augustine *De civitate Dei* 19.14; *La Cité de Dieu*, 5:118.

41. Augustine *Confessions* 3.8.15, BA 13:390.

42. Augustine *De Sermone Domini in monte* 2.9.32, *PL* 34:1283 [c], quoted from *Commentary of the Lord's Sermon on the Mount*, trans. Denis J. Kavanagh (New York: Fathers of the Church, 1951), 141; Augustine *De ordine* 2.8.25, BA 4:404.

43. Augustine *De civitate Dei* 9.22; *La Cité de Dieu*, 2:408; Augustine *De vera religione* 31.57, *PL* 34:147 [c]; Augustine *De diversis Quaestionibus* 83.741, *PL* 40:90 [d]; in a contrary sense, see Augustine, *Enarrationes in Psalmos* 36.3.5, 1:371.

44. Augustine, *De civitate Dei* 2.7; *La Cité de Dieu*, 1:326; 14.2, 1:346; 16, 1:350; 17, 1:352; 19, 1:362; 8.22, 1:378.

45. Ibid., 19.17; *La Cité de Dieu*, 5:128.

46. See, for example, Aquinas *Summa contra Gentiles* 3.134, p. 388b. This notion occurs in Gersonides *Mihamot ha-Shem* 2.1, p. 17b/97; see also ibid., 6.18, p. 61d/375.

47. Augustine *Enarrationes in Psalmos* 57.1, 2:708.

48. Ibid., 1.2, 1:1.

49. Augustine, Letter 217, *Epistolarum classis III*, 4.12, *PL* 33:983; see also Augustine *De civitate Dei* 20.28; *La Cité de Dieu*, 5:342; 21.16, 446.

50. Isidore of Seville *Etymologiae* 5.2. For the period between Augustine and Thomas Aquinas, see Chroust, "Philosophy of Law from Augustine to Aquinas."

51. Anselm of Canterbury, "Letter 210 to Pope Paschal," in *Opera Omnia*, ed. Franciscus Salesius Schmitt, 6 vols. (Edinburgh: Nelson, 1946–61), 4:106, 16; "Letter 324 to Baldwin of Jerusalem," in ibid., 5:255; "Letter 424 to Henry I," 5:370. I am relying here on Trego, "De la 'loi de Dieu' à la 'volonté de Dieu.'" See also Anselm *De voluntate Dei* 2, *PL* 158:582c.

52. See Padovani, *Perché chiedi il mio nome?*

53. *Die Summa des Stephanus Tornacensis über das Decretum Gratiani*, ed. Joh. Friedrich von Schulte (Giessen, 1891), 7. There are similar passages in John of Faenza (Johannes Faventinus), *Summa*, British Museum, MS Royal 9 E, VII, fol. 2, cited by Post, *Studies in Medieval Legal Thought*, 523 n. 63, and in Guido da Baysio, in Fassò, "Dio e la natura presso i decretisti ed i glossatori," 5.

54. See Gagnér, *Studien zur Ideengeschichte der Gesetzgebung*, 210–56 and, from another viewpoint, Brague, *La Sagesse du monde*, 161; *Wisdom of the World*, 138; Padovani, *Perché chiedi il mio nome?*, 57–60.

55. Spinoza, *Ethica*, IV, Preface, in Spinoza, *Opera*, 1:183: "The reason or cause why God or nature exists and the reason why he acts, are one and the same": *Improvement of the Understanding, Ethics and Correspondence*, trans. R. H. M. Elwes (New York and London: M. Walter Dunn, 1901), 190. See Tierney, *"Natura id est deus:* A Case of Juristic Panatheism?," and the very subtle remarks in Fassò, "Dio e la natura presso i decretisti ed i glossatori." Spinoza's real source may perhaps be Maimonides (see *Guide* 3.32, the first sentence), or Descartes, *Meditationes* 5, AT, vol. 9, 80, pp. 21–24. On the role of the Kabbalah in the formation of this expression, see Idel, *"Deus sive Natura."*

56. Roland of Cremona, MS. Paris Mazarine, 795, fol. 133v, col. A, in Lottin, *Psychologie et morale aux XIIe et XIIIe siècles;* Jean Gerson *De vita spirituali animae* 3, p. 142; Spinoza, *Tractatus politicus*, 2.4, in Spinoza, *Opera*, 2:6, quoted from *Political Treatise*, trans. Samuel Shirley, with an introduction and notes by Steven Barbone and Lee Rice (Indianapolis and Cambridge: Hackett, 2000), 38.

57. Marginal note to MS Avignon 288, fol. 155v (commentary of Peter of Tarentaise), in Lottin, *Psychologie et morale*, 60–63. I have been unable to find a reference in Averroes, *Middle Commentary on Aristotle's Nicomachean Ethics*, to "Commentator super 8 Ethicorum." There is a closely similar argument in Aquinas, *S. Thomae Aquinatis in decem libros Ethicorum Aristotelis ad Nicomachum expositis*, ed. Raimondo Spiazzi (Turin: Marietti, 1949), 5, lect. 12, par. 1019, p. 280a.

58. Manegold von Lautenbach *Opusculum contra Wolfelmum coloniensem* 22, *PL* 155:170b; Abelard *Theologia christiana* 2, *PL* 178:1179d; Guillaume d'Auxerre *Summa aurea* 3.7, chap. 1, d. 3, in Chroust, "Philosophy of Law from Augustine to Aquinas," 42; Aquinas *Summa Theologica* IIaIIae, q. 1–170; Roger Bacon, *Moralis philosophia*, ed. Eugenio Massa (Zurich: Thesauri Mundi, 1953), 3, d. 3–7; pp. 72–184.

59. Augustine, "Epistola CXX, Consentio ad questiones de Trinitate sibi Propostos,"

4.19, *PL* 35:461 [d], cols. 452–62, in Villey, *La Formation de la pensée juridique moderne*, 114; Bernard of Clairvaux *De diligendo Deo* 12.35, in Bernard, *Opera*, 3:149, quoted from *The Book of Saint Bernard on the Love of God*, ed., trans., with notes, by Edmund G. Gardner (London: J. M. Dent and Sons; New York: E. P. Dutton, n.d.), 121. For a resurgence of the idea in the modern age, see Malebranche, *Traité de morale*, 2.9, par. 12, in Malebranche, *Oeuvres*, 2:606.

60. *La Summa Institutionum "Iustiniani est in hoc opere"* (*manuscrit Pierpont Morgan 903*), ed. Pierre Legendre (Frankfurt: Klostermann, 1973), 1.1, p. 23; or *Fragmentum Pragense* 4.2, in Hermann Fitting, *Juristische Schriften des frühen Mittelaters* . . . (Halle, 1876), 216, in Quaglioni, *À une déesse inconnue*, 50; *Sachsenspiegel: Landrecht*, ed. Karl August Eckhardt (Göttingen: Musterschmidt, 1955), 51–55. Regarding Dante, see also Friedrich, *Die Rechtsmetaphysik der göttlichen Komödie*, 92; for the context, see Brunner, *Land und Herrschaft*, 133–36.

61. Bonaventure, *Collationes in Hexaemeron*, ed. Ferdinand Delorme (Quaracchi [Florence]: Collegiis Bonaventurae, 1934), 31.7, p. 236; in English translation by José de Vinck as *The Works of Bonaventure* (Paterson, N.J.: St. Antony Guild Press, 1970), vol. 5, *Collations on the Six Days*, 321–22.

62. Gratian *Decretum* Ia, d. 9, c. 11, col. 18: see H. Berman, *Law and Revolution*, 145.

63. John of Salisbury *Metalogicus* 1.9, *PL* 199:838a–b, in Post, *Medieval Legal Thought*, 1964, 519; John of Salisbury *Policraticus* 4.2, 1:237, who cites *Digest* 1.3.1–2; Otto Behrends et al., eds., *Corpus Iuris Civilis: Text und Übersetzung*, vol. 2: *Digesten* (Heidelberg: C. F. Müller, 1995), 111–12.

64. Alexander of Hales, *Summa Theologica*, originally called *Summa Fratris Alexandri*, 4 vols. (Quaracchi [Florence]: Collegii S. Bonaventurae, 1924–1999), vol. 4, *De legibus et praeceptis*, ed. Pacifico Maria Perantoni (1948), p. 350a (on which, see Lottin, *Le Droit naturel chez saint Thomas d'Aquin et ses prédécesseurs*, 88, which also gives the text of Peter of Tarentaise cited in n. 57 above); 1b, p. 351b. See a similar definition, at a later date, in Jean Gerson *De vita spirituali animae* 2, p. 130.

65. Augustine *Sermones* 355.4.5, *PL* 39:1572d: see Brague, *La Sagesse du monde*, 163 (*Wisdom of the World*, 140), where the reference to Gratian given in n. 88 is incorrect (I have not managed to locate the right one).

66. Yves de Chartres *Prologus in Decretum a se concinnatum*, *PL* 161:47d–48b. The same idea can be found in Henricus de Segusio (Hostiensis): see Cortese, *Il diritto nella storia medievale*, 2:79 n. 45; Grabmann, "Das Narurrecht der Scholastik von Gratian bis Thomas von Aquin," 69.

67. See the judgment of the Protestant jurist Rudolf von Jhering, *Der Zweck im Recht* (1877–83), 2d ed. (Leipzig: Breitkopf und Härtel, 1923), 2:125–26, in Chroust, "Philosophy of Law from Augustine to Aquinas," 29 and n. 17, or in Villey, *La Formation de la pensée juridique moderne*, 165. Jhering is available in English translation by Isaak Husik as *Law as a Means to an End* (New York: Macmillan, 1921).

68. Aquinas *Summa contra Gentiles* 3.114–18; Aquinas *Summa Theologica* IaIIae, q. 90–108: see Kühn, *Via caritatis*; Merks, *Theologische Grundlegung der sittlichen Autonomie*. For the importance of Thomas as the one who liberated human law from the burden of the divine laws, see Villey, *La Formation de la pensée juridique moderne*, 165.

69. Aquinas *Summa Theologica* IaIIae, q. 93 (the divine), 94 (the natural); 95–97 (the human); 98–108 (the divine, 98–100, the Old Covenant; 106–8, the New Covenant). Albertus Magnus divides the law into three categories, the natural, the Mosaic, and the law of grace: see Albertus Magnus *Summa de Bono* 5, q. 2, a. 2, p. 283a.

70. Yves of Chartres *Prologus in Decretum* . . . , *PL* 161:50a, in Grossi, *L'ordine giuridico medievale*, 121.

71. Aquinas *Summa Theologica* Ia, q. 21, a. 1, ad 2m, English translation, vol. 5, p. 75. See also Alexander of Hales, in Chroust, "Philosophy of Law from Augustine to Aquinas," 46: see also Kluxen, *Philosophische Ethik bei Thomas von Aquin,* 234.

72. Aquinas *Sententiarum* 3, d. 37, q. 1, a. 2b, c, in *S. Thomae Aquinatis Opera Omnia,* ed. Roberto Busa, 7 vols. (Stuttgart: Frommann-Holzboog, 1980), vol. 1, *In quattuor libros sententiarum,* p. 407b; Aristotle *Nicomachean Ethics* 10.8, 1178b8–20.

73. Aquinas *Summa Theologica* IIaIIae, q. 57, a. 1, ad. 3m.

74. Aquinas *Summa Theologica* IaIIae, respectively, q. 91, 1. 4 and 5; q. 98–108; q. 91, a. 1, ad 1m; a. 4, 1st objection; q. 93, a. 3, 1st objection; a. 5 c (*lex Dei*).

75. Aquinas, *Summa contra Gentiles* 1, par. 9, p. 8a. Treating the law within the framework of a treatise on providence is a novelty introduced by Thomas: see Kühn, *Via caritatis,* 89.

76. Aquinas *Summa contra Gentiles* 3, par. 111, p. 363a.

77. Ibid., III, par. 113, p. 365a. On Maimonides, see Maimonides *Guide* 2.40, p. 270, 7–22/306–7 and, for example, 1.74, p. 155, 10/434.

78. Aquinas *Summa contra Gentiles* 3, par. 113, pp. 365b–366a; Aquinas *De unitate intellectus contra Averroistas* 3, par. 216, in *Opuscula philosophica,* ed. Raimondo M. Spiazzi (Turin: Marietti, 1954), 76b. See also Brague, "Un modèle médiéval de la subjectivité," 60–61.

79. Aquinas *Summa contra Gentiles* 3, par. 70, p. 306b, Bourke trans., vol. 3, p. 237. See also Aquinas *De veritate* q. 11, a 1, c, vol. 1 of *Quaestiones Disputatae,* ed. Raimondo M. Spiazzi (Turin: Marietti, 1964), 225b.

80. Aquinas *Summa contra Gentiles* 3, par. 114. See above, p. 169.

81. Aquinas *Summa Theologica* IaIIae, q. 90, Introduction.

82. Ibid., IaIIae, q. 91, a. 4, c.

83. Ibid., IaIIae, q. 106, a. 1c. See also, for example, Aquinas *Quaestiones quodlibetales* 4.13. The expression quoted is from Heinrich Maria Christmann, cited in Kühn, *Via caritatis,* 192, 209, from whom I am borrowing my explanation.

84. Aquinas *Summa contra Gentiles* 3, par. 114, p. 366a; Bourke trans., 122.

85. Ibid., III, par. 115, p. 366b; Bourke trans., 124. See also Aquinas *Summa Theologica* IaIIae, q. 91, a. 1, c.

86. Aquinas *Summa contra Gentiles* 3, par. 115, p. 367a; Bourke trans., 124.

87. Kühn, *Via caritatis,* 60; 67.

88. On this concept, see Brague, "Note sur la traduction arabe de la *Politique* d'Aristote," 161–62; Brague, "Thomas d'Aquin et la 'loi divine.'"

89. Aquinas *Summa contra Gentiles* 3, par. 116, p. 367a–b; par. 97, p. 343b; par. 122, p. 373b; Bourke trans., 125, 126, 66, 143. Compare with Jer. 7:19, and Saadia Gaon, *Beliefs and Opinions* 4, par. 4, p. 158.

90. Aquinas *Summa contra Gentiles* 3, par. 69, p. 303b; Bourke trans., 303b.

91. On the translation of this term, see Brague, "Pour une topique de la morale chrétienne," 112–13.

92. Aquinas *Summa contra Gentiles* 3, par. 118, p. 368a; Bourke trans., 128. See also above, pp. 50–51, 119, 169–70.

93. Aquinas *Summa contra Gentiles* 3, par. 118, p. 368b; Bourke trans., 129. On truth as an object of faith, and on the goal of divine law according to Maimonides, see above, p. 200.

94. Aquinas *Summa contra Gentiles* 3, par. 121, p. 373a–b, and par. 128, p. 380a–b.

95. Aquinas *De regimine principum* 1.16.824, pp. 275b–276a, quoted from *On the Governance of Rulers,* 101–2. See Deut. 17:18–19.

96. See above, pp. 47–48.

Chapter 14

1. See above, pp. 62–63, 69–70, 129, 201, 211.

2. See, respectively: Cicero *De finibus bonorum et malorum* 3.7; Maimonides, Introduction to Helek, chap. 2, in Maimonides, *Introductions to the Mishnah*, pp. 361–62; Bernard of Clairvaux *De diligendo Deo* 8.23–10.29, in Bernard, *Opera*, 3:138–44, quoted from *The Book of Saint Bernard on the Love of God*, ed., trans., with notes, by Edmund G. Gardner (London: J. M. Dent and Sons; New York: E. P. Dutton, n.d.), 133.

3. See, for example, Maimonides, *Mishneh Torah, The Book of Knowledge*, "Foundations of the Law," 4.13, p. 39b; Meister Eckhart, *Die Rede der Underscheidunge*, 10, in Meister Eckhart, *Die deutschen und lateinischen Werke*, vol. 3, *Die deutschen Werke*, ed. Josef Quint (Stuttgart and Berlin: Kohlhammer, 1963), 221.

4. Manent, *Cours familier de philosophie politique*, 146, suggests the connection between interest and counsel.

5. Aristotle *Nicomachean Ethics* 6.8, 1141b33; Brague, *Aristote et la question du monde*, 111–15.

6. Montesquieu, *De l'esprit des Lois* 21.20, p. 673a, quoted from *The Spirit of the Laws*, 389–90.

7. See Besançon, *Les Origines intellectuelles du léninisme*, 144 (on Dostoevsky).

8. Francisco Suárez, *De legibus*, ed. Luciano Pereña et al. (Madrid: CSIC, 1971–), 1.1.7, vol. 1, p. 17; 12.4, vol. 2, pp. 68–69; 14.10–11, vol. 2, pp. 87–89.

9. Bodin, *Les Six Livres de la République* 1.8, p. 155, in Quaglioni, *À une déesse inconnue*, 120; Hobbes, *Leviathan* 2.26, p. 172; 1.15, p. 105. See also the first sentence in Austin, *The Province of Jurisprudence Determined*, 1.

10. See Manent, *La Cité de l'homme*, 46. On a possible origin of this representation in Luther, see Villey, *La Formation de la pensée juridique moderne*, 293.

11. See Brague, *La Sagesse du monde*, 234; *Wisdom of the World*, 203.

12. See Oakley, "Christian Theology and the Newtonian Science"; Milton, "The Origin and Development of the Concept of the 'Laws of Nature.'"

13. Plato *Timaeus* 83e5; Aristotle *On the Heavens* 1.1, 268a13–14; Lucretius *De rerum natura* 1, 586 (on which, see Cyril Bailey, ed., *De rerum natura*, 3 vols. [Oxford: Clarendon Press, 1947], 2:699: "Lucretius is not thinking of an observed uniformity in nature, but rather of the limits which nature imposes on the growth, life, powers, etc. of things"); 2, 302; 5, 310, 924; Augustine *De civitate Dei* 21.8.5; *La Cité de Dieu*, 5:418: see Hirzel, *Themis, Dike und Verwandtes*, 386–92.

14. Descartes, *Le monde* (1632), chap. 7; AT, 11, pp. 36–48.

15. Hooker, *Laws of Ecclesiastical Polity* 1, chap. 1, 2.1, p. 150. It is interesting that John Austin, two centuries later, calls the sumptuous English of Hooker's definition a "fustian description of law," no more than an example of stilted style and an inability to grasp "laws imperative and proper" in their true meaning. Austin includes in his criticism Blackstone's entire chapter on the law in general, which Blackstone defines as "a rule of action": see Blackstone, *Commentaries on the Laws of England*, Introduction, 2, pp. 38–62, quotation, p. 38. See Austin, *Province of Jurisprudence Determined* 5, p. 180.

16. A. M. Ramsay, *An Essay upon Civil Government . . . Translated from the French* (London, 1722), chap. 2, "Of the Law of Nature," 11, after Fénelon, *Essai philosophique sur le gouvernement civil*, in Fénelon, *Oeuvres*, 3 vols. (Paris: Didot, 1985), 3:353b.

17. Jean Bodin, *Colloquium Heptaplomeres*, ed. Ludwig Noack (Schwerin, 1857), 22, quoted from *Colloquium of the Seven about Secrets of the Sublime*, trans. and ed. Marion Leathers Daniels Kuntz (Princeton: Princeton University Press, 1975), 31: see Quaglioni, *À une déesse inconnue*, 118; Funkenstein, *Theology and the Scientific Imagination*, 133–229.

18. Descartes, Letter to Mersenne, 14 April 1630, AT, 1, p. 145, quoted from Descartes, *Philosophical Letters, Essays and Correspondence*, ed. Roger Ariew (Indianapolis and Cambridge: Hackett, 2000), 28. See also Hobbes, *De cive*, 3.33, in Hobbes, *Opera philosophica quae latine scripsit omnia*, 5 vols. (London, 1839–45; reprint, Aalen: Scientia, 1966), 2:198; Hobbes, *Leviathan*, 1.15, p. 105; David Hume, "Of Suicide," in Hume, *Essays Moral, Political, and Literary*, 2 vols. (London, 1875), 2:407.

19. Spinoza, *Tractatus theologico-politicus*, 4:139, in Spinoza, *Opera*, vol. 2.

20. Hobbes, *Leviathan*, 2.29, p. 212; 3.43, pp. 386.

21. Auguste Comte, *Discours préliminaire sur l'esprit positif*, ed. Paul Arbousse-Bastide (Paris: Plon, 1963), chap. 1, p. 43.

22. See Henri Bergson, *Les deux sources de la morale et de la religion*, in Bergson, *Oeuvres*, ed. André Robinet (Paris: PUF, 1959), 1:983–84; 2:1080.

23. Malebranche, *Traité de la nature et de la grâce*, 1er éclaircissement, 3, in Malebranche, *Oeuvres*, 2:138, quoted from *Treatise on Nature and Grace*, trans. Patrick Riley Cox (Oxford: Clarendon Press; New York: Oxford University Press, 1992), 196.

24. Malebranche, *Traité de la morale*, 1.1, par. 20, in Malebranche, *Oeuvres*, 2:432 and passim (such expressions are repeated some forty times), quoted from *Treatise on Ethics*, trans. by Craig Walton (Dordrecht and Boston: Kluwer, 1993), 49. See also Barone, *Teo-nomie*.

25. Examples of this shift can be found in Gratian *Decretum* 1, d. 9, c. 11, p. 18; Padovani, *Perché chiedi il mio nome?*, 103–4; Dante *De monarchia* 2.2.4, p. 120; Dante, *Divina Commedia: Il Paradiso*, 29.88; Friedrich, *Die Rechtsmetaphysik der göttlichen Komödie*, 93–99. See also Luscombe, "Natural Morality and Natural Law," and Bastit, *Naissance de la loi moderne*, whose remarks are based on courses that Michel Villey gave in the 1960s and that were published posthumously: see Villey, *La Formation de la pensée juridique moderne*.

26. Huldreich Zwingli, *De vera et falsa religione commentarius*, chap. 9, in *Corpus Reformatorum*, 90, in *H. Zwinglis Sämtliche Werke* (Leipzig: Heinsius), vol. 3 (1914), 707, quoted in Avis, "Moses and the Magistrate," 159, and quoted here from Zwingli, *Commentary on True and False Religion*, ed. Samuel McCauley Jackson and Clarence Nevin Letter (1927), reprint ed. (Durham, N.C.: Labyrinth, 1981), 137. See also Barrow, *Writings of Henry Barrow, 1587–1590*, ed. L. H. Carlson (London, 1962): p. 602: "God . . . is the onlie lawmaker," in Avis, "Moses and the Magistrate," 170.

27. See Villey, *La Formation de la pensée juridique moderne*, 231, 237.

28. See, for example, Luis de Léon, *De legibus, o, Tratado de las leyes* (1571), ed. Luciano Pereña (Madrid: CSIC, 1963), 1.3, p. 17. See also Gerson, *De vita spirituali animae* 2, p. 131.

29. See Courtenay, "The Critique of Natural Causality"; Rubio, *El "Ocasionalismo" de los teólogos especulativos del Islam*; Rudolph and Perler, *Occasionalismus*.

30. See Quillet, *D'une cité l'autre*, 113.

31. Kant, *Kritik der praktischen Vernunft*, 1.1, par. 7, Anm., in Kant, *Werke*, 4:143. The mocking suggestion regarding angels is from Schopenhauer, *Grundlage der Moral*, 2, par. 6, in Schopenhauer, *Sämtliche Werke*, ed. Wolfgang von Lohneysen, 5 vols. (Darmstadt: Wissenschaftliche Buchgesellschaft, 1968), 3:658.

32. Spinoza, *Tractatus theologico-politicus*, 4:135–36; *Theological-Political Treatise*, 103, quoted from Benedict de Spinoza, *The Political Works*, ed. A. G. Wernham (Oxford: Clarendon Press, 1958), 71. Compare with Maimonides *Guide* 2.40, p. 271, 24–29/311, quoted from *The Guide of the Perplexed*, 383. See also Spinoza, *Tractatus theologico-politicus*, 5:145.

33. Montesquieu, *De l'esprit des Lois* 21.20, pp. 672–73; Montesquieu, *Réponses et explications pour la faculté de théologie*, in *Oeuvres complètes*, p. 827a–b.

34. Montesquieu, *De l'esprit des Lois* 26.2, p. 710b.

35. Ibid., 1.1, p. 530a, *The Spirit of the Laws*, 3.

36. See above, pp. 218–19.

37. Montesquieu, *De l'esprit des Lois* 1.1, p. 530a; *The Spirit of the Laws*, 3.

38. Montesquieu may possibly have drawn this principle from Vico. When he was in Venice in 1728, he planned to buy the *Scienza nuova* when he went to Naples. Did he read Vico's work? See Montesquieu, *Voyages en Europe*, in *Oeuvres complètes*, 226a.

39. Montesquieu, *De l'esprit des Lois* 1.3, p. 532a; *The Spirit of the Laws*, 8.

40. Montesquieu, *Pensées*, par. 109, in *Oeuvres complètes*, p. 862. Montesquieu does his own translation of Cicero: ibid., par. 185, p. 874b. See Cicero *De legibus* 2.4.10, Keyes trans., 383.

41. See Brague, "Zur Vorgeschichte der Unterscheidung von Sein und Sollen."

42. Alexis de Tocqueville, *La Démocratie en Amérique*, 1.2.7; 2.4.6; *Democracy in America*, trans. Harvey C. Mansfield and Delba Winthrop (Chicago: University of Chicago Press, 2000).

43. See Foucault, *Surveiller et punir*, 186, 310.

44. Machiavelli, *Discorsi*, 1.11, in Machiavelli, *Opere*, 1:126–27, in English translation by Harvey C. Mansfield and Nathan Tarcov as *Discourses on Livy* (Chicago: University of Chicago Press, 1996), 35. The untranslatable play on the words *ordinare* (to bring to order) and *ordini* (orders, commands) is both highly telling and somewhat obscure.

45. Machiavelli, *Discorsi*, 1.9; in *Opere*, 1:120. See also Machiavelli, *L'Arte della guerra*, 6, in Machiavelli, *Opere*, 1:584.

46. Montesquieu, *Essai touchant les lois naturelles*, in *Oeuvres complètes*, 180b; Montesquieu, *Fragments non publiés de l'Esprit des Lois*, in *Oeuvres complètes*, 805a.

47. Rousseau, *Du contrat social*, 4.8, p. 468; *The Social Contract*, 151.

48. *Déclaration des droits de l'homme et du citoyen*, 26 August 1789, par. 17.

49. John Austin, *Province of Jurisprudence Determined*, "Analysis of Lectures," pp. 5–6; 3, pp. 69, 73; 4, pp. 104, 106; 5, pp. 124, 128; 6, p. 269. Blackstone is scarcely any more forthcoming regarding revealed laws: see *Commentaries*, Introduction, 2, 1:42.

50. Austin, *Province of Jurisprudence Determined*, 1, p. 5; 4, p. 106; 2, pp. 34–35. See also ibid., 5, pp. 128, 161.

51. Ibid., 2, pp. 37, 43, 53; 3, p. 80; 4, pp. 99, 104, 116; 5, pp. 162, 185; 6, pp. 230, 307.

52. See Blackstone, *Commentaries*, Introduction, 2, 1:40–41; John Stuart Mill, *Utilitarianism* (1861), ed. A. D. Lindsay (London: Dent, 1968), 20.

53. Austin, *Province of Jurisprudence Determined*, 5, p. 130; 6, p. 288; 4, pp. 84, 104; 5, p. 163; 2, pp. 51, 58; 3, p. 80.

54. Ibid., 5, p. 173.

55. Ibid., 1, p. 24; 2, p. 42; 4, p. 116; 5, pp. 160, 184. See also ibid., 5, p. 179 (against Montesquieu); 5, pp. 130, 164.

56. Ibid., 1, p. 10.

57. See Avis, "Moses and the Magistrate," 152, 160.

58. Tommaso Campanella, *La Città del Sole*, ed. Luigi Firpo (Bari: Laterza, 1997), 1220–24, p. 54, available in English translation, with introduction and notes by Daniel J. Donno, as *La città del sole, dialogo poetico = The City of the Sun: A Poetic Dialogue* (Berkeley and Los Angeles: University of California Press, 1981). See also Thomas More, *Utopia*, ed. George M. Logan et al., (Cambridge: Cambridge University Press, 1995), 2, pp. 218ff.

59. See Thomas Aquinas, *Quaestiones quodlibetales*, vol. 5 of Aquinas, *Questiones disputatae* (1927): see above, p. 216. See also Voltaire, *Traité sur la tolérance*, chap. 14, in English translation by Brian Masters as *Treatise on Tolerance* (Cambridge and New York: Cambridge University Press, 2000); Chateaubriand, *Le Génie du christianisme*, in *Essai sur les révolu-*

tions, Le Génie du christianisme, ed. Maurice Regard (Paris: Gallimard, 1978), 1.1.8, p. 500; 1.4.14, p. 599, in English translation as *The Genius of Christianity,* ed. Charles I. White (New York: Fertig, 1976).

60. Chateaubriand, *Mémoires d'outre-tombe,* ed. Pierre Clarac (Paris: Livre de Poche, 1973), 1.4.13, p. 137; Charles Baudelaire, "Anniversaire de la naissance de Shakespeare. À M. le rédacteur en chef du *Figaro,* 14 avril 1864," in Baudelaire, *Oeuvres complètes,* ed. Claude Pichois, 2 vols. (Paris: Gallimard, 1976), 2:229.

61. Kant, *Grundlegung zur Metaphysik der Sitten,* 3, in Kant, *Werke,* 4:78. See also Kant, *Metaphysik der Sitten,* 1, Introduction, in Kant, *Werke,* 4:325, in English translation as *The Moral Law: Groundwork of the Metaphysic of Morals,* trans. H. J. Paton (London and New York: Routledge, 1991).

62. Kant, *Kritik der praktischen Vernunft,* 2.2.5, in Kant, *Werke,* 4:261, quoted from *Critique of Practical Reason and Other Writings in Moral Philosophy,* trans. by Lewis White Beck (Chicago: University of Chicago Press, 1949), 232.

63. Kant, *Über Pädagogik,* in Kant, *Werke,* 6:756, quoted from *Education,* trans. Annette Churton (Ann Arbor: University of Michigan Press, 1960), 113. For what follows, see, for example, Hegel, *Fragmente über Volksreligion und Christentum,* in Hegel, *Werke,* 21 vols. (Frankfurt: Suhrkamp, 1969–79), 1:88.

64. Kant, *Die Religion innerhalb der Grenzen der blossen Vernunft,* 3.5, in Kant, *Werke,* 4:762–67.

65. Kant, *Die Religion,* 4.2, in Kant, *Werke,* 4:838, quoted from *Religion Within the Limits of Reason Alone,* 156. This is a final echo of the Jewish distinction between *mishpatim* and *huqqim,* or the scholastic distinction between *lex moralis* and *lex caeremonialis:* see above, p. 63.

66. Schleiermacher, *Über die Religion,* chap. 2, p. 25.

67. Chateaubriand, *Mémoires d'outre-tombe,* 4.44, p. 1789, quoted from *The Memoirs of François René, vicomte de Chateaubriand,* trans. Alexander Teixeira de Mattos, 6 vols. (New York: Putnam, 1902), 6:218.

68. Friedrich von Gentz to Adam Müller, 19 April 1819, in *Briefwechsel zwischen Friedrich Gentz und Adam Heinrich Müller, 1800–1829* (Stuttgart, 1857), no. 171, p. 274.

69. Joseph de Maistre, *Considérations sur la France,* 5, in de Maistre, *Écrits sur la Révolution,* ed. Jean-Louis Darcel (Paris: PUF, 1989), 135. See also de Maistre, *Les Soirées de Saint Pétersbourg,* 2 vols. (Paris: Garnier, 1929), 1, 1:32; 7, 2:47; 8, 2:99.

70. Joseph de Maistre, *De la souveraineté du peuple: Un anti-contrat social,* ed. Jean-Louis Darcel (Paris: PUF, 1992), 1.1, p. 93, quoted from *The Works of Joseph de Maistre,* selected, trans., with an introduction, by Jack Lively (New York: Macmillan; London: Collier-Macmillan, 1965), 94.

71. Auguste Comte, *Cours de philosophie positive,* Lesson 57, in Comte, *Sciences et politique: Les conclusions globales du cours de philosophie positive,* ed. Michel Bourdeau (Paris: Pocket, 2003), 253–369.

72. Friedrich Carl von Savigny, *Vom Beruf unsrer Zeit für Gesetzgebung und Rechtswissenschaft* (Heidelberg: Mohr und Zimmer, 1814), 5, in English translation by Abraham Hayward as *On the Vocation of our Age for Legislation and Jurisprudence* (New York: Arno, 1975), 22.

73. Henry Sumner Maine, *Ancient Law,* 1, p. 2; 5, p. 72; 3, p. 41; 9, p. 180; 6, p. 101.

74. Ibid., 4, pp. 51–52; 9, p. 182; 4, pp. 51, 53, 57.

75. Ibid., 3, pp. 29–31.

76. Ibid., 5, p. 74; 6, p. 108; 8, p. 159; 9, p. 184.

77. Ibid., 1, p. 11; 4, p. 45; 5, p. 93 (on marriage); 7, p. 132 (on protection of widows); 8, p. 168 (on prescription).

78. Ibid., 9, p. 182; 10, p. 218; 5, p. 100 (the final words in the chapter); 6, pp. 113–14.

79. John Jakob Bachofen, *Das Mutterrecht*, Introduction, xxixa, quoted from *Myth, Religion and Mother Right*, 113.

80. Ibid., par. 66, p. 139a–b, the latter quoted from *Myth, Religion, and Mother Right*, 185, 189.

81. Ibid., par. 66, p. 140a; par. 67, p. 140b; Introduction, p. xxixa; *Myth, Religion, and Mother Right*, 193.

82. Ibid., par. 37, p. 71a and b; par. 65, p. 135a; *Myth, Religion, and Mother Right*, 186.

83. Ibid., par. 66, p. 139a.

84. Fustel de Coulanges, *La cité antique*, Introduction, p. 2; Hobbes, *Leviathan* 2.29, p. 214.

85. Fustel de Coulanges, *La cité antique*, 3.11, pp. 218–26, quotations, pp. 218, 220, 221; quoted here from *The Ancient City*, 178, 180–81.

86. Fustel de Coulanges, *La cité antique*, 2.8, par. 1, p. 93; *The Ancient City*, 78.

87. Fustel de Coulanges, *La cité antique*, 3.7, par. 4, p. 194 (against Montesquieu); *The Ancient City*, 124. See also ibid., 3.17, p. 257; 3.3, pp. 149–50; 2.7, par. 2, pp. 82, and also 370, 373, 463.

88. Fustel de Coulanges, *La cité antique*, 4.9, pp. 363–75, quotation, p. 365; *The Ancient City*, 299–300.

Chapter 15

1. Moses Mendelssohn, *Jérusalem*, 1, pp. 65, 104; Rida, *Le Califat*, 13.

2. On Salvador, see Fleischmann, *Le Christianisme "mis à nu*," 54, 58, 62, 65. For other examples of the accusation of anomism, see, in a polemic tone, Benamozegh, *Morale juive et morale chrétienne*, 2, pp. 32–33; and, in a very moderate tone, Rosenzweig, *Der Stern der Erlösung*, 3.3, par. 436, p. 452.

3. For example, see Rosenzweig, *Der Stern der Erlösung*, 3.1, par. 321, p. 337. In much the same spirit, Rosenzweig and Martin Buber's German version of the Bible, *Die Schrift*, 4 vols. (Cologne: Hegner, 1966), translates the word *Torah* by *Weisung*.

4. See Heschel, *Theology of Ancient Judaism*,1:iv.

5. Emmanuel Lévinas, *Difficile liberté: Essais sur le judaïsme* (Paris: Albin Michel, 1963), 192–93; in English translation by Séan Hand as *Difficult Freedom: Essays on Judaism* (Baltimore: Johns Hopkins University Press, 1990), 142–45.

6. For a summary of this tendency, see von Balthasar, *In Gottes Einsatz Leben*, 77–83.

7. Mendelssohn, *Jérusalem*, 2, pp. 123, 136, quoted from *Jerusalem and Other Jewish Writings*, trans. Jospe, 61. See also Bourel, *Moses Mendelssohn*, 335–36.

8. Mendelssohn, *Jérusalem*, 2, pp. 160–61: see J. Maier, "'Gesetz' und 'Gnade,'" 139; Bourel, *Moses Mendelssohn*, 342.

9. Hermann Cohen, *Religion der Vernunft aus dem Quellen des Judentums*, Introduction, pp. 11–12; 24.

10. Ibid., 18, p. 476.

11. Rosenzweig, *Der Stern der Erlösung*, 2.2, par. 176, p. 210; 3.3, pars. 436, 451.

12. Ibid., 2.2, pars. 161–62, pp. 196–98; 2.3, p. 229.

13. Ibid., 3.3, par. 436, p. 45; pars. 440–42, pp. 454–57.

14. Franz Rosenzweig, "Die Bauleute: Über das Gesetz" (1923), in Rosenzweig, *Die Schrift; Aufsätze, Übertragungen und Briefe*, ed. Karl Thieme (Frankfurt: Europäische Verlagsanstalt, 1964), 143–58, esp. pp. 147, 153.

15. Rosenzweig, *Der Stern der Erlösung*, 3.1, par. 342, p. 352.

16. Emmanuel Lévinas, *En découvrant l'existence avec Husserl et Heidegger* (Paris: Vrin,

1949), 195; Lévinas, *Totalité et infini: Essai sur l'extériorité* (The Hague: Nijhoff, 1965), 267, in English translation by Alphonse Lingis as *Totality and Infinity: An Essay on Exteriority* (The Hague and Boston: Nijhoff, 1979), 290; Lévinas, *Difficile liberté*, 22, *Difficult Freedom*, 8. See also Lévinas, *Éthique et infini: Entretiens avec Philippe Nemo* (Paris: Fayard, 1982), 90, *Ethics and Infinity: Conversations with Philippe Nemo*, trans. Richard A. Cohen (Pittsburgh: Duquesne University Press, 1985), 89. I owe the substance of this paragraph to a report given by my student M. Magnichever-Cittanova.

17. Emmanuel Lévinas, *De Dieu qui vient à l'idée* (Paris: Vrin, 1982), p. 203 n. 6; Lévinas, *Ethique et infini*, 121–22, *Ethics and Infinity*, 113; Lévinas, *L'Au-delà du verset: Lectures et discours talmudiques* (Paris: Éditions de Minuit, 1982), 86; Lévinas, *Totalité et infini*, 223.

18. Emmanuel Lévinas, *Hors sujet* (Montpellier, Fata Morgana, 1987), 184, *Outside the Subject*, trans. Michael B. Smith (Stanford, Calif.: Stanford University Press, 1994), 122; Lévinas, *Difficile liberté*, 136; Lévinas, *Au-delà du verset*, 116, *Beyond the Verse: Talmudic Readings and Lectures*, trans. Gary D. Mole (London. Athione Press, 1994), 93.

19. For parallels with the Hindu religion, see Veyne, *Les Grecs ont-il cru à leurs mythes?*, 142 n. 13; for parallels with Buddhism, see de Lubac, *La Rencontre du bouddhisme et de l'Occident*, 235–37.

20. See Di Matteo, "Il 'tarîf' od alterazione della Bibbia secondo i musulmani," 252–58. On Ibn Hazm, see above, pp. 95, 124, 164; Rippin, "Interpreting the Bible through the Qur'ān," 254–56.

21. See E. Rosenthal, *Studia Semitica*, 2:173, 184.

22. Abderraziq, *L'Islam et les fondements du pouvoir*, 1.2.7, p. 69; 2.5.2, p. 100. For the Muslim version of the "God and Caesar" theme, see Goldziher, *Sur l'Islam*, 92–93; for the Jewish parallel, see Ravitzky, *History and Faith*, 67; Mendelssohn, *Jérusalem*, 2, p. 179, also refers to the formula.

23. Abderraziq, *L'Islam*, 2.6.5, p. 120; 1.2.7, p. 69; 2.6.8, p. 129; 3.9.12, p. 155.

24. Rida, *Le Califat*, 204–6.

25. See Rosenthal, *Studia Semitica*, 2:179, 190; Benkheira, *L'Amour de la Loi*, 207, 325.

26. On the notion of *sharia* being later than that of *shar'*, see above, p. 160. For examples of the historical legend, see Muhammad 'Abduh, *Rissalat al Tawhid*, 100, and Rida, *Le Califat*, 152–53.

27. Abderraziq, *L'Islam*, 3.7.4, p. 138; 9, 10, p. 154; Objections and responses, p. 159.

Conclusion

1. Dakhlia, *Le Divan des rois*, 99, 81.

2. See the texts of Ibn Qutayba and Nizām al-Mulk cited in von Grunebaum, *L'identité culturelle de l'Islam*, 26–27.

3. See, for example, H. Cohen, *Religion der Vernunft*, 16, p. 394.

4. Aside from the classic Arkoun, *Contribution à l'étude de l'humanisme arabe au IVe/Xe siècle*, see the two recent summaries of Gutas, "Ethische Schriften im Islam," and Vadet, *Les Idées morales dans l'islam*. The last remark is taken from Weiss, *The Search for God's Law*, 6.

5. See C. S. Lewis, *The Abolition of Man*.

6. See above, pp. 69–70.

7. Benjamin Constant, *Principes de politique*, 17, in Constant, *Oeuvres*, ed. Alfred Roulin (Paris: Gallimard, 1957), 1225; quoted from *Principles of Politics Applicable to all Governments*, ed. Étienne Hofmann, trans. Dennis O'Keefe (Indianapolis: Liberty Fund, 2003), 141, 142.

8. Friedrich Wilhelm Joseph von Schelling, *Philosophie der Offenbarung*, lesson 26, in his *Ausgewählte Werke*, 5 vols. (Darmstadt: Wissenschaftliche Buchgesellschaft, 1983,

reprint of 1858), 2:57. There is an unexpected echo of this in Leo Strauss, *Gesammelte Schriften*, 2:126, 428.

9. Rousseau, *Contrat social*, 4.8, p. 465; my emphasis, quoted from *The Social Contract and Other Late Political Writings*, 147.

10. Fustel de Coulanges, *La cité antique*, 5.3, p. 453; *The Ancient City*, 387.

11. *Epistle of Barnabas* 1.4 and 5.4, in *PA*; Clement I, *First Epistle to the Corinthians* 5.7, Biblioteca de autores cristianos, p. 359 For references and comparisons, see G. Stroumsa, *Barbarian Philosophy*, 249.

12. Augustine *Confessions* 10.29.40. The phrase is often cited, from Albertus Magnus *Summa de Bono* 5, q. 2, a. 2, p. 288a, for example, up to Rosenzweig, *Der Stern der Erlösung*, 2.3, par. 200, p. 239 (who substitutes *fac* for *da*, however).

13. See *PGL*, s.v. "*ephodion*," 588a. Other examples might include John Chrysostom, *Huit catéchèses baptismales inédites*, 8.1, critical edition, trans. with notes by Antoine Wenger (Paris: Cerf, 1970), SC no. 50bis, p. 218; in English translation by Paul W. Harkins as *Baptismal Instructions* (Westminster, Md.: Newman Press, 1963).

14. See above, p. viii.

15. Leszek Kolakowski, *God Owes Us Nothing: A Brief Remark on Pascal's Religion and on the Spirit of Jansenism* (Chicago: University of Chicago Press, 1995).

16. Montesquieu, *Pensées*, 12, par. 437, p. 901a: see Beauchamp, *D'une montagne à l'autre*, 33, 105–8.

17. Gauchet, *La Religion dans la démocratie*, 63.

18. Bodin, *Les Six Livres de la République*, 1.8, pp. 129, 131, 149–50, 152, 161, discussed and placed in its medieval context in Pennington, *The Prince and the Law*, 8 (the source of the quotations here).

19. Stephen Toulmin, *Cosmopolis: The Hidden Agenda of Modernity* (New York: The Free Press, 1990), from which I have borrowed nothing but the title.

20. See Butterworth, "Political Islam," 37b.

21. See Brague, *Europe, la voie romaine*, 178.

Selected Bibliography]&··

Reference Works, Multivolume Works, and Collections

ANET James B. Pritchard, ed., *Ancient Near Eastern Texts Relating to the Old Testament.* 2nd ed. Princeton: Princeton University Press, 1955.

AT Rene Descartes, *Oeuvres*, ed. Charles Adam and Paul Tannery (1897–1913). New ed., 2nd printing. 11 vols. Paris: Vrin, 1974–82.

BA Bibliothèque Augustinienne. *Oeuvres de saint Augustin.* Paris: Desclé de Brouwer, 1947.

BT Bibltiotheca scriptorium Graecorumn et Romanorum Teubneriana. Leipzig: Teubner.

CAG Commentaria in Aristotelem Graeca. Berlin: Reimer, 1882–1907.

CCCM Corpus Christianorum, Continuatio Medievalis.

CCSL Corpus Christianorum, Series Latina. Tournai: Brepols, 1953.

CSEL Corpus scriptorum ecclesiasticorum latinorum Vienna, 1866–.

CSIC Consejo Superior de Investigaciones Cientificas.

CTM A. J. Wensinck, *Concordance et indices des traditions musulmanes.* 8 vols. Leiden: Brill, 1933–88.

CUF Collection des Universités de France. Paris: Les Belles-Lettres, 1920–.

DK Hermann Diels and Walther Kranz, *Die Fragmente der Vorsokratiker* (in Greek and German). 11th ed. 3 vols. Zurich: Weidmann, 1964. In English translation by Kathleen Freeman as *Ancilla to the pre-Socratic Philosophers* (1948). Cambridge, Mass.: Harvard University Press, 1957.

EI *Encyclopédie de l'Islam*, ed. H. R. R. Gibbs et al. Leiden: Brill, 1960–.

EJ *Encyclopaedia Judaica.* 16 vols. Jerusalem: Keter, 1972. Corrected edition in 17 vols. Jerusalem Keter, 1996.

FPhG Freidrich Wilhelm August Mullach, *Fragmenta Philosophorum Graecorum.* 3 vols. Paris: Didot, 1860–80.

GAS Fuat Sezgin, *Geschichte des arabischen Schrifttums.* 12 vols. Leiden: Brill, 1967–2000.

HWPh *Historisches Wörterbuch der Philosophie*, ed. Joachim Ritter et al. 12 vols. Basel: Schwabe, 1971–2004.

LA *Lexicon der Ägyptologie*, ed. Maria Plantikow and Wolfgang Helck. Wiesbaden: Harrassowitz, 1914–.

LCL   Loeb Classical Library. Cambridge, Mass.: Harvard University Press; London: Heinemann, 1912–.

LM   *Lexikon des Mittelalters,* ed. Norbert Angermann. Munich and Zurich: Artemis, 1977.

MG   Miqrā'ōt gedlōlōt (1859). Jerusalem: Eshkol, 1976.

MT   Maimonides, *Mishneh Torah.* Edited by M. D. Rabinovitch, 12 vols. Jerusalem: Mosad Rav Kook, 1959–.

PA   *Padres apostólicos,* ed. and trans. Daniel Ruíz Bueno. 3rd ed. Madrid: Biblioteca de Autores Cristianos, 1985.

PG   *Patrologia cursus completus: Series Graeca,* ed. Jacques-Paul Migne. Paris, 1857–66.

PGL   *A Patristic Greek Lexicon,* ed. G. W. H. Lampe. Oxford: Clarendon Press, 1968.

PL   *Patrologia cursus completus: Series Latina,* ed. Jacques-Paul Migne. Paris, 1841–64.

PUF   Presses Universitaires de France.

RAVA   *Reallexikon der Assyriologie und der vorderasiatischen Archäologie,* ed. Erich Ebeling. Berlin and Leipzig: De Gruyter, 1928.

SB   Sahīh Bukhari. Translated into French by Octave Victor Houdas and William Marçais as *Les traditions islamiques.* 4 vols. Paris: Leroux, 1903–14.

SC   Sources chrétiennes. Paris: Éditions du Cerf, 1941–.

SPTB   *Social and Political Thought in Byzantium from Justinian I to the last Palaelogus: Passages from Byzantine Writers and Documents,* ed. and trans., with an introduction, by Ernest Barker (Oxford: Clarendon Press, 1957).

SVF   *Stoicorum Veterum Fragmenta,* ed. Hans Friedrich August von Arnim. 4 vols. Leipzig: Teubner, 1903–24.

TE   *Talmudic Encyclopedia.* A Digest of Halachic Literature and Jewish Law from the Tanaitic Period to the Present Time. Alphabetically arranged (in Hebrew). Jerusalem: Talmudic Encyclopedia Institute, 1975.

Works Cited

Abderraziq, Ali. *L'Islam et les fondements du pouvoir.* Translated into French, with an introduction, by Abdou Filali-Ansary. Paris: La Découverte, 1994.

'Abduh, Muhammad. *Rissalat al Tawhid: Exposé de la religion musulmane* (1897). Translated into French by B. Michel and Moustapha Abdel Razik. Paris: Geuthner, 1925.

Abraham bar Hiyya. *Hegyōn ha-Nefesh ha-'atsūvah.* Edited by Geoffrey Wigoder. Jerusalem: Mosad Byalik, 1971. In English translation, with an introduction, by Geoffrey Wigoder as *Meditation of the Sad Soul.* London: Routledge and Kegan Paul, 1969.

Abravanel, Isaac. *Peyrūsh.* 3 vols. Jerusalem: Torah ve-da'at, 1976.

Abū Yūsuf Ya'qūb. *Livre de l'impôt foncier.* Edited and translated by Edmond Fagnan. Paris: Geuthner, 1921.

Adang, Camilla. *Muslim Writers on Judaism and the Hebrew Bible: From Ibn Rabban to Ibn Hazm.* Leiden and New York: Brill, 1996.

Adler, William. "The Jews as Falsifier: Charges of Tendentious Emendations in Anti-Jewish Christian Polemics." In *Translations of Scriptures,* supplement to *Jewish Quarterly Review* (1990): 1–27.

Ahrweiler, Hélène. *L'Idéologie politique de l'Empire byzantin.* Paris: Presses Universitaires de France, 1975.

Albertus Magnus. *Summa de Bono.* Edited by Heinrich Kühle et al. In Albertus, *Opera Omnia,* vol. 28. Munster: Aschendorff, 1951.

Albo, Joseph. *Book of Principles.* Edited and translated by Isaak Husik. 5 vols. Philadelphia: The Jewish Publication Society, 1920.

Albrektson, Bertil. *History and the Gods: An Essay on the Idea of Historical Events as Divine Manifestations in the Ancient Near East and in Israel.* Lund: Gleerup, 1967.

Albright, William Foxwell. *From the Stone Age to Christianity: Monotheism and the Historical Process.* 2nd ed. New York: Doubleday, 1957; Baltimore: Johns Hopkins University Press, 1962.

Alfarabi. *Against John the Grammarian.* See Muhsin Mahdi, "Alfarabi Against Philoponus," *Journal of Near Eastern Studies* 26 (1967): 233–60.

———. *Al-Farabi on the Perfect State: Abū Nasr al-Fārābī's Mabādi'ārā'Ahl al-madina al-fādila.* Edited and translated by Richard Walzer. Oxford: Clarendom Press; New York: Oxford University Press, 1985. *Idées des habitants de la Cité vertueuse.* Translated into French from the Arabic, with introduction and notes, by Yusuf Karam et al. Beirut: Commission libanaise pour la traduction des chefs-d'oeuvre, 1980.

———. *Alfarabi's Book of Letters (Kitāb Al-Hurūf): Commentary on Aristotle's Metatphysics.* Edited and translated by Muhsin Mahdi. Beirut: Dar al-Mashreq, 1969.

———. *Alfarabi's Book of Religion and Related Texts.* Edited and translated by Muhsin Mahdi. Beirut: Dar al-Mashreq, 1967.

———. *Alfarabi's Philosophy of Plato and Aristotle.* Translated, with an introduction, by Muhsin Mahdi. New York: Macmillan/Free Press of Glencoe, 1962; rev. ed., Ithaca: Cornell University Press, 1969.

———. *Al-Mantīq 'inda al-Farabi.* Edited by Rafiq al-'Ajam and Majid Fakrhrī. 4 vols. Beirut: Dar al-Mashreq 1985–87.

———. *Al-Siyāsah al-Madaniyah* (The political regime). Edited by Fauzi M. Najjar. Beirut: Dar al-Mashreq, 1964.

———. *Catálogo de las ciencias.* Edited and translated by Angel González Palencía. 2nd ed. Madrid and Granada: CSIC, 1955.

———. *Fusūl Muntaza'ah* (Selected aphorisms). Edited by Fauzi M. Najjar. Beirut: Dar al-Mashreq, 1971.

———. *Kitāb al-Millah wa-nusūs ukkrá* (Alfarabi's book of religion and related texts). Edited by Muhsin Mahdi. Beirut: Dar al-Mashreq, 1968.

———. *The Philosophical Works* ("On the Attainment of Happiness"; "Note on the Path to Happiness"; "On the Truth of Astrology"; "Questions"; "Notes"). Edited by Ja'far Al-Yasin. Beirut: Dar al-Manahel, 1987, 1992–.

———. "Le sommaire du livre des 'Lois' de Platon (*Gawāmī'Kitāb al-Nawāmīs li-Aflatun*)." Critical edition, with an introduction, by Thérèse-Anne Druart. *Bulletin d'études orientales,* Institut Français de Damas 50 (1998): 109–55.

Allam, Schafik. "La problématique des quarante rouleaux de loi." In *Studien zur Sprache und Religion Ägyptens,* vol. 1: *Sprache: Zu Ehren von Wolfhart Westendorf,* 447–53. Göttingen: Seminar für Ägyptologie, 1984.

Alon, Ilai. "Farabi's Funny Flora: al-Nawabit as 'Opposition.'" *Journal of the Royal Asiatic Society* (1989): 222–51.

———. *Socrates in Mediaeval Arabic Literature.* Leiden: Brill, 1991. See also my critical review in *Les Études philosophiques* (1994): 409–12.

Alt, Albrecht. "Die Staatenbildung der Israeliten in Palästina" (1930). In *Kleine Schriften zur Geschichte des Volkes Israels,* 3 vols., ed. Martin Noth, 2:1–65. Munich: Beck, 1953. In English translation by R. A. Wilson as *Essays on Old Testament History and Religion.* Sheffield: JSOT Press, 1989.

————. "Die Ursprünge des israelitischen Rechts" (1934), in ibid., 2:278–332.

Altmann, Alexander. "Saadya's Conception of the Law." *Bulletin of the John Rylands Library* 28 (1944): 320–39.

Amir, Yehoshua. "Mose as Verfasser der Tora bei Philon." In *Der Hellenistische Gestalt des Judentum bei Philon von Alexandrien,* 77–106. Neukirches-Vluyn: Neukirchener Verlag, 1983.

Ammann, Ludwig. *Die Geburt des Islam: Historische Innovation durch Offenbarung.* Göttingen: Wallstein, 2001.

Antes, Peter. *Ethik und Politik im Islam.* Stuttgart: Kohlhammer, 1982.

Arberry, Arthur J. "An Arabic Treatise on Politics." *Islamic Quarterly* 2 (1955): 9–22.

Arendt, Hannah. *The Life of the Mind,* vol. 2: *Willing.* London: Secker and Warburg; New York: Harcourt Brace Jovanovich, 1978.

Aristotle. *Metaphysics.* Translated by Hugh Tredennick. 2 vols. LCL. Cambridge, Mass.: Harvard University Press; London: William Heinemann, 1958.

————. *Nicomachean Ethics.* Translated by H. Rackham. LCL. Cambridge, Mass.: Harvard University Press; London: William Heinemann, 1975.

————. *Politics.* Translated by H. Rackham. LCL. London and Cambridge, Mass.: Harvard University Press, 1972.

Arkoun, Mohammed. 1970. *Contribution à l'étude de l'humanisme arabe au IVe/Xe siècle: Miskawayh philosophe et historien.* Paris: Vrin, 1970.

Arnaldez, Roger. *Aspects de la pensée musulmane.* Paris: Vrin, 1987.

Arnold, Thomas Walker. *The Caliphate* (1924). 2nd ed. London: Routledge and Kegan Paul; New York: Barnes and Noble, 1966.

Asín Palacios, Miguel. "La tesis de la necesidad de la revelación en el islam y en la escolástica." *Al-Andalus* 3 (1935):345–89.

————. "El origen del lenguaje y problemas conexos, en Algazel, Ibn Sîda y Ibn Hazm." *Al-Andalus* 4 (1939): 235–81. Also in Asín Palacios, *Obras escogidas,* vol. 2–3: *De historia y filología arabe,* 357–88. Madrid: Maestre, 1948.

Assmann, Aleida. "Exkarnation: Gedanken zur Grenze zwischen Körper und Schrift." In Jörg Huber and Alois Martin Müller, eds., *Raum und Verfahren, Interventionen 2,* 135–55. Zurich: Museum für Gestaltung Zürich, 1993.

Assmann, Jan. *Ägypten: Eine Sinngeschichte.* Munich: Hanser, 1996. In English translation by Andrew Jenkins as *The Mind of Egypt: History and Meaning in the Time of the Pharaohs.* New York: Metropolitan Books, 2002.

————. *Herrschaft und Heil: Politische Theologie in Altägypten, Israel und Europa.* Munich: Hanser, 2000.

————. *Das kulturelle Gedächtnis: Schrift, Erinnerung und politische Identität in frühen Hochkulturen.* Munich: Beck, 1997.

————. *Ma'at: Gerechtigkeit und Unsterblichkeit im Alten Ägypten.* Munich: Beck, 1990.

————. *Maât: L'Égypte pharaonique et l'idée de justice sociale.* Paris: Juillard, 1989.

————. *Moses der Ägypter: Entzifferung einer Gedächtnisspur.* Munich: Hanser, 1998. In English translation as *Moses the Egyptian: The Memory of Egypt in Western Monotheism.* Cambridge, Mass.: Harvard University Press, 1997.

————. *Politische Theologie zwischen Ägypten und Israel.* Munich: Siemens Stiftung, 1992.

————. *Stein und Zeit: Mensch und Gesellschaft im alten Ägypten.* Munich: Fink, 1991.

Augustine. *Enarrationes in Psalmos.* Edited by Eligius Dekkers and Johannes Fraipont. CCSL, 38–40. 3 vols. Turnhut: Brepols, 1956. In English translation as *St. Augustine on the Psalms,* with annotations, by Scholastica Hebgin and Felicitas Corrigan. 2 vols. Westminster, Md.: Newman Press, 1960.

———. *La Cité de Dieu.* Edited by Bernhard Dombart and Alfons Kalb. Translated into French by Alfons Combès, 5 vols. Paris: Declée de Brouwer, 1959–60. In English translation by Henry Bettenson as *Concerning the City of God against the Pagans.* London and New York: Penguin, 2003.

Austin, John. *The Province of Jurisprudence Determined and The Uses of the Study of Jurisprudence.* Edited by H. L. A. Hart. Indianapolis: Hackett, 1998.

Averroes. *Averroes' Commentary on Plato's Republic.* Edited and translated by E. I. J. Rosenthal. Cambridge: Cambridge University Press, 1969.

———. *Averroes' Middle Commentary on Aristotle's Nicomachean Ethics in the Hebrew Version of Samuel ben Judah.* Edited and translated by Lawrence V. Berman. Jerusalem: The Israel Academy of Sciences and Humanities, 1999.

———. *Averroes on Plato's Republic.* Edited and translated, with an introduction and notes, by Ralph Lerner. Ithaca and London: Cornell University Press, 1974.

———. *Commentaire moyen à la Rhétorique d'Aristote.* Vol. 2. Edited by Maroun Aouad. 3 vols. Paris: Vrin, 2002.

———. *Kashfa ʿan manāhij al-adilla fīʾaqāʾid al-milla.* In *Falsafat Ibn Rushd,* 45–142. Beirut: Dar al-Afāq al-Jadīdah, 1982.

———. *Tafsīr mā baʿda al-tabīʿah: Grand commentaire de la Métaphyique d'Aristote.* Edited by Maurice Bouyges (1938–52). 2nd ed. 3 vols. Beirut: Dar al-Mashreq, 1967.

———. *Tahafot at-Tahafot: L'incohérence de l'incohérence.* Edited by Maurice Bouyges (1930). Beirut: Dar al-Mashreq, 1987. In English translation by Simon van den Bergh, with an introduction and notes, as *Tahafut al-tahafut (The Incoherence of the Incoherence).* London: Luzac, 1964.

———. *Traité décisif (Façl el-maqāl) sur l'accord de la religion et de la philosophie.* Arabic text edited and translated by Léon Gauthier. Paris: Vrin, 1983. In English translation, with notes and introduction by George F. Hourani as *On the Harmony of Reason and Philosophy.* London: Luzac, 1961.

Avicenna. *Al-Shifā, al-Ilāhiyyāt (Metaphysics).* Edited by Georges C. Anawati and S. Zaʾīd. Cairo: L'Organisation égyptienne générale du livre, 1960. In French translation by Georges C. Anawati as *La métaphysique du Shifaʾ Avicenne.* 2 vols. Paris: Vrin: 1978, 1985.

———. *Avicenna's De Anima, being the psychological part of Kitāb al-Shifā.* Edited by Fazlur Rahman. Oxford: Oxford University Press, 1959.

———. *Fi Ithbāt al-Nubuwwāt (Proof of Prophecies).* Edited by Michael E. Marmura (1968). Beirut: Dar an-Nahar, 1991.

———. *Tisʾrasāʾil fi al-hikmah wa-al-tabīʾiyāt.* Cairo: Dar al-Arab, n.d.

Avis, P. D. L. "Moses and the Magistrate: A Study in the Rise of Protestant Legalism." *Journal of Ecclesiastical History* 26 (1975): 149–72.

Bachofen, Johann Jakob. *Das Mutterrecht: Eine Untersuchung über die Gynaikokratie der alten Welt nach ihrer religiösen und rechtlichen Natur.* Stuttgart: Krais & Hofmann, 1861. In English translation by Ralph Manheim as *Myth, Religion, and Mother Right: Selected Writings of J. J. Bachofen.* Princeton: Princeton University Press, 1967.

Badawi, ʾAbd al-Rahman, ed. *Aflatun fi al-Islam: Nusus* (Plato in the land of Islam). Beirut: Dar al-Andaloss, 1980.

———. *Traités philosophiques (Rasaʾil falsafiyah) par al-Kindī, al-Farabi, Ibn Bājjah, Ibn ʿAdyy.* Benghazi, Libya: Publications de l'Université de Libye, 1973.

Baer, Yitzhak. 1986. *A History of the Jews in Christian Spain,* vol. 1: *From the Age of Reconquest to the Fourteenth Century.* Translated by Louis Schoffman. Philadelphia: The Jewish Publication Society of America, 1986.

Bahya ben Joseph ibn Paquda. *Al-Hidāja ̓īlā Farā ̓id al-Qulūb.* Edited and translated by A. S. Yahuda. Leiden: Brill, 1912. In English translation, with commentary, by Yaakov Feldman, as *The Duties of the Heart.* Northvale, N.J. and London: Jason Aronson, 1996.

Balthasar, Hans Urs von. *Herrlichkeit: Eine theologische Ästhetik.* vol. 3, pt. 2: *Theologie*, pt. 1: *Alter Bund.* Einsiedeln: Johannes Verlag, 1967. In English translation by Erasmo Leiva as *The Glory of the Lord: A Theological Aesthetics*, ed. Joseph Fessio and John Riches. 7 vols. San Francisco: Ignatius Press; New York: Crossroads, 1983–91.

———. *In Gottes Einsatz Leben.* Einsiedeln: Johannes Verlag, 1971.

———. *Kosmische Liturgie: Das Weltbild Maximus' des Bekenners.* Einseideln: Johannes Verlag, 1961. In English translation by Brian E. Daley as *Cosmic Liturgy: The Universe according to Maximus the Confessor.* San Francisco: Ignatius Press, 2003.

Barker, Ernest, ed. and trans. *Social and Political Thought in Byzantium from Justinian I to the last Palaelogus: Passages from Byzantine Writers and Documents.* Oxford: Clarendon Press, 1957.

Baron, Salo Wittmayer. *A Social and Religious History of the Jews.* 2nd ed. rev. and enlarged. *High Middle Ages, 500–1200*, vol. 6: *Laws, Homilies, and the Bible.* New York and Philadelphia: The Jewish Publication Society of America, 1958.

Barone, Elisabetta. *Teo-nomie: Metafisica dell'essere e mistica della legge in Nicolas Malebranche.* Naples: Edizioni Scientifiche Italiane, 1998.

Barone Adesi, Giorgio. *L'età della Lex Dei.* Naples: Jovene, 1992.

Bastit, Michel. *Naissance de la loi moderne: La pensée de la loi de saint Thomas à Suarez.* Paris: PUF, 1990.

Baumstark, Anton. "Das Problem eines vorislamischen christlich-kirchlichen Schrifttums in arabisher Sprache." *Islamica* 4 (1931): 562–75.

Beauchamp, Paul. *Création et séparation: Étude exégétique du chapitre premier de la Genèse.* Paris: Aubier-Montaigne, 1969; Paris: Éditions du Cerf, 2005.

———. *D'une montagne à l'autre: La loi de Dieu.* Paris: Éditions du Seuil, 1999.

———. *L'un et l'Autre Testament: Essai de lecture.* Paris: Éditions du Seuil, 1976.

Beck, Hans-Georg. *Nomos, Kanon und Staatsraison in Byzanz.* Philosophisch-historische Klasse, no. 384. Vienna: Österreichische Akademie der Wissenschaften, 1981.

Becker, Carl Heinrich. *Vom Werden und Wesen der islamischen Welt: Islamstudien* (1924). 2 vols. Hildesheim: Olms, 1967.

Bellini, Piero. "Il riformismo gregoriano fra pretese egemoniche imperiali e spiritualismo escatologico." In *Saggi di storia della esperienza canonistica*, 57–69. Turin: Giappichelli, 1991.

Bellomo, Manlio. *L'Europa del diritto comune.* Rome: Il Cigno Galileo Galilei, 1993. In English translation by Lydia G. Cochrane as *The Common Legal Past of Europe: 1000–1800.* Washington, D.C.: Catholic University of America Press, 1995.

Benamozegh, Elia. *Morale juive et morale chrétienne* (1867). Revised edition, Boudry-Neuchâtel: La Baconnière, 1946. In English translation as *Jewish and Christian Ethics, with a Criticism on Mahomedism.* San Francisco: Blochman, 1873.

Benardete, Seth. *Plato's "Laws": The Discovery of Being.* Chicago and London: University of Chicago Press, 2000.

Benkheira, Mohammed H. *L'Amour de la Loi: Essai sur la normativité en islam.* Paris: PUF, 1997.

Ben-Sasson, Jonah. "On the Doctrine of the Reasons for the Commandments in the *Guide for the Perplexed*" (in Hebrew). *Tarbiz* 29 (1960): 268–81.

Benveniste, Émile. *Le vocabulaire des institutions indo-européennes.* 2 vols. Paris: Éditions de Minuit, 1969.

Berman, Harold J. *Law and Revolution: The Formation of the Western Legal Tradition.* Cambridge, Mass.: Harvard University Press, 1983.

Berman, Lawrence. "Maimonides, the Disciple of Alfarabi." *Israel Oriental Studies* 4 (1974): 154–78.

———. "The Political Interpretation of the Maxim: 'The Purpose of Philosophy Is the Imitation of God.'" *Studia Islamica* 15 (1961): 53–61.

———. "A Re-examination of Maimonides' Statement on Political Science." *Journal of the American Oriental Society* 89 (1969): 106–11.

Berman, Lawrence, and Ilai Alon. "Socrates on Law and Philosophy." *Jerusalem Studies in Arabic and Islam* 2 (1980): 263–79.

Bernard of Clairvaux. *Opera.* Edited by Jean Leclercq et al. 8 vols. Rome: Editiones Cistercienses, 1957–77.

Besançon, Alain. *Les Origines intellectuelles du léninisme.* Paris: Calmann-Lévy, 1977. In English translation by Sarah Matthews as *The Rise of the Gulag: Intellectual Origins of Leninism.* New York: Continuum, 1981.

———. *Trois tentations dans l'Église.* Paris: Calmann-Lévy, 1996. Paris: Perrin, 2002.

Beyerlin, Walter. *Weisheitlich-kultische Heilsordnung: Studien zum 15. Psalm.* Neukirchen-Vluyn: Neukirchener Verlag, 1985.

Bible. *The New American Bible.* Chicago: Catholic Press, 1970.

Bickerman, Elias J. "Autonomia: Sur un passage de Thucydide (I, 144, 2)." In *Religions and Politics in the Hellenistic and Roman Periods,* ed. Emilio Gabba and Morton Smith, 421–52. Como: New Press, 1958.

Birkeland, Harris. *Old Muslim Opposition against Interpretation of the Koran.* Oslo: Jacob Dybwad, 1955.

al-Bīrūnī. *Chronologie orientalischer Völker.* Edited by Eduard Sachau. Leipzig: Brockhaus und Harrasowitz, 1923. In English translation as *The Chronology of Ancient Nations.* London: W. H. Allen, 1879.

———. *Taḥqīq mā li-'l-Hind min maqūla maqbū fī 'l-ʾaql aw mardūhla.* Edited by A. Safan. 3rd ed. Beirut: Alam al-Kutub, 1983. Extracts in French translation by Vincent-Mansour Monteil as *Le livre de l'Inde.* Arles: Actes Sud (Sinbad) UNESCO, 1996. In English translation, with notes and an index, by Edward C. Sachau as *Alberuni's India.* Delhi: S. Chand and Co., 1964.

Blackstone, William. *Commentaries on the Laws of England,* vol. 1: *Of the Rights of Persons.* Oxford: Clarendon Press, 1766. Chicago: University of Chicago Press, 1979.

Bland, Kalman P. "Moses and the Law According to Maimonides." In *Mystics, Philosophers and Politicians: Essays in Jewish Intellectual History in Honor of A. Altmann,* ed. Jehuda Reinharz et al., 49–66. Durham: Duke University Press, 1982.

Blass, Heinrich. *Gott und die Gesetze: Ein Beitrag zur Frage des Naturrechts bei Heraklit (Fragment 114).* Bonn: Bouvier, 1958.

Blidstein, Gerald J. *Political Concepts in Maimonidean Halakha* (in Hebrew). Ber Sheva: Bar Ilan University, 1983; Ramat-Gan: Bar-Ilan University, 1993.

Bloch, Marc. *Les Rois thaumaturges: Étude sur le caractère surnaturel attribué à la puissance royale particulièrement en France et en Angleterre* (1924). Paris: Colin, 1961. New edition, Paris: Gallimard, 1983. In English translation by J. E. Anderson as *The Royal Touch: Sacred Monarchy and Scrofula in England and France.* London: Routledge and Kegan Paul, 1973.

Blumenthal, Uta-Renate. *Der Investiturstreit.* Stuttgart: Kohlhammer, 1982. In English translation by the author as *The Investiture Controversy: Church and the Monarchy from the Ninth to the Twelfth Century.* Philadelphia: University of Pennsylvania Press, 1983.

Bodde, Derk, and Clarence Morris. *Law in Imperial China: Exemplified by 190 Ch'ing Dynasty Cases.* Cambridge, Mass.: Harvard University Press, 1967; Philadelphia: University of Pennsylvania Press, 1973.

Bodin, Jean. *Les Six Livres de la République de I. Bodon angevin.* Paris: Jacques du Puis, 1583. Aalen: Scientia, 1961.

Boochs, Wolfgang. "Zur Bedeutung der *hpw*." *Varia Aegyptiaca* 2, no. 2 (1986): 87–92.

Bori, Pier Cesare. "'Date a Cesare quel che è di Cesare' . . . (Mt 22, 21): Linee di storia dell'interpretazione antica." *Cristianesimo nella storia* 7 (1986): 451–64.

Bornkamm, Günther. "Gesetz und Natur: Röm 2, 14–16." In *Gesammelte Aufsätze,* vol. 2: *Studien zur Antike und Urchristentum,* 93–118. Munich: Kaiser, 1963.

———. "Wandelungen im alt- und neutestamentlichen Gesetzesverständnis." In *Gesammelte Aufzätze,* vol. 4: *Geschichte und Glaube.* pt. 2, 73–119. Munich: Kaiser, 1971.

Bottéro, Jean. *Mésopotamie: L'écriture, la raison et les dieux.* Paris: Gallimard, 1987. In English translation by Zainab Bahrani and Marc Van De Mieroop as *Mesopotamia: Writing, Reasoning, and the Gods.* Chicago: University of Chicago Press, 1992.

Bourel, Dominique. *Moses Mendelssohn: La naissance du judaïsme moderne.* Paris: Gallimard, 2004.

Brague, Rémi. *Aristote et la question du monde: Essai sur le contexte cosmologique et anthropologique de l'ontologie.* Paris: PUF, 1988.

———. "Athens, Jeruslem, Mecca: Leo Strauss' 'Muslim' Understanding of Greek Philosophy." *Poetics Today* 1, no. 19 (1998): 235–59.

———. "À tout péché miséricorde." *Revue catholique internationale Communio* 14 (1989): 18–27.

———. "Averroès et la *République*." In *Images de Platon et lectures de ses oeuvres: Les interprétations de Platon à travers les siècles,* ed. Ada Neschke-Hentschke, 99–114. Louvain and Paris: Peeters, 1998.

———. "Bible." In *Dictionnaire de philosophie politique,* 3rd ed., ed. Philippe Raynaud and Stéphane Rials, 62–69. Paris: PUF, 2003.

———. "Christianisme et liberté: Quelques remarques." In *Monothéismes et tolérance,* 87–95. Colloquium of the Centre international de recherche sur les Juifs de Maroc, under the direction of Michel Abitbol and Robert Assaraf. Paris: Albin Michel, 1998.

———. "Cosmological Mysticism: The Imitation of the Heavenly Bodies in Ibn Tufayl's *Hayy ibn Yaqzan.*" *Graduate Faculty Philosophy Journal,* New School for Social Research, New York, nos. 19/20 (1997): 91–102.

———. "Der Dschihad der Philosophen." In *Krieg im Mittalter,* ed. Hans-Henning Kortüm, 77–91. Berlin: Akademie Verlag, 2001.

———. "*Eorum praeclara ingenia*: Conscience de la nouveauté et prétention à la continuité chez Farabi et Maïmonide." In *Études de philosophie arabe,* proceedings of a conference, Bordeaux, 17–19 June 1994. *Bulletin d'études orientales* 48 (1996): 87–102.

———. *Europe, la voie romaine.* 3rd ed. Paris: Gallimard, 1999. In English translation by Samuel Lester as *Eccentric Culture: A Theory of Western Civilization.* South Bend, Ind.: St. Augustine's Press, 2002.

———. "L'impuissance du Verbe: Le Dieu qui a tout dit." *Diogène* 170 (1995): 49–74.

———. "Leo Strauss et Maïmonide." In *Maimonides and Philosophy: Papers Presented at the Sixth Jerusalem Philosophical Encounter, May 1985,* ed. Shlomo Pinès and Yirmihahu Yovel, 246–68. Dordrecht and Boston: Nijhoff, 1986.

———. "Maïmonide en français: Quelques ouvrages récents (1979–1996)." *Revue de Méta-physique et de Morale* 4 (1998): 585–603.

———. "Maimonides: Bibel als Philosophie." In *Philosophen des Mittelalters*, ed. Theo Kobusch, 96–110. Darmstadt: Primus, 2000.

———. "Un modèle médiéval de la subjectivité: La chair." In *Ibn Rochd, Maïmonide, saint Thomas, ou La filiation entre foi et raison: Le Colloque de Cordoue*, 36–62. Castelnau-le-Lez: Climats; Paris: Association freudienne internationale, 1994.

———. "Note sur la traduction arabe de la *Politique* d'Aristote: Derechef, qu'elle n'existe pas." In *Aristote politique: Études sur la Politique d'Aristote*, ed. Pierre Aubenque, 423–33. Paris: PUF, 1993.

———. "La porte de la nature: Note sur la nature et la loi selon Maïmonide." In *Maïmonide philosophe et savant*, ed. Tony Lévy, 193–208. Louvain: Peeters, 2004.

———. "Pour une topique de la morale chrétienne." *Le Supplément* 181 (1992): 91–116.

———. "Du prince au peuple: La sagesse politique dans la Bible." In *Le savoir du prince: Du Moyen Âge aux Lumières*, ed. Ran Halévi, 7–23. Paris: Fayard, 2002.

———. *La Sagesse du monde: Histoire de l'expérience humaine de l'univers*. Paris: Fayard, 1999; 2nd ed., Paris: Hachette, 2002. In English translation by Teresa Lavender Fagan as *The Wisdom of the World: The Human Experience of the Universe in Western Thought*. Chicago and London: University of Chicago Press, 2003.

———. "Le sérieux de l'incarnation." In *La France, l'Église, quinze siècles, déjà*, proceedings of a conference, ed. Marceau Long and François Monnier, 87–91. Geneva: Droz, 1997.

———. "Thomas d'Aquin et la 'loi divine': Notes sur *Summa contra Gentiles*, III, 113–129." *Le Trimestre psychanalytique* 1 (1995): 81–95.

———. "Trois regards musulmans sur la cité chrétienne." *Le Trimestre psychanalytique* 3 (1996): 17–28.

———. "Zur Vorgeschichte der Unterscheidung von Sein und Sollen." In *Die Normativität des Wirklichen: Über die Greuze zwischen Sein und Sollen, Festschift für Robert Spaemann*, ed. Thomas Buchheim, Rolf Schönberger, and Walter Schweidler, 21–34. Stuttgart: Klett-Cotta, 2002.

"Brethren of Purity." *Rasa'il Ihwan as-Safa'*. Edited by 'Abd Allāh Bustani. 4 vols. Beirut: Dar Beirut, 1937.

Brown, Peter. "Society and the Supernatural: A Medieval Change." *Daedalus* 104 (1975): 133–51.

Brunner, Otto. *Land und Herrschaft: Grundfragen der territorialen Verfassungsgeschichte Öster-reichs im Mittelalter*. 5th ed. Darmstadt: Wissenschaftliche Buchgesellschaft, 1965. In English translation from the 4th edition, revised, with an introduction, by Howard Kaminsky and James van Horn Melton as *Land and Lordship: Structures of Governance in Medieval Austria*. Philadelphia: University of Pennsylvania Press, 1992.

Brunner-Traut, Emma. *Frühformen der Erkenntnis: Aspektive im alten Ägypten*. 2nd ed. Darmstadt, Wissenschaftliche Buchgesellschaft, 1992. See my critical review in *Le temps des savoirs*, vol. 1: *La dénomination*, 2000, 251–54.

Brunschvig, Robert, and Gustav von Grunebaum. *Classicisme et déclin culturel dans l'histoire de l'Islam: Actes du symposium international d'histoire de la civilisation musulmane, Bordeaux, 25–29 juin 1956* (1957). Paris: Maisonneuve et Larose, 1977.

Buc, Philippe. *L'Ambiguïté du livre: Prince, pouvour et peuple dans les commentaires de la Bible au Moyen Âge*. Paris: Beauchesne, 1994.

Buccellatti, Giorgio. "Da Saul a Davide: Le origini della monarchia israelitica alla luce della storiografia contemporanea." *Bibbia e Oriente* 1 (1959): 99–128.

Buckley, J. J. "The Nizari Isma'ilites Abolishment of the Shari'a during the Great Resurrection of 1164 A.D. / 559 A.H." *Studia Islamica* 60 (1984): 137–65.

Buisson, Ludwig. "Die Entstehung des Kirchenrechts." *Zeitschrift der Savigny-Stiftung für Rechtsgeschichte, Kanonistische Abteilung* 52 (1966): 1–175.

al-Bukhari. *Sahīh.* Translated into French by Octave Victor Houdas and William Marçais as *Les traditions islamiques.* 4 vols. Paris: Leroux, 1903–14.

Bürgel, Johann Christoph. *Allmacht und Mächtigkeit: Religion und Welt im Islam.* Munich: Beck, 1991.

Burton, John. *The Collection of the Qu'rān.* Cambridge and New York: Cambridge University Press, 1977.

———. *An Introduction to the Hadith* (1977). Edinburgh: Edinburgh University Press, 1994.

Butterworth, Charles E. *Philosophy, Ethics and Virtuous Rule: A Study of Averroes' Commentary on Plato's "Republic."* Cairo papers in Social Science, vol. 9, monograph 1. Cairo: American University in Cairo Press, 1986.

———. "Political Islam: The Origins." In *The Annals of the American Academy of Political and Social Science,* no. 524 (1992), "Political Islam," ed. Charles E. Butterworth and I. William Zartman, 26–37.

Caetani, Leone. *Annali dell'islām.* 10 vols. Milan: Hoepli, 1905–26. Facsimile edition, Hildesheim and New York: Olms, 1972.

Cahen, Claude. "Note sur l'acceuil des chrétiens d'Orient à l'islam." *Revue de l'histoire des religions* 166 (1964): 51–58.

Calder, Norman. "The Barāhima: Literary Construct and Historical Reality." *Bulletin of the School of Oriental and African Studies* 57 (1994): 40–51.

———. *Studies in Early Muslim Jurisprudence.* Oxford: Clarendon Press, 1993.

Carmichael, Calum M. *The Spirit of Biblical Law.* Athens: University of Georgia Press, 1996.

Castoriadis, Cornelius. *Sur le "Politique" de Platon.* Paris: Éditions du Seuil, 1999.

Cazelles, Henri. "Dix paroles: Les origines du décalogue." In *Autour de l'Exode (Études),* 113–23. Paris: Gabalda, 1987.

Chabbi, Jacqueline. *Le Seigneur des Tribus: L'islam de Mahomet.* Paris: Noësis, 1997.

Chehata, Chafik. *Études de droit musulman.* 2 vols. Paris: PUF, 1971.

Chodorow, Stanley. *Christian Political Theory and Church Politics in the Mid-Twelfth Century: The Ecclesiology of Gratian's Decretum.* Berkeley and Los Angeles: University of California Press, 1972.

Chroust, Anton Hermann. "The Fundamental Ideas of St. Augustine's Philosophy of Law." *American Journal of Jurisprudence* 18 (1973): 57–79.

———. "The Philosophy of Law from St. Augustine to St. Thomas Aquinas." *New Scholasticism* 20 (1946): 26–71.

———. "The Philosophy of Law of St. Augustine." *Philosophical Review* 53 (1944): 195–202.

Cicero. *De finibus bonorum et malorum.* Translated by H. Rackham. LCL. Cambridge, Mass.: Harvard University Press; London: William Heinemann, 1983.

———. *De legibus.* Translated by Clinton Walker Keyes. LCL. Cambridge, Mass.: Harvard University Press; London: William Heinemann, 1943.

———. *De officiis.* Translated by Walter Miller. LCL. Cambridge, Mass.: Harvard University Press; London: William Heinemann, 1968.

Cohen, Hermann. *Religion der Vernunft aus dem Quellen des Judentums* (1919). Wiesbaden: Fourier, 1995.

Cohen, Mark R. *Jewish Self-Government in Medieval Egypt: The Origins of the Office of Head of the Jews, ca. 1065–1126.* Princeton: Princeton University Press, 1980.

Congar, Yves. "Le thème du 'don de la Loi' dans l'art paléochrétien." *Nouvelle Revue théologique* 84 (1962): 915–33.

Le Coran. Edited and translated into French by Denise Masson. Beirut: Dar al-Kitab al-Lubnani, n.d.

———. Translated into French by Régis Blachère. 3 vols. Paris: Maisonneuve, 1949–50. See also *Qur'an.*

Cortese, Ennio. *Il diritto nella storia medievale,* vol. 1: *L'alto medioevo;* vol. 2, *Il basso medioevo.* Rome: Il Cigno Galileo Galilei, 1995.

Courtenay, William J. "The Critique of Natural Causality in the Mutakallimun and Nominalism." *Harvard Theological Review* 55 (1973): 77–94.

Courtine, Jean-François. *Nature et empire de la loi: Études suaréziennes.* Paris: Vrin, 1999.

Crescas, Hasdai. *Light of the Lord* (in Hebrew). Edited by Shelomoh Yehonatan Yehudah Fisher. Jerusalem: Ramot, 1990.

Crone, Patricia. "Did al-Ghazālī Write 'A Mirror for Princes'? On the Authorship of the Nasîhat al-mulūk." *Jerusalem Studies in Arabic and Islam* 10 (1987): 167–91.

———. *Roman, Provincial and Islamic Law: The Origins of the Islamic Patronate.* Cambridge and New York: Cambridge University Press, 1987; new ed., 2002.

———. *Slaves on Horses: The Evolution of the Islamic Polity.* Cambridge and New York: Cambridge University Press, 1980.

Crone, Patricia, and Michael Cook. *Hagarism: The Making of the Islamic World.* Cambridge and New York: Cambridge University Press, 1977.

Crone, Patricia, and Martin Hinds. *God's Caliph: Religious Authority in the First Centuries of Islam.* Cambridge and New York: Cambridge University Press, 1986.

Crüsemann, Frank. *Der Widerstand gegen das Königstum: Die antiköniglichen Texte des Alten Testaments und der Kampf um den frühen israelitischen Staat.* Neukirchen-Vluyn: Neukirchener Verlag, 1978.

———. *Die Tora: Theologie und Sozialgeschischte des alttestamentlichen Gesetzes.* Munich: Kaiser, 1992. In English translation by Allan W. Mahnke as *The Torah: Theology and Social History of Old Testament Law.* Minneapolis: Fortress Press, 1996.

Crussol, Yolande de. *Le Rôle de la raison dans la réflexion éthique d'al-Muhāsibī: 'Aql et conversion chez al-Muhāsibī.* Paris: Consep, 2002.

Curtius, Ernst Robert. *Europäische Literatur und lateinisches Mittelalter* (1948). Berne: Francke, 1973. In English translation by Willard R. Trask as *European Literature and the Latin Middle Ages* (1953). Princeton: Princeton University Press, 1983, 1990.

Dagron, Gilbert. *Empereur et prêtre: Étude sur le "césaropapisme" byzantin.* Paris: Gallimard, 1996. In English translation as *Emperor and Priest: The Imperial Office in Byzantium.* Cambridge: Cambridge University Press, 2003.

Daiber, Hans. "The Ruler as Philosopher: A New Interpretation of al-Farabi's Views." In *Mededelingen der Koninklijke Nederlandse Akademie van Wetenschapen,* 5–18. Amsterdam: North Holland, 1986.

Dakhlia, Jocelyne. *Le Divan des rois: Le politique et le religieux dans l'islam.* Paris: Aubier, 1998.

Dante Alighieri. *De monarchia* (in Latin and German). Edited by Ruedi Imbach and Christoph Flüeler. Stuttgart: Reclam, 1989. In English translation by Prue Shaw as *Monarchy.* New York: Cambridge University Press, 1996.

Davidson, Herbert. "Maimonides' Shemonah Peraqim and Alfarabi's Fusūl al-Madani." *Proceedings of the American Academy for Jewish Research* 31 (1963): 33–50.

Davidson, Israel. *Saadia's Polemic against Hiwi al-Balkhi: A Fragment Edited from a Genizah Ms.* New York: Jewish Theological Seminary of America, 1915.

Décobert, Christian. *Le Mendiant et le combattant: L'institution de l'islam.* Paris: Éditions du Seuil, 1991.

Descartes, René. *Oeuvres.* Edited by Charles Adam and Paul Tannery (1897–1913). New ed., 2nd printing. 11 vols. Paris: Vrin, 1974–82.

Dienstag, Jacob I. "Natural Law in Maimonidean Thought and Scholarship (On *Mishneh Torah, Kings,* VIII, 11)." *Jewish Law Annual* 6 (1987): 64–77.

Di Matteo, Ignazio. "Il 'tarîf' od alterazione della Bibbia secondo i musulmani." *Bessarione* 26 (1922): 64–111, 223–60.

Djaït, Hichem. *La Grande Discorde: Religion et politique dans l'Islam des origines.* Paris: Gallimard, 1989.

Donahue, Charles. "The Interaction of Law and Religion in the Middle Ages." *Mercer Law Review* 31 (1980): 466–76.

———. "Malchus' Ear: Reflections on Classical Canon Law as a Religious Legal System." In *Lex et Romanitas: Essays for Alan Watson,* ed. Michael Hoeflich, 91–120. Berkeley: Robbins Collection, 2000.

Donner, Fred McGraw. *The Early Islamic Conquests.* Princeton: Princeton University Press, 1981.

Driver, Samuel Rolles. *Notes on the Hebrew Text and the Topography of the Books of Samuel.* 2nd ed. rev. Oxford: Clarendon Press, 1913.

Ducellier, Alain. *Les Byzantins: Histoire et culture.* Paris: Éditions du Seuil, 1988.

Dunlop, Douglas Morton. *The History of the Jewish Khazars.* Princeton: Princeton University Press, 1954. New York: Schocken, 1967.

Düring, Ingemar. *Aristotle in the Ancient Biographical Tradition.* Göteborg: Almqvist & Wiksell, 1957; New York: Garland, 1987.

Dvornik, Francis. *Early Christian and Byzantine Political Philosophy: Origins and Background.* 2 vols. Washington, D.C.: Dumbarton Oaks Studies, 1966.

Edmond, Michel-Pierre. *Le Philosophe roi: Platon et la politique.* Paris: Payot, 1991.

Ehrhardt, Arnold. *Politische Metaphysik von Solon bis Augustin.* 3 vols. Tübingen: Mohr, 1959–69.

Ellul, Jacques. "Loi et sacré, droit et divin: De la loi sacrée au droit divin." In *Le sacré: Études et recherches,* conference proceedings, ed. Enrico Castelli, 179–99. Paris: Aubier, 1974.

Emilia, Antonio d'. "Il diritto musulmano comparato con il bizantino dal punto di vista della tipologia del diritto." *Studia Islamica* 4 (1955): 57–76.

Eslin, Jean-Claude. *Dieu et le pouvoir: Théologie et politique en Occident.* Paris: Éditions du Seuil, 1999.

Ess, Josef van. "Some Fragments of the Mu'āradat al-Qur'ān Attributed to Ibn al-Muqaffa'." In *Studia Arabica et islamica: Festschrift für Ihsān 'Abbās,* ed. Wadādid al-Qādī, 151–63. Beirut: American University, 1981.

———. *Theologie und Gesellschaft in 2. und 3. Jahrhundert Hidschra: Eine Geschichte des religiösen Denkens im frühen Islam.* 6 vols. Berlin and New York: de Gruyter, 1991–97.

———. *Zwischen Hadît und Theologie: Studien zum Entstehen prädestinatianischer Überlieferung.* Berlin and New York: De Gruyter, 1975.

Falaturi, Abdoldjawad. "Das Fehlen einer Heilsgeschichte im Islam." *Miscellanea Medeaevalia,* no. 11 (1977), "Die Macht des Guten und Bösen," 72–80.

Falk, Ze'ev A. *Law and Religion: The Jewish Experience.* Jerusalem: Mesharim, 1981.

Fantappiè, Carlo. *Introduzione storica al diritto canonico.* Bologna: Il Mulino, 1999.

Fassò, Guido. "Dio e la natura presso i decretisti ed i glossatori." *Il diritto ecclesiastico* 67 (1956): 3–10.

Fattal, Antoine. *Le Statut légal des non-musulmans en pays d'Islam*. Beirut: Imprimerie Catholique, 1958.

Faur, José. "La doctrina de la ley natural en el pensamiento judio del medioevo." *Sefarad* 27 (1967): 239–68.

———. "The Origin of the Classification of Rational and Divine Commandments in Mediaeval Jewish Philosophy." *Augustinianum* 9 (1969): 299–304.

———. "The Source of the Obligatory Character of the Commandments in the Thought of Maimonides" (in Hebrew). *Tarbiz* 38 (1968): 43–53.

Figgis, John Neville. *The Divine Right of Kings* (1896). 2nd ed., Cambridge: Cambridge University Press, 1914; reprint, New York: Harper and Row, 1965.

———. *Political Thought from Gerson to Grotius: 1414–1625: Seven Studies* (1907). New York: Harper and Brothers, 1960.

Finkelstein, Louis. *Jewish Self-Government in the Middle Ages*. New York: Jewish Theological Seminary of America, 1924.

Fishbane, Michael. *Biblical Interpretation in Ancient Israel*. Oxford: Clarendon Press, 1985.

Fleischmann, Eugène. *Le Christianisme "mis à nu": La critique juive du christianisme*. Paris: Plon, 1970.

Flückiger, Felix. *Geschichte des Naturrechts*, vol. 1 (no further volumes published): *Altertum und Frühmittelalter*. Zollikon-Zurich: Evangelischer Verlag, 1954.

Foreville, Raymonde. "Le recours aux sources scriptuaires: À quel moment de l'histoire l'Écriture a-t-elle cessé d'être source directe du droit de l'Église?" *L'Année canonique* 21 (1977): 49–55.

Foucault, Michel. *Surveiller et punir: Naissance de la prison*. Paris: Gallimard, 1975. In English translation by Alan Sheridan as *Discipline and Punish: The Birth of the Prison*. New York: Pantheon, 1977.

Franck, Didier. *Nietzsche et l'ombre de Dieu*. Paris: PUF, 1998.

Frank, Richard M. "Reason and Revealed Law: A Sample of Parallels and Divergence." In *Recherches d'islamologie: Recueil d'articles offert à Georges C. Anawati et Louis Gardet par leurs collègues et amis*, 123–38. Louvain: Peeters, 1977.

Fränkel, Hermann. *Dichtung und Philosophie des frühen Griechentums: Eine Geschichte der griechischen Epik, Lyrik und Prosa bis zur Mitte des fünften Jahrhunderts* (1962). Munich: Beck, 1976. In English translation by Moses Hadas and James Willis as *Early Greek Poetry and Philosophy: A History of Greek Epic, Lyric, and Prose to the Middle of the Fifth Century*. New York: Harcourt, Brace Jovanovich, 1975.

Frantz, Alison. "Pagan Philosophers in Christian Athens." *Proceedings of the American Philosophical Society* 119 (1975): 29–38.

Friedrich, Hugo. *Die Rechtsmetaphysik der göttlichen Komödie: Francesca da Rimini*. Frankfurt: Klostermann, 1942.

Funkenstein, Amos. *Perceptions of Jewish History*. Berkeley and Los Angeles: University of California Press, 1993.

———. *Theology and the Scientific Imagination from the Late Middle Ages to the Seventeenth Century*. Princeton: Princeton University Press, 1986. In French translation by Jean-Pierre Rothschild as *Théologie et imagination scientifique du Moyen Âge au XVII siècle*. Paris: PUF, 1995.

Fustel de Coulanges. *La cité antique: Étude sur le culte, le droit, les institutions de la Grèce et de Rome* (1864). Paris: Flammarion, 1984. In English translation as *The Ancient City: A Study on the Religion, Laws, and Institutions of Greece and Rome*. Baltimore: Johns Hopkins University Press, 1980.

Gagnér, Sten. "Boniface VIII and Avicenna." In *Proceedings of the Second International Congress of Medieval Canon Law*, edited by Stephan Kuttner and J. Joseph Ryan, 261–79. Vatican City: S. Congregatio de seminariis et studiorum universitatibus, 1965.

———. *Studien zur Ideengeschichte der Gesetzgebung*. Stockholm: Almqvist & Wiksell, 1960.

Galston, Myriam. "Philosopher-King v. Prophet." *Israel Oriental Studies* 9 (1978): 204–18.

———. *Politics and Excellence: The Political Philosophy of Alfarabi*. Princeton: Princeton University Press, 1990.

———. "The Purpose of the Law according to Maimonides." *Jewish Quarterly Review* 69 (1978): 27–51.

———. "Realism and Idealism in Avicenna's Political Philosophy." *The Review of Politics* 41 (1979): 561–77.

Gandeul, Jean-Marie, and Robert Caspar. "Textes de la tradition musulmane concernant le *tahrīf* (falsification) des Écritures." *Islamochristiana* 6 (1980): 61–104.

García de la Fuente, Olegario. "Liturgias de entrada, normas de asilo o exhortaciones proféticas? A propósito de los Salmos 15 y 24." *Augustinianum* 9 (1969): 266–98.

García Gomez, Emilio. "Polémica religiosa entre Ibn Hazm y Ibn al-Nagrila." *Al-Andalus* 4 (1936/39): 7–23.

Gardet, Louis. *La Cité musulmane: Vie sociale et politique*. 3rd ed. Paris: Vrin, 1981.

———. *Dieu et la destinée de l'homme*. Les Grands Problèmes de la théologie musulmane, no. 9. Paris: Vrin, 1967.

Gauchet, Marcel. *Le Désenchantement du monde: Une histoire politique de la religion*. Paris: Gallimard, 1985. In English translation by Oscar Burge as *The Disenchantement of the World: A Political History of Religion*. Princeton: Princeton University Press, 1997.

———. *La Religion dans la démocratie: Parcours de la laïcité*. Paris: Gallimard, 1998.

Gaudemet, Jean. *Église et cité: Histoire du droit canonique*. Paris: Éditions du Cerf, 1994.

———. *La Formation du droit séculier et du droit de l'Église aux IVe et Ve siècles*. 2nd ed. Paris: Sirey, 1979.

———. *Les Sources du droit canonique, VIIIe–XXe siècle: Repères canoniques: Sources occidentales*. Paris: Éditions du Cerf, 1993.

———. *Les Sources du droit de l'Église en Occident du IIe au VIIe siècle*. Paris: Éditions du Cerf, 1985.

Genesis Rabbah: Midrash Bereshit Rabba. Critical edition with notes and commentary by Julius Theodor and Chanoch Albeck (in Hebrew). 2nd ed., with corrections. 3 vols. Jerusalem Wahrmann, 1965.

Gerson, Jean. *De vita spirituali animae*. In Gerson, *Oeuvres complètes*, ed. Palémon Glorieux, 3:113–202. 3 vols. Paris: Desclée, 1962.

Gersonides (Levi ben Geshom). *Mihamot ha-Shem* (The wars of the lord). Riva di Trento, 1560; Leipzig, 1866. In English translation by Seymour Feldman as *The Wars of the Lord*. 3 vols. Philadelphia: Jewish Publication Society of America, 1984–89.

al-Ghazali. *Al-Munqid min adalal (Erreur et délivrance)*. French translation, with an introduction and notes, by Farid Jabre. Beirut: Commission libanaise pour la traduction des chefs-d'oeuvre, 1969.

———. *Al-Mustafa min 'ilm al-usūl*. Edited by I. M. Ramadān. 2 vols. Beirut: Dar el-Arquam, n.d.

———. *Ihyā' 'ulūm al-Dīn* (Revival of the Religious Sciences). 5 vols. Beirut: Dar al-Kutub al-Ilmiyya, 1996.

———. *Streitschrift des Gazālī gegen die Batinijja-Sekte*. Edited by Ignaz Goldziher. Leiden: Brill, 1916.

———. *Die Streitschrift des Gazālī gegen die Ibāhīja im persichen Text*. Edited and translated by Otto Pretzl. Munich: Akademie der Wissenschaften Bayrischen, 1933.

Gigante, Marcello. *ΝΟΜΟΣ ΒΑΣΙΛΕΥΣ* [Nomos basileus]: *Con un appendice* (1956). Naples: Bibliopolis, 1993.

———, ed. *La scuola di Epicuro*. Naples: Bibliopolis, 1976.

Gimaret, Daniel. *La Doctrine d'Al-Ash'ar*. Paris: Éditions du Cerf, 1990.

———. *Les Noms divins en Islam: Exégèse lexicographique et théologique*. Paris: Éditions du Cerf, 1988.

Goetschel, Roland. *Isaac Abravanel, conseiller des princes et philosophe (1437–1508)*. Paris: Albin Michel, 1996.

Goitein, Salomon Dov Fritz. *Studies in Islamic History and Institutions*. Leiden: Brill, 1966.

Goldziher, Ignaz. *Gesammelte Schriften*. Edited by Joseph Desomogyi. 6 vols. Hildesheim: Olms, 1967–70.

———. *Muhammedanische Studien*. 2 vols. Halle: Niemeyer, 1889–90.

———. *Die Richtungen der islamischen Koranauslegung*. Leiden: Brill, 1920.

———. *Sur l'Islam: Origines de la théologie musulmane*. Paris: Desclée de Brouwer, 2003.

———. "Über muhammedanische Polemik gegen Ahl al-Kitāb" (1878). In *Gesammelte Schriften*, 2:1–47. Hildesheim: Olms, 1968.

———. *Die Zahiriten, ihr Lehrsystem und ihre Geschichte: Beitrag zur Geschichte der Muhammadanischen Theologie* (1884). Leipzig: Schulze; Hildesheim: Olds, 1967.

Golinski, Georg. *Das Wesen des Religionsgesetzes in der Philosophie des Bachja ibn Pakuda*. Inaugural diss. Würzburg and Berlin: Brandel, 1935.

Goodenough, Erwin R. *The Politics of Philo Judaeus: Practice and Theory*. New Haven: Yale University Press, 1938.

Grabmann, Martin. "Das Narurrecht der Scholastik von Gratian bis Thomas von Aquin" (1922–23). In *Mittelalterliches Geistesleben: Abhandlungen zur Geschichte der Scholastik und Mystik*, 1:65–103. Munich: Hueber, 1926; 3 vols. Hildesheim and New York: Olms, 1994.

Gräf, Erwin. "De Koran, Uit het Arbisch vertaalt door J. H. Kramers." Review of J. H. Kramers, *De taal van den Koran* (Leiden: Brill, 1940, 1956). *Oriens* 16 (1963): 364–68.

Gratian. *Decretum Magistri Gratiani*. Edited by A. L. Richter and E. Friedberg. Leipzig, 1879; *The Treatise on Laws (Decretum DD. 1–20)*, trans. Augustine Thompson, with *The Ordinary Gloss*, translation by James Gordley, introduction by Katherine Christensen. Washington, D.C.: Catholic University of America Press, 1993.

Greenberg, Moshe. "Jewish Conceptions of the Human Factor in Biblical Prophecy." In *Justice and the Holy: Essays in Honor of Walter Harrelson.*, ed. Douglas A. Knight and Peter J. Paris, 145–62. Atlanta: Scholars Press, 1989.

Griffiths, John Gwyn. *The Divine Verdict: A Study of Divine Judgement in the Ancient Religions*. Leiden and New York: Brill, 1991.

Grossi, Paolo. *L'ordine giuridico medievale*. Bari: Laterza, 1995.

Grunebaum, Gustave E. von. *L'identité culturelle de l'Islam*. Translated by Roger Stuvéras. Paris: Gallimard, 1973. Original German edition, *Studien zum Kulturbild und Selbsverstandnis des Islam*. Stuttgart: Artemis, 1969.

———. *Medieval Islam: A Study in Cultural Orientation*. Chicago: University of Chicago Press, 1946, 1953.

Guilland, Rodolphe. "Le droit divin à Byzance." In *Études byzantines*, 207–32. Paris: PUF, 1959.

Gundert, Hermann. "ΘΕΙΟΣ im politischen Denken Platons." In *Politeia und Res Publica:*

Beiträge zum Verständnis von Politik, Recht und Staat in der Antike: Dem Andenken Rudolf Starks gewidmet, ed. Peter Steinmetz, 91–107. Wiesbaden: Steiner, 1969.

Gutas, Dmitri. "Ethische Schriften im Islam." In *Neues Handbuch der Literaturwissenschaft*, ed. Klaus von See, vol. 5: *Orientalisches Mittelalter*, ed. W. Heinrichs, 346–65. Wiesbaden: Aula, 1990.

———. "Galen's Synopsis of Plato's Laws and Fārābī's Talkhīṣ." In *The Ancient Tradition in Christian and Islamic Hellenism: Studies on the Transmission of Greek Philosophy and Sciences, dedicated to H. J. Drossart Lulofs on His Ninetieth Birthday*, ed. Gerhard Endress and Remke Kruk, 101–19. Leiden: Research School CNWS, 1997.

Hadas-Lebel, Mireille. *Hillel: Un sage au temps de Jésus*. Paris: Albin Michel, 1999.

Halevi, Jehuda. *Kitāb al-Radd wa-ʾl-dadīl fī ʾl-dīn al-dhalīl: The Book of Refutation and Proof of the Despised Faith: The Book of the Khazars (known as the Kuzari)* (Hebrew). Edited by David Hartwig Baneth and Haggai Ben-Shammai. Jerusalem: Magnes, 1977. In French translation as *Le Kuzari: Apologie de la religion méprisée*, translated from the original Arabic compared with the Hebrew version and accompanied by an introduction and notes by Charles Touati. Louvain and Paris: Peeters, 1994.

Hallaq, Wael B. *A History of Islamic Legal Theories: An Introduction to the Sunnī uṣūl al-fiqh*. Cambridge: Cambridge University Press, 1997.

———. "Was al-Shāfiʿī the Master Architect of Islamic Jurisprudence?" *International Journal of Middle East Studies* 25 (1993): 587–605.

———. "Was the Gate of Ijtihad Closed?" *International Journal of Middle East Studies* 16 (1984): 3–41.

Harnack, Adolf von. *Marcion: Das Evangelium vom fremden Gott* (1924). In French translation by Bernard Lauret as *L'Évangile de Dieu étranger: Contribution à l'histoire de la fondation de l'Église catholique*. Paris: Éditions du Cerf, 2003.

Harvey, Steven. "The Hebrew Translation of Averroes' Prooemium to His Long Commentary on Aristotle's Physics." *Proceedings of the American Academy for Jewish Research* 52 (1985): 55–84.

Harvey, Warren Zeev. "Between Political Philosophy and Halakhah in the Teachings of Maimonides" (in Hebrew). *Iyyun* 29 (1981): 198–212.

———. "On Averroes, Maimonides, and the Ideal State" (in Hebrew). In *Reflections on Philosophical Themes: Essays presented on the Evening in Honor of S. Pines, on the Occasion of His 80th Birthday* (in Hebrew), 19–31. Jerusalem: Israeli Academy of Sciences and Humanities, 1992.

Heinemann, Issak. "Die Lehre vom ungeschriebenen Gesetz im jüdischen Schrifttum." *Hebrew Union College Annual* 4 (1927): 149–71.

———. *La Loi dans la pensée juive*. French adaptation of the following by Charles Touati. Paris: Albin Michel, 1962.

———. *Philons griechische und jüdische Bildung: Kulturvergleichende Untersuchungen zu Philons Darstellung der jüdischen Gesetze* (1932). Hildesheim: Olms, 1962.

Heinimann, Felix. *Nomos und Physis: Herkunft und Bedeutung einer Antithese im griechischen Denken des 5. Jahrhunderts* (1945). Darmstadt: Wissenschaftliche Buchgesellschaft, 1972.

Helmholz, Richard H. *The Spirit of Classical Canon Law*. Athens: University of Georgia Press, 1996.

Hengel, Martin. *War Jesus Revolutionär?* (1970). In French translation by C. V. Schönbrun and K. Kernal as *Jésus et la violence révolutionnaire*. Paris: Éditions du Cerf, 1973. In English translation as *Was Jesus a Revolutionist?* Philadelphia: Fortress Press, 1971.

———. *Die Zeloten: Untersuchungen zur jüdischen Freiheitsbewegung in der Zeit von Herodes I. bis 70 n. Chr.*, 2nd ed. Leiden and Cologne: Brill, 1976. In English translation by David Smith as *The Zealots: Investigation into the Freedom Movement in the Period from Herod I until 70 A.D.* Edinburgh: T. and T. Clark, 1989.

Heschel, Abraham Joshua. *Theology of Ancient Judaism* (in Hebrew). 2 vols. London and New York: Soncino Press. 1962, 1965.

Hirzel, Rudolf. *Agraphos Nomos.* Leipzig: Teubner, 1900.

———. *Themis, Dike und Verwandtes: Ein Beitrag zur Geschichte der Rechtsidee bei den Griechen.* Leipzig: Hierzel, 1907; Hildesheim: Olms, 1966.

Hobbes, Thomas. *Leviathan.* Edited by Michael Oakeshott. Oxford: Blackwell, 1957.

Hooker, Richard. *Of the Laws of Ecclesiastical Polity*, vol. 1 (Books I–IV). Edited by Christopher Morris. London: Dent; New York: Dutton, 1963.

Hoyland, Robert G. *Seeing Islam as Others Saw It: A Survey and Evaluation of Christian, Jewish and Zorostrian Writings on Early Islam.* Princeton: Darwin Press, 1997.

Humphreys, R. Stephen. *Islamic History: A Framework for Inquiry.* Rev. ed. Princeton: Princeton University Press, 1991.

Ibn Abī al-Rabīʿ. *The Political Philosophy of Ibn Abī al-Rabīʿ: With an Edition of His Sulūk al-Mālik fī Tadbīr al-Mamālik* (in Arabic). Edited by Naji Takriti. Beirut: Al-Andalus, 1983.

Ibn Bājjah. *Opera Metaphysica.* Edited and translated by Majid Fakhry. 2nd ed. Beirut: Dar an-Nahar, 1991.

———. *Philosophical Writings of Ibn Bājja* (in Arabic). Edited by Jamā al-Dīn ʿAlawī. Beirut: Dar al-Thaqāfah, 1983.

———. *El Régimen del solitario.* Translated by Joaquín Lomba Fuentes. Madrid: Trotta, 1997. In English translation by Miguel Asín Palacios as *Avempace, Conduct of the Solitary.* Madrid: n.p., 1946.

Ibn Daoud. *The Exalted Faith.* Translated, with commentary, by Norbert M. Samuelson, translation edited by Gershon Weiss. Rutherford, N.J.: Fairleigh Dickinson University Press; London: Associated University Presses, 1986.

Ibn Ezra, Abraham. *Reader: Annotated Texts with Introductions and Commentaries* (in Hebrew). Edited and translated by Israel Levin. New York and Tel-Aviv: I. Matz Hebrew Classics; I. E. Kiev Library Foundation, 1985.

Ibn Hazm. *Al-Fisal fī al-Milal wa-lʿahwāʾ wa-l-nihal.* Edited by Abul Kalem Shams ud-Dīn. 3 vols. Beirut: Dar al-Kutub al-Ilmiyya, 1999.

Ibn Hishām. *Al-Sirat al-Nabawiyyah li Ibn Hisham.* Edited by Mustafa Saqqā et al. 4 vols. Beirut: Dār Ihyāʾ al-Turath al-Arabī, n.d. In English translation by Alfred Guillaume as *The Life of Muhammad.* London: Oxford University Press, 1955, 1997.

Ibn Kammuna. *Saʿd b. Mansūr ibn Kammūnaʾs Examination of the Inquiries into the Three Faiths: A Thirteenth-Century Essay in Comparative Religion.* Edited and translated by Moshe Perlmann. Berkeley and Los Angeles: University of California Press, 1967. *Ibn Kammuna's Examination of the Three Faiths: A Thirteenth-Century Essay in the Comparative Study of Religions.* Translated by Moshe Perlmann. Berkeley and Los Angeles: University of California Press, 1971.

Ibn Khaldūn. *Prolégomènes d'Ebn Khaldoun, texte arabe publié d'après les manuscrits de la Bibliothèque impériale* (1858). Edited by Étienne Quatremère. 3 vols. Beirut: Librairie du Liban, 1996. In English translation by Franz Rosenthal as *The Muqaddimah: An Introduction to History.* 3 vols. New York: Pantheon Books, 1958.

Ibn al-Muqaffaʿ. *Conseilleur du Calife: Ibn al-Muqaffaʿ.* Edited by Charles Pellat. Paris: Maisonneuve et Larose, 1976.

Ibn Taymiyya. *Le Traité de droit public d'Ibn Taimīya: Traduction annotée de la Siyāsa sharʿīya.* Edited and translated by Henri Laoust. Beirut: Institut Français de Damas, 1948.

Ibn Tufayl. *Hayy ben Yaqdhān: Roman philosophique.* Arabic text with French translation by Léon Gauthier. 2nd ed. Beirut: Imprimerie Catholique, 1948.

Idel, Moshe. "The Concept of the Torah in Heikhalot Literature and Its Metamorphoses in Kabbalah" (in Hebrew). *Jerusalem Studies in Jewish Thought* 1 (1981): 23–84.

———. "*Deus sive Natura:* The Metamorphosis of a Dictum from Maimonides to Spinoza." In *Maimonides and the Sciences,* ed. Robert S. Cohen and Hillel Levine, 87–110. Dordrecht: Kluwer, 2000.

———. "Infinities of Torah in Kabbalah." In *Midrash and Literature,* ed. Godfrey H. Hartman and Sanford Budick, 141–57. New Haven: Yale University Press, 1986.

———. *Maïmonide et la mystique juive.* Translated from the Hebrew by Charles Mopsik. Paris: Éditions du Cerf, 1991.

Jackson, Bernard S. "The Concept of Religious Law in Judaism." In *Aufstieg und Niedergang der Römischen Welt: Geschichte und Kultur Roms im Spiegel der neuren Forschung,* vol. 2: *Principat. Religion,* ed. Hildegard Temporini and Wolfgang Haase (Judentum: allgemeines; palästinisches Judentum), 33–52. Berlin and New York: De Gruyter, 1979.

Jadaane, Fehmi. "Les conditions socio-culturelles de la philosophie islamique." *Studia Islamica* 38 (1973): 5–60.

Jaeger, Werner. "Solons Eunomie" (1926). In *Scripta Minora,* 1:315–37. Rome: Storia e Letteratura, 1960.

Jambet, Christian. *La Grande Résurrection d'Alamût: Les formes de la liberté dans le shīʿisme ismaélien.* Lagrasse: Verdier, 1990.

Jeffery, Arthur. *The Foreign Vocabulary of the Qurʾān.* Gaekwad Oriental Series, no. 79. Baroda: Oriental Institute, 1938; Lahore: al-Biruni, 1977.

———. *The Qurʾān as Scripture.* New York: Russel F. Moore, 1952.

Jeremias, Jörg. *Das Königtum Gottes in den Psalmen: Israels Begegnung mit dem kanaanäischen Mythos in den Jahwe-König-Psalmen.* Göttingen: Vandenhoeck und Ruprecht, 1987.

Johansen, Baber. *Contingency in a Sacred Law: Legal and Ethical Norms in the Muslim Fiqh.* Leiden and Boston: Brill, 1999.

John of Salisbury. *Ioannis Saresberiensis episcopi Carnotensis Policratici sive De nugis curialium et vestigiis philosophorum libri VIII.* [*Policraticus*]. Edited by Clement J. Webb. 2 vols. Oxford: Clarendon Press, 1909.

Josephus, Flavius. *Contre Apion.* Text established and annotated by Théodore Reinach and translated by Léon Blum. Paris: CUF, 1930. In English translation by H. St. J. Thackeray as *The Life; Against Apion.* Vol. 1 of *Josephus.* 9 vols. LCL. Cambridge, Mass.: Harvard University Press; London: William Heinemann, 1956.

Jospe, Raphael. *Torah and Sophia: The Life and Thought of Shem Tov ibn Falaquera.* Cincinnati: Hebrew Union College Press, 1988.

Justin Martyr. *Dialogue avec Tryphon.* Greek with French translation, introductions, notes, and index by Georges Archambault. 2 vols. Paris: Picard, 1909. In English translation by Thomas B. Falls as *Dialogue with Trypho,* revised, with a new introduction by Thomas P. Halton, edited by Michael Slusser. Washington, D.C.: Catholic University of America Press, 2003.

Justinian. *Corpus Juris Civilis,* vol. 3: *Novellae.* Edited by Rudolf Schöll and Wilhelm Kroll. 6th ed. Hildesheim: Weidmann, 1989–93.

Juwaynī. *El-Irchad.* Edited and translated by Jean-Dominique Luciani. Paris: Leroux, 1938.

Kant, Immanuel. *Die Religion innerhalb der Grenzen der blossen Vernunft.* In Kant, *Werke,*

4:647–879. In English translation, with introduction and notes, by Theodore M. Greene and Hoyt H. Hudson as *Religion within the Limits of Reason Alone.* London: Open Court, 1934; New York: Harper, 1960.

———. *Werke in sechs Bänden.* Edited by Wilhelm Weischedel. Darmstadt: Wissenschaftliche Buchgesellschaft, 1983.

Kantorowicz, Ernst H. *The King's Two Bodies: A Study in Mediaeval Political Theology.* Princeton: Princeton University Press, 1957; new ed., 1997. In French translation by Jean-Philippe Genet and Nicole Genet as *Les Deux Corps du roi: Essai sur la théologie politique au Moyen Age.* Paris: Gallimard, 1989.

Kasher, Hanna. "Maimonides' Philosophical Division of the Laws" (in Hebrew). *Hebrew Union College Annual* 56 (1985): 1–7.

Keddie, Nikkie R. "Symbol and Sincerity in Islam." *Studia Islamica* 19 (1963): 27–63.

Kern, Fritz. *Gottesgnadentum und Widerstandsrecht im früheren Mittelalter: Zur Entwicklungsgeshichte der Monoarchie.* Edited by Rudolf Buchner. 7th ed. Darmstadt: Wissenschaftliche Buchgesellschaft, 1960. In English translation, with an introduction, by S. B. Chrimes as *Kingship and Law in the Middle Ages,* vol. 1: *The Divine Right of Kings and the Right of Resistance in the Early Middle Ages,* vol. 2: *Law and Constitution in the Middle Ages.* Oxford: Blackwell, 1939.

al-Kindī. *Rasāʾil al-Kindī al-falsafiyah Haqqaqahā.* Edited by Muhammad ʾAbd al-Hādīʾ Abū Ridah. 2 vols. Cairo: Dar al-Fikr al-ʿArabī, 1950, 1953.

Kister, Moshe J. "*Haddithu an hani israʾila wa-la baraja:* A Study of an Early Tradition." *Israel Oriental Studies* 2 (1972): 215–39.

Klein-Braslavi, Sara. *King Solomon and Philosophical Esotericism in the Thought of Maimonides* (in Hebrew). Jerusalem: Magnes, 1996.

Kluxen, Wolfgang. *Philosophische Ethik bei Thomas von Aquin* (1964). 3rd ed. Hamburg: Meiner, 1998.

Koch, Klaus. "Tempeleinlassliturgien und Dekaloge." In *Studien zur Theologie der alttestamentlichen Überlieferungen,* ed. Rolf Rendtorff and Klaus Koch, 45–60. Neukirchen-Vluyn: Neukirchener Verlag, 1961.

Kohlbert, Etan. "Some Ināmī-Shīʿī Views on *taqiyya.*" *Journal of the American Oriental Society* 95 (1975): 395–402.

Kojève, Alexandre. *Esquisse d'une phénoménologie du droit: Exposé provisoire.* Paris: Gallimard, 1981. In English translation, with an introductory essay and notes, by Bryan-Paul Frost and Robert Howse, as *Outline of a Phenomenology of Right.* Lanham, Md.: Rowman and Littlefield, 2000.

Kollwitz, Johannes. "Christus als Lehrer und die Gesetzesübergabe an Petrus in der konstantinischen Kunst Roms." *Römische Quartalschrift für christliche Altertumskunde und für Kirchengeschichte* 44 (1936): 45–66.

Koran. See *Le Coran; Qurʾan.*

Kraemer, Joel L. "Alfarabi's *Opinions of the Virtuous City* and Maimonides' *Foundations of the Law.*" In *Studia Orientalia Memoriae D. H. Baneth dedicatae,* 107–53. Jerusalem: Magnes, 1979.

———. "Apostates, Rebels and Brigands." In "Religion and Government in the World of Islam," ed. Joel L. Kraemer and I. Alon. *Israel Oriental Studies* 10 (1980): 34–73.

———. *Humanism in the Renaissance of Islam: The Cultural Revival during the Buyid Age* (1986). 2nd ed., rev., Leiden: Brill, 1992.

———. "The Jihād of the Falāsifa." *Jerusalem Studies in Arabic and Islam* 10 (1987): 288–324.

———. "Namus and Shariʿa in Maimonides' Doctrine"(in Hebrew). *Teʿuda* 4 (1986): 288–324.

———. "Naturalism and Universalism in Maimonides' Political and Religious Thought." In *Me'ah She'arim: Studies in Medieval Jewish Spiritual Life in Memory of Isador Twersky*, ed. Ezra Fleischer et al., 47–81. Jerusalem: Magnes, 2001.

———. *Philosophy in the Renaissance of Islam: Abū Sulaymān al-Sijistānī and His Circle*. Leiden: Brill, 1986.

Kramer, Samuel Noah. "Ur-Nammu Law Code." *Orientalia* 23 (1954): 40–51.

Kreisel, Howard T. *Maimonides' Political Thought: Studies in Ethics, Law and the Human Ideal*. Albany: State University of New York Press, 1999. See my critical review in *Revue des études juives* 160 (2001): 525–26.

Kühn, Ulrich. *Via caritatis: Theologie des Gesetzes bei Thomas von Aquin*. Göttingen: Vandenhoeck & Ruprecht, 1965.

Kühneweg, Uwe. *Das neue Gesetz: Christus als Gesetzgeber und Gesetz: Studien zu den Anfängen christlicher Naturrechtslehre im 2. Jahrhundert*. Marbourg: Elwert, 1993.

Lachterman, David. "Torah and Logos." *The St. John's Review* 42 (1994): 5–25.

Laks, André. "L'utopie législative de Platon." *Revue philosophique* 4 (1991): 417–28.

Lambrecht, Jan. *"Eh bien! Moi je vous dis": Le disours programme de Jésus (Mt 5–7; Luc 6, 20–49)*. French translation from the Dutch. Paris: Éditions du Cerf, 1986.

Lambton, Ann K. S. *State and Government in Medieval Islam: An Introduction to the Study of Islamic Political Theory: The Jurists*. Oxford: Oxford University Press, 1981.

Laoust, Henri. *La Politique de Ghazali*. Paris: Geuthner, 1970.

Lapidus, Ira M. "The Separation of State and Religion in the Development of Early Islamic Society." *International Journal of Middle East Studies* 6 (1975): 365–85.

Latte, Kurt. *Heileges Recht: Untersuchungen zur Geschichte der sakralen Rechtsformen in Griechenland* (1920). Aalen: Scientia, 1964.

Laudage, Johannes. *Gregorianische Reform und Investiturstreit*. Darmstadt: Wissenschaftliche Buchgesellschaft, 1993.

Lazarus-Yafeh, Hava. *Intertwined Worlds: Medieval Islam and Bible Criticism*. Princeton: Princeton University Press, 1992.

———. *Studies in Al-Ghazzālī*. Jerusalem: Magnes, 1975.

Leaman, Oliver. "Ibn Bājja on Society and Philosophy." *Der Islam* 57 (1980): 129–19.

Leben, Charles. "L'interprétation du culte sacrificiel chez Maïmonide." *Pardès* 14 (1991): 129–45.

———. "La question du droit naturel dans le judaïsme." In *Libertés, justice, tolérance: Mélanges en hommage au Doyen Gérard Cohen-Jonathan*, 1109–23. Brussels: Bruylant, 2004.

Legendre, Pierre. *Le Crime du caporal Lortie: Traité sur le Père* (1989). Paris: Flammarion, 2000.

———. *Le Désir politique de Dieu: Étude sur les montages de l'État et du droit*. Paris: Fayard, 1988.

———. *Dieu au miroir: Étude sur l'institution des images*. Paris: Fayard, 1994.

———. *L'Empire de la vérité: Introduction aux espaces dogmatiques industriels*. Paris: Fayard, 1983.

Lerner, Ralph. *Maimonides' Empire of Light: Popular Enlightenment in an Age of Belief*. Chicago: University of Chicago Press, 2000.

———. "Maimonides' Governance of the Solitary." In *Perspectives on Maimonides: Philosophical and Historical Studies*, ed. Joel L. Kraemer, 33–46. Oxford and New York: Oxford University Press, 1994.

———. "Natural Law in Albo's Book of Roots." In *Ancients and Moderns: Essays on the Tradi-*

tion of Political Philosophy in Honor of Leo Strauss, ed. Joseph Cropsey, 132–47. New York: Basic Books, 1964.

Lettre d'Aristée à Philocrate. Introduction, critical text, translation, and notes, with a complete index of Greek words by André Pelletier. SC, no. 89. Paris: Éditions du Cerf, 1962.

Levi, Lionello. "Cinque lettere inedite di Emanuele Moscopulo (Cod. Marc. CL. XI, 15)." *Studi italiani di filologia classica* 10 (1902): 55–72.

Levin, Christoph. "Das vorstaatliche Israel." *Zeitschrift für Theologie und Kirche* 97 (2000): 385–403.

Lewis, Bernard. *The Political Language of Islam.* Chicago: University of Chicago Press, 1988. In French translation by O. Guitard as *Le Langage politique de l'islam.* Paris: Gallimard, 1988.

Lewis, C. S. *The Abolition of Man, or Reflections on Education with Reference to the Teaching in the Upper Forms of Schools* (1943). New York: Macmillan, 1947.

Liedke, Gerhard. *Gestalt und Bezeichnung alttestamentlicher Rechtssätze: Eine formgeschichtlich-terminologische Studie.* Neukirchen-Vluyn: Neukirchener Verlag, 1971.

Locke, John. *The Second Treatise of Government (An Essay Concerning the True Original, Extent and End of Civil Government)* and *A Letter Concerning Toleration.* Edited by J. W. Gough. Oxford: Blackwell, 1966.

Lohfink, Norbert. "Der Begriff des Gottesreichs vom Alten Testament her gesehen." In *Unterwegs zur Kirche: Alttestamentliche Konzeptionen,* ed. Josef Schreiner, 33–86. Freiburg im Breisgau: Herder, 1987.

Lombard, Maurice. *L'Islam dans sa première grandeur (VIIIe–XIe siècle).* Paris: Flammarion, 1971. In English translation by Joan Spencer as *The Golden Age of Islam.* Amsterdam: North-Holland; New York: Elsevier, 1975.

Long, A. A., and D. N. Sedley. *The Hellenistic Philosophers,* vol. 1: *Translations of the Principal Sources, with Philosophical Commentary.* Cambridge and New York: Cambridge University Press, 1987.

Lorberbaum, Menachem. *Politics and the Limits of Law: Secularizing the Political in Medieval Jewish Thought.* Stanford: Stanford University Press, 2001.

Lorton, David. "The King and the Law." *Varia Aegyptiaca* 2, no. 1 (1986).

———. "The Treatment of Criminals in Ancient Egypt through the New Kingdom." *Journal of the Economic and Social History of the Orient* 20 (1977): 2–64.

Lottin, Odon. *Le Droit naturel chez saint Thomas d'Aquin et ses prédécesseurs.* 2nd ed. Bruges: Beyaert, 1931.

———. *Psychologie et morale aux XIIe et XIIIe siècles,* vol. 2, pt. 1: *Problèmes de morale* (1948). 6 vols. in 7. Louvain: Abbaye du Mont-César, 1942–49.

Lubac, Henri de. *La Rencontre du bouddhisme et de l'Occident.* Paris: Aubier, 1952.

Luscombe, D. E. "Natural Morality and Natural Law." In *The Cambridge History of Later Medieval Philosophy,* ed. Norman Kretzmann et al., 705–19. Cambridge: Cambridge University Press, 1989.

Luxenberg, Christoph. *Die syro-aramäische Lesart des Koran: Ein Beitrag zur Entschlüsslung der Koransprache.* Berlin: Das Arabische Buch, 2000. See my critical review, "Le Coran, sortir du cercle?" *Critique* 671 (2003): 232–51.

Machiavelli, Niccolò. *Tutte le opere.* Edited by Francesco Flora and Carlo Cordiè. 2 vols. Milan: Mondadori, 1968.

Macy, Jeffrey. "The Rule of Law and the Rule of Wisdom in Plato, al-Farabi and Maimonides." In *Studies in Islamic and Jewish Traditions,* ed. William M. Brinner and Stephen David Ricks, 1:205–32. 2 vols. Atlanta: Scholars Press, 1986, 1989.

Maddox, Graham. *Religion and the Rise of Democracy.* London: Routledge, 1996.

Mahdi, Muhsin. "Al-Fārābī." In *Dictionary of Scientific Biography,* ed. Charles Coulston Gillispie, 4:523a–526b. New York: Scribners, 1970–.

———. "Alfarabi against Philoponus." *Journal of Near Eastern Studies* 26 (1967): 233–60.

———. "Alfarabi's Imperfect State." *Journal of the American Oriental Society* 110 (1990): 691–726.

———. *La Cité vertueuse d'Alfarabi: La fondation de la philosophie politique en Islam.* Translated by F. Zabbal. Paris: Albin Michel, 2000. In English translation as *Alfarabi and the Foundation of Islamic Political Philosophy.* Chicago: University of Chicago Press, 2001.

———. *Ibn Khaldūn's Philosophy of History: A Study in the Philosophic Foundation of the Science of Culture.* London: Allen and Unwin, 1957. Chicago: University of Chicago Press, 1964.

Maier, Hans. *Kritik der politischen Theologie.* Einsiedeln: Johannes Verlag, 1970.

Maier, Johann. "'Gesetz' und 'Gnade' im Wandel des Gesetzes-verständnisses der nachtalmudischen Zeit." *Judaica* 25 (1969): 64–176.

Maimonides. *Commentary on the Mishnah* (in Arabic). Edited by Joseph Qāfih. 6 vols. Jerusalem, 1968.

———. *Guide for the Perplexed* (in Arabic). Edited by Issachar Joël. Jerusalem: Junovitch, 1929. In French translation with notes by Solomon Munk as *Guide des égarés.* 3 vols. Paris: A. France, 1856–66; Paris: Maisonneuve, 1970. In English translation by Shlomo Pines, with introduction and notes, as *The Guide of the Perplexed.* Introductory essay by Leo Strauss. Chicago: University of Chicago Press, 1963.

———. *Igrot: Letters* (Letter to the Yemen; Treatise on the Resurrection; Letter on Persecution). Edited and translated by Josef Qāfih. Jerusalem: Mosad Rav Kook, 1994. Selected letters in English translation, edited and with notes by Leon D. Stitskin, as *Letters of Maimonides.* New York: Yeshiva University Press, (5737) 1977.

———. *Introductions to the Mishnah* (General introduction to the Mishnah; Introduction to the Heleq chapter; Introduction to the Pirke Avot; in Arabic). Edited by I. Shaylat. Ma'aley Adumim, 1991.

———. *Livre des commandements.* Translated into French by A. Gellner. Lausanne: L'Âge de l'homme, 1987. In English translation, with commentary, by Joseph Qāfih as *Sefer Hamitzvot: Book of Commandments.* Jerusalem: Mossad Harav Kook, 1971.

———. *Maimonides' Treatise on Resurrection.* Edited and translated by Joshua Finkel. New York: American Academy for Jewish Research, 1939.

———. *Mishneh Torah.* Edited by M. D. Rabinovitch, 12 vols. Jerusalem: Mosad Rav Kook, 1959–.

———. *Mishneh Torah, The Book of Knowledge.* Edited by Moses Hyamson. Jerusalem and New York: Feldheim, 1981. In French translation as *Livre de Connaissance* by Valentin Nikiprowetsky and André Zaoui. Paris: PUF, 1961; 2nd ed., 1990. Also in English translation by H. M. Russell and J. Weinberg as *The Book of Knowledge: From the Mishneh Torah of Maimonides.* New York: Ktav, 1983.

———. *Traité d'Éthique.* Translated from the Arabic, with an introduction and notes, by Rémi Brague. Paris: Desclée de Brouwer, 2001. In English translation by Craig Walton, with an introduction, as *Treatise on Ethics (1684).* Dordrecht, Boston, and London: Kluwer, 1993.

———. *Traité de Logique.* Translated from the Arabic, with an introduction and notes, by Rémi Brague. Paris: Desclée de Brouwer, 1996. In English translation by Israel Efros as *Maimonides' Treatise on Logic.* New York: American Academy for Jewish Research, 1938.

Maine, Henry Sumner. *Ancient Law: Its Connection with the Early History of Society and Its*

Relation to Modern Ideas (1861). Edited by J. H. Morgan. London: Dent, 1960; 14th ed., Holmes Beach, Fla.: Gaunt, 1999.

Makdisi, George. *Ibn ʾAqīl et la résurgence de l'Islam traditionaliste au XIe siècle, Ve siècle de l'Hégire.* Damascus: Institut Français de Damas, 1963. In English translation as *Ibn ʾAqil: Religion and Culture in Classical Islam.* Edinburgh: Edinburgh University Press, 1997.

Malebranche, Nicholas. *Oeuvres.* Edited by Geneviève Rodis-Lewis. 2 vols. Paris: Gallimard, 1979, 1992.

Manent, Pierre. *La Cité de l'homme.* Paris: Fayard, 1994. In English translation by Marc A. LePain as *The City of Man.* Princeton: Princeton University Press, 1998.

———. *Cours familier de philosophie politique.* Paris: Fayard, 2001.

———. *Histoire intellectuelle du libéralisme: Dix leçons.* Paris: Calmann-Lévy, 1987. In English translation by Rebecca Balinsky as *An Intellectual History of Liberalism.* Princeton: Princeton University Press, 1994.

Marquet, Yves. *La Philosophie des Ihwan al-Safaʾ: L'imam et la société.* Dakar: Faculté des Lettres, 1973.

Marsilius of Padua. *Der Verteidiger des Friedens (Defensor Pacis).* Edited by Horst Kusch on the basis of the translation by Walter Kunzmann. 2 vols. Darmstadt: Wissenschaftliche Buchgesellschaft, 1958. In English translation, with an introduction, by Alan Gewirth, as *Defensor Pacis.* Toronto: University of Toronto Press, in association with the Medieval Academy of America, 1980.

Marx, Alexander. "Texts by and about Maimonides." *Jewish Quarterly Review,* n.s. 25, no. 4 (1935): 371–428.

Massignon, Louis. *La Passion d'al-Husayn Ibn Mansūr al-Hallāj, martyr mystique de l'Islam* (1922). 4 vols. Paris: Gallimard, 1975. In English translation, with a biographical foreword, by Herbert Mason, as *The Passion of al-Hallāj: Mystic and Martyr of Islam.* 4 vols. Princeton: Princeton University Press, 1982.

Masson, Denise. *Monothéisme coranique et monothéisme biblique: Doctrines comparées.* Paris: Desclée de Brouwer, 1976.

al-Māwardī. *Adab ad-Dunyā wa-al-Dīn.* Edited by Mustafā Saqqā. Cairo, 1955.

———. *Al-Ahkām al-sultānīyah waʾl-walāyāt al-dīniyya.* Beirut, n.d. Edited and translated into French by Edmond Fagnan as *Les Statuts gouvernementaux; ou, Règles de droit public et administratif* (1915). Paris: Le Sycomore, 1982. In English translation by Wafaa H. Wahba as *The Ordinances of Government.* Reading, UK: Center for Muslim Contribution to Civilization; London: Garnet, 1996.

Meier, Heinrich. *Die Lehre Carl Schmitts: Vier Kapitel zur Unterscheidung Politischer Theologie und Politischer Philosophie.* Stuttgart: Metzler, 1994. In English translation as *The Lessons of Carl Schmitt: Four Chapters on the Distinction between Political Theory and Political Philosophy.* Chicago: University of Chicago Press, 1998.

———. *Das Theologisch-politische Problem: Zum Thema von Leo Strauss.* Stuttgart: Metzler, 2003.

Melamed, Avraham. "Aristotle's Politics in Medieval and Renaissance Jewish Thought" (in Hebrew). *Prʾamim* 51 (1992): 27–69.

———. "The Attitude towards Democracy in Medieval Jewish Philosophy." *Jewish Political Studies Review* 5 (1993): 33–56.

Mélèze Modrzejewski, Joseph. 1997. "La Septante comme *nomos:* Comment la Torah est devenue une 'loi civique' pour les Juifs d'Égypte." *Annali di scienze religiose* 2 (1997): 143–58.

Mendelssohn, Moses. *Jérusalem ou Pouvoir religieux et judaïsme.* Translated by Dominique

Bourel. Paris: Les Presses d'Aujourd'hui, 1982. In English translation by Alfred Jospe as *Jerusalem and Other Jewish Writings*. New York: Schocken Books, 1969.

Merks, Karl Wilhelm. *Theologische Grundlegung der sittlichen Autonomie: Strukturmomente eines, autonomn' Normbergründungsverständnisses im Lex-Traktat der Summa theologiae des Thomas von Aquin*. Düsseldorf: Patmos, 1978.

Milton, John R. "The Origin and Development of the Concept of the 'Laws of Nature.'" *Archives européennes de sociologie* 22 (1981): 173–95.

Miskawayh. *Le Petit Livre du Salut*. Edited by Sālih ʿUdaymah. In Arabic, with French translation by Roger Arnaldez . [Tunisia]: Maison Arabe du Livre, 1987.

———. *Tahdhīb al-Akhlāq wa Tathīr al-Aʾrāq*. Edited by Hasan Tamīm. Beirut: Dar Maktabat al-Hayāh, 1398 AH. In French translation by Mohammed Arkoun as *Traité d'éthique*. Damascus: Institut Français de Damas, 1988. In English translation by Constantine K. Zurayk as *The Refinement of Character*. Beirut: American University of Beirut, 1968.

Momigliano, Arnaldo. "Un'apologia del giudaismo: Il *Contro Apione* di Flavio Giuseppe" (1931). In *Pagine ebraiche*, ed. Silvia Berti, 63–71. Turin: Einaudi, 1987. In English translation by Maura Masella-Gayley as "An Apology of Judaism: The *Against Apion* by Flavius Josephus." In *Essays on Ancient and Modern Judaism*, ed., with an introduction by Silvia Berti, 58–66. Chicago: University of Chicago Press, 1994.

Monneret de Villard, Ugo. *Lo studio dell'islâm in Europa nel XII e nel XIII secolo*. Vatican City: Biblioteca Apostolica Vaticana 1944.

Monod, Jean-Claude. *La Querelle de la sécularisation: Théologie politique et philosophies de l'histoire de Hegel à Blumberg*. Paris: Vrin, 2002.

Montesquieu. *De l'esprit des Lois*. In Montesquieu, *Oeuvres complètes*, 528–795. Edited by Daniel Oster. Paris: Éditions du Seuil; New York: Macmillan, 1964. In English translation as *The Spirit of Laws*. Translated and edited by Anne M. Cohler, Basia Carolyn Muller, and Harold Samuel Stone. Cambridge and New York: Cambridge University Press, 1989.

Morabia, Alfred. *Le Gihād dans l'Islam médiéval*. Paris: Albin Michel, 1993.

Moraux, Paul. *Les Listes anciennes des ouvrages d'Aristote*. Louvain: Éditions Universitaires, 1951.

Morris, James W. "The Philosopher-Prophet in Avicenna's Political Philosophy." In *The Political Dimensions of Islamic Philosophy: Essays in Honor of Muhsin S. Madhi*, ed. Charles E. Butterworth, 152–98. Cambridge, Mass.: Harvard University Press, 1992.

Motzki, Harald. *Die Anfänge der islamischen Jurisprudenz und ihre Entwicklung in Mekka bus zur Mitte des 2./8. Jh*. Stuttgart: Steiner, 1991. In English translation by Marion H. Katz as *The Origins of Islamic Jurisprudence: Meccan fiqh Before the Classical Schools*. Leiden and Boston: Brill, 2002.

Mourelatos, Alexander P. D. "Heraclitus, fr. 114." *American Journal of Philology* 86 (1965): 258–66.

Mowinckel, Sigmund. *Le Décalogue*. Paris: Félix Alcan, 1927.

———. *Psalmenstudien*, vol. 1: *Das Thronbeseigungsfest Jahwäs und der Ursprung der Eschatologie*. Kristiania: Dybwad, 1921.

al-Muqammas. *Dāwūd ibn Marwān al-Muqammis's Twenty Chapters (ʿIshrūn Maqāla)*. Edited, translated, and annotated by Sarah Stroumsa. Leiden: Brill, 1989.

Muranyi, Miklos. *Die Prophetengenossen in der frühislamischen Geschichte*. Bonn: Selbstverlag des Orientalischen Seminars der Universität, 1973.

Nagel, Tilman. *Die Festung des Glaubens: Triumph und Scheitern des islamischen Rationalismus im 11. Jahrhundert*. Munich: Beck, 1988.

———. *Das islamische Recht: Eine Einfürung.* Westhofen: WVA Velag Skulima, 2001.

———. *Staat und Glaubensgemeinschaft im Islam: Geschichte der politischen Ordnunsvorstellungen der Muslime,* vol. 1: *Von den Anfängen bis ins 13. Jahrhundert;* vol. 2: *Vom Spätmittelalter bis zur Neuzeit.* Zurich: Artemis, 1981.

Nahmanides. *Torat Hashem temimah.* In *Kitvey Rabbenu Mosheh B. Nahman,* ed. Charles B. Chavel, 1:141–75. Jerusalem: Mosad Rav Kuk, 1963.

Najjar, Fawzi M. "Farabi's Political Philosophy and Shī'ism." *Studia Islamica* 15 (1961): 57–72.

Nasīr ad-Dīn Tūsī. *The Nasirean Ethics.* Translated by G. M. Wickens. London: George Allen and Unwin, 1964.

Nemo, Philippe. *Histoire des idées politiques dans l'Antiquité et au Moyen Âge.* Paris: PUF, 1998.

Neschke-Hentschke, Ada B. *Platonisme politique et théorie du droit naturel: Contributions à une archéologie de la culture politique européenne,* vol. 1: *Le Platonisme politique dans l'Antiquité.* Louvain and Paris: Peeters, 1995.

———. *Politik und Philosophie bei Platon und Aristoteles: Die Stellung der 'NOMOI' im Platonischen Gesamtwerk und die politische Theorie des Aristoteles.* Frankfurt: Klostermann, 1971.

Netton, Ian Richard. *Muslim Neoplatonists: An Introduction to the Thought of the Brethren of Purity, Ikhwā al-Safā'.* London and Boston: Allen and Unwin, 1982.

Nevo, Yehuda D. "Towards a Prehistory of Islam." *Jerusalem Studies in Arabic and Islam* 17 (1994): 108–41.

Nizām al-Mulk. *Siasset Namèh: Traité de gouvernement.* Translated by Charles Schefer. 2 vols. Paris: Leroux, 1891–97.

Nörr, Knut Wolfgang. "Recht und Religion: Über drei Schnittstellen im Recht der mittelalterlichen Kirche." *Zeitschrift der Savigny-Stuftung für Rechtsgeschichte, Kanonistische Abteilung* 79 (1993): 1–15.

Noth, Martin. *Das Gesetze im Pentateuch: Ihre Voraussetzungen und ihr Sinn* (1940). In *Gesammelte Studien zum Alten Testament,* 1–141. 3rd ed. Munich: Kaiser, 1961.

———. *The History of Israel.* New York: Harper, 1960. In French translation as *Histoire d'Israël.* Paris: Payot, 1970.

———. *Das System der zwölf Stämme Israels* (1930). Darmstadt: Wissenschaftliche Burgesellschaft, 1966.

Nwyia, Paul. *Exégèse coranique et langage mystique: Nouvel essai sur le lexique technique des mystiques musulmans.* Beirut: Dar el-Machreq, 1970.

Oakley, Francis. "Christian Theology and the Newtonian Science: The Rise of the Concept of the Laws of Nature." *Church History* 30 (1961): 433–57.

Ostwald, Martin. *Nomos and the Beginnings of the Athenian Democracy.* Oxford: Clarendon Press, 1969. Westport, Conn.: Greenwood Press, 1979.

———. "Was There a Concept *agraphos nomos* in Classical Greece?" In *Exegesis and Argument: Studies in Greek Philosophy Presented to Gregory Vlastos,* ed. E. N. Lee et al., 70–104. Assen: Van Gorcum, 1973.

Otto, Eberhard. "Prolegomena zur Frage der Gesetzgebung und Rechtssprechung in Ägypten." *Mitteilungen des deutschen Archäologischen Instituts, Abteilung Kairo* 14 (1956): 150–59.

Padovani, Andrea. *Perché chiedi il mio nome? Dio natura e diritto nel secolo XII.* Turin: Giappichelli, 1997.

Parens, Joshua. *Metaphysics as Rhetoric: Alfarabi's Summary of Plato's "Laws."* Albany: State University of New York Press, 1995.

Paret, Rudi. "Halifat Allah—Vicarius Dei: Ein differenzierender Vergleich." In *Mélanges d'islamologie: Volume dédié à la mémoire de Armand Abel par ses collégues, ses élèves et ses amis*, ed. Pierre Salmon, 224–32. Leiden: Brill, 1974.

——. "Toleranz und Intoleranz in Islam." *Saeculum* 21 (1970): 344–65.

Pelikan, Jaroslav. *The Christian Tradition: A History of the Development of Doctrine*. 5 vols. Chicago: University of Chicago Press, 1971–89. In French translation as *La Tradition chrétienne: Histoire du développement de la doctine*. 5 vols. Paris: PUF, 1994.

Pennington, Kenneth. *The Prince and the Law, 200–1600: Sovereignty and Rights in the Western Legal Tradition*. Berkeley and Los Angeles: University of California Press, 1993.

Peterson, Erik. *Theologische Traktate*. Munich: Kösel, 1951.

Piétri, Charles. "Mythe et réalité de l'Église constantinienne." *Les Quatre Fleuves* 3 (1974): 22–39.

Pines, Shlomo. *La Liberté de philosopher: De Maïmonide à Spinoza*. Translated by by Rémi Brague. Paris: Desclée de Brouwer, 1997.

——. *Studies in Arabic Versions of Greek Texts and in Medieval Science* (1977), vol. 2 of *The Collected Works of Shlomo Pinès*. Jerusalem: Magnes; Leiden: Brill, 1986.

——. *Studies in the History of Arabic Philosophy*, vol. 3 of *The Collected Works of Shlomo Pinès*. Jerusalem: Magnes, 1996.

——. *Studies in the History of Jewish Philosophy: The Transmission of Texts and Ideas* (in Hebrew). Jerusalem: Mosad Byalik, 1977.

——. *Studies in the History of Jewish Thought*, vol. 5 of *The Collected Works of Shlomo Pinès*. Jerusalem: Magnes, 1997.

——. *Studies in the History of Religion*, vol. 4 of *The Collected Works of Shlomo Pinès*. Jerusalem: Magnes, 1996.

Plato. *Laws*. Translated by R. G. Bury. 2 vols. LCL. London: William Heinemann; Cambridge, Mass.: Harvard University Press, 1961.

——. *Republic*. Translated by Paul Shorey. 2 vols. LCL. Cambridge, Mass.: Harvard University Press; London: William Heinemann, 1982.

——. *The Statesman; Philebus*. Translated by Harold N. Fowler. LCL. Cambridge, Mass.: Harvard University Press; London: William Heinemann, 1982.

Plotinus. *Opéra*. Edited by Paul Henry and Hans-Rudolf Schwyzer. 3 vols. Paris: Desclée de Brouwer; Brussels: L'Édition universelle, 1951–73. In English translation as *Complete Works*. 4 vols. London: Bell; Grantwood, N.J.: Comparative Literature Press, 1989.

Posener, Georges. *De la divinité du pharaon*. Paris: Société Asiatique, 1960.

Post, Gaines. *Studies in Medieval Legal Thought: Public Law and the State, 1100–1322* (1964). Princeton: Princeton University Press, 1988.

Post, Gaines, Kimon Giocarinis, and Richard May. "The Medieval Heritage of a Humanistic Ideal: *Scientia donum Dei est, unde vendi non potest*." *Traditio* 11 (1955): 195–234.

Power in Islamic Political Thought: Selected Texts and Readings Over a Thousand Years (in Arabic). Texts collected and presented, with prefaces, by Yūsuf Ibish. Beirut: Dar al-Hamrāʾ, 1994.

Powers, David S. "The Exegetical Genre nāsikh al-Qurʾān wa mansūkhuhu." In *Approaches to the History of the Interpretation of the Qurʾān*, ed. Andrew Rippin, 117–38. Oxford: Clarendon Press, 1988.

Prémare, Alfred-Louis de. *Les Fondations de l'Islam: Entre écriture et histoire*. Paris: Éditions du Seuil, 2002.

——. *Aux origines du Coran: Questions d'hier, approches d'aujourd'hui*. Paris: Téraèdre, 2004.

Pritchard, James Bennett, ed. *Ancient Near Eastern Texts Relating to the Old Testament*. 2nd ed. Princeton: Princeton University Press, 1955.

Prodi, Paolo. *Una storia della giustizia: Dal pluralismo dei fori al moderno dualismo tra coscienza e diritto.* Bologna: Il Mulino, 2000.

Puin, Gerd R. "Observations on Early Qur'an Manuscripts in San'a." In *The Qur'an as Text,* ed. Stefan Wild, 107–11. Leiden: Brill, 1996.

al-Qadi, Waddad. "The Term 'Khalīfa' in Early Exegetical Literature." *Welt des Islams* 28 (1988): 392–411.

al-Qasim Ibn Ibrahim, *La lotta tra l'islam e il manicheismo: Un libro di Ibn al-Muqaffa' contro il Corano confutato da al-Qāsim b. Ibrāhīm.* Arabic text and Italian translation, with notes and introduction by Michaelangelo Guidi. Rome: Reale Accademia Nazionale dei Lincei, 1927.

Quaglioni, Diego. *À une déesse inconnue: La conception pré-moderne de la justice.* Translated by Marie-Dominique Couzinet. Paris: Publications de la Sorbonne, 2003.

Quillet, Jeannine. *Les Clefs du pouvoir au Moyen Âge.* Paris: Flammarion, 1972.

———. *D'une cité l'autre: Problèmes de philosophie politique médiévale.* Paris: Champion, 2001.

The Qur'an: Translation. Translated by Abdullah Yusuf Ali. 13th ed. Elmhurst, N.Y.: Tahrike Tarsile Qur'an, 2004.

Qushayrī. *Al-Risāla al-Qushayriyya fi 'ilm al-atsawwuf.* Edited by Ma'ruf Zurayq and Ali 'Abd al-Hamid Balhahji. Beirut: Dar al-Jil, 1990. In German translation by Richard Gramlich as *Das Sendschreiben al-Qušaris über das Sufitum.* Stuttgart: Steiner, 1989.

Rahman, Fazlur. *Prophecy in Islam: Philosophy and Orthodoxy.* London: Allen and Unwin, 1958.

Räisänen, Heikki. *Paul and the Law.* Tübingen: Mohr, 1983.

Ravitsky, Aviezer. *History and Faith: Studies in Jewish Philosophy.* Amsterdam: Gieben, 1996.

———. *Religion and State in Jewish Philosophy: Models of Unity, Division, Collision and Subordination* (in Hebrew). Jerusalem: The Israel Democracy Institute, 2002.

Razi. *La Médecine spirituelle.* Translated from the Arabic, with introduction, notes, and bibliography, by Rémi Brague. Paris: Garnier-Flammarion, 2003.

———. *Opera Philosophica fragmentaque quae supersunt.* Edited by Paul Kraus. Cairo: n.p., 1939.

Reinhardt, Karl. "Poseidonios über Ursprung und Entartung: Interpretation zweier Kulturgeschichtlicher Fragmente" (1928). In *Vermächtnis der Antike: Gesammelte Essays zur Philosophie und Geschichtsschreibung,* 402–60. Göttingen: Vandenhoeck & Ruprecht, 1966.

Reinhart, A. Kevin. *Before Revelation: The Boundaries of Muslim Moral Thought.* Albany: State University of New York Press, 1995.

Les Religions du Proche-Orient asiatique: Textes babyloniens, ougaritiques, hittites. Edited and translated by René Labat et al. Paris: Fayard-Denoël, 1970.

Resnick, Irven M. "The Falsification of Scripture and Medieval Christian and Jewish Polemics." *Medieval Encounters* 2 (1996): 344–80.

Rials, Stéphane. "Veritas juris: La vérité du droit écrit: Critique philologique humaniste et culture juridique moderne de la forme." *Droits* 26 (1997): 101–82.

Richter, Gustav. *Studien zur Geschichte der älteren arabischen Fürstenspiegel.* Leipzig: Hinrichs, 1932.

Rida, Rashīd. *Le Califat dans la doctrine de Rasīd Ridā.* A translation, with notes, of *Al-Hilāfa au al-Imāma al 'uzmā (Le Califat ou l'Imāma suprême)* by Henri Laoust (1922) Beirut: Institut Français de Damas, 1938.

Rippin, Andrew. "Interpreting the Bible through the Qur'ān." In *Approaches to the Qur'ān,* ed. G. R. Hawting and Abdul-Kader A. Shareef, 249–59. London and New York: Routledge, 1993.

Rivlin, Josef Joel. *Gesetz im Koran: Kultus und Ritus.* Jerusalem: Bamberger & Wahrmann, 1934.

Rodinson, Maxime. *Mahomet* (1961, 1975). New ed. revised by the author. Paris: Éditions du Seuil, 1994.

Romilly, Jacqueline de. *La Loi dans la pensée grecque des origines à Aristote.* Paris: Les Belles-Lettres, 1971.

Rosen, Stanley. *Plato's "Statesman": The Web of Politics.* New Haven: Yale University Press, 1995.

Rosenstock-Huessy, Eugen. *Die europäischen Revolutionen und der Charakter der Nationen* (1960). Reprint, Moers: Brendow, 1987.

Rosenthal, Erwin I. J. *Political Thought in Medieval Islam: An Introductory Outline.* Cambridge: Cambridge University Press, 1958; Westport, Conn.: Greenwood Press, 1985.

———. *Studia Semitica,* vol. 1: *Jewish Themes;* vol. 2, *Islamic Themes.* Cambridge: Cambridge University Press, 1971.

Rosenthal, Franz. "From Arabic Books and Manuscripts, VI, Istanbul Materials for al-Kindī and as-Sharakhsī." *Journal of the American Oriental Society* 76 (1956): 27–31.

———. "Ibn ʿArabi between 'Philosophy' and 'Mysticism.'" *Oriens* 32 (1988): 1–35.

———. *The Muslim Concept of Freedom Prior to the Nineteenth Century.* Leiden: Brill, 1960.

Rosenzweig, Franz. *Der Stern der Erlösung* (1921). Frankfurt: Suhrkamp, 1990. In English translation by William Hallo as *The Star of Redemption.* New York: Holt, Rinehart and Winston, 1971; and by Barbara E. Galli as *The Star of Redemption.* Madison: University of Wisconsin Press, 2005.

Rössler, Dietrich. *Gesetz und Geschichte: Untersuchungen zur Theologie der jüdischen Apokalyptik und der pharisäischen Orthodoxie.* Neukirchen-Vluyn: Neukirchener Verlag, 1960.

Rothschild, Jean-Pierre. "Philosophie (gréco-arabe), 'philosophie' de la Loi, d'après les sources juives médiévales, dans la littérature latine: Un bilan provisoire." *Medioevo: Rivista di storia della filosofia medievale* 23 (1997): 473–513.

Rousseau, Jean-Jacques. *Du contrat social.* Vol. 3 of Rousseau, *Oeuvres complètes.* Edited by Bernard Gagnebin and Marcel Raymond. 5 vols. Paris: Gallimard, 1959–95. In English translation as *The Social Contract and Other Late Political Writings.* Edited and translated by Victor Gourevitch. Cambridge and New York: Cambridge University Press, 1977.

Rubio, Luciano. *El "Ocasionalismo" de los teólogos especulativos del Islam: Su posible influencia en Guillermo de Ockham y en los "ocasionalistas" de la Edad Moderna.* Salamanca: Ediciones Escurialenses, 1987.

Rudolph, Ulrich. *Al-Māturīdī und die sunnitische Theologie in Samarkand.* Leiden and New York: Brill, 1997.

Rudolph, Ulrich, and Dominik Perler. *Occasionalismus: Theorien der Kausalität im arabisch-islamischen und im europäischen Denken.* Göttingen: Vandenhoeck & Ruprecht, 2000.

Ryan, W. F., and Charles B. Schmitt, eds. *Pseudo-Aristotle, The Secret of Secrets: Sources and Influences.* London: Warburg Institute, 1982.

Saadia Gaon. *Book of Beliefs and Opinions* (in Hebrew). Arabic original and Hebrew translation by Joseph Qāfih. Jerusalem: Sura, 1970. In English translation by Samuel Rosenblatt as *The Book of Beliefs and Opinions.* New Haven: Yale University Press, 1948, 1976.

Saffrey, Henri-Dominique. "Allusions antichrétiennes chez Proclus le diadoque platonicien." *Revue des sciences philosophiques et théologiques* 59 (1975): 553–63.

al-Samau'al Maghribī. *Ifhām al-Yahūd: Silencing the Jews.* Edited and translated by Moshe Perlmann. New York: American Academy for Jewish Research, 1964.

Sanders, E. P. *Paul, the Law and the Jewish People.* Philadelphia: Fortress Press, 1983.

Schacht, Joseph. "Classicisme, traditionalisme et ankylose dans la loi religieuse de l'islam." In *Classicisme et déclin culturel dans l'histoire de l'islam,* Proceedings of a symposium organized by Robert Brunschvig and Gustave E. von Grunebaum, 141–61. Paris: Besson, Chantemerle, 1977.

———. *An Introduction to Islamic Law.* Oxford: Clarendon Press, 1964, 1979. In French translation by P. Kempf and A. M. Turki as *Introduction au droit musulman.* Paris: Maisonneuve et Larose, 1983.

———. *The Origins of Muhammadan Jurisprudence.* Oxford: Clarendon Press, 1950.

———. "Zur soziologischen Betrachtung des islamischen Rechts." *Der Islam* 22 (1935): 207–38.

Schäfer, Peter. "Die Torah der messianischen Zeit." *Zeitschrift für die neutestamentliche Wissenschaft und die Kunde der älteren Kirche* 65 (1974): 27–42.

Schimmel, Annemarie. *Mystische Dimensionen des Islam: Die Geschichte des Sufismus.* Cologne: Diederichs, 1985. In English translation as *Mystical Dimensions of Islam.* Chapel Hill: University of North Carolina Press, 1975.

———. *Und Muhammad ist sein Prophet: Die Verehrung des Propheten in der islamischen Frömmigheit* (1981). 2nd ed. Munich: Diderichs, 1989. In English translation as *And Muhammad Is His Messenger: The Veneration of the Prophet in Islamic Piety.* Chapel Hill: University of North Carolina Press, 1985.

Schleiermacher, Friedrich. *Über die Religion: Reden an die Gebildeten unter ihren Verächtern.* Edited by Hans Joachim Rothert. Hamburg: Meiner, 1958. In English translation as *On Religion: Speeches to Its Cultured Despisers.* Cambridge and New York: Cambridge University Press, 1996.

Schlier, Heinrich. *Der Zeit der Kirche: Exegetische Aufsätze und Vorträger.* Freiburg, Basel, and Vienna: Herder, 1966. In French translation by F. Corin as *Le Temps de l'Église: Recherches d'exégèse.* Tournai: Casterman, 1961.

Schmidt, Werner. *Königtum Gottes in Ugarit und Israel: Zur Herkunft der Königsprädikation Jahwes.* Berlin: Töpelmann, 1961.

Schoeps, Hans Joachim. *Theologie und Geschichte des Judenchristentums.* Tübingen: Mohr, 1949.

Schofield, Malcolm. *The Stoic Idea of the City.* Cambridge and New York: Cambridge University Press, 1991. With a new foreword by Martha C. Nussbaum and a new epilogue by the author. Chicago: University of Chicago Press, 1999.

Scholem, Gershom. *Kabbalah.* Jerusalem: Keter; New York: Quadrangle, 1974.

———. "Der Sinn der Tora in der jüdischen Mystik." In *Scholem, und ihrer Symbolik,* 49–116. Frankfurt: Suhrkamp, 1973. In English translation by Ralph Manheim as *On the Kabbalah and Its Symbolism.* Foreword by Bernard McGinn. New York: Schocken Books, 1996.

———. *Über einige Grundbegriffe des Judentums.* Frankfurt: Suhrkamp, 1970.

Schubert, Alois. *Augustins lex-aeterna-Lehre nach Inhald und Quellen.* Munster: Aschendorff, 1924.

Seidl, Erwin. *Einführung in die ägyptische Rechtsgeschichte bis zum Ende des neuen Reiches,* vol. 1: *Juristischer Teil.* Glückstadt: J. J. Augustin, 1939.

Sellheim, Rudolf. "Prophet, Chalif und Geschichte: Die Muhammed-Biographie des Ibn Ishāq." *Oriens* 18–19 (1967): 33–91.

Seneca. *Letters to Lucilius = Epistles.* Translated by Richard M. Gummere. 3 vols. LCL. Cambridge, Mass., and London: Harvard University Press, 2000.

Serjeant, R. B. "The *sunna jāi'ah,* Pacts with the Yathrib Jews, and the *tahrîm* of Yathrib: Analysis and Translation of the Documents Comprised in the So-called 'Constitution of Medina,'" *Bulletin of the School of Oriental and African Studies* 41 (1978): 1–42.

Shāfi'ī. *Islamic Jurisprudence: Shāfi'ī's Risāla.* Edited and translated, with notes and appendices, by Majid Khadduri. Baltimore: Johns Hopkins University Press, 1961.

Sirat, Colette. "The Political Ideas of Nissim ben Moses of Marseille" (in Hebrew). In *Shlomo Pines Jubilee Volume on the Occasion of His Eightieth Birthday,* 2:23–76. Jerusalem Studies in Jewish Thought, no. 9. 2 vols. Jerusalem: University of Jerusalem, 1988–90.

Smith, Wilfred Cantwell. "The Concept of Shari'a among some Mutakallimun." In *Arabic and Islamic Studies in Honor of Hamilton A. R. Gibb,* edited by George Makdisi, 581–602. Cambridge, Mass.: Harvard University Press, 1965.

Snouck Hurgronje, Christiaan. "Sur la nature du 'Droit' musulman" (1886). In Snouck Hurgronje, *Oeuvres choisies / Selected Works,* ed. G.-H. Bousquet and Joseph Schacht, 256–63. Leiden: Brill, 1957.

Sourdel, Dominique. "Un pamphlet musulman anonyme d'époque 'abbāside contre les chrétiens." *Revue des études islamiques* 34 (1966): 1–33.

Spiegelberg, Wilhelm. *Die sogenannte Demotische Chronik des Papyrus 215 der Bibliothèque Nationale zu Paris.* Edited and translated by Wilhelm Spiegelberg. Leipzig: Hinrich, 1914.

Spinoza, Baruch. *Opera, quotquot reporta sunt.* Edited by J. Van Vloten and J. P. N. Land. 4 vols. The Hague: Nijhoff, 1914. In English translation by Samuel Shirley as *Complete Works,* edited, with an introduction and notes, by Michael L. Morgan. Indianapolis: Hackett, 2002.

Steinschneider, Moritz. *Die arabischen Übersetzungen aus dem griechischen* (1889–96). 2 vols. Graz: Akademische Verlagsanstalt, 1960.

———. *Die hebräischen Übersetzungen des Mittelalters und die Juden als Dolmetscher* (1893). Graz: Akademische Verlagsanstalt, 1956.

Steinwenter, Arthur. "Νομος ἐψυος: Zur Geschichte einer politischen Theorie." *Anzeiger der Akademie der Wissenschaften in Wien: Philologisch-historische Klasse* 83 (1946): 250–68.

Stern, Menahem, ed. and trans., with commentary. *Greek and Latin Authors on Jews and Judaism: From Herodotus to Plutarch.* 3 vols. Jerusalem: Israel Academy of Sciences and Humanities, 1974.

Stieglecker, Hermann. *Die Glaubenslehren des Islam.* Paderborn: Schöningh, 1962.

Strauss, Leo. "Farabi's Plato." In *Louis Ginzberg Jubilee Volume on the Occasion of His 70th Birthday,* vol. 1: *English Section,* 357–93. New York: The American Academy for Jewish Research, 1945.

———. *Gesammelte Schriften,* vol. 2: *Philosophie und Gesetz: Frühe Schriften.* Edited by Heinrich Meier. Stuttgart: Matzler, 1996–97.

———. *Maïmonide.* Essays collected and translated by Rémi Brague. Paris: PUF, 1988.

———. *Natural Right and History.* Chicago: University of Chicago Press, 1953.

———. *Persecution and the Art of Writing.* New York: Free Press, 1952; Chicago: University of Chicago Press, 1980.

———. *The Rebirth of Classical Political Rationalism: An Introduction to the Thought of Leo Strauss: Essays and Lectures,* ed. Thomas L. Pangle. Chicago: University of Chicago Press, 1989.

———. *What Is Political Philosophy? And Other Studies.* Glencoe, Ill.: Free Press, 1959; Chicago: University of Chicago Press, 1988.

Stroumsa, Gedaliahu A. G. *Barbarian Philosophy: The Religious Revolution of Early Christianity.* Tübingen: Mohr Siebeck, 1999.

———. "John Spencer and the Roots of Idolatry." *History of Religions* 40 (2001): 1–23.

———. *Savoir et salut.* Paris: Éditions du Cerf, 1992.

Stroumsa, Sarah. "The Barahima in Early Kalām." *Jerusalem Studies in Arabic and Islam* 6 (1985): 229–41.

———. "Écritures alternatives? Tradition et autorité chez les libres-penseurs en Islam médiéval." In *Les Retours aux Écritures: Fondamentalisme présents et passés,* ed. Evelyne Patlagean and Alain Le Boulluec, 269–93. Louvain: Peeters, 1993.

———. "Entre Harrān et al-Maghreb: La théorie maïmonidienne de l'histoire des religions et ses sources arabes." In *Judíos y musulmanes en al-Andalus y el Maghreb: Contactos intelectuales,* ed. M. Fierro, 153–64. Madrid: Casa de Valázquez, 2002.

———. *Freethinkers of Medieval Islam: Ibn al-Rawāndī, Abū Bakr al-Rāzī and Their Impact on Islamic Thought.* Leiden and Boston: Brill, 1999.

———. "'Ravings': Maimonides' Concept of Pseudo-Science." *Aleph: Hisorical Studies in Science and Judaism* 1 (2001): 141–63.

Szabó-Bechstein, Brigitte. *Libertas ecclesiae: Ein Schüsselbegriff des Investitursstreits und seine Vorgeschichte, 4.–11. Jahrhundert.* Rome: Libreria Ateneo Salesiano, 1985.

Taubes, Jacob. *Die Politische Theologie des Paulus.* Munich: Fink, 1993. See my critical review of the French translation (Paris, 1999) in *Critique* 634 (2000): 214–20. In English translation by Dana Hollander as *The Political Theology of Paul,* ed. Aleida Assmann. Stanford: Stanford University Press, 2004.

Tawhīdī. *Kitab al-imtā 'wa-al-muanasah.* Edited by Ahmad Zeyn and Ahmad Armin. Beirut: Dar Maktaba al-Hayā, n.d.

Teicher, Jacob Leon. "Averroès, 'Paraphrase de la République de Platon.'" Review of E. I. J. Rosenthal's translation of *Avveroes' Commentary on Plato's Republic. Journal of Semitic Studies* 5 (1960): 176–95.

Tellenbach, Gerd. *Libertas: Kirche und Weltordnung im Zeitalter des Investitursstreits.* Stuttgart: Kohlhammer, 1936. In English translation by R. F. Bennett as *Church, State, and Christian Society at the Time of the Investiture Contest.* Oxford: Blackwell, 1940; Toronto and Buffalo: University of Toronto Press, 1991.

Théodoridès, Aristide. "À propos de la loi dans l'Égypte pharaonique." *Revue internationale des droits de l'Antiquité* 14 (1967): 107–52.

Thomas Aquinas. *De regimine principum.* In *Opuscula Philosophica,* edited by Raimondo M. Spiazzi, 257–358. Turin: Marietti, 1954. In English translation by James M. Blythe as *Ptolemy of Lucca,* with portions attributed to Thomas Aquinas, *On the Governance of Rulers: De regimine principum.* Philadelphia: University of Pennsylvania Press, 1997.

———. *Summa contra Gentiles.* Rome: Leonina Manualis, 1934. In English translation, with introduction and notes, as *Summa Contra Gentiles,* 4 vols. Notre Dame and London: University of Notre Dame Press, 1975.

———. *Summa Theologica.* 5 vols. Paris: Lethielleux, 1939. In English translation as *Summa Theologicae.* Latin text and English translation, with introductions and notes, appendices, and glossaries. 61 vols. Blackfriars, in conjunction with McGraw-Hill, New York, and Spottiswoode, London, n.d.

Tierney, Brian. "*Natura id est deus:* A Case of Juristic Panatheism?" *Journal of the History of Ideas* 24 (1963): 307–22.

Tirosh-Rothschild, Hava. "The Political Philosophy of Rabbi Abraham Shalom: The Platonic Tradition" (in Hebrew). In *Shlomo Pines Jubilee Volume on the Occasion of His Eightieth Birthday*, 1:988–90, 2:409–40. Jerusalem Studies in Jewish Thought, no. 9. 2 vols. Jerusalem: University of Jerusalem, 1988–90.

Touati, Charles. *La pensée philosophique et théologique de Gersonide*. Paris: Éditions de Minuit, 1973.

———. *Prophètes, talmudistes, philosophes*. Paris: Éditions du Cerf, 1990.

Trego, Kristell. "De la 'loi de Dieu' à la 'volonté de Dieu': L'être et son devoir chez Anselme de Cantorbéry." *Revue de théologie et de philosophie* 136 (2004): 113–29.

Twersky, Isadore. *Introduction to the Code of Maimonides (Mishneh Torah)*. New Haven: Yale University Press, 1980.

Tyan, Émile. *Institutions de droit public musulman*, vol. 1: *Le Califat*; vol. 2: *Sultanat et Califat*. Paris: Sirey, 1954, 1957.

Ullmann, Walter. *Principles of Government and Politics in the Middle Ages*. London and New York: Methuen, 1961, 2nd ed., 1966; New York: Barnes & Noble, 1974.

Urbach, Ephraim E. *The Sages: Their Concepts and Beliefs*. Translated from the Hebrew by Israel Abrahams. 2 vols. Jerusalem: Magnes, 1979.

———. "Die Staatsauffassung des Don Isaak Abravanel." *Monatsschrift zur Geschichte und Wissenschaft des Judentums* 81 (1937): 237–70.

Urvoy, Dominique. *Avveroès: Les ambitions d'un intellectuel musulman*. Paris: Flammarion, 1998.

———. "Ibn Haldūn et la notion d'altération des textes bibliques." In *Judíos y musulmanes en al-Andalus y el Maghreb: Contactos intelectuales*, ed. M. Fierro, 165–78. Madrid: Casa de Velázquez, 2002.

———. *Les Penseurs libres dans l'Islam médiéval: L'interrogation sur la religion chez les penseurs arabes indépendants*. Paris: Albin Michel, 1996.

Vadet, Jean-Claude. *Les Idées morales dans l'islam*. Paris: PUF, 1995.

Vajda, Georges. "D'une attestation peu connue du thème du Philosophe autodidacte." *Al-Andalus* 31 (1966): 379–82.

———. *Études de théologie et de philosophie arabo-islamiques à l'époque classique*, ed. Daniel Gimaret et al. London: Variorum Reprints, 1986.

———. "Juifs et musulmans selon le hadith." *Journal asiatique* 229 (1937): 57–127.

———. *Mélanges Georges Vajda: Études de pensée, de philosophie et de littérature juives et arabes in memoriam*, ed. G. E. Weil. Hildesheim: Olms, 1982.

———. *Recherches sur la philosophie et la Kabbale dans la pensée juive du Moyen Âge*. Paris and The Hague: Mouton, 1962.

Vaux, Roland de. *Les Institutions de l'Ancien Testament*. 2 vols. Paris: Éditions du Cerf, 1957, 1960. In English translation by John McHugh as *Ancient Israel: Its Life and Institutions*. 2 vols. New York: McGraw-Hill, 1961, 1965.

Vernant, Jean-Pierre. *Les Origines de la pensée grecque*. Paris: PUF, 1962. In English translation as *The Origins of Greek Thought*. Ithaca: Cornell University Press, 1982.

Verosta, Stephan. *Johannes Chrysostomus: Staatsphilosoph und Geschichtstheologe*. Graz: Styria, 1960.

Veyne, Paul. *Les Grecs ont-il cru à leurs mythes? Essai sur l'imagination constituante*. Paris: Éditions de Seuil, 1983. In English translation by Paul Wissing as *Did the Greeks Believe in their Myths? An Essay on the Constitutive Imagination*. Chicago: University of Chicago Press, 1988.

Villey, Michel. *La Formation de la pensée juridique moderne* (1968). Edited by Stéphane Rials. Paris: PUF, 2003.

Voegelin, Eric. *Order and History*, vol. 1: *Israel and Revelation*. Baton Rouge: Louisiana State University Press, 1956.

Walzer, Richard. "Early Islamic Philosophy." In *The Cambridge History of Later Greek and Early Medieval Philosophy*, ed. A. H. Armstrong, 643–69. Cambridge: Cambridge University Press, 1970; reprinted, with corrections, 1980.

———. *Galen on Jews and Christians*. Oxford: Oxford University Press, 1949.

Wansbrough, John E. *Quranic Studies: Sources and Methods of Scriptural Interpretation*. Oxford: Oxford University Press, 1977.

———. *The Sectarian Milieu: Content and Composition of Islamic Salvation History*. Oxford and New York: Oxford University Press, 1978.

Weigand, Rudolf. "Das göttliche Recht: Vorausserzung der mittelalterlichen Ordnung." In *Chiesa diritto e ordinamento della "societas christiana" nei secoli XI e XII*, 113–32. Conference proceedings. Milan: Vita e Pensiero, 1986.

Weiss, Bernard G. "Covenant and Law in Islam." In *Religion and Law: Biblical, Judaic and Islamic Perspectives*, ed. Edwin B. Fermage et al., 49–83. Conference papers. Winona Lake, Ind.: Eisenbrauns, 1990.

———. *The Search for God's Law: Islamic Jurisprudence in the Writings of Sayf al-Dīn al 'Amidī*. Salt Lake City: University of Utah Press, 1992.

———. *The Spirit of Islamic Law*. Athens: University of Georgia Press, 1998.

Wellhausen, Julius. *Das arabische Reich und sein Sturz*. Berlin: Reimer, 1902. In English translation as *The Arab Kingdom and Its Fall*. London and New York: Routledge, 2000.

Welton, William A. "Divine Inspiration and the Origins of the Laws in Plato's *Laws*." *Polis* 14 (1995): 53–83.

Wensinck, Arent Jan. *The Muslim Creed: Its Genesis and Historical Development*. Cambridge: Cambridge University Press, 1932. London: Frank Cass, 1965.

Werblowsky, R. J. Zwi. *Joseph Karo: Lawyer and Mystic*. Oxford: Oxford University Press, 1962.

Widengren, Geo. "The Sacral Kingship of Iran." In *The Sacral Kingship: Contributions to the Central Theme of the VIIIth Congress for the History of Religions, Rome, April 1955*, 242–58. Supplement to *Numen: International Review for the History of Religions*. Leiden: Brill, 1959.

Wilks, Michael. *The Problem of Sovereignty in the Later Middle Ages: The Papal Monarchy with Augustinus Triumphus and the Publicists*. Cambridge: Cambridge University Press, 1963.

Wilson, John A. *The Burden of Egypt: An Interpretation of Ancient Egyptian Culture*. Chicago: University of Chicago Press, 1951.

Wolf, Eric R. "The Social Organization of Mecca and the Origins of Islam." *Southwestern Journal of Anthropology* 7 (1951): 329–56.

Wolfson, Harry Austryn. *Philo: Foundations of Religious Philosophy in Judaism, Christianity and Islam*. 4th printing, rev. 2 vols. Cambridge, Mass.: Harvard University Press, 1968.

———. *The Philosophy of the Kalām*. Cambridge, Mass.: Harvard University Press, 1968.

Xenophon. *Cyropaedia*. Translated by Walter Miller. 2 vols. LCL. London: William Heinemann; Cambridge, Mass.: Harvard University Press (1914) 1983.

Zaehner, Richard Charles. *Mysticism, Sacred and Profane: An Inquiry into some Varieties of Praeternatural Experience*. Oxford: Oxford University Press, 1957. London and New York: Oxford University Press, 1971.

Zeitlin, Solomon. *Maimonides: A Biography.* New York: Bloch, 1935; 2nd ed., 1955.

Zonta, Mauro. *La filosofia antica nel Medioevo ebraico: Le traduzioni ebraiche medievali dei testi filosofici antichi.* Brescia: Paideia, 2002. See my critical review in *Bulletin de philosophie médiévale, II, Archives de philosophie* 61 (1998): 25–27.

Zuckerman, Arthur J. *A Jewish Princedom in Feudal France, 768–900.* New York and London: Columbia University Press, 1972.

Index